Courts, Law, and Judicial Processes

Edited by
S. Sidney Ulmer

THE FREE PRESS
A Division of Macmillan Publishing Co., Inc.
NEW YORK

Collier Macmillan Publishers
LONDON

For my daughters
Margaret, Susan, and Mary

The Free Press
A Division of Macmillan Publishing Co., Inc.
866 Third Avenue, New York, N.Y. 10022

Library of Congress Catalog Card Number: 80-1856

Printed in the United States of America

printing number

1 2 3 4 5 6 7 8 9 10

Library of Congress Cataloging in Publication Data

Main entry under title:

Courts, law, and judicial processes.

Includes index.
1. Courts—United States. 2. Judicial process
—United States. I. Ulmer, S. Sidney.
KF8700.A7C68   347.73′1   80-1856
ISBN 0-02-932980-9
ISBN 0-02-932970-1 (pbk.)

Contents

* Selections marked with asterisks have not been previously published.

Contents

Part VI   Current Problems in the Courts   521

Preface

This book is intended for use in teaching the American judicial process or related courses. In selecting materials for the book, we strove for a broad definition of the judicial process. While a good deal of attention has been given to the U.S. Supreme Court and its justices, an attempt has been made to enlarge the focus to include other participants in the process. We have been guided primarily by three considerations. The first is the discretion available to decision makers. The discretionary power of policemen, prosecutors, and judges is of prime importance in a democratic political system. While the use of such discretion is sometimes "system determined," our readings reveal many instances in which other explanations are necessary.

A second consideration pertains to the structure and purposes of judicial institutions and the place of each in a sociopolitical setting. We have sought to highlight roles that are either highly significant, newly assigned, or currently questioned. Illustrative here are the materials on law as social control, the selection of judges, and the delivery of legal services via private or public attorneys. Also of interest in this area are the relationships of judicial institutions and participants in the justice system to the environment in which they operate. It is in this area that system-determined behavior is most likely to be observed—although the term "system-influenced" may be a more accurate descriptor. The readings dealing with the role of the Supreme Court in the American system of government and the interaction of courts with their various publics are in point here.

The third interest reflected in our choice of readings has to do with current problems in the judicial system as well as with practical and theoretical controversies over the way in which that system functions. A number of our selections do not report research findings. Instead, they focus on problems in the system, suggested reforms, controversial Supreme Court policies, and the like. In that connection we have included, among others, the views of Raoul Berger on constitutionalism and the rule of law, Warren Burger on trial court advocacy, and Donald

Horowitz on courts as social policy makers. We have also included selections dealing with case load, case flow, and associated problems in the courts. Finally, we have felt free to mix selected Supreme Court opinions with research reports and theoretical argument, since our aim has been to provide broad rather than narrow perspectives on the American judicial process.

Although the three foci outlined here have guided the selection of items for the book, the materials are not segregated by these three headings. Any particular selection may illustrate one, two, or three of these perspectives. The effect is to avoid imposing a rigid editorial framework on those who use the book. By design we have left the instructor free to impose his or her own organization on the course. We have included eighty readings in the book (five not published previously)—a number large enough to permit the instructor considerable flexibility in that regard. Brief introductory statements in each part of the book promote the same end.

Because of the variety of sources and the diversity of authors, the pieces collected here naturally show variety and diversity of writing and editorial styles. Beyond basic typographics, no attempt has been made to impose any artificial consistency of style on this collection. Some reading titles and subheads have been altered for the sake of unity; however, the original numbering of tables and figures has been retained. With some exceptions, the original references within each article have been deleted; the reader is referred to the original source for these.

PART I

Courts and Law

The court system in the United States is a little more complicated than that found in many countries. This results from what is traditionally called "federalism." Unlike nations with a single government, our federal system consists of a central or federal government and fifty state governments. This fact has important consequences for the structure and organization of American courts. Instead of one court system, we have fifty-one. Within each state we find trial and appellate courts with variously defined jurisdictions and procedures. The great variety in these systems makes it difficult to generalize about state courts. In many of the state systems we find trial, intermediate appellate, and final appellate courts—i.e., the same format followed in the structure of the federal court system.

In the federal system, trials are conducted in U.S. district courts. Appeals from these courts lie to the U.S. courts of appeals. Final appellate authority is vested in the U.S. Supreme Court which also possesses some original jurisdiction.

Section One addresses a number of questions that flow from the coexistence of state and federal court systems. They include: (1) what is the relation of state to lower federal courts? (2) What is the relation of state and lower federal courts to the Supreme Court? and

1

most important (3) What are the consequences of the dual court
system in the United States?

Courts and judges—whether at state or federal levels—are engaged in resolving conflicts over law. The procedures employed and
the conclusions reached will be influenced by the kind of law at
issue. The student who masters Section One should have a good
grasp of the distinctions between common and statutory law, public
and private law, and criminal and civil law.

A major purpose of law is to influence people to do what we
think they should do and to refrain from doing that which we
think improper. Such a result may be obtained by reasoned appeal,
education, or other noncoercive measures, but we rely heavily on
a system of rewards and sanctions implemented through civil and
criminal proceedings in our courts. When we punish a person
through the enforcement of criminal sanctions, it is because of
certain beliefs about the effect of punishment on the person punished as well as on those who observe the punishment. The justification for punishment depends on the correctness of those beliefs.
However, as Section Two makes clear, the effect of punishment is
a controversial question.

The selection on Watergate and civil disobedience explores
some of the complex relations between legal rules and the response
of the public to those rules. The point is made that the felt duty to
obey laws is an essential ingredient in any political system. But such
a feeling may be undermined by social and political developments
within the system. The actions of courts in enforcing law and imposing sanctions or remedies must not transcend that realm in which
courts may act "legitimately." At the same time, judges must show
some sensitivity to community needs. Should these considerations
become unbalanced, the support for legal institutions may be im-
periled.

In Section Three, it is recognized that courts sometimes serve
as vehicles for the making of social and political policies. The extent to which judges should flout law, precedent, or other legal
restrictions in making policy, however, is a controversial matter.
J. Skelly Wright, the chief judge of the U.S. Court of Appeals for
the District of Columbia, has suggested that the courts should stop
trying to apply the laws in a neutral manner. Specifically, he believes that the Fourteenth Amendment should be used to "redress
the historical inbalance for disadvantaged minorities." [1] In Judge
Wright's view, "It is not embarrassing, or unjudicial, to notice whose

ox is being gored when assessing legislation or other action. We must know who is the victim and what class he belongs to." [2]

Most judges would probably not go so far, although many recognize that U.S. law sometimes impinges unfairly on certain segments of our population. Horowitz raises no fundamental objections to the equitable use of law when called for, but he argues that American courts have now exceeded their capacity to act effectively. He also thinks that many courts are now encroaching on policy realms that were thought barred to them.

Notes

1. *The National Law Journal,* October 29, 1979, p. 10.
2. Ibid.

The Structure and Function of American Courts

1

The Organization of Courts in the United States

Herbert Jacob

The structure of courts in the United States is complicated. Two separate court systems—federal and state—operate side by side. The structure is decentralized. Nevertheless, within this largely archaic structure the complex conflicts generated by twentieth-century life must be settled. To understand how judges, lawyers, and litigants operate, it is necessary to understand the labyrinthine environment in which they work.

• • •

The Structure of American Courts

From the beginning both the states and the federal government have maintained trial courts throughout the country. The network of state courts, however, remains by far the more extensive. Each state possesses several sets of trial courts.

Some state courts handle minor criminal and civil matters, such as traffic fines, local ordinance violations, and suits involving small amounts of money. These courts often exist in every large town of a county. Until very recently, the presiding official, called a justice of the peace, was an untrained layperson elected along with other county officials. Where the office of the justice of the peace still exists, he often remains in charge of these minor courts. In some states his functions have been limited to still more minor matters, and a professional magistrate or judge has been installed to hear criminal and civil suits. In most states, courts of minor jurisdiction may not hold jury trials. All matters that come before them are settled by the judge alone. If a jury trial is desired and permitted by law, the case must be transferred to another court.

Another tier of trial courts hears more important matters—felony trials where the defendant may be sentenced to a long prison term and civil suits that involve a greater sum of money, usually more than $1,000. Such courts are generally located only at the county seat. In some states several counties share a single court, which normally sits in one and visits the other counties of the circuit for short periods each year. Judges of these courts are always lawyers and normally serve for relatively long terms. All jury trials take place in these courts, although most cases are heard by the judge alone or are settled out of court.

Finally, many states have a set of specialized courts, which fit somewhere between the major and minor trial courts. Some of these—as in Ohio—deal with family matters, such as divorce and juvenile delinquency. Most larger cities have special traffic courts to handle the thousands of parking and driving violations that occur each year. Some cities also possess small-claims courts to handle monetary claims of less than $500; in small-claims courts, a lawyer is unnecessary and sometimes is not even allowed. Finally, larger cities often have special probate courts to handle the administration of wills and estates; in other locales, the major or minor trial courts handle the probate matters in addition to their other business.

No two states possess identical court structures, nor is the division of work between the courts of any state as symmetrical as would appear from the foregoing description. Without exception, the jurisdiction of lower and higher trial courts overlaps. The potential litigant is thus confronted with a maze of tribunals through which he and his lawyers must pass to attain their goals.

Federal trial courts are much more simply organized. For one thing, there are relatively few—ninety-two in the entire country. Each state has at least one. Called district courts, these courts normally operate over a large portion of a state. The court usually travels to the more important cities within its territory, visiting each for two weeks twice a year. Many district courts have several judges, each operating his own branch of the court. The court hears criminal matters involving the violation of a federal law, such as taking a stolen car across state boundaries or illegally dealing in narcotics. Civil matters heard in federal court range from large suits involving the citizens of two states to complicated antitrust complaints filed by the federal government. A single judge presides over each case. Although the Constitution guarantees the right to a jury trial for all criminal prosecutions and for many civil cases involving more than $20, only criminal trials make extensive use of juries. In 1975, for instance, litigants in civil trials waived their right to a jury in 68 percent of the trials. Criminal defendants waived a jury in only 36 percent of the trials. When no jury sits, the judge decides the case alone.

The federal government also maintains several specialized courts. Although some legal controversy exists over whether they have the same standing as constitutional courts, they operate like constitutional courts except that the jurisdiction is limited, they sit mostly in Washington, and they are assigned some quasi-legislative functions. These courts exist for custom and patent appeals and for claims against the federal government. They usually hear appeals of administrative decisions, much as the regular courts of appeals hear appeals from many regulatory agencies. The Supreme Court treats their decisions like those by courts of appeals.

Another extraordinary federal court is the three-man district court, which is an *ad hoc* tribunal specially convened in exceptional circumstances. Litigants who wish to use this court must make a special application to the senior judge of the district court. If he agrees to their request, the chief judge of the circuit convenes the court. It consists of three judges: at least one must be a district judge, and at least one must be a judge of the court of appeals. The court hears arguments and renders its decision. If the losing party wishes to appeal (and it usually does), the appeal goes directly to the United States Supreme Court. These three-man courts are used to hear some of the most controversial issues reaching the judiciary; they are intended to dispatch them more quickly and more authoritatively than a trial before an ordinary district court.

Trial courts settle most cases with finality, either by promoting out-of-court settlements or by a judgment resulting from a formal trial. Some litigants, however, wish to appeal the results of their trial, believing that the judge made prejudicial errors that robbed them of victory, or seek to win a change in policy through an appellate decision. For such appeals, special appellate tribunals exist in every state and in the federal court system. Twenty-four states have intermediate appellate courts as well as supreme courts; the remainder have only supreme courts to hear appeals. The federal judiciary has eleven intermediate appellate courts as well as its Supreme Court.

Where intermediate appellate courts exist, appeals usually must be directed to them before being taken to the appropriate supreme court. In almost every case the litigants have a *right* to one appeal. If they file their case properly, the appellate court is obliged to consider it, regardless of the legal merit of the appeal and the triviality or importance of the conflict. The intermediate appellate courts serve large portions of their state or, in the case of federal courts of appeals, several states. Like federal district judges, the judges of appellate courts ordinarily visit several major cities of their area, although most of their business takes place at the headquarters city. Unlike trial courts, each appellate court operates with several judges. There is no jury; a panel of three or more judges decides. Unlike most trial judges, appellate judges give reasons for their decisions in a written opinion, which is often published for future reference by lawyers and other judges.

Supreme courts make the final decision in the judicial process. State supreme courts render the final verdict for all cases involving state law; the federal Supreme Court renders the final judicial decision on all matters involving federal law or the federal Constitution. Some state supreme courts must hear every case appealed to them; other courts exercise a great deal of discretion in selecting the appeals that they will decide. The United States Supreme Court is the best-known example of the exercise of discretion. The Court receives requests to hear more than 5000 cases each year and dismisses nearly 90 percent of the appeals as unworthy of review. Among the state courts, Virginia and Louisiana are almost as selective. Courts like the Wisconsin Supreme Court hear almost all cases brought before them.

Three or more justices staff each of the supreme courts. They hear cases as a group, although in some states the court divides into panels in the same way as most federal courts of appeals. In a few states—Missouri is an especially conspicuous example—the court parcels cases out to "commissioners," who are appointed by the justices to act as their alternates. Although the decision of a commissioner does not become final until adopted by the court, in practice their decisions are seldom overruled.

The courts sit at the capital or in another large city of the state. Unlike other courts that go on circuit as a convenience for litigants, supreme courts demand that litigants come to them. As a result, the lawyers practicing before supreme courts often constitute a rather specialized group, who handle cases for their less experienced colleagues when an appeal is necessary.

The principal bridge between the state and federal courts is at the supreme court level. When a case involves federal statutes or rights under the federal Constitution, the decision of a state supreme court may be appealed to the United States Supreme Court. The federal Supreme Court either affirms the state's decision or reverses it. Reversals mean that the case is sent back to the state court system for the appropriate action—a dismissal, a rehearing, or a granting of the remedy that the litigant sought originally. Although constitutionally obliged to follow Supreme Court decisions, state courts in fact sometimes ignore them. They may simply react to the Court's decision with disbelief and interpret it away, or they may rehear the case and come to the same result as before, but on slightly different grounds. It would therefore be a mistake to describe the relationship between the state courts and the United States Supreme Court as that of subordinate and superior. It is more accurate to characterize the Supreme Court's position as being first among equals. In ordinary cases the Supreme Court's judgment is respected. In highly controversial ones, its decision is sometimes evaded by legalisms; for example, the state court may distinguish between cases on the basis of highly specific fact situations.

Consequences of the Dual Court System

The existence of the dual system of courts is not without substantive impact. It supplies alternative tribunals to which cases may be brought. The Southern black, for instance, may litigate to protect his civil rights in either a state or a federal court. As long as Southern legislatures ignored the desires of black citizens and as long as blacks could not vote for state judges, they were likely to prefer federal courts, which proved to be more receptive to their claims. Likewise, Southern whites were apt to go to a state court, where they were likely to have more influence.

A second consequence of the dual court system is that the interpretation of legal doctrine differs from state to state. Although several states may have identical or similar statutes and although most state courts operate in the same common-law tradition, none of them interprets the laws or their common-law heritage in exactly the same way. To some extent the resulting variation of law reflects different social conditions and different attitudes by the public toward similar problems. It may also represent experimentation by certain state courts in an effort to develop more effective ways of dealing with problems. Mostly, however, the diversity of legal doctrine is simply the consequence of a fragmented court system, representing neither conscious experimentation nor an explicit adaptation to peculiar social conditions. Consequently it is impossible to summarize the state of the law in the United States in brief form. What the law says about a particular matter depends not only upon the whims of fifty-one legislatures but also on the accidental development of judicial interpretation in fifty-one judicial systems.

The dual-court structure also provides a weapon for both the federal and state governments in their struggle to expand or retain their functions. State governments use their courts to resist what they regard as federal encroachments by asking state courts not to honor federal decisions. In turn, the federal government promotes litigation in its courts to extend the scope of its power. Thus in recent years Southern courts have been involved not only in the desegregation dispute but also in the larger issue of what powers each governmental level possesses. State courts in both the North and the South have on occasion sought to deny federal jurisdiction over a case to protect their state's sovereignty.

• • •

2

The Nature of Law
Henry J. Abraham

For centuries mankind has discussed the nature of law. In one way or another, it touches every citizen of every nation. The contact may be pleasant or unpleasant, tangible or intangible, direct or indirect, but it is nonetheless a constant force in the lives of people everywhere on the globe. It is essential that we have some understanding of its nature and of the human beings who interpret and administer it.

• • •

Common Law and Statutory Law

For our purposes, then, law—broadly speaking—represents the rules of conduct that pertain to a given political order of society, rules that are backed by the organized force of the community. As it has evolved through the centuries, law has been made either by the political repre-

From Henry J. Abraham, *The Judicial Process: An Introductory Analysis of the Courts of the United States, England, and France,* 3d ed. (Oxford University Press, 1975), pp. 4, 8–9, 16–17, 17–18, 18–19, 19, 19–21, 22, 22–23. Copyright © 1962, 1968, 1975 by Oxford University Press, Inc. Reprinted by permission. Footnotes have been omitted.

sentatives of the people—sometimes rather inaccurately styled "bar-made" law—or it has been "bench-made" by judges and justices. The former type is generally known as *statutory law,* the latter as *common law.* Both will bear close examination, but, at the risk of some oversimplification, the crucial distinction between the two is that between codified written law and unwritten law based on custom and tradition. (The terms "bar-made" and "bench-made" are never used in England; there they are called "statutory" and "judge-made.")

Common Law

Utilized by most English-speaking states, *common law* is variously known also as *English, Anglo-Saxon,* or *Anglo-American law.* Despite its conceptualization by Lord Coke as "the perfection of reason," it is indeed a vast and complex instrument of justice. Although at first glance it may well seem chaotic and abstruse, on closer examination it is readily possible to discern a logic which binds the many diverse components that comprise it into a comprehensive and comprehensible entity.

Common law is judge-made, bench-made, law rather than a fixed body of definite rules such as the modern civil law codes. In Roscoe Pound's words, it is a "mode of judicial and juristic thinking, a mode of treating legal problems." He might well have added "a mood." Often based on precedents, it embodies continuity in that it binds the present with the past.

Statutory Law

Despite the fact that the concept of *statutory law*—variously known as *code, written, Neo-Roman* or *Roman,* or *civil law*—comes to us from ancient Rome, its broad application is essentially a modern one. Whereas the common law has dealt traditionally with matters of a private character, with the relations between individuals, statutory law is more frequently concerned with society as a whole. It is law that originates with specifically designated, authoritative lawmaking bodies—presumably legislatures, but it also embraces executive-administrative decrees and ordinances, treaties and protocols, all of which are committed to paper.

● ● ●

"Mixing" Common and Statutory Law

England and the United States today have legal systems based on the common law that readily and naturally found its way across the Atlantic

Ocean from the Mother Country to the Colonies. But although it must be categorized as a common law system, the Anglo-American legal framework in effect now consists of a mixture of common *and* statutory law. A great deal of contemporary law is necessarily statutory; it is coded. However, this is a relatively recent development, for although statutes as a basis of Anglo-American law were not unknown, they played no really significant role until the second quarter of the nineteenth century.

The mixture came into its own largely, although certainly not exclusively, as a result of the perpetuating conservatism of the common law, particularly in the realm of the sanctity of private property, based on the overriding concept of economic *laisser faire*. With the advent of a rising spirit of common social consciousness and responsibility, and a gradual movement toward the service or welfare state on both sides of the ocean, legislative bodies everywhere—but considerably more slowly in the United States than in the United Kingdom—commenced to change or even displace the age-old concepts and practices of the common law in favor of what were viewed as primary considerations of necessary public interest.

Nonetheless, common law remained as an important basis of legislative motivations and actions, and often an enacted statute would—as indeed it still does today—simply spell out certain aspects of the grand sweep of common law. Furthermore, no legislative body—and sometimes not even the executive—is consistently, or even largely, capable of pinpointing in writing all the aspects and ramifications of a statute or order, nor would that necessarily be desirable even if it were possible.

• • •

Of course, there are certain areas of statutory law where little, if any, discretionary elements remain for the judge. The United States Criminal Code, for example, represents a compendium of laws that prescribe what shall constitute a crime and what the penalties shall be. A judge may have a modicum of leeway regarding the former, but the sole substantive discretion left to him in the realm of the latter is one specifically written into the code. Thus, a particular law may conceivably permit him to exercise his considered judgment as to the severity of a sentence which he is called upon to impose for a given criminal infraction, but this discretion will be strictly limited by the minimum and maximum penalties as provided in it. Moreover, it may well be limited by the nature of the verdict of the jury. Indeed, *criminal law* is becoming more and more codified everywhere among the common law lands, and hence is becoming statutory. The same applies to *public law* generally, although the great bulk of *private* law is still common law. A few words of explanation about these two types of law and some additional legal concepts are in order.

Some Additional Legal Definitions and Concepts

● ● ●

Private law governs the relationship between private citizens or persons; that is, it regulates the relations of individuals with each other. It is concerned with the definition, regulation, and enforcement of rights in cases where both the person in whom the right inheres and the person upon whom the obligation devolves are private individuals. Obvious examples of private law are the law governing contracts between individuals or corporations and that pertaining to marriage and divorce. In the sense that infractions of the legal obligations inherent in these areas are subject to adjudication by courts, the state is involved, of course, but it is neither the subject of the right nor the object of the duty.

Public law, on the other hand, is a branch or department of law which is very much concerned with the state in its political or sovereign capacities. . . . Public law deals with the definition, regulation, and enforcement of rights in those cases where the state *is* viewed as the subject of the right or the object of the duty, including criminal law and criminal procedure. In other words, it is that portion of law which is concerned with political conditions and situations—with the powers, rights, duties, capacities, and incapacities that are characteristic of and peculiar to both supreme and subordinate political authority.

Public law applies to and affects the entire people of a nation or state that adopts or enacts it—in contrast to private law, which affects and applies to only one or a few individuals—for it regulates both the relations between individuals and the state and the relations between the branches of the government. Thus, the vast majority of legislation enacted by Congress is in the category of public law—and its statutes are codified, preceded by the term "Public Law_____ [Number]." Social welfare, defense appropriations, subversive activities control, farm subsidies—all these areas of legislation represent illustrations of the vast, diversified content of public law.

Administrative law, which has quite naturally achieved ever increasing prominence over the past few decades, consists of those rules and regulations that are promulgated by the sundry administrative agencies of government that have been empowered to deal with the operation of government under the delegated rule-making authority of the legislative body. That branch of public law prescribes in detail the activities of the agencies involved—such as those concerned with the collection of revenue; regulation of competitive practices; coinage; public health, welfare, safety, and morals; sanitation; and regulation of the armed forces.

Constitutional law is the other great branch of public law. It determines the political organization of a state and its powers while also setting certain substantive and procedural limitations on the exercise of governing power. Because of its position and nature it stands legally above all other types of municipal law, public as well as private. In the United States, with its written Constitution, constitutional law consists of the application of fundamental principles of law based on that document, as finally interpreted by its highest judicial organ, the Supreme Court of the United States. A contemporary example is the famous *Steel Seizure Case*. Believing himself invested with the power to act in his capacity as Commander in Chief and endowed with what he and his advisers viewed as "inherent authority," President Truman seized the steel mills on April 8, 1952, in order to forestall a nation-wide strike in the midst of the Korean War. The owners filed for a writ to enjoin him, charging the absence of both constitutional and legislative authority for his actions. After a series of dramatic skirmishes in the lower federal courts, the United States Supreme Court received the case for adjudication—clearly a matter in the realm of constitutional law. On June 2, 1952, the Court rendered its decision, featured by seven different opinions! But six of the nine Justices did agree on *one* crucial point: that by *usurping legislative power* President Truman had violated the Constitution, and that the seizure of the steel mills was hence *ultra vires*—particularly so since Congress had expressly refused to enact a suggested amendment to the Taft-Hartley Act authorizing such governmental seizures in an emergency.

In brief, constitutional law prescribes generally the plan and method under which the public business of the political organ, known as the state, is conducted. And it differs further from the other types of law we have seen in that it is both enacted and changed either in an extraordinary manner by an ordinary legislative body or by an extraordinary body, such as a constitutional convention, constituted especially for that purpose.

• • •

Civil and Criminal Law

Another basic distinction of considerable importance which confronts the observer of the judicial and legal process is that between *civil law* and *criminal law*.

• • •

CIVIL LAW

A case at *civil law* is normally one between private persons and/or private organizations, for civil law governs the relations between individuals and defines their legal rights. A party bringing suit under it seeks legal redress in a *personal* interest, such as for a breach of contract, a divorce action, a defamation of character, the use of a copyrighted story without permission. Yet while suits at civil law far more often than not are suits among private persons, the government, too, may conceivably be involved. For example, under the Sherman Anti-Trust Act of 1890, as amended, the federal government in the United States is empowered to bring either civil or criminal action against an alleged offender. It has much more frequently brought civil than criminal actions under that statute, probably because the former are not so difficult to win and cause less of an uproar in the interested community.

CRIMINAL LAW

A case at *criminal law* is invariably brought by and in the name of the legally constituted government, no matter at what level—national, state, or local—it may arise. Chiefly statutory in the United States, criminal law defines crimes against the public order and provides for appropriate punishment. Prosecution brought under it by the proper governmental authority involves an accusation that the defendant has violated a specific provision of a law, an infraction for which a penalty has normally been provided by statute. Criminal cases comprise such felonies or major crimes as homicide, espionage, sabotage, rape, and perjury, to name but a few. The coverage is as extensive as the lawmakers choose to make it. Since the prosecuting authority in a criminal case is necessarily an agent of the sovereign, the latter's name appears in its title. Hence, assuming one Brown's indictment for murder in Pennsylvania, the case would be docketed for trial as either *The Commonwealth of Pennsylvania v. Brown,* or as *People v. Brown.* Moving to the federal level, one of the cases brought under the membership clause of the Smith Act of 1940 was entitled *United States v. Scales.* However, by far the largest volume of criminal law is still enacted at the state level in the United States and thus is enforced by state officials under state law. Unitary countries, such as France and the United Kingdom, are not confronted with that jurisdictional problem.

But in all cases and at all levels it is the jurists who render the decisions. Alexis de Tocqueville put it well: "Hardly any question arises in the United States that is not resolved sooner or later into a judicial question."

• • •

Law as Social Control

—————————— *3* ——————————

The General Preventive Effects Of Punishment

Johannes Andenaes

I. The Concept of General Prevention

In continental theories of criminal law, a basic distinction is made between the effects of punishment on the man being punished—individual prevention or special prevention—and the effects of punishment upon the members of society in general—general prevention. The characteristics of special prevention are termed "deterrence," "reformation" and "incapacitation," and these terms have meanings similar to their meanings in the English speaking world. General prevention, on the other hand, may be described as the *restraining influences emanating from the criminal law and the legal machinery.*

By means of the criminal law, and by means of specific applications of this law, "messages" are sent to members of a society. The criminal law lists those actions which are liable to prosecution, and it specifies the penalties involved. The decisions of the courts and actions by the police and prison officials transmit knowledge about the law, underlining the fact that criminal laws are not mere empty threats, and providing de-

From Johannes Andenaes, "The General Preventive Effects of Punishment," *University of Pennsylvania Law Review* 114 (May 1966) : 949, 951–953, 954, 955–957. Copyright © 1966 by the *University of Pennsylvania Law Review*. Reprinted by permission of the publisher and Fred B. Rothman & Company. Footnotes have been omitted.

tailed information as to what kind of penalty might be expected for violations of specific laws. To the extent that these stimuli restrain citizens from socially undesired actions which they might otherwise have committed, a general preventive effect is secured.

• • •

II. A Neglected Field of Research

General prevention has played a substantial part in the *philosophy of the criminal law*. It is mentioned in Greek philosophy, and it is basic in the writings of Beccaria, Bentham and Feuerbach. According to Feuerbach, for example, the function of punishment is to create a "psychological coercion" among the citizens. The threat of penalty, consequently, had to be specified so that, in the mind of the potential malefactor, the fear of punishment carried more weight than did the sacrifice involved in refraining from the offense. The use of punishment in individual cases could be justified only because punishment was necessary to render the threat effective. The earlier writers were concerned mainly with the purely deterrent effects of punishment, while the moral effect of punishment has been subjected to detailed analysis in more recent theories, especially in Germany and in the Scandinavian countries.

Notions of general prevention also have played a major part in *legislative actions*. This was especially apparent a hundred or a hundred and fifty years ago when the classical school was dominant. The Bavarian Penal Code of 1813, copied by many countries, was authored by Feuerbach and fashioned on his ideas. In more recent years, there has been an increasing tendency to emphasize special prevention. The judge now has greater discretion in deciding the length of sentences and he has at his disposal several alternatives to the classical prison sentence. But these changes have not altered the basic character of the system. Unlike mental health acts, penal laws are not designed as prescriptions for people who are in need of treatment because of personality troubles. While there are some exceptions, such as sexual psychopath acts and provisions in penal laws about specific measures to be used when dealing with mentally abnormal people or other special groups of delinquents, penal laws are primarily fashioned to *establish and defend social norms*. As a legislature tries to decide whether to extend or to restrict the area of punishable offenses, or to increase or mitigate the penalty, the focus of attention usually is on the ability of penal laws to modify patterns of behavior. This is the basic question in current debates about the legal treatment of homosexuality, abortion, public prostitution and drunken driving. From the point of view of sheer logic one must say that general prevention—*i.e.*, assurance that a minimum number of crimes will be committed—must have priority over special prevention—*i.e.,* impeding a particular criminal from future offenses. If general prevention were one hundred percent effective, there would obviously be no need for the imposition of penalties in individual cases.

Ideas about general prevention also have had great effects on the *sentencing policies of courts.* Sometimes this becomes manifest in a dramatic way. In September, 1958, international attention was aroused when the criminal court of Old Bailey sentenced nine young boys, six of them only seventeen years old, to four years of imprisonment for having taken part in race riots involving the use of force against colored people in the Notting Hill district in London. The sentences were considerably heavier than previous sentences in similar cases, and they were meant to be and were regarded as a strong warning to others. Another example occurred in 1945 when the Norwegian Supreme Court sentenced Quisling to death. The first voting judge expressed ideas of general prevention in the following words:

> In a country's hour of fate chaos must not be allowed to reign. And facing the present and the future it must be made clear that a man who, in a critical time in the nation's history, substitutes his own will for the will of constitutional institutions and consequently betrays his country, for him his country has no room.

Ordinarily, there is less drama in the sentencing activities of the courts. The individual decision generally remains within the established tradition of sentencing. But there is no doubt that considerations of general prevention have been important in establishing these patterns. In Norway, the Supreme Court is the court of last resort in matters of sentencing, and it gives reasons for its decisions. General prevention is frequently mentioned. For example, the Supreme Court has established the principle that for reasons of general prevention suspended sentences are not ordinarily imposed in cases involving the use of motor vehicles while in a state of intoxication or in cases involving the use of force against the police.

• • •

III. Some Erroneous Inferences About General Prevention

Certain untenable contentions are frequently introduced in various forms into discussions of general prevention, and it might be helpful to clear them away. . . .

• • •

*(1) "Our knowledge of criminals shows us that the
criminal law has no deterrent effects."*

The fallacy of this argument is obvious. If a man commits a crime, we
can only conclude that general prevention has not worked *in his case.*
If I interview a thousand prisoners, I collect information about a
thousand men in whose cases general prevention has failed. But I cannot
infer from this data that general prevention is ineffective in the cases of
all those who have *not* committed crimes. General prevention is more
concerned with the psychology of those obedient to the law than with the
psychology of criminals.

*(2) "The belief in general prevention rests on an untenable
rationalistic theory of behavior."*

It is true that the extreme theories of general prevention worked out
by people like Bentham and Feuerbach were based on a shallow psychological model in which the actions of men were regarded as the outcome of a rational choice whereby gains and losses were weighed against
each other. Similar simplified theories are sometimes expressed by police
officials and by authors of letters to newspaper editors asking for heavier
penalties. But if we discard such theories, it does not follow that we have
to discard the idea of general prevention. Just as fear enters the picture
when people take a calculated risk in committing an offense, fear may
also be an element in behavior which is not rationally motivated. As
mentioned earlier, modern theories of general prevention take into account both deterrence and moral influence, and they concede that the
effects involved may be "unconscious and emotional, drawing upon deep
rooted fears and aspirations." This does not mean that one's general
theory of motivation is of no consequence in assessing the effect of general prevention. The criminologist who believes that a great many people
walk about carrying an urge for punishment which may be satisfied by
committing crimes is likely to be more skeptical about the value of penal
threats than is another who believes that these cases are rare exceptions.
Similarly, a man who views human nature optimistically, is less inclined
to advocate repressive measures than a person who believes that man is
ruthless and egoistic by nature and kept in line only by means of fear.

*(3) "Legal history shows that general prevention has
always been overestimated."*

It is true that in the course of history there have been contentions
about general prevention which seem fantastic today. There was a time
when distinguished members of the House of Lords rose to warn their

countrymen that the security of property would be seriously endangered if the administration of justice were weakened by abolition of capital punishment for shoplifting of items having a value of five shillings. Even today, one might find people with exaggerated conceptions of what can be accomplished by means of strong threats of punishment. But the fact that the general preventive effects of punishment might have been exaggerated does not disprove the existence of such effects.

(4) "Because people generally refrain from crimes on moral grounds, threats of penalty have little influence."

The premise contains a large measure of truth, but it does not justify the conclusion. Three comments are necessary. (a) Even if people on the whole do not require the criminal law to keep them from committing more serious offenses, this is not true for offenses which are subject to little or no moral reprobation. (b) Even though moral inhibitions today are adequate enough to prevent the bulk of the population from committing serious crimes, it is a debatable question whether this would continue for long if the hazards of punishment were removed or drastically minimized. It is conceivable that only a small number of people would fall victim to temptation when the penalties were first abolished or greatly reduced, but that with the passage of time, crime would attract the weaker souls who had become demoralized by seeing offenses committed with impunity. The effects might gradually spread through the population in a chain reaction. (c) Even though it be conceded that law abiding conduct in certain areas predominantly depends upon nonlegal conditions, this does not mean that the effects of the legal machinery are not extremely valuable from a community point of view. Let us imagine a fictitious city which has a million adult male inhabitants who commit a hundred rapes annually. Suppose, then, that abolishing the crime of rape led to an increase in the number of rape cases to one thousand. From a social psychological point of view one might conclude that the legal measures were quite insignificant: 999,000 males do not commit rape even when the threat of penalty is absent. If observed from the view point of the legal machinery, however, the conclusion is entirely different. A catastrophic increase of serious cases of violence has occurred. In other words, the increase in rape has demonstrated the tremendous social importance of general prevention.

(5) "To believe in general prevention is to accept brutal penalties."

This reasoning is apparent in Zilboorg's statement that "if it is true that the punishment of the criminal must have a deterrent effect, then

the abolition of the drawing and quartering of criminals was both a
logical and penological mistake. Why make punishment milder and thus
diminish the deterrent effect of punishment?"

Here we find a mixture of empirical and ethical issues. It was never a
principle of criminal justice that crime should be prevented at all costs.
Ethical and social considerations will always determine which measures
are considered "proper." As Ball has expressed it: "[A] penalty may be
quite effective as a deterrent, yet undesirable." Even if it were possible to
prove that cutting off thieves' hands would effectively prevent theft,
proposals for such practice would scarcely win many adherents today.

• • •

——————————————— 4 ———————————————

Does Punishment Deter Crime?

William J. Chambliss

• • •

In the last analysis a legal system must be judged according to the impact
it has on the social order. If that impact is largely deleterious to the lives
of men, then maintaining the legal system can scarcely be justified. If, on
the other hand, the law contributes in some important ways to the goals
of society and its members, then there is justification for keeping it. And,
of course, if the legal system is useful in certain ways but deleterious in
others, then this condition cries out for changes to increase its effectiveness while maintaining those aspects found to have desirable consequences.

Not all of the presumed consequences of the law are equally amenable
to empirical verification. For example, the idea that if a person commits
a criminal act the state must punish him because this is the only way to
restore the balance of nature to its proper order is not amenable to sys-

From William J. Chambliss, "Types of Deviance and the Effectiveness of Legal
Sanctions," *Wisconsin Law Review* (1967): 703–708, 710–713. Reprinted by permission.
Footnotes have been omitted.

tematic investigation. Such a position rests, ultimately, on the purely philosophical assumption that retribution for wrongdoings is intrinsically valuable.

Such vague and ill-defined assertions about the consequences of the law have in recent years been relegated to a much less important place than the more directly demonstrable question of whether or not the presence of laws and the imposition of punishment acts as a deterrent to crime. As Schwartz and Skolnick point out:

> Legal thinking has moved increasingly toward a sociologically meaningful view of the legal system. Sanctions, in particular, have come to be regarded in functional terms. In criminal law, for instance, sanctions are said to be designed to prevent recidivism by rehabilitating, restraining or executing the offender. They are also said to be intended to deter others from the performance of similar acts and, sometimes, to provide a channel for the expression of retaliatory motives.

The social sciences have been concerned principally with the question of deterrence, for it is here that the impact of the legal system is most amenable to empirical and systematic evaluation.

I. The Deterrent Influence of Capital Punishment

The question of the deterrent influence of capital punishment has occupied the forefront in criminological research into deterrence for years. The preponderance of the evidence indicates that capital punishment does not act as a deterrent to murder. This general conclusion is based on a number of observations and researches that have demonstrated:

1. that murder rates have remained constant despite trends away from the use of capital punishment;
2. that within the United States where one state has abolished capital punishment and another has not, the murder rate is no higher in the abolition state than in the retention state; and
3. that apparently the possible consequences of the act of murder are not considered by the murderer at the time of the offense.

Some of the evidence substantiating these three conclusions is presented below.

There has been a very clear tendency throughout the Western World to eliminate capital punishment. In the United States this trend away from capital punishment has taken several forms. To begin with, there has been a rapid decline in the number of states where capital punishment is mandatory if an accused is found guilty; in 1924 the death penalty was mandatory in eight states, but by 1964 it was not mandatory in any. There has also been a tendency to impose the death sentence less and less frequently. Eighty percent of those persons sentenced to death in 1933–1934 were ultimately executed; the figure was 81 percent in 1940–1945. But from 1960 to 1964 only 34 percent of the persons sentenced to death have been executed.

There has also been a steady increase in the number of states that have abolished capital punishment for various crimes. In 1920 only six states had abolished capital punishment; by 1957 the number of such states had risen to eight; and by 1965, 13 states had formally abolished capital punishment. Perhaps even more significant is the rapid decline in the number of persons actually executed. In 1951 there were 105 executions in the United States. The number of executions has steadily and precipitously declined since that time, with 15 executions in 1964, 7 in 1965, and only 1 in 1966.

Thus we see in the United States a steady and rapid alteration in the propensity to administer capital punishment. From the standpoint of deterrence, the significance of this trend is that during this same period we find *no significant change* in the murder rate (see Table 1). It would seem that if the presence of capital punishment either in principle or in fact, were a deterrent to murder, then the murder rate should have gone up as both the potential and the actual use of capital punishment declined.

TABLE 1. Comparison of Prisoners Executed Under Civil Authority and Murder Rate, 1951–1966

YEAR	NUMBER OF PERSONS EXECUTED	MURDER RATE (PER 100,000 POPULATION)
1951	105	4.8
1952	83	5.0
1953	62	4.8
1954	81	4.8
1955	76	4.8
1956	65	4.9
1957	65	4.9
1958	49	4.7
1959	49	4.8
1960	56	5.1
1961	42	4.7
1962	47	4.5
1963	21	4.5
1964	15	4.8
1965	7	5.1
1966	1	5.6

A similar conclusion emerges when the murder rates of states that have retained the death penalty are compared with the murder rates of states that have abolished it. This general conclusion also holds true when one compares contiguous states—states that presumably are relatively homogeneous culturally, but where one state has retained the death penalty and the other has not (see Table 2).

The states that have *abolished* the death penalty do not show a substantially higher murder rate when compared with states that have retained it. In four of the five pairs of states included in the table, the abolition state has a lower murder rate. In one pair the abolition state has a higher rate. The differences are slight in every instance, and the only safe conclusion possible from this data is that there is no greater propensity to murder when capital punishment is not a possibility than when it is. The point is not that abolishing capital punishment decreases the murder rate; rather, since the murder rate does not increase, one must conclude that capital punishment is not an effective deterrent.

The same conclusion is also suggested by a study of the murder rate in Philadelphia immediately preceding and following particularly well-publicized executions. If executing someone for a capital crime is a deterrent, one would expect its influence to be at a peak when an execution was imminent or had just occurred. But Savitz found no difference in the murder rate immediately prior to and following such executions.

Some of these studies rest on the analysis of data that have serious limitations, and none of the data are as perfect as one would like. However, given the preponderance of evidence, it seems safe to conclude that capital punishment does not act as an effective deterrent to murder. This conclusion about capital punishment does not apply to punishment

TABLE 2.   Annual Average Murder Rates in Selected Contiguous States

	MURDER RATE 1959–1964
Rhode Island [a]	1.1
Connecticut [b]	1.5
Wisconsin [a]	1.3
Illinois [b]	5.1
Minnesota [a]	1.1
Iowa [b]	1.2
Wisconsin [a]	1.3
Iowa [b]	1.2
Michigan [a]	3.4
Indiana [b]	3.5

[a] abolition states
[b] death penalty states

generally since, as is well recognized, murder and other capital offenses are usually shrouded with a great deal of emotional involvement on the part of the offender. Thus, one might well expect punishment to be less effective precisely because such offenses are less dictated by "rational" considerations of gain or loss. Therefore, one must look at what the evidence indicates about different types of offenses.

II. Drug Addiction and the Law

There is a saying among drug addicts that "once the monkey's on your back, you never shake him off." The empirical research on drug addiction strongly supports this contention. In a study of 800 addicts who were followed after treatment, it was found that 81.6 percent of them had relapsed within the first year, 93.9 percent within three years and 96.7 percent within five years. The federally run hospitals at Lexington and Fort Worth report similar recidivism rates among persons treated at these hospitals. The President's Commission on Law Enforcement and Administration of Justice has also concluded that there is a high relapse rate.

Even among persons who are presumably the most likely to be rehabilitated through treatment, the recidivism rate is exceedingly high. Synanon, an organization for the treatment of drug addicts in Los Angeles, accepts only those addicts who volunteer for treatment. In addition to volunteering, the addicts must agree to undergo rather severe "hazing" policies in order to demonstrate the sincerity of their desire to abstain from drug use. Given these conditions, it is reasonable to presume that Synanon treats only those persons whose desire to "kick the habit" is very strong. But even with these persons, the proportion who fail to complete the treatment program is in excess of 70 percent of all those who initially apply.

For the question of the deterrent influence of punishment, the significance of these statistics comes from the realization that concomitant with this propensity to recidivate has been the constantly increasing effort of the federal government to punish drug users severely. The Bureau of Narcotics has increased its efforts at control, and the formal sanctions have drastically increased in severity. Under certain federal statutes, an offender can be sentenced to prison for six years with no possibility of parole, thus making drug use one of the most severely punished crimes in the United States.

This evidence, then, suggests that drug addiction, like murder, is relatively unaffected by the threat or the imposition of punishment. But one may still raise the question of whether it is justifiable to generalize these findings to all types of offenses. Indeed, at least in one respect, drug addiction and murder share in common something that is lacking in many other types of offenses. Both of these acts are "expressive"—the act is committed because it is pleasurable in and of itself and not because it is a route to some other goal.

• • •

III. The Snitch and Booster

Cameron's study of shoplifting throws still more light on the impact of punishment as a deterrent. Cameron points out that there are two types of shoplifters: the "Snitch" and the "Booster." The Booster is a professional thief whose principal form of theft is shoplifting. The Snitch (or pilferer), in contrast, is generally a respectable citizen (usually a middle-class housewife) who shoplifts in order to obtain goods she could not otherwise afford. Cameron was able to check on the recidivism of persons apprehended by careful examination of department store files. Once a person is apprehended by a store detective, a card is filed with her picture; every store in the city has access to this file. Thus it is quite likely that any previous arrest will be known. Cameron found that persons who were professional thieves invariably had prior arrest records in the stores' files but that the Snitches almost never did. For the Snitches, one arrest was almost always sufficient to insure that she would never be arrested again. It is possible, but quite unlikely, that the Snitch simply became more careful after having been arrested once. It is more likely that she was in fact deterred from further shoplifting by the experience.

Among pilferers who are apprehended and interrogated by the store police but set free without formal charge, there is *very little or no recidivism*. . . .

[O]nce arrested, interrogated, and in their own perspective, perhaps humiliated, pilferers apparently stop pilfering. The rate of recidivism is amazingly low. The reward of shoplifting, whatever it is, is not worth the cost to reputation and self-esteem. . . . One woman was observed who, thoroughly shaken as the realization of her predicament began to appear to her, interrupted her protestations of innocence from time to time, over-whelmed at the thought of how some particular person in her "in-group" would react to her arrest. Her conversation with the interrogator ran somewhat as follows: "I didn't intend to take the dress. I just wanted to see it in the daylght. [She had stuffed it into a shopping bag and carried it out of the store.] Oh, what will my husband do? I *did* intend to pay for it. It's all a mistake. Oh, my God, what will my mother say! I'll be glad to pay for it. See, I've got the money with me. Oh, my children! They can't find out I've been *arrested!* I'd never be able tc face them again! . . ."

The contrast in behavior between the pilferer and the recognized and self-admitted thief is striking. The experienced thief either already knows what to do or knows precisely where and how to find out. His emotional reactions may involve anger directed at himself or at features in the situation around him, but he is not at a loss for reactions. He follows the prescribed modes of behavior, and knows, either because of prior experience or through the vicarious experiences of acquaintances, what arrest involves by way of obligations and rights. He has some familiarity with bonding practice and either already has or knows how to find a lawyer who will act for him.

These findings suggest that the amateur shoplifter, or the Snitch, will be deterred from further criminality by the imposition of punishment, while the professional thief will be little affected by it.

The Cameron findings on professional thieves are also corroborated by other investigations. Lemert's study of the systematic check forger suggests that receiving an occasional jail sentence is merely part of the life of being a professional thief; it is accepted as one of the "hazards of the business," just as other occupational groups accept certain characteristics of their work as inevitable hazards. That arrest and jail sentence do not interrupt the ongoing interpersonal relations of professional thieves is undoubtedly an important element in rendering the punishment relatively ineffective.

But this fatalistic acceptance of imprisonment as an inevitability should not be interpreted to mean that the professional thief is wholly unresponsive to the threat of punishment. On the contrary, a much greater proportion of a thief's energy is devoted to avoiding capture and imprisonment than is devoted to stealing. Although serving an occasional sentence apparently does not deter the professional thief from crime, it must be remembered that, for a reasonably competent and skillful thief, prison sentences occur relatively infrequently.

IV. A Typology of Crime and Deterrence

The preceding summary of research findings on the deterrent influence of punishment on various types of crimes suggests some interesting contrasts. First is the contrast between acts that are "expressive" and acts that are "instrumental." Murder as an expressive act is quite resistant to punishment as a deterrent, as is drug addition; instrumental acts, such as violating parking regulations and shoplifting by middle-class housewives, are more likely to be influenced by the threat or imposition of punishment.

The other major distinction suggested by the research is between persons who are highly committed to crime as a way of life and persons whose commitment is low. Cameron talks about this distinction in contrasting the Booster and the Snitch. She argues that this distinction is essentially a difference in the group support for their transgressions perceived by these different categories of offenders. More generally, one could say that persons with a high commitment perceive group support, conceive of themselves as criminal, and pattern their way of life around their involvement in criminality. Persons with low commitment would, of course, exhibit the reverse of these characteristics.

By combining these two dimensions of criminality and offender, it is possible to construct a typology of criminal acts with clear implications for the likelihood that a combination of offender and offense will respond to punishment by reducing their involvement in crime. The hypothesis is that where a high commitment to crime as a way of life is combined with involvement in an act that is expressive, one finds the greatest resistance to deterrence through threat of punishment. At the other extreme are acts where commitment to crime is low and where the act is instrumental (such as the Snitch, the white-collar criminal, or the parking law violator). Here we would expect both general and specific deterrence to be maximally effective (see Table 3).

While we can assert with some confidence that the remaining two types—high commitment-instrumental and low commitment-expressive—will fall between the two polar types, it is somewhat more difficult to know which of these types will be more responsive to punishment. It seems likely, however, that the impulsive nature of expressive acts, even when commitment to crime is low, will make such acts less amenable to punishment than instrumental acts, even though commitment is high.

TABLE 3. Types of Deviance

		TYPE OF ACT	
		Instrumental	*Expressive*
Degree of Commitment to Crime as a Way of Life	*High*	Professional thief Booster Some check forgers Some murderers	Most drug addicts Some murderers Some sex offenders
	Low	Snitch Parking law violator White-collar criminal Some murderers	Most murderers Some drug addicts Most sex offenders

• • •

———————————————— 5 ————————————————

Watergate and The Limits of Civil Disobedience

Alexander M. Bickel

A definition of civil disobedience, applicable to our legal order, would be the following: Civil disobedience is the act of disobeying formally binding general law on grounds of moral or political principle without challenging the validity of the law; or the incidental disobedience of general law which is itself neither challenged as invalid nor disapproved of in the course of agitating for change in public policies, actions, or social conditions which are regarded as bad on grounds of moral or political principle—all in circumstances where the legal order makes no allowance for the disobedience. This last qualification has to be added because the First Amendment is construed as making some allowance for the sort of incidental disobedience referred to in the second half of the definition.

In purpose if not in effect, civil disobedience differs greatly from conscientious objection. The effect of the coincidence of multiple consciences objecting to a law and the effect of civil disobedience may be the same. But conscientious objection is a withdrawal. Civil disobedience is ineluctably an attempt to coerce the legal order, an exercise of power in the sense in which Burke defined it: "Liberty, when men act in bodies, is *power*." And it is not easy to make room for it, although I shall argue that our legal order does so. Thus not only the Hobbesian but the contractarian view of the nature and foundation of society can tolerate no civil disobedience at all. The contractarian view legitimates government as a compact among citizens, embodying the agreement of each to abide the judgment of all. The ends of government are substantially predetermined in the contractarian view, in that they are limited by timeless principles, the rights of man. Government is allowed some margin of error, but the premise is that it will normally act only in plausible pursuit of predetermined ends. If it should not, says Locke, the remedy is revolution, and there is a right to use force against the government. Short of the right of revolution, there is an absolute duty to obey. Rousseau held that the people, expressing themselves through universal suffrage, give voice to the general will, although he allowed that they might also not. The general will is the highest good, and when the people by majority vote give it voice, the individual owes absolute obedience, even unto death. If at times a minority has hold of the true general will it follows that absolute obedience is equally owed to it. This in fact, said Rousseau, only forces the individual to be free.

• • •

But there must be limits, both to conscientious objection and to civil disobedience, limits to be stated not as positive law imposed by the enforcement machinery of the legal order, but as a moral obligation, a duty to obey. For use of the enforcement machinery of the legal order denotes the point at which it has broken down. The test of a legal order is its self-executing capacity, its moral authority. In an extraordinarily sustained experience of civil disobedience and conscientious objection on the part of at least three distinct, sizable groups in the society over a period of some fifteen years, which perhaps no other society could have endured without a change of regime—in this sustained experience, I shall suggest, the limits were often transgressed. The experience started with white Southerners in the mid-50's; it was followed and overlapped by the civil-rights movement; and it ended with and was overlapped by the white-middle-class movement against the war, which bade fair for a while to take permanent shape as a movement addressing numerous other issues as well, from ecology up, down, and sideways to gay liberation. The limits, as I say, were transgressed, and in some measure, I am willing to suggest, Watergate is a replica of the transgressions.

A first and most easily stated limit was very clear to Lincoln when he opposed the *Dred Scott* decision. "We do not propose," he said, "that when Dred Scott has been decided to be a slave by the court, we as a mob will decide him to be free. . . . but we nevertheless do oppose that decision as a political rule which shall be binding. . . ." The line is thus drawn between the general law, the law of the land, as it is commonly called, enunciated in a judicial decision, or *mutatis mutandis* in legislation, and the judicial judgment addressed to the parties in an actual case. There is no moral duty always and invariably to obey the former. There is a moral duty to obey the latter.

This limit was transgressed repeatedly in the South during the 50's and 60's, by private and official persons, and by mobs who disobeyed or violated judicial decrees. It was transgressed as well by disruptive courtroom behavior on the part of the radical Left in the late 60's, which amounted to the same thing, denoting as it did a rejection of the process and necessarily, therefore, of its results. Both kinds of transgression were perhaps more spectacular than numerous, but they told.

Another sort of limit has to do with means. Violence must be a monopoly of the state. In private hands, whatever its possible misuses by the state, it is always an unjust weapon. It is inadmissible, but was of course widely used and excused. Only the other day the historian Gabriel Kolko said of the man who planted a bomb in 1970 at the University of Wisconsin's Mathematics Research Center, which killed one person and wounded four: "To condemn Karl Armstrong is to condemn a whole anguished generation. His intentions are more significant than the unanticipated consequences of his actions."

Some nonviolent interference with the justified and lawful activities and expectations of innocent third parties is an inevitable concomitant of civil disobedience, and if contained and civil, is to be borne, subject to other limits to which I shall come in a moment. But when the interference is massive, when it is not civil, when it borders on violence or threatens it, when it is coercive not in its ultimate intent, as all civil disobedience necessarily is, but in its immediate impact, when its imposition is not of inconvenience but of terror, then it is unacceptable. And yet we saw quantities of it.

• • •

Returning to civil disobedience, let me restate, in approaching yet another limit, the grounds on which the legitimacy of civil disobedience can be rested. It is because on most issues we command no definite answers grounded in solid and generally shared values that we value an open, responsive, varied, and continual process of law-formation and provide numerous stages of decision-making, most of them provisional, and numerous opportunities for revision and resistance, including civil disobedience. But not only do the outcomes of the law-formation process, however provisional, count for something; what is more important, in the middle distance, and if also provisionally then over a much longer term, so that for a time they have a relatively enduring aspect, we do as a legal order hold some values, some principles, by which we judge the process and even some of its outcomes. Unless these are defended against coercive political action, there is no legal order, or at any rate, there is not this one. Therefore, the use of civil disobedience, not to redress grievances on the assumption of the continued operation of the system and by plausible appeal to its own principles, but against it, ought not be tolerated. Civil disobedience is one thing, revolutionary activity quite another, and the difference between them is told not only by their manner, but also by their objectives.

• • •

Still another necessary limit of civil disobedience was transgressed. Like law itself, civil disobedience is habit-forming, and the habit it forms is destructive of the legal order. Disobedience, even if legitimate in every other way, must not be allowed to become epidemic. Individuals are under a duty to ration themselves, to assess occasions in terms of their relative as well as absolute importance. For disobedience is attended by the overhanging threat of anarchy. We did not ration ourselves, and those in authority in the universities in the late 60's imposed no rationing. Coming as the third wave of massive disobedience movements in fifteen years, the demonstrations of the late 60's, including the most peaceable and legitimate ones of all, carried the clear and present danger of anarchy. And their objectives were of course not restricted to stopping the war. They went on to ecology and to numberless other social and economic objectives.

~ The point may be put in another and more general way with reference not only to civil disobedience. In 1969, President Kingman Brewster of Yale charged a number of speakers about to appear at a Yale alumni seminar with addressing the subject, "What is happening to morality today?" My answer at the time, if I may quote myself, was: "It threatens to engulf us." The legal order heaved and groaned for years under a prodigality of moral causes, and if not broken, it is no wonder that it is badly bent. Vietnam, let us not forget, was not only a moral error, but for its authors, a moral urgency. The urgencies of "peace with honor," of the clean life, of patriotism—in a word, Watergate—were merely the last straws. It is ironic, but entirely natural, that "law-and-order" as a moral imperative should have clashed with the legal order.

The legal order, after all, is an accommodation. It cannot sustain the continuous assault of moral imperatives, not even the moral imperative of "law-and-order," which as a moral imperative has only a verbal resemblance to the ends of the legal order. No legal order can sustain such a bombardment, and the less so a federal constitutional order of separated and diffused powers. It is the premise of our legal order that its own complicated arangements, although subject to evolutionary change, are more important than any momentary objective. This premise must give way at times, of course, to accommodate inevitable change. And change which is significant, as Justice Brandeis once wrote, manifests itself more "in intellectual and moral conceptions than in material things." But our legal order cannot endure too rapid a pace of change in moral conceptions, and its fundamental premise is that its own stability is itself a high moral value, in most circumstances the highest. The legal order must be given time to absorb change, to accommodate it to itself as well as itself to it. If the pace is forced, there can be no law.

The assault upon the legal order by moral imperatives wasn't only or perhaps even the most effectively an assault from the outside. It came as well from within, in the Supreme Court headed for fifteen years by Earl Warren. The judicial hallmark of Chief Justice Warren was that when some lawyer would be standing before him arguing his side of a case on the basis of some legal doctrine or other, or making a procedural point, or contending that the Constitution allocated competence over a given issue to another branch of government than the Supreme Court or to the states rather than to the federal government, the Chief Justice would shake him off saying, "Yes, yes, yes, but is it [whatever the case exemplified about law or about the society] is it *right?* Is is *good?*" More than once, and in some of its most important actions, the Warren Court got over doctrinal difficulties or issues of the allocation of competences among various institutions by asking what it viewed as a decisive practical question: If the Court did not take a certain action which was *right* and *good,* would other institutions do so, given political realities? The Warren Court took the greatest pride in cutting through legal technicalities, in piercing through procedure to substance. But legal technicalities are the stuff of law, and piercing through a particular substance to get to procedures suitable to many substances is in fact what the task of law most often is.

From within and from without, then, the legal order was bombarded by moral imperatives, and was reduced to submission time and again. The derogators of procedure and of technicalities, and other anti-institutional forces, rode high, on the bench as well as off. These were the armies of conscience and of ideology. If it is paradoxical that they were also the armies of a new populism, it is not a paradox to wonder at, for it has occurred often before, not least of all in Rousseau, who may be counted the patron philosopher of the time. The paradox, of course, is that the people whom the populist exalts may well, will frequently, not vote for the results that conscience and ideology dictate. But then one can always hope, or identify the general will with the people despite their votes, and let the Supreme Court bespeak the people's general will when the vote comes out wrong.

It has been a time of populism to the Left and populism to the Right, strongly encouraged by the Supreme Court. There was a powerful strain of populism in the rhetoric by which the Court supported its one-man, one-vote doctrine, and after promulgating it the Court strove mightily to strike down all barriers, not only the poll tax, but duration of residence, all manner of special qualifications, and even in some measure, age, to the enlargement and true universalization of the franchise. In this the Court led successfully. It became irresistible dogma that no qualification for voting made any sense. It didn't matter that you were a transient—the election is a snapshot, and wherever it catches you, you vote with no questions asked. No connection to place is relevant, there is no room for balancing interests and places, no need to structure institutions so that they might rest on different electoral foundations and in the aggregate be better able to generate consent. Every impediment, every distortion, including the electoral college, must go. All that matters is the people, told by the head.

Here the connection with attitudes that at least contributed to Watergate is direct. It was utterly inevitable that such a populist fixation should tend toward the concentration of power in that single institution which has the most immediate link to the largest constituency. Naturally the consequence was a Gaullist Presidency, making war, making peace, spending, saving, being secret, being open, doing what is necessary, and needing no excuse for aggregating power to itself beside the excuse that it could do more effectively what other institutions, particularly Congress, did not do very rapidly or very well, or under particular political circumstances would not do at all. This was a leaf from the Warren Court's book, but the Presidency could undertake to act anti-institutionally in this fashion with more justification because, unlike the Court, it could claim not only a constituency, but the largest one. This Presidency acknowledged accountability only at quadrennial plebiscites, but not to other, less plebiscitary institutions, and certainly not to irresponsible private ones, or to something called "public opinion," which is led and formed in mysterious ways, rather than being told by the head.

The accumulation of power in the Presidency did not begin with Richard M. Nixon, of course, but it reached heights made possible by the populism of the day. There was a time there, soon after the election of 1972, when Mr. Nixon gave the impression that he thought the American political process had taken place, so to speak, that it was over for a while, and that he could simply rule. We know again now that an election is the beginning as well as the culmination of a political process, and that the President, separate, independent, and critically important as he is, is part of the process, not its ruler. We were being led to forget, however, and had it not been for Watergate, conceivably we might have forgotten.

● ● ●

Courts as Policy Makers

6

Social Policy and Judicial Capacity

Donald L. Horowitz

• • •

The Expansion of Judicial Responsibility

The last two decades have been a period of considerable expansion of judicial responsibility in the United States. Although the kinds of cases judges have long handled still occupy most of their time, the scope of judicial business has broadened. The result has been involvement of courts in decisions that would earlier have been thought unfit for adjudication. Judicial activity has extended to welfare administration, prison administration, and mental hospital administration, to education policy and employment policy, to road building and bridge building, to automotive safety standards, and to natural resource management.

In just the past few years, courts have struck down laws requiring a period of in-state residence as a condition of eligibility for welfare. They have invalidated presumptions of child support arising from the presence in the home of a "substitute father." Federal district courts have laid down elaborate standards for food handling, hospital operations, recreation facilities, inmate employment and education, sanitation, and laun-

---

dry, painting, lighting, plumbing, and renovation in some prisons; they have ordered other prisons closed. Courts have established equally comprehensive programs of care and treatment for the mentally ill confined in hospitals. They have ordered the equalization of school expenditures on teachers salaries, established hearing procedures for public school discipline cases, decided that bilingual education must be provided for Mexican-American children, and suspended the use by school boards of the National Teacher Examination and of comparable tests for school supervisors. They have eliminated a high school diploma as a requirement for a fireman's job. They have enjoined the construction of roads and bridges on environmental grounds and suspended performance requirements for automobile tires and air bags. They have told the Farmers Home Administration to restore a disaster loan program, the Forest Service to stop the clear-cutting of timber, and the Corps of Engineers to maintain the nation's non-navigable waterways. They have been, to put it mildly, very busy, laboring in unfamiliar territory.

What the judges have been doing is new in a special sense. Although no single feature of most of this litigation constitutes an abrupt departure, the aggregate of features distinguishes it sharply from the traditional exercise of the judicial function.

First of all, many wholly new areas of adjudication have been opened up. There was, for all practical purposes, no previous judge-made law of housing or welfare rights, for example. To some extent, the new areas of activity respond to invitations from Congress or, to a much lesser extent, from state legislatures. Sometimes these take the form of judicial review provisions written into new legislation. Sometimes they take the form of new legislation so broad, so vague, so indeterminate, as to pass the problem to the courts. They then have to deal with the inevitable litigation to determine the "intent of Congress," which, in such statutes, is of course nonexistent.

If some such developments result from legislative or even bureaucratic activity (interpretation of regulations, for example), then it is natural to see the expansion of judicial activity as a mere concomitant of the growth of the welfare state. As governmental activity in general expands, so will judicial activity.

But that is not all that is involved. Much judicial activity has occurred quite independent of Congress and the bureaucracy, and sometimes quite contrary to their announced policies. The very idea is sometimes to handle a problem unsatisfactorily resolved by another branch of government. In areas far from traditional development by case law, indeed in areas often covered densely by statutes and regulations, the courts have now seized the initiative in lawmaking. In such areas, the conventional formulation of the judicial role has it that courts are to "legislate" only interstitially. With the important exception of judicial decisions holding legislative or executive action unconstitutional, this convenional formulation of what used to be the judicial role is probably not far from what judges did in fact do. It is no longer an adequate formulation.

What the courts demand in such cases, by way of remedy, also tends to be different. Even building programs have been ordered by courts, and the character of some judicial decrees has made them, de facto, exercises of the appropriation power. A district court order rendered in Alabama had the effect of raising the state's annual expenditure on mental institutions from $14 million before suit was filed in 1971 to $58 million in 1973, a year after the decree was rendered. Decisions expanding welfare eligibility or ordering special education for disturbed, retarded, or hyperactive pupils have had similar budgetary effects. "For example, it is estimated that federal court decisions striking down various state restrictions on welfare payments, like residency requirements, made an additional 100,000 people eligible for assistance." It is no longer even approximately accurate to say that courts exercise only a veto. What is asked and what is awarded is often the doing of something, not just the stopping of something.

To be sure, courts have always had some say in the way public funds were spent. How else could they award damages against the government? But even in the aggregate, decisions ordering a municipality to pay for an injury sustained by someone who trips over a loose manhole cover are not generally important enough to influence the setting of public priorities. The recent decisions that require spending to achieve compliance with a newly articulated policy are something else again.

It is also true that both affirmative and negative relief (orders to do something and orders to stop doing something) have a long history in English equity jurisprudence. The hoary remedies of mandamus and specific performance both require affirmative action—but action of a very circumscribed, precise sort, the limits of which are known in advance of the decree. Mandamus traditionally lies to compel performance of an official duty of a clear and usually trivial sort; generally, compliance is measured by performance of one or two simple acts. Specific performance lies to compel compliance with certain kinds of contractual obligation, the exact nature of the obligation spelled out in the contract. But specific performance is not traditionally awarded to compel performance of a contract for personal services, one significant reason being that the courts would then find themselves deep in the management of a continuing relationship, perhaps a whole business enterprise.

Again, therefore, compelling the performance of certain affirmative acts is nothing new in principle, but it is new in degree. The decree of a federal district judge ordering mental hospitals to adhere to some eighty-four minimum standards of care and treatment represents an extreme in specificity, but it is representative of the trend toward demanding performance that cannot be measured in one or two simple acts but in a whole course of conduct, performance that tends to be open-ended in time and even in the identity of the parties to whom the performance will be owed. Remedies like these are reminiscent of the kinds of programs adopted by legislatures and executives. If they are to be translated into action, remedies of this kind often require the same kinds of supervision as other government programs do.

This leads to still another difference in degree between adjudication as it once was and as it now is. Litigation is now more explicitly problem-solving than grievance-answering. The individual litigant, though still necessary, has tended to fade a bit into the background. Courts sometimes take off from the individual cases before them to the more general problem the cases call up, and indeed they may assume—dubiously—that the litigants before them typify the problem.

Once again, of course, it is all too easy to fabricate an idealized judicial past that consigned judges merely to resolving individual disputes. It has not been that way. In articulating the law of negligence from one case to the next, judges have tried to lay down a standard of care calculated to reduce the incidence of personal injury and property damage without unduly raising the expense of doing so. Many other common-law rules could be described in similar terms, as much efforts to frame behavioral standards as to apply them. Some of the most formidable difficulties faced by common-law judges have arisen in cases that present the judges with an inescapable choice between doing justice in the individual case and doing justice in general.

For all that, however, the individual and his case remained indispensable. Courts paid particular attention to the interplay between the facts of the individual case and the facts of the class of cases they projected from it. Without the particular case, the task of framing standards was devoid of meaning. It is inconceivable, for example, that even a great, innovative common-law court like the New York Court of Appeals early in this century would have countenanced deciding a case that had become moot. That some issues might forever escape judicial scrutiny because of the doctrine that a moot case is not a case at all would have struck even bold judges of a few decades ago as entirely natural.

Today it is repellent to many judges. For the view has gained ground that the judicial power is, by and large, coterminous with the governmental power. One test of this is the withering of the mootness doctrine in the federal courts. The old prohibition on the decision of moot cases is now so riddled with exceptions that it is almost a matter of discretion whether to hear a moot case. The argument for deciding a case that has become moot is often the distinctly recent one that there is a public interest in the judicial resolution of important issues. In contrast, the earlier view was that there was a public interest in avoiding litigation. By the same token, dismissal for mootness has become a practice reserved for invocation when it is unimportant, inconvenient, or impolitic to decide the issues a case raises.

What this shift signifies is the increasing subordination of the individual case in judicial policymaking, as well as the expansion of judicial responsibility more nearly to overlap the responsibilities of other governmental institutions. The individual case and its peculiar facts have on occasion become mere vehicles for an exposition of more general policy problems. Consequently, somewhat less care can be devoted, by lawyers and judges alike, to the appropriateness of particular plaintiffs and to the details of their grievances.

At the same time, the courts have tended to move from the byways onto the highways of policymaking. Alexander M. Bickel has captured, albeit with hyperbole, the thrust of the new judicial ventures into social policy. "All too many federal judges," he has written, "have been induced to view themselves as holding roving commissions as problem solvers, and as charged with a duty to act when majoritarian institutions do not." The hyperbole is itself significant: many federal judges regard themselves as holding no such commission, yet even they have embarked on "problem-solving" ventures. This is the surest sign that the tendency is not idiosyncratic but systemic: it transcends, in some measure, individual judicial preference and calls for systematic explanation.

• • •

Legitimacy and Capacity

The appropriate scope of judicial power in the American system of government has periodically been debated, often intensely. For the most part, what has been challenged has been the power to declare legislative and executive action unconstitutional. Accordingly, the debate has been cast in terms of legitimacy. A polity accustomed to question unchecked power views with unease judicial authority to strike down laws enacted by democratically elected legislatures. Where, after all, is the accountability of life-tenured judges? This question of democratic theory has been raised insistently, especially in times of constitutional crisis, notably in the 1930s and again in the 1950s.

The last word has not been heard in these debates, and it will not soon be heard. The structure of American government guarantees the issue a long life. But, for the moment, the debate seems to have waned with the growing recognition that there are elements of overstatement in the case against judicial review. The courts are more democratically accountable, through a variety of formal and informal mechanisms, than they have been accused of being. Equally important, the other branches are in many ways less democratically accountable than they in turn were said to be by those who emphasized the special disabilities under which judges labor. Hence the many academic discussions of the need for "representative bureaucracy," for a less insular presidency, and for reform of the procedures and devices that make Congress undemocratic internally and unrepresentative externally. (That students of any single institution often tend to see that institution as the flawed one is a useful indication of the limited perspective that comes from singleminded attention to any one institution. It should properly make us chary of drawing inferences about the courts without an institutionally comparative frame of reference.)

As the debate over the democratic character of judicial review wanes, there is another set of issues in the offing. It relates not to legitimacy but to capacity, not to whether the courts *should* perform certain tasks but to whether they *can* perform them competently.

Of course, legitimacy and capacity are related. A court wholly without capacity may forfeit its claim to legitimacy. A court wholly without legitimacy will soon suffer from diminished capacity. The cases for and against judicial review have always rested in part on assessments of judicial capacity: on the one hand, the presumably superior ability of the courts "to build up a body of coherent and intelligible constitutional principle"; on the other, the presumably inferior ability of courts to make the political judgments on which exercises of the power of judicial review so often turn. If the separation of powers reflects a division of labor according to expertise, then relative institutional capacity becomes relevant to defining spheres of power and particular exercises of power.

The recent developments that I have described necessarily raise the previously subsidiary issue of capacity to a more prominent place. Although the assumption of new responsibilities can, as I have observed, be traced to exercises of the traditional power to declare laws unconstitutional, they now transcend that power. Traditional judicial review meant forbidding action, saying "no" to the other branches. Now the judicial function often means requiring action, and there is a difference between foreclosing an alternative and choosing one, between constraining and commanding. Among other things, it is this difference, and the problematic character of judicial resources to manage the task of commanding, that make the question of capacity so important.

Amendment from the Judgment Seat

Before proceeding any further, let me try to recapitulate what I have said so far and where it seems to me to lead. I have argued that judicial intervention in matters of social policy has greatly increased and will not soon decrease. This expansion of judicial responsibility means, first, a broadening of the sphere of judge-made law, into areas that might once have been called "social welfare" and were not considered "legal" at all. It also means an expansion of the scope for judicial initiative within these areas. Courts are no longer as confined to the interstices of legislation as they once were—now the statute is often a mere point of departure—and they are no longer as inhibited as they once were from delving into supervisory or administrative responsibilities in connection with the remedies they award. They are more often found requiring detailed, specific, and affirmative action than previously. They are less constrained, too, by the limitations of the cases and the litigants before them. More openly, self-consciously, and broadly than before, the courts are engaged in efforts to shape or control the behavior of identifiable social groups, groups not necessarily before the court: welfare administrators, employers, school officials, policemen. The expansion of the judicial sphere means there are more such groups whose behavior has become a subject of judicial attention.

This has not happened all at once, and the transition is anything but complete. Most courts, most of the time, are doing roughly what they did many years ago. Not a landslide but an erosion of some of the distinctive features of the judicial process is what seems to have been occurring.

What this means is that there is somewhat less institutional differentiation today than two decades ago. There is now more overlap between the courts and Congress in formulating policy and between the courts and the executive in both formulating and carrying out programs. That is, the types of decisions being made by the various institutions—their scope and level of generality—seem to be converging somewhat, though the processes by which the decisions are made and the outcomes of those processes may be quite different—as different as the groups who maneuver to place an issue before one set of decisionmakers rather than another, or who, defeated in one forum, turn hopefully to the next, believe them to be. Thus, to say that there is convergence in the business of courts and other institutions is not tantamount to saying that it makes no difference who decides a question. On the contrary, it matters a good deal, for the institutions are differently composed and organized. The real possibility of overlapping responsibilities but opposite outcomes makes the policy process a more complex and drawn-out affair than it once was.

The recency, the incompleteness, and the incremental history of these developments should not obscure their portentousness. It is just possible that these modifications in the scope of judicial power will one day amount to a major structural change. We regard as quaintly and unduly restrictive the medieval conception of legislation as mere restatement of customary law. Future generations may likewise view our distinctive association of adjudication with the grievances of individual litigants as an equally curious affectation.

It may be, of course, that something much less significant than this is in the offing. For the purposes of this discussion, it makes little difference. The changes of degree that are already visible are quite enough to raise important questions about the consequences of using the judicial process for the resolution of social policy issues.

If extensive judicial activity in matters of social policy is not a passing phenomenon, then Mansfield and Bentham have a new relevance for us. For we must confront Bentham's blunt assertion that "amendment from the judgment seat is confusion."

• • •

PART II

Participants in the Judicial Process

This part does not pretend to be an exhaustive coverage of all participants in the legal system. Instead, we focus on four types of decision makers: policemen, lawyers, juries, and judges. While these classifications by no means incorporate all those who contribute to judicial processes, they do delineate those who make the day-to-day decisions of greatest import for the judicial system. It may be noted that the materials dealing with judges in this section do not discuss Supreme Court justices since these justices are discussed in Part III.

The emphases of our selections vary with category of decision maker. But in each case the materials address problems of current interest to those who study these particular institutions. In the case of policemen and prosecutors, a major concern is the use of discretion. When to arrest, how to treat criminal suspects, and how vigorously to enforce particular laws are discretionary matters for the policeman on the street. Prosecutors, on the other hand, have even more discretionary power. They decide when to prosecute, when to dismiss a charge, what "deals" to make via plea bargaining, what sentences to recommend, and so on. It is important to com-

prehend the use of such discretionary powers in the judicial process if that process is to function in accord with our intentions.

The readings in Section Four indicate that the behavior of the policeman is influenced by his work environment, his sense of justice, and whether the expectations of the community are realistic or unrealistic. The point is made that an expectation of "full enforcement" of every law in every situation encourages surreptitious nonenforcement patterns of behavior. Section Four also includes excerpts from two major Supreme Court cases—Mapp v. Ohio (1961) and Miranda v. Arizona (1966). These cases placed specific limitations on the constitutionally permissible behavior of policmen in certain situations. Mapp tells us that if the policeman engages in an unreasonable search and seizure to secure criminal evidence in the field, he will not be able to employ such evidence for purposes of obtaining a criminal conviction; the case applied the well-known "exclusionary rule" to the states. Miranda, on the other hand, limits the discretion of policemen or other investigators who interrogate criminal suspects prior to trial.

Section Five examines the behavior of prosecutors. The readings in that section emphasize the necessity of granting wide discretionary authority to the prosecutorial office and of allowing prosecutors the leverage of plea bargaining to reduce the case load pressures on their offices. Bordenkircher v. Hayes underscores this point. In the reading by Friedman, we see how practice and theory diverge in the "real world" cases of Tokyo Rose and Spiro Agnew.

The material on lawyers in Section Six shifts focus from discretionary power to the multiplicity of roles that lawyers play in our society. The institutional linkages of private and public attorneys to the criminal justice system are spotligthed in interviews with prison inmates in Connecticut. The relationship between a lawyer's self-perceptions and client selection is noted. And the pressures that encourage the criminal lawyer to play the role of "confidence man" with his client are interestingly sketched by Blumberg. Finally, we are exposed to Chief Justice Burger's argument that a large number of trial advocates in the United States are unqualified if not grossly incompetent.

The two final sections in Part II deal with the selection of judges and the factors that influence decisions in litigated cases. The materials on selection focus primarily on the relatively new U.S. Circuit Judge Nominating Commissions. The implications of these new procedures are drawn and discussed. The impact of these proce-

dures on participants in the selection process is considered and the Carter emphasis on affirmative action in selecting federal judges is debated.

Lower court judges clearly exercise a high degree of discretion in decision making; the requirements of law and precedent are not always sufficiently restrictive to rule out discretionary decision making. The emphasis in this section is on the nonlegal factors that push the decisions of the judges in one direction or another. In that context, it is suggested that attitudes, role perceptions, social background, and situational variables of one kind or another impact on the decision-making process in both state and federal courts.

The American jury is considered at length in Section Nine. Here the emphasis is on the current debate over (1) whether to continue the use of the petit jury in the United States, and (2) if so, what modifications, if any, to make in the institution. Chief Justice Burger clearly believes that we should dispense with the jury in many instances and rely on a bench trial. If the jury is to be used, however, we must decide its overall size and the decision rule to be employed in reaching a verdict. The U.S. Supreme Court has said that a twelve-member jury is not required by the Sixth Amendment to the Constitution and that neither a 10–2 nor a 9–3 verdict violates a defendant's constitutional rights. But in 1978 and 1979, the Court held further that the minimum size required for a petit jury in a state criminal trial is six and that when that minimum size is used, the verdict must be unanimous. Whether these and other numbers "make a difference" is a question that continues to attract debate, as is the source of the numbers the Supreme Court has been selecting in deciding jury cases. Finally, Section Nine includes an excerpt on one additional controversial matter—the so-called "scientific jury selection" procedures used so successfully in some recent notorious cases. Scientific jury selection relies on demographic and psychological profiles of prospective jurors. A number of questions raised by such procedures is addressed by Saks in the paper from which our exccerpt is taken. In the material included in this reading, Saks effectively makes the point that such procedures have not been proved to be the cause of the successes noted.

Policemen

7

Police Behavior: Gradations in Law Enforcement

Joseph Goldstein

• • •

I

The police have a duty not to enforce the substantive law of crimes unless invocation of the process can be achieved within bounds set by constitution, statute, court decision, and possibly official pronouncements of the prosecutor. *Total enforcement,* were it possible, is thus precluded, by generally applicable due-process restrictions on such police procedures as arrest, search, seizure, and interrogation. *Total enforcement* is further precluded by such specific procedural restrictions as prohibitions on invoking an adultery statute unless the spouse of one of the parties complains, or an unlawful-possession-of-firearms statute if the offender surrenders his dangerous weapons during a statutory period of amnesty. Such restrictions of general and specific application mark the bounds, often ambiguously, of an area of *full enforcement* in which the police are not only authorized but expected to enforce fully the law of crimes. An

From Joseph Goldstein, "Police Discretion Not to Invoke the Criminal Process: Low Visibility Decisions in the Administration of Justice," *The Yale Law Journal* 69 (March 1960): 554–562, 563, 586–588. Reprinted by permission of The Yale Law Journal Company and Fred B. Rothman & Company. Footnotes have been omitted.

area of *no enforcement* lies, therefore, between the perimeter of *total enforcement* and the outer limits of *full enforcement.* In this *no enforcement* area, the police have no authority to invoke the criminal process.

Within the area of *full enforcement,* the police have not been delegated discretion not to invoke the criminal process. On the contrary, those state statutes providing for municipal police departments which define the responsibility of police provide:

> It shall be the duty of the police . . . under the direction of the mayor and chief of police and in conformity with the ordinances of the city, and the laws of the state, . . . to pursue and arrest any persons fleeing from justice . . . to apprehend any and all persons in the act of committing any offense against the laws of the state . . . and to take the offender forthwith before the proper court or magistrate, to be dealt with for the offense; to make complaints to the proper officers and magistrates of any person known or believed by them to be guilty of the violation of the ordinances of the city or the penal laws of the state; and at all times diligently and faithfully to enforce all such laws. . . .

Even in jurisdictions without such a specific statutory definition, declarations of the *full enforcement* mandate generally appear in municipal charters, ordinances or police manuals. Police manuals, for example, commonly provide, in sections detailing the duties at each level of the police hierarchy, that the captain, superintendent, lieutenant, or patrolman shall be responsible, so far as is in his power, for the prevention and detection of crime and the enforcement of all criminal laws and ordinances. Illustrative of the spirit and policy of *full enforcement* is this protestation from the introduction to the Rules and Regulations of the Atlanta, Georgia, Police Department:

> Enforcement of all Criminal Laws and City Ordinances, is my obligation. There are no specialties under the Law. My eyes must be open to traffic problems and disorders, though I move on other assignments, to slinking vice in back streets and dives though I have been directed elsewhere, to the suspicious appearance of evil wherever it is encountered. . . . I must be impartial because the Law surrounds, protects and applies to all alike, rich and poor, low and high, black and white. . . .

Minimally, then, *full enforcement,* so far as the police are concerned, means (1) the investigation of every disturbing event which is reported to or observed by them and which they have reason to suspect may be a violation of the criminal law; (2) following a determination that some crime has been committed, an effort to discover its perpetrators; and (3) the presentation of all information collected by them to the prosecutor for his determination of the appropriateness of further invoking the criminal process.

Full enforcement, however, is not a realistic expectation. In addition

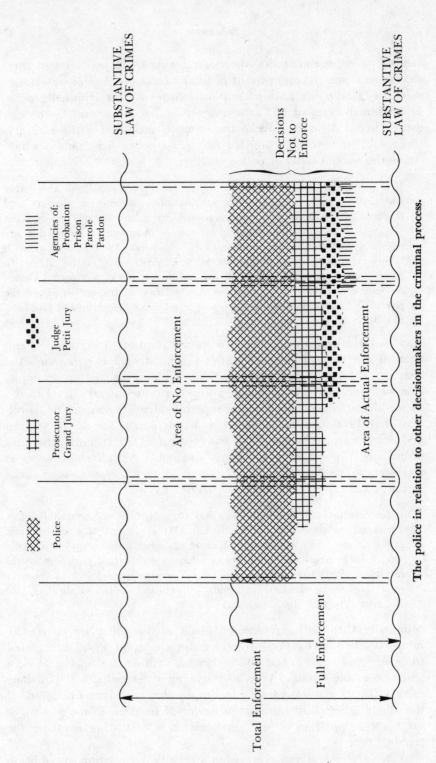

The police in relation to other decisionmakers in the criminal process.

to ambiguities in the definitions of both substantive offenses and due-process boundaries, countless limitations and pressures preclude the possibility of the police seeking or achieving *full enforcement.* Limitations of time, personnel, and investigative devices—all in part but not entirely functions of budget—force the development, by plan or default, of priorities of enforcement. Even if there were "enough police" adequately equipped and trained, pressures from within and without the department, which is after all a human institution, may force the police to invoke the criminal process selectively. By decisions not to invoke within the area of *full enforcement,* the police largely determine the outer limits of *actual enforcement* throughout the criminal process. This relationship of the police to the total administration of criminal justice can be seen in the diagram opposite this page. They may reinforce, or they may undermine, the legislature's objectives in designating certain conduct "criminal" and in authorizing the imposition of certain sanctions following conviction. A police decision to ignore a felonious assault "because the victim will not sign a complaint," usually precludes the prosecutor or grand jury from deciding whether to accuse, judge or jury from determining guilt or innocence, judge from imposing the most "appropriate" sentence, probation or correctional authorities from instituting the most "appropriate" restraint and rehabilitation programs, and finally parole or pardon authorities from determining the offender's readiness for release to the community.

• • •

II

The mandate of *full enforcement,* under circumstances which compel selective enforcement, has placed the municipal police in an intolerable position. As a result, nonenforcement programs have developed undercover, in a hit-or-miss fashion, and without regard to impact on the overall administration of justice or the basic objectives of the criminal law. Legislatures, therefore, ought to reconsider what discretion, if any, the police must or should have in invoking the criminal process, and what devices, if any, should be designed to increase visibility and hence reviewability of these police decisions.

The ultimate answer is that the police should not be delegated discretion not to invoke the criminal law. It is recognized, of course, that the exercise of discretion cannot be completely eliminated where human beings are involved. The frailties of human language and human perception will always admit of borderline cases (although none of the situations analyzed in this Article are "borderline"). But nonetheless, outside this margin of ambiguity, the police should operate in an atmosphere which exhorts and commands them to invoke impartially all criminal laws within the bounds of *full enforcement*. If a criminal law is ill-advised, poorly defined, or too costly to enforce, efforts by the police to achieve *full enforcement* should generate pressures for legislative action. Responsibility for the enactment, amendment, and repeal of the criminal laws will not, then, be abandoned to the whim of each police officer or department, but retained where it belongs in a democracy—with elected representatives.

Equating *actual enforcement* with *full enforcement,* however, would be neither workable nor humane nor humanly possible under present conditions in most, if not all, jurisdictions. Even if there were "enough police" (and there are not) to enforce all of the criminal laws, too many people have come to rely on the nonenforcement of too many "obsolete" laws to justify the embarrassment, discomfort, and misery which would follow implementation of *full enforcement* programs for every crime. *Full enforcement* is a program for the future, a program which could be initiated with the least hardship when the states, perhaps stimulated by the work of the American Law Institute, enact new criminal codes clearing the books of obsolete offenses.

• • •

8

Police Justice

Albert J. Reiss

• • •

Consider how a police officer typically handles a situation that may lead to an arrest. The officer invariably makes a judgment that some criminal statute has been violated, thereby satisfying the legal criterion of arrest on probable cause. But police officers in America do more than that, since there is a high probability an officer will not make an arrest when

From Albert J. Reiss, *The Public and the Police* (Yale University Press, 1971), pp. 134–135, 135–136, 137–140, 140–144. Copyright © 1971 by Yale University. Reprinted by permission. Footnotes have been omitted.

he satisfies probable cause. Our observations of citizen initiated encounters with the police, for example, show that officers decided not to make arrests of one or more suspects for 43 percent of all felonies and 52 percent of all misdemeanors judged by observers as situations where an arrest could have been made on probable cause. Something other than probable cause is required, then, for the officer to make an arrest.

For the police, that something else is a *moral belief* that the law should be enforced and the violation sanctioned by the criminal-justice system. The line officer usually reaches that decision by conducting an investigation to establish probable cause and by conducting a "trial" to determine who is guilty. His decision, therefore, is in an important sense judicial. This judicial determination will be influenced, as it is in the courts, by the deference and demeanor of the suspect, argument as to mitigating circumstances, complainant preferences for justice, and the willingness of the complainant to participate in seeing that it is done. All in all, an officer not only satisfies probable cause but also concludes after his careful evaluation that *the suspect is guilty and an arrest is therefore just.*

• • •

The experiences in the encounter create dilemmas for officers and set the stage for their conflict with other officials in the system of criminal justice. Given their investment in making a decision to arrest and a firm conviction that it is just, they believe that justice should be done by others as well. This belief in justice, of course, has been tempered by experience in the system and the full awareness that there is "bargain justice" played according to the lawyers' rules. Indeed the police often stereotype other participants in the system. Citizens "cop out"; defense lawyers have "clout"; the prosecutor "deals under the table"; judge X "throws the book." Indeed when an officer wants justice done, he may tailor his case accordingly. He may seek out a particular prosecutor or book for a particular court (if he has that option).

Sometimes an officer makes more than an ordinary investment in a case, and he becomes indignant when justice is not done. Several conditions give rise to high investment in seeing justice done. Moral indignation is one, particularly if it stems from the failure of an offender to grant deference to police authority. The officer, then, wants justice done to punish disrespectful demeanor toward *his* authority. Observation of police and citizen transactions show that an officer is more likely to arrest a juvenile or an adult offender when deference is withheld than when it is granted. Whether or not a complainant is present in citizen initiated encounters, the citizens who behave antagonistically toward the officer are more likely to be arrested than those who are civil or very deferential. Black reports that when complainants are present, 72 percent of the adults who behave antagonistically toward the police are arrested in the field while only 45 percent of those who are civil and 40 percent of those who are deferential toward the police are arrested. There is similar evidence that police arrest in response to antagonism from juveniles.

• • •

Patrol officers commonly regard juveniles as the most difficult class of citizens to police and the most leniently handled in the system of justice. Our survey interviews with officers in high-crime-rate precincts of Boston, Chicago, and Washington, D.C., disclose that 80 percent of all officers thought juveniles were harder to deal with now than formerly. This is almost double the percentage for dealing with "people in his precinct." The main ways in which officers perceived it to be harder to cope with juveniles were that they show less respect for law and authority (20 percent), they are more aggressive, defiant, and rebellious (24 percent), and they are more aware of restrictions on police conduct (22 percent). A considerable number of officers who policed in these areas also expressed negative judgments about the operating legal system; 54 percent of all officers, for example, regarded juvenile court judges as too lenient and only 16 percent thought the judges behaved in a fair or just manner. Similarly, 59 percent of all officers regarded municipal court judges as too lenient and only 26 percent saw them as on the whole fair or just. At times, officers in a police department may regard the juvenile court judges so negatively that an open attack on the court develops. During the spring of 1969, such an attack was waged by the police officers in Ypsilanti, Michigan, against the Washtenaw County Juvenile Court. The major complaint of the officers was that they could not control juveniles when the court continued to release them without formal sanctions. Regardless of their merit, such charges bring into the open the cleavage between the police and judges over issues of justice and the sanctioning of offenders.

The judgments of the police and of others in the legal system are intricately balanced in a commitment to justice. If, on the average, the officer's sense of justice is not confirmed, or if his moral commitments are not sustained by others, he loses his own moral commitment to the system. Where moral commitment is lost, subcultural practices take over. One such practice that exacerbates the relationship of the police with the public is harassment.

Police Harassment

Police resort to harassment under conditions where they are caught between their own, or others', expectations that they control unlawful conduct, while other levels of the system thwart such enforcement by failing to treat their arrests of citizens seriously. Actually, one can predict that harassment will become police policy or unofficial practice whenever citizen influence compels the police to make arrests that are systematically disregarded by others in the criminal-justice system. The harassment of juveniles, minorities, and even of those engaged in vice can be predicted, based on these factors.

It is altogether predictable that the police will harass citizens. In fact, it is a general strategy that citizens frequently use under similar conditions. For example, some citizens of Kew Gardens, Queens, New York, when disgruntled with what they regarded as failure to police homosexuals in a local park (a failure they attributed more to city control of the police than to the police as such) formed a vigilante committee to harass the homosexuals by "policing" the area with powerful flashlights and walkie-talkies. A Mr. Tashman reported to the *New York Times* that "when the homosexuals appeared, the men would surround them, shine the lights in their faces, and tell them to get out." As a final move, they cut down all shrubs and trees. Similarly, college students and civil rights workers found that harassment is an effective means of extralegal control, taking such forms as the sit-in, the mill-in, or disruption of ordered events by some other tactic.

The processing of cases in the system of criminal justice also frustrates officers and further encourages the creation of an officer culture of justice. Citizens and police, those who initiate inputs, characteristically assess the behavior of persons, while prosecutors and judges characteristically assess information to insure that justice is done. Paradoxically, those farthest removed from observing criminal behavior—the criminal court judges—make the final judgment about the behavior.

Often an officer views the judge's decision as justice subverted, because for him a case is not isolated. Rather it is a part of an order of behavior and events that he, the officer, is expected to control in a specified way. These seemingly different approaches in dealing with such matters encourage police subcultures to do their own justice, an extreme instance of which is illustrated by reports of police behavior in Brazil. There, it is reported, that the police have taken to murdering leaders in organized crime out of a conviction that the system of justice is unjust. A problem with any system of criminal justice, where the final decision rests outside the control of those who previously decided the matter, is to prevent their alienation.

Our system of criminal justice tends to alienate the police by accentuating status and prestige inequalities among officials in the system. By failing to show deference and by a condescending demeanor, lawyers, prosecutors, and judges often demean the status of the officer, by treating him as less professional. Furthermore, many officers become particularly sensitive when the bench fails to treat seriously a lack of deference to police authority while demanding total deference to judicial authority. Citizen behavior that the officer must tolerate, the judge will not. Many judges who regard contempt of police authority as part of the officer's job are quick to sanction defendants for far less serious infractions in court. Even more infuriating to the officer is how citizens change their behavior for the court from what it was when they made the arrest. The officer relives his experience with offenders and sees them as they were; the prosecutor or judge cannot.

Police subculture consists, then, in part, of developing standards of doing justice. Justice becomes necessary in the eyes of the police when deference is violated, when outcomes violate their sense of justice, when they are degraded in status, and when their efforts to control are subverted by other organizations in the subsystem.

• • •

Exemplary Police Conduct

The conduct of the police at work and as representatives of a moral order is as much at issue in our society as are the police standards for performing their official duties to arrest on probable cause and maintain order. The police, in short, are expected to fulfill the expectations of a "moral call" profession; they are expected to lead exemplary lives.

We shall deal only with their exemplary conduct while on duty, since little is known about their moral conduct when they are not on duty. The police are expected to violate no laws of moral or legal conduct while on duty. They also are expected to behave according to the department's code of "conduct becoming an officer" and to follow all rules and regulations. In considering an officer's conduct in upholding the law, it is clear that he often fails to arrest citizens for violations of the law. As previously noted, that lies within his sphere of discretion, since at law and by official policy he is permitted to exercise discretion in making an arrest. To be sure, he can be cited by the department for failure to exercise discretion properly or for lax enforcement, but the boundaries in these matters are far from clear.

An examination of the officer's conduct on duty must, therefore, be limited to considering his unlawful behavior and his failure to obey the department's rules and regulations. Unlawful conduct is of two kinds. The officer may use unlawful means in enforcing the law or he may engage in unlawful conduct by violating the laws that apply to all citizens. Infractions of department rules vary considerably in their seriousness. The more serious infractions are neglect of duty, drinking while on duty, and falsification of information, since these clearly affect the quality and performance of duty.

TABLE 3.1. Percentage Distributions of the Demeanor of Citizens and Conduct of Police Officers in 13,939 Citizen and Police Transactions

DEMEANOR OF CITIZEN TOWARD OFFICER	CONDUCT OF POLICE OFFICER TOWARD CITIZEN					
	Personal (2,133)*	Civil (10,092)	Demeaning (645)	Authoritarian (655)	Threatening, hostile, provocative (414)	TOTAL PERCENTAGE
PERCENTAGE BY DEMEANOR OF CITIZEN IN RESPONSE TO CONDUCT OF OFFICER						
Very deferential (1,647)*	26	64	4	3	3	100
Civil (11,143)	15	76	3	4	2	100
Antagonistic (1,149)	6	52	16	16	10	100
Total	15	72	5	5	3	100
PERCENTAGE BY CONDUCT OF OFFICER IN RESPONSE TO CITIZEN DEMEANOR						
Very deferential (1,647)	20	10	10	7	12	12
Civil (11,143)	77	84	61	65	61	80
Antagonistic (1,149)	3	6	29	28	27	8
Total	100	100	100	100	100	100

SOURCE: *Studies of Crime and Law Enforcement in Major Metropolitan Areas,* table 5.
* Figures in parentheses indicate number of transactions.

Unwarranted Use of Police Authority

The unwarranted use of authority toward citizens includes a variety of charges relative to the employment of illegal means such as the undue use of force and threats, harassment, uncivil treatment through abusive language and demeaning epithets, and the application of illegal means in investigation, e.g., illegal search and seizure of evidence.

Precise estimates of the extent to which the police engage in unwarranted conduct toward citizens are lacking. Available data come from three different methods of data collection: sample surveys of a cross-section of citizens, formal complaints to police authorities and boards or to civil review agencies, and observations of police and citizen transactions. A number of conclusions about the nature, extent, and causes of police misconduct toward citizens may be drawn from these studies.

The use of illegal means of investigation and of incivility toward citizens seems far more common than the misuse of force and threats in police contacts with citizens. Questioning of a sample of citizens in fifteen cities about police misconduct for the National Advisory Commission on Civil Disorders showed 22 percent of all Negroes and 6 percent of all whites reported they had been frisked or searched without good reason, and 20 percent of all Negroes and 9 percent of all whites said the police had been disrespectful or used insulting language. Smaller proportions, 7 percent of all Negroes and 2 percent of all whites, said they had been roughed up by the police at some time.

Evidence of a similar sort (table 3.1) is available from our observation of 13,939 citizens in 5,012 police and citizen transactions. Police officers openly ridiculed or belittled 5 percent of all citizens, and they were observed behaving in a brusque or authoritarian manner toward another 5 percent. Three percent of all citizens claimed the police behaved with threatening, hostile, or provocative conduct. Observers judged the use of force to be excessive for only about 3 in 1000 citizens in these encounters.

The rates from surveys based on citizen experiences are consistent with these data obtained from our own observations in showing that undue use of force is far less frequent than other forms of police misconduct toward citizens. Incivility toward citizens and illegal practices in law enforcement seem far [more] common. The high rates based on experiences seem reasonable if one simply assumes that over time police misconduct is directed toward different citizens.

9

Discretion and Occupational Environment
Jerome H. Skolnick

• • •

The across-the-board standards of the traffic warrant policeman—traceable to a relatively benign occupational environment—do not necessarily characterize all other policemen. Thus, the behavior of the policeman toward Blacks is likely to vary with his assignment within the department, always based on a foundation of strong racial bias. Hostility toward Blacks is apt to be revealed on the street, especially in situations inviting stereotyping. If police are looking for a robbery assailant, and have "nothing to go on" but a vague description of a Black male, innocent Black males will easily be assimilated to the policeman's stereotype of the suspect. The more ambiguous the information the police may have about the suspect, the more likely is it that large numbers of people will be treated as potential suspects. Along these lines, Kephart presents the interesting finding that white patrolmen tend grossly to overestimate the percentage of Negro arrests (in Philadelphia, circa 1955).

The policeman whose main job is to maintain the appearance of public order on the street has in several respects a more difficult task than the warrant policeman or the plainclothesman. A uniformed policeman is a conspicuous and visible target for subtle but unmistakable forms of insult such as sidelong glances, pursed lips, or loud sniffs.

• • •

The uniformed officer, in addition to being an object of hostility, has a further related problem. He is sometimes asked to move people from one place on the street to another. For this task he requires the cooperation and respect of the citizenry. Sanctions are the only backing with which the patrolman can command the respect of a hostile citzenry. Unlike the traffic warrant policeman, who has the power to make an arrest in his pocket, the uniformed officer has mainly the weapon of violence to prod reluctant citizens (although lately the police have developed more subtle weapons, such as "field contact" reports. When a policeman sees a "suspicious" looking individual he may stop and ask

From Jerome H. Skolnick, *Justice Without Trial*, 2d ed. (John Wiley & Sons, 1975), pp. 86–87, 87–88, 88, 89. Copyright © 1975 by John Wiley & Sons, Inc. Reprinted by permission of John Wiley & Sons, Inc. Footnotes have been omitted.

his name, birthdate, place of residence, and note identifying char-acteristics—height, weight, color, and clothing. He will also, likely, ask the man questions regarding his purpose for being where he is. As happens not infrequently, the policeman introduces such an interaction with a statement like "hey, boy," "burrhead," (or any of the other derog-atory terms now forbidden by the chief of police [in the departments studied by the author]). His assertion of authority is usually less than fully appreciated by those so approached.

The Black population is no longer so cowed as it once was, unfortu-nately for the patrol police. As one patrolman commented:

> It's harder to work in these neighborhoods now than it used to be be-cause we send the kids to school and teach them about rights and then put them back in the neighborhood. I think we ought to either get rid of these neighborhoods or stop teaching these kids about their rights.

When a policeman pushes a man who knows his rights, he receives an understandably hostile response. In an early period (but less than twenty years ago) the police used outright violence to maintain re-spect. It is now more difficult for them . . . to maintain control through these techniques because of the operation of civil rights groups, and the increased knowledgeability of the citizens most likely to talk back—the younger males. But it is not color that is necessarily the determining factor. The "uncooperative" white delinquent will be treated just as roughly as the Black. And woe to the white demonstrator who goes "limp" with others during a protest demonstration. For the police-man, this form of protest generates physical labor, hard and, in his view, unnecessary. When a citizen *makes* a policeman sweat to take him into custody, he has created the situation most apt to lead to police indigna-tion and anger.

● ● ●

Examining his occupational environment, we find it especially con-ducive to developing an evenhanded discretionary stance. First, since the warrant policeman is not required to direct the activities of citizens acting within the law, he does not tend to generate hostilities and counter-hostilities inflaming prejudice. Second, the offense he deals with is relatively minor, not the sort promoting strong feelings of danger to the community or to the policeman himself. Third, when he encounters repeated offenders, a relatively rare occurence, he may be on friendly terms with them, since they are neither dangerous violators of the law nor organized criminals. Finally, as an officer lawfully warranted to make an arrest which is virtually certain to be followed by a conviction, he does not anticipate the offender will meet with less punishment than he "deserves," according to the warrant policeman's standards. He is confident that his conception of justice will ultimately be served. Thus, the warrant policeman does not find it necessary to exceed his delegated discretion, nor to be especially punitive within its terms. There are of course some warrant officers who are more punitive than others, but the pattern described seems to hold as a rule.

10

Restricting Police Behavior in the Station House: *Miranda* v. *Arizona*

• • •

On March 13, 1963, petitioner, Ernesto Miranda, was arrested at his home and taken in custody to a Phoenix police station. He was there identified by the complaining witness. The police then took him to "Interrogation Room No. 2" of the detective bureau. There he was questioned by two police officers. The officers admitted at trial that Miranda was not advised that he had a right to have an attorney present. Two hours later, the officers emerged from the interrogation room with a written confession signed by Miranda. At the top of the statement was a typed paragraph stating that the confession was made voluntarily, without threats or promises of immunity and "with full knowledge of my legal rights, understanding any statement I make may be used against me."

At his trial before a jury, the written confession was admitted into evidence over the objection of defense counsel, and the officers testified to the prior oral confession made by Miranda during the interrogation. Miranda was found guilty of kidnapping and rape. He was sentenced to 20 to 30 years' imprisonment on each count, the sentences to run concurrently. On appeal, the Supreme Court of Arizona held that Miranda's constitutional rights were not violated in obtaining the confession and affirmed the conviction. 98 Ariz. 18, 401 P.2d 721. In reach-

From *Miranda* v. *Arizona, Supreme Court Reporter* 86 (1966): 1612, 1614–1615, 1616–1617, 1619, 1636–1637. Footnotes and most references have been omitted.
Note: One or more paragraphs have been transposed to increase clarity.

ing its decision, the court emphasized heavily the fact that Miranda did not specifically request counsel.

[*For the U.S. Supreme Court, Chief Justice Warren wrote as follows—*]

• • •

We reverse. From the testimony of the officers and by the admission of respondent, it is clear that Miranda was not in any way apprised of his right to consult with an attorney and to have one present during the interrogation, nor was his right not to be compelled to incriminate himself effectively protected in any other manner. Without these warnings the statements were inadmissible. The mere fact that he signed a statement which contained a typed-in clause stating that he had "full knowledge" of his "legal rights" does not approach the knowing and intelligent waiver required to relinquish constitutional rights.

• • •

[T]he modern practice of in-custody interrogation is psychologically rather than physically oriented. As we have stated before, "Since Chambers v. State of Florida, 309 U.S. 227, 60 SCt. 472, 84 L.Ed. 716, this Court has recognized that coercion can be mental as well as physical, and that the blood of the accused is not the only hallmark of an unconstitutional inquistion." Blackburn v. State of Alabama, 361 U.S. 199, 206, 80 S.Ct. 274, 279, 4 L.Ed.2d 242 (1960). Interrogation still takes place in privacy. Privacy results in secrecy and this in turn results in a gap in our knowledge as to what in fact goes on in the interrogation rooms. A valuable source of information about present police practices, however, may be found in various police manuals and texts which document procedures employed with success in the past, and which recommend various other effective tactics. These texts are used by law enforcement agencies themselves as guides It should be noted that these texts professedly present the most enlightened and effective means presently used to obtain statements through custodial interrogation. By considering these texts and other data, it is possible to describe procedures observed and noted around the country.

The officers are told by the manuals that the "principle psychological factor contributing to a successful interrogation is privacy—being alone with the person under interrogation." The efficacy of this tactic has been explained as follows:

"If at all practicable, the interrogation should take place in the investigator's office or at least in a room of his own choice. The subject should be deprived of every psychological advantage. In his own home he may be confident, indignant, or recalcitrant. He is more keenly aware of his rights and more reluctant to tell of his indiscretions or criminal behavior within the walls of his home. Moreover his family and other friends are nearby, their presence lending moral support. In his office, the investigator possesses all the advantages. The atmosphere suggests the invincibility of the forces of the law."

To highlight the isolation and unfamiliar surroundings, the manuals instruct the police to display an air of confidence in the suspect's guilt and from outward appearance to maintain only an interest in confirming certain details. The guilt of the subject is to be posited as a fact. The interrogator should direct his comments toward the reasons why the subject committed the act, rather than court failure by asking the subject whether he did it. Like other men, perhaps the subject has had a bad family life, had an unhappy childhood, had too much to drink, had an unrequited desire for women. The officers are instructed to minimize the moral seriousness of the offense, to cast blame on the victim or on society. These tactics are designed to put the subject in a psychological state where his story is but an elaboration of what the police purport to know already—that he is guilty. Explanations to the contrary are dismissed and discouraged.

The texts thus stress that the major qualities an interrogator should possess are patience and perseverance.

● ● ●

The interrogators sometimes are instructed to induce a confession out of trickery. The technique here is quite effective in crimes which require identification or which run in series. In the identification situation, the interrogator may take a break in his questioning to place the subject among a group of men in a line-up. "The witness or complainant (previously coached, if necessary) studies the line-up and confidently points out the subject as the guilty party." Then the questioning resumes "as though there were now no doubt about the guilt of the subject." A variation on this technique is called the "reverse line-up":

> "The accused is placed in a line-up, but this time he is identified by several fictitious witnesses or victims who associated him with different offenses. It is expected that the subject will become desperate and confess to the offense under investigation in order to escape from the false accusations."

The manuals also contain instructions for police on how to handle the individual who refuses to discuss the matter entirely, or who asks for an attorney or relatives. The examiner is to concede him the right to remain silent. "This usually has a very undermining effect. First of all, he is disappointed in his expectation of an unfavorable reaction on the part of the interrogator. Secondly, a concession of this right to remain silent impresses the subject with the apparent fairness of his interrogator."

After this psychological conditioning, however, the officer is told to point out the incriminating significance of the suspect's refusal to talk:

> "Joe, you have a right to remain silent. That's your privilege and I'm the last person in the world who'll try to take it away from you. If that's the way you want to leave this, O. K. But let me ask you this. Suppose you were in my shoes and I were in yours and you called me in to ask me about this and I told you, 'I don't want to answer any of your questions.' You'd think I had something to hide, and you'd probably be right in thinking that. That's exactly what I'll have to think about you, and so will everybody else. So let's sit here and talk this whole thing over."

Few will persist in their initial refusal to talk, it is said, if this monologue is employed correctly.

In the event that the subject wishes to speak to a relative or an attorney, the following advice is tendered:

> "[T]he interrogator should respond by suggesting that the subject first tell the truth to the interrogator himself rather than get anyone else involved in the matter. If the request is for an attorney, the interrogator may suggest that the subject save himself or his family the expense of any such professional service, particularly if he is innocent of the offense under investigation. The interrogator may also add, 'Joe, I'm only looking for the truth, and if you're telling the truth, that's it. You can handle this by yourself.' "

From these representative samples of interrogation techniques, the setting prescribed by the manuals and observed in practice becomes clear. In essence, it is this: To be alone with the subject is essential to prevent distraction and to deprive him of any outside support. The aura of confidence in his guilt undermines his will to resist. He merely confirms the preconceived story the police seek to have him describe. Patience and persistence, at times relentless questioning, are employed. To obtain a confession, the interrogator must "patiently maneuver himself or his quarry into a position from which the desired objective may be attained." When normal procedures fail to produce the needed result, the police may resort to deceptive stratagems such as giving false legal advice. It is important to keep the subject off balance, for example, by trading on his insecurity about himself or his surroundings. The police then persuade, trick, or cajole him out of exercising his constitutional rights.

• • •

It is obvious that such an interrogation environment is created for no purpose other than to subjugate the individual to the will of his examiner. This atmosphere carries its own badge of intimidation. To be sure, this is not physical intimidation, but it is equally destructive of human dignity. The current practice of incommunicado interrogation is at odds with one of our Nation's most cherished principles—that the individual may not be compelled to incriminate himself. Unless adequate protective devices are employed to dispel the compulsion inherent in custodial surroundings, no statement obtained from the defendant can truly be the product of his free choice.

• • •

Our holding is . . . this: the prosecution may not use statements, whether exculpatory or inculpatory, stemming from custodial interrogation of the defendant unless it demonstrates the use of procedural safeguards effective to secure the privilege against self-incrimination. By custodial interrogation, we mean questioning initiated by law enforcement officers after a person has been taken into custody or otherwise deprived of his freedom of action in any significant way. As for the procedural safeguards to be employed, unless other fully effective means are devised to inform accused persons of their right of silence and to assure a continuous opportunity to exercise it, the following measures are required. Prior to any questioning, the person must be warned that he has a right to remain silent, that any statement he does make may be used as evidence against him, and that he has a right to the presence of an attorney, either retained or appointed. The defendant may waive effectuation of these rights, provided the waiver is made voluntarily, knowingly and intelligently. If, however, he indicates in any manner and at any stage of the process that he wishes to consult with an attorney before speaking there can be no questioning. Likewise, if the individual is alone and indicates in any manner that he does not wish to be interrogated, the police may not question him. The mere fact that he may have answered some questions or volunteered some statements on his own does not deprive him of the right to refrain from answering any further inquires until he has consulted with an attorney and thereafter consents to be questioned.

• • •

—————————————————— 11 ——————————————————

Restricting Police Behavior
in the Field: *Mapp* v. *Ohio*

• • •

Mr. Justice CLARK delivered the opinion of the Court.

Appellant stands convicted of knowingly having had in her possession and under her control certain lewd and lascivious books, pictures, and photographs in violation of § 2905.34 of Ohio's Revised Code. As officially stated in the syllabus to its opinion, the Supreme Court of Ohio found that her conviction was valid though "based primarily upon the introduction in evidence of lewd and lascivious books and pictures unlawfully seized during an unlawful search of defendant's home. . . ." 170 Ohio St. 427–428, 166 N.E.2d 387, 388.

On May 23, 1957, three Cleveland police officers arrived at appellant's residence in that city pursuant to information that "a person [was] hiding out in the home, who was wanted for questioning in connection with a recent bombing, and that there was a large amount of policy paraphernalia being hidden in the home." Miss Mapp and her daughter by a former marriage lived on the top floor of the two-family dwelling. Upon their arrival at that house, the officers knocked on the door and demanded entrance but appellant, after telephoning her attorney, refused to admit them without a search warrant. They advised their headquarters of the situation and undertook a surveillance of the house.

The officers again sought entrance some three hours later when four or more additional officers arrived on the scene. When Miss Mapp did not come to the door immediately, at least one of the several doors to the house was forcibly opened and the policemen gained admittance. Meanwhile Miss Mapp's attorney arrived, but the officers, having secured their own entry, and continuing in their defiance of the law, would permit him neither to see Miss Mapp nor to enter the house. It appears that Miss Mapp was halfway down the stairs from the upper floor to the front door when the officers, in this highhanded manner, broke into the hall. She demanded to see the search warrant. A paper, claimed to be a warrant, was held up by one of the officers. She grabbed the "warrant" and placed it in her bosom. A struggle ensued in which the officers re-

—————————————

From *Mapp* v. *Ohio, Supreme Court Reporter* 81 (1961): 1685–1686, 1693, 1693–1694. Footnotes and most references have been omitted.

covered the piece of paper and as a result of which they handcuffed appellant because she had been "belligerent" in resisting their official rescue of the "warrant" from her person. Running roughshod over appellant, a policeman "grabbed" her, "twisted [her] hand," and she "yelled [and] pleaded with him" because "it was hurting." Appellant, in handcuffs, was then forcibly taken upstairs to her bedroom where the officers searched a dresser, a chest of drawers, a closet and some suitcases. They also looked into a photo album and through personal papers belonging to the appellant. The search spread to the rest of the second floor including the child's bedroom, the living room, the kitchen and a dinette. The basement of the building and a trunk found therein were also searched. The obscene materials for possession of which she was ultimately convicted were discovered in the course of that widespread search.

At the trial no search warrant was produced by the prosecution, nor was the failure to produce one explained or accounted for. At best, "There is, in the record, considerable doubt as to whether there ever was any warrant for the search of defendant's home." 170 Ohio St. at page 430, 166 N.E.2d at page 389. The Ohio Supreme Court believed a "reasonable argument" could be made that the conviction should be reversed "because the 'methods' employed to obtain the [evidence] were such as to 'offend "a sense of justice," ' " but the court found determinative the fact that the evidence had not been taken "from defentant's person by the use of brutal or offensive physical force against defendant." 170 Ohio St. at page 431, 166 N.E.2d at pages 389–390.

The State says that even if the search were made without authority, or otherwise unreasonably, it is not prevented from using the unconstitutionally seized evidence at trial, citing Wolf v. People of State of Colorado, 1949, 338 U.S. 25, at page 33, 69 S.Ct. 1359, at page 1364, 93 L.Ed. 1782, in which this Court did indeed hold "that in a prosecution in a State court for a State crime the Fourteenth Amendment does not forbid the admission of evidence obtained by an unreasonable search and seizure." On this appeal, of which we have noted probable jurisdiction, 364 U.S. 868, 81 S.Ct. 111, 5 L.Ed.2d 90, it is urged once again that we review that holding.

• • •

[T]hat the exclusionary rule is an essential part of both the Fourth and Fourteenth Amendments is not only the logical dictate of prior cases, but it also makes very good sense. There is no war between the Constitution and common sense. Presently, a federal prosecutor may make no use of evidence illegally seized, but a State's attorney across the street may, although he supposedly is operating under the enforceable prohibitions of the same Amendment. Thus the State, by admitting evidence unlawfully seized, serves to encourage disobedience to the Federal Constitution which it is bound to uphold.

• • •

There are those who say, as did Justice (then Judge) Cardozo, that under our constitutional exclusionary doctrine "[t]he criminal is to go free because the constable has blundered." People v. Defore, 242 N.Y. at page 21, 150 N.E. at page 587. In some cases this will undoubtedly be the result. But, as was said in Elkins, "there is another consideration— the imperative of judicial integrity." 364 U.S. at page 222, 80 S.Ct. at page 1447. The criminal goes free, if he must, but it is the law that sets him free. Nothing can destroy a government more quickly than its failure to observe its own laws, or worse, its disregard of the character of its own existence. As Mr. Justice Brandeis, dissenting, said in Olmstead v. United States, 1928, 277 U.S. 438, 485, 48 S.Ct. 564, 575, 72 L.Ed. 944: "Our government is the potent, the omnipresent teacher. For good or for ill, it teaches the whole people by its example. . . . If the government becomes a lawbreaker, it breeds contempt for law; it invites every man to become a law unto himself; it invites anarchy." Nor can it lightly be assumed that, as a practical matter, adoption of the exclusionary rule fetters law enforcement. Only last year this Court expressly considered that contention and found that "pragmatic evidence of a sort" to the contrary was not wanting. Elkins v. United States, supra, 364 U.S. at page 218, 80 S.Ct. at page 1444. The Court noted that

> "The federal courts themselves have operated under the exclusionary rule of Weeks for almost half a century; yet it has not been suggested either that the Federal Bureau of Investigation . . . has thereby been rendered ineffective, or that the administration of criminal justice in the federal courts has thereby been disrupted. Moreover, the experience of the states is impressive. . . . The movement towards the rule of exclusion has been halting but seemingly inexorable." Id., 364 U.S. at pages 218–219, 80 S.Ct. at pages 1444–1445.

The ignoble shortcut to conviction left open to the State tends to destroy the entire system of constitutional restraints on which the liberties of the people rest. Having once recognized that the right to privacy embodied in the Fourth Amendment is enforceable against the States, and that the right to be secure against rude invasions of privacy by state officers is, therefore, constitutional in origin, we can no longer permit that right to remain an empty promise. Because it is enforceable in the same manner and to like effect as other basic rights secured by the Due Process Clause, we can no longer permit it to be revocable at the whim of any police officer who, in the name of law enforcement itself, chooses to suspend its enjoyment. Our decision, founded on reason and truth, gives to the individual no more than that which the Constitution guarantees him, to the police officer no less than that to which honest law enforcement is entitled, and, to the courts, that judicial integrity so necessary in the true administration of justice.

The judgment of the Supreme Court of Ohio is reversed and the cause remanded for further proceedings not inconsistent with this opinion.

Reversed and remanded.

Prosecutors

—————————— 12 ——————————

Prosecutorial Discretion

William T. Pizzi

• • •

A. The Charging Decision

Consider a prosecutor faced with the task of drawing up an indictment against a defendant who has passed four forged checks over a two month period. Assume that the penalty for passing a forged check is a maximum sentence of ten years with no minimum, that the evidence against the defendant is relatively strong on each check, and that the prosecutor personally believes that based on what he knows about the defendant, a sentence of two or three years would seem appropriate. How should a prosecutor prepare the indictment?

If the prosecutor charges the defendant with four counts of passing a forged check, the defendant will be exposed to a possible sentence of as much as forty years in prison; if the prosecutor charges only one count, the sentence exposure is reduced to ten years, a term which comes closer to the prosecutor's view of the appropriate sentence. But should the prosecutor, in reaching a decision to indict, be guided either

From William T. Pizzi, "Prosecutorial Discretion, Plea Bargaining and the Supreme Court's Opinion in *Bordenkircher* v. *Hayes*," *Hastings Constitutional Law Quarterly* 6 (Fall 1978): 270–278. Reprinted by permission. Footnotes have been omitted.

by the total sentence exposure to which the defendent could be subjected, or by his own view of what sentence the case merits?

One view of the prosecutor's role which suggests indicting the defendent on all four offenses sees the prosecutor as an advocate for the state whose primary responsibility it to enforce the law against all offenders. Where the defendent has committed four separate offenses and the evidence is strong on each of them, each ought to be prosecuted. For the prosecutor to "bury" three of the offenses would simply not be consistent with the facts of the defendent's criminal activities. Whether the statutory penalties are too severe in the prosecutor's opinion is of no consequence; the prosecutor's duty is to enforce the laws as written, not to use discretion to soften the law.

The reply will certainly be that this position presents too narrow a view of the prosecutor's role. The prosecutor's responsibility is to enforce the law, but this responsibility is not to be carried out in a mechanical fashion. In American jurisdictions, unlike those on the European continent, prosecutors are given discretion over whether to prosecute and what charges to bring. We have come to expect prosecutors to consider a range of factors including the nature of the criminal act and the background of the offender in deciding whether to proceed and, if so, what charges to file. The need for broad discretion in the enforcement of criminal statutes is often attributed to the severity of American statutory penalties. While there are some conceptual problems in suggesting that a prosecutor's responsibility to enforce the law should yield in some cases because of the severity of the very law that the prosecutor has sworn to uphold, the American Bar Association Standards for the Prosecution Function adopt a broad view of prosecutorial discretion. The Standards state that a prosecutor "is not obligated to present all charges which the evidence might support," and also that one of the factors the prosecutor "may properly consider in exercising his discretion" is "the disproportion of the authorized punishment in relation to the particular offense of the offender." Presumably a prosecutor may give such disproportionate punishment consideration not only in deciding whether to charge but also in choosing the number of counts to be charged.

It has also been suggested that part of the role of the prosecutor is to fill gaps or deficiencies in a criminal code and to "individualize justice." Consider, for example, the following view on prosecutorial enforcement of the criminal code from the President's Commission on Law Enforcement and Administration of Justice:

> [A] criminal code has no way of describing the difference between a petty thief who is on his way to becoming an armed robber and a petty thief who succumbs once to a momentary impulse. The same criminal conduct may be the deliberate act of a professional criminal or an isolated aberration in the

behavior of a normally law abiding person. The criminal conduct describes
the existence of a problem, but not its nature or source. The system depends
on prosecutors to recognize these distinctions when bringing charges.

This statement concerns the initial decision to charge, not what to
charge. But if a prosecutor ought to consider carefully the prospective
defendent as an individual before bringing a charge of petty theft, the
same considerations would seem relevant when deciding whether to expose a defendant to a ten-year or a forty-year sentence.

This broad view of prosecutorial discretion has some disturbing
aspects. First, the notion that "the same criminal conduct" as defined
by the statute should be prosecuted differently based on factors quite
divorced from the crime in question seems to imply that the defendant
is being punished less for the crime than for these others factors. Is it
not inconsistent with justice, rather than "individualizing justice," to
apply a rule of law differently to different people for reasons not specified in the statute? And should justice be a matter of *discretion?*
Second, how does one tell when a petty thief "is on his way to becoming an armed robber"? If a criminal code has "no way of describing"
the differences among petty thieves, perhaps the problem lies not in the
limits of our language, but in the limits of our knowledge. Finally,
even if these distinctions should be made, why should it be the prosecutor who makes the controlling decision? After all, both petty thieves
will eventually come before a sentencing judge, and if the judge determines that in one case it is "an isolated aberration in the behavior of a
normally law abiding person," a very slight sentence or even no sentence may be imposed.

In the example of the check case, the prosecutor does not have
ultimate control over sentencing. It will be up to the court to decide
what sentence is appropriate. Given the broad sentencing discretion of
a trial judge, and the dominant sentencing philosophy which demands
the "punishment should fit the offender," why is it necessary that a
prosecutor also have some responsibility to see that the charges brought
"fit the offender" in terms of sentence exposure, especially where the
sentencing judge will have more information about the defendant when
it is time to impose a sentence? And although it sounds reassuring to
suggest that a prosecutor should temper the charges to insure an appropriate sentence, is such a role consistent with the prosecutor's role as an
advocate for the state? Certainly there are strong indications that many
prosecutors see their function in the sentencing process as that of an
advocate for a law enforcement point of view.

But even if our example is a proper case for the exercise of the
prosecutor's charging discretion, strategic considerations may make the
decision difficult. It many be significantly easier for a prosecutor to obtain a conviction on an indictment charging four forged checks than on

one charging a single violation. Four counts of check passing will undercut defenses stressing confusion or mistake and make jury sympathy in response to these defenses less likely. It may be easier for the jury to convict on individual counts where each count is seen as part of a pattern. And with four counts there may be room for jurors to compromise if deadlocks deveop as to the proper verdict. While a single count indictment does not foreclose proof of the other violations for certain evidentiary purposes, courts are nevertheless reluctant to admit "other crimes" evidence. The safer course for the prosecutor is to avoid having admissibility turn on a favorable evidentiary ruling and to indict on four counts, thus insuring that the evidence of all four checks is independently admissible. One can hardly blame a prosecutor for giving weight to such strategic matters in the charging decision. Before a prosecutor worries overly about a defendant's sentence exposure, the prosecutor must first be concerned with convicting the defendent. The realities of trial work and the requirement of proof beyond a reasonable doubt suggest that a prosecutor should be most reluctant to draw up an indictment that lessens the chances for conviction to any significant degree.

B. Plea Bargaining

Another strategic consideration that suggests indicting the defendant on all four counts is the realistic likelihood of plea bargaining. If the defendant is exposed to a possible sentence of up to forty years in prison, he or she may be tempted to enter a plea to minimize that exposure. While it may be unlikely that a judge would impose such a harsh sentence, there is little the defendant can do should the judge give a sentence that jolts expectations. If the prosecutor has a strong case, why should the defendant not remove any risk of a long sentence? Besides, a plea may move the court to some leniency. Perhaps the smart move for both the prosecutor and the defendant would be to agree to a plea to a single count. The prosecutor could further enhance the bargain by recommending a two or three year sentence.

If the prosecutor charges only a single count, however, there will be substantially less reason for the defendant to enter a plea. The sensible approach for a prosecutor who wants to obtain a plea would be to indict on all four counts, and then to compromise the case through plea bargaining with a result that both sides consider fair. As the Supreme Court noted in upholding the constitutionality of plea bargaining in *Brady v. United States,* "both the state and the defendant often find it advantageous to preclude the possibility of the maximum penalty authorized by law." Where the maximum penalty is very high, a plea yields what the Court termed a "mutuality of advantage," allowing the state to conserve prosecutorial and judicial resources while the defendant significantly reduces his sentence exposure.

Viewed in this way, plea bargaining appears to be a means of avoiding the problems which surround the charging decision by permitting the state and the defendant to reach a compromise that is satisfactory to both sides. From the defendant's point of view, a plea allows him to avoid the hazards of appearing before a judge who has sentencing discretion. The defendant gives up his chance for an acquittal, but the certainty of a lesser sentence may be well worth the exchange. From the prosecutor's point of view, the state is saved the expense of a trial and the defendant's acceptance of a single count provides some assurance that the sentence will be reasonable.

The problem with this model is that the plea bargain will yield a reasonable compromise only if the indictment prepared by the prosecutor is itself reasonable. The defendant's acceptance of the plea bargain does not justify the original charging decision. That the defendant may be sufficiently worried by a forty-year exposure to accept a plea bargain does not resolve the questionable propriety of using the four count indictment as the base of negotiations. Plea bargaining may yield a sensible compromise of the risks presented, but should a four count indictment have been one of these risks? And of course there may be no "compromise" if the defendant elects to go to trial. If the prosecutor has some obligation to see that the defendant's sentence exposure is reasonable, should that not be true even if the defendant elects to exercise his constitutional right to a trial?

The broad charging discretion of the prosecutor and the practice of plea bargaining has led to the frequent complaint that prosecutors "overcharge" in order to obtain plea bargaining leverage and thereby induce the defendant to plead guilty. One way prosecutors are claimed to overcharge is by "multiplying 'unreasonably' the number of accusations against a single defendant." In our example, if the prosecutor were to decide to file a four count indictment to gain plea bargaining leverage, this would constitute an example of such overcharging. Another form of overcharging occurs where a prosecutor charges "a single offense at a higher level than the circumstances of the case seem to warrant."

"Overcharging," at least as the term is used in this article, is not premised on the claim that there is insufficient evidence to support either the multiplied counts of the indictment or the aggravated level of a particular charge. There is no dispute that a prosecutor has an obligation to bring only those charges that can in good faith be supported by the evidence. Rather the vice of overcharging is thought to lie in the prosecutor's use of a high sentence exposure to induce a defendant to plead guilty. It is argued that if a prosecutor is willing to accept a plea to a single count or a lesser included offense because there remains an "adequate scope of punishment" for the defendant, this same reasoning should apply in the initial charging decision. The attack on over-charging is premised on the assumption that the same factors that move a prosecutor to accept a plea should have been considered in the decision to charge. But this depends on one's view of the prosecutor's role. For one could also say that plea bargaining forces a prosecutor to take on some of the responsibilities of a sentencing judge, and that in accepting a plea, a prosecutor is considering factors which properly are the concern of the judge in sentencing rather than the prosecutor in charging.

In a system where a prosecutor is required to bring all the charges which are reasonably supported by the evidence, the attack on over-charging is obviously without force. On the other hand, if the pro-secutor is obligated to consider the "appropriate" sentence for the defendant in deciding what to charge, charging solely for plea bargain-ing leverage is inconsistent with that obligation. In a system such as ours which relies on plea bargaining to dispose of close to ninety per-cent of its cases, it seems fair to say that the broad discretion granted prosecutors to limit the severity of the charges against a defendant is unlikely to be frequently exercised where it will undercut plea bargain-ing leverage. For this reason the attack on overcharging, if sustained by the Supreme Court, could have broad implications for it demands that in reaching a charging decision, a prosecutor not consider the stra-tegic advantage that certain counts would yield in subsequent plea bargaining.

• • •

―――――――――――――――――――――― 13 ――――――――――――――――――――――

Prosecutorial Leverage in Plea
Bargaining: *Bordenkircher* v. *Hayes*

I

• • •

The respondent, Paul Lewis Hayes, was indicted by a Fayette County, Ky., grand jury on a charge of uttering a forged instrument in the amount of $88.30, an offense then punishable by a term of 2 to 10 years in prison. Ky. Rev. Stat. § 434.130 (1973) (repealed 1975). After arraignment, Hayes, his retained counsel, and the Commonwealth's Attorney met in the presence of the Clerk of the Court to discuss a possible plea agreement. During these conferences the prosecutor offered to recommend a sentence of five years in prison if Hayes would plead guilty to the indictment. He also said that if Hayes did not plead guilty and "save the court the inconvenience and necessity of a trial," he would return to the grand jury to seek an indictment under the Kentucky Habitual Criminal Act, then Ky. Rev. Stat. § 431.190 (1973) (repealed 1975), which would subject Hayes to a mandatory sentence of life imprisonment by reason of his two prior felony convictions. Hayes chose not to plead guilty, and the prosecutor did obtain an indictment charging him under the Habitual Criminal Act. It is not disputed that the recidivist charge was fully justified by the evidence, that the prosecutor was in possession of this evidence at the time of the original indictment, and that Hayes' refusal to plead guilty to the original charge was what led to his indictment under the habitual criminal statute.

A jury found Hayes guilty on the principal charge of uttering a forged instrument and, in a separate proceeding, further found that he had twice before been convicted of felonies. As required by the habitual offender statute, he was sentenced to a life term in the penitentiary. The Kentucky Court of Appeals rejected Hayes' constitutional objections to the enhanced sentence, holding in an unpublished opinion that imprisonment for life with the possibility of parole was constitutionally permissible in light of the previous felonies of which Hayes had been convicted, and that the prosecutor's decision to indict him as a habitual offender was a legitimate use of available leverage in the plea bargaining process.

―――

From *Bordenkircher* v. *Hayes*, U.S. Reports 434 (1978): 358–360, 361–362, 363–365. Footnotes and most references have been omitted.

On Hayes' petition for a federal writ of habeas corpus, the United States District Court for the Eastern District of Kentucky agreed that there had been no constitutional violation in the sentence or the indictment procedure, and denied the writ. The Court of Appeals for the Sixth Circuit reversed the District Court's judgment. *Hayes* v. *Cowan,* 547 F. 2d 42. While recognizing "that plea bargaining now plays an important role in our criminal justice system," *id.,* at 43, the appellate court thought that the prosecutor's conduct during the bargaining negotiations had violated the principles of *Blackledge* v. *Perry,* 417 U. S. 21, which "protect[ed] defendants from the vindictive exercise of a prosecutor's discretion." 547 F. 2d, at 44. Accordingly, the court ordered that Hayes be discharged "except for his confinement under a lawful sentence imposed solely for the crime of uttering a forged instrument." *Id.,* at 45. We granted certiorari to consider a constitutional question of importance in the administration of criminal justice. 431 U. S. 953.

• • •

II

We have recently had occasion to observe that "[w]hatever might be the situation in an ideal world, the fact is that the guilty plea and the often concomitant plea bargain are important components of this country's criminal justice system. Properly administered, they can benefit all concerned." *Blackledge* v. *Allison,* 431 U.S. 63, 71. The open acknowledgment of this previously clandestine practice has led this Court to recognize the importance of counsel during plea negotiations, *Brady* v. *United States,* 397 U.S. 742, 758, the need for a public record indicating that a plea was knowingly and voluntarily made, *Boykin* v. *Alabama,* 395 U.S. 238, 242, and the requirement that a prosecutor's plea bargaining promise must be kept, *Santobello* v. *New York,* 404 U.S. 257, 262. The decision of the Court of Appeals in the present case, however, did not deal with considerations such as these, but held that the substance of the plea offer itself violated the limitations imposed by the Due Process Clause of the Fourteenth Amendment. Cf. *Brady* v. *United States, supra,* at 751 n. 8. For the reasons that follow, we have concluded that the Court of Appeals was mistaken in so ruling.

To punish a person because he has done what the law plainly allows him to do is a due process violation of the most basic sort, see *North Carolina* v. *Pearce, supra,* at 738 (opinion of Black, J.), and for an agent of the State to pursue a course of action whose objective is to penalize a person's reliance on his legal rights is "patently unconstitutional." *Chaffin* v. *Stynchcombe, supra,* at 32–33, n. 20. See *United States* v. *Jackson,* 390 U.S. 570. But in the "give-and-take" of plea bargaining, there is no such element of punishment or retaliation so long as the accused is free to accept or reject the prosecution's offer.

Plea bargaining flows from "the mutuality of advantage" to defendants and prosecutors, each with his own reasons for wanting to avoid trial. *Brady* v. *United States, supra,* at 752. Defendants advised by competent counsel and protected by other procedural safeguards are presumptively capable of intelligent choice in response to prosecutorial persuasion, and unlikely to be driven to false self-condemnation. 397 U.S., at 758. Indeed, acceptance of the basic legitimacy of plea bargaining necessarily implies rejection of any notion that a guilty plea is involuntary in a constitutional sense simply because it is the end result of the bargaining process. By hypothesis, the plea may have been induced by promises of a recommendation of a lenient sentence or a reduction of charges, and thus by fear of the possibility of a greater penalty upon conviction after a trial. See ABA Project on Standards for Criminal Justice, Pleas of Guilty § 3.1 (App. Draft 1968); Note, Plea Bargaining and the Transformation of the Criminal Process, 90 Harv. L. Rev. 564 (1977). Cf. *Brady* v. *United States, supra,* at 751; *North Carolina* v. *Alford,* 400 U.S. 25.

While confronting a defendant with the risk of more severe punishment clearly may have a "discouraging effect on the defendant's assertion of his trial rights, the imposition of these difficult choices [is] an inevitable"—and permissible—"attribute of any legitimate system which tolerates and encourages the negotiation of pleas." *Chaffin* v. *Stynchcombe, supra,* at 31. It follows that, by tolerating and encouraging the negotiation of pleas, this Court has necessarily accepted as constitutionally legitimate the simple reality that the prosecutor's interest at the bargaining table is to persuade the defendant to forgo his right to plead not guilty.

It is not disputed here that Hayes was properly chargeable under the recidivist statute, since he had in fact been convicted of two previous felonies. In our system, so long as the prosecutor has probable cause to believe that the accused committed an offense defined by statute, the decision whether or not to prosecute; and what charge to file or bring before a grand jury, generally rests entirely in his discretion. Within the limits set by the legislature's constitutionally valid definition of chargeable offenses, "the conscious exercise of some selectivity in enforcement is not in itself a federal constitutional violation" so long as "the selection was [not] deliberately based upon an unjustifiable standard such as race, religion, or other arbitrary classification." *Oyler* v. *Boles,* 368 U.S. 448, 456. To hold that the prosecutor's desire to induce a guilty plea is an "unjustifiable standard," which, like race or religion, may play no part in his charging decision, would contradict the very premises that underlie the concept of plea bargaining itself. Moreover, a rigid constitutional rule that would prohibit a prosecutor from acting forthrightly in his dealings with the defense could only invite unhealthy subterfuge that would drive the practice of plea bargaining back into the shadows from which it has so recently emerged. See *Blackledge* v. *Allison,* 431 U.S., at 76.

There is no doubt that the breadth of discretion that our country's legal system vests in prosecuting attorneys carries with it the potential for both individual and institutional abuse. And broad though that discretion may be, there are undoubtedly constitutional limits upon its exercise. We hold only that the course of conduct engaged in by the prosecutor in this case, which no more than openly presented the defendant with the unpleasant alternatives of forgoing trial or facing charges on which he was plainly subject to prosecution, did not violate the Due Process Clause of the Fourteenth Amendment.

Accordingly, the judgment of the Court of Appeals is *Reversed.*

14

Prosecutorial Decision Making in the "Real" World

Max Friedman

• • •

Both the decision to prosecute Tokyo Rose and the decision to accept Spiro Agnew's nolo contendere plea have been the subject of controversy and debate. It is suggested here that the antagonists in the debate are antagonists precisely because they approach prosecutorial function from different perspectives. . . .

In August 1973, then Vice President Agnew issued a statement to the effect that he was the subject of a criminal investigation being conducted by U.S. Attorney Beall. Kickbacks allegedly had been paid by contractors,

From Max Friedman, "The Prosecutor: A Model for Role and Function," *Washington University Law Quarterly* 109 (1978): 134, 134–137, 138–139. Copyrights © 1978 by the *Washington University Law Quarterly,* Washington University School of Law, St. Louis, Mo. Reprinted by permission. Most footnotes have been omitted.

architects, and engineers to various Maryland officials while Agnew was governor; certain campaign contributions also were at issue. On the day following this disclosure, the Vice President announced that he had no intention of resigning. The investigation proceeded and on August 10, federal investigators subpoenaed Agnew's records of his two years as governor. This and other material was given to a grand jury which proceeded to indict a Baltimore County executive on thirty-nine counts of bribery, extortion, and conspiracy.

During this period, Agnew discussed his possible resignation with President Nixon. These discussions turned eventually to negotiating an exchange of Agnew's resignation for a guilty plea to a minor offense. Finally, a deal was struck: there would be no prosecutions for criminal activity relating to the kickback schemes or campaign contributions in return for Agnew's nolo contendere plea to a charge of tax evasion and resignation of the Vice Presidency.

This agreement was formalized in three statements: one by the Attorney General requesting that the court accept the agreement; one by the Vice President; and one by the Judge. The vantage [point] analysis will be applied to these three statements.

Attorney General Richardson viewed the matter almost exclusively from a communitarian perspective. He noted that the decision must be "perceived [as] just and honorable, not simply to the parties but above all to the American people," and thought that providing information to the national community would aid in that evaluation. But Richardson's presentation of the information had implications for the integrity of the process, particularly for the role of the jury, because he released information that normally would be used in the process itself. Richardson unwittingly reflected these ramifications when he noted that "this evidence establishes . . ."—a statement which the jury alone was entitled to make. Richardson also implicated the process to the extent his statements reflected on the character of possible witnesses and the reliability of their statements, i.e., "None of the Government's major witnesses has been promised immunity from prosecution. . . ." Richardson adverted to the process (and conflated the criminal and impeachment processes) only to suggest that its purpose is to vindicate a defendant and, if the defendant wishes to forego such vindication, communitarian interests must be considered paramount. By assuming this narrow view of the process' accomplishments, Richardson ignored the community values which inhere in the process itself. Finally, his failure to consider other vantages and, particularly, his oversimplified treatment of the process perspective was reflected in his willingness to suggest an appropriate sentence. He thus minimized the process' importance in ultimately arriving at an appropriate sentence decision and simultaneously ignored the process' extensive, underlying role differentiations.

In simplifying the process' inherent values, Richardson adverted neither to the character of the negotiations that produced the deal (an internal, functional perspective) nor, except in passing, to the implied separation of powers notions. Both omissions were surprising. There had been an obvious departure from the standard bureaucratic process in the charge determination; Richardson had dramatically exercised his internal authority and supervisory functions. There was also an important degree of judicial abrogation to the executive.

Agnew's statement echoed and yet transformed Richardson's. He agreed that the point of departure was the community vantage, but did so in a peculiarly self-effacing manner, suggesting that community concern was better spent on other matters. He essentially dismissed process; but instead found the grand jury as the one relevant point in the traditional criminal process. He proceeded no further, and made it clear that any hypothesis as to the process' result was unnecessary because he had altruistically dispensed with the process itself. He failed to consider whether the process might serve community interests.

Judge Hoffman's response was analytically more complex. He began, from an internal vantage, with a discussion of the procedures that led to the agreement, but lapsed quickly into the prevailing sentiment when he spoke of community perceptions. He objected to the publication of the evidence, not because it usurped an essentially process function, but because it would have led to further community discussion. He addressed the process itself only at the end of his opinion, by discussing the propriety of a sentence rather than a fine.

The appropriate set of judicial considerations are more complex. It was the judge's responsibility to consider the fact and manner of negotiation: whether the deal was properly made and whether the prosecutor's office recognized the standards by which it was made. There is no reason to dispense with bureaucratic norms without justification; there is no reason the Attorney General should not be subject to standards in charge and plea decisions. The court should have more carefully considered process values in removing evidentiary doubt and vindicating either Agnew, Beall, or Richardson. Some discussion of community in that context also was warranted: the court should have considered whether the community would best be served by an ultimate resolution of the dispute by the proper process institution.

Independent of Agnew's political position, what are the process goals in this kind of prosecution? What are the separation of powers effects? Clearly passive concurrence in an agreement fashioned by the executive branch for one of its own raises issues with respect to the balance of power. Finally, there is the communitarian interest, which is represented by a desire to swiftly resolve the matter. Apart from the question of whether other means could be found to remove the uncertainty, *i.e.*, by appointing an acting Vice President, the court does not discuss the community interests at stake.

Essentially the same issues arise in the Tokyo Rose case. Iva Toquino was an American living in Japan during the Second World War. In 1942, she took a job as a typist with Radio Tokyo and became acquainted with two prisoners of war who worked there, in charge of a program called "Zero Hour." When they needed a female voice for the program, which consisted of light entertainment and propoganda directed at American forces in the Pacific, Iva agreed to be that voice.

After the war, Iva gave an interview about her job and noted that she once broadcast the following line: "You fellows are all without ships. What are you going to do about going home now?" This line was the crux of her subsequent trial on charges of treason. The United States Attorney decided initially not to prosecute because it would be difficult to locate the two corroborating witnesses required by the Constitution. This decision was heatedly attacked by the public, particularly Walter Winchell, who accused Attorney General Clark of laxness. The trial was marked by the introduction of questionable evidence and a hung jury eventually reached a guilty verdict following a "dynamite charge." [A "dynamite charge" is said to be given when a judge informs a jury that the case is important to the government and reminds the jury of the cost to the taxpayer that the prosecution entails.] . . . Because the Justice Department controlled decisionmaking, Iva Toquino was, in a sense, subject to double jeopardy. In normal circumstances, the prosecutor uses established standards in reaching a decision not to prosecute, and follows that determination unless further evidence is adduced. In Iva's case, there was no internal structure capable of reaching a determination and no standards available to reconsider the determination once made. It is also doubtful whether, in an office with articulated standards for prosecution, only one of a dozen Tokyo Roses would have been prosecuted. Selective prosecution does not seem appropriate to the offense of treason. These two points denote a clear normative position. They reflect nevertheless that the Tokyo Rose decision would have been analyzed differently if internal, administrative structure had been considered.

The criminal process vantage requires a consideration of whether the prosecution compromised process-related values. On the one hand, the character of her prosecution threatened the process' independence; on the other hand, an innocent Iva Toquino would have realized an important vindication of her loyalty.

The separation of powers perspective sheds more light on the matter. Perhaps prosecutions tinged by political controversy should be scrutinized more carefully by the judiciary. The political, primarily executive, process mode of self-correction, however—the pardon power—counters the argument for stricter scrutiny. Moreover, if treason is a crime against the state in its executive capacity as warmaker, executive and political controls are expected. Yet both the legislature and judiciary appear to have abrogated their responsibility in this case.

Finally, there is the communitarian perspective. There was a strong community desire to see Tokyo Rose prosecuted; unfortunately, the character of that community and whether it, in fact, represented majority sentiment, was not analyzed. Nor was the role of people like Walter Winchell analyzed to determine the proper community spokesmen. Perhaps some methodical inquiry into community sentiment could have been undertaken by the relevant actors. This care would have been consistent with the fact that treason is a constitutional offense and thus, unlike statutory offenses, reflects deep-seated notions of community needs and desires.

The final analysis of the Tokyo Rose decision leads to two fundamental perceptions. First, since community pressure was central to the progress of the prosecution, that pressure should have been analyzed more carefully. Second, the absence of internal bureaucratic structures made the prosecutorial decisionmaking process susceptible to community forces. It would be interesting to observe internal structures that were designed for control purposes to provide for community input and, at the same time, to ensure that the input did not altogether alter the decision-making process.

Lawyers

15

Attorneys for the Public

Herbert Jacob

Not all lawyers engaged in litigation are private entrepreneurs. Many are government employees. The government—whether the federal government, state government, or federal, state, or local agency—is frequently involved in litigation and must have its own representatives before the courts. The government plays a dominant role in criminal cases, for it prosecutes them. It participates in important civil litigation, for when cases involve public policy, the government is concerned.

Each level of government in the United States possesses its own legal agents. Their role in the judicial process varies with their formal functions and their informal position in the political system.

Lawyers for the Federal Government

As the scope of federal activity has grown in the twentieth century, the range of litigation involving the federal government has also increased. Now more than eighteen thousand lawyers work for the federal government. Some serve particular agencies, such as the regulatory commissions, the Department of Agriculture, and the Department of De-

From Herbert Jacob, *Justice in America: Courts, Lawyers, and the Judicial Process*, 3d ed. (Little, Brown and Company, 1978), pp. 79–86. Copyright © 1978, 1972, 1965 by Little, Brown and Company, Inc. Reprinted by permission. Footnotes have been omitted.

fense. The largest single civilian group works in the government's principal legal office, the Department of Justice.

The Justice Department was not organized until 1870, although its head, the Attorney General, was one of the original cabinet officials authorized by Congress in 1789. Until after the Civil War, litigation involving the federal government did not justify a separate department: the Attorney General could operate in a small office. Today, however, he supervises ninety-one United States Attorneys, one attached to each district court, an equal number of United States Marshals, the FBI, and several thousand attorneys in Washington.

The Justice Department's impact on the judiciary is manifold. The Attorney General is a key participant in the selection of federal judges. He supervises the prosecution of all violations of federal criminal law and the initiation of major civil litigation to carry out the President's antitrust and civil rights policies. Another official of the department, the Solicitor General, supervises the appeal of government cases to the Courts of Appeals and to the Supreme Court.

Since the Civil War the scope of criminal statutes passed by Congress has increased greatly. They prohibit: interfering with federal elections, transporting stolen cars over state lines, white slavery, bank robbery, mail fraud, kidnaping, tax fraud, and similar offenses. Whenever anyone is charged with a federal crime, he is arraigned before a federal magistrate, and his case is turned over to the United States Attorney attached to the United States district court, who functions much like a district attorney. He prepares the prosecution case; he negotiates with the defendant; and he conducts the trial.

United States Attorneys also handle a large number of civil cases for the federal government. The government initiates numerous suits over its contracts for materials and service, tax matters, and its regulatory programs. Private individuals also sue the government over such matters. Of the 117,320 civil cases begun in federal district courts in 1975, 27 percent involved the federal government as either plaintiff or defendant.

Many civil cases are handled by government attorneys employed by operating agencies rather than by the Justice Department. Some of their legal staffs are quite sizable and process thousands of claims. The legal staff of the Treasury Department, for instance, must litigate all challenges to its rulings before the tax court. It also must assist the Justice Department in preparing civil and criminal cases involving tax evasion. Such attorneys also handle many matters that never reach trial. They represent the government in bankruptcy proceedings in order to press the government's tax claims; they file claims before probate courts for payment of federal inheritance taxes. Similar services—though on a much smaller scale—are performed by the legal staff of other departments. Attorneys working for regulatory commissions play a key role in carrying out their programs. They investigate violations of the regulatory statutes; they conduct hearings before the commissions; and they prepare to defend the commissions' decisions when appeals are brought to the courts.

Most attorneys working for the government are civil servants who win a position through competitive examinations. Many make government work their career. Like most other federal civil servants, they may not participate in overt political activity. In the Justice Department, however, many attorneys are political appointees. This is true not only of the key policy-making officials in the department but also of the principal trial lawyers, the U.S. Attorneys.

The United States Attorneys are presidential political appointees. Each serves for a term of four years, although he may be asked to resign earlier. The term of office often coincides with the President's term, so that each President may appoint his own United States Attorneys. The post is one of the few patronage positions still available to the President for rewarding his political supporters. Consequently those appointed are often lawyers who have been active in their party's political affairs. The office allows its incumbent to become prominent on the local political scene; it is sometimes used as a steppingstone to a congressional seat, a judgeship, or a high state office. Few attorneys serve more than two terms before returning to private practice or proceeding to a higher public office.

Although United States Attorneys resemble prosecuting attorneys, they normally enjoy much less independence. The local prosecutor is usually an elected official operating without direct supervision, whereas the United States Attorney is part of the Justice Department's bureaucracy and has to carry out the orders he receives from Washington. In most instances Washington gives him considerable latitude in dealing with the ordinary cases that constitute most of his business. He apparently has as much latitude in dealing with a bank robber as the local prosecutor would have if the person had robbed a supermarket. However, those cases to which Washington attaches special importance are prosecuted according to instructions. When a prominent union leader like James Hoffa is on trial or when a major industrial firm is accused of violating the antitrust statutes, the United States Attorney operates under the close supervision of the Justice Department, which maintains specialists in Washington to assist United States Attorneys with their difficult cases. When a particularly important case arises, the department often sends a specialist to the trial court to help prosecute the case. Supervising such cases allows the Attorney General to use his field staff of United States Attorneys to promote particular policies through litigation. This is particularly important to the Attorney General, because some administration policies can only be promoted through litigation. The federal government, for instance, had few other means of assisting blacks in their attempts to register to vote in the South. Litigation is also the principal means of enforcing antitrust policies.

Moreover, control over the prosecution of a case is important in order to lay the proper groundwork for an appeal. Controversial policy issues are rarely settled at a trial; they are usually appealed to a Court of Appeals and to the Supreme Court. To win a favorable ruling, the government must be careful to raise the right questions during the trial so that an appellate court can later rule on them. It must avoid mistakes that would raise irrelevant questions on appeal.

The Justice Department exerts a much tighter control over appeals than over original prosecutions. Most appeals must be approved by the proper division of the Justice Department and the Solicitor General. Appeals are argued by a Justice Department lawyer from Washington rather than by the United States Attorney who originated the case. Still more centralized control is imposed on appeals to the Supreme Court. The Solicitor General passes on all such appeals. Although he is also a presidential appointee, he traditionally has remained somewhat independent of the Attorney General. He clears cases for appeal to the Supreme Court on the basis of his estimate of the government's chance of winning its case, the probable damage that would result if the government lost, the work load of the court, and the policy significance of a particular case.

Appeals to the Supreme Court and to Courts of Appeals are handled by the specialized staff of the Justice Department in Washington. The Antitrust Division supervises litigation on restraint-of-competition cases; the Civil Rights Division handles cases involving civil rights; ordinary civil actions are usually prepared by members of the Civil Division. The other sections of the department (Criminal Division, Internal Security Division, Land and Natural Resources Division, and Tax Division) operate similarly.

One important consequence of these activities by the Department of Justice is that it operates with a higher level of expertise than most private litigants. Many of the Justice Department's Washington lawyers are career officials. They specialize in a narrow range of conflicts and gain enormous experience with the appellate courts before which they appear. The Solicitor General's office is not staffed quite so heavily by career employees. It recruits top-ranking graduates from the leading law schools, who serve for a few years before moving to other positions in government or private practice. Although its lawyers are young, they argue more cases before the Supreme Court than anyone else. They learn through experience the personal proclivities of the justices and are then better prepared for unexpected questions that the justices pose during an oral argument.

Since the volume of government litigation is large, the Solicitor General can often choose to delay the appeal of an issue to the Supreme Court until the right case or the right moment comes. Most private litigants cannot do this, for they do not control a large enough volume of cases so that at any moment one can be chosen to submit a question to the Supreme Court.

The Justice Department's control over appellate cases has been used to advantage. It has gained the gratitude of the Supreme Court by helping the Court restrict its work load. While private requests for Supreme Court rulings (in the form of requests for a writ of certiorari) doubled between 1930 and 1960, the government's requests declined. Although the Supreme Court grants certiorari in less than 10 percent of all cases, it accepts more than two-thirds of the cases supported by the Solicitor General.

The Solicitor General's control over government suits that are appealed to the Supreme Court gives the Justice Department considerable influence over the kinds of cases that the Supreme Court decides. If the time does not appear propitious, the Solicitor General may decide to accept a lower court defeat that affects cases in only one circuit rather than to risk an unfavorable Supreme Court ruling that would affect the entire country. Not all cases, of course, are subject to review by the Solicitor General; private individuals may appeal their cases to the Supreme Court if they have lost in the lower courts, regardless of the Justice Department's desires. However, the Supreme Court accepts a much smaller proportion of such private appeals. In addition, since most policy issues involve the government, the Justice Department can either block review or oppose Supreme Court action on a private application for review. By restricting the flow of cases to the Court, the Justice Department influences the scope of judicial policy making.

Moreover, the Justice Department can prevent judicial review of certain government actions by advising·another agency to evade litigation. The Postal Service, for instance, sometimes stops the delivery of mail that it considers pornographic; when it does so, it acts as a censor. Its legal right to censor reading material is questionable under the First Amendment. Rather than risk judicial review of its policies, the service has often resumed the delivery of particular items as soon as it was sued in court. Such action moots the case and halts court action. Postal policy is not affected: the next shipment of pornographic literature may again be impounded.

In the same way that the Justice Department can block action by the courts, it can also promote judicial activity by initiating suits that will induce judicial declarations of policy. It may take the lead in forcing a judicial test of the constitutionality of a statute. It may support private test cases by submitting *amicus curiae* briefs.

Although litigation is a risky venture, the Justice Department's operations make it a more manageable tool of policy. Sometimes a President uses the department to enforce a particular policy—such as civil rights. On other occasions an administration may use litigation to suppress what it considers extremist opposition to its policies. Many observers gave this interpretation to the Nixon administration's decision to prosecute the Chicago Eight for allegedly crossing state lines to incite a riot at the 1968 Democratic National Convention in Chicago and to prosecute the "Berrigan Conspiracy," in which the Berrigan brothers and several others were accused of planning to kidnap presidential adviser Henry Kissinger and to blow up several heating tunnels in Washington to demonstrate their opposition to the Vietnam war.

In summary the federal government uses its lawyers for quite diverse purposes. It employs them to prosecute violations of federal laws and to defend the government in legal actions. The Justice Department also uses its staff to influence judicial policy making by promoting the appeal of some cases while blocking the appeal of others. Such a use of government attorneys helps to make the federal court system a weapon in the political arsenal of a President.

● ● ●

16

The Public Defender: Man in the Middle

Jonathan D. Casper

[*The following selection is based on interviews with 71 criminal defendants in Connecticut, 49 of whom were incarcerated in Connecticut correctional institutions.*]

From Jonathan D. Casper, *American Criminal Justice: The Defendant's Perspective* (Prentice-Hall, 1972), pp. 106–112, 112–115, Copyright © 1972 by Prentice-Hall, Inc. Reprinted by permission of Prentice-Hall, Inc., Englewood Cliffs, N.J. Footnotes have been omitted.

• • •

Nearly 70 percent of the men interviewed were represented by the public defender. They had little choice in the matter: they did not have the money to hire a lawyer, and the judge appointed the public defender to represent them. A defendant typically encountered his lawyer in the hallway or bullpen (lock-up) of the courthouse, or else he found himself before the judge with a man beside him who turned out to be his attorney. The typical defendant reported that he spent a total of five to ten minutes conferring with his attorney, usually in rapid, hushed conversations in the courthouse. Thus, a man who may receive five or ten years in prison spends five or ten minutes with the man who is supposed to supply the "guiding hand of counsel," to ensure that his rights are exercised and protected, to make certain that the "noble ideal" of a fair trial is protected.

What can a defendant talk about in five to ten minutes with "his" attorney? His social and psychological background? His motives for committing the crime, if he did indeed do it? The nature of police investigation and interrogation and possible legal defenses dealing with search and seizure and entrapment? His goals and treatment needs? Hardly. What he can talk about is the deal. Most of the men reported that among the first words uttered by their public defender were: "I can get you—— if you plead guilty." Perhaps they do not remember other words that came before, but certainly these were the most salient words the public defender uttered.

> You know, his name in superior court is known as "cop-out Kujawski." This what everybody in prison calls him cause that's the first thing as soon as he comes in your cell in superior court, that's the first thing he says—cop out, cop out, cop out. Through the past years everybody's known him as cop-out Kujawski. He's earned a name for himself.

• • •

> Well, he have the nickname of "cop-out Kujawski." That's all; it's the only thing that you hear from him: If you cop out, I get you this; if you cop out, I get you that. If you cop out, I get you a suspended sentence—that's the only thing he ever speak about. Other than that, he don't speak about—well, at first he might say, Well, I'm gonna try and do this for you—or do somethin like that; then maybe he might come back two or three weeks later, and he says, You cop out. That's what he always brings up—cop out—that's the first thing. If you cop out, I get you this—and that's it.

Thus, the public defender is not "their" lawyer, but an agent of the state. He is the surrogate of the prosecutor—a member of "their little syndicate"—rather than the defendant's representative.

> He seemed like he didn't care one way or the other. He just cop out, you know. Like, you see a police walking on the street writing a ticket out, you

know. He puts a ticket on the car. He don't care whose car it is. [The public defender] say, just, you know, You cop out to this, and you say no, and he says, I see if I can get a better deal. Then he brings another offer: You cop out to this. Just like that, you know. Just checking on the cop-outs.

• • •

A public defender is just like the prosecutors' assistant. Anything you tell this man, he's not gonna do anything but relay it back to the public defender [*sic;* he means the prosecutor]; they'll come to some sort of agreement, and that's the best you're gonna get. You know, whatever they come to and he brings you back the first time, well, you better accept it because you may get more.

• • •

He just playing a middle game. You know, you're the public defender; now, you don't care what happens to me, really. You don't know me, and I don't know you; this is your job, that's all; so you're gonna go up there and say a little bit, make it look like you're tryin to help me, but actually you don't give a damn.

• • •

It's just like you got a junkie there, and he needs a bag of dope, and you tell him, Well, here's the bag of dope if you want it, or you gotta suffer it out, if you want to, you know. I mean, here's the bag of dope if you want it; I mean, you don't have to take it, when you know damn well he gonna snatch at it, cause the man is sick, you know what I mean.

You say the public defender is like that?

Sure, [it's as if someone says to a junkie], Well, here's the bag of dope. If you want it, you can take it; if you don't. . . . Well, you say, Yeah, I want it, I want it, I'm sick, man. That's the way it is, man. It's nothing big to him. Like I say, he makes deals like this every day.

The public defender typically has access to police reports and knows the strength of the case against the defendant. Before any extended discussion with the defendant and the offer of a deal, he sometimes consults with the prosecutor and agrees on a tentative sentence in return for a plea. He knows what is "in the ballpark" for a particular offense given a man's record. He knows the man is guilty. He knows that failure to plead guilty will probably result in a conviction at trial and harsher punishment than can be obtained by a compromise and a guilty plea. He knows that his caseload is tremendous and that it is in the interest of the courts as a whole for most guilty men to plead guilty. He knows that he cannot spend as much time as he might like on any particular case.

Thus, the behavior of "their" attorney—especially if he is a public defender—contributes to the feeling that they are essentially standing alone without advice that they can rely upon to be impartial. This distrust of the public defender is terribly strong. Notice that in one of the excerpts reproduced above, a defendant said "public defender" when he meant to say "prosecutor." This mistake was common—at one point or another most of the men interviewed either called the public defender the prosecutor or called the prosecutor the public defender. This is a subtle but significant indicator of the confusion of roles that the defendants experienced—the near interchangeability of "their" lawyer with the prosecutor.

Unlike the private lawyer, who was viewed as giving advice, providing information and offering suggestions, most defendants felt that the public defender tried to tell them what to do. This is also a major source of dissatisfaction with the public defender. Another source of dissatisfaction stems from the lack of choice facing the typical defendant. The indigent defendant—except in those cities in which legal assistance lawyers handle criminal cases—is simply *given* the public defender. Most feel that they cannot *fire* their defender—he is simply given to them, and they have no control over the matter.

Although most defendants do not consider the possibility, they can in fact sometimes fire their public defender. Most either don't know that this is possible or think that they will simply get another of the same. Two of the men interviewed refused the services of the regular public defender and had special public defenders appointed from the private bar. These two men were somewhat more satisfied with their attorneys, though both were in prison. Both reported that they felt their attorney was on their side, though both were quite bitter about their convictions and sentences. Both felt that they had a reasonably good relationship with their attorney and that they exchanged ideas rather than simply received instructions about how they ought to behave. Their attorneys apparently were able to spend somewhat more time with them than the public defender usually does. The fact that the defendants had some voice in the selection of their attorneys also seems to have been important. Both knew that but for their choice, the attorney would not have received the case and the money that went with it, though the money was admittedly rather meager. We shall return to this theme later, for the notion of choice—of some control over the lawyer's getting the case—seems an important determinant of a defendant's evaluation of his attorney's services.

Another factor contributing to distrust of the public defender is the belief that most public defenders desire to become prosecutors (and then, eventually, judges). As two men suggested: "The more convictions he get . . . and the higher he can get"; "Most of the prosecutors—most of the public defenders go from public defender to prosecutor." There are no systematic data available describing career patterns of public defenders, but it is by no means unheard of for a public defender to join the prosecutor's staff. Such incidents become widely known and are cited frequently as indicating that the public defender must be working with the prosecution in order to further his own career ambitions.

Another factor is that the public defender really has no financial incentive for fighting hard for his clients. "He gets his money either way," was the common phrase—whether his client wins or loses. The ability of a "street lawyer" (private attorney) to get clients depends upon his reputation, and defendants believe that good reputations are built by winning cases. The public defender, on the other hand, does not have to depend upon his reputation to get clients—he receives them automatically, whether he wins many cases or loses many. Thus, from a defendant's vantage point, the public defender has nothing to gain (and perhaps, given his perceived career ambitions, something to lose) by vigorously defending clients.

> Public defenders usually don't want to fight a case in this state. They get the same amount of money if they win or lose; so why should they fight if they don't have to, if they got an easy way out?

Perhaps the most important factor affecting defendants' distrust of the public defender is his position as an employee of the state: "They got to be on the state's side in order that they can work for the state." Most of the men with whom I spoke approach life with a simple yet powerful premise. Put in abstract form, it might be stated as follows: any two or more persons receiving money from a common source must have common interests. In the context of defendant-public defender relations, it urges that since both the prosecutor and the public defender are employed by "the state," they *cannot* fight one another. He who pays the piper calls the tune in this world, and if the same source is paying the public defender and the prosecutor, the reasonable expectation is that they will work together. Thus, a crucial difference between a street lawyer and a public defender is that the street lawyer is *paid* by the client; the public defender is not:

> You're giving him [a street lawyer] something for you. I wasn't giving "Jones" [a legal assistance lawyer] nothing, and what they're paying him, they're gonna pay him that anyway. [With a private lawyer] if he doesn't go for you, you give him half salary; you don't have to pay him his other half. And I think that he'll look at that a lot, you know.

• • •

> *Why is it that [street lawyers] do a better job for you?*

> Well, first of all, you payin him; so you got a right to demand some things.

• • •

> Because I feel that if you are paying a lawyer—regardless whether you wrong or right—the person he's defending come first. By hiring a lawyer, he'll

take time cause I mean if you want to talk, he feel, Well, damn it, this man is paying me, he got a right to talk to me about it cause he want to know what's goin on, and you got to tell him. But on those terms you not payin him; so you really can't say nothin if you want to talk.

• • •

You're paying [the street lawyer]; you're given him money, you're putting food—in other words, you know, you're gonna buy his next suit or maybe his next house. The public defender just can't possibly get—the one I got, he must not got too much pay from the state. I know he wasn't gettin no hundred dollars. Since, you know, he ain't making much money. If I only had a thousand dollars hidden in my sock and I asked and I brung it out, he would have went and helped me more, you know.

Thus, paying a lawyer not only provides some assurance that he is on the defendant's side, but also gives the defendant a sense of leverage over his attorney, a sense that he is in a position of some autonomy. Most of the men had never had street lawyers and were simply expressing a faith that this is the way that it would be; the key to their analysis was the notion of a financial transaction between lawyer and client. By paying an attorney, you can make sure that he is "yours."

• • •

The importance of money and of financial transactions reflects the general socialization into a market economy that the defendants, like all Americans, have experienced. In this sense the defendants were very "good" Americans, for they were very accepting of the ethic of the market-place. For example, although most felt that the poor fare worse than the rich in the legal system, they also believe that this cannot be changed. When asked whether they felt that a "society in which there weren't any rich and weren't any poor, but everybody had about the same" would be better or worse, a majority felt that it would be worse (or was, given human nature, unattainable). They want the opportunity to get rich themselves, to enjoy the benefits of life that others enjoy, and tend to associate equality with moving everyone down to the lowest common denominator.

Likewise, almost all—even those convicted of property crimes—were accepting and supportive of laws against taking property from others. After all, they reasoned, when I get rich I don't want someone taking it away from me. With only a couple of exceptions, none of the men was a modern-day Robin Hood taking from the rich to aid the poor (except in an individualistic sense—aiding himself), or a "radical" who believed that the rich had no "right" to possess what the poor cannot have. Most *wanted* what the rich have, but almost none felt that this made it morally right to steal from the rich. Indeed, the men seemed to have strongly internalized the marketplace ethic of our society. They believe that you get what you pay for and that what costs more is probably better than (or at least as good as) what costs less.

It is not surprising, then, that defendants who didn't have the money to purchase an attorney's services think that the "merchandise" which they were provided by the state was inferior to that available on the open market. In many ways, the crucial difference between the public defender and street lawyers lies not only in how they behave toward their clients—how much time they give them, how concerned they appear to be, how the case comes out—but also in the nature of the transaction between lawyer and client. Money talks:

Suppose you'd said to your public defender, "Here's a hundred dollars if you can get me a suspended sentence." Do you think he'd have fought any harder for you?

I'm almost positive he would. If you were a public defender—now you're only gettin paid by the state—and a guy said, "Look, if you can beat this case, I'll give you an extra hundred dollars on the side". . . . I mean, it's a hundred dollars, and all you gotta do is put a little more effort into it— just like anybody else would do, cause it's the next hundred dollars, and that's what he's tryin to do: he's trying to make as much money as he can.

Some of the men I spoke with had been represented by public defenders and had received suspended sentences. They were, not unnaturally, somewhat more satisfied with the quality of representation they had been afforded, though all expressed a preference in future cases for a street lawyer rather than a public defender. Moreover, they tended to attribute the "good" outcome not to their lawyer but to their own efforts ("I talked up to the judge and told him I was in the methadone program") or to luck. They generally refused to believe that their own attorneys were responsible for the outcome, for they did not really trust the public defender. Thus, even when the public defender did well for a client, he did not seem able to convince him that he had adequately represented him.

The common view among all men represented by the public defender was, then, "If only I'd had a street lawyer, I'd have come out much better." Yet looking at the charges against the defendants, their reports of the evidence against them, their past records, and the like, this expectation often appeared to be somewhat unrealistic, for many seemed to have come out fairly well. Men who expressed this desire for a street lawyer were asked whether they had ever had one. Most had not and were simply expressing blind faith in street lawyers and distrust of the public defender:

If you got in trouble again, would you like to be represented by this man [a public defender]?

No! I'm gettin a lawyer this time. I'm payin for a lawyer.

Well, a lot of guys tell me that they think that street lawyers do a better job for them than a public defender. Why do you think that's true?

Because you pay . . . I mean, like this guy [a private attorney with whom the defendant had had contact] said if I paid the three hundred dollars, he said he might of got me off on probation. He might have.

How do you think he could have done that if the public defender couldn't have?

I don't know!

Others, though, did have experiences with street lawyers, but the stories they told were quite mixed. A few spoke of "sure" convictions beaten by wily and dedicated street lawyers. Many described cases in which they appeared to have fared only moderately well—the outcome was about what one could expect—but which had cost them substantial sums of money. Some related stories in which it appeared that they had been exploited—their sentences were harsh, and the fee seemed exorbitant. But in almost all situations, even the last, the defendants spoke with a kind of satisfaction about the quality of their representation. Not that the outcome was always desirable, but at least they had *paid* the lawyer— he depended upon them for his money—and hence he must have been on their side.

The importance of money and of the financial exchange also emerged in the defendants' notions of the ideal relationship between lawyer and client. Most seemed to desire a contingent fee arrangement. A defendant would retain an attorney for a small fee and would pay him a further fee based on the outcome of the case (e.g., a thousand dollars for an acquittal or dismissal; five hundred dollars for a suspended sentence; three hundred dollars for a one-to-three-year sentence; one hundred dollars for a two-to-five). Such an arrangement may not make much economic sense, for the outcome may not vary directly with the amount of time spent on a case, but it indicates that defendants tend to associate the size of the exchange with the efforts of the attorney.

The relationship of public defender to client seems to the defendants another perversion of the symbols of the criminal justice system. The gamelike nature of the proceeding extends even to the defendant's *own* lawyer, for he is himself playing a game, mediating between prosecutor and defendant, pursuing interpersonal and professional goals that are seen as contrary to the goals of the defendant, whom the lawyer is supposed to be representing.

• • •

———————————— 17 ————————————

Supreme Court Lawyers

Jonathan D. Casper

[*The following selection is taken from a study of lawyers appearing before the Supreme Court during the tenure of Chief Justice
Earl Warren.*]

• • •

There is a variety of ways of conceptualizing what a lawyer is trying to
achieve in his litigation. We might talk about *goals,* referring to what
particular outcome the lawyer was trying to achieve (to win? to win on a
particular point of law? to secure some social or political policy?). The
notion of *role* might be useful, for self-expectations and those of others
may be very important in shaping the lawyer's perception of his case and
his notions of how he ought to approach it. Another useful concept might
be *reference groups or individuals,* for there may be particular individuals or groups whose expectations and preferences are particularly important to the lawyer. Finally, we could use the concept of *clientele,*
which deals with the set of persons (ranging from an individual to all of
society) that the lawyer perceives as having a stake in the case and as
being likely to be affected importantly by its outcome.

Most of the concepts suggested above are theoretically distinct and
separable, but all are related to some extent. One of these concepts,
clientele, is the focus of this study.

• • •

The term "clientele" is not used here in the restricted sense usually
applied to the principal for whom the lawyer acts as agent. The clientele
of a lawyer (as distinguished from his client) is not simply the person,
group, or organization that formally retains and pays him. Rather, clientele is defined by the lawyer's perceptions of what group or interest he is
serving. Obviously, a lawyer's clientele in a particular case may be his
client, but the two need not be the same. In fact, a lawyer's clientele
could range along a continuum from one person (usually his client) to
all of society. In analyzing the responses to questions designed to tap the

From Jonathan D. Casper, *Lawyers Before the Warren Court* (University of
Illinois Press, 1972), pp. 71–72, 72–75. Copyright © 1972 by The Board of Trustees of
The University of Illinois. Reprinted by permission. Footnotes have been omitted.

respondent's clientele, lawyers with three different classes of clienteles were distinguished: the *Advocate,* the *Group Advocate,* and the *Civil Libertarian.*

The Advocate is close to the paradigm often associated with the legal profession. He uses his training and skills in litigation on behalf of his client. He is concerned simply with winning the case for his client, and he will use any legal and ethical means, raise any issue, seek any satisfactory result (e.g., agree to plea bargain before trial, be satisfied with winning an appeal on a technicality or with a remand to a lower court for further proceedings). The Advocate is essentially indifferent about whom he represents; the characteristics of his client are of little interest to him. The Advocate views his own policy preferences as irrelevant to his activity as an attorney, and the ramifications of his case for others in society are also of little concern, unless they affect directly his chances for winning. The Advocate's clientele is his client.

The Group Advocate sees himself as a representative of some particular group and uses his skills in the case he argues to further the aims of that group. This is not to imply that the Group Advocate is simply an Advocate with a group as his client. Rather, the Group Advocate perceives himself as having long-term commitments to the group involved, and, more important, the group may not even be a formal party to the litigation. In a sense, then, the Group Advocate is serving *his* group in litigation (though he may not formally be a member of the group—e.g., the white civil rights lawyer representing black clients). Thus the Group Advocate's clientele is somewhat wider than that of the Advocate, but it still numbers less than all of society. The Group Advocate perceives himself as a member of a specific group and his activity in litigation as representative of the group interest.

The Civil Libertarian views his clientele as all of society and his case as a vehicle by which democratic principles important to all of society may be vindicated. The principles are general: "freedom of religion" or "freedom of speech." The lawyer is something of a gadfly, using his expertise to promote democratic principles. The ACLU is an organization—staffed largely by lawyers—dedicated to using litigation to promote such principles. The Civil Libertarian, like other lawyers, is involved in litigation that affects specific individuals, but he is primarily concerned with the results of the litigation upon society generally—not "free speech for John Doe" or "free speech for those with whom I am associated" but "free speech for all."

The distinction between the Advocate and the Group Advocate and Civil Libertarian is sharper than that between the Group Advocate and the Civil Libertarian. This is especially true because some of the cases in which Group Advocates have become involved—those dealing with racial discrimination, speech and association rights of political radicals, and reapportionment—do appear to involve principles obviously important to the whole society. But the key to the distinction between the Group Advocate and the Civil Libertarian is not the *issue* that appears to be involved in the case but the lawyer's perception of the group interest at stake. As is pointed out in some detail in the discussions of Group Advocates and Civil Libertarians, this is not meant to imply that Group Advocates are indifferent to the effects of their cases upon society generally, but simply that their primary concern deals with the effects upon a particular group rather than upon society at large.

The distinction between the Group Advocate and the Civil Libertarian may be further illuminated by contrasting two litigating interest groups, the NAACP Legal Defense Fund (LDF) and the ACLU. Lawyers of both organizations become involved in litigation dealing with similar issues. For the LDF the operative factor in its involvement has typically been the presence of an issue involving black people (i.e., an issue affecting this *particular* group of people); for the ACLU the operative factor has been the presence of some democratic principle. The services of the LDF have, in a sense, not been available to all, for the organization was set up and has functioned primarily as an advocate for a particular minority. The ACLU, on the other hand, has professed to be indifferent to the characteristics of its clients—ACLU lawyers have represented fascists and Communists, blacks and white racists. For the one organization, a particular group of people has brought it into action, for the other, a type of principle. The differences between the activities of the two organizations correspond rather closely to the distinction between the Group Advocate and the Civil Libertarian.

• • •

——————————————— 18 ———————————————

The Lawyer as Agent-Mediator
Abraham S. Blumberg

● ● ●

The Practice of Law as a Confidence Game

The real key to understanding the role of defense counsel in a criminal case is the fixing and collection of his fee. It is a problem which influences to a significant degree the criminal court process itself, not just the relationship of the lawyer and his client. In essence, a lawyer-client "confidence game" is played.

In many "server-served" relationships for a fee—which include not only the practice of law, medicine, or dentistry but also plumbing—there is not always a visible end-product or tangible service involved. A plumber, for example, will usually be able to show that he has performed a service by unstopping a drain, repairing a leaky faucet or pipe—and therefore merits his fee. He has rendered a tangible benefit for his client in return for the requested fee. On the other hand, a physician who has not performed some visible surgery or otherwise discernible procedure may be accused by the patient of having "done nothing" for him. Doctors may even prescribe or administer by injection a placebo to overcome a patient's potential dissatisfaction in paying a fee "for nothing."

The lawyer has a special problem in this regard, no matter what his status or prestige. Much legal work is intangible, because it is simply a few words of advice, some preventive action, a telephone call, negotiation of some kind, a form filled out and filed, a hurried conference with another attorney or an official of a government agency, a letter or opinion written, or a countless variety of seemingly innocuous and even prosaic procedures and actions. These are the basic activities of almost all lawyers at all levels of practice. They represent not precise professional skills but rather the acts of a broker, agent, sales representative, or lobbyist. The lawyer pursues someone else's interests and designs.

The large-scale law firm may not speak as openly of its "contacts" and "fixing" abilities as does the lower-level lawyer. It trades instead upon the facade of thick carpeting, walnut paneling, genteel low pressure, and

———————

From Abraham S. Blumberg, *Criminal Justice* (Quadrangle Books, 1967), pp. 110–115. Reprinted by permission of author. Footnotes have been omitted.

superficialities of traditional legal professionalism. But even the large firm may be challenged because the services rendered or results obtained do not appear to merit the fee asked. Thus there is a recurrent problem in the legal profession in fixing the fee and justifying it.

In a criminal case, the defendant is soon parted from the spoils he may have acquired from his illicit activities. Not infrequently, the returns from his larceny are sequestered by a defense lawyer in payment of fee. Inevitably, the amount of the fee is close to the dollar value of the crime committed. On occasion, defendants have been known to commit additional offenses while at liberty on bail, in order to get money for payment of legal fees. Defense lawyers make sure that even the most obtuse clients know there is a firm connection between fee payment and the zealous exercise of professional expertise, secret knowledge, and organizational "connections" in their behalf. They try to keep their clients at the precise edge of anxiety calculated to encourage prompt payment of fee. The client's attitude in this relationship is often a precarious admixture of hostility, mistrust, dependence, and sycophancy. By playing upon his client's anxieties and establishing a seemingly causal relationship between the fee and the accused's extrication from his difficulties, the lawyer establishes the necessary groundwork to assure a minimum of haggling over the fee and its eventual payment.

The lawyer must then be sure to manipulate the client and stage manage the case so that help and service at least *appear* to be rendered. This is accomplished in several ways. At the outset, the lawyer uses a measure of sales puff which may range from unbounding self-confidence to complete arrogance. This will be supplemented by a studied, faultless mode of personal attire. In the larger firms, the furnishings and office trappings will serve as the backdrop for impressing and intimidating the client. In all firms, solo or large scale, an access to secret knowledge and to the seats of power and influence is implied as the basic vendible commodity.

The special complication of the criminal lawyer is that an accused always "loses," even when he has been exonerated by an acquittal, discharge, or dismissal. His hostility is directed, by means of displacement, toward his lawyer, and in this sense a criminal lawyer never really "wins" a case. The really satisfied client is rare, because even an accused's vindication leaves him with some degree of dissatisfaction and hostility. The man who is sentenced to jail may of course be a singularly unappreciative client.

Bearing these attitudes in mind, the criminal lawyer collects his fee *in advance*. Often, because the lawyer and the accused both have questionable designs upon each other, the lawyer plays the confidence game. First, he must arrange for his fee; second, he must prepare his client for defeat (a highly likely contingency) and then, if necessary, "cool him out"; third, he must satisfy the court organization that he has adequately negotiated the plea so as to preclude an embarrassing incident which might invite "outside" scrutiny.

If the accused is himself unable to pay more than a token fee, the lawyer must involve as many of the accused's kin group as possible in the situation. This is especially so if he hopes to collect a significant part of a proposed substantial fee. It is not uncommon for several relatives to contribute toward the fee. The larger the group, the greater the possibility that the lawyer will collect a sizable fee by exacting several contributions.

A fee for a felony case which ultimately results in a plea, rather than a trial, may ordinarily range anywhere from $500 to $1,500. Should the case go to trial, the fee will be proportionately larger, depending upon the length of the trial. But the larger the fee the lawyer wishes to exact, the more impressive his performance must be; he must show himself to be of great influence and power in the court organization. To some extent court personnel will aid the lawyer in creating and maintaining an image. This is the partial basis for the quid pro quo that exists between the lawyer and the court organization. It is the continuing basis for the lawyer's higher loyalty to the organization; his relationship with his client, in contrast, is transient, ephemeral, and often superficial.

The lawyer has often been accused of stirring up unnecessary litigation, especially in the field of negligence. He is said to acquire a vested interest in an action or claim which would otherwise never have developed. The criminal lawyer develops a vested interest of a different nature: not to promote the litigation but to limit its scope and duration. Only in this way can a case be "profitable." Thus he enlists the aid of relatives not only to assure payment of his fee but to help him in his agent-mediator role of convincing the accused to plead guilty, and ultimately to help him in "cooling out" the accused, if necessary.

The fee is often collected in stages, each installment payable before a necessary court appearance during an accused's career journey. At each stage, in his interviews and communications with the accused (and with members of his kin group, if they are helping with the fee payment), the lawyer employs an air of professional confidence and "inside-dopesterism" to assuage anxieties on all sides. He makes the necessary bland assurances and in effect manipulates his client, who is usually willing to do and say the things—true or not—that will help his attorney extricate him. Because what he is selling is not measurable, the lawyer can make extravagant claims of influence and secret knowledge with impunity. But, as in a genuine confidence game, the victim who has participated is loath to do anything that will upset the lesser plea which his lawyer has "conned" him into accepting.

In his role as double agent, the criminal lawyer performs an extremely vital and delicate mission for the court organization and the accused.

Both principals are anxious to terminate the litigation with a minimum of expense and damage. No one else in the court structure is more strategically located, more ideally suited to do so than the lawyer. In recognition of this, judges will cooperate with attorneys in many important ways. For example, they will recess the case of an accused who is in jail awaiting plea or sentence if the attorney requests such action. Overtly this may be done for some innocuous and seemingly valid reason, but the real purpose is to permit the attorney to press for the collection of his fee, which he knows he will probably not get if the case is concluded. Judges are aware of this tactic, but they will go along with it on the grounds that important ends are being served.

The judge may also lend the official aura of his office and courtroom so that a lawyer can stage manage an "all-out" performance for the accused in justification of his fee. The judge and other court personnel will serve as backdrop for a scene charged with dramatic fire, in which the accused's lawyer makes a stirring appeal in his behalf. With a show of restrained passion, the lawyer will intone the virtues of the accused and recite the social deprivations that have reduced him to his present state. The speech varies somewhat, depending on whether the accused has been convicted after trial or has pleaded guilty. In the main, however, the incongruity, superficiality, and ritualistic character of the total performance is understood by a visibly impassive, almost bored reaction on the part of the judge and other members of the court retinue. Afterward, there is a hearty exchange of pleasantries between the lawyer and district attorney, wholly out of context with the supposed adversary nature of the preceding events. The fiery passion is gone, and lawyers for both sides resume their offstage relations, chatting amiably and perhaps including the judge in their restrained banter. No other aspect of their visible conduct so effectively puts even a casual observer on notice that these individuals have claims upon each other. In intricacy and depth, their relations range far beyond the priorities or claims of a particular defendant.

Criminal law is a unique form of private law practice. It simply *appears* to be private practice. Actually, it is bureaucratic practice, because of the lawyer's role in the authority, discipline, and perspectives of the court organization. Private practice, in a professional sense, supposedly involves the maintenance of an organized, disciplined body of knowledge and learning; the lawyer is imbued with a spirit of autonomy and service, the earning of a livelihood being incidental. But the lawyer in the criminal court is a double agent, serving higher organizational rather than professional ends. The lawyer-client "confidence game," in addition to its other functions, helps to conceal this fact.

● ● ●

——————————————— **19** ———————————————

The Lawyer as Advocate

Warren E. Burger

• • •

Time does not allow a recital of the myriad points of substantive law and procedure that an advocate in criminal cases should know in order to perform his or her task. Suffice it to say that in the past dozen or more years a whole range of new developments has drastically altered the trial of a criminal case. To give adequate representation, an advocate must be intimately familiar with these recent developments, most of them deriving from case law.

Whether we measure the recent changes in terms of one decade or three, we see that the litigation volume, particularly in criminal cases, has escalated swiftly. The Criminal Justice Act and the Bail Reform Act, the extension of new federal standards to state courts, rising population, increased crime rates, creation of new causes of action and expanded civil remedies have contributed to the literal flood of cases in state and federal courts.

Whatever the legal issues or claims, the indispensable element in the trial of a case is a minimally adequate advocate for each litigant. Many judges in general jurisdiction trial courts have stated to me that fewer than 25 percent of the lawyers appearing before them are genuinely qualified; other judges go as high as 75 percent. I draw this from conversations extending over the past 12 to 15 years at judicial meetings and seminars, with literally hundreds of judges and experienced lawyers. It would be safer to pick a middle ground and accept as a working hypothesis that from one-third to one-half of the lawyers who appear in the serious cases are not really qualified to render fully adequate representation. The trial of a "serious" case, whether for damages or for infringement of civil rights, or for a criminal felony, calls for the kind of special skills and experience that insurance companies, for example, seek out to defend damage claims.

Let me try to put some flesh on the bones of these generalizations concerning the function and quality of advocates. I will try to do this by

From Warren E. Burger, "The Special Skills of Advocacy," (Fourth John F. Sonnett Memorial Lecture, Fordham Law School, New York, N.Y., November 26, 1973), pp. 10–14. Reprinted by permission of the author. Footnotes have been omitted.

way of a few examples observed when I sat by assignment as a trial judge, while serving on the U.S. Court of Appeals:

1. The thousands of trial transcripts I have reviewed show that a majority of the lawyers have never learned the seemingly simple but actually difficult art of asking questions so as to develop concrete images for the fact triers and to do so in conformity with rules of evidence.

2. Few lawyers have really learned the art of cross-examination, including the high art of when not to cross-examine.

3. The rules of evidence generally forbid leading questions, but when there are simple undisputed facts, the leading questions rule need not apply. Inexperienced lawyers waste time making wooden objections to simple, acceptable questions, on uncontested factual matters.

4. Inexperienced lawyers are often unaware that "inflammatory" exhibits such as weapons or bloody clothes should not be exposed to jurors' sight until they are offered in evidence.

5. An inexperienced prosecutor wasted an hour on the historical development of the fingerprint identification process discovered by the Frenchman Bertillon until it finally developed that there was no contested fingerprint issue. Such examples could be multiplied almost without limit.

Another aspect of inadequate advocacy—and one quite as important as familiarity with the rules of practice—is the failure of lawyers to observe the rules of professional manners and professional etiquette that are essential for effective trial advocacy.

Jurors who have been interviewed after jury service, and some who have written articles based on their service, express dismay at the distr[a]cting effect of personal clashes between the lawyers. There is no place in a properly run courtroom for the shouting matches and other absurd antics of lawyers sometimes seen on television shows and in the movies. From many centuries of experience, the ablest lawyers and judges have found that certain quite fixed rules of etiquette and manners are the lubricant to keep the focus of the courtroom contest on issues and facts and away from distracting personal clashes and irrelevancies.

A truly qualified advocate—like every genuine professional—resembles a seamless garment in the sense that legal knowledge, forensic skills, professional ethics, courtroom etiquette and manners are blended in the total person as their use is blended in the performance of the function.

There are some few lawyers who scoff at the idea that manners and etiquette form any part of the necessary equipment of the courtroom advocate. Yet, if one were to undertake a list of the truly great advocates of the past 100 years, I suggest he would find a common denominator: they were all intensely individualistic, but each was a lawyer for whom courtroom manners were a key weapon in his arsenal. Whether engaged in the destruction of adverse witnesses or undermining damaging evidence or final argument, the performance was characterized by coolness, poise and graphic clarity, without shouting or ranting, and without baiting witnesses, opponents or the judge. We cannot all be great advocates, but as every lawyer seeks to emulate such tactics, he can approach, if not achieve, superior skill as an advocate.

What is essential is that certain standards of total advocacy performance be established and that we develop means to measure those standards to the end that important cases have advocates who can give adequate representation. Law school students are adults who can contribute once they are persuaded of the need for training in this area. Rather than being "lectured" on ethics, they should be invited to discuss with the faculty and the best advocates the ethical element in the practice of law so as to impress them with the reality that courtroom ethics and etiquette are crucial to the lawyer's role in society—and indispensable to a rational system of justice. Woven into the seamless fabric of effective advocacy, professional ethics and professional manners are no less important than technical skills.

Lawyers are—or should be—society's peacemakers, problem solvers, and stabilizers. The English historian Plucknett suggests that England and America have been largely spared cataclysmic revolutions for two centuries, in part because the common law system lends itself to gradual evolutionary change to meet the changing needs of people. Lawyers can fulfill that high mission only if they are properly trained.

● ● ●

Lower Court Judges: Selection

20

Judicial Election and the Missouri Plan

Patrick Winston Dunn

• • •

Elective Judicial Selection

The case for elective judicial selection centers on two principal arguments: the open nature of elections and the appeal of political competition. Citing America's tradition of republican government, proponents of judicial elections claim that the process of electing judges is the most open and straightforward method of selection, and further, that popular participation at the polls produces the beneficial result of a judiciary which is both representative of and accountable to the electorate. It is argued as well that since judges are part of our political life, the competitive political election serves as the best mechanism by which to educate the public about judicial candidates and insure that judges are responsible to the people.

The arguments for elective judicial selection are theoretically appealing but, in fact, misleading.

From Patrick Winston Dunn, "Judicial Selection in the States: A Critical Study with Proposals for Reform," *Hofstra Law Review* 4 (1976): 285, 286, 289, 290, 293–295, 295, 296–298, 299–300, 301–302, 302, 303. Copyright © 1976 by the Hofstra Law Review Association. Reprinted by permission. Footnotes have been omitted.

• • •

[T]he assumption that the election of judges is an open method of selection has little basis in fact. In many instances, the theoretical process of free judicial elections does not, in practice, exist. What does exist more often is a system of judicial appointment dominated by party and government leaders and supported, often unwittingly, by the organized bar and the judges themselves.

In many jurisdictions, for example, the vacation of a judgeship before the end of a term transfers to the executive the right to appoint an interim successor. This has two major ramifications: it oftentimes allows the executive to make unrestricted appointments, and it confers upon the appointee the status of incumbent, which in elective judicial contests is practically tantamount to victory in the next election. Likewise, in non-incumbent elections, it is common practice for political parties to combine their forces informally, divide prospective seats among themselves and cross-endorse their precontracted contestants. True competition is thus substantially diminished and victory for the pre-arranged judicial candidates is virtually assured.

• • •

A major fault of the elective system is that the political recruitment of judicial candidates tends to be based not on character qualifications but, instead, on individual service to the party.

• • •

Political activity can basically be divided into two types: that which involves the development of governmental policies responsive to the needs of a heterogeneous society and that which seeks to widen a power base primarily for the sake of increasing political control. Although we are inclined to condone the former and condemn the latter, these tasks are by no means mutually exclusive. The judicial candidate who is a loyal and hardworking party member may make a competent public official. However, if party servitude is all that is required of judicial contestants, there is no guarantee—and, in fact, little hope—that they will meet . . . the . . . qualitative criteria established . . . to identify the proficient judge.

Once they become candidates, prospective judges are then faced with the ordeal of a campaign. Not only must judicial candidates solicit financial contributions for their own campaigns, but they are often requested to make a monetary donation to the party in anticipation of the well-paying job to come. Both of these practices encourage serious problems of undue influence and conflict of interest.

• • •

TABLE II. A Synthesis of the Results of an Elmo Roper and Associates Survey of Voter Awareness of Judicial Elections During the 1954 Statewide Elections in New York.

OF THOSE WHO HAD VOTED AT ALL, THE PERCENTAGE THAT	NEW YORK CITY	BUFFALO	CAYUGA COUNTY
• voted for any judicial candidate	75%	88%	80%
• paid attention to judicial candidates before the election	39%	52%	25%
• could name one or more judicial candidate voted for	19%	30%	4%
• could name a judicial candidate they had not voted for	0%	less than 1%	less than 1%
• could name a court for which judges had been elected	20%	11%	14%
• either paid no attention to the election at all or merely voted for the straight party ticket	78%	62%	84%

Assuming, however, that voters are given every theoretical advantage in an election—how likely is it that they would be willing and able to select the most qualified judges? The answer would seem to be: not very. In fact, surveys have shown that the electorate knows and cares substantially less about judicial candidates than any others on the ballot. One of the most revealing of these surveys was conducted in 1954 by Elmo Roper and Associates in New York State within a ten-day period immediately following a statewide election. The poll was conducted in New York City, a metropolis; Buffalo, an upstate municipality; and rural Cayuga County (see Table II). If more voters paid closer attention to judicial elections or could name the judicial candidates for whom they voted, it is conceivable that party leaders would be more inclined to insure that their judicial political activities were responsive to the needs of the publc.

Although the flow of information in judicial elections is stifled by ethical restraints, there is no particular reason to assume that a lengthy and unfettered discussion of complicated court cases would inspire the apathetic, nor would it benefit the average voter who is unschooled in the intricacies of legal and judicial affairs.

• • •

The election of judges does not, therefore, effectively or consistently serve its intended purpose which is to place responsible and responsive public servants on the bench.

• • •

Missouri Plan

The elective system's major rival is the Missouri plan. Supporters of
the latter say that its greatest accomplishment has been to remove the
judiciary from the contamination of politics by placing the power of
judicial selection in the hands of a committee properly structured for the
task. There is general support throughout the legal profession for this
view and for the Missouri plan itself. The selection committee, defenders
assert, is able actively to recruit candidates for the bench, to examine
their qualifications thoroughly, and to compare them critically as the
field is narrowed. It is further claimed that once a nominee is placed on
the bench, this selection system substantially guarantees the judge's independence from the deleterious political influences present under the
elective aproach. It is also suggested that the committee, composed of a
judge, three members of the bar, and three lay appointees of the governor, provides the proper combination of citizen representation and
legal expertise for active deliberations and resolutions based on quality.
Since the committee is a permanent body, its expertise can be refined by
on-going educational programs, its own experience, and the advice of a
professional staff. In fact, proponents assert that the mere presence of a
screening committee is adequate to deter those candidates who are clearly
unqualified. In addition, under this plan, if the electorate decides later
that the committee and the governor have made an improper choice, it
has the option to vote for dismissal in a special election held after the
appointed judge has been on the bench for one year. The voters may
further choose not to approve a judge for a future term.

The legal community, regrettably, has failed to utilize its own resources and those of other disciplines—especially political science, sociology, and history—to examine closely the operation and ramifications
of this plan. Lawyers seem to be reticent to identify shortcomings in a
program which in the United States is offered as the only practical alternative to the elective system. This "hands-off" treatment of the Missouri plan has seriously retarded efforts to reform the judicial selection
process.

●　●　●

With very little analysis available comparing the various selection
systems and the judges they produce, it is impossible to respond with any
certainty to the claim that the Missouri plan provides for elitist control
of the judiciary. Recent data on judicial selection committees, as is discussed below, indicate that these committees are narrowly based and
suggest that the question of elitist control should be the subject of future
inquiry. In defense of the Missouri system, however, it is important to

note that in their exhaustive study of its operation in the State of Missouri in the 1960's, Richard Watson and Ronald Downing found (as summarized by the U.S. Advisory Commission) that:

Contrary to expectations, there is a greater tendency for graduates of night law schools—not of prestigious institutions—to ascend to the bench than under the preceding elective system.

Appointees are essentially "locals" rather than "cosmopolitans."

The majority are affiliated with the majority party.

They are older, more mature than judges previously selected by election.

Appellate judges selected have had more service at the lower levels than previously.

Appointees tend to have prior experience in law enforcement, particularly as prosecutors.

They are not more conservative than those chosen by election.

They are better judges than their predecessors in terms of knowledge of the law, open-mindedness, common sense, courtesy, and hard work.

Closely related to the charge that the Missouri plan is elitist, is the suggestion that the Missouri selection committees are unable to produce a judiciary which is representative of the pluralistic interests of the society-at-large.

• • •

Allan Ashman and James J. Alfini's important study of Missouri plan judicial selection committees throughout the country found their composition to be highly unrepresentative. Of the 371 committee members who responded to their survey, 97.8 percent were white and 89.6 percent were male. Certainly the paucity of women and blacks in the legal profession largely accounts for these figures, but it does not explain why only 3.3 percent of the lay commissioners were non-white and only 22.3 percent were women. In addition, among the lay members of the selection committees surveyed, business and banking executives predominated (27.1 percent) with less input by educators (7.8 percent), journalists (4.8 percent), and medical professionals (3.6 percent). The prevalence of these particular interests on the selection committees raises very serious doubts about the commissions' ability to produce a judiciary sensitive to all interests of the general public.

• • •

Moreover, there is evidence to show that the lay members who theoretically represent the general public during deliberations tend to defer to the views of the governor who appointed them and are often intimidated by lawyer members. This then allows the bar and the governor further to dominate the proceedings. Watson and Downing as well as

Ashman and Alfini discovered this problem to exist under the Missouri plan and recommended the inclusion of strong, independent lay members on the selection committees and energetic lawyer-lay interaction during the selection process.

• • •

Finally, there is general agreement that the Missouri plan has not eliminated politics from the selection process but only altered its form. The Governor's choice of committee members and final appointive power is not immune from political pressures; the bar, in its selection of commissioners, is similarly subject to political rivalries. It is equally impossible for the committee itself to be entirely isolated from the political realities of the outside world. The ultimate question is not, however, whether politics should play a part in judicial selection, for it will under any system except divine revelation, but rather whether the Missouri plan so channels today's political energy as to select the best possible judiciary.

• • •

21

The U.S. Circuit Judge Nominating Commission

Larry Berkson

For years, one of the main prerogatives of a U.S. Senator was to "recommend" judges to the President, provided that the senator belonged to the same party as the chief executive. But that situation changed, at least in part, when Jimmy Carter became President. On February 17, 1977, he announced the establishment of the U.S. Circuit Judge Nominating Commission to aid him in filling vacancies on the courts of ap-

---

From Larry Berkson, "The United States Circuit Judge Nominating Commission: The Candidates' Perspective," *Judicature* 62 (May 1979): 466, 466–468, 469. Reprinted by permission of the author. Footnotes have been omitted.

peals. (Carter left intact the senators' power to recommend district judges.)

Under his plan, the Commission is divided into 13 panels, one for each judicial circuit and two for the geographically large Fifth and Ninth Circuits. Once the President activates a panel, it is required to give public notice of the vacancy, conduct inquiries and report to the President the names of persons deemed "best qualified" for the position. The President then makes the final choice.

Several studies have now been published analyzing the Commission's operations and procedures, but none so far has examined the characteristics of the candidates who have been recommended. . . .

To obtain this information, a questionnaire was mailed to the 74 candidates recommended to the White House between February 1, 1977, and September 1, 1978. During that period, 10 panels were convened 13 times to assist the President in filling 17 vacancies (see Figure 1). They were asked for biographical data, impressions about the panel before which they appeared, attitudes about the propriety of the questions they were asked, and ways the process could be improved. Altogether, the survey contained 35 closed and open-ended questions. Sixty-three of the 74 candidates responded (85 per cent).

Qualifications for Office

The Executive Order creating the Commission established standards which candidates must meet before they can be recommended to the President. All prospective nominees must be members in good standing of a state bar or the District of Columbia bar. They must possess, and have reputations for, integrity and good character; possess and have demonstrated outstanding legal ability and commitment to equal justice under law; and be of sound health. Their demeanor, character and personality must indicate that they will exhibit judicial temperament if appointed to the bench. Moreover, their training, experience and expertise must meet the needs of the court of appeals where the vacancy exists.

The supplemental instructions elaborate on these standards. The candidates must be free of physical, mental or emotional problems. They must have experience in at least two of five enumerated areas of law, and they must be able to work collegially with their fellow judges. Moreover, they must be free of biases against any class of citizens or any religious or racial group.

Candidates are disqualified from consideration if they have been convicted of a felony or a misdemeanor other than a minor traffic violation. They are also disqualified if they use narcotics, have been guilty of professionally unethical conduct or are not U.S. citizens.

A Profile of the Candidates

One of the principal purposes of the nominating commission survey was to discover the kinds of people who were recommended to the President for the Courts of Appeals. Here is a summary of what was found.

SEX AND RACE.

The 63 respondents in the survey included 45 white males, nine black males and nine white women. (Thus, the sample was highly representative of the entire group of candidates, which included 52 white males, 10 black males, one Asian-American male and 11 white females.)

OCCUPATION.

Those who answered the survey included 23 practicing attorneys; 17 state judges; 16 federal judges; and six law professors. (The whole group consisted of 26 practicing attorneys; 17 state judges; 19 federal judges, including four District of Columbia Superior Court judges; and 12 professors and deans, including one university chancellor.)

PARTY.

Fifty-five of the respondents were Democrats; eight were Republicans. (In the whole group, there were 63 Democrats, nine Republicans, one independent and one who claimed no party affiliation.)

AGE.

Most of the respondents were between the ages of 41 and 60.

RELIGION.

Thirty-one of the 63 respondents reported being Protestant, 13 Jewish and 12 Catholic.

INCOME.

Nearly all of the respondents reported substantial incomes. Fifty-nine (95 per cent) earned more than $40,000; forty-seven (76 per cent) stated that their earnings were over $50,000; twenty-five (40 per cent) stated that their income exceeded $60,000; and eighteen (29 per cent) claimed to earn more than $70,000. Only three earned less than $40,000.

Since the salary of a circuit judge is currently $57,500, it appears that about 40 per cent of the applicants would experience a reduction in income if selected, whereas nearly 60 per cent would either maintain an equivalent income or experience an increase.

EDUCATION.

The respondents attended a wide variety of colleges and universities. As undergraduates they earned degrees from 43 different schools. Eleven candidates received degrees from Ivy League schools, 21 from other private schools and 27 from state colleges and universities.

Twenty-two received their law degrees from Columbia, Harvard, Pennsylvania or Yale. Six others attended such prestigious law schools as the University of Chicago, University of Michigan and Stanford. The other 34 earned their law degrees from a variety of other state and private universities. Additionally, eight reported earning graduate degrees in law.

PARTISAN ACTIVITY.

Most of the respondents had not been active in partisan politics. Over 90 per cent had never sought party office and none had held a paid party position. Only four had served as volunteers on the staff of a political party. Fifty-six per cent of the candidates claimed not to have made a party contribution within the past five years. The 23 who did contribute, however, gave to the Democratic Party. One gave to both parties.

POLITICAL IDEOLOGY.

Twenty-five respondents (42 per cent) claimed to be liberal or very liberal; thirty-three (55 per cent) claimed to be moderate; and two (3 per cent) claimed to be conservative. No one considered himself very conservative. Of the eight Republicans, six claimed to be moderate, one claimed to be liberal, and one, conservative.

——————————————— 22 ———————————————

Should There Be Affirmative Action for the Judiciary?

Sheldon Goldman

The Carter Administration has jolted the legal community with its outspoken and widely-publicized affirmative action policy of placing women and ethnic minorities on the federal bench. Many of the arguments raised against the implementation of affirmative action programs elsewhere are now being heard with regard to the judiciary along with arguments attuned to the special status of the federal bench. But after considering the nature of the Administration's efforts and successes in implementing judicial affirmative action, I have concluded that the legal profession ought to applaud President Carter and Attorney General Bell.

As I see it, six major objections can be raised against an affirmative action approach to federal judicial selection. Each, I believe, can be persuasively answered. I would like to discuss these objections briefly and the rejoinders I find convincing.

1. THE DANGERS OF CLASSIFYING PEOPLE.

Affirmative action inevitably leads government agencies to define race, critics argue, and it leads government officials to make judgments about racial characteristics. Is an individual with one black grandparent or great-grandparent (say, Homer Plessy) to be classified as black? What about someone with one black parent who was raised by white foster parents? Is an American-born individual with an American father and Mexican mother Hispanic? The argument, essentially, is that it is dangerous for government to make any racial classifications. Such activities stir memories of the racial laws of Nazi Germany and run counter to the value Americans have traditionally placed on treating individuals on the basis of their personal qualities and not their racial attributes.

RESPONSE.

While many (including myself) are uncomfortable with government concern with race/ethnicity, I believe there is a crucial and fundamental

From Sheldon Goldman, "Should There Be Affirmative Action for the Judiciary?" *Judicature* 62 (May 1979): 489–494, 494. Copyright © by Sheldon Goldman. Reprinted by permission of the author. Footnotes have been omitted.

distinction between America's official racial consciousness for purposes of affirmative action and the racial classifications of totalitarian regimes. America's purpose is to aid definable classes of persons who have historically suffered from official discrimination. Racial classifications in Nazi Germany were, of course, for ghastly purposes and in more contemporary totalitarian societies ethnic designations on identity cards and other records form the basis for official discrimination.

The federal judiciary has been and still is an overwhelmingly white, male institution, for many reasons. America's long-standing racism and sexism, for example, have historically limited opportunities in the judiciary for women, blacks and Hispanics. It does not seem unreasonable to make special efforts to recruit from these groupings of Americans for federal judgeships. Deliberate considerations of race and sex should not be given negative connotations so long as the government demonstrates positive, anti-racist, anti-sexist motives and purposes.

2. The Threat of Reverse Discrimination.

The real result of affirmative action, opponents argue, is reverse discrimination. Government selects a group or groups of persons for favored treatment, thereby putting all others at a disadvantage. This is reminiscent of George Orwell's *Animal Farm* where all animals are equal but some are more equal than others. On an individual basis this produces reverse discrimination; individuals are ruled out of consideration *because* they are the "wrong" race or sex. Furthermore, when it comes to judicial selection, those women, blacks and Hispanics who are favored for judgeships are frequently from the same social class and similar backgrounds as competing white males and their careers have not necessarily suffered from discrimination. Why then should they have an advantage?

Response.

I cannot be persuaded that affirmative action is reverse discrimination—at least when the objective is *not* to give minorities a majority hold. I have not seen evidence that any affirmative action program of any kind in the United States has seriously threatened the majority status of white males in government, industry, the professions or academia. Certainly the type of affirmative action that the Carter Administration is promoting for the judiciary in no way threatens the overwhelming majority status of white males.

Although the Administration's efforts thus far to place women, blacks, and Hispanics on the federal bench have been spectacular when compared with the record of previous administrations, taken alone the results of the Carter Administration's affirmative action policy are actually very modest. About 12 per cent of the Carter nominees have been black and about the same proportion have been women. In terms of the entire federal bench, the proportions of blacks and women are exceedingly small and for Hispanics almost non-existent.

At the individual level, the charge of reverse discrimination potentially can be more troublesome, as it was in the *Bakke* case. But we do not have to be concerned with this since judicial selection traditionally has involved numerous variables. The addition of racial/ethnic and sexual considerations is in no way inconsistent with the host of other considerations that have been involved in judicial selection, including geography, party affiliation, party activity, sponsorship by senators and other key politicians, professional connections, ideological or policy outlook, and so on. Race/ethnicity and sex are today politically relevant variables and they have been added to other political type variables in a selection process that historically has been political.

3. The Error of Focusing on Group Affiliation.

No matter how worthy an objective it may be, critics say, affirmative action is inconsistent with the professed goal of merit selection which many judicial reformers and the Carter Administration itself espouse. How can one accept the principle that only the best qualified should be given judgeships and then decree that women, blacks, and Hispanics are to be given special preference? Merit selection emphasizes individual qualities; affirmative action stresses group affiliation.

Response.

It does a disservice to women, blacks and Hispanics to suggest that they do not ordinarily possess as strong a set of professional credentials as white males do, but I will not dwell on this obvious rejoinder. What I find persuasive is the fact that, based on my own extensive research and that of others, we never had, we do not now have, and we probably never will have a judicial selection method based solely on professional merits. The professional credentials of candidates do play a part in judicial selection, but rarely have they been the determining factor. Of course it is important to have qualified persons sitting on the bench and there is no question in my mind that Attorney General Bell, under affirmative action, is recommending to the President only persons with the professional credentials essential to perform the job.

Ironically, affirmative action may provide a more potent push towards merit selection than anything else that has ever been done. By searching for well qualified women, blacks and Hispanics, the Administration and Democratic senators are downplaying party activity and political connections. This breaks with the past judges-as-patronage syndrome that historically characterized much of judicial selection.

Let me add for the record that the Administration's so-called merit selection of appeals judges is not merit selection in fact. As recent issues of *Judicature* have shown, mostly Democrats (including large numbers of Carter loyalists) have chosen mostly other Democrats for placement on the lists given the President. Other Democrats then lobby the Democratic President as to which Democrats to choose.

However, the selection process has become more open in large part due to institution of merit commissions and the affirmative action push. It is highly unrealistic to expect a civil service type merit approach to judicial selection ever to be established. Even assuming that an effective merit selection process could be instituted, I would have to be persuaded that the sorts of people chosen were better suited for the bench than the sorts of people chosen through our traditional political processes.

4. The Need for Government Neutrality, not Favoritism.

Affirmative action is a remedy to right a proven constitutional wrong, critics emphasize. Even if it could be proven that racism and sexism served to exclude blacks, women and Hispanics from the judiciary, that would not justify affirmative action in choosing the highest officials of the federal government. It would only justify efforts to ensure that these groups were no longer deliberately excluded.

Blacks prevented from voting were eventually protected by federal legislation and action to enable them to exercise the franchise, but they were not given the right to elect so many black congressmen or black state representatives. Women given the right to vote in 1920 were not given the right to have a specific number of women in high elective or appointive office. Isn't it sufficient that the judicial selection process be non-discriminatory? Isn't affirmative action inappropriate here?

Response.

The racial and sexual make-up of the judiciary, past and present, speaks for itself. It is clear that all-pervasive societal attitudes toward women, blacks, Hispanics, and indeed other groups such as Asian-Americans and American Indians severely limited their opportunities in the law and that they were, in fact, routinely and systematically excluded from federal judgeships. Justice Department officials and senators were not necessarily themselves racist or sexist. It is simply that within the framework of political reality and racist and sexist belief systems in the larger society, appointments of women, blacks, and some other ethnic groups were impossible.

But leaving aside the difficult questions of proof, and, indeed, whether constitutional wrongs were committed in the past, it can be argued that government can serve as a teacher by setting a good example and structuring situations in which learning and personal growth can occur. Clearly, the widespread racist and sexist attitudes of the past and the discrimination so widely practiced were moral, if not constitutional, wrongs. We should seize this opportunity to correct them.

By seeking out and appointing to federal judgeships a visible number of qualified women and minorities, government is teaching the nation that racial and sexual stereotypes are invalid. Government is also teaching young women, young blacks and young Hispanics that it no longer recognizes as political reality the racial and sexual biases of the past, and that individual accomplishment and achievement are more important than race and sex.

Yes, it is ironic that affirmative action which recognizes race and sex is necessary in order to hasten the time when race and sex will be irrelevant, and when racism and sexism are virtually non-existent. Perhaps most importantly, by voluntarily undertaking affirmative action, the government is practicing what it preaches (although, make no mistake about it, the Carter Administration is responding to its own political needs and commitments). We ought to welcome any diminution of government hypocrisy.

5. The Problem of Quotas.

Affirmative action in practice results in a quota system, opponents contend, and quotas are dysfunctional for the workings of American institutions. Quotas based on group affiliation and not individual merit can work grave hardship on well-qualified individuals who are in excess of their group's quota, and, in general, quotas tend to promote mediocrity. Quotas can exclude superior qualified persons who have the wrong sex, race, religion, or ethnic affiliation; they can include not only the marginally qualified, but even unqualified persons. Affirmative action is the first step on the road to the balkanization of America, and the courts—our prized palladiums of justice—should be the last place where this concept is imposed.

Response.

Affirmative action programs have existed for close to a decade, and I am not persuaded that the parade of horrors suggested above has even begun to come about. I see no movement within the United States for each ethnic or religious grouping to claim a quota of public or private jobs. Most Americans accept individual merit as the proper basis for school admissions and employment opportunities.

Although the distinction may be fuzzy, I do see a difference between affirmative action and a quota system. Affirmative action does not have a rigid numerical goal; it retains flexibility yet is a good faith effort to widen the recruitment net, indeed to vigorously recruit, and pay particular attention to women and disadvantaged racial/ethnic groups. Affirmative action also means selecting the individual from the previously discriminated-against group when all else is approximately equal.

I have not heard or read the word "quota" in connection with the Carter Administration's affirmative action objectives for judicial selection. I would oppose the use of a quota system as unnecessarily rigid and singularly inappropriate for the judiciary, but this is not at issue. The Carter Administration itself, as I understand it, is making strenuous efforts to recruit, or have selection commissions and senators recruit, qualified women, blacks, and Hispanic candidates. The Administration, as I also under it, is quite concerned with the qualifications of minority and women candidates.

If the politics of federal judicial selection today make it unlikely that incompetent white males will go on the bench, the politics of affirmative action requires that only competent minorities and women be appointed. The surest way to sabotage affirmative action is to link it with incompetency. The Carter Administration's record of minority and women appointments thus far has been excellent . . . and there is every reason to believe that the concern with credentials of minority and women candidates will continue to yield well-qualified judges.

6. An Inappropriate Program for the Judiciary.

No matter what the merits of affirmative action may be for other spheres of American life, critics insist, it is highly inappropriate for the judicial branch. Even though merit may not actually be the sole criterion for judicial selection, it is recognized as ideally the basis for choosing judges, and leading professional groups have been working to make progress towards that goal. But if a criterion other than individual merit gains legitimacy, it becomes all the more difficult to assign to oblivion the "extraneous" political considerations that have traditionally "polluted" the process. And it becomes more difficult to win support for a partisan-free merit selection process.

Part of the justification for merit selection is that a federal judge must be highly skilled since the federal courts are the fastest legal tracks in town. We need the best people for the job; would we select a surgeon to perform a highly complex and delicate operation on any basis other than the best person available? Why should we do less with the judiciary?

We need the best people on the bench regardless of race, sex or national origin. In the words of the President, "Why not the best?"

RESPONSE.

This is a slippery argument to counter. To be sure, there must be highly competent judges to service the trial and appellate courts of the nation. Official recognition of race and sex does appear at first blush to detract from the goal of a non-discriminatory process for obtaining the best qualified persons to serve. But a closer look at the job of federal judges should make it clear that our judges have always been involved in the major political controversies of the day. As Tocqueville so perceptively observed over 140 years ago, "Scarcely any political question arises in the United States that is not resolved, sooner or later, into a judicial question."

Today, racial and sexual discrimination are major legal issues before the courts. A judge who is a member of a racial minority or a woman cannot help but bring to the bench a certain sensitivity—indeed, certain qualities of the heart and mind—that may be particularly helpful in dealing with these issues. This is not to say that white judges are necessarily insensitive to issues of racial discrimination or that male judges cannot cope with issues of sexual discrimination. But the presence on the bench in visible numbers of well qualified judges drawn from the minorities and women cannot help but add a new dimension of justice to our courts in most instances.

These judges cannot help but educate their colleagues by the example they set, by the creation of precedents, and by informal as well as formal interchange. They are likely the "best" people to fill certain of the vacancies and new judgeships.

Yes, we ought to aspire to obtaining the "best" people for our judiciary—but the "best" bench may be one composed of persons of all races and both sexes with diverse backgrounds and experiences and not necessarily only those who were editors of the Harvard and Yale law reviews. It is difficult to define—much less find—the "best." Despite occasional mistakes, the current selection process with its political sensitivity has served the nation well. But affirmative action of the sort advocated and being practiced by the Carter Administration should strengthen the federal bench. And perhaps most significantly, it may be that by searching for the best possible women and minority candidates a precedent will be established for emphasizing the individual professional merits of all candidates for judgeships, regardless of race and sex.

—————————————— **23** ——————————————

The Changing Role of the
Senate Judiciary Committee
in Judicial Selection

Elliot E. Slotnick

• • •

The Judiciary Committee's Role

Central to any consideration of the process that is being followed in the current recruitment effort is the role of the Senate Judiciary Committee under the leadership of its new chairman, Senator Edward Kennedy. It is the constitutional duty of the Senate to advise and consent to federal judicial appointments and, except in rare and unusual instances of bitter floor fights (generally in more visible and controversial Supreme Court appointments), the Senate's role has been played out primarily in the committee's deliberations and ultimate recommendations to the entire chamber.

• • •

The Blue Slip Tradition

Perhaps the implications of the transition from the Eastland to the Kennedy stewardship of the Judiciary Committee is most clearly evident in the changes being initiated in the traditional prerogatives of senatorial courtesy and the blue slip procedure. The custom of senatorial courtesy usually insures that senators will support a colleague who objects to a federal appointment being made by the President in his state as long as the objecting senator is a member of the President's party.

Over time, the Judiciary Committee formally institutionalized and extended the concept of senatorial courtesy through the blue slip procedure "whereby the Judiciary Committee formally invites senators from

From Elliot E. Slotnick, "The Changing Role of the Senate Judiciary Committee in Judicial Selection," *Judicature* 62 (May 1979): 503, 504–506, 506–508, 509. Reprinted by permission of the author. Footnotes have been omitted.

a nominee's home state to disclose opinions and information concerning the nomination." The original understanding of the blue slip procedure was that objecting senators would make their negative views known on the blue slip. The blue slip itself states, "Under a rule of the committee, unless a reply is received from you within a week from this date, it will be assumed that you have no objection to this nomination."

In practice, however, the blue slip has operated as a potential "pocket veto" of judicial appointments by home state senators. That is, when the blue slip is *not* returned, the assumption is made that a home state senator objects to a nomination and, "in fact, no hearing is scheduled on a nominee in the absence of a returned blue slip. Thus, senatorial courtesy is institutionalized within the committee as an automatic and mechanical one-member veto of nominees." Of particular note is the fact that committee practice has resulted in the distribution of blue slips to all home state senators regardless of party affiliation. In effect, the potential veto of Presidential appointments could be exercised by senators who are *not* members of the President's party and who were never traditionally considered within the gambit of senatorial courtesy.

The blue slip procedure has surfaced as an issue symbolic of the conservative and often hidden forces which have long controlled the judicial selection process in the Senate. Consequently, it has become a question of great public controversy. Commenting on the blue slip tradition at the January committee hearing, Charles Halpern of the Judicial Selection Project asserted that the "privilege in its pristine force should be rejected." David Cohen of Common Cause asserted at the same hearing: "It's not only secret, but it becomes an act of personal political self-indulgence which damages the institution. It damages the institution."

Reforming the Blue Slip Procedure

Senator Kennedy publicly placed himself squarely on the side of reforming the blue slip procedure in his opening remarks at the committee hearing and, it appears, initiated a substantial change in the process.

> I will not unilaterally table a nomination simply because a blue slip is not returned by a colleague. . . . I have instructed the committee staff to send to each senator from a nominee's state a blue slip requesting the senator's opinion and information concerning the nominee. If the blue slip is not returned within a reasonable time, rather than letting the nomination die, I will place before the committee a motion to determine whether it wishes to proceed to a hearing on the nomination, notwithstanding the absence of the blue slip. The committee, and ultimately the Senate, can work its will.

In effect, Kennedy has created a situation in which, with the support of his committee, the silent veto of the blue slip can be overridden at the

United States Senate
Committee on the Judiciary

_____ , 197___

Dear Senator,

 Will you kindly give me, for the use of the Committee, your opinion
and information concerning the nomination of

 Under a rule of the Committee, unless a reply is received from you
within a week from this date, it will be assumed that you have no objection
to this nomination.

Respectfully,

Chairman

To Hon. _____
U.S. Senate

Reply

_____

_____

_____

_____

_____

The Senate's blue slip.

committee stage of the process. Indirectly, the reform will severely damage the potential of minority party senators to affect judicial appointments made by the opposition party President. It has been reported that "Kennedy's stand has been greeted by virtually solid opposition from the seven Republicans on the 17-member committee." Countering Kennedy's position at the Judiciary Committee's hearing most forcefully was Republican Senator Paul Laxalt.

> There's an erroneous perception about senators with great delight utilizing the device of a blue slip. . . . I suspect first of all it has been rarely utilized. And secondly, I would suspect also that a senator driven to that . . . finds it to be a very onerous responsibility.
>
> I personally think that it would be a sad day in the committee and in the Senate for there not to be insured a senatorial prerogative—not from the standpoint of preempting anybody—but from assuming our responsibilities. That's way we're here as senators. And that's to call these tough shots within our states . . .
>
> I feel strongly about the blue slip process since it hasn't been abused . . . I hope personally that I never have to utilize it, but I never want to foreclose myself or any of my colleagues in the right case from being able to do that.

• • •

A Separate Questionnaire

A second area in which the Judiciary Committee has substantially altered its procedures in handling judicial nominations is in instituting an in-depth personal questionnaire, drafted and designed for its use. In the past, the committee relied heavily on the questionnaire designed by the ABA Standing Committee on Federal Judiciary for developing a profile of nominees. In addition, the committee chairman and, perhaps selected committee members were privy to information generated by FBI investigations of judicial candidates.

While such information has often proven to be valuable, the committee was limited to information deemed important by outside agencies aproaching the appointment process from their own unique perspectives. A cursory glance at the questionnaire drafted for the committee's use demonstrates that new areas of inquiry have been opened up, and that candidates will now be asked several new questions which could prove central to the Senate's exercise of advice and consent.

For example, the questionnaire demands detailed financial data, including a full listing of assets and liabilities, a five-year income report, a list of businesses or enterprises with which the candidate has been connected during the past decade or has a continuing financial interest in, a list of deferred compensation agreements and stock options the candidate has entered into, and a list of political contributions and contributions accepted.

The candidate is also asked to identify potential conflict of interest situations and, further, to state how he would resolve them. And in assembling a biographical profile of the nominee, the questionnaire seeks copies of every speech the candidate has made in the last five years. It is little wonder that Senator Alan Simpson labelled the questionnaire "searing" at the Judiciary Committee's hearing.

The Committee's Own Judgment

Perhaps the most novel, significant, and potentially controversial section of the questionnaire focuses on the nominee's ability to document that he "possesses and has demonstrated commitment to equal justice under law." This selection criterion is drawn from President Carter's November 8th Executive Order which outlined qualifications for the federal bench. The questionnaire asks a candidate:

1. In what specific ways have you demonstrated a commitment to equal justice during your career?

2. Canon 2 of the American Bar Association's Code of Professional Responsibility states: "Every lawyer, regardless of professional prominence or professional workload, should find time to participate in serving the disadvantaged." Describe what you have done to fulfill this responsibility.

3. Do you belong to any organizations or clubs which exclude persons or discriminate on the basis of race, sex, or religion? List, with dates of membership. Have you been involved in efforts to change such policies?

It is too early to comment on what independent role the committee will play in assuring that the President's nominees meet the President's own standards for selection. But the centrality of these questions in the committee's own questionnaire suggests that it will reach its *own* judgment concerning a candidate's commitment to equal justice and that the questionnaire responses could provide a basis for the committee and the Senate as a whole to exercise an aggressive, activist, and independent advice and consent role in judicial recruitment.

It should also be noted that the questionnaire even solicits the candidate's perceptions of his experiences, if any, with merit commissions that might have led to his eventual selection. Thus, it appears that the committee will attempt, to some degree, to examine the *process* by which candidates were chosen in addition to the *qualifications* of the chosen few.

A final change in Judiciary Committee recruitment processes worthy of mention is the internal development of an investigatory capacity of its own. The committee has established an investigative staff and no longer will the Senate find itself totally at the mercy of information from sources outside of the chamber. Clearly, there could be questions and concerns of unique interest to senators performing their recruitment role and now, for the first time, a mechanism exists to seek answers to those questions.

Opening Up the Process

If there is one concept which best summarizes the thrust of the Judiciary Committee's activity in the judicial recruitment arena since the convening of the 96th Congress, it is clearly the attempt to foster a spirit of "openness" in the process. Such openness was evident both in the symbolic act of holding a public hearing on January 25th as well as in the nature of the witnesses heard and the bones of contention raised.

Two themes dominated the session in addition to the committee's consideration of the Senate's own role and function in the selection process: the unique role of the American Bar Association in judicial selection and the place of affirmative action in future appointments. These are two areas of controversy with which the committee must come to grips in the coming months.

THE ABA's ROLE.

It is evident that the Bar committee will continue to be the target of criticisms from more broadly defined "public interest" groups such as the Judicial Selection Project. Charles Halpern phrased his unhappiness most succinctly at the hearing:

> We object . . . to the quasi-official status that is sometimes given to that committee and to its recommendations. . . . We were troubled . . . by the testimony of Attorney General Bell which seemed to think that the success of a judicial selection process could be measured by how many of the names submitted to the Senate have been [given a] very well qualified or exceptionally well qualified ABA imprimatur.

It is also evident that the ABA Committee role will be subjected to greater scrutiny by some members of the Judiciary Committee itself. Thus, as Senator Patrick Leahy stated in his opening remarks at the committee hearing:

> With all due respect to the American Bar Association there have been some . . . who have suggested that their very significant role in determining the qualifications of judges has been on some occasions like Jack the Ripper determining the qualifications of surgeons in 19th century England.

Addressing comments to Robert Raven, chairman of the ABA's Standing Committee on Federal Judiciary, Senator Howard Metzenbaum described his understanding of the ABA's procedures.

> One person from each circuit. That person really does all of this investigation . . . That one individual talks to everybody and then writes up the report. If that person has a pre-conceived idea, isn't there an element of subjectivity in that person, in that kind of investigation?
>
> Don't we all hear what we want to hear and reject that which we don't want to hear? How do you assure yourself that the individual that has all the limitations that each of us has doesn't inject into the matter his own reaction as a practicing lawyer? . . . How do you protect yourself against that?
>
> I must tell you that I practiced law all the time until I came to this body. . . . To this moment I haven't the slightest idea of who the individual is or did I ever know who the individual was that represented the American Bar Association in the circuit in which I lived.

And, further, Senator Kennedy questioned whether the ABA process assured an "old boy network" outcome, disadvantaged minority candidates because of the emphasis placed on judicial experience, or took into account a potential nominee's activity in public law concerns, such as poverty or environmental law.

● ● ●

A More Independent Role

In the final analysis, the questions addressed at the Senate Judiciary Committee's January hearing have raised the possibility of an increased, independent role for the committee and the Senate in federal judicial recruitment. It is also possible, however, that the spirit of openness dominating the hearing could result in even greater frustration for those unhappy with the traditional recruitment process if the committee reforms are not carried through or do not have their intended consequences.

Lower Court Judges: Decision Making

———— 24 ————

The Judicial Gatekeeping Function

Lawrence Baum

[G]atekeeping powers may be defined as those with which courts help to determine which demands they will address and how fully they will consider those that they do address. This rather broad and ambiguous definition requires some explication. Litigants may be considered political actors who wish to obtain favorable responses to their demands. To achieve this end, they seek first to get these demands before judges and to have them considered fully and officially. Gatekeeping powers represent means by which courts help to determine litigants' success in achieving this intermediate goal. The decision whether or not to hear a case, the shunting of some cases to a category receiving limited consideration, the establishment of rules of access to the court, and the encouragement of litigation or of alternative paths of action all constitute types of gatekeeping. To understand the nature of judicial gatekeeping, it will be useful to examine briefly some major forms of judicial activity which may be classified as gatekeeping practices.

From Lawrence Baum, "The Judicial Gatekeeping Function: A General Analysis and a Study of the California Supreme Court" (Paper delivered at the Annual Meeting of the American Political Science Association, San Francisco, Ca., September 1975), pp. 3–10. Reprinted by permission of the American Political Science Association and the author. Footnotes have been omitted.

1. DISCRETIONARY JURISDICTION

Perhaps the most clearly delineated form of judicial gatekeeping is the exercise of discretionary jurisdiction. The Supreme Court's *certiorari* power has its counterpart in most of the states, where the highest appellate courts possess the power to refuse decision on the merits to some or all classes of appeals. In states with intermediate appellate courts (N-23), typically the supreme court is required to hear certain kinds of appeals but has discretionary jurisdiction over most appeals from the intermediate level. Several states without intermediate appellate courts give their supreme courts discretion in the hearing of some cases; most notably, Virginia and West Virginia allow no appeals as a matter of right. Procedures for decision on the acceptance of cases and the proportions of cases accepted both vary considerably. In each court, however, discretionary jurisdiction serves as a device by which a large number of appellants are denied formal consideration of their demands on the merits.

2. SUMMARY DISPOSITION

Siblings of discretionary jurisdiction, some of illegitimate birth, are the practices of summary dismissal of appeals and summary affirmance of lower-court decisions in cases which appellate courts legally must hear. These practices are widespread as means by which appellate judges dispose rapidly of appeals which they do not wish to accord full consideration. The federal courts of appeals have used statutory powers as bases for summary dismissal of *habeas corpus* cases involving state prisoners and of pauper appeals, and under court rules some have adopted procedures for summary disposition of other appeals. The Supreme Court summarily affirms and dismisses appeals under its mandatory jurisdiction in a procedure similar to its *certiorari* decisions. Some state supreme courts have adopted similar procedures. In Nebraska, for instance, the appellee may move for summary affirmance under court rule. Summary disposition differs in legal form from discretionary jurisdiction, but its impact on appellants is virtually the same.

3. TRUNCATED PROCEDURE

Cousins of the first two forms are the procedures increasingly used by appellate courts to classify certain cases as worthy of less than the court's full procedure for their consideration. In some state courts, a staff director classifies some appeals as easy to decide and assigns them to a staff member, who writes a memorandum on the case, proposes the court's decision, and writes a draft *per curiam* opinion for the court. These materials then go to the judges responsible for the case, who reach final decision without oral argument. Other kinds of truncated procedure, with and without extensive staff involvement, exist in both federal and state systems.

Like summary disposition, truncated procedure represents a kind of substitute for discretionary jurisdiction, but it constitutes a more ambiguous form of gatekeeping. It involves gatekeeping in two senses. First, most of the "easy" cases assigned to the group receiving limited consideration inevitably will be those in which the appellant's demand is perceived as having little merit, so that the assignment in itself serves as a signal to limit the seriousness with which that demand is considered. Second, the adoption of truncated procedure, particularly the avoidance of oral argument, limits the appellant's ability to overcome the presumption of lower-court correctness. In contrast with discretionary jurisdiction and summary disposition, however, the appellant retains a chance for victory even if his case has been screened out of the mainstream.

4. ENCOURAGING SETTLEMENT

The most important form of gatekeeping in trial courts is the encouragement of pretrial settlements by judges. In criminal cases nearly all judges facilitate plea-bargaining, supplementing other pressures for bargaining with their own. This process is well understood by students of the judiciary. In civil litigation judges use pretrial and "settlement" conferences as means to obtain the settlement of cases. Because negotiation has greater legitimacy in civil cases than in criminal, judges tend to take a more active role in helping to reach settlement in civil litigation. One important difference between civil and criminal settlements lies in the fact that after a bargain is achieved in a criminal case the judge still plays an important decisional role in the sentencing process. A judge's pressure for settlement may be consistent or inconsistent with the parties' own preferences; in contrast with the devices already discussed, many litigants *want* the judge to play a gatekeeping role. Another difference with these devices lies in the fact that the court only influences the parties' own determination as to whether full decision will be obtained, rather than making that determination himself. Nevertheless, pressure for settlement of cases represents a clear and significant form of gatekeeping.

5. MANIPULATION OF COSTS

Both trial and appellate courts can manipulate the financial costs of litigation, costs which may be crucial in a potential litigant's decision whether to go to court. Thus, the relaxation of rules of form for appeals by indigent appellants in the Supreme Court and other courts has eliminated a major financial barrier to the appeal of criminal convictions. An example of another kind is the imposition of financial penalties for appeals judged frivolous in the intermediate appellate courts of California, intended to discourage groundless appeals. Whether directed specifically at indigents or at the general population, the manipulation of financial costs inevitably has a differential impact on groups of different economic status. What serves as an important gatekeeping device in regard to some segments of the population may have no effect on others.

6. MANIPULATION OF COURTS' RIGHT TO DECIDE

A variety of characteristics of a case may deprive a court of the legal power to hear and to decide it, including lack of jurisdiction, mootness, and lack of adversariness. Many of the rules establishing restriction on courts' power to decide cases were created by courts themselves. Moreover, those "imposed" on the courts by constitutions and legislatures are subject to considerable leeway in their interpretation. As a result, these rules have served as judicial gatekeeping devices, manipulated in their general form and in individual cases to open or close access to litigants. The Supreme Court's use of such devices as rules of standing and the doctrine of political questions as gatekeeping procedures is part of the folklore of the judiciary. Thus, for instance, the requirement of adversariness is adhered to when the Court wishes to avoid decision, relaxed when the Court wishes to decide.

Manipulation of rules concerning a court's right to decide cases serves two rather separate gatekeeping functions. The rules in themselves constitute factors influencing potential litigants' decision whether to go to court. In addition, their application in particular cases allows courts to determine whether particular litigants will obtain full consideration. The two functions together make this a significant form of gatekeeping.

These six forms of judicial gatekeeping, probably the most significant, provide a basis for some general conclusions about this form of judicial action. First, gatekeeping powers are used primarily to narrow access to judicial decision. Courts may relax or fortify barriers to litigants, and many gatekeeping powers are used for both purposes. But the emphasis of gatekeeping activity is one of making it more difficult for litigants to go to court and to obtain full consideration of their demands. This emphasis follows from the major purposes for the adoption of gatekeeping practices, the limitation of court workloads to improve court functioning and to ease judges' responsibilities.

Second, the possession of significant gatekeeping powers is not limited to a small number of fortunate courts. Relatively few courts possess highly formal, explicit gatekeeping powers like discretionary jurisdiction, but judges on other courts have made use of less explicit powers to achieve the same ends. Gatekeeping should be seen as a nearly universal function in the judicial system, an integral part of the judicial process at all levels.

Third, gatekeeping practices differ in some significant characteristics. One is the identity of the ultimate decision-maker in the gatekeeping process. In "court-centered" gatekeeping like the exercise of discretionary jurisdiction, the court determines whether or not each case will receive full consideration. In "court-litigant" gatekeeping, exemplified by encouragement of pretrial settlement, the court influences the *litigant's* decision whether to seek court decision. As noted earlier, manipulation of the courts' right to decide cases involves both types of gatekeeping.

Another distinction among gatekeeping practices concerns the impact of the gatekeeping decision. In most forms of gatekeeping this action determines whether a case will be decided on the merits or dropped. In this sense the impact of gatekeeping is "absolute." Truncated appellate procedure and pressure for settlement of criminal cases are devices of "limited" impact; even after a case is screened out a decision on the merits—in criminal trials, on sentencing—remains to be made.

The gatekeeping devices which have been discussed may be characterized on these two dimensions in the way shown in Table 1.

It is difficult to make categorical statements about the effect of judicial gatekeeping activities on litigants' ability to obtain favorable outcomes in court. This effect surely varies with such factors as the form of gatekeeping involved and the frequency with which gatekeeping powers are used to limit access. Moreover, there are serious problems in measuring the impact of most gatekeeping devices. We cannot easily determine

TABLE 1.   Characteristics of Major Forms of Judicial Gatekeeping

		IMPACT	
		Absolute	*Limited*
	Court-centered	Discretionary jurisdiction Summary disposition	Truncated procedure
Locus of decisionmaking	*Combined*	Manipulation of right to decide	
	Court-litigant	Manipulation of costs Encouraging civil settlement	Encouraging criminal settlement

the number of litigants deterred by jurisdictional rules or the number of settlements induced by judicial pressure.

On a more general level, however, it is clear that judicial gatekeeping creates barriers to success for litigants. This fact is clearest in the case of discretionary jurisdiction, by which some courts turn back the vast majority of demands which are brought to them. But it is also true of very different forms of gatekeeping such as the manipulation of financial costs. Litigants face other barriers to success in the courts—including, of course, judges' decisions on the merits in those cases which get past the gatekeeping stage. The existence of gatekeeping powers simply adds to the difficulty of getting to court and securing favorable outcomes. The agenda-setting powers of courts are real and significant, and students of the litigation process must take these powers into account in examining the tasks faced by those who would use the courts for political or other action.

25

Political Orientations, Social Backgrounds, and Role Perceptions of State Supreme Court Judges

John T. Wold

Previous studies of the judicial "role" have not attempted to explore systematically the origins of judges' role perceptions. This paper seeks to do so in terms of jurists' political ideologies and their background experiences. It focuses specifically upon the basic political outlooks and social backgrounds of judges in four state supreme courts, and relates these variables to the jurists' perceptions concerning judicial lawmaking. The concluding section analyzes the implications of our findings for the study of judicial behavior and of political behavior as a whole.

From John T. Wold, "Political Orientations, Social Backgrounds, and Role Perceptions of State Supreme Court Judges," *Western Political Quarterly* 27 (1974): 239–248. Reprinted by permission of the University of Utah, Copyright Holder. Footnotes have been omitted.

Role Orientations

To determine judges' perceptions of the judicial role we interviewed members of the highest courts of Delaware, Maryland, New York, and Virginia. The jurists' most striking reactions came in response to the following question: "What do you think of the controversy over whether appellate judges should act as law interpreters or lawmakers?" The replies fell into three distinct categories: law interpreter; lawmaker; and eclectic, reflecting a middle position between the other two approaches.

Law Interpreter

Over half of the judges strongly believed they should restrict themselves almost exclusively to "interpreting" the law. Judicial legislating, they felt, should be confined to the "interstices" of the existing law. Most had a strong attachment to the concept of "judicial restraint": they perceived their job to be almost solely one of following legal precedent and the will of the legislature.

Lawmaker

A striking contrast was provided by the views of three New York jurists, all of whom were firm believers in judicial "activism." Although they felt that lawmaking was primarily the prerogative of the legislature, they were apparently not averse to creating new law when convinced that circumstances warranted it. "We should make the law creative," declared one. "Where there has been social change and where the legislature has abdicated its responsibilities, I think we have a right to intervene." These "lawmakers" likewise seemed more willing than other judges to disregard or abandon legal precedent.

Eclectic

The remaining jurists refused to commit themselves fully to either the concept of law interpreting or lawmaking. Theirs was an eclectic approach; they felt the function of the court depended upon the particular case before it. Although most expressed the sentiment that ". . . basic policy changes should be made by the legislature," many also claimed, in the words of one judge, that ". . . under the guise of interpretation there is a lot of lawmaking going on."

Table 1 presents the distribution of responses by state and judicial

TABLE 1. Distribution of Law Interpreters, Lawmakers, and Eclectics

ORIENTATION	ELECTIVE RECRUITMENT		APPOINTIVE RECRUITMENT		
	Maryland	*New York*	*Virginia*	*Delaware*	*N*
Law Interpreter	4	1	6	1	12
Eclectic	3	2	0	2	7
Lawmaker	0	3	0	0	3
N	7	6	6	3	22

selection system. The data indicate the strong support given to the law-interpreter position and the rather sparing support given to the law-maker orientation. They also reveal substantial intercourt differences, differences which were more significant within than between the two recruitment systems.

The respondents clearly disagreed on whether it was permissible for appellate jurists to be innovators or sponsors of legal change. Two opposing views regarding decisional creativity appeared to be vying for the judges' allegiance—a deferential, precedent-oriented view and an innovative, policy-oriented view. To determine the basis for the disagreement, we will examine a series of attitudinal and background variables which might help explain the variance in responses.

Political Orientations and Role Perceptions

One possible explanation of the disagreements is that these differences merely reflected the political orientations of the individual jurists. In other words, the judges' perceptions of the judicial role may have been primarily a function of their personal ideological leanings.

In order to test this hypothesis, we asked each respondent: "Before you became a judge, how did you classify yourself according to political beliefs or values?" The judges proved to be highly receptive to this type of questioning. They generally classified themselves as "conservatives," "moderates," or "liberals," and the few who used other terms were classifiable into one of these three categories. The distribution of responses provided evidence of distinct variations among the political environments of the four states. In Maryland, four judges described themselves as "conservatives," two termed themselves "moderates," and one termed himself a "liberal." In New York, five classified themselves as "liberals" and one described himself as a "moderate." All six Virginia justices classified themselves as "conservatives." All three Delaware justices described themselves as "moderates."

Table 2 shows the relationship between the judges' political orienta-

TABLE 2.   Relationship of Political Orientations to Law-Interpreter, Eclectic, and Lawmaker Orientations

POLITICAL ORIENTATION	ROLE ORIENTATION			
	Law Interpreters	Eclectic	Lawmaker	N
Conservative	10	0	0	10
Moderate	1	4	1	6
Liberal	1	3	2	6
N	12	7	3	22

tions and the law-interpreter, eclectic, and lawmaker positions. The data strongly indicate there was a close relationship between the jurists' policy values and their role perceptions. Every political conservative adopted the law-interpreter position, while moderates were strongly attracted to the eclectic orientation. More political liberals adopted the lawmaker orientation than did the members of either of the other groups, and one-half of the liberals took the ecletic position.

Hence, the antecedent political ideologies of these appellate judges appeared to be closely related to the ways in which they conceived of the judicial role. Can the same be said of social background variables?

Social Backgrounds and Role Perceptions

An alternative explanation of the variance in responses is that the judges' perceptions of their role were conditioned by various personal and cultural background factors. The judges' early lives, their training and professional careers may have instilled in them certain viewpoints regarding questions of public policy and may have strongly influenced their ultimate role concepts. During their law school years, for instance, they presumably were exposed to traditional definitions of the role of the judge. Their subsequent law practices may have further molded their views concerning the proper judicial function. Other individual factors, such as bar activeness and party affiliation, may have also predisposed the potential jurists toward particular sets of role perceptions.

Having ascended the bench, the judges' perceptions of the judicial role may have been further modified. On-the-bench factors, such as their continuous interaction with fellow judges, may have reinforced existing conceptions or resulted in alteration of these views.

In sum, the judges' personal backgrounds, training, and experiences (both off and on the bench) perhaps led them to adopt given sets of role perceptions in regard to their everyday work.

Although it is the *cumulative* impact of background variables which we consider potentially influential in molding role conceptions, for convenience, several background variables will be related independently to individual role perceptions in this analysis. We will attempt to determine the relationship between each of fifteen background factors and judges' tendencies to adopt the law-interpreter, lawmaker, or eclectic orientation.

Areal, Class, Partisan, and Religious Backgrounds

We first asked each judge a number of questions relating to his early life and his partisan and religious affiliations. Our preliminary assumption was that the more innovative role orientations (lawmaker or eclectic) would be closely associated with an urban or suburban upbringing, a lower socioeconomic class background, and affiliation with the Democratic party, and Roman Catholic or Jewish denomination. Table 3 presents our findings.

The areal and religious variables both related to the role categories in the expected manner. Although the relationship was a weak one, judges with urban backgrounds tended to have more innovative role orientations than judges with rural upbringings. The relationship between religion and role orientations was stronger. Protestant judges tended to take a much more restrictive view of their role than either Catholic or Jewish jurists.

Despite these findings, there was evidence that areal backgrounds, religious affiliations, and role categories were all more intimately related

TABLE 3. Relationship of Areal, Class, Partisan, and Religious Variables to Role Orientations

	ROLE ORIENTATION			
BACKGROUND VARIABLE	*Law Interpreter*	*Eclectic*	*Lawmaker*	*N*
Area *				
Rural/small town	7	3	0	10
Urban/suburban	5	3	3	11
Class †				
Upper/upper-middle	2	3	0	5
Middle-middle	5	2	2	9
Lower/lower-middle	2	2	1	5
Political Party				
Republican	2	3	1	6
Democratic	10	4	2	16
Religion				
Protestant	10	4	0	14
Catholic	1	2	2	5
Jewish	1	1	1	3

* Areal background of one respondent unknown.
† Class background of three respondents unknown.

to political orientations that they were to each other. Seven (70 percent) of the judges who were brought up in small towns, for example, were also political conservatives, while only three (27 percent) of those with urban or suburban backgrounds so classified themselves.

Likewise, *every* Protestant who took the law-interpreter position also described himself as a political conservative. Over one-half of the Catholic and Jewish judges were political liberals, and none of the members of either denomination termed himself a conservative.

Class and partisan variables did not relate to the role orientations as expected. Republicans actually showed more innovative tendencies than Democrats. This finding, too, may have been related to the ideological leanings of the particular judges interviewed for this report. Half of the sixteen Democrats were political conservatives from southern or border states, and half of the six Republicans were liberal New Yorkers. Thus in terms of political orientations the judges probably did not comprise a representative sample of the leadership or elites of the two major parties. Use of a more representative sample may have yielded more "successful" results.

Educational and Career Backgrounds

Every jurist was also asked several questions relating to his formal education and his previous career. We expected to find a close relationship between the more creative role orientations and each of the following background factors: graduation from a college or university of high standing; graduation from a law school of high standing; an urban law practice or a practice of substantial size; and previous governmental experience (excluding another judgeship). Although the judges were asked about previous judgeships, we made no assumptions concerning prior judicial experience.

Underlying these expectations was the belief that judges who had attended schools of high standing had received a more sophisticated training than those who had not, training which was thought to have predisposed them to accept a nontraditional view of the judicial role. Jurists whose law practice had been either of substantial size or located in an urban setting were also presumed to have been less conditioned to accept only traditional conceptions of role. Those who had served in other governmental posts were thought to have become more oriented toward policy making than those who had not so served, and hence more willing to adopt an innovative view of their job.

As Table 4 shows, our data provided a limited amount of support for two of our expectations. Judges from prestigious law schools were slightly

TABLE 4. **Relationship of Educational and Career Variables to Role Orientations**

BACKGROUND VARIABLE	ROLE ORIENTATION			
	Law Interpreter	Eclectic	Lawmaker	N
Education				
Undergraduate				
College/university of average standing	6	4	2	12
College/university of high standing	4	3	1	8
No college training	2	0	0	2
Legal				
Law school of average standing	8	4	1	13
Law school of high standing	4	3	2	9
Career				
Law practice (size) *				
Moderate	4	3	2	9
Substantial	8	3	1	12
Law practice (setting) †				
Nonurban	6	3	0	9
Urban	6	3	3	12
Government posts ‡				
Did not hold	3	2	1	6
Held	9	4	2	15
Judgeships				
Did not hold	5	3	0	8
Held	7	4	3	14

* Size of law practice of one respondent unknown.
† Setting of law practice of one respondent unknown.
‡ Unknown whether one respondent held government posts.

more inclined to accept an innovative position than those from other schools, and those who had practiced law in urban settings were likewise distinguishable from jurists who had practiced in nonurban surroundings.

Partisan and Bar Association Activeness

We were also interested in the effects of partisan activeness and bar association activeness upon the judges' choice of role concepts. Our findings clearly indicated that neither activeness nor inactiveness in a political party or bar association related to the judges' role orientations. Leadership in either type of organization apparently did not incline the jurists to adopt a particular view of their role.

Age and Appellate Experience

The remaining variables related to the ages of the judges upon elevation to the supreme court, their ages at the time of the interview, and the length of their service in their respective courts. Our preliminary expectation was that the younger and relatively inexperienced jurists would tend to be less encumbered than their seniors with traditional notions of the judicial function. We thus expected them to be more willing to conceive of their task in creative terms. Specifically, we assumed that jurists in each of the following categories would have a greater tendency to adopt the innovative orientations than judges in the opposite category: those who were under fifty-five years of age when first appointed or elected; those who were under sixty years of age at the time of their interview; those who had served on their respective courts for less than five years.

The data did not support any of our assumptions, as Table 5 clearly shows. Neither age at appointment nor length of service related at all to the variance in role perceptions. The judges' ages at present were so related, but in the opposite direction from that which we had expected.

There was evidence that the latter relationship resulted more from the ideological leanings of the judges than from the factor of individual age. Six (75 percent) of the judges under sixty years of age were political conservatives, while ten (71 percent) of those over that age were either political liberals or moderates. Once again, therefore, the data suggested

TABLE 5. Relationship of Age and Appellate Experience to Role Orientations

	Role Orientation			
Variable	Law Interpreter	Eclectic	Lawmaker	N
Age at Elevation				
Under 55	6	4	1	11
Over 55	6	3	2	11
Age at Present				
Under 60	6	1	1	8
Over 60	6	6	2	14
Length of Service				
Under five years	6	3	2	11
Over five years	6	4	1	11

that political orientations were more closely associated than background factors with judges' perceptions of the judicial role.

Summary and Conclusions

This study uncovered a basic division among state supreme court judges concerning the permissible degree of innovation in judicial decision making. We found conspicuous disagreement regarding whether judges should act as law interpreters, lawmakers, or as both. This disagreement, also found in other studies of the judicial role, indicated that two conceptions of role were in competition concerning decisional creativity—a deferential, precedent-oriented view and an innovative, policy-oriented view.

The dissimilarities between the two views of course should not be exaggerated. Regardless of his feelings about judicial creativity, no jurist advocated an unrestrained policy-making role for his court. Even the lawmakers believed that sponsorship of change in public policy was chiefly the prerogative of the legislature, and only secondarily that of the judge. Thus although many judges disagreed concerning the legitimacy of decisional innovation, their differences never appeared to be wholly antithetical.

We also found that individual political values—wholly personal factors—related much more strongly to the judges' orientations toward judicial lawmaking than did social background characteristics or recruitment methods. Political conservatives uniformly adopted the law-interpreter position, and political moderates were strongly attracted to the eclectic position. More political liberals adopted the lawmaker orientation than did the members of either of the other two groups, and one-half of them took the eclectic position. Social background variables which appeared to relate strongly to role perceptions, e.g., urban or rural upbringing, religion, and current age, related closely to the ideological variable as well. Methods of judicial selection appeared to be unrelated to the judges' choices of role perceptions. Hence, within the assumptions of our data, the jurists' antecedent political orientations appeared to exert a considerable influence upon their conceptions of their role.

These findings contain several implications for the study of judicial behavior. One is that the competition between role conceptions has enlarged the range of personal discretion within state supreme courts. Subject to whatever constraints their colleagues' attitudes may place upon them, state appellate jurists apparently are relatively free to adopt a restrictive, an innovative, or an eclectic, approach to their decisional tasks.

Thus it is not suprising that our respondents tended to embrace views of their job which reflected their policy values. Confronted with ambiguous demands of role, they apparently tended merely to follow the dictates of their personal convictions.

A further implication of our findings is that descriptions of the judicial role simply in terms of attachment to legal precedent are inadequate. Almost one-half of our respondents perceived some degree of innovation and sponsorship of legal change to be either a necessary or proper part of their job, and even some interpreters admitted the necessity of legislating in the "interstices" of the law. If attachment to precedent constituted the sole "objective" role of a judge, presumably few respondents would have conceived of decisional creativity as an integral part of their task.

Our findings also tended to confirm the view of Herbert McClosky, Angus Campbell and other political scientists concerning the potency of ideology among political elites. However irrelevant it may be to the political beliefs of mass publics, ideology apparently is a potent consideration for elites—among members of the state high bench as elsewhere. This is not to say that the verbalized role perceptions reported here are the equivalent of judicial behavior. Much further work will be needed to determine the linkages between judges' perceptions of their role and their conduct. Our findings do indicate, however, that, for all the efforts to make it otherwise, political ideology pervades the world of state supreme court judges as well as the world of other political elites.

26

Judicial Incentives
Greg Caldeira

• • •

Incentive theory springs from several lines of research relating personal motivation to political activity.

• • •

Underlying incentive theory is a basic premise, that "participants behave in a manner consistent with their incentives." To be more exact, "other things being equal, men will act in a manner which satisfies their basic needs." If one can uncover the motivations of political actors, he can then predict their behavior more accurately; and, if one knows the incentives of political actors, one can offer a substantial explanation of group and individual behavior within an institution or political system. Given a similar set of environmental constraints, men with different incentives will behave differently. An institution or system dominated by politicians of one incentive type will perform in a much different manner than institutions in which another incentive pattern prevails.

In their research over the last few years, Payne and Woshinsky have generated seven incentive types: Program, Game, Obligation, Conviviality, Mission, Status, and Adulation. From the text of a personal interview in which the respondent indicates his primary area of satisfaction (in addition to numerous other traits and attitudes) one determines the incentive of a particular political actor:

> The interview reveals, first, the central interest or concern of the participant. He talks about this subject more than any other; he is enthusiastic and knowledgeable about it; and he voluntarily returns to it during the interview. Because a persons' attention focuses upon objects relevant to his satisfaction, these foci indicate his area of satisfaction. This area of central concern is the main identifying characteristic of the incentive.

• • •

From Greg Caldeira, "Judicial Incentives: Some Evidence From Urban Trial Courts," *Iustitia* 4 (1977): 4, 5, 7, 8, 11–12, 15, 16, 19, 20–23. Reprinted by permission. Footnotes have been omitted.

Data and Design

The present paper reports the findings of a study of state trial judges in heavily urbanized cities in New Jersey. Its purpose is twofold: (1) identification and description of trial judge's incentives; and (2) examination of the relationships between motivational bases for judicial participation and the attitudes and behavior of trial judges. The main source of data is a set of personal interviews conducted with twenty-six Superior Court and County Court judges in the winter of 1973 and the summer of 1975. These are the basic trial courts of general jurisdiction in New Jersey and handle both civil and criminal matters. The choice of New Jersey as a research site was dictated by its geographical proximity.

• • •

Judicial Incentives in Urban Trial Courts

In their research thus far, as noted earlier, Payne and his associates have encountered seven different incentive types. In the present study, however, I found only game, status, program, and obligation judges.

• • •

The Game Judge

The trial judge with a game incentive derives his emotional satisfaction from applying and exhibiting his skills in a structured, challenging, and competitive situation; he perceives the judicial process as a complex game. Unlike the program judge, he is not attracted to the bench by a desire to piece together specific bits of law into a coherent mass; nor is he attempting to gain position or prestige. His motivation "lies . . . simply in his desire to take an active part in an ongoing, exciting series of events involving a complex mixture of human interactions."

• • •

The Program Judge

The individual holding a program incentive enjoys the role of the trial judge, by and large, because it allows him to work on and solve challenging problems in the administration of justice. The motivation is similar to that of Barber's Lawmakers. Unlike the program politicians that Payne and Woshinsky have encountered, however, the trial judge whose incentive is programmatic does not usually *enter* politics in order to participate in debate on specific issues or the formulation of public policies. For the most part, the program judge enters public life because of the nature of private law practice.

• • •

The Status Judge

The status participant is in politics to demonstrate to himself and others that he is indeed an adequate human being. To prove his adequacy, he seeks the social prestige inhering in political positions—he seeks respect and deference from others. His focus is on the judgments of worth or "success" made by society at large, not on particular policies, issues or cases. For the status judge, the bench is of value because of the social prestige attached to it, not the latitude it affords in problem-solving, game-playing, or conscience-soothing. He is abnormally preoccupied with getting and keeping positions, his own personal political history, and the strategy and tactics of campaigning and politicking. A cool attitude is taken toward leaders because they are *above* him, and he resents any possibility of being controlled. Moreover, in discussing the motives of others, he projects upon them evil and selfish designs. Though he may claim to enjoy politics, the status judge does not. For the status judge, then, life in the world of politics is "nasty, poor, brutish, and short." He feels that other men are to be stepped on or stepped over; cooperation is not possible.

• • •

The Obligation Judge

The trial judge who is moved by an obligation incentive resembles closely the "Purist" Wildavsky found in his analysis of the 1964 Republican Convention and the "Reluctant" Barber developed in his study of freshmen legislators. The desire to fulfill a social obligation characterizes this type. For the obligation judge, political activity helps to relieve feelings of guilt he possesses. His anxiety is brought about by the perception of a "discrepancy between his normative beliefs and his failure to act upon them." The decision to enter politics is a moral one for him.

• • •

Role Perceptions

The normative concept of a role "is a pleasing notion in that it immediately explains in an intuitive manner much of the conflict that has occurred among judges" and scholars concerning the proper behavior of common-law judges in a democratic polity.

• • •

Each of the judges interviewed in this study was presented two batteries of statements concerning his role vis-a-vis his colleagues, past and present, and the public. Because of his desire to demonstrate to others his own power and prestige, I hypothesized that status judges would be most willing to approve a creative role for judging at the trial level. The obligation judge, because he is concerned with the normative style of decision-making, should be most begrudging of the exercise of discretion. Program judges are interested in concrete policy accomplishments, so they should closely resemble the status judges in terms of precedent orientation. Because he is acutely aware of the importance of following the "rules of the game," the game judge should more closely resemble the obligation judge.

The responses to the precedent scale, presented in Table 2, show mixed results. First of all, there is a relatively high regard for precedent throughout the sample. Contrary to expectation, status judges demonstrate "high" regard for precedent as an element in decision-making. There is, however, no readily apparent reason for such a pattern; and reexamination of the interviews discloses no clues. Perhaps status judges find other areas of the judicial turf better outlets for their anxieties. In line with my hypothesis, obligation judges showed a high degree of respect for precedent. Unexpectedly, however, game judges are more like program, not obligation, judges. From a reading of the interviews, it is my impression that game judges, despite an acute awareness of the "rules," are more tolerant of the ambiguities inherent in any decisional process than are their obligation-oriented colleagues. That most program judges are also precedent-oriented is not, as it first seems, a paradox. Once again drawing on the interview data, I gather that the program judge believes that, even if he follows precedent in a religious fashion, there are still enough interstices to permit a considerable amount of policy accomplishment.

The obligation judge, because of his strict feelings about internal decisional criteria, should be more oriented toward the individual than

TABLE 2. Precedent Orientations of Trial Judges

	GAME	PROGRAM	STATUS	OBLIGATION
High	67%	70%	100%	100%
Low	33%	30%	0%	0%
N	6	10	6	4

the community. Geared to results and not decisional rules, program judges should steer a middle-course. The status judge, since his primary source of satisfaction is the respect and deference of others, should be more public-regarding than other trial judges. Game judges, concerned with process and not result, should bear close resemblance to their obligation colleagues.

"Public orientations" of the trial judges appear in Table 3. The results, once again, are mixed. First of all, the obligation judges split on the individual-community dimension. Upon reconsideration, this finding is not unreasonable. Different judges feel different sorts of obligations. In the present sample, some are deeply committed to serving their individual conceptions of right; others, to serving the public's conception of right—but both of these commitments are "internalized." Though not all status judges focus on the community, the relationship is the correct direction. Program judges, following expectation, divide their attention about evenly between the individual and the community. Finally, in accord with the hypothesis, game judges focus more on the individual than on the community.

By constructing a fourfold table with two variables, precedent- and public-orientation, one comes up with four ideal role types. The Law Applier is characterized by the high regard he has for precedent; neither societal needs nor social consequences of his decisions are legitimate criteria in choice-making. The Law Extender, like his colleague, the Law Applier, feels that nearly all cases can be decided using precedent. Unlike the Law Applier, he is clearly conscious of societal needs and the social consequences of his decisions. Following Walker, one might say that he is both public-regarding and law-regarding. The Mediator places low on both scales; he is not sanguine about finding clear and relevant precedents in every case he decides; nor does he seek to conform his decisions to public needs. He is, as Flango and associates observe, "inclined to rely largely on his own common sense and understanding of the meaning of justice to reach his decision," rather than on public needs or desires. Placing low on precedent orientation and high on public orientation, the Policymaker feels that he should be making socially-relevant decisions, not engaging in mere dispute settlement. He is expected to be a proponent of the explicitly political functions of courts.

TABLE 3. Public Orientations of Trial Judges

	GAME	PROGRAM	STATUS	OBLIGATION
Individual	67%	40%	33%	50%
Community	33%	60%	67%	50%
N	6	10	6	4

Table 4 presents the distribution of role perceptions among the trial judges in this sample. The results do not coincide completely with what one might expect, but the relationships are in the correct directions. Game judges, expected to be dominated by Mediators, instead perceive themselves as Law Appliers. (There are, in fact, no Mediators in the sample.) But the distributions of role perceptions among game and status judges are quite different. Though several program judges are Law Appliers, more than half are either Law Extenders or Policymakers. The status judges, following expected patterns, are more discretion-oriented and individual-oriented. Some of the obligation judges, as I noted earlier, feel strongly that their internalized decisional criteria should be those of the public. Thus, contrary to expectation, these judges conceptualize their role as Law Extender.

The Independence of Trial Judges

Up until quite recently, the power of the trial judge in his own court was absolute; he was sovereign on his own turf. But no longer. The independent trial judge, as Cook said of one-judge courts, "is going the way of the one-room schoolhouse. Structural change is forcing established judges to adjust their role definitions and performance to suit the requirements" of modern administrative controls. The pressure of litigation, the increasing complexity of cases, and insufficient budgeting have forced increased restrictions on the discretion of the "independent trial judge." It is no secret that many trial judges chafe under modern administrative controls.

From several closed-ended and open-ended items, I have determined each judge's orientation to administrative control. There are two basic types, "traditionals" and "moderns." The first, traditionals, feel strongly that administrative controls usurp their prerogatives and threaten independence of substantive judicial decision-making. Moderns, on the other hand, feel that some restrictions on judicial discretion are both necessary and sometimes helpful.

I had certain expectations concerning the relationship between ju-

TABLE 4. Distribution of Judicial Role Perceptions

	GAME	PROGRAM	STATUS	OBLIGATION
Law Applier	67%	40%	33%	50%
Mediator	0%	0%	0%	0%
Law Extender	0%	30%	67%	50%
Policy Maker	33%	30%	0%	0%
N	6	10	6	4

TABLE 5. The Independence of Trial Judges

	GAME	PROGRAM	STATUS	OBLIGATION
Traditionals	67%	40%	100%	100%
Moderns	33%	60%	0%	0%
N	6	10	6	4

dicial incentive and modernism-traditionalism. First, because of his desire to demonstrate his power to others, to maximize his own discretion, the status judge should take on a traditional orientation. The obligation judge—also desirous of maximum discretion, because of his conscience, not recognition—should also be traditional in his orientation. Third, both program and game judges are tolerant of structural limitations, so one should expect both to be moderns; but, because of a greater need for manipulative scope, the game judges will also have a tendency to feel circumscribed by administrative controls.

The results, presented in Table 5, fit expectations quite well. First, game and program judges are more tolerant of limits on their discretion, and the game judges are more jealous of their prerogatives. Second, both status and obligation judges are "traditionals," wed to classical notions of judicial independence.

Conclusion

Incentive theory, I observed earlier, is a particularly interesting and fruitful method of studying the motivations of trial judges. Though the study presented here is exploratory, I believe nonetheless that the results justify my optimism. There is no doubt that incentive analysis has a rich descriptive power, capturing the multi-faceted nature of trial judging more adequately than other approaches. The data marshalled here suggest, too, that incentive theory has considerable explanatory or predictive power.

• • •

————————————— 27 —————————————

Judges' Role Orientations, Attitudes, and Decisions

James L. Gibson

[After finding that the attitudes of Iowa trial court judges do not explain sufficiently the severity of the sentences they hand down, Professor Gibson—in the following pages—explores the possibility that the role orientations of the judges affect the extent to which attitudes are predictors of sentencing behavior.]

• • •

Role Orientation as an Intervening Variable

The correlations between the judges' attitudes and the severity of their sentencing behavior are less than spectacular. This is not entirely surprising: nonjudicial experimental research on the relationship between attitudes and behavior have reported similarly unsubstantial correlations. However, these same experimental studies have also made some significant advances in dissecting the nature of the low correlations. Several scholars have suggested that the relationship between attitudes and behavior is probably mediated by situational intervening variables. That is, the relationship between attitudes and behavior is modified by the situational context of the behavior. Reference group variables, the subject's definition of the situation, social participation, need for approval, social constraints and social distance, the consequences of behavior, and a wide variety of other variables have been identified as significant contextual variables.

The most relevant formulation of the role of intervening variables, however, is found in Campbell's notion of situational thresholds. . . . Similar attitudes may result in different overt behaviors due to situational pressures which inhibit the expression of behavior consistent with the attitude. The impetus for a response must be strong enough to overcome situational forces inhibiting the response. Consequently, we can

———
From James L. Gibson, "Judges' Role Orientations, Attitudes, and Decisions: An Interactive Model," *American Political Science Review* (1978): 917, 918–919, 919. Reprinted by permission. Footnotes have been omitted.

predict that an individual would give a discriminatory response to a questionnaire item (low threshold) but fail to discriminate in face-to-face situations (high threshold). Thus, there is little question that the actor's assessment of the context of behavior affects the degree of relationship between attitudes and behavior.

Situational variables can be summarized most usefully by the concept "role expectations." Individuals who interact with role occupants have conceptions of what constitutes "proper" role behavior for the role occupant. These are norms of behavior which constrain the activities of the role occupant. Situational constraints and "contingent consistency" are concepts highly related to role expectations. While expectations affect almost all social behavior, they are especially salient for actors in positions subject to relatively unambiguous, institutionalized role expectations. A role orientation is a psychological construct which is the combination of the occupant's perception of the role expectations of significant others and his or her own norms and expectations of proper behavior for a judge.

The concept of role orientation plays a central function in this analysis. Role orientation is essentially a summary variable which defines for the role occupant the range of appropriate behavioral alternatives in any given situation. As such, role orientations are very similar to many of the situational intervening variables identified above and are almost identical to Rokeach's (1968) notion "attitude toward situation" (A_s). Role orientations are also similar to Campbell's situational threshold. In order for an attitude to find expression in behavior, the behavior consistent with the attitude must lie within the range of acceptable behaviors, i.e., be defined as situationally appropriate.

While many judicial researchers have investigated judicial role orientations, none has done so from this perspective. Most studies have been content to develop empirically based typologies.

• • •

While these scholars seem to agree that the judge's orientation toward precedents is an important intervening variable, none has been successful in developing an empirical model integrating attitudes, role orientations, and behavior. . . .

At least a portion of the difficulty in relating role orientations to decision behavior stems from the inadequacy of the present conceptualization of role concepts. Judges' role orientations are their beliefs about the kind of behavior proper for a judge. In the case of decisional role orientations, the beliefs concern what constitutes proper decision-making behavior. "Proper" does not, however, refer as much to the kind of policy which is made as it does to the kind of stimuli which influence policy making. The basic function of decision-making role orientations is to specify what variables can legitimately be allowed to influence decision making, and in the case of conflict, what priorities to assign to different decisional criteria. Some judges may believe it proper to be influenced by a particular stimulus while other judges may regard the stimulus as improper.

There are good reasons for conceptualizing role orientations in this way. A central expectation of judicial and legal traditions concerns the criteria of decision making employed by judges. For instance, "equality before the law" is not an empirical statement; it does not assert that individual litigants are in fact equal. Rather the phrase is an exhortation to ignore the variables (stimuli), such as power, on which litigants are unequal and to render decisions only on variables which provide for equality. As an additional illustration, it is generally regarded as illegitimate to discriminate on the basis of race in sentencing. This means that it is illegitimate to allow the race of the defendant to influence the decision. Race is not viewed as a proper decisional criterion. Similarly, even such concepts as the presumption of innocence in criminal cases are merely expectations that court officials will not allow empirical stimuli relating to the factual guilt of the defendant to influence their pretrial decisions (e.g., bail). The presumption of innocence is a norm which defines some criteria of decision making as proper and others as improper. . . .

Thus, role orientations specify the criteria upon which decisions are made. A generalized role orientation might concern the legitimacy of allowing criteria which have no strictly legal base to influence decision making. A "broad" role orientation restrains the use of other criteria very little. The "narrow" orientation is more restrictive in the use of "nonlegal" criteria. What is important to note, however, is that the role orientation does not indicate whether judges' policy decisions will be liberal or conservative, but instead indicates the criteria upon which their decisions will be based. For a decision to be liberal, the theory predicts that the criterion upon which the judge bases a decision must itself predict a liberal decision. Two factors must therefore be known in order to predict decisions: (1) what criteria the judge considers to be legitimate determinants of decisions, and (2) whether the criteria themselves predict liberal or conservative decisions.

There is no logically *necessary* basis for expecting judges with "broad" role orientations to make "liberal" decisions unless the decisional criteria employed by "broad" judges are liberal. One might imagine, for instance, that judges with "broad" role orientations would grant greater legitimacy to allowing their own values and sense of justice to influence their decisions than would "narrow" judges. If the values are liberal (as in the case of William O. Douglas, for instance), then the decisions will be liberal. If the values are conservative, however, then the decisions will be conservative (as illustrated by William Rehnquist). Obviously, this suggests that "activism" can just as well be conservative "activism" (e.g., the Hughes Court) as liberal activism. Similarly, a "narrow" orientation does not necessarily lead to conservative decisions. If "narrow" judges tend to grant greater legitimacy to criteria with a strictly legal base (e.g., precedents, statutes, and "strict construction" of constitutions), and if those criteria were liberal, then a "narrow" judge would make liberal decisions. For instance, the Burger Court, if it were acting "narrowly," with strong regard for Warren Court precedents, would make liberal decisions. Further, a "strict construction" of the First Amendment prohibition on laws restricting freedom of speech would result in very liberal decisions (at least up to the question of "symbolic speech"). Thus, role orientations should not directly predict decisions but, in combination with the decisional criteria a relationship should exist.

Consequently, role orientations, attitudes and behavior can be integrated into one model; attitudes are related to behavior only insofar as the judge's role orientation allows it. Judges viewing attitudes as having a legitimate role in decision making allow their personal values to influence their decision making. This formulation is amenable to direct empirical evaluation.

Regression residuals can provide a good measure of the extent to which individual judges' attitudes predict their behavior. Using . . . nine attitudinal measures as independent variables and the sentence severity scores as the dependent variable, I calculated these residuals. A small (absolute value) residual indicates that the attitudes are strong predictors of sentence severity; a large residual indicates that attitudes are weak

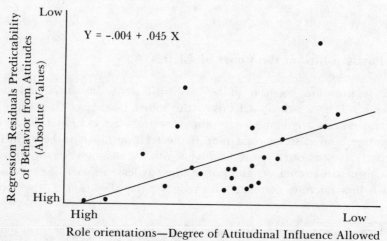

FIGURE 1.   Scattergram of role orientations and regression residuals.

predictors of severity. Thus, the hypothesis is that the judge's role orientation is related to the degree to which behavior is influenced by attitudes (the residuals).

• • •

Figure 1 shows the plot of the regression residuals and the role orientation factor scores. The Pearson correlation is .51. The results are just as hypothesized: role orientations are acting as an intervening variable mediating the attitude-behavior relationship. Attitudes are good predictors of behavior only for those judges with "broad" role orientations. Role orientations do *not* predict the severity (policy content) of the sentences ($r = .29$); they do, however, predict how much influence certain criteria will have on behavior.

• • •

──────────────── 28 ────────────────

Partisanship on an Apolitical Court
Justin J. Green

• • •

V. Partisanship on the Court of Claims

The relationship between judges' political party affiliation and their votes has been a principal focus of the judicial behavior literature. No generalizations are immediately apparent from an examination of the literature, and it seems clear that, if the relationship is to be identified precisely, more courts must be investigated. Previous research suggests that three situational variables determine, at least in part, the extent to which judicial votes correlate with judges' party affiliation: 1) the extent

───────────
From Justin J. Green, "Partisanship on an Apolitical Court: The United States Court of Claims," *Pepperdine Law Review* 6 (1979): 399–404, 404–405, 406. Reprinted by permission. Footnotes have been omitted.

to which the court is politicized, 2) the physical structure of the court, and 3) the types of cases that the court decides.

Adamany speculated that the involvement of the court in partisan politics would affect the voting behavior of the judges. He tested the accuracy of his observation by comparing the Supreme Courts of Wisconsin and Michigan. The Michigan court was widely recognized as a politicized institution, and studies by Feeley, Schubert, and Ulmer reported partisan affiliation to be an axis of division. The Wisconsin Supreme Court is less closely related to partisan politics, particularly insofar as judicial selection is concerned, and party affiliation explains less of the variance in voting behavior than in Michigan. Beiser and Silberman, reporting on the New York Court of Appeals, draw conclusions similar to those of Adamany for the same general reason: the level of politicization. The lower federal courts, including the Court of Claims, would certainly qualify as partisan in nature, primarily because of the distinctive relationship between party and judicial selection. Goldman, studying the United States Court of Appeals from 1961 to 1964, found a correlation between partisan affiliation and decisions in several areas. Walker, analyzing the decisions of district court judges, did not find partisan influences in civil liberties cases, but did not investigate the civil areas in which Goldman found most of the significant associations. Thus, the political attributes of the court must be the starting point for developing a general statement concerning the relationship between party affiliation and judicial decisions.

After observing the differences between the Wisconsin and Michigan Supreme Courts in terms of the party variable, Adamany speculated that the physical environs of the decision making process are material to the existence of the relationship. He argued that on a court such as the Wisconsin Supreme Court in which the members frequently interact, conflicts are resolved more often than on "loner" collegial courts such as the Michigan Supreme Court, hence stifling party based disagreement. It appears that although physical arrangements might be relevant to the level of dissent on a court, they are at best tangentially related to the type of disagreement. Through frequent informal consultation and the imposition of stringent deadlines for the filing of dissenting opinions, a court might acquire unanimity in nearly all of its decisions, but, when dissenting judges fail to form blocs based on party affiliation the physical structure of the court is not an immediately obvious cause. Thus, Canon and Jaros might profitably have included such a variable in their analysis of the level of dissent on state supreme courts, but any correlation with partisan voting would be fortuitous.

The third factor in the analysis of this particular aspect of judicial behavior regarding the types of cases decided by the courts is more descriptive of the research design employed than of the courts involved.

Such considerations may well affect the conclusions drawn and thus should be noted. With the success that students of judicial behavior have experienced in the scaling and bloc analysis of United States Supreme Court civil liberty decisions, it seems odd that whenever criminal or civil liberty decisions of any court are examined for evidence of partisan influence, the search is often fruitless. Because judicial analysts have generally confined their research designs to one or two types of cases, their conclusions about judicial behavior are content specific. Relationships seem to appear and vanish depending upon the manner in which cases are chosen. For example, Goldman and Nagel found evidence of partisan influence only in certain types of economic cases. These peculiarities of research design make it difficult to derive a generalization, a problem Adamany claims can be resolved only by "more careful conceptualization and more rigorous testing of a provocative hypothesis."

The Court of Claims presents an intriguing combination of variables and, therefore, possesses considerable potential for a useful and productive investigation of the issue. Since the partisan nature of the court has changed between each of the three time periods, the Court of Claims is a superb source of data to test Adamany's conclusions about the role of partisanship. The court is also a collegial body similar to the Wisconsin Supreme Court. Although often divided into panels, it sits together and the members have frequent formal and informal contact with each other. The biographies written by Judge Bennett often refer to the spirit of collegiality on the court and the friendship and respect which the judges have for each other. Fortunately, the court hears only those cases involving economic issues which are likely to display a correlation between partisan affiliation and voting behavior. Every case pits a claimant against the federal government. Using the concept of partisanship elaborated upon by Schubert early in the study of judicial behavior, it seems reasonable to expect the following manifestations of partisanship in judicial voting: Democratic judges are expected to vote in support of suits by private individuals and against business claims. However, the type of hypothesis to be tested is more ambiguous. In general, because of the relatively nonpartisan and highly collegial nature of the bench in Period I [1964–66], an association between party affiliation and judicial voting is *not* expected. It is more likely that a relationship will appear in Periods II [1969–71] and III [1975–76] due to the change in the court's personnel. Hence, it is hypothesized that the relationship between party affiliation and judicial voting will increase over time.

The method of testing such hypotheses has also been considered in the literature. Nagel simply calculated the number of times that each judge voted in the expected direction and then evaluated the scores in terms of a court mean. Democrats were expected to cluster to one side of the mean, Republicans to the other. Adamany found this approach to be inadequate. Adamany prefers the attitudinal scaling approach of Ulmer, Schubert, and others, but argues strongly that the techniques used to study collegial courts can be borrowed from research on legislative behavior. However, a problem arises in that the data may not be amenable to such highly sophisticated statistical manipulations, *i.e.*, the technique must be appropriate for the data.

Using the Nagel approach, pro-business and pro-individual support scores were calculated for each judge. Table 5 . . . displays these as a percentage of the votes cast in all cases to which each type of plaintiff was a party. For convenience, the judges are listed in order of seniority and the party affiliation of each judge is indicated.

As indicated above, the first hypothesis was that there would be no relationship between party affiliation and voting behavior in Period I. Table 5 shows conclusively that this hypothesis should be accepted. The mean support scores in business cases for Democrats and Republicans are virtually identical and the difference in cases involving individuals as plaintiffs is not significant. Furthermore, in the latter category, the scores are in the opposite direction from that predicted by the hypothesis: both Democratic judges voted for the individual less often than did the two Republican judges. It seems obvious that partisan affiliation is not correlated with judicial voting behavior in Period I.

The hypothesis specified that the party/voting behavior correlation would be higher in the second time period because the bench consisted of a Democratic majority and included at least one additional judge with a background as an active partisan. Again, however, the table displays little evidence of a relationship between the two variables. Contrary to expectations the mean support score for Democratic judges is higher than for Republicans in business cases and a Democrat, Collins, has the highest support rate. The means for cases brought by individuals are as expected but are so similar that party identification is not associated with voting behavior.

Period III presents more complicated patterns. Eighteen of the twenty *en banc* cases heard during the period were brought by businesses. An examination of the votes in these cases reveals a very high relationship between party and voting behavior. The means for each party are significantly different and, as expected, the three Republican judges favored the claim most often whereas the three Democratic judges least often. Although the bench was evenly divided between the parties, at least four judges had partisan backgrounds. Examination of *en banc* cases shows that this increased level of politicization is identifiable in the judges' votes.

Votes cast by members of panels do not fall into such an identifiable pattern. In business cases, a Democrat (Nichols) was more supportive than expected, and a Republican (Bennett) was far less inclined to

TABLE 5. Plaintiff Support Scores (In percentages)

Judge	Pro-Business				Pro-Individual			
	Period I (1964–66)	Period II (1969–71)	Period III* (1975–76)	Period III** (1975–76)	Period I (1964–66)	Period II (1969–71)	Period III* (1975–76)	Period III* (1975–76)
Cowen (D)	48.6	53.6	53.3	37.5	32.8	43.8		34.8
Laramore (R)	48.8	51.8		50.0[1]	33.2	42.2		33.3[3]
Durfee (R)	46.6	53.6	62.5	36.4[2]	33.5	42.2		33.3[4]
Davis (I)	47.7	51.4		56.3	33.1	42.2		48.0
Collins (D)	46.4	56.5			32.2	45.3		29.6
Skelton (D)		53.6	44.4	32.3		43.8		27.6
Nichols (D)		52.6	64.7	52.2		39.1		41.2
Kunzig (R)			72.2	47.1				35.0
Kashiwa (R)			76.5	44.4				35.7
Bennett (R)			72.2	34.3				30.7
Democratic Mean	47.5	54.1	54.1	40.7	32.5	43.0		37.3
Republican Mean	47.7	52.7	73.6	41.9	33.4	42.2		36.0
Court Mean	47.6	53.3	63.7	43.4	33.0	42.7		

* En banc cases only (N = 18), all filed by businesses

** Panel cases only

1 Sat by designation in 10 cases

2 Sat by designation in 22 cases

3 Sat by designation in 9 cases

4 Sat by designation in 15 cases

support the claim than either of his colleagues. Hence, although the means differ in the expected direction, the amount of the difference is too small to support the conclusion that party affiliation is a relevant variable. In cases brought by individuals, the mean support scores are significantly different, but in the opposite direction than was expected. It must therefore be concluded that the relationship between party identification and voting behavior, so clearly manifested in *en banc* cases, did not exist in cases heard by panels. Thus, in general, when using this type of analysis, the Court of Claims is not a court in which party affiliation and voting behavior are related.

Simply put, the Court of Claims appears to be a very harmonious court. In Period I, nearly all of the dissenting votes were cast by retired Court of Claims Judge Samuel E. Whitaker sitting by designation. The dissent rate for the five appointed judges was .3 percent. In Period II, the effects of politicization might be demonstrated by the dissent rate which increased substantially to 7.4 percent. The two new judges, Nichols and Skelton, were most active with dissent rates of 4.0 percent and 3.5 percent, respectively. In nearly all cases, their dissents were solitary which is most unusual for new judges on collegial courts. Typically, they do not draw attention to themselves by casting the sole dissenting vote, indeed, the prospect of a solitary dissent appears to present strong psychological and social barriers to be overcome. In Period III, there were a total of 21 cases in which one or more dissenting votes were cast. However, only eleven of these cases were heard by panels even though panels hear 89.6 percent of the cases. Clearly, the pressures against solitary dissents are very strong on the Court of Claims as they are on all other three member courts. As the data in Table 5 suggest, the dissenting votes in *en banc* cases fall into patterns related to party affiliation, but due to the relatively small number of votes involved, a more intensive analysis appears appropriate.

Conclusion

• • •

With respect to the basic focus of the research, the role of the party variable, the Court of Claims leaves few unanswered questions. Partisanship was not a factor in the court's decisions, indeed, Judge Bennett's renunciation of partisan activity when he became a Commissioner of the court appears to reflect a strongly felt court norm. The data contradict Adamany's expectation that partisanship in judicial recruitment is associated with partisanship in judicial voting. Alternatively, Adamany is accurate in his claim that, if future research on the "provocative hypothesis" is to be fruitful, then more innovative operationalizations of the party variable are essential preconditions. This study of the Court of Claims may be a significant source of ideas for the completion of that task.

29

The Effect of
Past Judicial Behavior on
Subsequent Decision-Making

Sheldon Goldman

The proposition that an individual's past behavior provides the best guide to predicting subsequent behavior given similar circumstances or stimuli is well accepted by social psychologists and by most students of politics. However, traditional students of the law, insofar as judicial decision-making is concerned, never accepted this. For them, it was court precedent that guided individual behavior. More sophisticated legal scholars recognized the importance of individual contributions to the development of *the law* but political, social, and economic stimuli were considered outside the realm of decision-making. It remained for the judicial behavior school to provide a wealth of studies to demonstrate that judges respond not only to legal stimuli but also to a wide range of political or public policy stimuli. The inference was irresistible that a judge's attitudes and values play a major role in judicial decision-making Other studies have tested and uncovered some relationships between judges' attributes and their judicial behavior. Thus it is now generally accepted by political scientists (although still meeting skepticism from some legal circles) that judges respond to *political* stimuli, that certain

From Sheldon Goldman, "The Effect of Past Judicial Behavior on Subsequent Decision-Making," *Jurimetrics Journal* 19 (Spring 1979): 208–217. Reprinted by permission of the Section of Science and Technology (American Bar Association) from their publication *Jurimetrics Journal*. Copyright © 1979. Footnotes have been omitted.

of their attributes are linked in some ways to their decision-making and that knowledge of past behavior is the best predictor of future behavior, given similar political stimuli. However, the literature is surprisingly barren of precise tests that suggest *how much* of the variance of subsequent decisional behavior can be linked to past behavior and how much more of the variance of subsequent behavior does past behavior explain as compared to certain attribute variables. This research note seeks to answer these questions with regard to judges serving on the United States Courts of Appeals over a ten year period beginning in 1961.

Data Set

Data were collected concerning selected background or attribute characteristics of a group of seventy-four federal appeals court judges and their judicial voting behavior during two consecutive time periods. The judges were those in active service who sat on one of the eleven federal courts of appeals during part or all of the period between fiscal 1962 (July 1, 1961) and fiscal 1966 (June 30, 1966), hereafter called *time period one* and during part or all of the period between fiscal 1967 (July 1, 1966) and fiscal 1971 (June 30, 1971), hereafter called *time period two*. The cases selected for analysis were those nonunanimously decided by a panel of three judges or (infrequently) the entire appeals court sitting en banc. There were 2,911 cases in the sample.

Variables

Ten behavioral dimensions were measured in both time periods:

1. *Criminal Procedures*—the propensity to favor the claims of criminal defendants and prisoners *excluding* selective service violators and white collar (business) crime such as income tax evasion, fraud, embezzlement;
2. *Civil Liberties*—the tendency to support the civil rights claims of Black Americans and civil libertarian claims of selective service violators and others;
3. *Political Liberalism*—support for the criminal procedure and civil liberties claims from the previous categories as well as support for the claims of white collar criminal defendants and prisoners;
4. *Private Economic*—support for the claims of such economic underdogs as the insured in disputes with an insurance company, the small businessman or subcontractor when opposed by larger busi-

ness or contractor, the alleged victim in private anti-trust disputes and for the tenant, debtor, bankrupt, stockholder, and consumer;

5. *Labor*—propensity to favor the claims of labor in disputes with management and to favor enforcement of pro-labor NLRB rulings;

6. *Injured Persons*—for the claims or injured workers and other injured persons (or their estates) in accident and/or federal tort cases;

7. *Economic Liberalism*—support for the private economic, labor, and injured persons claims from the previous categories as well as the claims of government in business regulation cases;

8. *Activism*—for federal court jurisdiction and the imposition of federal standards on the states in criminal procedures and other cases;

9. *Government Fiscal*—for the government in tax, eminent domain, and other fiscal cases; and

10. *Dissents*—propensity to cast a dissenting vote.

Judicial voting behavior was quantified by assigning the value of 2.0 to the propensities outlined above and a value of 0.0 to the contrary voting positions. Where the judges in a case were split three ways, a value of 1.0 was given to the middle position. The arithmetic mean of the total for each judge's votes constituted that judge's score on each of the ten behavioral dimensions. A minimum of five cases for each dimension during each time period was required before a score would be calculated, thus, the number of judges scored on each dimension differed ranging from fifteen judges for Private Economic to seventy-four judges on the Dissents dimension. Political Liberalism with fifty-seven judges and Economic Liberalism with sixty-two along with Dissents were the dimensions with the most participation of judges. All 2,911 cases in the sample were coded on the Dissents dimension *and* other dimensions as appropriate. Judicial behavior was measured on the ten dimensions for each of the two consecutive five year time periods.

The judicial attribute (or background) variables tested were: (1) Judge's political party affiliation; (2) age as of July 1, 1966; (3) religious origin or affiliation; (4) prior candidacy for public office; (5) previous judicial experience before ascending the appeals court bench; (6) prior prosecutorial experience—federal, state, or local; and (7) number of years of service on the appeals courts as of January 1, 1971.

Stepwise multiple regression and partial correlation analyses of judicial behavior during time period two were conducted. Voting behavior on the ten dimensions for time period two constituted the dependent variables. The independent variables consisted of the voting behavior from time period one and the seven attribute (background) variables. For example, the Criminal Procedures dimension for time period two was one of the ten dependent variables. It was tested with the seven attribute variables and the Criminal Procedures scores from time period one.

Findings

The findings presented in Table 1 . . . reveal a number of noteworthy relationships. First, the correlations between the votes (scores) in time period two to the votes (scores) in time period one varied by dimension. The highest correlations were on the Labor (.9), Political Liberalism (.8), Activism (.8), and Injured Persons (.8) dimensions. All but three of the remaining dimensions had correlations of .7. Private Economic voting had a .6 correlation between the two time periods which is perhaps higher than might have been expected given the wide variety of economic disputes encompassed within the dimension. Government Fiscal had a .5 correlation that perhaps also reflects the varied nature of the disputes as well as their changing character over the two time periods. Thus at the outset it should be emphasized that, as expected, a high degree of voting consistency was found. Consistency was found even though the dimensions were defined in terms of political stimuli and not according to narrow legal categories.

The lowest correlation between the voting in the first and second time periods was on the Dissents dimension (.4). If dissent behavior were a personality variable, we would expect to find a high correlation between dissent during the two time periods. Propensity to dissent regardless of the issue but perhaps in response to certain disliked colleagues or personal irritability would then be relatively constant over the two time periods. But the literature suggests otherwise. Atkins found that dissent behavior is policy oriented. Since the Dissent dimension utilized here did not take into account the policy issues involved but was simply a measure of propensity to dissent, a high correlation of dissent behavior in time period one to time period two would call into question Atkins' finding. Conversely, a low correlation would suggest that a multitude of attitudes and issues are involved so that no simple propensity to dissent is discernible. The fact that the lowest correlation was indeed found for the Dissents dimension therefore provides at least some support for dissent as policy oriented.

The most striking finding revealed by the partial correlation analysis was the clear superiority of previous behavior over the background variables. The Political and Economic Liberalism dimensions for which the largest numbers of judges were tested (of all the policy oriented dimensions) best demonstrates this. With Political Liberalism, previous voting behavior explained over 67 percent of the variation in behavior during time period two whereas none of the attribute variables individ-

TABLE 1. Stepwise Multiple Regression and Correlation Analysis of Background Variables and Previous Voting During Time Period One to the Scores for Time Period Two

DIMENSION	INDEPENDENT VARIABLE	Multiple R	% of Explained Variance	TIME PERIOD TWO Zero-Order Correlation	Partial Corr. (Sixth Order)	% of Expl. Variance
Criminal Procedures	Political Party	.250	6.3	.250	.086	0.7
	Age	.263	6.9	−.109	.048	0.2
	Religion	.263	6.9	−.062	.101	1.0
	Candidate	.263	6.9	−.037	−.099	0.9
	Prior Judicial	.266	7.1	−.059	−.011	0.0
	Years on Appeals	.281	7.9	−.074	−.185	3.4
	Prosecutorial Exper.	.281	7.9	−.031	−.002	0.0
	Previous Voting (T.P. 1)	.791	62.6	.772	.770	59.3
Civil Liberties	Age	.162	2.6	−.162	−.337	11.4
	Political Party	.169	2.8	.105	−.137	1.8
	Religion	.321	10.3	−.288	−.228	5.2
	Candidate	.410	16.8	−.282	−.087	0.8
	Years on Appeals	.442	19.5	.137	−.081	0.6
	Prosecutorial Exper.	.454	20.6	−.177	−.069	0.5
	Prior Judicial	.525	27.5	.088	.230	5.3
	Previous Voting (T.P. 1)	.845	71.4	.774	.778	60.5
Labor	Political Party	.474	22.5	.474	.447	19.9
	Age	.546	29.8	−.340	−.294	8.6
	Religion	.693	48.0	−.546	−.162	2.6
	Prior Judicial	.693	48.0	.045	−.026	0.1
	Candidate	.695	48.3	−.156	.441	19.4
	Years on Appeals	.704	49.6	−.216	.139	1.9
	Prosecutorial Exper.	.714	51.0	.115	.328	10.8
	Previous Voting (T.P. 1)	.938	88.0	.884	.869	75.5

Private Economic	Political Party	.285	8.1	.285	.441	19.4
	Age	.440	19.4	.260	−.062	0.4
	Religion	.537	28.8	−.417	.081	0.7
	Prior Judicial	.554	30.7	.054	−.009	0.0
	Candidate	.664	44.0	.545	.635	40.3
	Years on Appeals	.709	50.2	.184	.271	7.3
	Prosecutorial Exper.	.771	59.4	.112	.656	43.0
	Previous Voting (T.P. 1)	.898	80.7	.634	.724	52.4
Government Fiscal	Political Party	.371	13.8	−.371	−.138	1.9
	Age	.381	14.5	−.118	.164	2.7
	Candidate	.530	28.1	−.468	−.530	28.1
	Religion	.533	28.4	.211	−.326	10.6
	Prior Judicial	.533	28.4	−.168	−.205	4.2
	Years on Appeals	.579	33.6	−.209	−.163	2.7
	Prosecutorial Exper.	.580	33.6	−.137	−.048	0.2
	Previous Voting (T.P. 1)	.741	54.9	.492	.566	32.0
Injured Persons	Political Party	.523	27.3	.523	.077	0.6
	Age	.525	27.6	−.054	.107	1.1
	Religion	.620	38.5	−.526	−.108	1.2
	Candidate	.644	41.5	−.146	−.269	7.2
	Prior Judicial	.646	41.7	.224	.033	0.1
	Years on Appeals	.669	44.8	−.128	−.424	17.9
	Prosecutorial Exper.	.690	47.7	−.141	−.423	17.9
	Previous Voting (T.P. 1)	.868	75.3	.789	.726	52.7
Political Liberalism	Political Party	.247	6.1	.247	.053	0.3
	Age	.280	7.8	−.162	−.109	1.2
	Religion	.280	7.9	−.101	.074	0.5
	Candidate	.280	7.9	−.059	−.087	0.8
	Prior Judicial	.281	7.9	−.040	.139	1.9
	Years on Appeals	.281	7.9	−.067	−.052	0.3
	Prosecutorial Exper.	.303	9.2	−.130	−.052	0.3
	Previous Voting (T.P. 1)	.839	70.4	.826	.821	67.4

TABLE 1. (*continued*)

Dimension	Independent Variable	Time Period Two				
		Multiple R	% of Explained Variance	Zero-Order Correlation	Partial Corr. (Sixth Order)	% of Expl. Variance
Economic Liberalism	Political Party	.372	13.8	.372	.081	0.7
	Age	.391	15.3	−.184	−.169	2.9
	Religion	.445	19.8	−.314	−.129	1.7
	Candidate	.450	20.2	−.006	.019	0.0
	Prior Judicial	.465	21.7	−.119	−.061	0.4
	Years on Appeals	.481	23.1	.067	.086	0.7
	Prosecutorial Exper.	.481	23.2	−.060	.139	1.9
	Previous Voting (T.P. 1)	.745	55.5	.714	.649	42.1
Activism	Age	.079	0.6	.079	−.214	4.6
	Political Party	.104	1.1	.054	−.121	1.5
	Religion	.117	1.4	.014	.083	0.7
	Candidate	.133	1.8	.090	.082	0.8
	Prior Judicial	.272	7.4	.230	.167	2.8
	Prosecutorial Exper.	.339	11.5	−.118	−.022	0.1
	Years on Appeals	.355	12.6	−.059	−.094	0.9
	Previous Voting (T.P. 1)	.844	71.3	.811	.819	67.1
Dissents	Political Party	.106	1.1	.106	−.033	0.1
	Age	.263	6.9	.219	.147	2.2
	Religion	.347	12.0	−.278	−.305	9.3
	Prior Judicial	.373	13.9	−.078	−.130	1.7
	Candidate	.380	14.4	−.088	−.072	0.5
	Years on Appeals	.404	16.3	.260	.123	1.5
	Prosecutorial Exper.	.416	17.3	.112	.148	2.2
	Previous Dissent Score	.605	36.6	.430	.483	23.3

Note that Democrats, Protestants, candidates, those with prior judicial experience, and those with previous prosecutorial experience were assigned a higher numerical value than those who were not in those groups.

166

ually explained more than 2 percent. With Economic Liberalism similar findings appeared. For the other dimensions as well, voting behavior during time period one was superior for explanatory purposes than any of the attribute variables.

In terms of which attribute variables exhibited the most potency, the partial correlation analysis suggested that political party affiliation was relatively important for two of the economic categories—Labor and Private Economic (with Democrats voting more "liberal" than Republicans) but of negligible important elsewhere. Age was relatively important for Civil Liberties voting (older judges voting more "conservative") but not on the other issues. Religion was of relatively minor importance on the Government Fiscal and Dissents dimensions (non-Protestants had a slight tendency to be more antigovernment and to dissent more). Those who were candidates for public office had a tendency to support organized labor, to be anti-government in the fiscal cases, and to support the economic underdog on the Private Economic dimension. Those with prosecutorial experience had a slight tendency to support labor, to support the economic underdog, but to oppose the injured. Those with the longest tenure on the appeals courts also had a tendency to be relatively unsympathetic to the injured.

On two dimensions, Labor and Private Economic, the background variables alone explained over half the variance. The three key variables were party, candidacy for public office and prosecutorial experience. It is of interest to observe that candidacy and prosecutorial experience were likely to have occurred sometime in the two + decades preceding 1960 when certain kinds of economic issues (but not civil liberties issues) were linked to American politics. Candidacy and prosecutorial experience are the variables along with party affiliation that seem to be closest to being political system variables. Thus the findings for Labor and Private Economic can perhaps be attributed to their special linkages with electoral politics.

The stepwise multiple regression analysis suggests that attribute variables contributed proportionately more of the variance on the economic oriented dimensions than on the noneconomic dimensions. Political Liberalism and the allied Criminal Procedures and Civil Liberties along with the Activism dimensions had past behavior contributing proportionately more of the variance than on the economic-oriented dimensions. Attribute variables thus appear to be of greater import and are likely to be of greater explanatory value with certain kinds of economic policy-making issues than with the issues of noneconomic political rights.

The most striking finding of the stepwise multiple regression analysis, however, is that, although past behavior is responsible for the large portion of the explained variance, the combination of attributes and attitudes on all dimensions but Dissents explains from about 55 percent of the variance (Government Fiscal and Economic Liberalism) to 88 percent (Labor).

Conclusions

Results from the test of the effect of past judicial voting behavior on subsequent voting behavior lead to several conclusions. First, as expected, there was stability of the direction of voting behavior over the two consecutive five year periods. This implies that judicial attitudes, at least in the short run, remain relatively stable. The Judge who in the first time period tended to be sympathetic to the claims of criminal defendants or organized labor tended to remain so through the second time period.

Second, although nine policy-oriented dimensions were cast in sociopolitical terms and not narrow legal categories, the independent variables were able to explain the large portion of the variance. This suggests, particularly to those in the law schools and legal profession who have resisted the sort of analysis employed here, that socio-political categorization of court cases is a useful and potentially insightful tool for the analysis of certain legal phenomena.

Finally although past behavior proved superior to attributes, the findings demonstrated that together both can explain more of the variance than either alone.

The American Jury

— 30 —

A Jury Is Better!

Charles W. Joiner

I am a strong believer in the jury system. This conviction is bottomed on the various avenues of exposure I have had with jury trials. I have tried jury cases as a lawyer. I have taught procedure, trial, and appellate practice, and have been the chairman and principal draftsman of the revised Michigan Procedural Rules. I have also been a member of the Advisory Committees on Civil Procedure and Evidence of the Judicial Conference of the United States; and in 1962, prior to becoming a Judge, I wrote a small essay . . . on the civil jury.

• • •

As a judge, I have presided over jury trials about two-thirds of my time in court. These trials, on the criminal side, involve a broad variety of federal crimes, including serious narcotics violations, bank robberies, frauds against the government, civil rights violations, interstate gambling conspiracy, and forgery. On the civil side, a whole range of problems have been presented to juries in my court, including personal injury matters, contract violations, copyright matters, antitrust cases and civil rights.

In my jury trials, I have made a special effort to communicate with

From Charles W. Joiner, "From the Bench," in *The Jury System in America: A Critical Overview*, ed. Rita Simon (Sage Publications, 1975), pp. 145, 145–146, 146, 148–149, 150–151, 152, 153, 154–155, 155, 155–156. Copyright © 1975 by Sage Publications, Inc. Reprinted by permission of the publisher, Sage Publications, Inc. (Beverly Hills/ London) . Footnotes have been omitted.

the jury and to make certain they feel they are a part of the system of administering justice.

I make an effort to inform them of what is happening at every stage of the trial and to answer any questions they may have about the procedure. I instruct them in advance of the voir dire about their place in the trial and again, in advance of the opening statement, about the trial, the lawyer's duties, the jurors' duties, and sometimes—in complicated cases in which the issues are difficult but defined—I give them instructions on the law of the issues they will have to decide. I tell them about the function of all of the actors in the courtroom drama, about the reasons for excusing individual jurors as well as the reasons for the sidebar conference. I give them notepaper and pencils for their discretionary use, and I give them a written copy of the charge when they retire. In other words, I try to let them know of their importance and the fact that I believe they can only do their task if they understand the whole process. When I release them for lunch or in the evening, I try to make certain there are no unanswered procedural questions about their activities, their duties, or about the occurrences of the day. These steps, of course, are taken by many judges, but I believe they are essential to making the system work.

• • •

Deliberation: The Principal Value of the Jury

Sitting as a trial judge has reinforced my view that the greatest value of the jury is its ability to decide cases correctly. I have generally, but not always, agreed with the jury verdict at the time it was rendered. But in each instance, except one, on reflection and on deeper analysis, I have decided the jury was correct. My reflection involved an effort to expose myself to my biases and attempt to counteract them in my mind. I have concluded that the process of deliberation did this for my jury and their decision was correct.

• • •

Juror Quality

Our jurors come from voter lists drawn broadly from our district. I have been favorably impressed with the quality of the persons I have seen on the juries. They are far superior to the jurors I saw in practice in Iowa. They appear to be a reasonable cross-section of a significant portion of our society. Many have not gone to college. A few have not completed high school. Some are young; some are old. Many have raised families. In most instances, all jurors have achieved in their own way and are performing responsible tasks in our society.

On the whole, the juries I have selected appear to include men and women I would enjoy arguing with about the decision of a case, and persons who are interested in doing the right thing. The jurors seem to be the same sort of men and women who are involved in community government, who are teaching our children in our schools or our Sunday schools, who are raising their own children as our neighbors, who are repairing our phones, our television sets, our automobiles, who are driving the trucks, typing the letters, selling us merchandise in our stores, and doing all of the other thousands of tasks that make society operate. In doing these tasks, all of them in their own way have developed some system of making decisions, of listening and seeing and screening and evaluating. In many instances these are highly sophisticated systems. In others, they are relatively simple. But when you put a number of these different systems of evaluation and screening together and tell them to reach a result, according to certain rules and standards given to them, generally a good result is reached. It is important, of course, to make certain the judge and the lawyers relate to the experience of the jurors. When they do, the aggregate decision is likely to be better than that of a single person.

• • •

Ability to Follow Law

Generally, my experience with juries following the law has been good. I take careful pains to help them in this respect. One of the mistakes many persons make, including some judges and lawyers, is to become too refined in their view of the law and to expect ordinary behavior to reflect this refinement. The law should be as simple as possible, and the behavior of persons should be judged by relatively broad, understandable statements of legal principle. I think this is all that can be expected of the normal person in our society. As activity becomes more specialized and refined, of course the legal doctrines surrounding that activity may become more specialized and refined as well; but, in general, too much detail and too many qualifications, too many exceptions, cannot be absorbed by the rank and file of our citizens in their decision-making behavior. It is not fruitful to attempt to apply overly refined doctrine to activity and persons not capable of conforming their lives to such detailed statements. Thus, in instructing juries on the law in general, my standard approach is to paint with a relatively broad brush.

• • •

Jury Esprit

Jurors come to jury service with mixed feelings. A few resent being required to participate in the judicial process. The majority, however, are excited and interested at being asked to perform this public duty.

• • •

I have noticed when I am attentive and listening carefully, not bored, the jury is likewise. They are not listening because I am, but because we both, independently, are interested in what is going on between the witness and the lawyers. On occasion when I become bored, because it seems to me that the proceedings are not very relevant or important or material, I find that members of the jury are acting in the same way. I find their attention span is on the whole as good as mine, but not any better.

• • •

In summary, I believe jurors come for service properly motivated. They want to do what is right according to the standards set by the court. If this spirit fails or decreases, it is because the courts do not handle the jurors correctly by providing adequate facilities and accommodations, adequate detailed instructions explaining jury service and how to act, and adequate attention to the common civilities appropriately due to an outside person who is invited to come and help solve problems. When courts have good facilities, accommodations, court personnel including lawyers and judges, and remember that people thrust into strange situations feel uncomfortable until they know the rules and constantly pay attention to help the jurors understand, the spirit of wanting to do what is right will not lessen.

Conclusion

I do not suggest that all is perfect with the jury system. It takes a lot of work on the part of the judge and lawyers to make the system work; but when both try, I believe good results are reached. On the other hand, when lawyers are not prepared or when they are unequal in ability, the judge carries an especially heavy obligation to help the jury and to keep it from becoming confused. When the judge does not work at helping the jury, the system does not work well.

• • •

1. I believe the decisions by juries properly instructed and taught are better than decisions by a single judge.

2. The principal reason for this is that the process of deliberation is a process through which the biases of individual jurors are exposed and isolated or controlled, and it is an ideal teaching procedure continuing throughout the decisional process.

3. Juries are better today than they were thirty years ago, largely as a result of the effort to make them represent a reasonably fair cross-section of the voting community, and as a result of the impact that television and easier transportation have had on their knowledge and experience.

4. Judges, lawyers, and court staff have a heavy burden to make the system work. All of them must make jurors feel at home in the strange environment of the court house by making certain the jurors understand everything they are asked to do.

5. Lawyers must not ask jurors to do more than they are capable of doing; in particular, jury trials of an extended case—unless it has major issues or matters of great moment or involves substantial personal liberty—should be avoided, because individual jurors have difficulty understanding why their lives should be disrupted for such substantial periods of time on matters that do not seem to be important to them.

31

A Judge Is Better?

Warren E. Burger

• • •

When the framers of the Constitution were engaged in the practice of law in the colonies, they were not dealing with the kinds of complex cases which are the daily fare of the courts in the second half of the twentieth century. The performance of those draftsmen in anticipating problems of the future and casting the Constitution in broad, flexible

From "Remarks of Warren E. Burger" (Meeting of the Conference of Chief Justices, Flagstaff, Ariz., August 7, 1979), pp. 1–10. Reprinted by permission of the author. Most footnotes have been omitted.

terms was extraordinary. But it would be asking too much to suggest that they should have anticipated today's litigation involving a host of new problems unknown to the lawyers of 1787. The change in litigation patterns in recent decades boggles the mind of man and numerous cases document this reality.

We know now that in both state and federal courts, with a higher incidence in the federal courts, we have civil cases which last not merely two weeks or one month, but two, six, eight months and even longer. What are the factors to be taken into account with respect to the use of lay jurors in these protracted cases?

First, experienced business and professional people, accountants, professors of economics, statisticians, or others competent to cope with complex economic or scientific questions rarely survive challenges in the jury selection process if they are not excused for cause. The jury actually selected is rarely a true cross-section, as we are so fond of repeating.

Second, the factual issues are likely to be of enormous complexity. The analysis of documents, of expert testimony, of charts, graphs and other visual aids, and the comprehension of those elements, present problems which often only a sophisticated businessman, an economist, or another expert could grasp;

Third, the legal issues, which must be explained to jurors by the trial judge, may take not hours, but days, to present by way of instructions;

Fourth, there is a limit to the capacity of any of us—jurors or even a judge—to understand and remember complicated transactions described in a long trial;

Fifth, there is an enormous—inordinate—impact on the life of each of 12 to 15 lay jurors thrust for weeks and months into a totally strange environment and confronted with the burden of decisions in areas in which they have no experience.

There is a marked increase in the length of trials in the federal districts courts. From 1970 to 1978, the total of trial days of civil cases lasting more than one month more than doubled.[1]

Thirty years ago in his book *Courts on Trial,* Jerome Frank, then a judge of the United States Court of Appeals, after describing a series of bizarre results reached by juries, had this to say:

"Are jurors to blame when they decide cases in the ways I have described? I think not. In the first place, often they cannot understand what the judge told them about the legal rules. To comprehend the meaning of many a legal rule requires special training. It is inconceivable that a body of twelve ordinary [jurors], casually gathered together for a few days, could, merely from listening to the instructions of the judge, gain the knowledge necessary to grasp the true import of the judge's words." P. 116, Frank, *Courts on Trial.*

Note that Jerome Frank was talking about the *ordinary* case tried in "a few days," not the protracted or complicated case which runs for weeks or months and often involves testimony incomprehensible to all but a trained expert. Such a case is likely to have a multitude of exhibits which fall into the same category.

Simon Rifkind, formerly a federal trial judge, in his address to the "Pound Conference" in 1976 had this to say:

> "A trial is a medium of communication and every such medium, whether it be a newspaper, a broadcast, or a play, has learned to accommodate itself to an effective size. Trials are no exception."

The legal issues in the long case, of course, are not the primary responsibility of the jury, but of the judge. Yet, each individual juror is presumed, in one of those fictions we lawyers love, to understand the instructions on the law and to be able to apply them to a factual setting. But the legal issues are sometimes such that it may take not two, four, or six hours, but several days for the judge to give the instructions which the jurors are directed to apply to the facts.

The discussions concerning the use of lay juries in such cases is not advanced by the cliches about "the common sense of the common man" and the jury as the "bulwark against oppression." But the "common sense" of the common man—which is, of course, important—cannot be brought to bear unless there is comprehension of the facts and the law. And, of course, the jury acts as the "bulwark against oppression" in chiefly criminal cases, not civil.

Even Jefferson would be appalled at the prospect of a dozen of his yeomen and artisans trying to cope with some of today's complex litigation in a trial lasting many weeks or months.

Overwhelmingly, as every trial judge and trial lawyer knows, a great many of the people best qualified to sit on juries are those most eager to escape jury duty—and they are largely successful in doing so—under existing practices.

There is an enormous impact on the life of the individual who is asked to leave his or her private affairs, family or business to devote five or even six days each week for months to a single case. This is quite different from being called from the farm, factory, or home for several weeks to decide simple negligence cases or claims of breach of contract. Such routine cases (even when tried by lawyers who may take twice as much time as ought to be taken) can be completed within days or, at most, weeks. The disruption to personal and family life and business or professional occupations in these routine cases is minimal. Moreover, this is an obligation of citizenship. But apart from all the other flaws, it borders on cruelty to draft people to sit for long periods trying to cope with issues largely beyond their grasp. Some day the claim may be made by a plumber or electrician that to compel him to serve on a jury for five to six months at thirty dollars per day when he customarily earns at least one-hundred dollars a day, deprives him of property without due process and just compensation. Far more unusual claims have been made to the courts in recent times.

In his book, *Trial Techniques,* Goldstein urges trial lawyers, when selecting juries, to seek the type of juror who "will most naturally respond to an emotional appeal." He goes on to say that lawyers, particularly for the plaintiff, should make every effort to exclude from the jury anyone who is particularly experienced in the field of endeavor which is the basis of the lawsuit. Parenthetically, I find it somewhat amusing when he also makes the point that, by and large, juries try the lawyers rather than the clients, accepting and crediting evidence and arguments offered by the lawyer whose personality appeals to them. This concept was expressed vividly by Balzac when he characterized a jury as "twelve men chosen to decide who has the better lawyer."

Let me turn now to one concrete example which, although it occurred in the context of a criminal antitrust prosecution [*United States* v. *United States Gypsum Co.*], could just have easily occurred in any complex, protracted civil trial. I draw first on the Supreme Court's recital of the relevant facts:

> "After hearing a mass of testimony for nearly five months, the jurors were sequestered when deliberations commenced. On the second and third days of deliberations, supplemental instructions were given in response to jury questions; on the fourth day, the hours of deliberations were shortened because of reported nervous tension among the jurors; on the fifth day, the judge *sua sponte* delivered what amounted to a modified *Allen* charge[*] in the course of providing further answers to questions from the jury; and on the sixth day, the modified *Allen* charge was repeated this time in response to a note from the jury that it was unable to reach a verdict. Against this background of internal pressures and apparent disagreements and confusion among the jurors, the jury foreman, on the morning of the seventh day of deliberations, requested a meeting with the judge 'to discuss the condition of the jury and further guidance.' "

Now I ask your indulgence to allow a reading of part of the transcript of the discussion between the trial judge and the jury foreman. Bear in mind, as I proceed, that at the conclusion of this colloquy I will put to each of you this question: if the interests at stake were yours—on one side or the other—would you want such complex issues of a *civil* case

---

* An instruction to pay deference to the views of other jurors, to be predisposed to be convinced by the arguments of other jurors. Variously called a dynamite charge, a shotgun, or third degree instruction.

determined by jurors whose state of mind is so graphically described by the material I now present?

APPENDIX

[Present: The foreman of the jury and the Court.]

THE COURT: What is your problem, sir?

MR. RUSSELL: I have two problems. And first of all, if I refer to a juror with a sexual gender, I would like it struck, because I would like to say juror.

THE COURT: In other words, if he says he or she, make it neutral.

MR. RUSSELL. The two problems are health and the status of the court. (sic) [count].

THE COURT: You can't tell me that now.

MR. RUSSELL: I am not going to tell you what the status is in no way. In fact, I can't tell you, because I can't remember.

THE COURT: All right.

MR. RUSSELL: But first of all, I would like to thank you for that 6:30 adjournment because I don't think you would have a jury left. I am not a doctor, but these people are getting very distraught. It is not that they go into a depression and stay there; they go into a depression and they're coming out high. Now I would say at least eight of the jurors are taking some kind of pill. Some of the pills have been issued by the doctor downstairs. I am not a doctor and I can't judge these things, but I have seen one of these jurors at one time I thought she was going to jump out the window. And I, just for my own sake, without telling you this, I cannot take the responsibility that this could happen. I know this is part of Mr. Keene's job, but like I say, they go high and low, and sometimes by the time I get to Mr. Keene and get him down there, they are perfectly normal again.

In fact, one of the instances was when I saw this one girl—

THE COURT: May I ask this: If we discharged—we can excuse one juror for health reasons. Is there any juror we could excuse that would help the situation? If it is more than that, there is no point.

MR. RUSSELL: I think there is more than that, Judge. I am not a doctor, so I can't say. I'm not even sure these are true sicknesses. They seem—I mean, with the high and low, they seem induced, but when a person thinks they are sick, they're generally sick.

THE COURT: It is just as bad, if they think they are.

MR. RUSSELL: As I say, I am not a doctor. I don't like to be a judge, but I think for my own sake, my feelings, it is my responsibility as foreman to tell you these things. I do not want to be responsible for anybody's health.

THE COURT: I don't, either.

You recall, though, that before—when I had two alternate jurors, I asked all the jurors if there was anybody who was not physically able to go ahead and everybody wanted to do it.

MR. RUSSELL: I realize that. I think every juror out there wants to do their duty.

THE COURT: See, we have tried this case now for four months.

MR. RUSSELL: This is part of it, I will grant you, but it is not the whole part of it. There is some personality conflicts on the jury that have led to certain situations and I think we have overcome those.

THE COURT: If we continue to deliberate from 9 to 6:30, with a lunch hour, for a while longer—

MR. RUSSELL: What I want to tell you next is—and that is, again, my opinion—and you can tell me I am wrong—and I have to look at it in a different way. We have taken enough ballots now, and we have had enough discussions, and the way it is divided is not going to be settled by any document, any remembrance of testimony. It is based on a belief and even if they—even if they would sign a document today, and you would ask me to get up in the jury box and swear I think this is a true and just verdict, I would have to say no, because I believe in the twelve or multiple system of a jury; that if we are to decide beyond a reasonable doubt, when you get twelve, or whatever the number has to be—

THE COURT: That is what you have to decide.

MR. RUSSELL: ——it proves it beyond a shadow of a doubt.

THE COURT: Not beyond a shadow of a doubt.

MR. RUSSELL: I know. Each individual proves it to himself, but for a man to be convicted guilty, or the company, we do it beyond a reasonable doubt, but if you have twelve, you know it is beyond a shadow of a doubt and you cannot have any conscience over it as far as a juror or anything else. That is the way I feel, Judge.

THE COURT: What are you suggesting?

MR. RUSSELL: I am asking you what I should do. I am to the point——

THE COURT: I would like this jury to deliberate longer. I say that because, as I say, we have tried it for a considerable period of time.

MR. RUSSELL: Everybody realizes that and I do.

THE COURT: We have individual people here who are concerned and the jury has now deliberated—they deliberated three full days, Wednesday, Thursday and Friday. They deliberated a half a day on Saturday and a half day on Sunday. They are not deliberating a full day, because jurors usually deliberate until eleven or ten at night.

MR. RUSSELL: We know that and we want to thank you.

THE COURT: You have not deliberated that long yet.

MR. RUSSELL: I know that is the way you would like it, but what I am trying to tell you is I don't think deliberation is going to change it. It is not a matter of time anymore.

THE COURT: Are you telling me this jury is hopelessly deadlocked and will never reach a verdict?

MR. RUSSELL: In my opinion, it is. I have to rely on that. I have no experience in this kind of thing. I don't know what people go through in a jury. This is the first time I have ever served on one and it is a new experience and I will never forget it. But it is a terrible responsibility and what I said, if it was a matter of finding a document or finding a part of a testimony that would convince somebody, I would say sure, and good.

THE COURT: All right.

For the time being continue your deliberations. I will take into consideration what you have told me.

MR. RUSSELL: As I said, the health problem is something that I think has to be looked at. I don't know how you are going to judge this or whether you call Mr. Keene and ask him or the Marshal's opinion, but I think something ought to be done.

THE COURT: All right. I will take it into consideration. I have to talk to counsel.

MR. RUSSELL: I appreciate that. I didn't expect a decision, but I would like some kind of guidance.

THE COURT: I would like to ask the jurors to continue their deliberations and I will take into consideration what you have told me. That is all I can say.

MR. RUSSELL: I appreciate it. It is a situation I don't know how to help you get what you are after.

THE COURT: Oh, I am not after anything.

MR. RUSSELL: You are after a verdict one way or the other.

THE COURT: Which way it goes doesn't make any difference to me.

MR. RUSSELL: They keep saying, "If you will tell him what the situation is, he might accept it."

I said, "He doesn't want to know. He told me that he doesn't want to know what the decision is."

THE COURT: No, I don't want to know that. It would not be proper for me to know.

MR. RUSSELL: You may imply something from what I said.

THE COURT: I can imply something from just watching, but I don't want you to tell me. That would be a breach of your duty.

MR. RUSSELL: I have told you as best I can.

THE COURT: Thank you. You tell them to keep deliberating and see if they can come to a verdict.

[At 12:04 P.M. the jury foreman returned to the deliberation room.]
Certified true and correct transcript.

/s/ MARION C. WIKE
Marion C. Wike
Official Reporter

[Joint App. 1837–1846.]

I now waive any response as to whether you would want any case of yours decided by a jury in these circumstances.

It is nearly 25 years now since Professor Leon Green, writing in the *Yale Law Journal*, put his finger on the essence of the problem that I press upon you today.

"As long as civil cases remained simple, and the issues were in the domain of the understanding of the everyday citizens, jury trial both in England and in this country was relatively satisfactory. But as civil cases became more complex and litigation brought within its vortex the interests of an expanding commercial and industrial economy; as the significance of these interests outran the understanding of laymen; as population multiplied and became mobile, so that strangers infiltrated every precinct; as business activities became organized into great enterprises that overflowed their local and even state boundaries; as many activities came to depend on dangerous machines that counted their victims by the thousands; as insurance companies assumed the liability and took over the role of the defense; as the experts and their methods in all the fields of science were called upon to provide proof; and as the courts through which the swelling tides of litigation were channeled grew in number and overlapped in jurisdiction, many serious conflicts have arisen within the jury process."

We know that many years before England abolished juries in virtually all civil cases, English judges increasingly treated complex civil cases as cases in equity for trial without a jury. When the results of that practice came to be fully understood, England took the final step and in 1937 abolished juries in all civil cases except libel and fraud.

We need not go so far as Jerome Frank advocated or accept Professor Green's analysis—or go so far as England has gone—to justify the need for a careful study of a more selective use of juries in certain categories of civil cases. It is enough for now that we inquire into the possibility of some alternatives to jury trial for the protracted trials of issues which baffle all but the rarest of jurors.

• • •

Note

1. From 1017 trial days to 2195 trial days. State court statistics are not available for all states, but I venture a guess—and it is only a partially informed guess—that about 200 state court civil cases each year run more than a month.

32

Twelve Is Just!

Hans Zeisel

There is a movement abroad in the land to diminish the size of the American jury from 12 members to six. Such a movement, if successful, would, in my opinion, not only result in a diminution of the size of the jury, but would also result in a diminution of the quality of justice—at least if such reduction were made without the most painstaking studies of the alternatives. Unfortunately, such studies have not been made.

The argument for reducing the size of the jury from 12 to six is two-fold:

- Such a move would save money and allegedly time.
- Such a reduction would not interfere with the quality of justice, because there is no difference between the verdicts of 12-member and six-member juries.

As to saving money, the case is clear enough: It has been estimated that in the federal system, with its relatively high per diem rate of $20, reducing all juries from 12 to six would save about $4 million. This is a substantial sum; still it is only a little more than 2% of the total federal judicial budget and a little more than the thousandth part of 1% of the total federal budget.

As to the amount of time saved, the best estimates arrive at a negligible quantity, primarily because the voir dire proceedings are not markedly affected by the reduction. In most federal courts the core of voir dire questioning is done by the judge simultaneously for all jurors, and it makes little difference whether 12 or six jurors listen and answer. Nevertheless, a minor, insignificant amount of time might well be saved at the voir dire level.

There is no hard evidence that the six-member jury would deliberate less than the 12-member jury. And if it turned out to do that, it would be doubtful whether this shortening should be entered on the credit side of the proposed reform.

As to whether adjudication by a six-member jury is the same as by a 12-member jury, the US Supreme Court has said twice that the evidence

From Hans Zeisel, "Twelve Is Just," *Trial* magazine 10 (Nov./Dec. 1974): 12, 12–14. Reprinted by permission of The Association of Trial Lawyers of America. Footnotes have been omitted.

before the Court showed that there is no difference between the verdicts of a 12-member jury and those of a six-member jury. With all due respect to the judges who composed the majority of the Court in these cases— on this point they were simply wrong. The Court's so-called evidence proved nothing of the sort. Moreover, there is good evidence indicating that the reduction from 12 to six will affect the verdicts.

• • •

Now, what, if any, effect will the jury reduction from 12 to six in civil cases have? The jury's preeminent function is to represent the community in the judicial process. If you reduce the jury's size from 12 to six, the first effect will be on the jury itself: You will make it less representative of the community from which it was drawn. To be sure, everybody knows that 12 jurors cannot really represent the whole community; but however poorly they do it, six jurors would do it less well. An example will make this clear. Think of a 10% minority of the population. You might think of the blacks, but you may also think of the Jews, or of very poor people, or of very educated people. You then ask yourself: What are the chances in a random selection of jurors from this population, of having at least one member of this ten percent minority on the jury? Simple calculus reveals that, on the average, 72 out of 100 randomly selected 12-member juries will have at least one such minority member. But among 100 juries of six-members, only 47 will have such a minority representative. Hence, less frequent representation of minorities on our juries is one inevitable result of cutting down their size from 12 to six. This reduced representation of minorities on our juries is probably a bad thing in itself.

But this less representative character of the six-member jury is bound to also have an effect on the verdicts of these juries: It increases the gamble the litigants take by bringing their case into court. Again, by way of example, it will help if we think of the jury decision in personal injury cases, which form the bulk of the business that comes before our civil juries. In these cases, the individual jurors' differences in perception and evaluation express themselves in different ideas of what constitutes negligence, of how much an injury hurts, and of what an injury is worth. And we know that the final verdict in a case will be somewhere in the middle, some kind of average, of these different evaluations of the individual jurors.

An elementary statistical calculation again reveals that these averages of juror evaluations in comparable cases will fluctuate more in six-member juries than they do in 12-member juries. The analogy with the Gallup Poll will help. We know that the smaller the size of a sample, the greater will be its margin of error. And here again we learn from calculus that reducing the sample size by one-half (e.g., from 1500 to 750

—but also from 12 to six) will increase the margin of error by some 41%. Translated into our jury problem, "margin of error" means wider fluctuations, and hence reduced predictability, and greater gamble, all by a margin of 41%, for the litigants that come to court.

And what is true for the size of the damage award is equally true for the verdict on liability: It will be more of a gamble all around. I might add here that reports from trial lawyers indicate that the reduced jury size affects also the relationship between counsel and jury: It is likely to become somewhat more personal, too personal, some of these lawyers feel.

The lawyers who now must try their cases before six-man juries know in their bones that the gamble is too great. And with the trial judge's consent, they are finding a way out of the difficulty. In at least two federal circuits, cases have been tried with eight jurors. You will ask how. Trust lawyers' ingenuity. They selected two alternate jurors and at the end of the trial, stipulated that the two alternates may join the six regular jurors in their deliberations.

In this context I should like to say a word on the proposition collateral to the reduction of the jury's size, namely the proposal to reduce also the number of peremptory challenges available to each side. It seems reasonable enough to assume that if we have six jurors instead of 12, we may as well also curtail the number of available challenges. In view of what the jury-size reduction does to the representative character of the jury, I wonder whether one could not argue under these circumstances for an expansion, or at least against a reduction of the present number of available challenges, so as to allow at least for this correction of the mode by which chance will produce odd compositions of the six-member jury.

On balance, it might seem that the legislators considering the issue would have to weigh the savings of some $4 million annually against the less representative character of the jury and the resulting increase in the gamble the litigants take in bringing their case to court. But this would be a myopic, limited view. One must see the reduction of the jury size in civil cases in the federal courts as but one move in a major attack on the jury system that began in the "law-and-order days," when it was thought that the jury, as we have known it since the founding of the Republic, might stand in the way of law enforcement.

To see the whole picture, you must see that we already have a six-man jury in criminal cases in some of our state courts, and that following the Supreme Court's decision in *Williams v. Florida,* there is already a Senate bill proposing the six-member criminal jury for federal trials. Nor is this all: Majority verdicts in jury trials, well established in civil cases in some state courts, are being proposed for criminal trials. So we may soon have in our courts what we have for the time being only in a remote corner of our law, the military court-martial: a six-member criminal jury that can reach a verdict with a majority of five or four jurors.

After what I have said, it might appear that I am an advocate of the traditional jury. Allow me to correct this view. I obtained my first legal education in Austria, one of the many countries that know juries only for trials of a small number of major crimes, and never had a jury in civil cases. The jury in civil trials has now become almost an American specialty, and I am not at all convinced that it will or should forever remain on our laws books. But this is a very serious question that will require much study of how the jury operates and also of what judges are doing.

What we must consider today is whether now is the right moment to single out the jury for diminution. Our system of justice is at a moment of crisis; aspersions are being cast on almost every part of that system, from the policeman on the beat to the very highest officials in the land. I said on almost every part, for has anyone heard any criticism of the jury lately? I think not.

Much has been said and written in recent months about reestablishing the authority of Congress vis-a-vis the Executive. But what about the restablishment of the authority of Congress vis-a-vis the Judiciary? Why doesn't Congress help those district courts who so far have refused to cut the size of their juries? In sum, why doesn't the Congress pass a bill that reestablishes the 12-member jury in all federal courts? Why not share our view that $4 million is perhaps not the right price for abandoning half of the American jury?

33

Conviction By Five Is Not Enough!
Burch v. *Louisiana*

• • •

Petitioners, an individual and a Louisiana corporation, were jointly charged in two counts with the exhibition of two obscene motion pictures. Pursuant to Louisiana law, they were tried before a six-person jury, which found both petitioners guilty as charged. A poll of the jury after verdict indicated that the jury had voted unanimously to convict petitioner Wrestle, Inc. and had voted 5–1 to convict petitioner Burch. Burch was sentenced to two consecutive 7-month prison terms, which were suspended, and fined $1,000; Wrestle, Inc. was fined $600 on each count.

• • •

Petitioners appealed their convictions to the Supreme Court of Louisiana, where they argued that the provisions of Louisiana law permitting conviction by a nonunanimous six-member jury violated the rights of persons accused of nonpetty criminal offenses to trial by jury guaranteed by the Sixth and Fourteenth Amendments. Though acknowledging that the issue was "close," the court held that conviction by a nonunanimous six-person jury did not offend the Constitution. 360 So. 2d 381, 838 (1978). The court concluded that none of this Court's decisions precluded use of a nonunanimous six-person jury. " 'If 75 percent concurrence (9/12) was enough for a verdict as determined in *Johnson* v. *Louisiana,* 406 U.S. 356 (1972), then requiring 83 percent concurrence (5/6) ought to be within the permissible limits of *Johnson.*' " *Ibid.,* quoting Hargrove. The Declaration of Rights of the Louisiana Constitution of 1974, 35 La. L. Rev. 1, 56 n. 300 (1974). And our recent decision in *Ballew* v. *Georgia,* 435 U.S. 223 (1978), striking down a Georgia law allowing conviction by a unanimous five-person jury in nonpetty criminal cases, was distinguishable in the Louisiana Supreme Court's view:

"[I]n *Williams* [v. *Florida,* 399 U. S. 78 (1970)] the court held that a *six-*person jury was of sufficient size to promote adequate group deliberation, to

From *Burch* v. *Louisiana, The United States Law Week* 47 (1979): 4393–4395. *The United States Law Week* is a publication of The Bureau of National Affairs, Inc. Reprinted by permission. Footnotes have been omitted.

insulate members from outside intimidation, and to provide a representative cross-section of the community. These values which *Ballew* held a five-person jury is inadequate to serve, are not necessarily defeated because the six-person jury's verdict may be rendered by five instead of by six persons." 360 So. 2d, at 838.

Since the Louisiana Supreme Court believed that conviction by a non-unanimous six-person jury was not necessarily foreclosed by this Court's decisions, it stated that it preferred to "indulg[e] in the presumption of federal constitutionality which must be afforded to provisions of our state constitution." 360 So. 2d, at 838.

We agree with the Louisiana Supreme Court that the question presented is a "close" one. Nonetheless, we believe that conviction by a non-unanimous six-member jury in a state criminal trial for a nonpetty offense deprives an accused of his constitutional right to trial by jury.

Only in relatively recent years has this Court had to consider the practices of the several States relating to jury size and unanimity. *Duncan* v. *Louisiana* 391 U.S. 145 (1968), marked the beginning of our involvement with such questions. The Court in *Duncan* held that because trial by jury in "serious" criminal cases is "fundamental to the American scheme of justice" and essential to due process of law, the Fourteenth Amendment guarantees a state criminal defendant the right to a jury trial in any case, which, if tried in a federal court, would require a jury under the Sixth Amendment. *Id.,* at 149, 158–159.

Two Terms later in *Williams* v. *Florida,* 399 U.S. 78, 86 (1970), the Court held that this constitutional guarantee of trial by jury did not require a State to provide an accused with a jury of 12 members and that Florida did not violate the jury trial rights of criminal defendants charged with nonpetty offenses by affording them jury panels comprised of only six persons. After canvassing the common-law development of the jury and the constitutional history of the jury trial right, the Court concluded that the 12-person requirement was "a historical accident" and that there was no indication that the Framers intended to preserve in the Constitution the features of the jury system as it existed at common law. *Id.,* at 89–90. Thus freed from strictly historical considerations, the Court turned to examine the function that this particular feature performs and its relation to the purposes of jury trial. *Id.,* at 99–100. The purpose of trial by jury, as noted in *Duncan,* is to prevent Government oppression by providing a "safeguard against the corrupt or overzealous prosecutor and against the compliant, biased, or eccentric judge." 391 U.S., at 156. Given this purpose, the *Williams* Court observed that the jury's essential feature lies in the "interposition between the accused and his accuser of the commonsense judgment of a group of laymen and in the community participation and shared responsibility that results from that group's determination of guilt or innocence." 399 U.S., at 100. These purposes could be fulfilled, the Court believed, so long as the jury was of a sufficient size to promote group deliberation, free from outside intimidation, and to provide a fair possibility that a cross-section of the community would be represented on it. *Ibid.* The Court concluded, however, that there is "little reason to think that these goals are in any meaningful sense less likely to be achieved when the jury numbers six, than when it numbers 12—*particularly if the requirement of unanimity is retained." Ibid.* (emphasis added).

A similar analysis led us to conclude in 1972 that a jury's verdict need not be unanimous to satisfy constitutional requirements, even though unanimity had been the rule at common law. Thus, in *Apodaca* v. *Oregon,* 406 U.S. 404 (1972), we upheld a state statute providing that only 10 members of a 12-person jury need concur to render a verdict in certain noncapital cases. In terms of the role of the jury as a safeguard against oppression, the plurality opinion perceived no difference between those juries required to act unanimously and those permitted to act by votes of 10 to two. 406 U.S., at 411. Nor was unanimity viewed by the plurality as contributing materially to the exercise of the jury's common-sense judgment or as a necessary precondition to effective application of the requirement that jury panels represent a fair cross-section of the community. *Id.,* at 410, 412.

Last Term in *Ballew* v. *Georgia* 435 U.S. 223 (1978) we considered whether a jury of less than six members passes constitutional scrutiny, a question that was explicitly reserved in *Williams* v. *Florida.* See 399 U.S., at 91 n. 28. The Court, in separate opinions, held that conviction by a unanimous five-person jury for a nonpetty offense deprives an accused of his right to trial by jury. While readily admitting that the line between six members and five was not altogether easy to justify, at least five Members of the Court believed that reducing a jury to five persons in nonpetty cases raised sufficiently substantial doubts as to fairness of the proceeding and proper functioning of the jury to warrant drawing the line at six. See 435 U.S., at 239 (opinion of BLACKMUN, J.); *id.,* at 245–246 (opinion of POWELL, J.).

We thus have held that the Constitution permits juries of less than 12 members, but that it requires at least six. *Ballew* v. *Georgia, supra; Williams* v. *Florida,* supra. And we have approved the use of certain non-unanimous verdicts in cases involving 12-person juries. *Apodaca* v. *Oregon, supra* (10–2); *Johnson* v. *Louisiana,* 406 U.S. 356 (1972) (9–3). These principles are not questioned here. Rather, this case lies at the intersection of our decisions concerning jury size and unanimity. As in *Ballew,* we do not pretend the ability to discern *a priori* a bright line below which the number of jurors participating in the trial or in the verdict would not permit the jury to function in the manner required by our prior cases. 435 U.S., at 231–232 (opinion of BLACKMUN, J.); *id.*, at 245–246 (opinion of POWELL, J.); see *Williams* v. *Florida, supra,* at 100. But having already departed from the strictly historical requirements of jury trial, it is inevitable that lines must be drawn somewhere if the substance of the jury trial right is to be preserved. Cf. *Scott* v. *Illinois,* —— U.S. ——, —— (1979); *Baldwin* v. *New York,* 399 U.S. 66, 72–73 (1970) (plurality opinion); *Duncan* v. *Louisiana,* 391 U.S., at 161. Even the State concedes as much. Tr. of Oral Arg. 26–27.

This line drawing process, "although essential, cannot be wholly satisfactory, for · it requires attaching different consequences to events which, when they lie near the line, actually differ very little." *Duncan* v. *Louisiana, supra,* at 161; see *Baldwin* v. *New York, supra* at 72–73 (plurality opinion). However, much the same reasons that led us in *Ballew* to decide that use of a five-member jury threatened the fairness of the proceeding and the proper role of the jury, lead us to conclude now that conviction for a nonpetty offense by only five members of a six-person jury presents a similar threat to preservation of the substance of the jury trial guarantee and justifies our requiring verdicts rendered by six-person juries to be unanimous. We are buttressed in this view by the current jury practices of the several States. It appears that of those States that utilize six-member juries in trials of nonpetty offenses, only two, including Louisiana, also allow nonunanimous verdicts. We think that this near-uniform judgment of the Nation provides a useful guide in delimiting the line between those jury practices that are constitutionally permissible and those that are not. See *Baldwin* v. *New York, supra,* at 70–72 (plurality opinion); *Duncan* v. *Louisiana, supra,* at 161; *District of Columbia* v. *Clawans,* 300 U.S. 617, 628 (1937).

The State seeks to justify its use of nonunanimous six-person juries on the basis of the "considerable time" savings that it claims results from trying cases in this manner. It asserts that under its system, juror deliberation time is shortened and the number of hung juries is reduced. Brief of Respondent 14. Undoubtedly, the State has a substantial interest in reducing the time and expense associated with the administration of its system of criminal justice. But that interest cannot prevail here. First, on this record, any benefits that might accrue by allowing five members of a six-person jury to render a verdict, as compared with requiring unanimity of a six-member jury, are speculative, at best. More importantly, we think that when a State has reduced the size of its juries to the minimum number of jurors permitted by the Constitution, the additional authorization of nonunanimous verdicts by such juries sufficiently threatens the constitutional principles that led to the establishment of the size threshold that any countervailing interest of the State should yield.

The judgment of the Louisiana Supreme Court affirming the convic-

tion of petitioner Burch is, therefore, reversed and its judgment affirming the conviction of petitioner Wrestle, Inc. is affirmed. The case is
remanded to the Louisiana Supreme Court for proceedings not inconsistent with this opinion.

   It is so ordered.

34

The Limits of Scientific Jury Selection

Michael J. Saks

• • •

The law provides for a two-stage process for the selection of jurors. From
the eligible population, known as the venire, a pool of prospective jurors
is drawn. The pool is intended to be a representative cross-section of the
population and usually comes from voter registration lists. Persons who
would be overburdened by serving or who are not able to perform the
juror role competently (such as a person who does not speak English) are
"excused." On the other hand, a good many Supreme Court decisions
have asserted that no groups of citizens may be arbitrarily denied the
opportunity to serve.

   From this pool will be drawn the jurors for each trial, be it civil or
criminal. Jurors are subjected to *voir dire* examination where they are
questioned—sometimes by the judge, sometimes by the prosecuting and
defense attorneys; sometimes with statutory questions, sometimes with
a wider range of questions—in an effort to determine their fitness to
serve. Prospective jurors will be impaneled for the trial unless a challenge
is made against them. The respective attorneys may challenge for cause,
where the judge is asked to exclude the prospective juror for reasons put
forth by the challenging attorney and if the judge agrees, the juror is

---

excluded from that case. Or the attorneys may use one of a limited number of peremptory challenges with which to exclude a juror without having to state reasons and without requiring the judge's consent. The defense is usually given a larger number of peremptory challenges than the prosecution.

It is through these challenges that attorneys can influence the composition of the jury that is finally impaneled. The purpose of *voir dire* is to eliminate jurors whose biases may interfere with a fair consideration of the evidence, thus insuring—or trying to—an impartial jury. Of course, both advocates try to find and impanel jurors who are most favorable to their side. Literally for centuries, lawyers have relied upon intuition, superstition, past personal experience, old wives' tales, and various combinations of these to try to figure out which prospective jurors will be most favorable to their side. Scientific jury selection allows these decisions to be made with the benefit of knowledge acquired through the use of systematic empirical (i.e., "scientific") methods.

Schulman and his associates have given a lucid account of the procedures they used in the Harrisburg Seven trial. Taking into consideration the issues on which the case is likely to hinge, the social scientists design questionnaires which include:

- scales previously developed and validated to measure attitudes related to the crucial issues of the case, such as a Trust in government measure;
- new attitude and information items written for the particular case at hand, such as knowledge of the defendants and their case;
- measures of background characteristics including:
  - personality measures, such as the F-scale (which measures authoritarianism);
  - demographic characteristics, such as sex, occupation, race, education, socioeconomic status, etc.;
  - media contact and preferences;
  - spare time activities, organizational memberships, etc.

Interviewers use these questionnaires to collect data from a sample of the population from which the juror pool is drawn. They do not approach any of the prospective jurors themselves. By correlating the background characteristics with the attitude measures, it is possible to uncover the important predictor variables for the population's attitudes. It might be found, for example, that females are more favorable to the defense than males; young people more than older people; egalitarians more than authoritarians; readers of the New York Times more than readers of the Daily News; Elks more than Masons; and that level of education, introversion, age, political affiliation, and two dozen other things are not at all related to the critical attitudes.

The reason for surveying the local jurisdiction rather than looking up data on national trends is that each community may have its own unusual circumstances which make, say, women more defense prone in Harrisburg but men more defense prone in Gainesville. It is best to know what is happening in a particular community where the case is being tried instead of relying on general trends which may not hold in that locality. Moreover, these things change not only with geography but with the passage of time or a new case which activates new issues.

Socio-psychological surveys of the population can be useful to defense attorneys for purposes other than jury selection. If the jury venire proves to be unrepresentative of the community, the constitutionality of selection procedures can be challenged. And if the case is lost, the survey data can form the basis for an appeal.

Social scientists can become quite fancy and rather precise with disarming ease, thanks to computers. With about five seconds' extra human effort, the computer can be instructed to perform a "multiple regression analysis." A number of variables can thereby be taken into account simultaneously instead of one at a time, and the relative importance of the several best predictors can be incorporated into a "prediction equation." The best predictor variables are identified, weighted, and combined to maximize predictive power. Should you have to choose between an old female and a young male, the prediction equation would take into account how old is old, and the fact that sex has 31.7 percent more predictive power than age, and tell you which of the two is a safer bet.

One benefit of obtaining demographic correlates of trial-related attitudes is that during *voir dire,* jurors sometimes lie. They may say they are not biased against protesting priests when they actually are and want to be on the jury to punish the defendant. But background characteristics cannot be falsified. If the juror is a 54-year-old male registered Republican who is the proprietor of a sporting goods store, your printouts will tell you what he is likely to believe, even if he won't. On the other hand, your data will tell you only about the probabilities for the population, not how any particular 54-year-old male Republican entrepreneur will vote. Like a baseball manager deciding on which pinch hitter to use, you cannot know if on *this* occasion player A will outhit player B. But you can know that against this type of pitcher player A, on the average, does better than player B and you play the percentages because in the long run you will come out ahead. And, more important, because there really is no better information available to go on.

• • •

These techniques, and others still to be developed, are worrying many lawyers, social scientists, and others concerned with the health of the jury system. What about their concerns that the new jury selection technology raises questions about the integrity of the jury system, and perhaps ultimately will destroy this uniquely democratic institution, and that the only real beneficiaries will be a few wealthy and prominent defendants and many prosecutors, once they hire social scientists to help them?

● ● ●

No evidence exists to support the apparently widely held belief that scientific jury selection is a powerful tool. What has most people upset about the technique is the fact that no one who has used it has lost a case. By the usual standards for evaluating empirical evidence, the same standards used by the social and behavioral scientists who developed the basic principles for the technique, this seemingly impressive evidence is really no evidence at all. The venerated scientific method usually calls for a control group, that is, a comparison group to tell you what an observation really means. To elucidate, suppose there were a control group. Suppose each of the cases had been tried before two juries—one selected the scientific way and one selected the old way. We could then compare the verdicts delivered by the scientific juries with those delivered by the conventional juries (the control juries). We know that all of the scientifically selected juries refused to convict. What would the conventionally selected juries have done? The answer to this question is absolutely essential to an assessment of how effective scientific jury selection is or even whether it works at all. Without such comparisons it simply is impossible to know. If a significant number of control juries convicted we would know that the use of scientific jury selection techniques helped the defense effort.

● ● ●

None of this is to say that scientific jury selection did not have an important effect on verdicts in the cases where it was used. It says only that we cannot know what the impact was because the necessary comparisons could not be made. The social scientists at Harrisburg understood all of this and, true to their training, they endeavored to measure the effectiveness of their selections. While the actual jury was deliberating, they re-interviewed a subsample of people from their original survey of the community. Fifty-four percent revealed a high presumption of the defendant's guilt. In contrast, only 17 percent (two of twelve) of the actual jurors voted to convict. The major weakness of these data is that the surveyed citizens differed from the selected jurors in a very important way. The surveyed citizens had not heard the evidence—or lack of it.

More interesting and more complete data are available to help inform our *understanding of the impact* of scientific jury selection.

In popular (i.e., nontechnical) reports of the findings and doings of social scientists working in the jury selection area, you will read, for instance, that females were more favorable to the defense than males. Does that mean that 0 percent of females would vote to convict while 100 percent of males would? Or does it mean that 65 percent of females were conviction prone while 67 percent of males were similarly disposed? The difference is important for a realistic understanding of scientific jury selection. In the first illustration your selections are a certainty. The second shows more correctly how you are really engaged in probabilistic decision-making. You will do better than if you did not have the knowledge, but you will not make flawless selections. This is especially evident when you consider that Male Juror A may be one of the 33 percent of males who would acquit and Female Juror B is one of the 65 percent of females who would convict. You would pick juror B because she was your best bet, but you would lose. Scientific jury selection helps one make educated bets. It is not magic. In fact, it appears to be a relatively weak device, and most social and behavioral scientists would expect it to be. Before explaining why this is so, let's be sure we appreciate how weak the available data show it to be.

Warning to Trial Lawyers: Do not uncritically use the following data to select your juries. The findings may not be applicable in the jurisdiction where you practice.

In one of the most extensive studies of jurors and their decision making behavior, Rita James Simon studied jurors in Chicago, St. Louis, and Minneapolis. She looked at the relationship between a juror's vote and his/her education, occupation, sex income, religion, ethnicity, and age. Only education and ethnicity were able to predict jurors' votes (in two experimental cases where defendants were pleading Not Guilty by reason of Insanity (NGI).

In one case (the housebreaking case), if you selected your jurors at random, 66 percent would have voted NGI. If you knew that people with less than college education were more inclined that way, and selected only those, you would have a group of whom about 72 percent would vote NGI—an improvement of about six percentage points. Knowing the effect of ethnicity and consequently choosing only blacks, you would increase the likelihood of obtaining an NGI juror to 85 percent—an increase of 19 percentage points. These reductions in uncertainty, incidentally, cannot simply be added together, so that the two pieces of knowledge improve your accuracy by up to 25 percent, because there will be a lot of overlap. Many of the blacks chosen will have less than college education, so that the first cut will already filter out many jurors who are undesirable on the remaining criteria. In the other case (the incest case), a random selection of jurors would consist of people of whom 33 percent voted NGI. Your knowledge of education effects would improve your selection in this case by two percentage points, and ethnicity again would improve it by 19 percentage points. That is not insubstantial improvement. But the most powerful difference of all was the effect of the type of case: the housebreaking case produced 66 percent NGI voters compared to only 33 percent of the incest case—a difference of 33 percentage points. None of the demographic characteristics of the jurors approached that figure.

Looking at the relationship of jurors' attitudes about issues vital to the cases, Simon found even less of importance. She concluded:

> The sharp lack of findings reported in this chapter rival in interest any data we have. Three efforts were made to relate attitudes to verdict and each ended in failure.
>
> Had we reported the responses to the attitude items separately, and not compared them with the jurors' verdicts, we think that most researchers would have expected and would have been prepared to use them as good predictors of verdicts. It may be some comfort to the trial lawyer who is prevented from asking these kinds of questions to learn that such information would give him no advantage.

I studied 480 jurors in Columbus, Ohio. Each was shown the same videotaped trial, deliberated in a jury, and rendered a verdict. Predictor variables examined included many things, from attitudes toward criminals and jurors' personal value systems to their socioeconomic status and level of education to whether they were left or right handed. These predictors were correlated with their degree of certainty of guilt prior to deliberation, and their certainty after deliberation, and their vote to convict or acquit. Out of the 27 predictors, the single best was whether jurors believed crime was mainly the product of "bad people" or "bad social conditions." Those holding the latter belief were more likely to regard the defendant as guilty. (Yes, guilty.) The best predictor could account for only 9 percent of the variance in the jurors' judgments. Using a multiple predictor format, the four best predictors in linear combination (belief that crime is caused by bad people versus social conditions, how much they value obedience, how much they value leadership, and political party preference) combined to account for less than 13 percent of the variance. None of the remaining variables could add as much as 1 percent to the predictive accuracy.

Robert Buckhout, director of the Center for Responsive Psychology in New York, studied a sample of municipal court jurors in California. He compared the demographic and personality characteristics of jurors voting guilty to those voting not guilty. He found no significant differences in age, income, education, or on such personality measures as Need for Social Approval, Dogmatism, or Machiavellianism. The only significant discriminator of jurors voting guilty and those voting not guilty was the effective rating of the prosecutor. Those voting guilty liked him more than those voting not guilty. Such an index does not seem likely to be useful in selecting jurors. In court, face to face with the prosecutor and defense attorneys, jurors are not likely to candidly state their preferences even if the judge allowed the question to be asked.

Research by Herman Mitchell and Donn Byrne, fairly often cited of late by social scientists interested in jury behavior, found that measures of authoritarianism did not distinguish conviction-prone jurors from acquittal-prone. They found instead that high authoritarians were more likely to acquit defendants they saw as similar to themselves and convict those they saw as different, while low authoritarians did not respond with such see-saw preferences. The problem for the defendant, then, may not be to select non-authoritarians from the jury pool (because there was no overall difference in the way authoritarians and egalitarians voted). The problem is: do you take authoritarians and hope they'll like you rather than dislike you, or do you go with egalitarians and know that their personal reaction to you will not affect their decision. Even for authoritarians, though, their feelings toward the defendant determined less than 14 percent of the variance in their certainty of his guilt. The effect (on authoritarians' certainty of guilt) of perceiving the defendant as similar rather than dissimilar amounted to only about half a point on a seven-point scale.

All of the findings reported thus far and to be reported are "statistically significant," which means that the effects found are highly unlikely to be the product of chance. That is, they are real. But they are, nevertheless, not strong. What this means is that scientific jury selection can help, but it is not going to come close to absolutely determining the outcome of a trial. If the evidence against a defendant is very strong or very weak, it isn't going to matter who is on the jury. If the evidence is close, then the jury selection could make the difference. You wouldn't be wasting your money or your time if you employed scientific jury selection, but if you did at at the expense of building a strong case out of evidence, you would be making a serious mistake.

• • •

Social and behavioral scientists are generally not surprised by any of this. While in our culture it has been popularly believed for a long time that personal characteristics make the major difference in people's behavior, that apparently is not correct. However important genetics, personality, and attitudes may be, they are generally not as important as situational factors. This realization came only after decades of research on personality variables which turned out to have little relationship to actual behavior, and attitudes measures which were about as bad. Stimulus characteristics of situations account for most of the difference in people's behavior. The old Freudian theory that we have a core personality which manifests itself throughout our behavior, across different

situations and circumstances in which we find ourselves, is either inadequate, relatively trivial, or simply wrong. After decades of looking for
the core personality types, and finding none, it began to occur to the
searchers that perhaps little was there to be found. Behavior changes
dramatically from situation to situation. One would therefore be more
effective by controlling the key stimulus characteristics of the situation
(the evidence) rather than the characteristics of the people in the situation. This is essentially why Skinnerian Behavior Modification has been
more effective in producing psychotherapeutic change than psycho-
dynamic-analytic approaches. The former change the situation; the latter
try to change the personality. The stimulus of stating these notions is
upsetting to many people because they take them to mean that we are
not unique individuals with our own autonomous direction in life, that
we instead are impotent rats responding to environmental stimuli. The
nicer way of stating the case, and the least upsetting to people, is that we
are all unique individuals, but our differences are vastly overshadowed
by our similarities. Moreover, the range of situations we are likely to
encounter is far more varied than the range of human beings who will
encounter them. Put that way, the Skinnerian view is, I think, a quite
humanistic view of human nature. And from the viewpoint of one concerned about the fate of our system of justice and the jury's place in that
system, it is optimistic. It means that jurors have been and will continue
to be much more responsive to the evidence placed before them than to
their own personalities and attitudes.

• • •

PART III

The Supreme Court

The primary function of the Supreme Court is to interpret the Constitution. Just exactly what that means has been the focal point of a debate that is now almost 200 years old. As those who compile dictionaries know, it is difficult if not impossible to saddle a word with a single, precise meaning. The difficulty is no less in interpreting a Constitution. Of course some words in the document—such as senator, president, and congress—present no problem. And some particular provisions are no less clear. When the Constitution provides that each state shall have two senators or that every bill must be signed by the president before it can become law, we all know what the framers intended. Throughout the Constitution, however, we find words and phrases such as due process, equal protection, bill of attainder, capitation or direct tax, war, peace, ex post facto, and so on. Not only must the Supreme Court decide the legal meaning of such terms, it must decide from time to time whether actions, events, and social or political developments, of which the framers never dreamt, are covered by the Constitution and if so consequences of that coverage. Does the Fourteenth Amendment require school busing to achieve racial desegregation? Is a "police action" a war, thereby requiring the approval of Congress?

Does the Constitution guarantee the right to an abortion? These are questions the framers of the Constitution never confronted. Yet, they illustrate the kind of question the Supreme Court is frequently called on to answer.

Obviously the power to interpret words is the power to give meanings never intended. Such a power can be used to incorporate into the law of the land the personal policy preferences of the justices. At the same time, such flexibility has a positive aspect. It enables the Court to view the Constitution as a constantly evolving document, to allow the system which that document regulates to grow, to change, to remain a viable, dynamic system capable of coping with domestic and international needs as they arise. While some may say that the Constitution should be interpreted strictly in terms of the framers' intent, most disagreement is over the consequences of this or that interpretation. If the Court strays too far from the path of strict interpretation, it may undermine the support accorded it by the political branches of the government and the various publics served by the Court. But even those, like Raoul Berger, who argue that the Court has no right to "do justice" or to substitute its views for those of the Constitution concede that innovation or change is essential at times.

Historically, how has the Court employed its interpretative powers? One suggestion is that in using its power to review the constitutionality of congressional and executive actions, the Court legitimizes those actions. Adamany argues that the proposition is far from proven. Another suggestion is that the Court defends minorities from excesses of majorities. But Dahl shows that viewed historically, the evidence is to the contrary. He provides support for the proposition that lawmaking majorities in the Congress will ultimately have their way with the Court, particularly where important policies are concerned. Even so, the Court has on occasion been able to delay policy preferred by Congress for a quarter of a century.

As for the executive, the president interacts with the Court on a fairly constant basis and in a number of different ways. First of all, with the consent of the Senate, he appoints the justices. In so doing he consults broadly and frequently includes the chief justice and other sitting justices in his consultations. The president almost always seeks to seat men who are basically competent lawyers but who are also sympathetic to the policy preferences of the administration or of the president personally. Historical research shows that presi-

dents have usually chosen Protestant lawyers from politically active business and professional families. The nominees almost inevitably come from the president's own political party. In making his selections, the president is essentially predicting the future behavior of his nominees from their social background and past behavior. While presidents have more often been right than wrong in these predictions, none of the factors mentioned above has been associated with superior judicial performance. Walker and Hulbary, however, suggest several valid generalizations in this area: e.g., that Jewish justices perform at a higher level of competence than non-Jewish justices, academic lawyers do better than nonacademic lawyers, and those without prior bench experience are more likely to provide superior service than those who possess such experience. Our increasing understanding of human behavior in recent decades suggests that future presidents will be even more successful in choosing nominees who perform as anticipated.

Of course, presidents are by no means restricted to the nominating process in trying to influence Court outputs. Steven Puro directs our attention to the amicus curiae *procedure through which the President is constantly communicating the preferences of his administration to the Court. As Puro's research makes clear, the executive is unusually successful in getting the Court to decide cases of interest to the federal government in the way preferred by the government. When these successes are added to those of the government when a direct party to litigation, we see that the executive branch—in one way or another—has a vital impact on the way the Supreme Court interprets the law.*

The crucial stage for Senate consent to Supreme Court nominations is the hearing usually held by the Senate Committee on the Judiciary. If presidents seek nominees with particular philosophies, we may expect the Committee to probe for these philosophies when the nominee presents him or herself for questioning. But, as the exchange with Rehnquist makes clear, getting the required answers may not be such a simple matter.

The final role of the Supreme Court addressed in this section pertains to its gatekeeping function. A number of devices are available that enable the Court to pick and choose the cases it will hear and decide with full opinion. The use of these devices allows the Court to regulate case flow and to determine those questions that warrant attention at the national level. Since the Court does not identify the factors that assure selection or rejection of cases for review, political scientists have developed and tested various theories. The work of Tanenhaus reveals that the characteristics of litigants and the presence of other situational variables impact on the selection process. When the federal government is the petitioner, review is likely to be granted. And sociopolitical "underdogs" are less likely to have their cases reviewed than are parties possessing the resources and influence that go with higher sociopolitical status. Such a distinction is explained as a response of the Court to its role in the governmental and political system. Some writers have even suggested that in certain kinds of cases, the Court plays a "game" in deciding which cases to review. The reading selection by Berger is illustrative of this point of view.

After formal review has been granted, the Court hears oral argument and receives a full briefing (in writing) of the issues at stake. Having done all this, the substantive issue in a case may still be sidestepped. Such an evasive action may be taken for political reasons; perhaps the timing of the question is considered inappropriate, or for any number of reasons, the question no longer seems to call for resolution at the national level. Illustrations of this phenomenon are provided by Rathjen and Spaeth. These authors suggest that the attitudes and predispostions of the justices toward access have much to do with such decisions. They also report that the current trend is toward restricting access to Supreme Court resolution of selected issues.

In general, it is evident that the Supreme Court is an institution whose actions are shaped by its justices, while at the same time its functioning is subject to the constraints that flow from its place in a governmental and political system.

The Political System and the Court's Role in It

35

Government By Judiciary

Raoul Berger

• • •

When Howard Jay Graham acknowledged that the Framers excluded segregation from the compass of "equal protection," but concluded that we dare not be bound by their "imperfect understanding," he premised that the Court, as it had done in *Brown* v. *Board of Education* (1954), should strike the "chains of the Constitution." The demands of justice, in short, must rise above the law, or, as libertarians put it, humanitarian goals must override what they regard as arid legalism. To dismiss adherence to "the rule of law," observance of the limitations imposed by a written Constitution, is to strike at the very root of our democratic system. History confirms Justice Black's statement that the struggle for a written constitution was "to make certain that men in power would be governed by *law*, not the arbitrary fiat of the man or men in power," "according to the 'law of the land,' " not by the "law of judges." The Framers, as will appear, had no stomach for the dispensation of "justice" by a kadi under a tree. Justice, to be sure, is the aim of a democratic

From Raoul Berger, *Government by Judiciary: The Transformation of the Fourteenth Amendment* (Harvard University Press, 1977), pp. 288–290, 291–292, 292–293, 293, 295, 296, 297–298. Copyright © 1977 by the President and Fellows of Harvard College. Reprinted by permission. Footnotes have been omitted.

state, but there can be no justice without a government of laws, least of all when power is uncurbed. It is for this reason, I suggest, that judges are not required by Article VI, §3, to take an oath to do justice but rather "to support this Constitution." Our system is committed to "Equal Justice *Under* Law," not to "Justices Above the Law." They were not authorized to revise the Constitution in the interests of "justice."

Mechanical repetition over the years—like a child's unthinking daily pledge of allegiance—has dulled the significance of the rule of law; it has been called a "useful fiction." For the Framers, however, it was the essence of constitutional government. "The government of the United States," said Chief Justice Marshall in one of his earliest decisions, "has been emphatically termed a government of laws and not of men."

• • •

The Constitution represents fundamental choices that have been made by the people, and the task of the Courts is to effectuate them, "not [to] construct new rights." When the judiciary substitutes its own value choices for those of the people it subverts the Constitution by usurpation of power. No dispensation was given to the Court to step outside its powers; it is no less bound by constitutional limits than are the other branches, as the historical evidence makes plain. First, it was clearly excluded from participation in the making of policy, the function of the legislature.

• • •

Second, as Chief Justice Warren recognized, "We are oath-bound to defend the Constitution. This obligation requires that congressional enactments be judged by the standards of the Constitution." Substituted judicial made-to-order "standards" are not really the "standards of the Constitution," as the State "reapportionment" cases plainly evidence.

• • •

Third, conclusive evidence that the judiciary was designed only to police constitutional boundaries, not to exercise supraconstitutional policymaking functions, was furnished by Hamilton. In Federalist No. 78 he stressed that the courts were to serve as "bulwarks of a limited Constitution against legislative encroachments"—a note repeatedly sounded in the subsequent Ratification Conventions.

• • •

Today there is a tendency to reduce the Constitution to the status of a "symbol" of continuity and unity, but for the Founders it was a living reality. They swore the President to "preserve and defend the Constitution" because it represented a "bulwark" of their liberties, not a mere symbol. They indited a charter which delegates power to the "servants and agents of the people," with "limits," "checks and balances" to guard against its abuse. It bears witness to the creation of a *government by consent* of the sovereign people; "just government," stated the Declaration of Independence "is founded on the consent of the governed." The terms of that consent are spelled out in the Constitution.

• • •

We must therefore reject, I submit, Charles Evans Hughes' dictum that "the Constitution is what the Supreme Court says it is." No power to revise the Constitution under the guise of "interpretation" was conferred on the Court; it does so only because the people have not grasped the reality—an unsafe foundation for power in a government by consent.

• • •

Like Chief Justice Burger and Justices Douglas and Frankfurter, I assert the right to look at the Constitution itself, stripped of judicial incrustations, as the index of constitutional law and to affirm that the Supreme Court has no authority to substitute an "unwritten Constitution" for the written Constitution the Founders gave us and the people ratified.

• • •

36

The Court As A Legitimate Institution

Archibald Cox

• • •

The most important quality of law in a free society is the power to command acceptance and support from the community so as to render force unnecessary, or necessary only upon a small scale against a few recalcitrants. I call this quality the 'power of legitimacy' because it appears to

From Archibald Cox, *The Role of the Supreme Court in American Government* (Oxford University Press, 1976), pp. 103–105, 105–108, 109–110. Copyright © 1976 by Oxford University Press, Inc. Reprinted by permission. Footnotes have been omitted.

attach to those commands of established organs of government which are
seen to result from their performance in an authorized fashion of the
functions assigned to them. Such commands, and only such, are legitimate.

The Judicial Branch is uniquely dependent upon the power of legitimacy when engaged in constitutional adjudication; and belief in the
legitimacy of its constitutional decisions is therefore a matter of prime
importance. The rulings thwart powerful interests. The issues arouse the
deepest political emotions. Although the courts control neither the purse
nor the sword, their decrees often run against the Executive, set aside the
will of the Congress, and dictate to a State. Compliance results from the
belief that in such cases the courts are legitimately performing the function assigned to them, and that it is important that the function be
preserved. It was the power of legitimacy that produced the public outcry which in turn compelled obedience when President Nixon announced
his intention to disregard Judge Sirica's order to produce the Watergate Tapes despite its affirmation by the Court of Appeals. It is to the
same power that we must look to induce other branches of government
to give support when necessary even to constitutional decisions of which
they disapprove.

Without the power of legitimacy, moreover, the Judicial Branch
would be exceedingly vulnerable to assaults and reprisals from other
branches of government. In *Marbury* v. *Madison* the Secretary of State,
following the directions of President Jefferson, ignored the process served
upon him. Shortly before, Congress changed the dates of the Supreme
Court's terms in order to prevent a timely ruling upon a constitutional
question. After the Civil War the Court was deprived of a portion of its
appellate jurisdiction in order to prevent its ruling upon the actions
of military authority. In the 1950s bills gathered congressional support,
although they never became law, looking to sharp curtailment of the
Court's jurisdiction in areas in which it had recently rendered unpopular decisions. President Nixon's anti-busing legislation was another direct
attack upon the Court's authority which was barely defeated. President
Franklin Roosevelt unsuccessfully sought legislation enabling him to
pack the Court with new Justices committed to his constitutional philosophy.

The power of the Supreme Court to command acceptance and support not only for its decisions but also for its role in government seems
to depend upon a sufficiently widespread conviction that it is acting legitimately, that is, performing the functions assigned to it, and only
those functions, in the manner assigned. The conviction of which I speak
is the resultant of many voices, not all carrying equal weight: of the opinion of the legal profession, of attitudes in the Executive and in Congress,
of the response in State governments, of the press, and of public opinion.

But since judicial supremacy upon constitutional questions is a product of institutional development rather than deliberate mandate, the Framers provided no charter by which to measure the legitimate scope and nature of constitutional adjudication. Anyone seeking to determine what role the Supreme Court may play legitimately is driven to examine the sources of acceptance and support in the Nation, upon which reliance must be ultimately placed to give legitimacy to constitutional rulings thwarting other branches of government and even the expressed wish of a majority of the people.

Surely history is the chief source of legitimacy for the basic idea of constitutional adjudication. The Court has long had to decide some constitutional questions, chiefly those arising out of our federalism, . . . and its performance has proved acceptable. Whether it is because of 'the dull traditional habit of mankind' or for some other reason, 'yesterday's institutions are,' as Bagehot said, 'accepted as the best for today,' all other things being equal, 'and the most easy to get obeyed because they inherit the reverence which others must win.' To this we may link the general acceptance of the courts as forums for resolving a wide variety of judicially cognizable cases and controversies—a role to which constitutional adjudication is readily acceptable as an appendage, provided that we do not make the mistake of severing the two, or of making the tail so big that it wags the dog. But history will not make a new role legitimate in the eyes of the judge, nor a radically and observably new role legitimate in the eyes of the people. Here the 'dull traditional habit of mankind' may aid those who challenge decisions as usurpations.

There is a school of political scientists in the United States that likens the Court to purely political agencies. The Court should do whatever it can—they say—to carry out the policies it deems desirable. Like other politicians the Court should consciously build a coalition of interest-groups, dependent upon judicial aid because they are under-represented elsewhere in government but strong enough collectively to sustain the Court against attacks. As the Court is a clientele agency, we should expect it to follow the pattern of other clientele agencies in acting to create and reinforce its own supporting interests. Part of the clientele is said to be the bench and bar, another part the 'interest-groups' naïve enough to keep on believing the 'judicial myth' that judges are influenced by law and sincerely seek unbiased decisions referrable as often as possible to general and more or less objective standards. 'If the myth of the Court is destroyed in the law schools, the Court loses power,' it is said; '. . . the real problem is how the Supreme Court can pursue its policy goals without violating those popular and professional expectations of neutrality, which are an important factor in our legal tradition and a principal source of the Court's prestige.'

Although it may fit the jargon of sociology to describe as an interest-group those who share a common belief in the integrity of the judicial process, surely there is for the judge himself as well as for the people a vast difference between, on the one hand, pursuing the goals of impartial justice *under law* to the satisfaction of those who share this aspiration and, on the other hand, arranging airline routes, highway subsidies, and television allotments to the satisfaction of those who enjoy the benefits. Nor is it possible to keep the 'myth of the Court' alive without living by it enough of the time to give it some reality. Law professors cannot keep a myth alive if political scientists are able to expose the fiction because of their greater candour or truer perception.

But the real vice in substituting a manipulative for a moral view of the judge's role lies much deeper. At the core of the Court's strength is impartiality and independence, and the Justices' freedom from every form of commitment or self-interest. I am not speaking only of freedom from the crasser forms of obligation and ambition, but of a cast of mind free so far as humanly possible from the ties of personal and group loyalties and implied commitments. Nothing can hurt the Court more than for a Justice to continue to maintain political or professional ties with members of the Executive or Legislative Branch or with private organizations. To seek to serve the interests of a clientele—the liberal press, the black, the poor, the extreme political groups, the American Civil Liberties Union, the Office of Economic Opportunity lawyers—is not the same as to seek to find and serve our society's long-range fundamental values appropriately expressed in constitutional law. Serving a clientele implies a degree of commitment apart from merit. Clientele interests and long-range societal values do not *always* overlap. Nor does one get near to describing a Holmes, a Brandeis, a Black, a Warren, or a Harlan by saying that he served a clientele of group-interests that reinforced the Court's position.

Similarly, although the general outlook of an appointee may often be predictable enough and would be taken into account by any President, 'value-packing' the Court in the sense of appointing men so committed to one set of values that all would vote together on a variety of issues in predictable ways would soon raise questions of legitimacy, and thus undermine both the Court and the impact of its decisions. One of the chief dangers of excessive politicization is its tendency to feed upon itself. If constitutional decisions lose their roots in law, such pressures as there are to appoint Justices steeped in the legal tradition would diminish, the decisions would become more political, and the descending spiral accelerate.

●　●　●

The use of constitutional adjudication as an instrument of reform intensifies the difficulty of explaining constitutional decisions by reference to accepted sources of law. A nay-saying court engaged in invalidating novel legislation upon constitutional grounds has little need to overrule previous decisions. A reforming court is constantly overturning settled precedents. The costs are illustrated by *Brown* v. *Board of Education*. The failure to follow *Plessy* v. *Ferguson* and other cases upholding racial segregation in equal facilities damaged the principle of legitimacy because men disappointed by the new decision were able to excuse disobedience by saying, 'The desegregation ruling is not law, but the dictate of nine men. In time, with nine different men, the Court will return to its earlier decisions.' The strain thus put upon the Court's position, in terms of the capacity to do one of the major jobs assigned to law, did not pass unobserved in subsequent litigation.

I am far from suggesting that the decision in the school desegregation cases was wrong even in the most technical sense. To have adhered to the doctrine of 'separate but equal' would have ignored not only the revolution sweeping the world, but the moral sense of civilization. Law must be binding even upon the highest court, but it must also meet the needs of men and match their ethical sensibilities. The dilemma lies at the root of Anglo-American jurisprudence. There have always been occasions when the courts, to shape the law to these objectives, have had to pay the price of revealing that judges sometimes make law to suit the occasion. Nor should we forget that not to pay that price may even defeat the object of obtaining voluntary compliance, because law, to command consent, must deserve it.

• • •

37

The Court As A Legitimizer
of Governmental Policy

David Adamany

• • •

Whether the legitimacy-conferring function justifies judicial review or judicial self-restraint, it rests on an assumption about the facts: That the Supreme Court has the capacity to and does throw the cloak of legitimacy over governmental actions. Yet none who bottom their arguments on the Court's legitimacy-conferring capacity offer the slightest empirical basis for its reality. Perhaps the doubter should be content to move for a directed verdict, the proponents having failed utterly to adduce even a scintilla of evidence, much less a preponderance, in support of their plea.

Without assuming the burden of disproof, I do wish to review the bits and pieces of evidence that reenforce doubt and, indeed, suggest the Court's *incapacity* to legitimize governmental action. Only one study, by Professor Walter F. Murphy and Joseph Tanenhaus has directly probed the Court's legitimacy-conferring capacity. Acknowledging that "[l]egitimation is an elusive concept," they nonetheless postulate the prerequisites for judicial legitimization, . . .

> [F]or people who meet three conditions, a high probability exists that a judicial decision could legitimate a regime change. The first condition is that the constitutional court be perceived. Major decisions cannot have a direct—though they may have an indirect—legitimating impact if they are not visible. There is no necessity, of course, that public understanding be sophisticated or articulated into a coherent ideology. The second condition is a recognition that it is a proper judicial function to interpret and apply the fundamental principles underlying the polity—acceptance, that is, of judges as guardians of the chastity of the constitution. The third condition is that the court be regarded as carrying out its responsibilities in an impartial and competent manner. People who believe specific decisions are wrong, even wrong-headed, and individual judges unworthy of their office may still meet this last condition if they respect the court as an institution that is generally impartial, just, and competent.

From David Adamany, "Legitimacy, Realigning Elections and the Supreme Court," *Wisconsin Law Review* (1973): 807, 807–812. Reprinted by permission. Footnotes have been omitted.

The Supreme Court met the first of these conditions for 46.2 percent of poll respondents, the second for 39.7 percent, and the third for 37 percent. In only a small group, 12.8 percent, did these three conditions converge to make legitimization feasible.

A. Popular Awareness of the Court and its Decisions

There is supporting evidence for the view that the Supreme Court and its decisions have such low salience as to render improbable popular acceptance of governmental action because of public knowledge that policies have been approved by the justices. Ignorance of the Court as an institution was reflected in early polls showing that 17.3 percent of respondents did not even know what the nation's highest court was and that 60 percent did not know the number of justices. Chief Justice Earl Warren was correctly identified in 1964 more often (63 percent) than Secretary General U Thant (40 percent) or Senator J. William Fulbright (31 percent), but less often than General DeGaulle (71 percent). Only five percent of respondents knew the number of justices from each party on the bench in 1945, on Justice Roberts' retirement, when there was an outcry for the appointment of a Republican to maintain some degree of partisan balance. In 1966 only 49 percent of those polled knew the name of at least one justice of the Supreme Court.

The low visibility of the Court as an institution has a tangential implication: It raises grave doubts about Bickel's assertion that the legitimacy-conferring capacity rests on public respect for the justices' distinguished public service and age and on public appreciation of the continuity of the Court's membership. It seems likely that few Americans know these details or that they attach any significance to whatever facts they may fleetingly grasp from the news media.

More important for the larger argument that the public has too little information to know of legitimizing actions by the judiciary is the overwhelming evidence that its knowledge of Supreme Court decisions is slight. Fifty-nine percent of respondents to a Survey Research Center (SRC) poll gave negative answers to the question "[h]ave you had time to pay any attention to what the Supreme Court of the United States has been doing in the past few years?" John Kessell, who sampled attitudes of Seattle residents about the Court, concluded that "[t]he comments . . . reveal a fairly low level of informational support for these attitudes." Twenty-one percent of his respondents were unable to give any answer even to the broad question "speaking generally, how would you describe your own feelings about the Supreme Court?" And "[n]early two-thirds of these individuals stated frankly that they didn't feel they knew enough to have an opinion." Of those who did express an opinion, "[t]he largest category of feelings . . . can best be described as generalized approval." Among the 53.6 percent who had affirmative impressions of the Court, 26.9 percent fell in the group who "were not specific in their discussions." Similarly, Kenneth M. Dolbeare and Phillip H. Hammond reported that 79 percent of Wisconsin survey respondents evaluated the Court, but that only 19 percent could cite any lines of cases or area of judicial activity that influenced their opinions.

Equally important is the shallowness of knowledge even among those who were able to give an "informed" answer about judicial decisions. Only 24.2 percent of the Murphy and Tanenhaus sample could name more than one Supreme Court decision or policy they liked or disliked; the remaining 22 percent of the "knowledgeable" cited only a single decision. A retabulation of Kessel's data shows that while 61 percent knew something of Court decisions about civil rights, school prayers, redistricting, or internal security, only 13 percent of them knew something about more than one of these subjects. Similarly, among the 41.4 percent of 1964 SRC respondents who knew of any Court rulings, 60 percent recalled only one subject of decision, 31.2 percent two, and 8.8 percent three or more.

Even when questions were structured rather than open-ended, thus inviting guesses and jarring respondents' memories, knowledge was scanty. The Wisconsin Survey Research Laboratory inquired whether the Supreme Court had in recent years made decisions in eight specified subject areas; in four the Court had actually rendered decisions and in four it had not. Fifty percent of respondents gave two or fewer correct answers, another 36 percent gave three or four correct answers, and only 15 percent were right more than half the time. And all that was asked here was whether the Court had made a decision, not what its content was. A precondition for legitimization is, of course, not merely that people know something about the Court, but rather that they know quite a lot. They must be aware at least of the several major areas in which the justices validate policies of the popular branches. Public knowledge in this depth seems utterly lacking.

There is one other aspect of the Court's visibility that raises doubts about its legitimacy-conferring capacity, namely, the kinds of decisions the public knows about. Of the two-fifths in the 1964 SRC survey who specified some Court action they like or disliked, 79.5 percent mentioned civil rights, school prayers, law enforcement-defendant's rights, or reapportionment. Kessel's respondents followed the same pattern: 42 percent mentioned civil rights, 19.6 percent school prayers, 8 percent redistricting and 4.5 percent internal security. Of the mere 19 percent of the Wisconsin sample who could cite any specific decision or policy as the basis for their evaluation of the Court, virtually all favorable responses were about civil rights and the most numerous negative com-

ments were on the school prayer cases. These most salient Supreme
Court decisions all invalidate the actions of other policymakers, either
state or federal. Charles Black conceded that "[t]he legitimating process
has been one that works quietly; the drama is found in the clash of
power implicit in the checking function." But this seems a prodigious
understatement, for the public's meager knowledge of judicial activity is
almost exclusively about checking cases. Apparently, judicial validation
works so "quietly" that it is not even a whisper, much less a resounding
legitimizing chord, in the public ear.

B. Popular Opinion and the Court's Constitutional Role

There is little additional evidence bearing on the second condition for
judicial legitimization: The public's recognition of the Court as the interpreter and guardian of the Constitution. Although Murphy and
Tanenhaus identify 39.7 percent of their respondents as holding this
constitutional perspective of the Court's work, other surveys put this
number at about half the population. When asked whether "the judges of
the U.S. Supreme Court decide cases strictly on the basis of what the
Constitution says" or "on the basis of what they think is right for the
country," 48 percent of the Wisconsin sample took the mechanical view
of constitutional adjudication and 38 percent the policymaking perspective. Another highly structured query drew a large "Constitution-
oriented" response: In the specific context of the school prayer cases,
49.5 percent of a sample in "Eastville-Westville" agreed, more or less intensely, that "[a]lthough we may disagree, we must accept what the
Court has said, since it has traditionally had the job of telling us what
the Constitution means." Dissenting were 33.6 percent. The Seattle survey asked open-endedly, "[w]hat do you think the job of the Supreme
Court should be?" The reporting of responses does not distinguish
sharply between constitutional and other functions, but as many as 40
percent gave answers falling into Constitution-related categories such as
"[i]nterpret the Law or the Constitution" (30.7 percent), "[p]rotect our
Freedoms" (5.4 percent), and "check other branches" (3.9 percent).

C. Popular Support for the Court as an Impartial Institution

Most surprising among the supplementary survey data is the Court's
lukewarm standing with the public, which bears on the third prerequi-
site for legitimization by raising doubts whether the justices are regarded

as so "impartial, just, and competent" that their decisions confer legitimacy on the other branches and their actions. A 1967 Gallup poll asked, "[d]o you think the Supreme Court has been impartial in its decisions or do you think it has tended to favor one group more than another?" Fully 30 percent of respondents thought the Court biased while 47 percent deemed it impartial; the remaining 23 percent were without opinion. The Eastville-Westville survey found that 27.9 percent thought that "Supreme Court judges [gave] preference to certain special interests such as labor unions or big business," 27.2 percent disagreed, and 44.9 percent offered no opinion.

The same lack of confidence in the Court emerges from polls asking for evaluation of the three branches of the national government. A 1964 survey asked "how much trust and confidence do you have in the Executive Branch, headed by the President (the Judicial branch, headed by the U.S. Supreme Court) (the Legislative branch, made up of the Senate and House of Representatives)?" Respondents made their judgments on a "ladder" ranging from zero to 10, the high numbers reflecting trust and confidence. The average rates were 7.43 for the President, 6.89 for the Supreme Court and 7.23 for the Congress. The Wisconsin survey asked "[w]ould you be likely to think the right thing had been done in Washington if the action had been taken by the Supreme Court (President) (Congress)?" The Legislature held the confidence of 50 percent of respondents, the Executive 35 percent, the Supreme Court 28 percent. Thirty-nine percent gave negative responses to the Court, while 33 percent lacked faith in the President and 16 percent in Congress.

Even the most charitable view of these findings, one which emphasizes that the Court does not substantially trail the other branches in public support, weakens the case for the Court's legitimacy-conferring capacity. The Court must be viewed generally, rather than by bare majorities or substantial minorities, as an impartial voice of constitutional interpretation. It must tower over the other branches in public confidence if their unpopular actions are to be made legitimate by its imprimatur. Indeed, since the Court lags behind the other branches in public support, it is as plausible to suggest that the popular branches legitimize judicial actions—particularly when they obey decisions which are highly unpopular, such as the recent school prayer and defendants' rights cases—as to insist that those branches rely on the justices for public acceptance of their policies.

● ● ●

—————————————— 38 ——————————————

The Supreme Court and Majority Control
Robert A. Dahl

• • •

Does the power of judicial review entail a nondemocratic, an aristocratic, even an oligarchic principle of government?

• • •

What does the record of the Supreme Court reveal? In the course of its one hundred and sixty-seven years, in eighty-five cases, the Court has struck down ninety-four different provisions of federal law as unconstitutional, and by interpretation it has significantly modified a good many more. It might be argued that in all or in a very large number of these cases the Court was, in fact, defending the legitimate constitutional rights of some minority against a "tyrannical" majority. There are, however, some exceedingly serious difficulties with this interpretation of the Court's activities.

• • •

In the absence of relatively direct information, we are thrown back on indirect tests. The ninety-four provisions of federal law that have been declared unconstitutional were, of course, initially passed by majorities of those voting in the Senate and in the House. They also had the President's formal approval. One could, therefore, speak of a majority of those voting in the House and Senate, together with the President, as a "law-making majority." It is not easy to determine whether a law-making majority actually coincides with the preferences of a majority of American adults, or even with the preferences of a majority of that half of the adult population which, on the average, votes in congressional elections. Such evidence as we have from opinion polls suggests that Congress is not markedly out of line with public opinion, or at any rate with such public opinion as there is after one discards the answers of people who fall into the category, often large, labelled "no response" or "don't know." If we may, on these somewhat uncertain grounds, take a law-making majority as equivalent to a "national majority," then it is

From Robert A. Dahl, *Pluralist Democracy in the U.S.* (Rand McNally, 1967), pp. 150, 154–155, 155, 155–163. Reprinted by permission of the author. Footnotes have been omitted.

possible to test the hypothesis that the Supreme Court is shield and buckler for minorities against tyrannical national majorities.

Under any reasonable assumptions about the nature of the political process, it would appear to be somewhat naive to assume that the Supreme Court either would or could play the role of Galahad. Over the whole history of the Court, one new Justice has been appointed on the average of every twenty-three months. Thus a President can expect to appoint two new Justices during one term of office; and if this were not enough to tip the balance on a normally divided Court, he would be almost certain to succeed in two terms. For example, Hoover made three appointments; Roosevelt, nine; Truman, four; Eisenhower, five; Kennedy in his brief tenure, two. Presidents are not famous for appointing Justices hostile to their own views on public policy; nor could they expect to secure confirmation of a man whose stance on key questions was flagrantly at odds with that of the dominant majority in the Senate. Typically, Justices are men who, prior to appointment, have engaged in public life and have committed themselves publicly on the great questions of the day. As the late Mr. Justice Frankfurter pointed out, a surprisingly large proportion of the Justices, particularly of the great Justices who have left their stamp upon the decisions of the Court, have had little or no prior judicial experience. Nor have the Justices—certainly not the great Justices—been timid men with a passion for anonymity. Indeed, it is not too much to say that if Justices were appointed primarily for their "judicial" qualities without regard to their basic attitudes on fundamental questions of public policy, the Court could not play the influential role in the American political system that it does in reality play.

It is reasonable to conclude, then, that the policy views dominant on the Court will never be out of line for very long with the policy views dominant among the law-making majorities of the United States. And it would be most unrealistic to suppose that the Court would, for more than a few years at most, stand against any major alternatives sought by a law-making majority. The judicial agonies of the New Deal will, of course, come quickly to mind; but President Franklin D. Roosevelt's difficulties with the Court were truly exceptional. Generalizing over the whole history of the Court, one can say that the chances are about two out of five that a President will make one appointment to the Court in less than a year, two out of three that he will make one within two years, and three out of four that he will make one within three years (Table 6.1). President Roosevelt had unusually bad luck: he had to wait four years for his first appointment; the odds against this long interval are about five to one. With average luck, his battle with the Court would never have occurred; even as it was, although his "court-packing" proposal did formally fail, by the end of his second term in 1940 Roosevelt had appointed five new Justices and he gained three more the following year:

TABLE 6.1. The Interval Between Appointments to the Supreme Court, 1789–1965

INTERVAL IN YEARS	NUMBER OF APPOINTMENTS	PERCENTAGE OF TOTAL	CUMULATIVE PERCENTAGE
Less than 1 year	38	41	41
1	22	24	65
2	10	11	76
3	9	10	86
4	6	6.5	92.5
5	6	6.5	99
12	1	1	100
Total	92	100	100

Note: The table excludes six Justices appointed in 1789. It includes only Justices who were appointed and confirmed and served on the Court. All data through 1964 are from *Congress and the Nation*, 1452–1453.

Thus by the end of 1941, Mr. Justice Roberts was the only remaining holdover from the pre-Roosevelt era.

It is to be expected, then, that the Court would be least successful in blocking a determined and persistent law-making majority on a major policy. Conversely, the Court is most likely to succeed against "weak" law-making majorities: transient majorities in Congress, fragile coalitions, coalitions weakly united upon a policy of subordinate importance or congressional coalitions no longer in existence, as might be the case when a law struck down by the Court had been passed several years earlier.

The Record

An examination of the cases in which the Court has held federal legislation unconstitutional confirms these expectations. Over the whole history of the Court, about half the decisions have been rendered more than four years after the legislation was passed (Table 6.2). Thus the congressional majorities that passed these laws went through at least two elections before the decision was handed down and may well have weakened or disappeared in the interval. In these cases, then, the Court was probably not directly challenging current law-making majorities.

Of the twenty-four laws held unconstitutional within two years, eleven were measures enacted in the early years of the New Deal. Indeed,

TABLE 6.2. Supreme Court Cases Holding Federal Legislation Unconstitutional: by time between legislation and decision.

	SUPREME COURT CASES INVOLVING:					
	NEW DEAL LEGISLATION		OTHER		ALL FEDERAL LEGISLATION	
NUMBER OF YEARS	N.	%	N.	%	N.	%
2 or less	11	92	13	17.5	24	28
3–4	1	8	13	17.5	14	16
5–8	0	0	20	27	20	24
9–12	0	0	10	14	10	12
13–16	0	0	7	10	7	8
17–20	0	0	2	3	2	2
21 or more	0	0	8	11	8	10
Total	12	100%	73	100%	85	100%

New Deal measures comprise nearly a third of all the legislation that has ever been declared unconstitutional within four years of enactment.

It is illuminating to examine the cases where the Court has acted on legislation within four years of enactment—where the presumption is, that is to say, that the law-making majority is not a dead one. Of the twelve New Deal cases, two were, from a policy point of view, trivial; and two although perhaps not trivial, were of minor importance to the New Deal program. A fifth involved the NRA, which was to expire within three weeks of the decision. Insofar as the unconstitutional provisions allowed "codes of fair competition" to be established by industrial groups, it is fair to say that President Roosevelt and his advisers were relieved by the Court's decision of a policy that they had come to find increasingly embarrassing. In view of the tenacity with which FDR held to his major program, there can hardly be any doubt that, had he wanted to pursue the policy objective involved in the NRA codes, as he did for example with the labor provisions, he would not have been stopped by the Court's special theory of the Constitution. As to the seven other cases, it is entirely correct to say, I think, that whatever some of the eminent Justices might have thought during their fleeting moments of glory, they did not succeed in interposing a barrier to the achievement of the objectives of the legislation; and in a few years most of the constitutional dogma on which they rested their opposition to the New Deal had been unceremoniously swept under the rug.

The remainder of the thirty-eight cases where the Court has declared legislation unconstitutional within four years of enactment tend to fall into two rather distinct groups: those involving legislation that could reasonably be regarded as important *from the point of view of the law-making majority* and those involving minor legislation. Although the one category merges into the other, so that some legislation must be

TABLE 6.3. Number of Cases Involving Legislative Policy Other than Those Arising Under New Deal Legislation Holding Legislation Unconstitutional Within Four Years After Enactment.

INTERVAL IN YEARS	MAJOR POLICY	MINOR POLICY	TOTAL
2 or less	11	2	13
3 to 4	4	9	13
Total	15	11	26

classified rather arbitrarily, probably there will be little disagreement with classifying the specific legislative provisions involved in eleven cases as essentially minor from the point of view of the law-making majority (however important they may have been as constitutional interpretations). The specific legislative provisions involved in the remaining fifteen cases are by no means of uniform importance, but with one or two possible exceptions it seems reasonable to classify them as major policy issues from the point of view of the law-making majority. We would expect that cases involving major legislative policy would be propelled to the Court much more rapidly than cases involving minor policy, and, as the table above shows, this is in fact what happens (Table 6.3).

Thus a law-making majority with major policy objectives in mind usually has an opportunity to seek ways of overcoming the Court's veto. It is an interesting and highly significant fact that Congress and the President do generally succeed in overcoming a hostile Court on major policy issues (Table 6.4). It is particularly instructive to examine the cases involving major policy. In two cases involving legislation enacted by radical Republican Congresses to punish supporters of the Confed-

TABLE 6.4. Type of Congressional Action Following Supreme Court Decisions Holding Legislation Unconstitutional Within Four Years After Enactment (Other than New Deal Legislation).

CONGRESSIONAL ACTION	MAJOR POLICY	MINOR POLICY	TOTAL
Reverses Court's Policy	10 [a]	2 [d]	12
Changes Own Policy	2 [b]	0	2
None	0	8 [e]	8
Unclear	3 [c]	1 [f]	4
Total	15	11	26

eracy during the Civil War, the Court faced a rapid crumbling majority whose death knell as an effective national force was sounded after the election of 1876. Three cases are difficult to classify and I have labelled them "unclear." Of these, two were decisions made in 1921 involving a 1919 amendment to the Lever Act to control prices. The legislation was important, and the provision in question was clearly struck down, but the Lever Act terminated three days after the decision and Congress did not return to the subject of price control until the Second World War, when it experienced no constitutional difficulties arising from these cases (which were primarily concerned with the lack of an ascertainable standard of guilt). The third case in this category successfully eliminated stock dividends from the scope of the Sixteenth Amendment, although a year later Congress enacted legislation taxing the actual income from such stocks.

The remaining ten cases were ultimately followed by a reversal of the actual policy results of the Court's action, although not necessarily of the specific constitutional interpretation. In four cases, the policy consequences of the Court's decision were overcome in less than a year. The other six required a long struggle. Workmen's compensation for longshoremen and harbor workers was invalidated by the Court in 1920; in 1922 Congress passed a new law which was, in its turn, knocked down by the Court in 1924; in 1927 Congress passed a third law, which was finally upheld in 1932. The notorious income tax cases of 1895 were first somewhat narrowed by the Court itself; the Sixteenth Amendment was recommended by President Taft in 1909 and was ratified in 1913, some eighteen years after the Court's decisions. The two child labor cases represent the most effective battle ever waged by the Court against legislative policy-makers. The original legislation outlawing child labor, based on the commerce clause, was passed in 1916 as part of Wilson's New Freedom. Like Franklin Roosevelt later, Wilson was somewhat unlucky in his Supreme Court appointments; he made only three appointments during his eight years, and one of these was wasted, from a policy point of view, on Mr. Justice McReynolds. Had McReynolds voted "right," the subsequent struggle over the problem of child labor need not have occurred, for the decision in 1918 was by a Court divided five to four, McReynolds voting with the majority. Congress moved at once to circumvent the decision by means of the tax power, but in 1922 the Court blocked that approach. In 1924, Congress returned to the engagement with a constitutional amendment that was rapidly endorsed by a number of state legislatures before it began to meet so much resistance in the states remaining that the enterprise miscarried. In 1938, under a second reformist President, new legislation was passed twenty-two years after the first; this a Court with a New Deal majority finally

TABLE 6.5. Type of Congressional Action After Supreme Court Decisions Holding Legislation Unconstitutional Within Four Years After Enactment (Including New Deal Legislation).

Congressional Action	Major Policy	Minor Policy	Total
Reverses Court's Policy	17	2	19
None	0	12	12
Other	6 *	1	7
Total	23	15	38

* In addition to the actions in Table 6.4 under "Changes Own Policy" and "Unclear," this figure includes the NRA legislation affected by the *Schechter Poultry* case.

accepted in 1941, and thereby brought to an end a battle that had lasted a full quarter-century.

The entire record of the duel between the Court and the law-making majority, in cases where the Court has held legislation unconstitutional within four years after enactment, is summarized in Table 6.5.

A consideration of the role of the Court as defender of minorities, then, suggests the following conclusions:

First, judicial review is surely inconsistent with democracy to the extent that the Court simply protects the policies of minorities from reversal or regulation by national majorities acting through regular law-making procedures.

Second, however, the frequency and nature of appointments to the Court inhibits it from playing this role, or otherwise protecting minorities against national law-making majorities. National law-making majorities—i.e., coalitions of the President and a majority of each house of Congress—generally have their way.

Third, although the court evidently cannot hold out indefinitely against a persistent law-making majority, in a very small number of important cases it has succeeded in delaying the application of a policy for as long as twenty-five years.

•   •   •

—————————————————— 39 ——————————————————

The United States As *Amicus Curiae*

Steven Puro

I. Introduction

Since the early part of the 20th century interest groups have frequently used *amicus curiae* briefs to enter United States Supreme Court cases. The *amicus* brief has become an important means of access for many organizations and individuals. An *amicus curiae*—"friend of the court" —is a participant, other than the parties, who brings additional information or viewpoints to the court.

The *amicus* may be interested in the Supreme Court's decisions because of the immediate or future effects upon him or his organization. Moreover, the amicus may assist the Supreme Court by providing novel or distinct legal arguments which "set the agenda" for dispute resolution or demonstrate symbolic support or opposition for the parties or issues in the case.

This study will examine the United States' participation as *amicus curiae* in political cases[1]—generally cases involving provisions of the first eight and the fourteenth amendments to the U.S. Constitution— between the 1920 through 1973 United States Supreme Court Terms. The U.S.'s *amicus* behavior is an important part of its litigation strategy in the Supreme Court. This study will examine several aspects of that behavior: the selection of cases, the frequency of participation, the ideological position, and the degree of concordance with Supreme Court decisions.

II. Methodology

The United States *amicus* behavior was examined in two separate ways. First, the United States Supreme Court Reports from 1920 through 1973 terms were used to discover the United States' frequency of participation, types of arguments and types of cases entered as *amicus*. Since it would

From Steven Puro, "Political Change and the United States Amicus Participation in the U.S. Supreme Court" (Paper delivered at the Annual Meeting of the American Political Science Association, Chicago, Ill. September 1971), pp. 1–23, *passim*. Reprinted by permission of the American Political Science Association and the author. Updated and revised version. Most footnotes have been omitted.

be impossible to explain an organization's rationale for using *amicus* briefs from the Supreme Court Reports alone, this information was supplemented through interviews with leading members of the U.S. Solicitor General's Office from the 1950's through 1972 (e.g., Solicitors General, First and Second Assistants to the Solicitor General). Moreover, the appellate division chiefs of the Department of Justice who participated most frequently in amicus activities were also interviewed. The interviews dealt with these officials' perceptions concerning their activities as *amicus* and their reasons for using the briefs.

III. Solicitor General's Decision to File an *Amicus* Brief

There are two different paths that the Solicitor General can follow in deciding to file an *amicus* brief: First, he may choose a case from those currently before the Supreme Court and second, the Supreme Court can "invite" him to file an *amicus* brief. In the first area there are close parallels between the Solicitor General's decision to enter a case as a party and as an *amicus*. The Solicitor General carefully selects the cases he will present to the Supreme Court because he and the members of his office believe they have an obligation to, and are expected by the Court to control their client and to enter only cases which present broad legal issues. . . . Robert L. Stern, a former acting Solicitor General, indicates the role of the Solicitor General in the Supreme Court: "the Solicitor General regards himself—and the Supreme Court regards him—not only as an officer of the executive branch but also as an officer of the Court. . . . The Solicitor General regards himself as a filter when deciding to file an *amicus* brief. He declines to take a position in the Supreme Court if the case is not substantial and thereby indicates to the Supreme Court which cases he believes are important. The main question the members of the Solicitor General's office consider when deciding to participate as *amicus* is: Is this case valuable in presenting the United States' arguments to the Court? In this way the Solicitor General attempts to explain executive policy to the Supreme Court. In addition, the Solicitor General's office, either as *amicus* or a party, can provide the Supreme Court with expertise in many fields of law and can often aid the Court in resolving problems concerning the importance of a case. Thus, the U.S.'s decision to file an *amicus* brief indicates to the Court its belief that this case is particularly important.

Another major factor in the Solicitor General's decision to file an *amicus* brief may be the Supreme Court's invitation. Anthony Lewis argues that "one reason for the Supreme Court's frequent invitation to the Federal Government to participate in non-Government cases is that the Solicitor General . . . provides a degree of expertise and responsibility in advocacy that few private counsel can match". . . . An Assistant to the Solicitor General indicated another dimension of the U.S.'s assistance to the Court when it is invited *amicus*. He said:

> Sometimes when we act as *amicus curiae* we are helping the Court and not helping ourselves. This is especially true when the Court asks for our views. They cannot tell if the case is important or not, and they rely on our supposedly disinterested answer.

In addition, the Court can frequently determine the current status of an issue within the federal government by inviting the Solicitor General's *amicus* brief. The Solicitor General has used unpublished government studies, reports on current executive negotiations with other agencies and indications of the future direction of federal policy in his *amicus* arguments. This information allows the Court to weigh the probability of executive or legislative action. The Court's invitation to the U.S. to file an *amicus* brief receives the highest priority in the Solicitor General's office. A former Solicitor General states the U.S.'s stance when requested to file by the Supreme Court:

> We do not file just to make an appearance. We file so that our voice would be heard because in many cases the Court wants to have the views of the United States before it.

The President and the Solicitor General maintain frequent contacts about the issues currently or potentially before the United States Supreme Court. Three examples will illustrate the process. First, President Franklin D. Roosevelt's papers show frequent exchanges between Roosevelt and Solicitors General Stanley Reed and Robert Jackson about pending constitutional questions and legislative matters. In addition, these Solicitors General also maintained frequent contacts with President Roosevelt's closest advisors. Second, President Eisenhower's reported neutrality in *Brown* v. *Board of Education*, 347 U.S. 483 (1954), is belied by his contacts with Solicitor General J. Lee Rankin. In this case President Eisenhower personally reviewed the U.S. *amicus* brief—which was invited by the Supreme Court—in order to insure compliance with his Administration's position. Two of my respondents indicated that Eisenhower made minor changes in the U.S.'s *amicus* brief. Branyan and Larsen, in their documentary history of the Eisenhower Administration, argue that Eisenhower moved quickly to implement the U.S. Supreme Court's decision rejecting segregated schools in the District of Columbia. . . . Third, Victor Navasky's examination of Justice Department files revealed frequent contacts between Solicitor General Archibald Cox and President John F. Kennedy, as well as contacts between Cox and Kennedy's chief presidential aides on many issues, including educational policy and apportionment.

IV. U.S. Participation and Success as *Amicus*

The United States has sharply increased its reliance on *amicus* briefs in political cases since the Warren Court's first term in 1953 (see Table 1). The twenty year period between 1953 and 1973 accounts for 71% of the United States *amicus'* briefs since 1920. In addition, within the first part of that twenty year period there was a rapid acceleration of the United States' use of *amicus* briefs. From the beginning of the Warren Court (1953) until 1966 the United States filed more *amicus* briefs (57 briefs) in political cases than it had in the previous thirty-three years. An Assistant to the Solicitor General offered an explanation for this rapid increase:

> The number of *amicus* briefs which the government has filed has increased rapidly (since the start of the Warren Court). This occurred basically because it was thought the government should play a more active role where the government would have a stake in the case such as cases involving broad scale public issues, e.g., one man, one vote.

The United States filed more briefs (161) in Supreme Court political cases than any other group or individual except the national ACLU (178 briefs) between 1920 and 1973. The U.S. as *amicus* had a high rate of success (i.e., supported the winning party) across a wide variety of cases. In political cases, it was successful in almost three quarters (74%) of its

TABLE 1. Number of United States *Amicus* Briefs in Political Cases in United States Supreme Court, by Time Period

TYPE OF CASE	1920–1936	1937–1952	1953–1973
Civil Liberties n = 59	1	8	50
Political Provisions of U.S. Constitution n = 19	10	4	5
Jurisdiction & Procedure of the Courts n = 32	5	11	16
Naturalization and Aliens n = 2	0	1	1
Civil Rights n = 40	0	1	39
International Law & Treaties n = 4	0	0	4
Other, Political Cases n = 5	1	4	0
Total n = 161	17	29	115

appearances [see Table 2]. The U.S.'s success as *amicus* in political cases was surpassed only by the NAACP which was successful more than four of five times (84 per cent or 22 of 26 cases). The U.S.'s rate of success exceeded 80 per cent in three types of cases: 1) civil rights, 2) civil liberties, and 3) political provisions of the U.S. Constitution (see Table 2). The only area where the U.S.'s success as *amicus* was below 60 per cent was in naturalization and alien cases.

The dominant pattern of the U.S.'s *amicus* briefs was support for individuals' positions against those of state and local government agencies, and corporations which sought to infringe individuals' civil liberties. In the entire period, 1920–1973, the U.S. supported individuals in 61 per cent of its *amicus* briefs, and opposed "state governments" and corporations in 66 per cent of its briefs (see Table 3). The only major divergence from the U.S.'s dominant pattern occurred during the Nixon Administration. From the 1969 through the 1973 Supreme Court Terms the U.S.'s *amicus* briefs increasingly supported state and local government agencies against private individuals. Eighteen of the twenty-six times that U.S. *amicus* briefs supported "state governments" occurred in these five terms. Prior to the 1969 term the U.S. *amicus* briefs had supported individuals in 65 per cent of its briefs and opposed "state governments" and corporations in 68 per cent. In the latter four terms the U.S. gave its greatest support for "state governments" in cases concerning criminal procedures and state regulation of social welfare programs. The U.S.'s rate of success did not diminish (with one exception which is discussed below) when the Nixon Administration adopted these new positions. The U.S.'s sup-

TABLE 2.   United States' Success as *Amici* in the U.S. Supreme Court in Political Cases 1920–1973

TYPE OF CASE	WON	LOST	No POSITION	Do NOT KNOW
Civil Liberties (n = 59)	48	9	2	0
Political Provisions of U.S. Constitution (n = 19)	15	3	0	1
Jurisdiction & Procedure of the Courts (n = 32)	14	8	6	4
Naturalization and Aliens (n = 2)	1	1	0	0
Civil Rights (n = 40)	32	7	1	0
International Law and Treaties (n = 4)	4	0	0	0
Other, Political Cases (n = 5)	3	2	0	0
Total (n = 161)	117	30	9	5

TABLE 3. United States' *Amicus* Support and Opposition for Parties in Political Cases, 1920–1973

TYPE OF PARTY	U.S. SUPPORT		U.S. OPPOSITION	
	No. of Times U.S. as Amicus Supported Party	% of Total U.S. Participation n = 136	No. of Times U.S. as Amicus Opposed Party	% of Total U.S. Participation n = 136
United States Government:				
All Branches & Agencies except the Independent Reg. Commissions	6	4.4%	4	2.9%
Independent Reg. Commissions	1	0.7	0	0.0
State Governments:				
Executive Agencies	5	3.7	15	11.0
Administrative Agencies	11	8.1	16	11.8
Political Subdivisions	10	7.4	38	28.0
Private Parties:				
Trade Associations	1	0.7	0	0.0
Labor Organizations	3	2.2	1	0.7
Private Individuals	83	61.0	38	28.0
Private Corporations	11	8.1	21	15.4
Other	5	3.7	3	2.2
Total	136	100.0*	136	100.0*

* Numbers were rounded to nearest tenth of a percent

port as *amicus* helped the parties by lending prestige and legitimacy to their positions and frequently strengthening their weak arguments.

V. Ideological Position

An important indicator of *amicus'* positions is the liberal-conservative continuum. This continuum classifies briefs into four categories: politically liberal, politically conservative, economically liberal, and economically conservative.[2]

The United States as *amicus* most frequently took a politically liberal position; it did so in 77.7 per cent of the cases (84 out of 108 cases), . . . The U.S. had a higher percentage of politically liberal positions prior to the Nixon Administration; that administration changed the U.S.'s ideological positions by substantially increasing its emphasis on politically conservative briefs. Between 1969 and 1973, 40% (13 of 32 cases) of the U.S.'s positions in political cases were politically conservative while in the period between 1920 and 1968 only 8% (6 of 70 cases) were. Between 1969 and 1973 the U.S. took politically conservative positions most often in cases involving criminal procedures (6 cases) and racial discrimination in educational facilities (4 cases, but 3 of these cases were connected to the *Swann* case *(Swann* v. *Charlotte-Mecklenburg Board of Education,* 402 U.S. 1 [1970]). The U.S.'s shift to a politically conservative position between 1969 and 1973 is indicated in Table 4. Eight of the ten politically conservative positions in civil liberties cases and four of the six politically conservative positions in civil rights cases for the entire period under investigation occurred during these four years. The shift is reflected in the *Swann* case where the U.S. as *amicus* adopted an unaccustomed position of supporting Southern officials against Negroes' desegre-

TABLE 4. United States Ideological Positions as *Amicus* in the U.S. Supreme Court Political Cases 1969–1973

	IDEOLOGICAL POSITIONS		
TYPE OF CASE	Political Liberal	Political Conservative	NA
Civil Liberties (n = 18)	10	8	
Political Provisions of U.S. Constitution (n = 3)		1	2
Jurisdiction Procedure of the Courts (n = 6)			6
Civil Rights (n = 16)	10	4	2
Total (n = 43)	20	13	10

TABLE 5.   United States Ideological Postion as *Amicus* and United States Supreme Court's Ideological Position in Political Cases, 1920–1973

		IDEOLOGICAL POSITION OF SUPREME COURT'S DECISION	
		Political Liberal (*n = 81*)	*Political Conservative* (*n = 22*)
Ideological Position of U.S. as *Amicus*	*Political Liberal* (*n = 84*)	74	10
	Political Conservative (*n = 19*)	7	12

Kendall's Q = .855

gation claims and in *Dutton* v. *Evans*, 400 U.S. 74 (1970), where the U.S. argued for limitations upon the 6th Amendment rights of confrontation of witnesses. When it adopted politically conservative positions, the U.S. was successful in 9 of 13 cases between 1969 and 1973 and in only 3 of 6 cases between 1920 and 1968. For the entire period under study the U.S. had a success rate of 63.1 per cent (12 out of 19 times) when it took a politically conservative position and 85.7 per cent (74 out of 84 times) when it argued in politically liberal terms (see Table 5).

An analysis of the liberal-conservative continuum shows there is a high degree of concordance between the United States ideological positions as *amicus* and the Court's ideological positions in political cases (see Table 5). For the entire period under study, the matrix of ideological positions shows only seventeen instances where the United States and the Court had different positions.

VI. Conclusion

The United States has used its *amicus* briefs in political cases predominantly to support private individuals against institutionalized political authority (i.e., states and localities). Thus, it has usually taken liberal positions when acting as *amicus*. . . . As *amicus* the United States most frequently supported private individuals and most frequently opposed the states' attempts to infringe upon an individual's rights, e.g., *Takahashi* v. *Fish and Games Commission of California*, 334 U.S. 410 (1948), *McLauren* v. *Oklahoma Board of Regents*, 339 U.S. 637 (1950), *Arger-*

singer v. *Hamlin, Sheriff,* 407 U.S. 25 (1971). With the exception of the Nixon Administration, the Solicitor General of the United States—as spokesman for the Executive—has consistently urged the Court to support the "underdog" position in the case. The U.S. took a politically liberal position as *amicus* in slightly more than three of four cases for the entire period under investigation. However, during the 1968 through 1973 terms the U.S. took politically liberal positions in slightly less than two out of three cases.

The Solicitor General's success can be partially measured by his ability to prevail in almost 75 per cent of his *amicus* appearances. The Solicitor General has participated as *amicus* in almost every major domestic question since World War II where it could not bring its own suit. The Solicitor General maintains his credibility as spokesman for the executive branch by filing only in significant cases, and by trying to reflect accurately the feelings of the executive on a given issue. The Court knows that any case brought to it by the Solicitor General is one which is perceived to be significant by at least some members of the executive branch of the United States. . . . This analysis indicates that the United States government as *amicus* is a major interest group in the United States Supreme Court and further the Justices are responsive to the demands of the United States. The consideration of the United States as a major interest group in political cases should allow us to reevaluate the extent and effect of interest group participation in the United States Supreme Court's environment, the basis of the Court's legitimacy, and the Court's ability to obtain compliance with its decisions.

The *amicus* brief can be an important way for the executive to communicate his desires to the Court. As *amicus,* the executive can indicate his willingness to support the Court's decision and explain its policy on statutory or constitutional questions. The Court may want to gauge the importance of an issue to the executive. Thus, frequently the Court will ask for the Solicitor General's opinion in an *amicus* brief if he does not come forward himself; in part, this invitation can be viewed as an attempt to ascertain if the executive or federal government as a whole has a real stake in the outcome of a case. If we follow Walter Murphy's analysis of Supreme Court Justices as "policy-making judges"—i.e., as trying to achieve positive action or to prevent or minimize hostile action—then it becomes important for the Justice(s) to have constant information from the Executive. This information becomes even more significant in cases concerning major political issues. In these circumstances when the U.S. is not a party to the case the *amicus* brief is a major means of communication between the Executive and the Supreme Court. . . . Dahl argues that the Supreme Court endangers its legitimacy when it opposes strongly held positions by one of the other components of the national lawmaking majority—i.e., the Executive or Congress. . . . In a later work Scigliano argues that the Executive, rather than Congress, is the principal support for the Supreme Court. . . . Thus, we could suggest that the Executive's position before the Court is a significant component of the Court's role as part of the national lawmaking majority and as a policy-making institution.

The executive's position helps the Court to assess the difficulties of policy implementation or the degree of compliance that will be given to their decision. In these instances, the executive branch indicates to the Court that it will support the Court's decision and not permit the Court to be faced with a situation similar to President Jackson's famous ulti-matum. The classic example of the United States giving such support occurred in *Brown* v. *Board of Education*. . . . In this case, the execu-tive as *amicus curiae* indicated that it would commit its support and resources to carry out the Court's decision. The United States also pro-vided this support for the Court in *Baker* v. *Carr*. The government's sup-port for new constitutional approaches legitimizes the importance of these approaches to the Court and eases placing the issue(s) on the Court's agenda.

The United States has also used its *amicus* briefs to indicate the in-ability or unwillingness of other governmental institutions to deal with pressing political problems. In this way the U.S. as *amicus* may be urging the Court, as the last hope for "out" groups, to espouse socially unpopu-lar views it would be politically risky for the executive to adopt. In this way, such "unpopular" or "progressive" views are transformed into pub-lic policy but the onus of having made the decisions rests on the Court and not upon the executive.

Notes

1. The cases in which *amici* participated were divided into two major categories: political and economic. Cases involving the following issues were considered essentially political: jurisdiction and procedure of the Courts, aliens, sub-versive organizations, civil rights, international law, internal governance of federal administrative and executive agencies, civil liberties, and constitu-tional provisions concerning the following political issues: a) executive powers—general scope, b) legislative powers—general scope, c) the amending process of the Constitution, d) the full faith and credit clause, e) the supremacy clause, and f) the "federal police power." The civil liberties category includes those cases decided upon the First through Eighth Amend-ments to the United States Constitution plus the provisions of the Fourteenth Amendment especially equal protection of the laws and due process.
2. The economic poles are as defined in G. A. Schubert, "Judicial Attitudes and Voting Behavior: The 1961 Term of the Supreme Court," *Law and Contemp-orary Problems*, Vol. 48 (1963), pp. 100–142; upholding individual workers over unions is defined as economically liberal. The political poles are defined generally as support for individual (liberal) or government (conservative) in conflicts over personal rights.

Selection of
Supreme Court Justices

40

Selection of Capable Justices

Thomas G. Walker and William E. Hulbary

It is difficult to underestimate the importance of those who assume positions on the United States Supreme Court. The decisions they render
have numerous and far-reaching consequences for the country; the rulings they hand down have a profound impact on the politics, laws, and
moral life of the nation. Consequently, it is important for the nation to
select the best possible individuals to sit on the Court. Indeed, it is especially important because those recruited to positions on the Supreme
Court serve for life, virtually immune from removal from office. A justice
appointed in the 1970s may well be influencing our laws and customs
long well [*sic*] after the year 2000. When a poorly qualified person is selected for the Court and serves for a period of more than a quarter-century, the nation may suffer in uncountable ways. While we cannot hope to
choose a Marshall or a Brandeis for every Court vacancy, we certainly
should avoid the elevation of those who will not carry their weight.

With each nomination to the Supreme Court the president is making
a prediction. Regardless of the criteria he employs in determining his
appointments, the president attempts to nominate individuals who will

From Thomas G. Walker and William E. Hulbary, "Selection of Capable Justices,"
in *The First One Hundred Justices*, ed. A. P. Blaustein and Roy M. Mersky (Ham-
den, Conn.: Archon Books/The Shoe String Press, 1978), pp. 52–53, 53, 54, 54–55,
55–66, 66–71. Reprinted by permission. Most footnotes have been omitted.

be productive and positive members of the Court. Similarly, when the Senate deliberates on the president's nomination, it attempts to use its confirmation power to eliminate those who, like Nixon's appointee, George Harrold Carswell, lack the capacity to become contributing members of the nation's highest tribunal. Historically, persons involved in the Supreme Court selection process have chosen rather well. However, it appears most difficult to predict with a great deal of accuracy the level of competence which will be exhibited by a person who is nominated for the Court. There is always a degree of uncertainty. No foolproof formula exists for selecting the best possible jurists.

• • •

Analyzing Personal Characteristics and Judicial Ability

In order to examine the relationships between certain personal characteristics and judicial ability, we began with ability ratings. . . . Each of the justices who served on the Court from 1789 to 1969 (John Jay through Thurgood Marshall) was given a numerical score based upon his rated ability level.[1] "Greats" were assigned the score of 5, "near greats" received a score of 4, "average" justices were given a 3, "below average" judges a 2, and the Court's "failures" were assigned a 1. Designating numerical values for each level of judicial ability allows us to compute "average ability scores" for various subgroups of justices. By doing so we are able to compare the ability ratings of justices with certain characteristics against justices with different traits. For example, we can compare justices with prior judicial experience with those who did not have prior judicial experience. Such a comparison permits us to evaluate a frequently expressed claim—that those justices with experience on the lower courts are more capable Supreme Court justices than those without lower court experience. By conducting an analysis such as this over a wide range of background factors we can determine whether the presence of certain characteristics in a justice's past indicates a tendency to demonstrate a given level of performance on the Court.

The average ability score for the first ninety-six justices was 3.18, indicating that the typical justice performed at a slightly above-average level. We confined our analysis to the first ninety-six justices on the grounds that Justices Burger, Blackmun, Powell, Rehnquist, and Stevens have not yet been on the Court a sufficient period of time to establish an accurate record of performance.

For each of the justices studied we compiled information on a large number of background characteristics. These characteristics can be loosely grouped into three broad categories: family background factors, personal traits, and career experiences. If certain individual characteristics are associated with levels of judicial ability, we should see evidence of it in the following pages.

Family Background and Judicial Ability

. . . Supreme Court justices are not typical of the population as a whole. They are different from the average citizen in terms of several factors: rather than coming from a wide range of socio-economic backgrounds, Supreme Court justices have come for the most part from prominent, well-to-do families. Relatively few individuals from humble family origins have achieved a position on the bench. When we compared the eighty-one justices whose backgrounds indicated roots in more affluent and prestigious families against those fifteen justices with lower socio-economic origins, we obtained the following results:

Family Status	Number of Justices	Average Ability Score
High Socio-economic Status	81	3.22
Low Socio-economic Status	15	2.93

At best we can say that slight differences appear. The justices who came from higher class families achieved a level of performance which was slightly higher than average; whereas, the justices from lower socio-economic origins performed at a slightly below-average level of judicial quality. The differences, however, are not so great as to allow us to make any sweeping generalizations regarding the influence of family origins on subsequent judicial ability.

Another indication of a justice's family origins is the occupation through which the family gained its livelihood. A family's values and life styles are often closely related to the father's means of making a living. For this reason we examined the justices and their later ability levels according to paternal occupation. The results offer some interesting differences:

Father's Occupation	Number of Justices	Average Ability Score
Farming	29	2.90
Business	16	3.47
Professional	41	3.22
Labor	5	3.80
Other/Unknown	2	2.50

First, over the long history of the Court a majority of the justices have had fathers engaged in business or the professions. A good number have also been raised in farming families, but the bulk of these justices were appointed during the earlier years of the nation's history when farming was the country's primary occupation. Relatively few justices have come from working class families. These differences quite probably are due not only to the relative advantage of business and professional people in terms of economic assets, but also because business and professional people tend to place a higher value on intellectual activities and transfer this importance to their children.

The second major finding obvious from the paternal occupation analysis is that there appears to be a relationship between the father's occupational category and the justice's subsequent performance. The business and professional categories are associated with above-average performance. So, too, are those justices who have come from working class families, but their number is small and any generalization should be viewed as extremely tentative. Justices from agricultural backgrounds, however, perform at a below-average level.

We also examined the role politics played in the early learning of the justices, studying whether or not the justice's fathers engaged in political activity. We thought that justices who grew up in a political environment might well perform differently than justices who acquired their initial political experiences later in life. The evidence shows that more of the members of the Supreme Court have come from politically active families:

Father's Political Activity	Number of Justices	Average Ability Score
Politically Active	55	3.07
Politically Inactive	41	3.32

By learning about politics early in life an individual will often place a high value on politics and begin his own political career earlier than those individuals who do not come from politically active families. In addition, individuals raised in families of which members are participants in the governmental process often make early political contacts which aid them in their careers. While persons with politically active fathers tend to have a higher probability of being appointed to the Supreme Court, such a background does not appear to affect the level of performance once on the Court. In fact, those justices who have come from politically inactive families have slightly higher levels of performance. The differences, however, are not large.

Finally, we analyzed the justices who have served on the Supreme Court in terms of whether their families had a tradition of judicial service. It is interesting that more than a quarter of the justices have been raised in families in which a close relative had served in a judicial capacity. It appears that judges tend to beget judges and that a child at an early age may learn to aspire to become a member of the judiciary. The ability levels of those individuals from judicial families were also slightly higher than persons coming from families without such a tradition of service. Once again, however, the differences are quite small.

Family Judicial Service	Number of Justices	Average Ability Score
Judicial Tradition in Family	25	3.36
No Judicial Tradition in Family	71	3.11

Based upon what we have found it does not appear likely that the antecedents of judicial ability can be found in a justice's family origins. Admittedly, the factors which we examined were rather crude indicators and it is possible that other family traits, more subtle and less observable, have an impact on a person's subsequent professional performance. Nonetheless, among those factors examined here none clearly distinguish the superior justices from their less-qualified counterparts.

PERSONAL TRAITS AND JUDICIAL ABILITY

There is at least some reason to suspect that if a person's background characteristics affect his subsequent behavior, there may be a greater likelihood of finding such relationships among an individual's personal traits than his family origins. Obviously family characteristics are quite remote from what a justice may do forty or fifty years after he leaves the home of his parents. The impact of his family may be weakened over the years. But an individual's personal traits are both more specific to his own development as well as more proximate to the performance we are interested in understanding. We, therefore, examined several personal characteristics of the justices of the Supreme Court—characteristics ranging from where they were raised to their educational experiences.

First, we examined the type of environment in which the justice was born and raised. An often-articulated theory states that the values and way of life in America's rural areas tend to produce strong individuals with high levels of patriotism. Similarly, American culture tends to idealize life in small towns, which are often identified as the cradle of American democracy, while urban environments are rarely discussed in terms such as these. Among the ninety-six men who have served on the Supreme Court a substantial number have come from each of the three environments, but small town origins appear to be the most prominent.

Early Childhood Environment	Number of Justices	Average Ability Score
Rural Areas	21	3.10
Small Towns	41	3.07
Urban Areas	34	3.35

Contrary to popular images, those justices who have been raised in an urban environment performed at a higher average level than those raised in either small town or rural areas. The differences are not so great as to prompt us to propose that presidents ignore less densely populated areas in making future appointments, but modest differences do appear to be associated with the conditions under which the judges were raised.

Perhaps closely related to the environment in which a justice was raised is the region of the country in which he spent most of his life. Cultural differences often have been associated with the various regions, having been even more pronounced in the past than they are at the present time. It is possible that we find that judges coming from certain areas perform at levels superior to those raised in other sections of the country. We categorized each of the justices according to the region from which he was appointed and compared average ability ratings on the basis of such regional groupings.

Region	Number of Justices	Average Ability Score
East	36	3.60
West	6	3.33
South and Border	35	2.97
Midwest	20	2.75

The eastern and southern states have dominated the appointments to the Supreme Court followed closely by the justices who have come from the midwestern region. The West clearly trails other regions in the number of representatives on the Court. These differences, of course, are due primarily to the way in which the nation developed. Presidents have been quite responsive to geographical demands and have been quick to appoint individuals to the Supreme Court to represent the later developing sections of the country.

However, more than any other factor discussed up to this point, region seems to have an impact on the level of judicial performance. Justices who have come from the eastern region have produced records superior to those of justices from the other regions. The South and Midwest particularly have tended to produce justices of less than average caliber. The superiority of the East is probably due to the fact that the northeastern United States has always been the center of the nation's best law firms and institutions of legal education. Therefore, when the president wishes to fill an "Eastern seat" on the Court he has a great many qualified attorneys from which to choose. The pool of potentially excellent judges is simply greater in the East than in any other region.

We also inquired into the justice's ethnic origins. All of the ninety-six Supreme Court justices appointed before 1970, save Thurgood Marshall, could trace their ancestry to European beginnings. The overwhelming majority of Court members had backgrounds steeped in the traditions of the British Commonwealth countries. A smaller number have had roots extending to countries in continental Europe. It is this final category of judges who demonstrated the highest average ability score. The solidly above-average performance of these judges is particularly impressive when compared to the justices of Scottish or Irish descent who as a group had a below-average mean ability score.

Ethnic Group	Number of Justices	Average Ability Score
English/Welsh	55	3.22
Scottish/Irish	27	2.89
Continental European	13	3.60
African	1	3.00

Religious affiliation is another personal trait which may have a good deal of influence on personal development, values, and attitudes. Historically, politics has been at least partially dependent upon religious interests. Appointments to political positions, including the Supreme Court, have often been made to placate certain religious groups or to insure representation for the various religious communities in the United States. Most of the justices who have served on the Supreme Court have been members of the Protestant faith and most frequently affiliated with "high church" Protestant denominations such as Episcopalian, Congregational, Presbyterian, and Unitarian sects. "Low church" Protestant members (for example, Baptist, Lutheran, and Methodist) have accounted for the second largest number of justices appointed to the Court. In addition to the majority Protestant members, there have been six Catholics and five Jews who have served on the nation's highest Court. As can be seen in the figures below there is a substantial relationship between religious affiliation and judicial performance:

Religious Affiliation	Number of Justices	Average Ability Score
High Protestant	59	3.13
Low Protestant	15	2.93
Catholic	6	3.33
Jewish	5	4.40
Other	3	3.00

The high church Protestants generally performed at a level approximating the average for the entire history of the Court. The low church Protestants, however, performed at a relatively low level. The most remarkable results concern the representatives of the "minority" religious faiths. The Catholic justices have performed at a level above that of either of the Protestant groups and the Jewish members of the Court earned a phenomenally high 4.40 average ability score. This should be no surprise if we recall the Jewish members of the Court—Brandeis, Cardozo, Frankfurter, Goldberg, and Fortas—all of whom made important contributions to the development of United States jurisprudence.

Given the fact that Supreme Court duties require intellectual ability and legal scholarship, we might expect a justice's performance to be related to the quality of his educational experiences. Therefore, we examined the justices' pre-legal and legal educations. The majority of members of the Supreme Court have enjoyed excellent educational opportunities. Largely due to the relatively high socio-economic status of their families, Supreme Court justices have attended institutions of pre-legal education which had high academic standings. By studying at such prestige institutions the future justices undoubtedly made important political and professional contacts, received superior educations, and obtained a boost in the building of their early careers. As well as helping them attain their high station, it also aided their performance when serving on the Court.

Pre-Legal Education	Number of Justices	Average Ability Score
Tutor	12	2.83
School of Average Standing	28	3.00
School of High Standing	56	3.34

In the past there was much greater diversity in the legal educations of men who have become members of the Court, ranging from those justices who taught themselves to those who attended prestigious institutions. This reflects the growth and development of legal education over the last 200 years. Our evidence indicates that the quality of legal education is in fact associated with the quality of service on the bench. Those justices who received the best legal education of the day have performed at a superior level.

Justices who were trained at universities of high standing or educated by attorneys of high reputation earned average ability scores in excess of 3.00; in contrast, Supreme Court judges who studied at average law schools or under average attorneys performed at below-average levels.

As expected, the personal traits of the ninety-six justices who have served on the Court were more closely related to their subsequent con-

Legal Education	Number of Justices	Average Ability Score
Self Taught	2	3.50
Apprenticeship from Prominent Attorney	32	3.13
Apprenticeship from Average Attorney	11	2.73
Law School of High Standing	38	3.45
Law School of Average Standing	13	2.85

tributions on the bench than were the family origin characteristics. The studies of regional, ethnic, religious, and education factors produced some evidence that justices with certain personal characteristics tend to perform at particular levels of quality.

CAREER EXPERIENCES AND JUDICIAL ABILITY

Among those background characteristics which a justice brings with him to the Court, the most proximate to his service are those relating to his career. We would expect these to have an influence on the way the justice conducts himself on the bench. Since service on the Court requires dealing with political and legal questions of substantial importance, we examined aspects of the justices' careers which were both political and legal in nature.

We first studied the political party affiliation of the justices. Party membership often affects the careers of those involved in public service. It not only shapes or reinforces a person's views and attitudes on political matters, but it also influences the political contacts he will make and the political opportunities made available to him. As noted in chapter one, presidents usually confine their choices for the bench to potential nominees of the same political persuasion. We categorized each of the ninety-six justices according to his party affiliation in order to determine whether certain political movements have produced judges with superior records of achievement. The results showed that political party affiliation did not sharply distinguish the justices according to ability.

Political Party Membership	Number of Justices	Average Ability Score
Federalists	13	3.00
Democratic-Republicans	7	3.29
Whig	1	4.00
Republican	33	3.27
Democrat	42	3.10

The average ability scores of the various political parties are closely grouped. None of the parties can lay claim to producing the most superior justices, nor does any party significantly lag behind others in terms of the representatives they have sent to the Supreme Court.

Almost all of the nation's Supreme Court justices have devoted a considerable proportion of their pre-Court lives to public service. Usually this has taken the form of holding public office of various kinds. The backgrounds of the justices reveal a diversified list of positions held. We divided the ninety-six justices according to the type of public service in which they were engaged prior to their Court appointments. We were particularly interested in comparing justices whose political careers were primarily in state government with those who were primarily active in politics at the federal level. The majority of the justices had careers chiefly in the federal level of government, although over one-third were primarily state officials. If one were to break down this information historically he would find that in the earlier years of the nation, state politics was the most frequent avenue to a Supreme Court appointment. Over the years, however, experience at the federal level has increasingly become the more frequent road to the Court. If we are interested in judicial performance, the level of a potential nominee's political activity appears to be an unimportant criterion. The average performance of those justices who were primarily state politicians is only slightly higher than the average ability of those who spent the bulk of their political careers in the United States government.

Level of Political Activity	Number of Justices	Average Ability Score
State Government	35	3.23
Federal Government	54	3.13
Other/Non-Political	7	3.29

While there is no formal requirement that Supreme Court justices be attorneys, all of the members of the Supreme Court have been members of the bar and all have practiced law in some form during their pre-Court years. We were interested in whether a justice's legal career could be linked with his subsequent Supreme Court performance. For this reason we classified each of the justices according to the way he spent the greatest part of his legal career. The bulk of the justices practiced law only minimally. They were usually engaged in law as a means of being active in politics. For them law was a natural path to political office rather than an end in itself. However, about a third of the justices could be classified primarily as corporate lawyers and a lesser number practiced as teachers in law schools. While there were only four justices who could be classified as primarily academic lawyers, the average performance score of this group was clearly superior to the other categories. It appears that if a person is able to distinguish himself in legal scholarship within a university, the same talents will serve him well while on the Court.

Type of Law Practice	Number of Justices	Average Ability Score
Lawyer/Politician	55	3.07
Corporate Lawyer	31	3.23
Academic Lawyer	4	4.50
Other	6	3.00

We now come to one of the most controversial relationships between career experiences and judicial performance—the question of judicial experience. . . . Many individuals have argued that Congress should impose the requirement that nominees for the Supreme Court first serve on the lower state or federal courts. To these critics of the current judicial selection procedures, candidates for the Court should have substantial judicial experience: they argue that it is unwise to elevate someone to the nation's highest tribunal who has never before sat on the bench. Opponents, such as Justice Frankfurter, have responded that there is no tangible evidence that prior judicial experience makes a person better qualified to sit on the Supreme Court. Quite the contrary, Frankfurter argued, some of history's most outstanding justices have come to the Court without any previous experience as judges. Given the long standing nature of this debate, we were extremely curious to see how the ninety-six justices would compare on the basis of their prior judicial experience. We divided the justices into three categories: those with no prior bench service, those with some judicial experience, and those who had extensive records of prior judicial service. The results clearly supported the position that previous training as a judge has no bearing on the ability of a justice to carry out his responsibilities on the Supreme Court. In fact, the group of justices with the highest performance scores were those who had no judicial service prior to assuming a position on the Court.

Judicial Experience	Number of Justices	Average Ability Score
None	37	3.43
Some	21	3.00
Extensive	38	3.03

Next, we examined the justices grouped according to their age at appointment. Presidents have often been quite vocal about using age as a criterion for the selection of Supreme Court justices. For the most part, presidents have preferred their nominees to be in the mid- to late-fifties. A person in this age group, so the rationale goes, is experienced enough to have developed stable political values and to have achieved a public record which reflects those values, and yet is young enough to have a reasonable life expectancy on the Court. Presidents have shied away from those potential nominees of advanced years for fear the impact the justice would have would be extremely short lived. Younger persons have similarly been rejected by many presidents on the grounds that their values and attitudes might not yet be firmly anchored. Given the importance placed on age, we analyzed the justices' ability scores based upon three groupings: justices appointed under the age of fifty-one, between their fifty-first and sixtieth years, and after their sixtieth birthday. The results were surprising:

Age at Appointment	Number of Justices	Average Ability Score
Under 51 years	23	3.45
51–60 years	53	2.94
Over 60 years	10	3.50

The preference for justices in their fifties is clearly demonstrated. More than half of the justices in the Court's history attained their positions at this stage of their lives. However, more than one-third of the justices fell into the category of being considered either too old or too young. What is interesting is that the justices who were appointed between their fifty-first and sixtieth years earned ability scores inferior to those of both the older and younger groups. It appears possible that the common presidential practice of choosing justices in their middle years works against the selection of superior jurists.

Finally, we looked at the justices' lengths of tenure. On this factor we found interesting, although not surprising, results. The table below clearly suggests that quality of performance increases as length of tenure increases. The longer a justice serves the greater likelihood that he will make significant contributions to the Court. It obviously takes a substantial length of time for a justice to begin making positive contributions. Based upon our evidence it seems that a major line of demarcation occurs with the fifteenth year of service. Justices in the tenure categories in excess of fifteen years produced records of above-average performance; in contrast, justices who served less than fifteen years earned below-average mean ratings. In fact, the ratings for the justices who served less than five years were the lowest average ability scores of any group of justices found in our study.

Tenure on Court	Number of Justices	Average Ability Score
Less than 5 years	9	2.44
5–14 years	40	2.98
15–24 years	27	3.30
25 or more years	20	3.75

The career experiences of the justices add several useful pieces of information to our knowledge of performance on the Supreme Court.

242   The Supreme Court

Two of the factors we examined are important because they are *unre-lated* to judicial ability; neither party affiliation nor prior judicial ex-perience appeared to influence the performance levels of the justices. Clearly, no political persuasion holds a monopoly over the production of superior justices; nor does the training of individuals in lower court judgeships appear to give them a head start in becoming outstanding jurists. Two other factors are especially interesting because of the man-ner in which they are related to judicial ability. The relationship between judicial ability and age at appointment seems to question con-ventional wisdom and traditional preconceptions of a number of presi-dents. Those justices appointed when they are between fifty-one and sixty years of age—judged by many to be the ideal age for a Court ap-pointee—tend to be less able Supreme Court justices than those who are either younger or older when appointed. Equally interesting is the re-lationship between tenure on the Court and judicial performance; the longer the period of service, the greater is the probability that a justice will make a positive contribution. Indeed, it appears that a maturing process of fifteen years or more on the Court is typically necessary before an individual begins to gain above-average ratings.

Conclusion

We have studied the backgrounds of the men who have served on the United States Supreme Court in order to determine if certain charac-teristics are associated with specific levels of judicial performance. Our analysis has not uncovered any one trait which clearly distinguishes the capable from the incapable. Nonetheless, certain patterns tend to emerge. On one hand, if we were to develop a profile of an individual with a strong likelihood of becoming an excellent jurist, he would be a person raised in a northeastern urban area as a member of a business-oriented family. His ethnic roots could be traced back to the European continent and he would be Jewish. He would have received his education from high-quality institutions and would have experience in the academic community as a legal scholar. He would have been appointed to the Court at a relatively early age, without prior judicial experience, and serve in that institution for more than twenty-five years. On the other hand, if we were to describe the background of a typical Supreme Court "failure," he would be a man from the midwestern United States, raised in a small town and from a family engaged in farming. His ethnic origins would be Scottish or Irish and he would be affiliated with a "low church" Protestant denomination. He would have attended mediocre educational institutions and his career would have been closely tied to partisan political activities. His appointment to the Court would have occurred during his mid-fifties and he would serve less than five years. These, of course, are general profiles. There are exceptions to every broad generalization, as attested to by the fact that McReynolds served more than a quarter-century and Cardozo but six years. Yet McReynolds is universally rated a "failure" and Cardozo a "great."

Some of the specific background factors studied are worthy of special attention. Interestingly, the prior judicial experience factor produced results in direct contradiction to the arguments of proponents of lower court apprenticeships. While the differences were not great, justices without lower court experience outperformed those who had previous training. While the specific explanation for the direction of these differences may be difficult to establish, it is clear that the supporters of lower court experience requirement are left with a shallow case.

The length of tenure factor is also of particular significance, largely because of the rather dramatic differences which emerged. Of the twelve "great" justices only Cardozo served less than ten years and only two others, Chief Justices Warren and Hughes, served less than two decades. While longevity does not insure greatness (e.g., McReynolds, Van Devanter, Washington, McLean, Wayne), it is reasonable to conclude that a justice will have difficulty establishing a record of excellence without spending a relatively long period on the Court.

Similarly, the age at appointment appears to be an important factor. While it may be difficult to explain with complete satisfaction, the historical facts are clear. A comparison of the "great" and "failure" categories is illustrative. Among the eight "failures," seven were appointed between their fifty-first and fifty-eighth years (the lone exception being James Byrnes who was sixty-two); but only three of the twelve "greats" (Stone, Black, and Frankfurter) were nominated during this period of their lives.

Our analysis does not provide an unerring formula for the selection of capable jurists. But it does illustrate some interesting relationships which have stood the test of almost two hundred years of Supreme Court history. Given some of the more substantial linkages between backgrounds and judicial ability, it is interesting to speculate upon the potentials of the five most recent appointees to the Court.

After examining their backgrounds we found that two of the five justices, Lewis Powell and William Rehnquist, possessed a number of characteristics which in the past have been associated with above-average performance. Both come from urban areas, received high quality prelegal and legal educations, and had no previous judicial experience. Powell was appointed at a relatively old age and Rehnquist in a reasonably youthful period of his life. The only significant factors associated with low-level performances possessed by these two men are Powell's southern background and Rehnquist's practice as a politically oriented lawyer. If our analysis has relevance for the future, then history probably has reserved a place in the "average" category for Harry Blackmun and John Paul Stevens. Both possess the highly-rated characteristics of receiving excellent educations and both had been corporate lawyers with part-time law school professorship experience. However, Blackmun and Stevens share a midwestern background, prior judicial experience, and Protestant religious affiliations. In addition, Blackmun has a small town background and Stevens was appointed when fifty-five years old. Among the most recent five, Chief Justice Burger appears to have the most strikes against him. While his age at appointment (62) and ethnic background (Swiss/German) are similar to those justices who have served well in the past, his family origins (rural, farming), region (midwestern), religion (Protestant), education (University of Minnesota and St. Paul College of Law), and judicial experience (thirteen years) are factors which, over the history of the Court, have been associated with less than distinguished levels of performance.

Obviously there are a number of factors which influence the performance of a judge. Many of these are personal characteristics peculiar to the individual himself, factors which do not fall into the gross categories we have used in this chapter. However, there does appear to be a general association between a judge's background experiences and his demonstrated ability on the Court. This fact alone enhances our understanding of the judicial process and it is hoped, will encourage others to focus their research efforts on the question of selecting capable jurists.

Note

1. R. L. Siegel and C. Rocco, "Rating the Justices," in A.P. Blaustein and R.M. Mersky (eds.), *The First One Hundred Justices* (Archon Books 1978), 32–51.

--- **41** ---

How They Get There

Henry J. Abraham

Studies of biographical and autobiographical data, which have become increasingly available during the past two or three decades, make it clear that Presidents do sporadically consult with Supreme Court Justices—

From Henry J. Abraham, *Justices and Presidents: A Political History of Appointments to the Supreme Court* (Oxford University Press, 1974), 20–22, 22–23, 23, 27, 27–30, 31. Copyright © 1974 by Oxford University Press, Inc. Reprinted by permission. Footnotes have been omitted.

most frequently with the Chief Justice—for advice on future appointments. The initiative usually lies with the Chief Executive; yet it may
also emanate from the Justices, as a mid-nineteenth-century event illus-
trates: in 1853 Associate Justices John Catron and Benjamin R. Curtis
not only personally urged President Pierce to nominate John A. Campbell but accompanied their plea with supportive letters from all of the
remaining sitting Justices (regardless of political or sectional persuasion).
Other Justices who lobbied prominently and successfully with Presidents
in the last century include Robert C. Grier (for William Strong, 1870);
Noah H. Swayne (for Joseph P. Bradley, also 1870); Morrison R. Waite
(for William B. Woods, 1880); Samuel F. Miller (for David J. Brewer,
1889); and Henry B. Brown (for Howell E. Jackson, 1893). The Presidents involved were, respectively, Ulysses S. Grant (twice), Rutherford B.
Hayes, Grover Cleveland, and Benjamin Harrison.

The champion influencer to date has unquestionably been William
Howard Taft, the only person to have served both as President (1901–13)
and as Chief Justice of the United States (1921–30). Taft actually coveted
the latter post more than the Presidency, but he was not about to relinquish his place as a leader of America's bar simply because of his elevation to the highest court. He had, after all, appointed six of its members
while he was President, two of whom were still serving when he reached
the Court. And Mr. Chief Justice Edward D. White, whom Taft ultimately succeeded, had been elevated by him to that post in 1910. Taft,
on leaving the Presidency in 1913, began to establish a long record of
rendering both solicited and unsolicited advice on judicial candidates,
literally bombarding the Executive Branch with suggestions, and he as-
suredly did not stop when President Harding nominated him as Chief
Justice in 1921.

Indeed, it is no exaggeration to maintain that Taft, rather than Harding, was basically responsible for selecting—or at the very least approving—three of the four individuals whom Harding sent to the Supreme
Court before his death in 1923: George Sutherland (1922), Pierce Butler
(1922), and William Howard Taft! Taft merely acquiesced in the President's choice of the fourth, Edward T. Sanford. Taft's lobbying activities
in his own behalf were perhaps matched only by his efforts on behalf of
Pierce Butler—a classic illustration of Taft's influence over Harding, who
seemed almost to fear him at times. Harding's Attorney General, Harry
M. Daugherty, a Taft ally and no mean special-interest lobbyist himself,
thus told Taft's brother, Henry, that the President "would not approve
of anybody for appointment who was not approved by [the Chief Jus-
tice]." And among those whom Taft successfully blocked as not having
"sound views" or being of "our kind" was the great Judge Learned Hand
of New York, whom Harding wanted to appoint to the Supreme Court
in 1922. Taft himself had appointed Judge Hand to the U.S. District
Court in 1909 (and would back his promotion by President Coolidge to

the U.S. Court of Appeals for the Second Circuit in 1924). Another Taft victim was Benjamin N. Cardozo, who might "herd," or so Taft feared, with Justices Holmes and Brandeis. Cardozo did become a Supreme Court Justice—but not until after Taft's death in 1932. On the other hand, despite Herculean (and nasty) efforts Taft failed to block President Wilson's contentious appointment of Louis Dembitz Brandeis in 1916.

While Taft's power to influence the selection of jurists has been unmatched, other Justices have also been influential, notable among them three Chiefs: Hughes, Stone, and Warren. Thus Charles Evans Hughes successfully urged F.D.R. to promote Associate Justice Harlan F. Stone to Chief Justice when he stepped down in 1941. And President Truman asked Hughes (then retired) to come to the White House to talk with him about a successor to Stone when the latter died in 1946. When Oliver Wendell Holmes stepped down in 1931, President Hoover consulted him on the candidacy of Stone's fellow New Yorker, Judge Benjamin N. Cardozo. Hoover, a reluctant dragon indeed on the Cardozo nomination, also asked Justice Stone for additional names, "just in case." Judge Learned Hand and Woodrow Wilson's Secretary of War, Newton D. Baker, were Stone's alternate choices. But Stone was convinced of Cardozo's superior qualifications and, suspecting the President's motives, sent him a string of memoranda and editorials extolling Cardozo in preference to the other two. He also tried hard to allay Hoover's political reservations concerning another "Brandeis co-religionist" on the Court. In fact, Stone went so far as to offer to resign from the Court in order to make room for Cardozo. But Hoover yielded. F.D.R. consulted with Stone before selecting Professor Felix Frankfurter and Truman did likewise before he named Senator Harold H. Burton (R.-Ohio). Mr. Chief Justice Earl Warren was an influential participant in President Kennedy's decision to nominate Secretary of Labor Arthur J. Goldberg to succeed Mr. Justice Frankfurter on the bench—a choice evidently discussed with and fully approved by Frankfurter as well. Warren was also heavily involved in President Johnson's unsuccessful selection of Abe Fortas to succeed him in 1968—although L.B.J. was so completely committed to his long-time friend and confidant that any adverse reaction from the outgoing Chief would hardly have deterred him.

[Another] factor to influence the process of judicial selection is the enormously influential role played by the Standing Committee on Federal Judiciary of the American Bar Association (A.B.A.). Established during President Truman's initial incumbency in 1945–46 as the Special Committee on Federal Judiciary, its role in the selection of jurists was more or less formalized at the end of the Truman Administration through the determined efforts of Deputy Attorney General Ross B. Malone. The Committee has been utilized in varying degree by all Presidents since then, and its work represents a significant attempt to complement, if not replace, the "political" aspects of judicial selection with "professional" input; that is, input from the organized bar. The attempt has been crowned with considerable success. An obvious measure was Deputy Attorney General Richard H. Kleindienst's announcement to the A.B.A. convention in August 1969 that the Nixon Administration had "accorded" the Association's Federal Judiciary Committee absolute veto power over all federal candidates to the bench (Supreme Court excepted) whom it considered unqualified.

• • •

The American Bar Association represents less than half of the nation's lawyers, and a relatively narrow segment of the "legal establishment" has traditionally dominated its Judiciary Committee, although an effort to become more representative seems to be under way. To date, however, almost all of the Committee's members have been successful lawyers, partners in large, big-city firms, veterans of local bar-association politics. They tend to be older men. This is not to say that the Committee is inevitably conservative, for it has had prominent members with liberal tendencies, such as Bernard G. Segal, President of the A.B.A. in 1969–70. Nor is it to say that the Committee suffers from components dominated by seasoned, cautious, prestigious professional members—not at all. But it does re-raise a crucial question: should a limited, private-interest group be accorded power of such magnitude that, in the words of Mr. Kleindienst, "the White House will never submit a nomination when the A.B.A.'s federal judiciary committee has issued a not qualified rating."

• • •

[T]he role of the A.B.A. Committee differs materially in the case of potential Supreme Court nominees, who have always been regarded as the President's own choice. . . . Indeed, the Committee's services were not enlisted in that connection until President Eisenhower nominated William J. Bennan, Jr., to the Court in 1956, and only then *after* the nominee's identity had been made public and transmitted to the Senate Judiciary Committee for action. Thus the A.B.A. Committee preferred to commit itself only to the rankings of "qualified" or "unqualified." This procedure was followed in each of the Supreme Court nominations following Brennan's until Blackmun was appointed in the spring of 1970: nominees Whittaker, Stewart, White, Goldberg, Fortas, Marshall, Fortas again (the aborted promotion), Thornberry (not acted upon by the Senate because its refusal to promote Fortas resulted in Warren's withdrawal of his resignation, hence negating the vacancy), Burger, and Haynsworth and Carswell (both rejected). The Committee stuck to the classification of "qualified" in all but a few instances: in 1963 it ranked Goldberg "highly acceptable" but considered it inappropriate to express ". . . an opinion to the degree of qualification." Yet it did express just such an opinion in the case of Judge Haynsworth in 1969—first and unanimously "highly qualified," then on reconsideration "highly qualified," but only by an 8:4 vote. In the Carswell case the Committee returned to its "qualified" designation (although more than a few observers wondered how he merited that).

In response to a storm of criticism following its actions in endorsing Haynsworth and Carswell (the former twice), the Committee's chairman Lawrence E. Walsh, a Nixon ally and the President's number-two representative at the Paris Peace Talks for some months, announced an impending change in the Committee's Supreme Court nomination classification system. Beginning with the nomination of Judge Blackmun early in 1970, the Committee adopted a new top classification of "high standards of integrity, judicial temperament, and professional competence" and substituted categories of "not opposed" or "not qualified" for the erstwhile dichotomy of "qualified" or "unqualified." It signified a tacit admission that under the latter system almost anyone could have been rated as "qualified." Evidently pleased with the Committee's new classification and its endorsement of Blackmun with the new top category, Attorney General Mitchell yielded to the importunities of Chairman Walsh. On July 23, 1970, Mitchell wrote him that henceforth the Nixon Administration would allow the A.B.A. Committee to screen potential nominees for the Supreme Court *in advance* of their submittal to the Senate Judiciary Committee. Considerable approbation in otherwise critical circles followed the announcement, for it also had become evident that its investigation of Blackmun, in sharp contrast to the sketchy report the Committee had rendered to the Senate in just six days in the Carswell case, had been rigorous: it had interviewed some 200 presumably knowledgeable individuals, including upward of 100 judges and lawyers, and had reviewed all of Judge Blackmun's court opinions in an effort to determine the candidate's qualifications in terms of "integrity . . . judicial temperament and professional competence. . . ."

Yet the era of "good tone" was destined to be short-lived. When Justices Hugo L. Black and John Marshall Harlan announced their resignations in September 1971, the Administration moved rapidly to submit possible nominees to the A.B.A. Committee, starting with Richard H. Poff, Republican Congressman from Virginia. The A.B.A. Committee, after interviewing almost 400 individuals, awarded Congressman Poff the A.B.A.'s highest recommendation. After Poff withdrew there came the much-publicized candidacy of "The Six," whose names reached the press and public even before the Walsh Committee went to work on them. The Attorney General in submitting the names of "The Six" urged speed— the Court had already begun its October 1971 term with but seven sitting members—and requested concentration on the Administration's two top choices, Mrs. Lillie and Mr. Friday. Apparently little or no work was done on the other four candidates, giving rise to later suspicions that they were but decoys.

The A.B.A. Committee, now working almost constantly, interviewed another 400 people in connection with each of the two nominees. The results were distressing. Whatever qualifications Judge Lillie and Lawyer Friday possessed, they were at best marginal in terms of what is required for service on the Supreme Court of the United States. The Committee responded with a unanimous vote of "not qualified" for Mrs. Lillie and a 6:6 tie (6 votes "not qualified," 6 votes "not opposed") for Mr. Friday. The fat was in the fire. When the A.B.A.'s actions, complete with votes, reached the news media only an hour or so after the Attorney General had received them, the Administration barely attempted to conceal its anger. Just who was responsible for the leak is difficult to establish, but the author is satisfied that it did not come from the A.B.A. Committee itself: either it was from personnel in the Justice Department or from members or staff of the Senate Judiciary Committee. There is some evidence that it came from both sources, with the initial divulgence made by the Justice Department. Within a matter of days Attorney General Mitchell addressed a sizzling letter to A.B.A. President Leon Jaworski and Chairman Walsh of the Committee informing them that at least the incumbent Administration would no longer apply to the Committee for its advice on nominees to the Supreme Court, that it would return to the practice of sending nominees directly to the Senate:

> The events of the past week have made it clear that our concern of confidentiality of communications between Justice and the Committee was well founded, and I can only conclude that there is no practical way to avoid unauthorized disclosure of the names submitted and the advice of your committee with respect thereto despite the best efforts of the committee. . . . Like you, I had hoped that the new procedure would be useful and productive. However, under the circumstances, I have concluded that the only fair and proper course is to resume the long-standing practice of submitting the Attorney General's recommendations directly to the President. . . .

The letter ended on a conciliatory note in recognizing the Committee's "wholehearted cooperation," and was signed "Yours sincerely, John," but there was no mistaking its bitter tone. The Committee was equally bitter. It would neither simply accept the blame nor cease its evaluations of Supreme Court nominees—even though that would have to be made at the Senate stage once again. A plainly miffed Chairman Walsh made the latter quite clear: when the President subsequently announced his selections of Messrs. Powell and Rehnquist for the two vacancies (he did not send the Lillie and Friday nominations to the Senate at all) the A.B.A. Committee sprang to action. After its normal investigation it submitted its report to Chairman Eastland of the Senate

Judiciary Committee: Powell, unanimously approved with the highest of the three classifications; Rehnquist, with eight votes for the highest classification and four "not opposed" votes. As noted, their confirmation by the Senate in December, 1971 came by votes of 89:1 and 68:26, respectively. One year later the A.B.A. formally requested Mr. Mitchell's successor, Richard G. Kleindienst, not only to revert to the Department's pre-"The Six" arrangements with the Committee, but to broaden the latter's role in advising Presidents on nominations.

•   •   •

The work of the A.B.A. Committee is but one piece—albeit a prominently perceived one—in a rather large mosaic. Its contribution is indeed essential, yet it should never become controlling. One of its most distinguished contemporary members noted perceptively that the Committee "performs a very significant function of saying 'no' to the political muscleboys . . . and it also plays an enormously important one in taking flak for the Senators." But as the Committee sheepishly conceded in its Carswell report "many other factors of a broad political and ideological nature" remain outside its competence. In sum, the bar can be of inestimable help in assessing professional qualifications of judicial nominees, but it must not, on any level, be accorded a veto power. For there remains the crucial constitutional cum political fact of governance under our representative democracy that judicial nominations are the President's to make and the Senate's to confirm.

───────────────────── 42 ─────────────────────

Some Theoretical Perspectives on Packing the Supreme Court

S. Sidney Ulmer

I

The selection procedure established in Article III of the Constitution seems designed to impede the conscious insertion of partisan bias into the Supreme Court via the appointment of partisan justices. Note that I

say impede, not prevent. Certainly the procedure has deterred the placement of presidential puppets on the Court or, if placed, the pulling of
their strings. Nevertheless, presidents have frequently sought to appoint
justices who shared their views on the controversial questions of the day.
Evidence for this can be seen in the political party affiliations of those
receiving Supreme Court appointments. Until Abraham Lincoln's presidency, no appointee was a member of the opposing political party.
Lincoln named five men to the Court between 1862 and 1864, one of
whom, Stephen J. Field, was a Democrat. Since the Lincoln exception
in 1863, there have been only nine others—the last being Nixon's selection in 1971 of Democrat Lewis F. Powell. Thus, of 101 men who have
served, 91 have been members of the appointing president's political
party.

II

This is not to suggest that presidents are likely to be satisfied with knowledge of political party affiliation alone. Given the wide range of views
that can be found in both major parties, additional inquiries are usually
made. The literature is replete with examples of presidential concern
over the policy preferences of prospective nominees. Woodrow Wilson
wanted Joseph Clarke because he would give the law a "liberal and enlightened interpretation." Lincoln thought that "We cannot ask a man
what he will do, and if we should, and he should answer us, we should
despise him for it." [1] Nevertheless, and as a consequence, he wanted to
appoint to the Court men whose opinions were known. Consistent with
such an approach, Lincoln defended his nomination of Salmon Chase
for chief justice on the ground that Chase would sustain the emancipa-
tion of Negro slaves.

Teddy Roosevelt was even more focussed. In considering Horace H.
Lurton (later appointed to the Court by President Taft), Roosevelt told
Senator Lodge that Lurton is "right on the Negro question; he is right
on the power of the federal government; he is right on the insular question; he is right about corporations; and he is right about labor. On
every question that would come before the bench he has shown himself
to be in much closer touch with the policies in which you and I believe
than even White [Edward D.] because he has been right about corporations, where White has been wrong." [2]

His cousin Franklin Roosevelt was equally anxious to get justices
friendly to the New Deal and declined to give his first appointment to
his Senate majority leader—Joseph Robinson—because Robinson's support had not been sufficiently intense.

Presidents have not, of course, proceeded in such a fashion with each and every one of their appointments. Herbert Hoover does not generally appear to have done so. One of his three appointees was a Democrat (Brandeis) and none was of Hoover's political cast. Others have done so with some nominations but not with others. The catalyst for the highly partisan approach seems to be three-pronged: namely, whether the country is beset with serious problems or controversies, whether the president has clear-cut policy positions from which to deal with the crises, and whether the Court as contemporaneously constituted is friendly, hostile, or uncertain as to these policy preferences.[3] Given the first two conditions and a hostile Court, almost any president can be expected to utilize the partisan approach for ameliorating his administration's difficulties.

III

The partisan approach, when tried, has not always been successful. The best known disappointments, perhaps, were those of Teddy Roosevelt with Oliver Wendell Holmes and Dwight Eisenhower with Earl Warren. After assuring himself that Holmes was sympathetic to his views, Roosevelt was bitterly disappointed when Holmes ruled against the government in the Northern Securities Case. Although the United States won this antitrust case by a 5–4 vote, Holmes' ringing dissent did not exactly endear him to the man who gave him his job. Indeed, Roosevelt said he could carve out of a banana a justice with more backbone than that. He even considered excluding Holmes from the White House as punishment for his misdeed. The justice thought this rather foolish. But, in any event, he said: "I never cared a damn whether I went there or not."[4]

After satisfying himself via personal interview that Earl Warren's basic philosophy was in tune with that of the president, Eisenhower made Warren a Chief Justice. Later, he is reported to have said: "Biggest damn fool mistake I ever made." While this may be apocryphal, Eisenhower's autobiography, published in 1963, suggests a general disappointment with Warren's performance.

The reasons why the partisan approach, when used, has not always been successful, are clear enough. They do not include Senate interference with presidential appointments since a persevering President will eventually get approval for his choices. Nor do they include the fact that some prospective nominees will decline the nomination as did Representative Poff of Virginia when solicited by Richard Nixon. A fundamental reason for failure is the life tenure provided in Article III of the Constitution. Once appointed, the political leverage of a president on his nominee is virtually nonexistent. Similarity of viewpoint may occur, however, regardless of any influence emanating from the White House. Presidents have always understood this; the framers of the Constitution, certainly, were no less astute. While they did not seek the elimination of any semblance of presidential views in Court-made policy, it is unlikely that they believed a single president or a succession of presidents should be allowed to pack the Court with partisans holding a single directing philosophy on the substantive questions of the day.

We have been able to rely on three factors other than life tenure to prevent such a development. First, the probable frequency distribution of appointments. Historically, presidents have been able to make a Supreme Court appointment once every twenty-two months. When that pattern holds, it is difficult to pack the Court because a president would have to serve nine years in order to appoint a majority of its members. A single directing philosophy *could* be established across the terms of two or more presidents who hold similar philosophical outlooks. One protection against this is the probability of such an occurrence. In the last 130 years, the same political party has occupied the White House more than eight years in succession only four times while the converse has occurred twice as often. Only one president has served more than eight years in the same period. Because presidents are now limited by the Constitution to eight years of service, we have additional protection on that dimension.

In a like view, given the great disparity of viewpoints within our political parties and among presidents of the same party, it is by no means certain that successive representatives of the same party will seek similar directing philosophies in the Supreme Court. In any event, the framers of the Constitution had a third defensive measure available to them— the fallibility of presidents in selecting justices with preferred and unchanging views across tenures of up to 35 years. Thus, for a combination of reasons, we have generally avoided single directing philosophies in the Court. There have, of course, been near exceptions. One can point to the early federalist courts, those of the late nineteenth and early twentieth centuries, or to the more recent Warren Court, but in general the Court has not been characterized by single directing philosophies— though smaller groups of justices might have been.

IV

It may be argued that there are now new elements in the situation that threaten to change the picture we have described. While the framers and earlier statesmen had some understanding of human behavior and its antecedents, their knowledge was no match for that now available to us through the research undertaken in psychology, sociology, political and other social sciences. Certainly the establishment of single directing philosophies is more probable now than in the past, given a willingness to exploit our recent theoretical advances in behavioral science. Failure

to recognize that the theory-knowledge base for the selection of Supreme
Court justices has been fundamentally altered in recent decades is to
risk a faulty interpretation of selection processes. One commentator has
recently written that "Republican Presidents have consistently considered the Court as a law court, members of which should have past
experience on lower federal or state courts. Democratic Presidents have
seen the Court as a policy Court and have consistently appointed to it
men from public life with substantial political experience." [5] The facts
that support this inference are these: Since 1937, only five of seventeen
Democratic nominees had been judges and two of these for very brief
periods. Of twelve Republican nominees, eight were sitting judges in
federal courts of appeals at time of nomination and a ninth was on the
Supreme Court of New Jersey.

One may surmise that Republicans are motivated by the thought that
prior judicial experience makes for more successful judges. Studies by
Felix Frankfurter and others, however, have failed to turn up any positive
correlation between such prior experience and success as a Supreme
Court justice. Indeed, Stuart Nagel has reported a negative association
between prior judicial experience and historical greatness as a Supreme
Court justice.[6]

An alternative reading of the facts we have described may be more
appealing—a reading derived from a theoretical framework not available
to the framers of the Constitution. I refer here to theories of cognitive
structure. These theories are built around three basic concepts: attitude,
dissonance, and commitment.

V

In 1787, as now, a notion was prevalent that a man's behavior reflected
his views and that knowing his views one could predict his behavior. That
is precisely why Lincoln said, "We want a man whose opinions are
known." But today we know that opinions are functions of attitudes and
that attitudes predict both opinions *and* behavior.

Moreover, opinions and behavior can be used to infer attitudes. In a
section of the Federal Tax Return Auditor's Handbook, the Internal
Revenue Service tells its agents that fraud is a matter of intent but that
"the things done or said by a person are assumed to be the natural consequences of the person's intentions." Similarly, the behavior and expressed opinions of prospective Supreme Court nominees can be used to
infer attitudinal structure which modern research has shown to be a crucial factor in decision making.

The theory of cognitive dissonance posits that a person is uncomfortable when any pair of cognitions is psychologically inconsistent. This is

similar to the idea of cross-pressure, a concept familiar to all political scientists. An example of dissonance can be seen in Hugo Black not too long after his first election to the Senate. Black believed that senators should not compromise themselves by engaging in activities that might give interested parties political leverage. But after election to the Senate, he continued to practice law and before long his jury verdicts for plaint-iffs jumped dramatically. Black wondered whether these obliging jurors might want favors from the senator and he didn't have to wait too long to find out. This created serious cognititive dissonance which, consistent with the theory, Black was motivated to reduce. He did so simply by giving up the practice of law.

Commitment—our third concept—is defined as the pledging or bind-ing of the individual to behavioral acts. If one only *believed* in main-taining the integrity of the Senate but was *committed* to the practice of law, dissonance reduction would be likely to involve some operation on the belief side. In the situation described above, we infer that Black was committed to maintaining the integrity of the Senate but not to the practice of law.

Experiments within a framework set by commitment theory have pro-duced some interesting propositions. One is that, in the face of increas-ing incentive, resistance to change varies with strength of commitment. Another is that resistance to change is greater if the commitment to cur-rent behavior is public rather than if commitment is private. If we com-mit ourselves to stop smoking, for instance, it is much easier to resume the habit if we have told no one else of our commitment. One who is committed is also bound by previous behavior, i.e., repetition of a be-havioral act increases the resistance to new evidence that otherwise might suggest behavior modification. And an attack upon one's commitment is likely to intensify the resistance to change. This is the so-called "boom-erang effect," an effect also associated with forewarning one of an attack upon one's commitments.

From the point of view of an appointing president, commitment theory suggests that he seek nominees whose commitments can be easily discovered, whose commitments have been frequently reinforced over a long period of time, whose commitments are public rather than anony-mous—nominees whose commitments are congruous with those of the president himself. If the theories of cognitive structure are valid, presi-dents who are guided by them in staffing the Supreme Court should improve their chances of biasing Court output and establishing single directing philosophies which they find appealing. Cognitive structure theories, moreover, can provide us with an interpretation of the Re-publican preference for judges that differs from that suggested earlier. Indeed, they provide us with a better explanation since prior judicial experience is not related to success on the high bench. That being the case, it would be rather ungenerous to base the Republican preference for judges on a discredited theory. The better explanation is that the conditions for staffing the Court consistent with theories of cognitive structure are best met by looking for nominees in the lower appellate courts.

Over the long run, as Burton Atkins has pointed out,[7] the judge in such a court is engaged in dissonance reduction—in working out a suitable level of consistency between beliefs and beliefs but also between beliefs and behavior. This resolution is reflected in the votes and opinions of each judge—all of which are easily accessible in a printed public record. Since these courts are producing hundreds of decisions and opinions each year, commitments are made frequently and reinforced repeatedly. Much of the reinforcement occurs in published opinions and this represents public commitment of the most compelling kind. A president may simply go to the record and with appropriate analysis discern the attitudes of any judge toward the issues of the day. If properly done, it permits a president to predict not only how a nominee might respond to issues he has faced before but also what to expect on new issues that tap previously identified attitudinal dimensions. And it gives him considerable confidence that future behavior will be consistent with past behavior.

In short, it is the focus on cognitive structure that distinguishes current theory and knowledge of behavior from that available to the framers and earlier presidents. And it may be hypothesized that it is the exploitation of these developments for partisan purposes that distinguishes the Republican and Democratic approaches to selecting Supreme Court nominees.

In sum, we now have a theory-knowledge base that lends itself to the systematic introduction of philosophical bias into the Supreme Court through the process by which we select the Court's justices. This development does not impact on two of the safeguards mentioned earlier—the infrequency of Supreme Court vacancies and the philosophical disparities that characterize our political parties and their presidential representatives. But the fallibility of the appointing officer in identifying a nominee with preferred philosophical perspectives and in predicting the nominee's future behavior can be reduced considerably by a systematic exploitation of the structures we have articulated. As a consequence, a threat by a presidential candidate to redirect Court policy via the appointment of new justices—however it might have been viewed earlier—is not to be dismissed lightly.

Notes

1. Quoted in Leo Pfeffer, *This Honorable Court* (Boston: Beacon Press, 1965), p. 165.

2. Henry Cabot Lodge, *Selections From the Correspondence of Theodore Roosevelt and Henry Cabot Lodge,* Vol. 2 (New York: Scribner, 1925), p. 228.

3. Robert Scigliano, *The Supreme Court and the Presidency* (New York: The Free Press, 1971), pp. 117–120.

4. Mark Dewolfe Howe, ed., *Holmes-Pollock Letters.,* Vol. 2 (Cambridge: Harvard University Press, 1941), pp. 63–64.

5. C. Herman Pritchett, "High Court Selection," *The New York Times,* January 12, 1976, p. L27.

6. Stuart S. Nagel, "Characteristics of Supreme Court Greatness," *American Bar Association Journal* 56 (October 1970): 957–959.

7. Burton Atkins, "Chief Justice Burger and the Criminal Offender in the U.S. Supreme Court: Or the Deterministic Source of Freewill Perspective" (Paper presented at the Annual Meeting of the Midwest Political Science Association, Chicago, April 29–May 1, 1971).

43

Nomination of
William H. Rehnquist:
The Senate Inquires

SENATOR HART: Now, the question of the Senate's proper role in this advice and consent procedure has been discussed rather thoroughly in the last few years, and some general ground rules are established.

I think I agree with Senator McClellan on the general definition of some of those rules. We can agree that the nominee should be a man of evident excellence, with outstanding capacity however he may have demonstrated that excellence. Moreover, those characteristics should be evident and recognized by the nominee's brethren at the bar. I hope we are never again confronted with nominees where you have to strain to find it.

You, Mr. Rehnquist, and this is also true of Mr. Powell, can have it said of you that you do clearly have such a record of ability.

Another fairly clear-cut hurdle is the possibility of disqualification

Nominations of William H. Rehnquist and Lewis F. Powell, Jr., Hearing before the Committee on the Judiciary of the U.S. Senate, 92d Congress, 1st Session (November 3–10, 1971). Footnotes have been omitted.

because of significant conflicts or similar activities which might compel opposition because of the effect the nomination would have upon the Court and its stature in our society.

One purpose of these hearings, of course, is to explore any issues of that nature, if they arise.

Then there is a group of more difficult considerations which have been explored in past hearings. First, there is a nominee's judicial philosophy. By that I mean his view of the role of the Court in our system of Government and the duty of a Justice in interpreting and safeguarding our Constitution, because let us not blink it, we do interpret the Constitution. It is not a slot machine where we put in a law and push a button to see if it is constitutional.

Second, there is a nominee's apparent willingness to enforce the great constitutional guarantees in the protections of which the Court has played a unique role throughout our history.

And third, there is a less tangible consideration of a man's breadth of vision, his compassion, his awareness, and understanding of the problem of our society to which the broad provisions of the Constitution must be applied.

In the past, as one Senator, I have acknowledged hesitancy to oppose a nominee with judicial experience merely because I might disagree with the results he had reached in specific cases.

However, I have also indicated my reservation about sending anyone to the Court whose overall record suggests a lack of sensitivity to the protection of individual rights and liberties—an insensitivity so clearly manifested that his elevation to the Court would place a cloud over the Constitution's promise of justice to the poor, the weak, and the unpopular, who must look to the Court for their protection.

As a predecessor of Senator Hruska, Senator Norris of Nebraska, put it, we ought to know how the nominee approaches these great questions of human liberty.

But it is easier to explain what we should find out than to put a handle on how you do it.

Finally, some observers have noted that when the Executive specifically chooses candidates in part because of their particular philosophy, rather than these more general credentials, the Senate, as constitutional coequal in the process of filling vacancies on the Court, must review carefully the implications of the Executive's expressly chosen criteria. I am sure that these matters, too, will be examined in these hearings. On some of these questions the nominees, themselves, will be able to offer the committee the benefit of their thoughts.

Now, Mr. Rehnquist, I would not ask you whether you agree or disagree with me that you possess both excellence and competency, but I would like to explore with you this matter of the Senate's role in regard to the nominee's philosophy and his views on the great issues of the people before the Court. I know you have written on that question. The question is a little less academic now than when you wrote. Have you given it any further thought?

MR. REHNQUIST: I have given it some further thought, Senator, and I would say that I have no reservation at all about what I said from the point of view of the Senate.

I think I did not fully appreciate the difficulty of the position that the nominee is in.

[Laughter.]

I say that not entirely facetiously, because the nominee is in an extraordinarily difficult position. He cannot answer a question which would try to engage him in predictions as to what he would do on a specific fact situation or a particular doctrine after it reaches the Court. And yet, any member of the committee is clearly entitled to probe as to what might be called, for lack of better words, the judicial philosophy of the nominee. I think that is the right and prerogative of any Senator who feels that is an appropriate test, and it would be presumptuous of me, perhaps, to even say that.

But, I have no disagreement at all with my earlier statement in the Harvard Law Record that it certainly is a legitimate concern of the Senate if it chooses to make it so, what the judicial philosophy of the nominee is.

SENATOR HART: Well, can you describe for us what your judicial philosophy is? My question just underscores the difficulty of the committee, let alone the nominee in such an inquiry.

MR. REHNQUIST: It is so difficult to do it in meaningful terms.

SENATOR HART: Well, let me see, if I can push a little bit. The President has told the country that he has selected you and Mr. Powell because you were "judicial conservatives." Now, I cannot ask you to put yourself in his position, but that is what he is telling us.

He then explained that by "judicial conservative" he meant a judge who was not too much of an activist, who interpreted the Constitution strictly and did not try to include his decisions toward a particular political or social view he thought desirable.

And on the other hand, the President went on to offer another qualification to being a "judicial conservative" as he used it. He indicated that to be a true judicial conservative one must also be a judge who will swing the pendulum more to the side of the forces of Government, and away from the protection of the individual rights of the accused.

He did not put it in those exact words, but that is in essence what he said. Now, I am wondering if, in your consideration of judicial philosophy, you see any inherent inconsistency between these two definitions of judicial conservative.

In other words, how can a nominee be put on the Court for the express purpose of tipping the balance more toward the Government and still be a nominee placed on the Court to follow strictly the mandates of the Constitution, without regard to a personal philosophy of law and order, or desired results in a particular area of the law?

Help us on that one.

MR. REHNQUIST: As you suggest, Senator, I cannot speak for the President on the subject. I can give you my own observations. I suppose it is conceivable that one might feel that the two were consistent if he also felt from his own study of decided cases that the pendulum had been swung too far toward the accused not by virtue of a fair reading of the Constitution but by virtue of what was conceived to be some outside influences such as the personal philosophy of one or more of the Justices.

SENATOR HART: You would not have a personal philosophy if you became a Justice?

MR. REHNQUIST: I would certainly expect that I would have a personal philosophy. I mean, I have lived 47 years.

• • •

SENATOR KENNEDY: Going back to the statement that the President made about the appointment, Mr. Rehnquist, what do you think troubles the President, and why do you think that the President makes the statement about comparing the peace forces and the criminal forces and says that he believes, and I think that I am stating it reasonably accurately, that the public interests have to be better protected than they have in the past, and it is important that he nominate to the Court, as he pledged he would during the last campaign, someone whose judicial philosophy is close to his own?

Why do you think the President believes that your appointment there will move the Court closer to the peace forces and away from the accused?

MR. REHNQUIST: I think it would be inappropriate for me to comment on what the President's thought processes were, if I knew them.

SENATOR KENNEDY: Well, I suppose he says he believes your judicial philosophy is that you are a judicial conservative, is what it gets down to. Do you feel so?

MR. REHNQUIST: Well, if by judicial conservative is meant one who will attempt to ——

SENATOR KENNEDY: What do you think he meant by that?

THE CHAIRMAN: Wait a minute. Let him answer the question.

MR. REHNQUIST: I simply cannot speak for him, Senator.

• • •

SENATOR MATHIAS: In an effort to get at this question of judicial philosophy, maybe we ought to look at some specific areas of the Constitution which would necessarily, I think, be embraced in a judicial philosophy, but which due to their very nature are not susceptible of strict construction: Words such as "unreasonable" in the fourth amendment "excessive" in the eighth, "due process" in the fifth and fourteenth amendments. I think these are areas which refer to rights which are not clear and absolute so that they have to be qualified and interpreted in protecting the freedoms and privileges, assessing the liabilities that the Constitution addressed itself to.

What would you consider, for example, to be reasonable searches and seizures as contemplated by the fourth amendment?

MR. REHNQUIST: Senator, I honestly think that is too specific a question for me to answer. I know there are several cases pending up there now and I would anticipate that there would be a number in the future.

SENATOR MATHIAS: Would you feel that you could give the committee your ideas on what you think excessive bail would be? Some broad definition which you could apply the word "excessive" to.

MR. REHNQUIST: I do not believe I ought to, Senator.

SENATOR MATHIAS: Well, I am not trying to put you in a position where you would prejudice your usefulness to your colleagues in the future, but I think this question may be important in the future as to which defendants or classes of defendants would be suited for bail. This is an area which would be of concern to the Senate, to the courts, and to the country.

What about due process?

MR. REHNQUIST: I just think it would be inappropriate for me to try to now advance some sort of definition of a term which may well, if I were confirmed, come before me and on which I would hear argument and read briefs and have the benefit of discussion in the conference room.

• • •

SENATOR HRUSKA: Mr. Rehnquist, the President in his comments on your nomination designated you, I believe, as a judicial conservative. Is my recollection correct?

MR. REHNQUIST: I believe it is, Senator.

SENATOR HRUSKA: Have you ever discussed with the President personally whether you are a judicial conservative or not, in the context of the nomination for the Supreme Court?

MR. REHNQUIST: It is not that I have any hesitancy in answering the question, except as to the propriety of repeating any discussion with the President. Since there was none here, I suppose I need have no hesitancy; no, he did not.

SENATOR HRUSKA: Then, obviously the President, in referring to you and describing you as a judicial conservative, resorted to the same type of information that is presently available to the committee, to wit: Your testimony before committees, your statements, your articles, opinions that you have written and the observations and the contacts and recommendations of different people who know you. Wouldn't that follow?

MR. REHNQUIST: Certainly those sources were available to him.

SENATOR HRUSKA: Yes. Presumably he did consult all or some of these sources. We know, at least as much as he knew when he determined your philosophy. I submit we can do the same.

Now, as to the interest, the very intense interest, of some members of this committee in some expression from you as to your personal philosophy, I would venture the suggestion that this is a rather newfound interest. I recall very well in the committee room when another nominee for the Supreme Court was occupying the nominee's chair which you now occupy. I think for the better part of 2 days the Senator from North Carolina repeated question after question almost without limit, requesting insight into his personal philosophy on various subjects. The answer was always the same. And at one juncture, the nominee said:

MR. SENATOR: I have talked to no one, no place, no how at no time about anything since I received this nomination.

Now, that was Thurgood Marshall.

I heard no expression of interest on the part of some other members of this committee in following up that line of questions with that nominee. Always before when a nominee has declined to answer a question when, in his own mind, for whatever reason, it has appeared inappropriate, this committee has honored that decision. This nominee should be treated no differently.

To require answers, aside from the attorney-client privilege, would not be fair to his future colleagues on the Court, assuming confirmation; it would not be fair to the litigants in the Court or to their respective counsel.

And so even if we have a letter here from all of the people of the United States saying it is all right for you to talk, Mr. Rehnquist, those considerations would not be solved, would they?

MR. REHNQUIST: No; I don't believe they would.

SENATOR HRUSKA: And that has been my experience, reaching back to the time of Justice Brennan's confirmation. That has been the standard answer, and it has been accepted by this committee. I do not believe that there is much hope of getting away from the immutable fact that there is a limit beyond which no nominee can in good conscience go in expressing opinions either personal or legal in character at this particular juncture.

As to the waiver, I don't see how you can get a waiver. There is no particular way it can be received nor issued.

MR. REHNQUIST: Certainly past nominations have generally taken that position, and I think their refusals to answer that sort of question were probably justified.

SENATOR HRUSKA: They certainly have, and I think upon the reading of any of the prior hearings, that same decision, that same answer, will be found. It has always been accepted by the committee and also by the Senate.

I think you have been more liberal than some of the nominees before us in the extent that you have answered many questions. I would have asserted the answer, the historical answer, much sooner than you have done.

• • •

SECTION TWELVE

Access to the Supreme Court

<hr/>

44

Denying Access in Plenary Cases: The Burger Court

Gregory J. Rathjen and Harold J. Spaeth

• • •

Because of confusion about the meaning of the term "access," we deem it important to specify the sense in which we use the concept. While some scholars, not inappropriately, confine their definition of access to the narrow gatekeeping function performed by the Supreme Court at the "decision to decide" stage—i.e., whether or not to accept a case for decision . . . our analysis focuses instead on the formal public policy made by the Supreme Court limiting or expanding the requirements litigants must meet to bring suit—to gain access—to any level of the federal court system. Our concern, then, is not the "Rule of Four" of the Supreme Court's conference, but rather the technical requirements, such as standing, mootness, exhaustion of remedies, and the like, that are the basis of a substantial number of the Court's formally decided cases. The formal doctrinal rules contained in the cases shape the tech-

From Gregory J. Rathjen and Harold J. Spaeth, "Access to the Federal Courts: An Analysis of Burger Court Policy Making," *American Journal of Political Science* 23 (May 1979): 360–364, 367–368, 368–369, 369–371, 372–374, 374, 376, 379–380. Copyright © 1979 by The University of Texas Press. Reprinted by permission of The University of Texas Press, publisher. Footnotes and some references have been omitted.

nical requirements that determine who has "access" to the judicial forum at all levels of the federal court system.

Since 1973, the relatively open access that the Warren Court had established in such notable decisions as *Baker* v. *Carr,* 369 U.S. 186 (1962), *Hardin* v. *Kentucky Utilities Co.,* 390 U.S. 1, (1968), *Flast* v. *Cohen,* 392 U.S. 83 (1968), and *Powell* v. *McCormack* 395 U.S. 486 (1969), has been displaced by "a movement away from . . . liberalization toward a raising of barriers against plaintiffs in Federal Court." . . . This movement did not begin with the inception of the Burger Court. Rather, the Burger Court initially appeared to be following and even advancing further the access trends of the Warren Court. Such decisions as *Data Processing,* 397 U.S. 150 (1970), *Barlow* v. *Collins,* 397 U.S. 159 (1970), and *Trafficante* v. *Metropolitan Life Insurance Co.,* 409 U.S. 205 (1972), supported this observation. So also *Sierra Club* v. *Morton,* 405 U.S. 727 (1972), and *United States* v. *S.C.R.A.P.,* 412 U.S. 669 (1973), which, though ruling against the plaintiffs at bar, altered the test governing standing to sue to provide easier access. But since 1973 the newsworthy access decisions have been those that restricted *entrée* to the federal courts.

Thus, for example, in *Linda R.S.* v. *Richard D.,* 410 U.S. 614 (1973), the Court asserted that in order to have standing to sue one must show a direct relationship between the injury and the claim sought to be adjudicated. This requirement of "causation" emerged full force in *Simon* v. *Eastern Kentucky Welfare Rights Organization,* 426 U.S. 26 (1976), wherein the Court held that standing to challenge government administrative action be granted only where the plaintiff can show that the injury is caused by government and the court action will indeed remedy the problem. The Court thereby appeared to take the stand that "injury" is not injury unless it can be redressed directly (Wolff, 1976, p. 673).

Two 1974 decisions strictly limited taxpayer access to the federal courts. Both cases concerned the applicability of the *Flast* v. *Cohen* "nexus" test in suits brought by taxpayers to challenge the constitutionality of congressional action. The test first required the taxpayer to "establish a logical link" between his status as a taxpayer "and the type of legislative enactment attacked." Second, the taxpayer "must show that the challenged enactment exceeds specific constitutional limitations. . . ." 392 U.S. 83 (1968), at 102–103. In *Flast,* the Court held that the expenditure of federal funds to finance instruction in religious schools was limited by the establishment of religion clause of the First Amendment and that the plaintiffs consequently could invoke the jurisdiction of the federal courts for an adjudication on the merits. In the first of the 1974 cases, *United States* v. *Richardson,* 418 U.S. 166 (1974), the court rigorously construed the nexus test as limited to statutes that emanated directly from Congress' taxing and spending power—i.e., Article I, Section 8 of the Constitution. Because Richardson had challenged the failure of Congress to publish detailed budgetary information on the CIA as required by Section 9 rather than Section 8 of Article I, he lacked standing. In the second case, *Schlesinger* v. *Reservists Committee,* 418 U.S. 208 (1974), the Court categorically denied federal taxpayers the right to challenge the membership of several congresspersons in the military reserves. The basis for the majority's decision was that the action complained of not only did not concern Congresss' power to tax and spend money, it did not pertain to Congress at all, but rather to action of the executive branch permitting members of Congress to maintain their reserve status.

Nor has the Burger Court adhered to its own initial liberalism as established in *Data Processing* and *Barlow* v. *Collins.* Efforts by blacks in Cairo, Illinois, to halt an alleged conspiracy against them by local law enforcement officials came to naught when the Court ruled that none of the named plaintiffs had been injured or threatened with injury. Hence, they had no standing to address the merits of the matter (*O'Shea* v. *Littleton,* 414 U.S. 488 [1974]). The Court similarly found no injury suffered by blacks, taxpayers, home builders, or a civic association because of restrictive zoning ordinances in a wealthy, white suburb (*Warth* v. *Seldin,* 422 U.S. 490 [1975]). Nor did the Court limit access only to racial minorities and the underprivileged. Substantial direct injury must also be suffered by the affluent. Thus, a potential investor who did not take advantage of a misleading stock offer could not sue the seller because he had falsely depreciated the value of the shares in the corporation's prospectus (*Blue Chips Stamps* v. *Manor Drug Stores,* 421 U.S. 723 [1975]).

Aside from using the requirements of standing to close access, the Burger Court has proceeded to accomplish much the same objective by demanding stricter attention to abstention, exhaustion of remedies, jurisdiction, and the like. These concerns are not directed at the plaintiff's eligibility, but rather concern the propriety of federal courts as decision makers. In general, federal courts are expected to await the decisions of and grant due respect to the jurisdiction and authority of other courts, particularly state courts. Under the rubric of what might be called a "new federalism," it appears that the Burger Court is shutting the door left ajar by the Warren Court in these areas.

With regard to federal court interference (usually injunctive) in pending or already progressing state prosecutions, the Burger Court in *Younger* v. *Harris,* 401 U.S. 37 (1971), narrowed the liberal Warren Court decision in *Dombrowski* v. *Pfister,* 380 U.S. 479 (1965). In *Dombrowski,* the Warren Court allowed injunctive relief in a fairly blatant case of state prosecutional abuse of a civil rights organization. In *Younger,* the Burger Court limited *Dombrowski*-like intrusions into state court actions to all but the most extreme circumstances. The Court, as well, has extended the *Younger* policy to state-initiated civil proceedings (*Huffman* v. *Pursue,* 420 U.S. 592 [1975]). While the *Younger* position closes off access to a degree, the Court has allowed some federal injunctive relief where such relief is authorized by statute. In the civil rights areas the Court allowed, for instance, the use of injunctive relief to halt a pattern of harrassment, arrest, and jailing of farmworkers by the Texas Rangers (*Allee* v. *Medrano,* 416 U.S. 802 [1974]). While this opening initially seemed encouraging, the Court quickly required a *Younger*-like "exceptional circumstance" to be established before the *Allee* ruling could be invoked in the denial of a request for a similar form of relief (*Rizzo* v. *Goode,* 423 U.S. 362 [1976]).

Adhering to its general policy of "new federalism," the Burger Court has proceeded to narrow the circumstances under which lower federal courts can review state convictions via the writ of *habeas corpus.* The Warren Court had expanded the writ's use ostensibly as a means to monitor state criminal procedures (*Fay* v. *Noia,* 372 U.S. 391 [1963]). The Burger Court, in *Picard* v. *Connor,* 404 U.S. 270 (1971) and *Francis* v. *Henderson,* 425 U.S. 536 (1976), denied *habeas corpus* relief to two state prisoners who were alleging discrimination in the composition of the grand jury because both prisoners had failed to raise the issue in a timely fashion in the state courts below. And, in its most far reaching *habeas corpus* decision to date, the Court, in *Stone* v. *Powell,* 428 U.S. 465 (1976), circumscribed the lower court's option to entertain petitions in which the allegation regarding unconstitutional imprisonment involves the Fourth Amendment and state court failure to adhere strictly to the exclusionary rule. Not only has the Court invoked stricter adherence to abstention, exhaustion of remedies, and *habeas corpus* in the area of criminal justice, it has also placed similar restrictions in other areas as well (*Askew* v. *Hargrave,* 401 U.S. 476 [1971]; *Harris County Commissioners* v. *Moore,* 420 U.S. 77 [1975]; *Colorado Conservation District* v. *United States,* 424 U.S. 800 [1976]).

• • •

[We provide] . . . three equally plausible explanations of Burger Court policy shifts in the access area. On one level we offer the reasonable contention that the Justices vote to open or close access on the basis of administrative/legal motivations. On another level, we assert that the Justices' votes in the access area are based on orientations toward substantive political considerations. And yet, on another level, we note the arguably reasonable view that both motivations interact in such a way as to create an overall orientation toward access per se which itself motivates the Justices' choices. In all of this, we are left with the question of which of these alternatives most appropriately reflects the motivations of the present Court. In the remainder of this paper we attempt to ascertain empirically which of these equally plausible motivations serves as the primary factor affecting the access behaviors of the Burger Court Justices.

To this end, rather than argue an absolutist position, we believe it more reasonable to maintain that in reality a Justice's access behaviors are a function of an interaction between administrative/legal attitudes toward access and political attitudes toward the merits in which the access stimulus arises. In this light, the essence of our concern becomes the determination of the relative degree of primacy or dominance of one attitude over the other to explain Burger Court access choices. Thus, we hypothesize the following:

H_1:   The access behaviors of Burger Court Justices are primarily a function of an overriding attitude toward access per se.

H_2:   The access behaviors of Burger Court Justices are primarily a function of a set of administrative/legal attitudes toward access.

H_3:   The access behaviors of Burger Court Justices are primarily a function of a set of attitudes toward the merits of cases in which access questions are subsumed.

III

To determine the extent to which the access behaviors of the Burger Court Justices conform to or fail to conform to one or the other of these hypotheses, we analyzed all the formally decided cases of the first seven terms of the Burger Court (1969–1976). . . .

• • •

[Available is] . . . a data set of 177 cases.

The cases and each participating Justice's votes are scored as pro (+) or anti (−) access. Where a Justice addresses himself both to the merits of a controversy and to the question of access, his vote on the latter controls. Where one or more of the Justices disagree with the access policy enunciated in the majority's opinion, and it is not possible to determine whose policy is more supportive or opposed to access, the Justices are scored as in agreement with one another.

• • •

To test our hypotheses we rely on cumulative scaling as the operational measure of attitude. Employing Spaeth's techniques of scale construction, . . . we first created an overall access scale containing all 177 decisions. Mindful that access issues have been subject only to taxonomic and doctrinal analysis, we subscaled the overall access scale for the purpose of testing H_2 without any preconceptions of how the cases *ought* to be subdivided. Our reading of the access decisions revealed that they all contained two mutually exclusive issues: whether the litigants were proper parties or whether the parties were in the proper forum. The 177 access decisions were accordingly placed in one or the other of these subscales. The proper party $(N = 57)$ and proper forum $(N = 120)$ subscales, in turn, lent themselves to further subdivision. Proper party was broken into standing $(N = 34)$ and mootness $(N = 23)$ components; proper forum into six exhaustive subscales: courts of first instance jurisdiction $(N = 22)$: i.e., the jurisdictional competency of the federal district courts and the Court of Claims to hear or decide cases; courts of appellate jurisdiction $(N = 23)$: i.e., the jurisdictional competency of the federal appellate courts, primary jurisdiction $(N = 19)$: i.e., whether the federal courts or administrative agencies are the proper forum for the resolution of certain conflicts; exhaustion of remedies $(N = 12)$: i.e., the applicability of the rule that administrative remedies be exhausted before resort to the courts may be had; the abstention doctrine $(N = 29)$: i.e., whether or not the federal courts should avoid intruding themselves into ongoing state judicial proceedings; and habeas corpus $(N = 15)$: i.e., the use of the writ of *habeas corpus* as a means whereby persons convicted under state law may have their convictions reviewed in the federal courts.

To test H_3 we subdivided the overall access scale on the basis of the merits contained in the 177 cases. Because of the great variety of substantive issues subsumed in the decisions we were not able to achieve nearly as much content refinement in these subscales as we desired. As a result, the subscales needed to test H_3 are general rather than specific. They are: criminal justice/due process $(N = 36)$, First Amendment $(N = 29)$, equality $(N = 52)$, environmental/consumer protection $(N = 17)$, business $(N = 28)$, unions $(N = 15)$.

Although twelve Justices sat on the Court during the first seven terms of the Burger Court, analysis of access choices excludes Black, Harlan, and Stevens simply because they participated in too few decisions: Stevens in only eight, black and Harlan in 47. The votes of these Justices are considered, however, in the following decision rules regarding the acceptance or rejection of hypotheses H_1, H_2, and H_3 with the exception of rules 1b and 2b:

1. to accept H_1 we require that:
   a. the overall access scale attains a Coefficient of Reproducibility $(CR) \geq .95$
   b. the CR not be an artifact of the marginal distribution: CR − Minimum Marginal Reproductibility (MMR) must be $\geq .10$;
   c. the scale be composed of inconsistencies which are randomly distributed;
   d. the subscaling, per administrative/legal content and/or political content, cannot result in significant error reduction (error reduction ≥ 50 percent).

2. to accept H_2 or H_3 we require that:
   a. a $CR \geq .95$ be obtained in the majority of subscales created;
   b. CR's not be an artifact of the subscale marginals (the majority of $CR - MMR's \geq .10$);
   c. errors within subscales be randomly distributed;
   d. subscaling must result in a significant reduction (≥ 50 percent) of overall access scale errors.

• • •

IV

Table 1 presents the results of the scale analyses. As is evident, the scale designed to determine the existence of an overall access attitude does not meet the standards outlined in our first decision rule. The CR is above Guttman's .90 standard of unidimensionality, but it does not attain our more stringent .95 requirement. The scale does reveal clear improvement over what would be expected given the marginals ($CR - MMR = .161$), but since the errors prove not to be randomly distributed (of the errors in the overall access scale 62 percent are shared by Brennan, Blackmun, Stewart, and White alone) and the CR requirement is not met, we must conclude that H_1 is not supported by the data. As a quick perusal of Table 1 shows, this conclusion garners support by virtue of the fact that substantial error reduction emerges as a result of subscaling (though not in excess of the 50 percent requirement). While the hypothesis in its strict form is not supported by the data, we do believe the evidence suggests partial support for the assertion that access behaviors are, in part, a function of an underlying attitude toward access per se.

As noted earlier, our initial effort to test H_2 (administrative/legal dominance) entailed crudely dividing the overall access scale between the two broad categories of proper forum and proper party. This division proved only partially successful. The proper party category scaled quite satisfactorily ($CR = .942$, $CR - MMR > .10$, inconsistencies randomly distributed) though not up to the decision rule standards, while the proper forum subscale, as an aggregate scale, failed to reveal an underlying dimension motivating access choice. Rather than take this evidence as the basis for rejection of H_2, we subscaled both into more refined categories. Table 1 shows the results of these subscalings as well. It is apparent that subscaling substantially improves the findings revealed by the overall proper forum scale, while providing little improvement among proper party cases. Proper forum subscales reveal an average CR of .939, as opposed to the overall proper forum CR of .894, and result in only 28 inconsistencies against 48 in the broad proper forum scale, a reduction of 42 percent. In contrast, by subscaling proper party into two

TABLE 1.   Access Scale and Subscales

Overall Access Scale
$N = 177; CR = .903; MMR = .762$
$CR - MMR = .161; n$ of incon $= 63$

ADMINISTRATIVE/LEGAL		POLITICAL

ADMINISTRATIVE/LEGAL

Proper Forum Scale
$N = 120, CR = .894, MMR = .730$
$CR - MMR = .172, n$ of incon $= 48$

First Instance Juris Scale
$N = 22, CR = .919, MMR = .742$
$CR - MMR = .169, n$ of incon $= 6$

Appellate Juris Scale
$N = 23, CR = .898, MMR = .742$
$CR - MMR = .156, n$ of incon $= 7$

Primary Juris Scale
$N = 19, CR = .937, MMR = .754$
$CR - MMR = .183, n$ of incon $= 5$

Exhaustion of Remedies Scale
$N = 12, CR = .980, MMR = .832$
$CR - MMR = .148, n$ of incon $= 1$

Abstention Scale
$N = 29, CR = .929, MMR = .782$
$CR - MMR = .147, n$ of incon $= 6$

Habeas Corpus Scale
$N = 15, CR = .972, MMR = .779$
$CR - MMR = .193, n$ of incon $= 3$

Proper Party Scale
$N = 57, CR = .942, MMR = .836$
$CR - MMR = .106, n$ of incon $= 11$

Standing Scale
$N = 34, CR = .948, MMR = .844$
$CR - MMR = .104, n$ of incon $= 8$

Mootness Scale
$N = 23, CR = .943, MMR = .840$
$CR - MMR = .103, n$ of incon $= 2$

POLITICAL

Equality Scale
$N = 52, CR = .956, MMR = .808$
$CR - MMR = .148, n$ of incon $= 10$

First Amendment Scale
$N = 29, CR = .954, MMR = .811$
$CR - MMR = .143, n$ of incon $= 4$

Criminal Justice/Due Process Scale
$N = 36, CR = .928, MMR = .777$
$CR - MMR = .151, n$ of incon $= 11$

Environmentalism/Consumerism Scale
$N = 17, CR = .899, MMR = .806$
$CR - MMR = .093, n$ of incon $= 7$

Business Scale
$N = 28, CR = .924, MMR = .739$
$CR - MMR = .185, n$ of incon $= 5$

Unions Scale
$N = 15, CR = .912, MMR = .701$
$CR - MMR = .211, n$ of incon $= 5$

subscales, standing and mootness, only one error is reduced (9 percent reduction) and the average subscale CR is only a slight improvement over the CR for the overall proper party scale. Despite the obvious improvement in unidimensionality and error reduction by virtue of this administrative/legal subscaling, none of the findings meet the strict requirements of our second decision rule for specifying dominance, and, thus, we must conclude that H_2 is unsupported. Again, though, while failing to meet the requirements, the data do indicate that access behaviors are, at least in part, a function of administrative/legal predispositions.

To test the viability of H_3 (political dominance) we categorized the entire set of 177 access cases on the basis of the content of the merits of each case without regard to the access question raised. As the data on the right side of Table 1 indicates, the political subscaling does not meet the standards for confirmation. . . . It is clear, though, that by political subscaling we do substantially improve the findings in the aggregate access scale. On the average, the political subscale CR is .929 and error reduction amounts to 33 percent. While we believe that the data support the assertion that the merits of an access case do play a role in determining access behavior, we cannot say that the political differentiation apparent here is sufficient to conclude that it is the primary factor motivating the Justices' votes.

• • •

VI

The results of this empirical investigation of Burger Court access behavior lead us to conclude that none of the hypothesized influences served as the controlling factor in explaining the access policy choices of the Court as a whole. However, we find that these three influences alone, and in combination, do operate to affect the choices of individual Justices and do so differently. More precisely in this regard the data show:

1. three Justices (Burger, Rehnquist, and Powell) willing (and ostensibly anxious) to close access, one of them (Burger) motivated by an overall access attitude, another (Rehnquist) motivated primarily by administrative/legal attitudes, and the third (Powell) motivated by an admixture of administrative legal attitudes and an overall access attitude;

2. three Justices (Stewart, Blackmun, and White) leaning generally toward access closure (but less so than Burger, Rehnquist, and Powell), one of them (Stewart) motivated by administrative/legal attitudes, with the remaining two by an admixture of administrative/legal and overall access attitudinal influences, and

3. three Justices (Marshall, Brennan, and Douglas) generally willing (with Douglas apparently anxious) to open access, one of them (Marshall) influenced by an admixture of administrative/legal attitudes and overall access attitude, and the remaining two by an admixture of administrative/legal and political attitudes.

As this delineation of individual access policy ought to make clear, it is little wonder that legal scholars have been bemoaning the obfuscatory nature of the Court's access policies. Given five quite distinct attitudinal orientations with varied behavior patterns emerging vis-à-vis each, it would be nothing short of miraculous if a coherent, clear-cut set of access policies were to emerge. While there may be an absence of coherence in the policy content, and an absence of congruity among members of the Court regarding the "why" of these access policy matters, there is no mistaking that the data show a general tendency and willingness on the part of those on the Court to close access to the federal courts, the ultimate implications of which must await further study.

45

The Supreme Court's Certiorari Jurisdiction: Cue Theory

Joseph Tanenhaus, Marvin Schick,
Matthew Muraskin, Daniel Rosen

• • •

The cue theory of certiorari maintains that the justices of the Supreme Court employ cues as a means of separating those petitions worthy of scrutiny from those that may be discarded without further study. If the theory is valid, it should follow that:

From Joseph Tanenhaus, Marvin Schick, Matthew Muraskin, and Daniel Rosen, "The Supreme Court's Certiorari Jurisdiction: Cue Theory," in *Judicial Decision-Making*, ed. Glendon A. Schubert (The Free Press of Glencoe, 1963), pp. 121–126, 126, 126–127, 127–130. Copyright © 1963 by The Free Press of Glencoe, a Division of The Macmillan Company. Reprinted by permission of Macmillan Publishing Co., Inc. Footnotes have been omitted.

Proposition I: Petitions that contain no cues will be denied.

Proposition II: Petitions that contain one or more cues will be studied carefully, and 25 to 43 per cent of them granted.

We estimate the percentage of petitions which contain cues and which are granted in the following manner. Previously cited statements by the members of the Court lead us to believe that 40 to 60 per cent of the appellate docket petitions have some merit, and therefore receive more or less careful attention. Since, furthermore, the Court grants the writ in 15 to 17 per cent of all appellate docket petitions, those granted should constitute from 25 per cent to 43 per cent of all meritorious certioraris.

It hardly needs to be said that we cannot expect to find the requirements of the cue theory completely fulfilled, if only because not all the hypothesized cues have been included in our analysis. But if we have accounted for most of the major cues, these requirements should be fairly well satisfied. At the very least we should find a sizable and statistically significant correlation between the presence of one or more cues and the granting of certiorari. Before this relationship can be measured, however, it is necessary to determine whether each of the several possible cues about which we have collected data can properly be regarded as a cue. One method of doing this is to take cases involving none of the hypothesized cues and compare them in turn with those cases containing a given cue but no other. If a given cue is present, the likelihood of certiorari should be greater (to a statistically significant degree) than when none of the cues is involved. Whenever this turns out in fact to be the case, we shall accept it as satisfactory evidence that the hypothesized cue does exist. Because the large number of petitions involved causes rather small differences to produce large chi squares, we have set the confidence level necessary to accept an hypothesis at 0.001.

The hypothesis concerning the several cues we wish to test may be stated as follows:

A. *Party as a Cue.* When the federal government seeks review, but no other cue is involved, the likelihood of certiorari is greater (to a statistically significant degree) than when other parties seek review and no other cue is involved.

B. *Dissension as a Cue.* When dissension has been indicated among the judges of the court immediately below, or between two or more courts and agencies in a given case, but no other cue is involved, the likelihood of certiorari is greater (to a statistically significant degree) than when no such dissension is present and no other cue is involved.

C. *Civil Liberties Issues as Cues.* When a civil liberties issue is present, but no other cue is involved, the likelihood of certiorari is greater (to a statistically significant degree) than when no civil liberties issue is present and no other cue is involved.

D. *Economic Issues as Cues.* When an economic issue is present, but no other cue is involved, the likelihood of review is greater (to a statistically significant degree) than when no economic issue is present and no other cue is involved.

We turn now to our reasons for selecting each of these hypotheses for testing, the procedures used in classifying the petitions, and the data we have developed.

Hypothesis A: Party as a Cue

This hypothesis finds some support in the literature. Frankfurter and Landis, in two of their early articles, observed that the Solicitor General speaks with special authority. They pointed out that during the 1929 and 1930 Terms the federal government was extremely successful in having certiorari granted when it was appellant and denied when it was respondent. More recently Justice Harlan and the authors of a law review note made similar observations.

There are several reasons why the position of the federal government may be regarded as an important cue. For one thing, many of the persons who prepare petitions for certiorari are sorely lacking in the required expertise. This is decidedly not the case with the Solicitor General's staff and the other government attorneys who practice before the Court. They have the talent, the resources, and the experience fully to exploit the strong aspects of their own cases, and in reply briefs to expose the most glaring weaknesses of their opponents. We do not mean to imply that government attorneys are grossly unfair in seeking or opposing writs of certiorari. In fact we place credence in the widely circulated gossip that when a clerk or justice wants to get to the nub of a complex case in a hurry he turns to the government's brief. Still, it is surely not invidious to suggest that government attorneys generally turn their assets to the government's advantage.

Another consequence of the government lawyers' expertise is its tendency to prevent them from deluging the Court with applications that they know the Court has no interest in reviewing.

Still another reason why the petitions for review submitted by the lawyers for the government tend to be meritorious is that only rarely are they under pressure to carry cases to the Court solely to satisfy a client who insists upon leaving no stone unturned in his search for vindication. Nor is the government lawyer tempted to pursue a case regardless of merit in the hope that he may gain the prestige of having argued once before the highest court in the land.

Finally, we suspect that the Court's deference for the opinions of the executive branch tends to make it especially solicitous of the government's judgment that particular cases do or do not warrant review.

TABLE 3.   Party as a Cue

	CERTIORARI GRANTED		CERTIORARI DENIED		TOTAL	
	N	Percentage	N	Percentage	N	Percentage
Federal Government Favored Certiorari;						
Cue Involved	8	47.1	9	52.9	17	100.0
No Cues Involved	39	5.8	637	94.2	676	100.0
Total:	47	6.8	646	93.2	693	100.0

$\phi = +0.25$ $x^2 = 44.72$ $P < 0.001$

The data used to test Hypothesis A appear in Table 3. We have included in the group of cases "federal government favors review" not only those in which the United States and its agencies and officials were petitioners, but also others if they clearly indicated that review should be granted—e.g., official declarations that review would not be opposed, and cases in which the federal government intervened on the side of the appellant. Cases involving the District of Columbia and the territories were not included unless a federal judge was a party. Cases dismissed for technical reasons, such as the petitioner withdrawing the case or mootness, and cases for which data on the parties were inadequate have been excluded from the analysis altogether.

The data reveal that when the federal government favored review and no other cue was involved the writ was issued 47.1 per cent of the time. On the other hand, when all other parties sought review, and no other cue was involved, only 5.8 per cent of the petitions were granted. Since these differences are statistically significant at the .001 level of confidence, Hypothesis A is confirmed. We accept these data as satisfactory evidence that party is a cue.

Hypothesis B: Dissension as a Cue

Hypothesis B was formulated to determine whether dissension may be regarded as a cue. By dissension we mean disagreement among the judges in the court immediately below (one or more concurring opinions, dissenting votes, or dissenting opinions) or disagreement between two or more courts and agencies in a given case. We have employed the term dissension rather than conflict to avoid any possible confusion between the concept we are testing and conflict in circuits. We have not sought to test conflict in circuits, not because we do not regard it as an important cue, but because there was no systematic way to assemble the

TABLE 4. Dissension as a Cue

	Certiorari Granted		Certiorari Denied		Total	
	N	Percentage	N	Percentage	N	Percentage
Dissension only cue present	37	12.8	253	87.2	290	100.0
No cues involved	39	5.8	637	94.2	676	100.0
Total:	76	7.9	890	92.1	966	100.0

$\phi = +0.12$ $x^2 = 13.69$ $P < 0.001$

necessary data without going to the certiorari papers themselves. And this we were not in a position to do.

The justification for deciding to test dissension as a cue was suggested by Chief Justice Vinson when he said: "Our discretionary jurisdiction encompasses, for the most part, only the borderline cases—those in which there is a conflict among the lower courts or widespread uncertainty regarding problems of national importance." When lower court judges and quasi-judicial administrators disagree strongly enough officially to reveal their differences, petitions for certiorari concerned with these disagreements are, we think, bound to be studied closely by the members of the highest appellate tribunal in the land. This feeling was buttressed by an examination of the certiorari cases decided with full opinion during the 1947–1958 Terms. At least 52 majority opinions during that period contained specific references to dissension within the court immediately below.

Table 4 contains the data used to test Hypothesis *B*. All appellate docket applications for certiorari were included, except the handful decided on the technical grounds referred to just above.

The data disclose that 12.8 per cent of the petitions in which dissension, but no other cue, was present were granted. As earlier noted, certiorari was granted in only 5.8 per cent of the petitions without any cue at all. While the phi coefficient shows that the correlation between the presence of dissension and the grant of certiorari is rather weak, these differences are significant at the .001 level of confidence, and Hypothesis *B* is confirmed. We accept these data as satisfactory evidence that dissension is a cue.

Hypotheses C and D: Civil Liberties and Economic Issues as Cues

Hypotheses *C* and *D* were formulated to determine whether certain types of subject matter can be regarded as cues. They will be considered together.

The supposition that subject matter is a major ingredient of what the Court refers to as "important" has been made so frequently that hypothesizing it as a cue needs no special justification. In fact, much data about subject matter appear in the literature. Petitions for certiorari granted and denied have been classified by subject matter by Frankfurter and his associates for the 1929–1938 Terms, by Harper for the 1952 Term, and by the editors of the *Harvard Law Review* for all terms since 1955.

We settled upon two subject matter groups (with four subcategories each) as the most likely to attract the interest of the justices when scanning the mountainous piles of certiorari papers. In the civil liberties group we included petitions pertaining to (1) alien deportation, (2) racial discrimination, (3) military justice, and (4) miscellaneous civil liberties. Our second group, economic issues, contains (5) labor, (6) regulation of economic life, (7) financial interest of the federal government, and (8) benefit and welfare legislation. Some of these categories are self-explanatory; others require a comment.

Miscellaneous civil liberties includes church-state relations, permits and licenses for the use of the streets and parks, postal and movie censorship, state and local censorship of reading matter, loyalty oaths, problems arising from the investigations of legislative committees, disbarment proceedings, regulation of occupations and professions, picketing, free speech, and right to work litigation. The financial interest of the federal government includes excise, gift, income, and excess profit tax cases, and government contract disputes in time of peace and war. The benefit and welfare category refers to litigation concerned with civil service rights, wage statutes, the Federal Employers Liability Act, seamen and longshoremen welfare legislation, servicemen's benefits, workmen's compensation, social security legislation, tort claims, agricultural benefit regulations, and unemployment insurance. About 1 per cent of the applications for certiorari could not be classified with satisfactory precision because insufficient data were available. These cases have been omitted from the analysis.

Table 5 contains the data used to test the civil liberties issue hypothesis (Hypothesis *C*). These data show that about one petition in every three containing a civil liberties cue, but no other, was granted. The differences between the treatment of petitions with civil liberties cues and petitions without any cues are significant at the 0.001 level of confidence. Hypothesis *C* is therefore confirmed, and we accept these data as satisfactory evidence that the presence of a civil liberties issue constitutes a cue.

The data used to test Hypothesis *D* (economic issue as a cue) appear in Table 6. As the contents of this table make clear, the likelihood of review when only an economic issue is present is not much greater than

TABLE 5.   Civil Liberties as a Cue

	Certiorari Granted		Certiorari Denied		Total	
	N	Percentage	N	Percentage	N	Percentage
Civil Liberties Issue						
Only Cue Present	57	32.9	116	67.1	173	100.0
No Cues Involved	39	5.8	637	94.2	676	100.0
Total:	96	11.3	753	88.7	849	100.0

$\phi = +0.35$ $x^2 = 101.46$ $P < 0.001$

when no cue at all is involved. The phi coefficient shows that the correlation between the presence of an economic issue and the grant of certiorari is only slightly positive. Nor can a chi square of the magnitude attained be regarded as impressive for an N of nearly 1400 cases. Hypothesis D is not confirmed, and we cannot regard the presence of an economic issue as a cue.

Now that we have determined that party, dissension, and civil liberties issues are cues we can return to the two propositions set forth [earlier.] . . . We . . . pointed out that if the cue theory were valid, it should follow that: *(Proposition I)* petitions which cointain no cue will be denied, and *(Proposition II)* petitions which contain one or more cues will be studied carefully and 25 to 43 per cent of them granted. Data giving some indication of the extent to which these propositions are satisfied by the data in our sample appear in Table 7.

Table 7 makes it quite evident that the requirements of *Proposition II* are satisfied. Of the petitions containing at least one cue, 27.5 per cent were granted. In addition, the petitions containing cues constituted 47.2 per cent of all appellate docket petitions. This falls within the estimate that 40 to 60 per cent of all appellate docket petitions contain some merit.

TABLE 6.   Economic Issue as a Cue

	Certiorari Granted		Certiorari Denied		Total	
	N	Percentage	N	Percentage	N	Percentage
Economic Issue Only						
Cue Present	59	8.5	637	91.5	696	100.0
No Cues Involved	39	5.8	637	94.2	676	100.0
Total:	98	7.1	1274	92.9	1372	100.0

$\phi = +0.05$ $x^2 = 4.11$ $0.05 < P < 0.01$

TABLE 7. Petitions Containing One or More Cues and Petitions Containing No Cue Compared

	CERTIORARI GRANTED		CERTIORARI DENIED		TOTAL	
	N	Percentage	N	Percentage	N	Percentage
One or More Cues	337	27.5	889	72.5	1226	100.0
No Cues	98	7.1	1274	92.9	1372	100.0
Total:	435	16.7	2163	83.3	2598	100.0

$\phi = +0.27$ $x^2 = 192.20$ $P < 0.001$

Proposition I is not fully supported, since 98 petitions containing no cues (7.1 per cent) were granted. But these 98 deviant cases do not in our judgment invalidate the cue theory, since all hypothesized cues have not been tested. Our judgment is reinforced by reading the opinions of the Court in those deviant cases decided with full opinion. In 19 instances the Court specifically pointed to a conflict in circuits, a cue we were unable to test. In one case, the Court pointed to dissents by intermediate appellate judges, and in another to the fact that the federal government did not oppose review. Still another case had civil liberties overtones which had been missed when the case was coded. More painstaking analysis would, we are convinced, still further reduce the number of deviant cases not readily accounted for by the cue theory.

We feel justified in concluding, therefore, that the cue theory of certiorari is valid.

As indicated [earlier,] . . . we had no theoretical or empirical bases for hypothesizing in advance of data processing about the interrelationships among the several cues and their usefulness as predictors of what the Court will do with sets of certiorari petitions containing given characteristics.

Insofar as the cue theory itself is concerned, the relative magnitude of the correlations between established cues and the grant or denial of certiorari (outcome) is of no particular consequence. All the cue theory requires is that the presence of a cue is enough to insure that a petition for certiorari will be studied with care. Hence, the presence of more than one cue, or for that matter the fact that one established cue may be more or less strongly correlated with outcome than another, will not alter the likelihood that a petition will be scrutinized. However, these relationships do have enough intrinsic interest to warrant analysis.

In testing Hypotheses *A, B,* and *C,* ϕ coefficients were computed and included in the appropriate tables. The correlation between outcome and party was +0.25, outcome and dissension +0.12, and outcome and civil liberties +0.35. But these correlations are not very adequate measures of the relationship between the individual cues and outcome because cases containing more than one cue were not taken into account. A more satis-factory method for determining the magnitude of the association between outcome and any given cue, when all other cues are held constant, is to compute the portion of the variance explained by each. The portion of the variance accounted for by a given cue is obtained by multiplying the coefficient of correlation between outcome and the cue by its standard partial regression (β) coefficient.

The β's were obtained by Doolittle's method and appear, together with the data necessary for their computation, in Table 8. Since only cases for which adequate information about all three cues were avail-able could be utilized, the number of cases used in this analysis was 2293.

As the data in Table 8 show, 7.4 per cent of the variance is explained by the party cue, 3.9 per cent by the civil liberties cue, and 2.4 per cent by the dissension cue. In our sample, therefore, party was relatively three times as important as dissension and almost twice as important as civil liberties in explaining outcome. Since the several contributions to the variance are additive, one may quickly determine the relative importance of the several cues in combination. For example, party alone was slightly more important than dissension and civil liberties combined, and all three cues taken together account for nearly twice as much of the vari-ance (13.7 per cent) as party taken alone.

However, these data on the percentage of the variance explained by

TABLE 8. Multiple Correlation and Regression Data

		x_1	x_2	x_3	x_4
	x_1	. . .	0.28	0.17	0.19
	x_2	0.28	. . .	0.16	−0.03
Intercorrelations					
	x_3	0.17	0.16	. . .	−0.06
	x_4	0.19	−0.03	−0.06	. . .
		x_1	x_2	x_3	x_4
M		0.176	0.076	0.401	0.116
σ		0.379	0.266	0.490	0.319

$\beta_2 = 0.264$ $B_2 = 0.375$ $A = 0.076$
$\beta_3 = 0.140$ $B_3 = 0.108$
$\beta_1 = 0.206$ $B_4 = 0.245$
$r^2 1.234 = 0.138$
$(\beta_2)(\phi 12) = 0.074$
$(\beta_3)(\phi 13) = 0.024$ $r1.234 = 0.37$
$(\beta_4)(\phi 14) = 0.039$
$x_1 = 0.375x_2 + 0.108x_3 + 0.245x_4 + 0.076$

LEGEND FOR VARIABLES
x_1 = Outcome (certiorari granted vs. certiorari denied)
x_2 = Party (federal government favored certiorari vs. other cases)
x_3 = Dissension
x_4 = Civil liberties issue

the three cues, independently and in combination, do not in themselves enable us to predict the likelihood of certiorari grants in sets of cases containing various assumed proportions of cues. Such predictions are made possible by solving the regression equation $x_1 = B_2 x_2 + B_3 x_3 + B_4 x_4 + A$, where outcome is the dependent variable (x_1) and the independent variables are party (x_2), dissension (x_3) and civil liberties issues (x_4). The equation and the data used in computing it appear in Table 8.

One can now substitute any set of means desired for the independent variables in the regression equation and solve for outcome. To illustrate, if in a given set of certiorari petitions the federal government sought review in 75 per cent, dissension was present in 50 per cent, and civil liberties issues were involved in 40 per cent, the following substitutions would be made:

$$x_1 = 0.375 \ (0.75) + (0.108) \ (0.50) + (0.245) \ (0.40) + 0.076.$$

Solving for outcome, $x_1 = 0.434$. Therefore, 43 per cent of the set of petitions will be granted.

Since our particular interest is to determine the predictive powers of the cues if every case in a set contains them in a given combination, we need to substitute 1.00 if we wish to include a cue and 0.00 if we wish to exclude it. For example, for a set in which every case contains all three cues, the following substitutions are made:

$$x_1 = (0.375) \ (1.00) + (0.108) \ (1.00) + (0.245) \ (1.00) + 0.076$$

Therefore, $x_1 = 0.804$, and 80 per cent of the petitions in the set will be granted. Similar substitutions provided the other results reported in Table 9.

We consider it important to re-emphasize that the relationships dis-

TABLE 9. Predicted Percentages of Certiorari Petitions That Will Be Granted When All Cases in a Set Contain Indicated Cues

	CUES		PREDICTED PERCENTAGE OF CERTIORARIS TO BE GRANTED
Party	Civil Liberties	Dissension	
+	+	+	80
+	+	0	70
+	0	+	56
+	0	0	45
0	+	+	43
0	+	0	32
0	0	+	18
0	0	0	7

LEGEND

0 = absence of a cue in all cases in set   + = presence of a cue in all cases in set

cussed in Section VII, unlike those in Sections IV-VI, were not hypothesized in advance of processing. As a result, we do not regard them as established, but only as useful bases for formulating hypotheses that need to be tested with fresh data.

Summary

Proceeding from assumptions based on what we consider to be established and relevant knowledge about the Supreme Court and its certiorari practice, we hypothesized the existence of a method of separating the petitions for certiorari requiring serious attention from those that are so frivolous as to be unworthy of careful study. We further hypothesized that a group of readily identifiable cues exists to serve this purpose. The presence of any one of these cues would warn a justice that a petition deserved scrutiny. If, on the other hand, no cue was present, a justice could safely discard a petition without further expenditure of time and energy. Careful study by a justice of the petitions containing cues could then be made to determine which should be denied because of jurisdictional defects, inadequacies in the records, lack of ripeness, tactical inadvisability, etc., and which should be allotted some of the limited time available for oral argument, research, and the preparation of full opinions. Those remaining could then be disposed of by denying certiorari, or by granting it and summarily affirming or reversing the courts below. This cluster of working hypotheses we labeled the cue theory.

Two propositions and four research hypotheses were developed to test the cue theory. Three of the hypotheses and both propositions were strongly enough supported by the data assembled to test them that we feel justified in considering the cue theory valid—at least until evidence is developed which casts doubt upon it.

––––––––––––––––––– 46 –––––––––––––––––––

Selecting Cases for
Supreme Court Review:
Litigant Status in the
Warren and Burger Courts

S. Sidney Ulmer

• • •

Commentators have often noted that political context is salient for
Supreme Court decision making in plenary cases. Less attention has been
devoted to the processes by which such plenary cases or issues are chosen
for consideration in the first place. Yet, no process in the Court is more
political than that by which policy issues are chosen for review and
resolution. That process is ultimately political because it is ultimately
discretionary; the Court grants jurisdiction to those seeking to overturn
lower court decisions if as many as four justices are of a mind to do so.
No reasons are required or given. Indeed, each justice may vote to grant
or deny plenary review for different and distinct reasons. And since,
theoretically, such votes are subject to any imaginable influence, the
context of the act is inevitably political.

The act of choice itself can be related to acts of a similar nature in
other decision-making arenas. Cobb and Elder (1972) characterize such
acts as "agenda building"—i.e., how the issues to be given serious consideration in a socio-political system are selected from all possible alternatives. Defining an issue as ". . . a conflict between two or more identifiable groups over procedural or substantive matters relating to the
distribution of positions or resources," they suggest that ". . . how an issue
comes to be on a formal agenda for authoritative decision making is a
crucial aspect of the overall governing process" (p. 13).

Conceptualizing case/issue selection in the Supreme Court as agenda
building, the author is presently engaged in a large scale study of the

––––––––––––––
From S. Sidney Ulmer, "Selecting Cases for Supreme Court Review: Litigant Status
in the Warren and Burger Courts" (Paper delivered at the Annual Meeting of the
American Political Science Association, Washington, D.C., September 1979), pp. 2–3,
3–10, 10–19, 20. Reprinted by permission of the American Political Science Association.
Footnotes and most references have been omitted.

processes by which items from the Court's Jurisdictional Agenda are selected for inclusion in the Court's Plenary Case Agenda. That effort is . . . being pursued within a theoretical framework which incorporates a number of possible influences on issue selection. In the present paper, we focus on one of these factors—the social status of the litigants petitioning or appealing for plenary review. Our orienting question is this: To what extent does variation in the status of litigants requesting plenary review explain variation in the Court's granting of such requests?

Earlier Work Related to the Inquiry

It is reasonable to ask why one might hypothesize such a relationship. Pritchett (1954) observed quite a while ago that in plenary cases certain Supreme Court justices were motivated by sympathy for underdog litigants. Howard (1968) has underscored the same point in reference to a single justice—Murphy—saying: "Justice Murphy just seemed incapable of voting against underdogs" (p. 341). Underdogs for Pritchett included aliens, racial and religious minorities, defendants in criminal trials, American Indians, common laborers, and the unpopular in general. Snyder (1956) established for the period 1921–1953 that, in plenary cases, litigants with "superior" social status received a far greater percentage of favorable opinions from the Court than did litigants with "inferior" status. Snyder's status scale ran from (1) the federal government and its agencies, to (2) state government and its agencies, to (3) local government and its agencies, to (4) corporations, to (5) labor unions, to (6) employees, individuals, minority group members, aliens, and criminal defendants. Her data consisted of over 10,000 Supreme Court opinions.

At the level of the individual justice, one might mention Justice Black's explanation for his vote to void the Alabama statute in *Cloverleaf Butter v. Patterson* (1942). According to Frankfurter, Black said that, when he was a boy, he worked in a grocery store and he learned that the poor people down there could only buy the kind of renovated butter that the statute barred. Assuming Frankfurter's allegation to be valid, it appears that Black was motivated more by the social (and economic) status of the poor than by the requirements of state or federal law.

Other studies (Ulmer, 1975; Canon, 1972; Tanenhaus, 1960) have shown that federal agencies get favorable treatment from the Court in plenary cases at a rate disproportionate to their case participation. This holds when the government is a direct party. It also holds when the government is participating as Amicus Curiae. Puro (1974) reports that in the period 1923–1973, the Solicitor General of the United States participated in 58 civil liberty cases as Amicus. In only eight of these cases was the Court's decision contrary to the position favored by the Government. In political cases, only 30 of 155 plenary decisions were disappointing to the government.

Given this picture at the level of plenary case decisions, it is not surprising that litigant status has been found to be associated with grant/deny patterns at the jurisdictional level. Tanenhaus (1963) and his associates established that when the federal government, a particularly high status litigant, requests plenary review, the chances the request will be honored are enhanced. More specifically, a regression analysis of cases involving civil liberty questions and dissension in the lower courts predicted a grant rate of 80% for government petitions as against a rate of 43% for non-government applicants. This finding was reaffirmed in a follow-up study controlling for cases that went to Conference and those decided without Conference attention (Ulmer, 1972). Another study of fifteen Supreme Court justices revealed that "federal government as petitioning party" explained a significant proportion of the variance in jurisdictional decisions for nine (Ulmer, 1973).

More recent research points in the same general direction. Provine (1978) reports that in the period 1947–57, the Court agreed to review 66% of the cases in which the federal government was the petitioning party. In cases in which the federal government was the respondent, however, plenary review was granted only 15% of the time. In a study published last September, it was found that liberal justices tend to favor Underdogs and conservatives Upperdogs in selecting cases for plenary review (Ulmer, 1978). And in a paper presented at the 1979 Annual Meeting of the Midwest Political Science Association, it was reported that the Supreme Court is much more likely to transform or operate on the issues presented for review by Underdogs than on those posed by Upperdogs (Ulmer, 1979). A particular finding of interest in that study was that in making jurisdictional decisions the Court frequently transformed issues posited by Underdogs. At the same time it left *all* issues posed by the federal government intact.

Theoretical Considerations

There are also sound theoretical reasons why the Court might favor high status over low status litigants in making both plenary and jurisdictional decisions. These reasons are related to avoidance of undue system stress. The principle cause of stress in a political system is inadequate support for the system and its institutions. Support—Easton (1965) tell us—is the "major variable linking a system to its environment" (p. 165). Without support, *authorities* cannot process demands into outputs, *regimes* cannot maintain stability in rules and structures, and the *politi-*

cal community cannot maintain the necessary cohesion within its membership.

A major function performed by the Supreme Court is to process demands in such a way as to promote solidarity around these political objects of authority, regime, and political community. We postulate that the Court selects demands/issues with its major system function in mind and consciously attempts to keep system stress at some acceptable level. We think system stress likely to be exacerbated when the Court inadequately responds to the demands/needs of high status system members For it is precisely such "elites" who can cause serious erosion in support for the Court. And while the "needs" of such elites may be met via appropriate rulings in plenary cases, such rulings cannot be forthcoming if high status litigants are unsuccessful in placing their issues on the Plenary Case Agenda in the first place.

We do not imply, of course, that litigant status is the only or primary consideration in determining the Court's choices. We do suggest that such a factor is an important element in the selection process.

Questions to Be Addressed

While earlier work in this area is provocative and important, it does not address the questions we wish to evaluate here. The earlier research rests heavily on data drawn from the pre-1960 terms of the Court and much of it has dealt with individual justices rather than with the Court as an institution. But, be that as it may, the earlier work informs and stimulates the specific inquiries we shall make in this paper. Those inquiries are:

1. Does the Court differentiate Underdogs and Upperdogs in granting and denying jurisdiction to those who request it?
2. If differentiation is discovered, is the Court consistent in regard to direction of differentiation?
3. If differentiation is discovered, are any trends in Court behavior across time observed?

The Data Base

These questions will be evaluated with data drawn essentially from post-1960 terms. Specifically, the cases to be used represent a 5 to 10% sample of "paid" cases on the Court's Jurisdictional Agenda in the 1954, 1961, 1968, 1971, 1973, and 1975 terms. Unpaid or In Forma Pauperis cases are excluded.

Variation in the sample size for paid cases results from the conditions imposed on the data in the larger study from which the cases are drawn. We are collecting data on jurisdictional decision making for the thirty Court terms—1946–1975. A 5% sample is being drawn from each of these terms. Where certain key characteristics are not adequately represented in any given term, the sample is increased in size up to 10%. The particular Court terms chosen for analysis in this paper were determined by (1) the availability of the data and (2) a desire to represent the Warren and Burger Courts adequately in the data set.

For present purposes, Underdogs are conceptualized as having less socio-political power (status) than Upperdogs. We include aliens, criminal defendants, minority group members, labor unions, employees, and individuals in the Underdog classification. Upperdogs, on the other hand, are defined as federal, state, and local governments or their agencies, and business corporations. This follows the format employed in my 1978 study which was adapted from the work of Snyder (1956) and Pritchett (1954).

Data Analysis

The Basic Relationship

In our data base, we have identified 1,061 instances in which Underdogs confronted Upperdogs as petitioners/appellants for review or as respondents opposing such applications. In 358 instances in which the petitioning/appealing party was an Upperdog, plenary review was granted 279 times—a rate of 78%. Underdogs, on the other hand were successful in their applications 331 times in 703 opportunities—a rate of only 47%. The raw data is arrayed in Table I:

TABLE I. Petitioner/Appellant

	UPPERDOG	UNDERDOG
Review Granted	279	331
Review Denied	79	372

The Gamma for this table is .597. This can be interpreted to mean that there is 60% greater agreement than disagreement in the rankings on our two variables. Or that 60% of the variation in jurisdictional decisions can be accounted for by variation in Dogclass. This degree of association is statistically significant at better than .001. Our initial inference, therefore, is that our first question must be answered in the affirmative. The Court does distinguish Underdogs and Upperdogs in making its jurisdictional decisions.

It is entirely possible that the association we have portrayed is weaker or stronger than indicated or is being affected by other influences on the Court. To explore that possibility we have identified four control variables, as follows: (1) dissension in the lower courts—defined as disagreement across courts or within the collegial court immediately below, (2) the presence or absence of a constitutional issue, (3) the presence or absence of a criminal law issue, and (4) the level of the court immediately below—i.e., state or federal court. Dissension below as a meaningful variable in jurisdictional decision making was reported in 1963 by Tanenhaus. Given that the time of the Court is severely limited and its primary responsibility is to interpret the Constitution, one may surmise that Constitutional issues are more likely to receive plenary review than non-constitutional issues. Since the enforcement of criminal law is primarily a function of the states and state courts, one might expect a higher incidence of review in non-criminal cases—at least in so far as the paid cases are concerned. As for court level, higher prestige federal court decisions should be less likely to be reviewed than lower prestige state court decisions. By controlling for criminal law, we are controlling largely for what political scientists frequently identify as "Civil Liberty Issues."

The Basic Relationship Under Controlled Conditions

The first order partial gamma has been calculated for the relationship between Dogclass and Jurisdictional Decisions—holding each intervening variable constant in turn. The results have no appreciable effect on the primary association. The zero order gamma, it may be recalled, is .597. The first order partial for Court Level is slightly higher (.609). Controlling for Constitutional Issue, the partial is exactly .597. It is slightly lower when Dissension and Criminal Law are controlled—.552 and .555 respectively. It may be that the control variables taken collectively have an impact that is masked when taken one at the time. The fourth order partial gamma turns out to be .480—11 percentage points below the zero order gamma. Thus, some impact is evident. Nevertheless, there is still 48% greater agreement than disagreement in the rankings on our two primary variables. In response to our first question, therefore, we continue to infer that the Court differentiates between Underdogs and Upperdogs in making its jurisdictional decisions.

Possible Explanations

What is the explanation for the results reported? It has been argued in the literature (Pritchett, 1954; Ulmer, 1978) that sympathy for Underdogs—or variation on that dimension—accounts to some extent for the support given certain litigants by certain justices. We have suggested in this paper that servicing the system requires the Court to pay heed to status differentials. A third view is that differences in the quality of the legal work reflected in review applications influences the selection of cases and issues by the Court. A related argument (Provine, 1978) is that litigants differ in their capacity to deduce review criteria.

• • •

Applying such thinking to jurisdictional decision making, one might expect litigants with financial and other resources to employ better legal talent. Superior talent should be able to fathom review criteria and to present a stronger case for review than litigants lacking superior legal assistance. This assumes, of course, that fathomable criteria exist and can be identified given sufficient analytical skills. After studying jurisdictional decision making across a decade, Provine (1978) asserts that "those interested in decision criteria can only guess at why the Court chooses most of the cases it does for decision on the merits" (p. 56). My own work over the past eight years convinces me that if decisional criteria exist, they have not yet been fathomed to a sufficient degree— though this is not to say that they cannot be nor that no progress has been made. Clearly the court has no strong wish to have criteria clearly understood by litigants seeking review. Such an inference is forced by the failure of the institution to take any action designed to reduce the guesswork for litigating parties. And, as Provine points out, the Court has not deigned to penalize those who waste its time with frivolous applications.

In spite of such comments, the quality of application argument requires some assessment. It has inherent plausibility for those not overly familiar with research in this area. It can be used to disarm critics who might suggest that the Court is using decision criteria of an unacceptable nature. Moreover, it is an alternative explanation to the one suggested in this paper—that the Court favors Upperdog litigants for system maintenance reasons. The question, conveniently, can be explored in the context of our second inquiry: How consistent has the Court been in differentiating Underdogs and Upperdogs in making its jurisdictional decisions?

Consistency in the Court

Upperdogs have been favored over Underdogs in the period 1954–1975 taken in the aggregate. Perfect consistency would imply that the same pattern of differentiation manifests itself across the Warren and Burger

TABLE II.   Petitioner/Appellant

	UPPERDOG	UNDERDOG
Review Granted	48	184
Review Denied	34	151

Warren Court

Courts as well as in each of the six terms represented in our data set. And if quality of application is responsible for litigant differentiation, Upperdogs should be favored substantially over Underdogs in any particular segment of the data.

Of the 1,750 cases in our sample, 730 were acted on during the Warren Court terms, 1954, 1961, and 1968. The remaining 1,020 cases were decided in the Burger Court era, 1971, 1973, and 1975. In the Warren period, 417 confrontations between Underdogs and Upperdogs were identified. For the Burger period, confrontations numbered 616. The success rate for Upperdog applicants in the Warren Court was 59%. In the Burger Court that rate jumped to 83%. Underdogs, on the other hand, succeeded as petitioners or appellants 55% of the time in the Warren Court but only 39% of the time in the Burger period. The raw data for the Warren era is presented in Table II.

The zero order gamma for this table is .073. Thus, there is only 7% greater agreement than disagreement in rankings assigned our two variables—and the association is not statistically significant.

Table III arrays the data for the Burger Court.

The Gamma for Table III is .77. It measures an association that is highly significant in the statistical sense. It is also an unusually strong relationship since approximately 77% of the variation in decisional outcome is accounted for by litigant status. In comparing Tables II and III, we infer that while the Burger Court differentiated Upperdogs and Underdogs in making it's jurisdictional decisions, the Warren Court did not. The differentiation identified when looking at both Courts combined, then, is due primarily to that associated with the Burger terms.

In response to our second inquiry—the two Courts have not been consistent in differentiating Upperdogs and Underdogs. That being the case, consistency in the direction of differentiation is moot.

TABLE III.   Petitioner/Appellant

	UPPERDOG	UNDERDOG
Review Granted	212	142
Review Denied	43	219

Burger Court

The results portrayed in Tables II and III also enable us to assess the "quality of application" hypothesis. Assume the following:

1. the quality of applications for review is higher for Upperdog than for Underdog applicants.
2. Qualitative disparities in applications are constant over time.
3. Qualitative variation in applications accounts for the variation observed in jurisdictional decisions.

Then, Ceteris Paribus, differentiation should occur in both Courts and in favor of the Upperdog. That it does not is evidence tending to refute the claim that differentiation is a function of superior legal talent or other resources employed by Upperdogs as reflected in the quality of Upperdog presentations to the Court. This is not to say that such considerations have no impact. But the qualitative disparity generalization is too simple an explanation for a complex question—particularly in view of the fact that no one has established that "quality of presentation" has any systematic consequence for jurisdictional decision making.

Approaching the question of consistency from the standpoint of Court terms, we find that the Warren Court was inconsistent across the three terms studied. It differentiated Upperdogs and Underdogs in only two of the terms (1961 the exception). Moreover, the Warren Court differentiated petitioners in favor of Underdogs only in the first of the three terms. The Burger Court, however, differentiated applicants in all three terms and always in favor of the Upperdog petitioner or appellant. Table IV arrays the appropriate data.

The Gammas reported in Table IV reflect differentiation between Upperdog and Underdog applicants in 5 of 6 terms. And the Court has consistently differentiated such applicants in the last four terms in our data set. However, a controlled analysis may change the picture. Table V summarizes such an analysis for the Warren Court period, by Court and by term.

As reflected in the aggregate analysis, the Warren Court did not dif-

TABLE IV.

TERM	GRANTS AS % OF APPLICATIONS		ZERO ORDER GAMMA
	Upperdogs	Underdogs	
1954	21%	56%	−.650
1961	57	52	.089
1968	78	56	.382
1971	77	40	.665
1973	82	38	.746
1975	88	40	.853

TABLE V.   Controlled Analysis: The Warren Court

VARIABLE CONTROLLED	TERM	FIRST ORDER PARTIAL G	FOURTH ORDER PARTIAL G	ZERO ORDER PARTIAL G
Const. Issue	1954	−.699		−.649
	1961	.155		.089
	1968	.376		.387
Court Level	1954	−.659		−.649
	1961	.279		.089
	1968	.238		.381
Dissension	1954	−.685		−.649
	1961	−.134		.089
	1968	.457		.387
Criminal Law	1954	−.723		−.649
	1961	.072		.089
	1968	.386		.387
All	1954		−.680	−.649
	1961		.075	.089
	1968		.245	.381
Const. Issue	1954–1968	.019		.048
Court Level	1954–1968	.035		.044
Dissension	1954–1968	−.003		.048
Criminal Law	1954–1968	.021		.048
All	1954–1968		−.051	.048

ferentiate Upperdogs and Underdogs in the 1961 term. The first order and fourth order partial Gammas underscore that point. The Warren Court did distinguish these litigant classes in the 1954 term. The partial Gammas are 10 to 50 points higher than the zero order Gamma in each instance. Thus, the inference of differentiation for that term is justified. We also infer differentiation in the 1968 term since the fourth order partial shows that the prediction of concordant and discordant pairings can be improved by 25% given knowledge of Dogclass. This is equivalent to saying that 25% of the variation in jurisdictional decisions can be accounted for by variation in litigant status. While this figure does not compare well with the extremely high statistic of 65% reached in the 1954 term, it is nevertheless substantial. As for the Warren Court across all three terms combined, the controlled analysis continues to show that the Court did not exhibit differentiation in this period—a result directly attributable to performance in the 1961 term.

In Table VI, we present the results of the controlled analysis for the Burger Court. Here the picture is striking indeed. All analyses show that the Burger Court differentiated Upperdogs and Underdogs in each term and across all terms combined. For all three terms collectively, the

TABLE VI.   Controlled Analysis: The Burger Court

VARIABLE CONTROLLED	TERM	FIRST ORDER PARTIAL G	FOURTH ORDER PARTIAL G	ZERO ORDER PARTIAL G
Const. Issue	1971	.674		.664
	1973	.740		.746
	1975	.841		.843
Court Level	1971	.667		.659
	1973	.775		.749
	1975	.846		.850
Dissension	1971	.599		.659
	1973	.725		.753
	1975	.815		.840
Criminal Law	1971	.645		.659
	1973	.724		.753
	1975	.789		.840
All	1971		.590	.664
	1973		.719	.746
	1975		.710	.853
Const. Issue	1971–1975	.781		.779
Court Level	1971–1975	.791		.782
Dissension	1971–1975	.748		.778
Criminal Law	1971–1975	.743		.778
All	1971–1975		.713	.784

reduction in predictive error is 71.3%. For the individual terms, the reductions range from 59 to 71%. Such strong associations are rarely exhibited in research on judicial variables.

Comparing Tables V and VI, we see that the control variable with the greatest impact on the two Courts is Court Level (1968 term) and Dissension (1971 term) respectively. But the drop in the Burger term is less than in the Warren term. Indeed, the differences among the zero, first order, and fourth order partials in the Burger Court are relatively miniscule across the board. This serves to strengthen our initial inference that litigant status is a telling factor for the making of jurisdictional decisions in the Burger Court.

Trends in Differentiation

Since 1954, the Court has exhibited an increasing skew in favor of Upperdogs. Thus, support for Upperdog applications increased from 21% in 1954 to 88% in 1975. Underdog applications were accepted at a fairly steady rate of 55% in the Warren period and at an equally stable but lower rate of about 40% in the Burger terms.

The ability of the Warren Court to steadily increase the percentage of grants to Upperdogs while continuing to accept about 55% of the applications forwarded by Underdogs implies either a drop in the number of petitions coming to the Court or a willingness to accept more paid cases for the plenary case agenda. Investigation of this matter shows that Upperdog petitions did not decrease across the three terms. Indeed, they increased 110% between 1954 and 1968. Underdog applications also increased 47% in the same period. Thus, the Court apparently decided to accept more paid cases for plenary review. The Burger Court also saw more Upperdog cases. Upperdog applications increased 101% between 1971 and 1975. While this was occurring, Underdog cases on the paid docket declined 8.5%. Whether these variations indicate that both Courts took on more or less work can be determined by looking at cases granted plenary consideration on the unpaid docket.

While the Warren Court maintained its support for paid Underdog applications between 1954 and 1968, it also increased the percentage of grants to unpaid Underdogs about one third. In the Burger Court, on the other hand, while Underdog grants as a percentage of paid Underdog applications remained the same between 1971 and 1975, the percentage of Underdog grants from the unpaid docket declined almost by half. Thus, change in the level of grants to Upperdogs in the Warren period was made at slight or no cost to Underdogs. That associated with the Burger period, however, was made at substantial cost to Underdog litigants.

Subjected to controls, a trend is observed in the Gammas beginning with the 1961 term. For the five succeeding terms, the fourth order partial Gammas went from .075 to .245 to .590 to .719 to .710. This is not quite as striking as the progression revealed in Table IV. Nevertheless, there is no question that from the later stages of the Warren era to the present, Upperdog applicants for plenary review have fared better and better on the paid case docket.

Summary and Conclusions

In general, we conclude that in making jurisdictional decisions, the Supreme Court tends to differentiate Upperdog and Underdog applicants for plenary review. Comparing the Warren and Burger Courts, this generalization did not hold. But the failure of the Warren Court to reflect differentiation was due to the actions taken in the 1961 term alone. Looking at each of six terms studied, we found differentiation in five of the six. Thus, the 1961 term may be viewed as an exception to the generalization.

As to direction of differentiation, we infer that in making jurisdictional decisions, the Court—in some periods—consistently differentiates in favor of the same litigant class. This qualified inference is due to the fact that while the Burger Court differentiated in favor of Upperdogs in each of its three terms, the Warren Court differentiated once in favor of Upperdogs, once in favor of Underdogs and in one term did not differentiate at all. Beginning with the 1961 term, however, a trend toward greater and greater support for Upperdog applicants is clearly evident.

• • •

As for alternative explanations—what can be said at this point? First of all, at the level of the Court, the "sympathy for the Underdog" argument seems to have no validity in recent years. This is evidenced by the fact that not since 1954 has the Court differentiated applications for plenary review in favor of Underdog applicants. This may be a little surprising given the reputation of the Warren Court as a great protector of Underdog interests. But the data do not lie. It may be said, of course, that the explanation for differentiation is "sympathy for the Upperdog." But somehow that theory seems less appealing than the theory of "system servicing" via catering to the needs of Upperdog applicants.

• • •

The "quality of presentation" argument has been damaged by the failure of Upperdogs to gain differentiation in their favor in two of the six terms studied. But it has not finally been put to rest. To assess the hypothesis adequately will require an analysis of the association between quality of presentation, directly measured, and grant/deny rates.

References

Books and Articles

ADAMANY, DAVID (1973). "Legitimacy, Realigning Elections, and the Supreme Court." *Wisconsin Law Review*, pp. 780–846.

ATKINS, BURTON (1976) and H. R. Glick. "Environmental and Structural Variables As Determinants of Issues in State Courts of Last Resort." *American Journal of Political Science* 20: 97–115.

BAUM, LAWRENCE (1975). "The Judicial Gatekeeping Function: A General Analysis." In Sheldon Goldman and Austin Sarat (eds.), *American Court Systems.* San Francisco: W. H. Freeman and Co., pp. 125–129.

BICKEL, ALEXANDER (1962). *The Least Dangerous Branch.* Indianapolis: The Bobbs-Merrill Co.

CANON, BRADLEY C. and M. GILES (1972). "Recurring Litigants: Federal Agencies Before the Supreme Court." *Western Political Quarterly* 25: 183–191.

CANON, BRADLEY C. and S. SIDNEY ULMER (1976). "The Supreme Court and Critical Elections: A Dissent." *American Political Science Review* 70:1218–1221.

CASPER, JONATHAN D. (1976). "The Supreme Court and National Policy Making." *American Political Science Review* 70: 50–63.

COBB, ROGER W. and C. D. ELDER (1972). *Participation in American Politics: The Dynamics of Agenda Building.* Boston: Allyn & Bacon.

COOK, BEVERLY B. (1977). "Public Opinion and Federal Judicial Policy." *American Journal of Political Science* 21: 567–600.

DAHL, ROBERT A. (1967). *Pluralist Democracy in the United States.* Chicago: Rand-McNally, pp. 155–164.

EASTON, DAVID (1965). *A Systems Analysis of Political Life.* Chicago: Wiley & Sons.

FUNSTON, RICHARD Y. (1975). "The Supreme Court and Critical Elections." *American Political Science Review* 69: 795–811.

GROSSMAN, JOEL and A. SARAT (1975). "Litigation in the Federal Courts: A Comparative Perspective." *Law and Society Review* 9: 321–346.

HOROWITZ, D. (1977). *The Courts and Social Policy.* Washington: The Brookings Institution.

HOWARD, J. WOODFORD (1968). *Mr. Justice Murphy.* Princeton: Princeton University Press.

KIRKPATRICK, SAMUEL A. (1974). *Quantitative Analysis of Political Data.* Columbus: Charles E. Merrill.

KRISLOV, SAMUEL (1965). *The Supreme Court in the Political Process.* New York: Macmillan.

MURPHY, WALTER (1977). "The Judicial Process and Judicial Papers: of Privilege, Prospect, Accountability, and Understanding" (Unpublished).

PRITCHETT, C. HERMAN (1954). *Civil Liberties and the Vinson Court.* Chicago: University of Chicago Press.

—— (1968). "Public Law and Judicial Behavior." *Journal of Politics* 30: 480–509.

PROVINE, DAVIS MARIE LONG (1978). "Case Selection in the United States Supreme Court" (Ph.D. Dissertation, Cornell University).

PURO, STEVEN (1974). "The United States As Amicus in the U.S. Supreme Court" (Unpublished paper).

SNYDER, ELOISE (1956). "A Quantitative Analysis of Supreme Court Opinions from 1921–1953: A Study of the Responses of an Institution Engaged in Resolving Social Conflict" (Ph.D. Dissertation, Pennsylvania State University), pp. 34–38.

TANENHAUS, JOSEPH (1960). "Supreme Court Attitudes Toward Federal Administrative Agencies." *Journal of Politics* 22: 502–24.

TANENHAUS, JOSEPH, M. SCHICK, M. MURASKIN, D. ROSEN (1963). "The Supreme Court's Certiorari Jurisdiction: Cue Theory." In G. Schubert (ed.), *Judicial Decision Making.* Glencoe: The Free Press, pp. 111–132.

ULMER, S. SIDNEY, L. KIRKLOSKY, W. HINTZ (1972). "The Decision to Grant or
Deny Certiorari: Further Considerations of Cue Theory." *Law and Society
Review* 6: 637–43.

—— (1973). "Revising the Jurisdiction of the Supreme Court: Mere Administrative Reform or Substantive Policy Change." *Minnesota Law Review*
58: 121–155.

—— and J. STOOKEY (1975). "Nixon's Legacy to the Supreme Court: A Statistical Analysis." *Florida State Law Review* 3: 331–47.

—— (1978). "Selecting Cases for Supreme Court Review: An Underdog
Model." *American Political Science Review* 72: 902–910.

—— (1979). "Issue Fluidity in the U.S. Supreme Court: An Exploration in
Agenda Building" (Paper presented at the Annual Meeting of the Midwest
Political Science Association, Chicago, Illinois, April 18–21, 1979).

WASBY, STEPHEN L. (1978). *The Supreme Court in the Federal Judicial System.*
New York: Holt, Rinehart and Winston.

—— (1979). "Accountability of the Courts." In Scott Greer (ed.), *Accountability in Urban Society: Public Agencies Under Fire.* Beverly Hills, CA: Sage
Publishing Co., pp. 143–168.

Cases

Cloverleaf Butter Co. v. *Patterson,* 315 U.S. 148 (1942).

——————————— 47 ———————————

The New Certiorari Game

Saul Brenner

Twenty years ago political scientist Glendon Schubert introduced the
Certiorari Game. Schubert examined the Federal Employees' Liability
evidentiary cases from 1942 to 1948 terms of the Supreme Court. He
found that a bloc of four justices (Black, Douglas, Murphy, Rutledge), by
voting for certiorari when the Court of Appeals had reversed a District

From Saul Brenner, "The New Certiorari Game," *Journal of Politics* 41 (1979):
649–655. Reprinted by permission. Footnotes have been omitted.

Court decision favoring the railroad workers, were successful 92% of the time in securing a decision of the Court in support of the workers. A limitation of Schubert's research is that it is not based upon the actual certiorari voting. Rather, Schubert inferred how the justices voted on cert mainly by looking at how they voted on the final vote on the merits. It would be better, of course, to investigate the success of the justices voting to grant certiorari by inspecting the cert vote as well. The cert voting has already been used to show significant relationships between the vote on certiorari and the final on the merits. It has not, however, been employed to demonstrate or to suggest that Supreme Court justices calculate the possible costs and benefits to themselves prior to deciding how to vote on certiorari.

In presenting his certiorari game Schubert made the right decision in focusing upon certiorari voting by four justices, for when there are four and only four votes for certiorari, the vote of each and every justice is necessary for cert to be granted, but even if all four justices seek the same result their votes would be insufficient to control the decision of the Court. In other words, Schubert had identified a situation in which those who voted for certiorari had an incentive to determine if their vote for cert would further their goals. Recently a reporter covering the Court noted that the liberal justices on the Burger Court often voted to deny cert even though they opposed the decision of the lower court because they feared that that decision would be affirmed by the more authoritative Supreme Court. Justices who vote to grant cert, when there are four votes for cert, can be perceived as gamblers both in the game theory and literal meaning of that term. Instead of accepting the decision of the court below (the intermediate position) these justices wager that their most preferred position will prevail at the risk that their least preferred position will win.

Hypotheses

When does it pay for these justices to gamble? Two factors are relevant: (1) the possible advantages and disadvantages to them of the Court's deciding the case on the merits (or, in other words, the odds) and, (2) the probability that the disposition they favor will triumph. If the four justices who vote to grant cert are rational decision-makers they will estimate the odds and their chances of winning prior to voting for certiorari. Justices can be expected to calculate with a high degree of accuracy for they have the motivation, ability, and opportunity to do so.

It cannot be anticipated, however, that these justices will achieve the same measure of success under all conditions. Justices who want the Court to affirm the decision below have much less to gain and much more to lose than justices who seek a reversal of the lower court's decision. At best, the justices who desire that the Court affirm can obtain a decision in agreement with their position at a higher and more authoritative level. At worst, their choice will be overturned. For justices who seek a reversal, on the other hand, the odds are very different. They may secure a reversal at the possible cost of the lower court's decision being affirmed by the more authoritative Supreme Court. Since the possible benefits and losses differ, different rates of success can be expected. Thus, it can be hypothesized:

H_1:   When there are four votes for certiorari, justices who vote for cert and want the Court to affirm will have a higher success rate than justices who vote for cert and wish that the Court reverses.

There is a possible rival explanation for the greater success potential of the justices who want the Court to affirm: they supply a greater number of votes for certiorari. If, for example, in a particular case three justices wish that the Court affirms and one justice seeks a reversal, the three are more likely to win because their votes will contribute to their own success. To control for this explanation, it is necessary to break down the data concerning the above hypothesis on the basis of the number of justices who support a particular outcome.

In addition, it is possible that justices who want the Court to affirm will be more successful because justices who fail to vote for certiorari tend to agree with the decision of the court below. To control for this explanation one ought to compare the success rates of the justices who vote for cert when there are four votes for cert with the success rates of the justices who vote to grant cert when there are more than four votes for cert but no group of pro-cert justices controls the final vote on the merits. The latter occurs, for example, when five justices vote for cert, three of whom want the Court to affirm and two want it to reverse. It can be expected that justices will be more successful when their votes are needed to grant cert (i.e., when there are four votes for cert) than when they lack such control. In the latter circumstance an individual justice has little incentive to calculate the odds and his chances of winning, for certiorari will be granted whether he votes for it or not. Thus:

H_2:   Justices who vote for cert when there are four votes for cert will have a higher success rate than justices who vote for cert when there are more than four votes for cert but no group of justices of those who vote to grant cert controls the final vote on the merits.

Data and Methods

For the purposes of this study the goals of the justices at the cert vote will be inferred by inspecting how they voted at the original vote on the merits. At times, of course, justices will have different aims at the original vote on the merits than they had at the cert vote. Indeed, it is possible that some justices usually vote to grant cert not because they seek a particular Court disposition, but because they believe that the Court ought to hear and decide the case. But most justices on most occasions vote to grant certiorari mainly because they desire a particular outcome. And the best evidence of the result they favor at cert is their vote at the original vote on the merits, for there is no systematic data as to the outcomes favored by the justices at the cert stage.

Data was obtained as to the certiorari vote and as to the original vote on the merits from Justice Harold Burton's docket books. Justice Burton was on the Court during the 1945 to 1957 terms. It is possible that Burton misrecorded some of these votes, but there is no alternative to using private papers as the source of this information for there is no official or unofficial publication of these votes. The final vote on the merits was recorded by Burton as well, but the *U.S. Reports* was used instead because it is likely to be more accurate.

The votes of the justices were obtained for all non-per curiam cases of the 1946, 1947, 1949, 1950, 1954, and 1955 terms of the Court. The terms selected were the first two terms of all three "natural" courts in the 1945–58 period which lasted more than one year. A natural court is a court in which only a given nine justices sit. The natural court was chosen so that the same justices would be voting in all three votes. Since the 1954 and 1955 Court was of two years duration, a two-year period for the other natural courts was selected as well. Only those cases in which all three votes were cast in the two-year period in question were included. There were 213 votes and 87 cases in the data set when there were four votes to grant certiorari and 361 votes and 129 cases when there were more than four votes but no group of justices of those who voted for certiorari controlled the vote on the merits.

Findings and Conclusion

It was stated in the first hypothesis that when there were four votes for cert, the justices who wanted the Court to affirm would be more successful in obtaining the outcome they desired than the justices who wanted the Court to reverse. The results, set forth in Table 1 below, clearly and unambiguously support this hypothesis.

But support for this hypothesis is insufficient to show that the four justices were calculating utilities prior to voting to grant certiorari. It had to be demonstrated, in addition, that justices who controlled the cert vote would be more successful than justices who lacked such control. This second hypothesis was confirmed when the justices wished the Court to affirm. Indeed, the differences between the two rates of success

TABLE 1. Success Rates of Justices Vote for Cert Under Various Conditions

OUTCOME DESIRED	4 VOTES FOR CERT No. of Justices Who Sought the Outcome				MORE THAN 4 VOTES FOR CERT No. of Justices Who Sought the Outcome			
	1	2	3	4	1	2	3	4
Affirm	N* 43% (14)	N* 83% (12)	N* 100% (8)	N* 100% (3)	N* 5% (20)	N* 42% (12)	N* 60% (15)	N* 80% (15)
Reverse	0% (6)	28% (14)	47% (15)	73% (15)	0% (5)	20% (10)	48% (21)	87% (31)

* N of cases   N = 87   N = 129

To test for significance Fisher's exact test was used. The results were as follows:

4 VOTES FOR CERT (AFFIRM v REVERSE)

1	2	3	4
Significant at .077 Level	Significant at .007 Level	Significant at .013 Level	*

4 VOTES FOR CERT v MORE THAN 4 VOTES FOR CERT

	1	2	3	4
Affirm	Significant at .012 Level	Significant at .045 Level	Significant at .017 Level	*
Reverse	*	*	*	*

* Not significant

when the justices wanted the Court to affirm are dramatic. (see Table 1) No support for this hypothesis was found, however, when the justices sought a reversal of the decision below, for the differences in the success rates between the four votes for cert and the greater than four votes situations are not significant. (see Table 1)

Why it is that justices who seek a reversal are no more successful when they control the cert vote than when they lack such control? Why don't they take advantage of their dominance of this vote to vote for cert only when their chances of winning are very high? Perhaps, the odds are so favorable to these justices (i.e., they have so much to gain and so little to lose) that it is not worth their time and effort to calculate their chances of winning. With a heavy caseload and with the Court reversing in two out of three cases during most of the period of this study, this failure to calculate can be perceived as rational.

The behavior of the justices who want the Court to affirm in the four votes for cert situation can be explained even more easily. Because of the poor odds these justices tend to vote for cert only when they believe that they have an excellent chance of winning. Their high success rate, then, can be interpreted as a consequence of their accurate calculation. These justices can justifiably be perceived as skillful players in the new certiorari game.

PART IV

Deciding the Issues in Plenary Cases

The U.S. Supreme Court makes many different kinds of decisions in disposing of the cases brought to its attention. For example, it decides whether to accept cases for plenary review—i.e., for decision on the substantive legal issues after full briefing and oral argument, such decision to be accompanied by a written opinion explaining the Court's action; what issue in the plenary case to decide and how to decide it; if the case is not accepted for plenary review, whether to decide it summarily—i.e., without oral argument and briefing, or simply to reject it; and what the summary decision shall be if that is the Court's choice.

Historically, most research attention has been focussed on plenary decision-making processes. This is understandable since such decisions allocate goods and values between litigants and provide social, economic, and social policies for the nation as a whole. The research problem usually specified is to determine why one party loses and another wins or, more importantly, why one social policy is adopted and another rejected.

A familiar decision-making model in the legal profession is the model of stare decisis—a latin phrase meaning "let the decision stand." The model requires a judge deciding a case with a particular set of facts and law to make his decision consistent with decisions in past cases on similar facts and law. The problem with this approach is that while law may be unchanged between two cases, the facts are never identical. Thus, the judge must always decide whether the similarities in the facts are sufficient for decision in the earlier case to control decision in the later case. Since such a procedure gives the judge considerable discretion as to when or when not to follow precedent, many commentators find the stare decisis model inadequate.

The breakdown of stare decisis leads to a search for other explanations. Fred Kort has argued that in many kinds of situations the Supreme Court is merely responding to certain kinds of facts. Such a model has been found to be a good predictor of Supreme Court action in right to counsel, coerced confession, and other cases. The approach is illustrated in Section thirteen by the paper on jury selection. But such models fail to explain why the Court chooses certain facts as relevant. Martin Shapiro's discussion of "incrementalism" suggests a partial answer to this question—i.e., the Court adopts those facts that will support a small or incremental change in the law, assuming that some change is indicated. This does not tell us, however, when the Court will find a need for change.

Another factor in Supreme Court decision making is the interpretive propensity of each justice. When the Court strays from strict interpretation of Constitution or statute, reaches out to decide issues whose resolution is not essential, or gives a strained meaning to words, it is likely to be criticized as "activist." The counter appellation—greatly admired by some—is "judicial restraint." Whether a particular justice shows activist or restraintist tendencies depends on his conception of the Court's role in the American governmental system. If he feels the Court is obligated to "do justice," he will be less restricted by Constitution or statute than if he thinks the Court is merely to "interpret" the laws made by others without regard to social consequences. While the Supreme Court under Chief Justice Warren was generally labeled activist, the Burger Court is exhibiting both activist and restraintist propensities. The zoning cases discussed by Lamb illustrate one area in which the Burger Court is showing its restraintist proclivities.

The cases following the Lamb reading illustrate activism and restraint in action. In Roe v. Wade, Justice Blackmun raises and decides a number of detailed issues that could have been left undecided. He articulates a number of prescriptions that cannot be traced directly to any Constitutional provision. A more restrained justice might agree with the dissenting opinion of Justice White in which he declares: "I find nothing in the language or history of the Court to support the Court's judgements." This is not to deny, of course, that the Court's holding in Roe may be good social policy.

In the short excerpt from Justice Holmes' dissent in Northern Securities v. U.S., we get one man's guide to the interpretation of statutes. The Holmes approach is decidedly restraintist. It is easy to think that in Kaiser v. Weber, Holmes would have joined the Burger or Rehnquist dissent rather than the activist position represented by the majority opinion.

The reaction of Congressman Ashbrook to Weber—i.e., that it is difficult ". . . to imagine a more direct challenge to our prerogatives that its [the Court's] rewriting of our legislation while we were actually in session less than a block away" shows a preference for a more restrained approach. But, of course, other congressional reactions supporting the Court's approach could easily be found.

In Section fifteen, the selections emphasize the influence of small group factors on judicial decision making. It is a well-known fact that a group context may produce decisions that differ from those that might be taken in an individual setting. This results from interaction among group members, the sharing of risk in certain situations, and the diffusion of responsibilty if the decision is likely to be unpopular. Collegial bodies frequently show a propensity to split into cliques or factions. Collegial courts are certainly no exception to such a generalization.

Murphy discusses some of the research relating group factors to the behavior of Supreme Court justices. The following reading relates leadership in the Court to group structural arrangments and attempts to reveal how the principles of small group theory are reflected in actual decision-making behavior. The point made is that Justice Warren's influence on the decision and opinion in Brown v. Board of Education (1955) was not divorced from the leadership role which is structured into the decision-making process for the Chief Justice.

Some of the consequences of interaction among the justices are vividly portrayed by Howard in discussing the fluidity of judicial choice. Clearly, we cannot know from judicial votes alone all those factors that go into the formulation of the vote. Just as clearly, many of these factors are related to the give and take among the justices prior to publicized decision. Overall, the materials in

Section fifteen pin down the point that the collegial or group context of decision making does make a difference.

Finally, Section sixteen calls attention to the impact of idiosyncratic factors on Supreme Court decision making. We should not be surprised to find that one or more justices can get "hung up" on a single word or concept, as indicated in the selection from The Brethren. *The Court, after all, is composed of nine unique individuals—each of whom brings to the Court a unique set of values, attitudes, predispositions and social backgrounds. Research on the Court has determined that all these factors influence decision-making processes and outcomes. Indeed, other things being equal, such matters are undoubtedly probative in some cases. Taking that observation as a point of departure, the reading on William O. Douglas reveals that the value preferences reflected in the voting behavior of a justice are subject to change over time. Thus—to comprehend fully the well springs of decision-making behavior, we must seek to learn not only the values and attitudes found in past and present behavior patterns but also the changes that may be occurring in those patterns and the trends, if any, that underlie those changes.*

SECTION THIRTEEN

Facts, Law, and Precedent

48

The Breakdown of *Stare Decisis*

Martin Shapiro

Perhaps the most important distinction that has been traditionally drawn between courts and administrative agencies, or indeed all other political agencies, has to do with what is frequently called "the taught tradition" in law. Judges are men trained in the law. They inherit a historically sanctioned method of thought—legal reasoning. They apply this peculiar—peculiarly well-tested and successful—analytical method to the problems brought before them. Thus they contribute a unique element to political decision making.

It would be extremely difficult to summarize briefly just what this taught style is. That, however, is not to question its existence. Basically it seems to consist of three elements. The first and foremost is really not a logical operation at all but a doctrine of common law, *stare decisis*. No matter how abstractly the rules of legal reasoning are put, in the end they reduce themselves to little more than a description of the way *stare decisis* is *supposed* to work translated from the lore of common law into the vocabulary of judicial thought. Perhaps this explains why the rules of "legal reasoning" are so difficult to summarize briefly. For tremendous floods of ink have been spilled in attempts to state exactly what *stare decisis* is and how it ought to be applied in various situations. There is

From Martin Shapiro, *The Supreme Court and Administrative Agencies* (The Free Press, 1968), pp. 67–71. Copyright © 1968 by The Free Press, a Division of The Macmillan Company. Reprinted by permission of Macmillan Publishing Co., Inc. Footnotes have been omitted.

not space here to follow this tortured path, particularly since I believe it to be basically a false one. What I am about to say may appear only a parody of the debate to those who still defend *stare decisis*, but it provides a sufficient starting point for my purposes, and one that can be supported by considerable reasoning and authority should the need arise.

Stare decisis means that a judge should decide a present case as a past case was decided. This would be simple if the facts in the two cases were absolutely identical. But they rarely are. Thus the judge must decide whether any fact in the present case is so different and so relevant that this case should not be decided the same way as the last. To do this he must discover what the "principle" was upon which the last case was decided or what *ratio decidendi*—what rationale of deciding—the last judge used. Let us suppose the principle was "long-haired men go to jail" or the ratio was "long-haired men constitute a danger to society— this man has long hair—this man goes to jail." Then in the present case the fact that the man has black hair, while in the past case he had red, makes no difference, and the new case can be decided as was the old. On the other hand, let us suppose that in the previous case the principle was "men belonging to a religious sect sworn to murder all unbelievers go to jail," and the *ratio* was, "the only men in our society who wear their hair long and dye it red are those who belong to murder sects; this man wears his hair long and dyes it red; therefore he is a member of a murder sect, therefore he goes to jail." Then the fact that the long-haired man in the present case has black hair is very relevant and will cause this case to be decided differently from the last one.

Various difficulties, however, arise in discovering the principle or *ratio* of a previous case. First the earlier judge may not have clearly explained what he was doing. He may not have clearly stated which facts he considered relevant and decisive and which he did not, or he may not have set down precisely what logical steps led him from the facts to his decision. Secondly, the judge may have stated a *ratio* which is either patently unsound in logic or one which is so vague and general that it would lead either to the decision he reached or precisely the opposite one. Thirdly, we may discover fifteen previous cases, all with roughly the same facts and all with roughly the same decision. Yet each of the judges in each of the cases may provide a quite different *ratio* than each of the others.

To overcome these difficulties it is necessary to argue that the *ratio* of a previous case is not how the judge said he got from the facts to the decision, but how logically he must have gotten from the facts to the decision. This is where the major element of fantasy enters *stare decisis*. We are no longer concerned with how previous judges actually decided cases, but how they ought to have decided them if they had clearly and correctly followed the rules of *stare decisis*.

Two new problems now arise. The first concerns facts. One determines the *ratio* of a given case by lining up all the facts, choosing the relevant ones, and then looking at the decision. The *ratio* is whatever series of logical stepping-stones will lead you from the relevant facts to the final decision. But you cannot know what facts are relevant until you know the ratio. In our earlier example you cannot know whether hair color is a relevant fact until you know whether the ratio is that long-haired men are dangerous or that religious fanatics who do certain things to their hair are dangerous. Unless you know what facts are relevant you cannot know from where to where the stepping-stones go, and unless you know from where to where the stepping-stones go you do not know what facts are relevant. This chicken-and-egg problem endlessly bedevils those attempting to pin down the single correct *ratio* in a single case. For every different choice of relevant facts a different *ratio* will appear, and for every ratio a different subset of the total facts will appear relevant.

The second problem concerns the *ratio* itself. Even supposing that we could hold the relevant facts fixed, the rules of Aristotelian logic under which lawyers purport to operate do not really demand that there be a single line of stepping-stones from the facts to the decision. In many instances it is quite possible to construct two or more equally plausible lines of logic that will connect a given set of facts and a given result. Which is the true *ratio?*

Because of these difficulties some legal scholars have argued that a *ratio* cannot be found in a single case, but one can be found for a line of cases. If we take a group of cases, all in roughly the same area, we should be able to identify a group of central facts common to all of them, and also some fact elements which, when they vary from case to case, cause the results to vary. There are, then, the relevant facts. Moreover if we take this same group of cases and list all the possible *ratios* in each, we should, by a process like canceling in fractions, be able to find a lowest-common-denominator *ratio* that will work on all of them and allow us to arrive at a single *ratio* summarizing all of these cases.

In fact, grouping cases will not entirely overcome the problems to be found in deriving a *ratio* from an individual case because the same chicken-and-egg problem arises. Unless you know what the criteria of relevance and *ratio* are in each case, you don't know what cases to group together as having enough in common to be considered together, and unless you have a group you cannot discover what criteria of relevance and ratio they have in common. Nevertheless, grouping will give a kind of rough-and-ready result or educated guess about *ratio* which is far better than the results to be obtained from a single case.

The difficulty that now arises is that by grouping different cases you can get different results and that very frequently two or even more lines of precedent came into existence on the same question as cases which do not fit neatly into one group are bunched to create a second. When two or more lines of precedent exist, it is literally impossible to follow the previous case. Moreover, new cases inevitably bring new facts. The identification of the *ratio,* and thus the determination of what is relevant and what is not in previous cases, is always of a rather rough ordering even when only a single line of precedent exists. Thus it is always possible to argue that a given decision either is or is not in line with past precedent in light of the new facts.

Thus the theory of *stare decisis* as an exact and rigorously logical mode of thought resulting in absolutely certain and predictable decisions has broken down, and as the theory has dissolved so has the judge's claim to bringing a unique form of analysis to political problems. For if *stare decisis* does not dictate automatic results, judges would seem to exercise a level of political discretion similar to that of other politicians, and particularly to that of other subordinate lawmakers who are expected to govern themselves at least generally by the existing statutes. It must be stressed that the breakdown in the theory of *stare decisis* does not mean that legal decision making is a form of free play in which every judge can do exactly what he pleases. It is now clear, however, that the judge is not subject to a unique constraint on his thought processes that makes him far different from the rest of us. Instead, like the bureaucrat, he is constrained by the previous state of the law insofar as it is clear. Because it is never entirely clear he always has some discretion. And he is likely to find the law less and less clear and exercise more and more discretion as he finds that old law is giving bad results in new circumstances.

• • •

—————————— **49** ——————————

Incremental Decision Making
Martin Shapiro

• • •

There is, however, an even more fundamental phenomenon linking courts and administrative agencies, indeed linking all political decision makers. This phenomenon tends to exhibit itself in the courts in the language of *stare decisis* although it is essentially the same phenomenon there as elsewhere. It is easiest to perceive this identity between the concern for precedent in courts and the general character of political decision making if we examine the general phenomenon first and then see how it operates in the specific setting of the courts.

This general phenomenon might be labeled incrementalism. It has been described in two recent works, each by a pair of authors. Richard Cyert and James March, and David Braybrooke and Charles Lindblom. Both have recently presented theories of decision making that might apply to both political and economic decisions and particularly to the peculiar mixture of politics and economics that typically occurs in what we call the "public policy" sphere. Courts are very frequently involved in just such mixed questions of politics and economics. Both sets of authors are seeking to present a method of decision making that proceeds by a series of incremental judgments as opposed to a single judgment made on the basis of rational manipulation of all the ideally relevant considerations.

It is easiest to explain what incrementalism is by way of what it isn't, or rather what it is in reaction against. For a long time the ideal type for decisions in economics or politics was "rational decision making" in which all relevant data were to be considered in the light of all relevant goals, the goals themselves to be precisely weighted according to the decision maker's valuational priorities. The basic sticking point with rational decision-making theories is that real decision makers just did not act this way. The economists found that firms did not act rationally— that is, so as to maximize their profits. The political scientists found that political decision-making bodies, particularly highly bureaucratized ones, tended toward decisions that compromised the conflicting interests of various participants on an ad hoc basis without agreement on either the facts or the priority of goals. This collision of rational decision-making theories with hard facts is marked by the popularity of such notions as "satisficing" rather than maximizing and definitions of public interest in terms of legitimizing processes rather than substantive policies. At this point it might have been said that propositions about how decisions ought to be made were simply at odds with how decisions were in fact made. But then economists began to tell us that the marginal cost involved in gathering every piece of pertinent data and checking it against every available alternative policy in terms of all approved values would frequently itself be irrational in terms of input-output ratios. And students of politics began to urge that the self-preservation of a given political agency and/or the political process as a whole necessitated mediational decisions. It is not quite rational to destroy cherished institutions in the process of making "correct" public policy. Thus deviations from rational decision-making models not only did occur but ought to occur. Incrementalism is the formal statement of this dissatisfaction with conventional models of decision making.

Let me briefly describe the tactics of incrementalism as presented by Lindblom. Lindblom begins with propositions about "margin-dependent choice." The decision maker starts from the status quo and compares alternatives which are typically marginal variations from the status quo. Formulation and choice among alternatives are derived largely from historical and contemporary experience. It follows that rather than all rationally conceivable alternatives only a restricted number are considered. Moreover, only a restricted number of the consequences of any given alternative are considered. And those that are chosen for consideration are not necessarily the most immediate or important but those that fall most clearly within the formal sphere of competence of the analyst and with which he feels most technically competent to deal.

In the traditional rational model of decision making, means are adjusted to ends, but the incrementalist often adjusts what he wants to the means available. Similarly, he constantly restructures both his data and values. He uses "themes" rather than "rules." That is he does not say "if factor X is present, decision Y must follow," but "factor X is an important consideration." Lindblom's next rubric is "serial analysis and evaluation"—the notion that policy is usually made by following a long series of steps. Rather than attempting to solve the problem in one fell swoop the decision maker whittles away at it. Indeed the analyst is likely to "identify . . . ills from which to move away rather than goals toward which to move." Finally, analysis of a given policy area is likely to be carried on by several different agencies or institutions with constantly differing world views.

Cyert and March working independently of Lindblom and drawing their theory largely from observation of private firms rather than government arrive at startlingly similar conclusions. I shall restate their theoretically more elegant but rather cryptic conclusions in more everyday language.

Decisions for large organizations are not made by one man but come about through compromise among the various parts of the organization. Since each part has different goals and values, the organization itself has multiple goals and usually defines the "right" solution not in terms of an abstract best but of a solution which is at least minimally acceptable to each of the parts. In searching for this solution, the organization usually considers only one alternative at a time, and the first one to be discovered that is minimally acceptable to all parts will be adopted. Where the status quo policy is acceptable to all, there is little search for alternatives. But where the existing policy fails, then search will be intensified.

Organizations are not only concerned with finding good or "best" policies. They are also vitally concerned with their interval stability. It is necessary, therefore, to make sure that the process of finding and selecting new alternatives is not conducted with such enthusiasm and preoccupation as to shatter the structure or distract attention from the vital job of maintaining the existing machinery. Just such results are likely to occur if the too vigorous search for alternatives to the status quo were to lead to excessive uncertainty among executives as to what was going to happen next. Thus even organizations very actively engaged in searching for new solutions are likely to stress the following of regular procedures in day-to-day operations. Moreover, to avoid excessive disruption of these operations it is likely to make very small-step changes, waiting for the results of each to become clear before making another. The feedback resulting from each change puts the organization in a much better position to predict exactly what will result from the next. Predicting the future environment and then choosing the major change that ideally suits the prediction might seem rationally best, but it will lead to a tremendous shock to the system if the world does not indeed turn out the way you predicted it would. Making a small change and seeing how it works out before making another may always leave the organization a bit short of ideal adjustment to changing times, but it also reduces losses if the guess was wrong. Moreover the constant feedback or new information that the decision maker gets from observing what happens after each small change helps in producing better guesses in the future.

An organization not only attempts to minimize the uncertainties resulting from decision making—i.e., choice among alternatives; it also seeks to minimize uncertainties within the decisional process itself. "It tends to use standard operating procedures and rules of thumb to make and implement choices. In the short run these procedures dominate the decisions made."

• • •

Now it seems to me that if we examine the decisional behavior of courts, where the concern with precedent and the vocabulary of *stare decisis* are ever-present even though the theory has long since broken down, what we find is incrementalism pure and simple dressed up in the peculiar language of the law. Courts are not distinguishable by a peculiar tradition of thinking or decision making. Instead they, along with bureaucrats and business managers, are very central practitioners of incrementalism. Only the technical vocabulary for expressing this incrementalism sets the courts apart.

The key feature of *stare decisis* is, after all, concern for the status quo. Let the previous decision stand unless it fails to adequately meet new conditions. If it fails, search for a new decision. In considering such alternatives, begin by testing those which are closest to the old—i.e., try marginal changes first. Judicial lawmaking is typically accompanied by a great concern for fitting new decisions into older patterns and showing that the changes being made are only minor and compatible variations on the old law. Most of what seems essentially false in judges' opinions— the repeated insistence that they are not changing the law at all when they obviously are—is simply a sort of conventional overstatement of the point that they are choosing that workable alternative closest to the old law.

To some readers it may appear misleading to assign the legal status quo to one of the two contending parties when judicial lawmaking occurs. For in such instances the judge is often confronted with two rival interpretations of a statute which may be said to have no status quo since it is vague enough to admit the rival interpretations. Just how frequently an appellate judge chooses the interpretation that "changes" the statute because that interpretation will yield better results, rather than choosing the interpretation that he believes would maintain the status quo, is a matter for investigation. Yet while we do not know just how often this occurs, we do know that it does occur, for at least the most extreme instances—those in which a court overrules one of its previous decisions— are readily observable.

However, even in the classic instances of rival interpretations of an existing statute, each of which is equally plausible in terms of the wording of the statute and its past interpretations, the decisional situation is still basically one of marginal choice based on the status quo. The status quo is the statute's general intention, and counsel for each party argues that his specific interpretation more appropriately relates the statute to the circumstances. In a sense the judge does not face a choice between status quo and change, since if there has been no previous authoritative interpretation of the statute on all fours with the new situation, whatever he decides will be new. Yet neither judge nor counsel is free to propose any interpretation they like. All potential interpreters are constrained by both technical canons of statutory interpretations and common-sense rules of logic to stay relatively close to the statutory language. The status quo here becomes the rather vague one of the very statutory intent that is in dispute. But vague as it is, it remains an anchor around which cluster various marginal choices. While we may argue whether the value of limestone or cement ought to be used in calculating depletion allowances under a statute allowing such calculation on the basis of "the commercially marketable mineral product," no one is going to argue that the value of the bridge eventually made out of the cement should be the basis of calculation.

The constant concern of lawyers and judges to narrow the issues and decide only that issue crucial to the case before them is also typical of incrementalism. If each case is the vehicle for decision on a single issue, and only the narrowest one possible to decide the case, then a major and wide-ranging problem is not considered all at once and in all its facets. Instead it unfolds step by step over time as a series of cases bring up first one aspect of the problem and then another. Thus at any given moment the court considers only a restricted number of alternatives, but the process as a whole constitutes just that serial analysis and evaluation and sequential consideration of alternatives that marks incrementalism.

The great virtue of common law is, after all, alleged to be the case by case development of a solution to a social problem by the gradual inclusion and exclusion of various alternatives. Courts do not make long-range forecasts about social conditions. Instead they attempt to handle each problem as it arises and with a tentative solution. The results of that small step can then be observed and help to inform the court's next decision. This is the much touted flexibility of judicial decision making. Instead of grand solutions that may become grand disasters, courts feel their way, seeking to benefit from accumulated experience with a past step before moving on to the next. Thus the great emphasis in courts on benefiting from historical experience. Here again there is a kind of conventional overexpression in which judges frequently say that they are only the passive utterers of the lessons of past experience embodied in *stare decisis*. But, stripped of the rhetoric, all this seems to boil down to is that judges like other incrementalists prefer the feedback–small-change–feedback–small-change style of decision making rather than great leaps forward.

If we run through the rest of the catalog of incrementalism, we shall also find the judge at every point. Judges do consider only a restricted number of consequences even for the restricted number of alternatives they handle. Another of the peculiar virtues of judicial decision making is supposed to be that because judges always decide in the context of a concrete case, they can see the real and immediate consequences of any given decision rather than making general decisions on the basis of vague and speculative assessments of what results are likely to follow. In short, a judge does not consider all the consequences to all the persons at all the future times that may follow from a given decision, although undeniably the decision may have consequences far beyond those in the given case. The judge trades the rationality that would come with calculating the probabilities of all future consequences under all foreseeable circumstances for the ease and relative certainty of sticking to the probable results in the immediate case. This point should not be pushed too far, however. Judges, like other incrementalists, are likely to look beyond the absolutely immediate consequences, since they know that their decisions will have more wide-ranging consequences if for no other reason than that under the traditions of *stare decisis* they will become precedents. The incrementalist does not rigorously exclude all but immediate consequences. He simply gives greater weight to those he is sure about because they are here and now than to those he is not sure about because they are there and later. The judge does concern himself with what results the principle he announces now will have later, but he tends to test the principle concretely by the results it will achieve now in the case before him.

Judges also share with other incrementalists a tendency to consider those consequences that lie within their immediate jurisdiction rather than those that fall in someone else's. This is precisely why jurisdictional questions are so vital in administrative law. Debates over jurisdiction are in fact debates about what consequences a judge should concern himself with and which he should leave to others. At least superficially the judge more than any other incremental decision maker cuts himself off from consideration outside his jurisdiction. In reality, of course, there is an interaction between consequences and jurisdiction in which jurisdictional lines are in part drawn on the basis of what consequences are so interrelated that they cannot be considered separately. Nevertheless a judge hearing a slum-clearance case is likely to consider the effect of his decision on the rights of property owners, and on the city's housing program, and perhaps on the future prosperity of the city, but he is unlikely to consider its effect on the gross national product or patterns of migratory bird flight for which his responsibility is minimal.

Cyert and March's emphasis on multiple goals as a characteristic of incrementalism is also confirmed in judicial decision making. Indeed, judges more openly announce that policy decisions inevitably rest on balancing various and conflicting interests or values than do any other group of decision makers. I am speaking here not only of the balancing doctrine in the First Amendment, which in fact frequently covered an inattention to certain important goals, but also of the rather consistent rhetoric of modern court opinions in many areas of both constitutional and administrative law, which acknowledges that many cases involve conflicting goals and that a judge's job is to choose which goal ought to be favored in each particular instance. For instance, in Southern Railroad *v.* North Carolina the Supreme Court argued that one goal of national transportation policy was to maintain the health of the railroads, but another was to move passengers conveniently, that the two might sometimes be in conflict and that in determining when to allow a railroad to abandon a passenger service, railroad revenues and convenience to passengers must both be taken into account.

This sort of approach is so much the stock and trade of appellate judging that few lawyers would need to be convinced that judges typically decide on the basis of multiple goals. There is always the risk, however, that the rhetoric of opinions does not accurately reflect the judge's actual thought processes. Recent attitudinal data might be naïvely interpreted to suggest that some judges always favor one goal or interest and do not really give any weight to other conflicting goals. In fact these data show, and indeed so those presenting the data have argued, that while a group of judges may be placed at different points along a scale between two conflicting goals, with each judge giving different relative weights to each goal, it is extremely rare to find a judge who favors one of the goals to the total exclusion of the others.

Lindblom speaks of "adjustment of objectives to policies" as one of the key aspects of incrementalism. His basic point here is that considerations of availability of means often and necessarily affect, and indeed partially define, what goals we are going to pursue. This point has, I think, always been evident in many of the more "routine" areas of law. The need to pursue certain legal goals within the context of what the real situation will bear is attested to by such concepts as "the reasonably prudent man," "innocent third-party purchaser," and "last clear chance." All of these concepts represent compromises between certain ideal goals and what can actually be expected of imperfect human beings in an imperfect society. Movements toward and away from absolute warranty, for instance, have always focused on what manufacturing and marketing conditions would bear rather than notions of absolute fairness or responsibility. In these areas judges are quite accustomed to modifying their goals and cutting their losses under the impact of the real world. Indeed, such adaptation of judicial behavior to reality is generally applauded and encouraged.

Another feature of incrementalism which Lindblom calls "reconstruction" also strikes home immediately in the judicial process. "Fact-systems are reconstructed as new ones are discovered. Policy proposals are redesigned as new views of the facts are adopted." At the most elementary level, any experienced reader of cases has many times been struck by the way in which, in a given case, the facts look so much different in the majority opinion than in the dissent. The majority's frightened child, shivering in his cell, cut off from his loving parents, and confessing in loneliness and desperation, may become the dissenters' hardened juvenile delinquent, refusing to see his mother and confessing as a final gesture of defiance. The poor little Seventh Day Adventist, who, forbidden by her conscience to work on Saturday, is struck off the unemployment compensation rolls, moves my heart precisely because I almost instinctively think in terms of an economic system in which there are plenty of five-day jobs. She moves my heart slightly less when a dissenter shows that, in the Southern town in which she lives, practically the only employment for women is in the textile mills which work a six-day week. Thus the lady's religion conveniently allows her to refuse every available job and continue to live off the taxpayers indefinitely. I am not saying that judges necessarily pick and choose their facts to support their decisions, but that judges typically decide on the basis of some model or abstraction from the facts and that the way they construct this model affects their decisions. As judges become aware of new facts, they are led to change the model. For example, the model of free employer and free employee freely bargaining about wages and working conditions which many judges used to decide early cases involving economic regulation changed under the impact of the facts about real working conditions in real laundries, bakeries, and clothing factories. That is precisely why lawyers have in recent years devoted so much space in their briefs to facts and are likely to emphasize changing conditions when they wish to obtain changes in the judge-made law.

Another of Lindblom's propositions—that incremental decisions are remedially oriented—should strike a familiar note with those who are acquainted with modern jurisprudential writings. He says "The characteristics of the strategy . . . encourage the analyst to identify . . . ills from which to move away rather than goals toward which to move." Edmond Cahn in his *Sense of Injustice* and *The Moral Decision* has put forward exactly this proposition to explain and rationalize the decisions of courts confronted by situations in which the mechanical application of existing law does not seem to yield just results. Cahn argues that courts do make decisions based on considerations of justice and morality in spite of their inability to articulate a rational set of moral principles or a systematic answer to the question, What is justice? He shows that courts are sensitized by the injustice or social failure they see in a given legal situation and move away from that situation even when they cannot formulate an abstract, complete, and ideal legal rule to cover the problem.

The old lawyers saw that "hard cases make bad law" also comes down to this. Where the old law (the status quo) yields at least minimally acceptable results, it will be retained. Where a concrete case shows that the old law is yielding intolerable social results—hard cases where men seem to be technically in violation of the law but morally and socially blameless—courts will move from the old law even if they cannot formulate exactly what the new law should be. Hard cases make not bad law but new, and therefore frequently incomplete, law.

Courts too typically alternate between themes and rules of thumb just as other incremental decision makers do. In many instances the courts do use a rule of thumb which specifies that, all other things being roughly equal, if X is present Y follows.

The Supreme Court holds that if violence or the immediate threat of violence is present in a labor-management dispute, the state may intervene in matters that would otherwise be the sole concern of the National Labor Relations Board—the so-called violence exception to the primary jurisdiction of the N.L.R.B. Where courts must determine whether a given crime involves moral turpitude, they almost invariably hold that where fraud was an element in the offense the crime does involve turpitude.

On the other hand, courts frequently take precisely the thematic tack Lindblom describes, simply naming various factors all of which they will consider but none of which they will bind themselves to treat as decisive. A clear example is the now largely defunct fair-trial rule under which no given lapse in criminal procedure in and of itself rendered a trial unfair, but the Supreme Court was, in each instance, to determine whether the trial was fundamentally fair as a whole. Courts very frequently instruct regulatory commissions that they must consider a number of factors and reach a decision representing a balanced appraisal of all the relevant factors involved. Courts will frequently reverse agencies on the ground that insufficient weight has been given to a certain factor even while specifically holding that that factor alone is not decisive.

In short, courts, like other political decision makers, sometimes find it convenient to appear to bind themselves closely by the rules of decision and sometimes wish to emphasize their sensitivity to multiple factors.

Perhaps the most dramatic examples of the alteration and mixture of rule of thumb and thematic techniques and the tactical advantages of each to various courts and litigants are to be found in those areas, particularly labor and anti-trust law, where per se rules are much in fashion. In such areas disputes about whether courts should or should not adopt per se rules are in effect disputes about whether they should use the rule or thematic approach. And, of course, courts have sometimes adopted and sometimes rejected the per se approach. Per se rules, however, offer an extreme example. Probably most common is the situation in which a court's doctrine is relatively clear and predictable—in other words, is a rule of thumb or standing operating procedure—but nevertheless is sufficiently imprecise to allow the judge some of the freedom of the thematic approach particularly through his choice of emphasis on particular portions of the relevant law and facts.

On the whole, Cyert and March's emphasis on the use of standard operating procedures and rules of thumb, which in the short run dominate the decisional process, is strikingly applicable to the legal process. The terminology is slightly different in law. But legal doctrines or rules are precisely those standard operating procedures or rules of thumb by which judicial decision makers dispose of most of the cases that come before them. The clear-and-present-danger rule is a familiar example, but it is hardly necessary to belabor the point that, in every field of law, doctrines which fall somewhere between the status of fixed elements in the law and random dicta by individual judges play an important part in the decision of cases. We know that in the short run most decisions are going to be routinely determined by the given state of doctrine. We also know that in the long run the doctrine is going to change. Cyert and March's proposition neatly fits that strange paradox of law in which we can at one and the same time be almost absolutely sure that the case tomorrow will be decided according to doctrine X and that ten years from now doctrine X will have disappeared. The rest of incrementalism explains how and why it disappears.

Finally, Cyert and March's description of organizations as seeking "to avoid uncertainty by following regular procedures," even in the midst of the multiple uncertainties of incremental decision making, is also strikingly applicable to courts. Lawyers have always insisted that regularity of procedure, not substance, was the essential virtue of law and the vital safeguard of individual rights. The enormous concern and acrimonious squabbling over procedure which frequently makes the layman impatient is defended by lawyers and judges precisely because certainty of procedure reduces the degree of uncertainty in a form of decision making marked by a relatively high rate of change and thus uncertainty at the substantive level.

To sum up then: courts, rather than being set apart by a peculiar style of decision making or a unique taught tradition of *stare decisis,* are firmly within the incremental style of decision making generally shared by political and other organizational decision makers.

It is in the end hardly surprising that courts make incremental decisions given the nature of American politics. As we have already noted, incrementalism is intimately associated with the multidecision-maker process which is the central feature of American government and politics, and courts are an integral part of this process. Each court of appeals and the Supreme Court is a multidecision-maker court. With their hierarchy of trial and appellate tribunals, the courts considered by themselves constitute a system of multidecision makers. As subordinate lawmakers the courts considered collectively are one of the multidecision makers in the lawmaking process. Given this integration of individual judge, individual court and whole court system into a process of widely shared decision making, it would indeed be remarkable if courts did not decide incrementally, since none of the decision makers in this process is free to effectuate independent, global decisions fully consistent with his own goals even if his internal rationality were great enough to allow him to make such decisions.

There is a peculiar paradox at work in the traditional separation of courts from other political decision makers on the grounds of their peculiar thought processes. For what is peculiar about courts is that they have always been openly, consciously, and formally incremental, and have even developed a special language and lore of *stare decisis* to express that incrementalism. But this very language and lore has been used to set them apart from other government agencies which, striving at least to appear to satisfy an unrealistic norm of rationality, were not fully conscious of their own incrementalism and certainly not anxious to openly announce it as the courts were doing. In other words, it is precisely because other agencies have always considered themselves to be rational while courts have been stressing incrementalism (reaching right decisions through the case-by-case process of inclusion and exclusion according to the technique of *stare decisis*) as their own peculiar virtue that a gap has appeared to exist. Once it is recognized that other agencies too act incrementally, then the gap disappears.

Courts then are not distinguished by a peculiar taught tradition, style, or technique of decision making. Basically they share the technique of incrementalism just as they share nearly all their characteristics with other political agencies in general and with their fellow subordinate lawmakers, the administrative agencies, in particular.

● ● ●

Quantitative Analysis of Fact-Patterns in Cases
Fred Kort

Studying the dependence of court decisions on facts can be clearly associated with traditional conceptions of the judicial process. There are, however, salient problems in the relationship between facts and decisions which cannot be solved by conventional methods. Such problems must be attacked by mathematical and statistical methods which have been extensively employed in the behavioral sciences. These methods are not limited to research on social backgrounds of judges, their values, and their individual positions as members of appellate courts. It has recently been suggested that the process of decision-making on the basis of relevant facts involves an attitude of the judge toward his responsibility which may be examined in the same manner as other judicial attitudes. If this view is accepted, the study of the dependence of decisions on facts could rely on methods that are also appropriate for the study of other aspects of judicial behavior. But even if traditional conceptions of the relationship of court decisions to facts are preferred, mathematical and statistical methods provide insights which otherwise cannot be obtained.

The use of mathematical and statistical methods yields such insights in areas of law where comprehensive sets of facts have been specified by appellate courts as relevant and controlling for reaching decisions. In such areas of law, it has been stated by courts that some combinations of the facts would lead to decisions in favor of one party to the dispute and that other combinations would result in decisions for the opposing party. Beyond the association of *some* combinations of facts with decisions which already have been reached, it is not known, however, what decisions can be expected on the basis of *other* combinations of the specified facts. For example, in the involuntary confession cases under the due process clause of the fourteenth amendment, the Supreme Court has clearly stated that each decision depends on the particular circumstances surrounding the interrogation of each petitioner. Workmen's compensation cases provide another example: reviewing courts have indicated that an award or denial of compensation must be decided on the basis of such facts as the nature of the injury, the circumstances under which the accident occurred and became known, and the health record

From Fred Kort, "Quantitative Analysis of Fact-Patterns in Cases and Their Impact on Judicial Decisions," *Harvard Law Review* 79 (1966): 1595–1598, 1598, 1598–1599, 1599–1601, 1601–1603. Copyright © 1966 by the Harvard Law Review Association. Reprinted by permission. Footnotes have been omitted.

of the claimant prior to the injury. In both of these areas of adjudication recurring relationships between certain fact configurations and decisional patterns can be identified. A more difficult question is to predict the decisions that other combinations of these facts would justify.

In recent years several studies have attempted to predict decisions by using mathematical and statistical techniques. But a serious problem confronts the scholar in this area: he must identify which facts appellate courts accept as controlling from lower court records and appellate briefs. The problem thus presents two aspects: (1) the acceptance or rejection of facts by appellate courts from lower court records and appellate briefs, and (2) the dependence of the decisions of appellate courts on facts that have been accepted as controlling.

I. The Acceptance or Rejection of Facts That Control Judicial Decisions From Lower Court Records and Appellate Briefs

Many legal realists argue that the acceptance or rejection of facts by appellate courts cannot be reduced to regular patterns. If the contrary can be shown, however, the prediction of the acceptance or rejection of facts, and ultimately the prediction of decisions, will become possible. As an initial hypothesis, it can be stated that the acceptance of a fact by an appellate court depends upon identifiable conditions surrounding the presentation of the fact in the briefs and record below. These conditions can be stated as follows: the appellate court will accept the fact *if and only if* it appears at one or more of the stages which the lower court records and appellate briefs represent, *or* is not denied at one or more of these stages, *or* one or a combination of other facts also is accepted by the appellate court. A specific application of this compound statement may be exemplified by the involuntary confession cases decided by the Supreme Court. The alleged fact that the defendant had not been advised of his right to remain silent is accepted by the Supreme Court *if and only if* (a) the fact appears in a dissenting opinion of the lower appellate court *and* in the respondent's brief to the Supreme Court *and* is not denied in the allegations of the respondent in the transcript of the record *and* in the opinion of the lower court, *or* (b) it appears in the allegations of the respondent in the transcript of the record *and* in a dissenting opinion of the lower court *and* in the brief of the petitioner to the Supreme Court *and* is not denied in the respondent's brief, *or* (c) it appears in the petitioner's brief to the Supreme Court *and* is not denied in the opinion of the lower court *and* in a dissenting opinion, *and* the alleged fact that the petitioner was not advised of his rights to counsel also is accepted by the Supreme Court.

The complexity of this statement directs attention to the need for a more concise formulation. Such a formulation can be obtained by using the algebraic notation devised by the nineteenth century British mathematician George Boole—Boolean algebra—first applied to the analysis of judicial decisions by Reed C. Lawlor. The notation also can be regarded as a form of symbolic logic. The purpose of the concise formulation is not merely the convenience of relative brevity, but the important objective of reducing the compound statement to a form which permits further analysis.

The compound statement which specifies the conditions under which a fact is accepted by an appellate court—the acceptance rule—can vary considerably for different facts. Initially it is not known which combination of appearances, nonappearances, or denials of a fact, as well as the acceptance of other facts, provides the acceptance rule for the fact.

• • •

Although not every possible combination needs to be examined to determine which compound statement can be correctly inferred for each fact from the applicable case, the number of combinations which must be examined makes human inspection prohibitive. However, the systematic search for the applicable compound statement can be performed by a digital computer. . . .

• • •

Although the compound statements identify the possible conditions for the acceptance or rejection of relevant facts by appellate courts, and thus provide a basis for prediction, two limitations must be noted. One is that the statements cannot feasibly take into account multiple manifestations of the appearance or denial of a fact, such as several accidents in a workmen's compensation case, some or all of which could be denied at various stages. Another limitation is that a direct statistical significance test for the compound statements is not available. The need for such a test becomes crucial when prediction of acceptance or rejection is attempted. For these reasons, another method has to be considered.

This other method employs a system of equations. Each case is represented by an equation, in which an index denoting the acceptance or rejection of a fact by an appellate court is set equal to the combination of appearances, nonappearances, and denials of the fact at the preceding stages. The weights of the fact at the various stages—in the sense of how persuasive its appearance at the respective stages is toward its acceptance by the appellate court—are the *unknowns* in the equations. As the equations are solved, the weights are determined. To be sure, the complex procedures which are required for the solution of the equations again necessitate the use of a computer, especially because there is a separate system of equations for each fact. By using the weights in a case not previously encountered, one can predict for each fact an acceptance or rejection that would be consistent with the established pattern of past cases. Although it may not be possible to predict every acceptance or rejection correctly, a statistical test for determining whether or not the predicted results are significant is available.

• • •

II. The Dependence of Appellate Court Decisions on Facts That Have Been Accepted as Controlling

The methods which can be used for analyzing the acceptance or rejection of facts by appellate courts also can be employed in examining the dependence of the decisions of these courts on the facts that they have accepted as controlling. The initial approach is essentially the same. Starting from the hypothesis that a decision in favor of the aggrieved party requires the occurrence of specified conditions regarding the facts accepted by the appellate court, the following compound statement can be formulated. The decision is in favor of the aggrieved party *if and only if* facts in one of several specified combinations have been accepted by the appellate court. In its specific applications this compound statement can assume forms amounting to several billions. But, through the use of a computer, it becomes possible to provide a basis for predicting decisions by deriving the correct compound statement from past cases.

The alternative method of a system of equations also has to be considered here. Again, each case is represented by an equation. In this instance, an index which denotes the decision (in favor or against the party seeking redress) is set equal to the combination of facts that have been accepted by the appellate court. The weights of the accepted facts—in the sense of how persuasive they are toward a decision in favor of the aggrieved party—are the *unknowns* in the equations. It may be impossible, for want of sufficient available data, to solve these equations. This problem can be attacked, however, by restating the facts in terms of *factors*, and by employing *factor analysis*. In the involuntary confession cases, for example, some of the facts which have been accepted as controlling by the Supreme Court include a delay in the formal presentation of charges, the incommunicado detention of the defendant, and the failure to advise the defendant of his right to remain silent or his right to counsel. These facts can be restated in terms of a factor described as "a tactic to keep the defendant in isolation and uninformed about the preceeding against him." This would be an example of the intuitive meaning of restating facts in terms of factors. It should be noted, however, that applicable factors actually are found by relying *exclusively* on the mathematical technique which factor analysis employs. It also should be noted that—in addition to solving the problem encountered in the original equations—factor analysis fully explores the mutual dependence or independence of the facts. For this reason, it always is advisable to attempt to restate the facts in terms of factors. For the same reason, it also would be irrelevant to say that factor analysis does not increase the predictability of the decisions.

On the basis of the restatement of the accepted facts in terms of factors, the original equations now can be restated as new equations, with indices denoting the decisions set equal to the various combinations of factors in the cases. The weights of the factors—again in the sense of how persuasive they are toward a decision in favor or against the aggrieved party—are the *unknowns* in the equations. The weights of the factors are found by solving the equations. As new cases arise, the applicable facts can be reduced to the factors which have been identified, and the decisions can be predicted.

Of primary interest to the present discussion is the combination of the methods for analyzing the acceptance of facts and the methods for exploring the dependence of decisions on facts. Such a combination of methods makes it possible to predict first the acceptance or rejection of facts by appellate courts from lower court records and appellate briefs, and then the decisions of the appellate courts on the basis of the accepted facts.

• • •

III. Purposes, Limitations, and Implications of the Proposed Methods

The purposes of the proposed methods must be understood not only in terms of their effective combination for prediction, but also in terms of their potentials for analyzing separately the two aspects of the problem under discussion. With regard to the acceptance and rejection of facts by appellate courts, the methods offer insights into matters about which there has been considerable speculation. Since the emergence of "fact-skepticism" in the framework of legal realism, there has been a widespread belief that courts pay relatively little attention to facts. The application of the proposed methods has refuted such a belief in at least some areas of law.

With regard to the dependence of decisions on facts, the proposed methods provide a precise and exhaustive distinction between combinations of facts that lead to decisions in favor of one party to the dispute and combinations of facts that lead to decisions in favor of the opposing party. Thus, the methods offer information about the content and the application of rules of law which verbal statements of these rules do not provide. The given examples show that courts employ rules which state that the decisions shall be made on the basis of combinations of facts. The verbal statements of these rules specify which facts shall be regarded as relevant but do not specify which combinations of these facts call for a decision in favor of the party seeking redress and which do not. This is the information which the proposed methods can provide.

It already has been seen that prediction is another purpose of the proposed methods. Prediction is possible only if it can be assumed that the patterns of consistency in past cases—with regard to the acceptance of facts as well as with regard to the decisions—will continue in the future. The proposed methods are not designed to predict doctrinal changes and the adoption of new rules of law. Furthermore, prediction does not apply to a case in which a fact *not previously encountered* appears, although a series of such cases provides a basis for the prediction of subsequent decisions. Thus the methods can demonstrate their validity, provided that their limitations are clearly recognized and understood, and that claims never made on their behalf are not carelessly attributed to them.

It should be noted that, in examining past cases by means of the proposed methods, no assumption is made regarding the existence or nonexistence of consistent patterns in the acceptance of facts or in decisions based on facts. Whether or not consistency does exist in a given area of adjudication is determined by the use of the methods. If consistent patterns cannot be identified, it must be concluded that judicial action in the given area of law cannot be understood in terms of the dependence of decisions on facts. If, on the other hand, consistent patterns are found, an important implication of the proposed methods is apparent. Should it be possible to predict only later cases from earlier cases, the underlying pattern of consistency could be explained in terms of stare decisis. But if earlier cases could be predicted from later ones, adherence to precedent would have to be explained in terms of an independent—although convergent—recognition and acceptance of similar standards of justice by different judges at different times. Thus not only the existence of consistent patterns but also the basis for their consistency can be evaluated.

Where patterns of consistency in the acceptance of facts and in corresponding decisions appear to be absent, other explanations of judicial action obviously must be given. Such explanations could be obtained from studies concerned with other aspects of the judicial process, such as the characteristics and changes in the attitudes and values of judges, their social backgrounds, and their indidivual positions as members of appellate courts. The possibility of effective coordination of these various endeavors remains an open question. Gustav Bergmann called attention to the fact that free-falling bodies, the inclined plane, and the pendulum originally were explained in terms of three separate empirical laws. Later, these three phenomena were regarded as special cases of a set of general laws—the laws of mechanics—and a scientific theory replaced the empirical laws. It is not inconceivable that similar developments will eventually lead to a scientific theory of the judicial process.

51

The Supreme Court and "Jury Selection" Facts

S. Sidney Ulmer

I. Introduction

While some Supreme Court decisions are determined by law and some by the idiosyncratic characteristics of a particular set of justices, some are heavily influenced by the factual circumstances in which a legal issue arises. This is not to say that judicial attitudes have no effect on the choice of "relevant" facts. Clearly they have. Nevertheless, it is instructive on occasion to delineate the factual patterns that the justices associate with outcomes in certain areas of the law. If some regularity in such patterns can be established, the necessity for continuity in decision making imposes some restraint on the Court regardless of why certain facts were characterized as legally significant in the first place.

One problem that can be better understood via factual analysis is associated with the selection of grand and petit juries in the American states. The key word here is "selection" since it implies that not all can serve. The problem arises because there has been a tendency in some parts of the system to exclude Negroes, Mexican Americans, and women to a disproportionate degree. It is created by requirements imposed on jury selection by the Fifth, Sixth, and Fourteenth Amendments to the Constitution. The Sixth Amendment establishes a federal right to trial by an impartial jury in criminal cases; the Fifth a right to indictment by grand jury in the federal system for capital or other infamous crimes; the Fourteenth extends the federal protections to the states with some exceptions. The grand jury is not required at the state level but in using grand and petit juries, due process and equal protection provisions of the Fourteenth Amendment must be honored.

In addition, the Court has held that petit juries must be representative; an impartial jury should be drawn from a cross section of the community. For the grand jury, the situation is somewhat different. A state defendant is not entitled to a grand jury at all and thus is clearly not entitled to one that represents a fair cross section of the community. But if used, the Fourteenth Amendment governs selection procedures.

In applying these amendments to the factual situations presented to it, the Court has generally held that Negroes, Mexican Americans, and women (more recently) cannot be intentionally and systematically excluded from either grand or petit jury systems solely on the basis of sexual or ethnic characteristics. The problem, however, is how to determine when intentional and systematic exclusion based solely on ethnic or sexual characteristics exists. The inference is one drawn from particular configurations of fact.

From an examination of jury exclusion cases in the period 1935–1960, it was found that the Court frequently referred to "chance" as a possible explanation for racial disparities in the jury system.[1] It was inferred from these comments that such discrepancies are significant for Fourteenth Amendment purposes only in situations in which the disparity cannot be attributed to chance using appropriate statistical models. The collectives relevant for comparison between 1935 and 1960 totaled a dozen or more. In one instance, the Court compared the percentage of Negroes in the raw population with the proportion of blacks on a grand jury. Or, another time, the comparison was between percentages of blacks on a tax roll and in a jury box. Other comparisons included such couplings as males/jury list, poll tax register/grand jury, jury list/grand jury, and jury pool/jury list.

These comparisons may be conceptualized as those between populations and samples with relevant population in one instance being a relevant sample in another, and vice versa. The examination of thirteen jury discrimination cases in the period 1935–1960 revealed that the Court found a violation of the Fourteenth Amendment (1) any time the disparity between the percentage of Negroes in a population and sample would be expected by chance less than five times in a hundred, and (2) any time Negroes had been systematically and totally excluded from a to be consistent with decisional outcome in twelve of the thirteen cases jury system over a long period of time. These generalizations were found examined. We may ask whether such generalizations have explanatory power when applied to jury exclusion cases falling in the years 1961–1977.

II. A Decision Model for Jury Discrimination Cases

For the analysis here, we have identified ten jury discrimination cases, in each of which the Court confronted and ruled upon a charge of invidious discrimination in the selection of grand or petit juries. One of the cases dealt with discrimination against Mexican Americans, two involved sex discrimination, and seven charged local officials with discrimination against Negroes. In each of these ten cases, we have isolated each set of numerical comparisons on which the Court commented and in regard to which the figures necessary to determine the magnitude of the disparity were provided. In all, nineteen comparisons were found with number per case ranging from one to six. In each instance, the comparison is between a pair of percentages. Thus, if sex discrimination is the issue, the comparison might be between the percentage of women in the population and the percentage on the jury venire.

In order to evaluate the probability that any difference in percentages is due to chance at the .05 level, the binomial expansion, with Yates correction for large samples has been used. The justification for the binomial approach to inference is two-pronged. First of all, it was employed with apparent success in the 1962 study. Furthermore, the method has been cited approvingly by Finkelstein in a lengthy discussion of jury discrimination and decision models which appeared in the *Harvard Law Review* in 1966.[2] But of greatest importance is the posture of the Court itself on the question of appropriate statistical models for evaluating percentage disparities in jury cases.

Prior to the 1962 paper, the Court had never indicated any awareness of the binomial model or its analytical value in jury exclusion cases. Nor did it do so between 1962 and the appearance of Finkelstein's article in 1966. As late as 1972 we find a majority of the justices asserting that, "The court has never announced mathematical standards for the demonstration of 'systematic' exclusion of blacks but has, rather, emphasized that a factual inquiry is necessary in each case that takes into account all possible explanatory factors." But, announced or not, if *some* magnitude of percentage disparity is legal and constitutional, some numerical standard for separating the prima facie case from that in which discrimination is not established must exist. It may very well be some such standard as that suggested in 1962. Indeed, the Court has often compared the magnitude of a discrepancy in one case with that in another in order to determine whether a similarity in degree of disparity warrants similar decision in the two cases. Moreover, within a year of the Finkelstein paper, a majority opinion writer cited probability theory approvingly as a means of determining purposeful discrimination in jury exclusion cases. In doing so, the Court was clearly not ready to base a decision on a statistical model. But its interest apparently had been piqued as reflected in a Clark footnote to the majority opinion in *Whitus* v. *Georgia*. That note declared that, "While unnecessary to our disposition of the instant case, it is interesting to note the 'probability' involved in the situation before the Court. The record does not indicate how many Negroes were actually on the 'revised' jury list of approximately 600 names. One jury commissioner, however, said his best estimate was 25% to 30%, which is in close proximity to the 27.1% who were admittedly on the tax digest for 1964. Assuming that 27% of the list was made up of names of qualified Negroes, the mathematical probability of having seven Negroes on a venire of 90 is .000006."

Clark's authority for this calculation is Finkelstein. In his *Harvard Law Review* paper, Finkelstein discusses both binomial and chi square models. Clark's footnote does not indicate which of these was used to reach the result he reports. Five years later, in the same case in which the majority denied the Court had ever "announced" a mathematical standard, another footnote indicated that the Court's interest in statistical probability models was still alive. Writing for the majority in *Alexander* v. *Louisiana*, Justice White took note ". . . as we did in *Whitus* v. *Georgia* . . . of petitioner's demonstration that under one statistical technique of calculating probabilities, the chances that 27 Negroes would have been selected at random for the 400 member final jury list, when 1,015 out of 7,374 questionnaires returned were from Negroes, are one in 20,000."

The demonstration to which White referred appeared in a petitioner's brief. The statistical model employed there, however, was not the binomial expansion but a modified version of a chi square model. A book explaining the method and "written for laymen without mathematical training" was deposited with the Supreme Court Clerk ". . . for the convenience of the Court." Since the Court reference in *Alexander*, therefore, was to a chi square model, it was not clear at that time whether the binomial or the chi square method was preferred. A hint, perhaps, was inherent in the reference to the chi square model as "one statistical technique." In any event, the matter was cleared up considerably in *Castaneda* v. *Partida*, decided March 23, 1977.

There is strong indication in *Castaneda* that the Court has finally recognized the importance of statistical probability models in deciding whether the facts show invidious discrimination. The footnotes to the Court's opinion are heavy with numbers of all kinds. But, for our purposes, footnotes 7 and 17 are particularly significant. Note 7 includes a chart of grand jury lists for each of eleven years, 1962–1972. The list reflects, for each year, the number of persons on the grand jury list, the average number of persons with Spanish surnames, and the percentage of such persons per list. It tells us that of 870 persons summoned for grand jury service during the eleven years, 339 or 39% were Mexican

Americans. It discusses gaps in the data and tells us that the Court accepts some figures and rejects others.

Footnote 17 is even more revealing. In the text of the majority opinion, the Court agrees ". . . with the District Court and the Court of Appeals that the proof in this case was enough to establish a prima facie case of discrimination against the Mexican-Americans in the Hidalgo County grand jury selection." The authority for this conclusion is provided in footnote 17, which, inter alia, is the most sophisticated comment the Court has offered on the appropriate statistical model in jury discrimination cases. The note clears up any ambiguity about the applicability of binomial models in such situations saying: "If the jurors were drawn randomly from the general population, then the number of Mexican-Americans in the sample could be modeled by a binomial distribution."

In addition to Finkelstein, the Court here cites Hoel's *Introduction to Mathematical Statistics* and Mosteller's *Probability With Statistical Applications,* giving page numbers where discussions of the binomial model may be found. The note explains how one calculates probabilities with the model and then provides the calculations for eleven-year and two-and-one-half-year periods. For the first, the Court reports that such a substantial departure of the number of Mexican Americans observed to serve from the number expected to serve, given a population 79.1 percent Mexican American, "would occur by chance less than 1 (time) in 10^{140}." For the shorter period, comparable calculations show the probability as "less than 1 (time) in 10^{25}." Since the footnote is to an opinion joined by five justices, one must think the Court now finds the binomial model acceptable if not preferred in situations of this kind.

As for the four dissenters, they challenge the figures used by the majority in making its statistical calculations, arguing that "eligible jurors" rather than general population should have been used, that one cannot equate number of persons with Spanish surnames with number of Mexican Americans, and so on. But no objection is raised to the binomial statistical model or its appropriateness for inferential purposes. Thus, putting all this together, one may be justified in concluding that all nine justices think a binomial model quite suitable for evaluating the disparities in percentages on which we focus in our analysis.

III. Analysis and Findings

The results of analysis with a binomial model are summarized in Table I. Probabilities of occurrence given random selection are provided for each of nineteen disparities. Since we are dealing with ten cases, we obviously report multiple comparisons for some cases. These multiple comparisons make it clear that the Court may comment in a single case on disparities that are both significant and insignificant in the statistical sense. Thus, in *Alexander* v. *Louisiana,* the Court compared six different sets of percentages, but only three were statistically significant. The mixing of such large and small disparities in opinion discussion suggests a modification of the earlier generalizations, as follows:

TABLE 1. Binomial Probabilities Associated with Sex or Ethnic Representational Differences in Selected Jury Collectives in Cases Decided by the U.S. Supreme Court, 1961–1977

CASE	REP. IN POPULATION %	REP. IN SAMPLE %	PROB. OF DIFFERENCE	DIRECTION OF DECISION
Hoyt v. *Florida*	40 [4]	.1 [3]	.0001	—
Arnold v. *N.C.* *	30.9 [3]	.3 [5]	.0001	+
Swain v. *Alabama*	26.1 [1]	0000 [5]	.0001	—
Swain v. *Alabama*	26.1 [1]	13.6 [2]	.0515	
Whitus v. *Georgia*	27.1 [2]	5.3 [5]	.284	+
Whitus v. *Georgia*	27.1 [2]	7.8 [2]	.0001	
Jones v. *Georgia* **	20 [3]	5 [2]	.000	+
Sims v. *Georgia* **	24.4 [3]	4.7 [2]	.0001	+
Turner v. *Fouche*	60 [4]	36.4 [2]	.0001	+
Turner v. *Fouche*	60 [4]	26.1 [5]	.0005	
Alexander v. *Louisiana*	21 [4]	7 [2]	.0001	+
Alexander v. *Louisiana*	21 [4]	14 [6]	.0001	
Alexander v. *Louisiana*	21 [4]	5 [2]	.040	
Alexander v. *Louisiana*	14 [6]	7 [2]	.0001	
Alexander v. *Louisiana*	14 [6]	5 [2]	.123	
Alexander v. *Louisiana*	7 [2]	5 [2]	.363	
Taylor v. *La.*	53 [1]	.7 [2]	<.0001	+
Castaneda v. *Partida*	79.1 [4]	38.9 [5]	<.0001	+
Castaneda v. *Partida*	79.1 [4]	45.4 [5]	<.0001	

Decision code: + = Violation of Fourteenth Amendment found.
            − = Violation of Fourteenth Amendment not found.
Subscripts to percentages: 1 = Eligible jurors
                             2 = Jury list, panel, pool, or venire
                             3 = Tax list, digest, or register
                             4 = County or other population
                             5 = Grand or petit jury
                             6 = Jury Questionnaires
* Number of grand jurors across 24 years not given. At least 12 each year or 288 assumed for purposes of comparison.
** Number of persons on the jury venire not given. Ninety is assumed on the basis of figures given in the related case of *Whitus* v. *Georgia.*

Hy. 1: In jury discrimination cases, the Supreme Court will infer a prima
facie case of invidious discrimination whenever the percentage of
class members in any relevant jury system population differs from
the percentage of class members in any relevant jury system sample
by a magnitude expected by random selection less than five times in
a hundred.

The modification is justified by the fact that the Court only needs a
single discrepancy to find for a jury discrimination claimant. Additional
discrepancies, significant or not, are neither necessary nor essential for
such a holding. Nor do they detract from it. The hypothesis asserts, in
effect, that a single significant disparity is sufficient for the inference of
prima facie discrimination. If the Court is basing its inference on a significant discrepancy, one might ask why it bothers to discuss insignificant
differences. The answer is unclear. But in the absence of detailed statistical calculations (which, apparently, have been carried out only recently)
a statistical disparity may not always be recognized for what it is. Moreover, the Court may feel that the sum of all disparities is more probative
with one or more of its "Publics" than focus on a single discrepancy
would be.

To evaluate our hypothesis, we need to look at the instances in which
the Court has inferred prima facie discrimination. In ten recent cases, the
Court drew such an inference in eight. The inference was not drawn
from the facts presented in *Hoyt* v. *Florida* and *Swain* v. *Alabama*. Each
of these exceptions deserves a comment since in each at least one disparity in relevant percentages was significant at .0001. One of the two cases
was somewhat unique on the facts. In *Swain*, a nineteen-year-old Negro
male was convicted of raping a seventeen-year-old white girl in Talladega
County, Alabama, and sentenced to death. In the county, there had not
been a Negro on a petit jury in fifteen years. According to Bobby Swain's
attorney, this was due to the systematic practices of county prosecutors in
eliminating prospective Negro jurors via peremptory challenges. The
Court did not think this bare fact in a county 26.1 percent black was
sufficient to establish prima facie discrimination.

Three dissenting justices (Warren, Douglas, and Goldberg) suggested
that ". . . if a Negro defendant proves that Negroes constitute a substantial segment of the population, that Negroes are qualified to serve
as jurors, and that none or only a token number has served on juries over
an extended period of time, a prima facie case of the exclusion of Negroes from juries is then made out." This was certainly no "far out" position in 1965 since the Court had held as much in examining the total
exclusion of Negroes from petit juries in *Norris* v. *Alabama,* decided in
1932, and in *Patton* v. *Mississippi,* decided in 1947.

It might be said in fairness to the majority that "4 or 5" Negroes on
the grand jury panel of thirty-three that indicted *Swain* was not such a

departure from the expected value as to warrant a conclusion of discrimination. As we indicate in Table I, the probability of a departure of such magnitude is less than .0515. But this does not speak to the total absence of Negroes from petit juries over a substantial number of years. It appears, as the dissenting justices argued, that this conflict with past precedent was essentially a function of the majority's desire to save the system of peremptory challenges inherited from English Common Law and now used in all state and federal jurisdictions.

The second exception—*Hoyt* v. *Florida*—is inconsistent with our hypothesis as well as with the principles that have governed invidious discrimination in race cases. In sex discrimination cases generally, the Court has displayed some uncertainty as to whether racial and sexual discrimination are analagous. Many years prior to *Hoyt,* the justices ruled that the representation of women on state juries was based on changing views of women's rights and responsibilities and not required by the Constitution. In the last decade, however, the Court has struck, as unconstitutional, a state law giving men preference over women for purposes of estate administration, a Utah statute mandating different ages of majority for males and females, a federal rule requiring females but not males to prove spousal dependency in order to become eligible for increased federal benefits, statutory discharge provisions allowing a disparity in terms of military service for males and females, and a section of the Social Security Act providing survivor's benefits to the widow of a deceased husband but not to the widower of a deceased wife. At the same time, the Court has upheld a Florida statute granting a $500 property tax exemption to widows but not to widowers on the grounds that the statute was reasonably shaped to benefit the sex on which spousal loss impacts most severely. Thus it appears that sex-based discrimination is permissible if designed to promote certain kinds of social goals. The key seems to be whether the discriminatory provision is remedial—that is, designed to remedy past discrimination or sex-based disparities.

Sensitivity to sex discrimination in jury cases came late to the Court and has undoubtedly been influenced by other Court decisions involving sex discrimination in recent years. These decisions have in turn been just as clearly related to developments in our social and political systems regarding the rights of women. *Hoyt* and *Taylor* v. *Louisiana* remind us that law, even constitutional law, does change and that the Court decides when and under what conditions new law is to be announced, as well as the magnitude of any breaks with the past it may adopt.

Few will be surprised to learn that over time some change has occurred in the law of jury discrimination. But the consistency of the Court in inferring prima facie discrimination from statistical disparities over four decades (1935–1977) is remarkable. Even more remarkable is that the .05 hypothesis explains twenty of twenty-three cases decided in the period, and two of the three exceptions possessed unusual factual characteristics which made them "hard" cases for the Court. The .05 cutting point and the binomial decision model would appear to have considerable applicability in explaining how the Court develops the prima facie inference. The .05 level of significance to determine when the magnitude of percentage discrepancies is sufficient for the inference has not been mentioned, much less specifically adopted by the Court. Yet analysis shows that "it works." Indeed, in the most recent period, the Court has only reviewed cases in which the probability was considerably less than .05. Thus, via the selection of cases, the Court may be trying to communicate a more severe standard than that used earlier. In any event, the Court's remark in *Castaneda* that social scientists find the randomness hypothesis "suspect" when the disparity between expected and observed values is greater than two or three standard deviations is suggestive of movement toward a social science approach to inference and perhaps some minimal acceptable level of difference—whether .05 or less.

Rebuttal Theory

Rebuttal Theory holds that once a prima facie case of invidious discrimination is inferred, the state may rebut the inference with appropriate evidence. *Swain* presents a situation in which such a theory may have been applied. The Court could have inferred a prima facie case of discrimination from the statistics. Alabama could have established in rebuttal that the disparity reflected the practice of defense attorneys in eliminating Negroes via peremptory challenges. The Court might then have ruled the rebuttal sufficient. Yet the Court in *Swain* declined to draw the discrimination inference in the first place saying that earlier principles for developing the inference could not be "woodenly applied" where the peremptory challenge was the ostensible cause of the deficiency. This suggests that the "rebuttal theory" may be little more than that. In fact, in the period 1961–77, a state never successfully rebutted the prima facie inference. The two cases won by a state in this period were both cases in which the Court did not infer prima facie discrimination in the first place.

In the earlier period (1935–60), when the prima facie rebuttal distinction was not as clearly drawn, the only case in which rebuttal evidence won the day was *Speller* v. *Allen*. In that case, the Court indicated it could not accept a disparity between 38 percent Negroes on a taxpayer list and 7 percent Negroes in a jury box. However, when the clerk of the jury commission indicated he selected those with "the most property," the Court agreed that economics might well account for the disparity and therefore that discrimination based solely on race was not proved.

Nevertheless, when rebuttal evidence is successful only once in twenty-three cases over forty-two years, one may not be well advised to depend on it where the statistical disparities fall within what we have suggested as the crucial range.

Conclusion

Given what we have learned in our studies of jury discrimination cases in the period 1935–1977, hypothesis #1 stated above and generally validated in the discussion that followed may be restated—to wit:

> Hy. 2: The Supreme Court will find a violation of the Fourteenth Amendment in the selection of grand or petit jurors when the percentage of class members in any relevant jury system population differs from the percentage of class members in any relevant jury system sample by a magnitude expected by random selection less than five times in one hundred.

The restated hypothesis ignores the theory of rebuttal to which the Court has devoted many words since rebuttal evidence does not appear to have been of much consequence in shaping decisional outcomes over the past forty-two years. As applied to twenty-three cases between 1935 and 1977, Hypothesis #2 would mispredict *Speller* v. *Allen, Swain* v. *Alabama,* and *Hoyt* v. *Florida* for an accuracy rate of 87 percent. In future cases, the hypothesis may do even better since the "error" in Hoyt is not likely to be repeated given the "correction": in *Taylor* v. *Louisiana. Speller* and *Swain* are conceptualized more readily as inconsistencies per se which can occur anytime the Court is insensitive to precedent. They are set off from *Hoyt* by the fact that the Court deliberately overruled that case, thus admitting its earlier mistake. Speller is simply an anomaly and *Swain* reflects the Court's commitment to certain traditional practices.

Notes

1. S. Sidney Ulmer, "Supreme Court Behavior in Racial Exclusion Cases," *American Political Science Review* 56 (1962):325–330.
2. M. O. Finkelstein, "The Application of Statistical Decision Theory to Jury Discrimination Cases," 80 *Harvard Law Review* (1966):338–376.

Judicial Activism
and Restraint

—————————— 52 ——————————

The Burger Court, Exclusionary Zoning,
and the Activist-Restraint Debate

Charles M. Lamb and Mitchell S. Lustig

I. Introduction

Over the years the United States Supreme Court has played a key role in
the American legal and political systems, functioning to varying degrees
as a court of law and as a social policymaker. The Burger Court is no
exception. Among other things, Burger Court decisions reflect a mixture
of the law and politics of the 1970's, the diverse attitudes and experiences of the particular Justices on the Court, differing legal backgrounds
and capabilities, and conflicting conceptions of the Court's proper governmental role.

This last consideration, the Court's "proper role" in the political system, has been particularly controversial during the twentieth century.
Many applauded and many condemned the conservative activism of the
Hughes Court and the liberal activism of the Warren Court. Few informed observers remained neutral. It is of course the latter period of ac-

From Charles M. Lamb and Mitchell S. Lustig, "The Burger Court, Exclusionary
Zoning, and the Activist-Restraint Debate," *University of Pittsburgh Law Review* 40
(1979): 169, 171–174, 197, 198–204. Reprinted by permission. Footnotes have been
omitted.

tivism that we remember most vividly. In response to Warren Court decisions, Richard Nixon campaigned for the White House in 1968 by emphasizing the need for judicial restraint and "strict constructionist" Justices for the Supreme Court.

Sufficient time has passed since Nixon's first term in office to reach solid conclusions concerning the impact of his four appointees on Supreme Court trends. However, a brief survey of the literature demonstrates that there remain significant differences of opinion concerning the type of role the Burger Court has assumed. Although conclusions are mixed, most commentators seem to believe that Nixon made good his campaign pledge.

● ● ●

Yet there are a number of scholars who disagree, asserting that in specific areas the Burger Court has not been exercising restraint but instead has been conservatively and selectively activist. Jonathan D. Casper's 1975 article suggests that the Burger Court has not exercised restraint in reapportionment, obscenity, and criminal justice cases. Casper notes that Burger Court decisions in these areas "suggest modifications in policy to some extent congruent with the demands of [Warren] Court opponents." In other words, the Burger Court has chipped away at certain Warren Court precedents as many expected.

Although judicial restraint normally refers to a Court's recognition of and deference to the law-making functions of the legislative branch, it does not preclude a Court's upholding its predecessor's decisions. Indeed, the rule of stare decisis is fundamental to the philosophy of restraint. In this sense some have observed instances of activism on the part of the Burger Court which contrasted sharply with Warren Court policy. Justice Arthur Goldberg has therefore argued that the Warren Court's activism in defense of individual rights was warranted, while Burger Court activism to overturn decisions of the Warren era is unjustified. Goldberg writes that:

> stare decisis applies with uneven force—that when the Supreme Court seeks to overrule in order to cut back the individual's fundamental, constitutional protections against governmental interference, the commands of stare decisis are all but absolute; yet when a court overrules to expand personal liberties, the doctrine interposes a markedly less restrictive caution.

With respect to criminal procedure, Leonard Levy has made the strongest case for the Burger Court's being activist. Levy particularly sees Burger as a "conservative activist," although Levy admits that such a label "probably obscures as much as it reveals." Archibald Cox notes that in view of decisions such as those involving abortions, "the new Justices are not restrained by a modest conception of the judicial function but

342

Deciding the Issues in Plenary Cases

will be activists when a statute offends their policy preferences." Raoul
Berger, among others, believes that by tossing out the traditional requirement for a twelve member jury in *Williams* v. *Florida,* the Burger Court
was clearly functioning in an activist mode. Donald Horowitz interprets
the Court's civil rights decisions in *Griggs* v. *Duke Power Company* and
Lau v. *Nichols* as activist in nature. Various other commentators have
pointed out a general retreat in civil rights. Likewise, in the fields of
labor law and federal securities law, other authors argue that the Burger
Court is handing down activist decisions. By substantially reducing
access to the Court, Chief Justice Burger and his conservative brethren
are often seen as activists when contrasted to their predecessors. Thus,
after eight years of Burger Court decisions, Laurence Tribe noted that
"[n]o great acumen is required to detect in recent decisions of the
United States Supreme Court a retreat from the vigorous defense of
liberty and equality."

And so the debate continues. These illustrations, interpreting the
Burger Court as exercising both restraint and activism, could easily be
multiplied. The overall conclusion seems to be that the Burger Court is
far less predictable than the Warren Court. Some Burger Court decisions
fit the restraint mold while others reflect activism. At the same time, as
Walter Murphy and C. Herman Pritchett have noted, the Supreme
Court's decisions have been equally as "political" under the leadership
of Warren Burger as they were under John Marshall, Charles Evans
Hughes, and Earl Warren. This Article thus accepts as given the fact
that the Burger Court has acted and will continue to act as a political
body. At times it will display restraint; at other times it will use its
power of judicial review or discretionary interpretations to make policy
in politically sensitive questions. Yet it remains to be shown how applicable the activist-restraint labels are to Burger Court decisions in a
number of specific issue areas.

• • •

[*Subsequent to this passage, the author proceeds to discuss several
Supreme Court decisions pertaining to exclusionary zoning. Here
we reprint, in part, the discussion of a single case—*Arlington
Heights v. Metropolitan Housing Development Corporation *429
U.S. 252 (1977).*]

II

Arlington Heights v. *Metropolitan Housing Development Corp* . . . was
the first instance in which the Court directly addressed the substantive
equal protection issue in exclusionary zoning litigation, and its decision

implies that the fourteenth amendment will be of little future value, at least during the Burger Court era, to plaintiffs challenging exclusionary zoning practices in federal courts.

• • •

The *Arlington Heights* case involved a challenge to the refusal of the Village of Arlington Heights, an affluent Chicago suburb, to rezone certain property from a single-family to a multi-family classification so that a low- and moderate-income housing project could be erected. The Metropolitan Housing Development Corporation (MHDC), a nonprofit developer which had constructed similar housing projects in the Chicago metropolitan area, planned to build federally subsidized townhouse units in the predominantly white suburb so that low- and moderate-income tenants—including racial minorities—might reside there. After a series of heavily attended public meetings at which MHDC unsuccessfully attempted to persuade Arlington Heights of the desirability of the housing project, the Village Plan Commission recommended that the zoning request be rejected because it allegedly did not comport with the Village's buffer policy for multiple-unit dwellings. The Village Board of Trustees, by a 6 to 1 vote, upheld the Commission's recommendation.

Shortly thereafter MHDC and three blacks, representing low- and moderate-income minorities who desired to work and live in Arlington Heights but could not find reasonably priced housing, filed suit in federal district court. They contended that the Village's refusal to rezone perpetuated segregation, was motivated at least in part by racial discrimination, and denied plaintiff developer of the right to use its property in a reasonable fashion under the fourteenth amendment. The plaintiffs further asserted a violation of individual rights under the fourteenth amendment, sections 1981, 1982 and 1983 of Title 42 of the U.S. Code, and the Fair Housing Act of 1968. The district court held that the Village's refusal to rezone was not motivated by racial discrimination or an intent to discriminate against indigent minorities. Rather, the court concluded that the refusal was due to a desire "to protect property values and the integrity of the Village's zoning plan."

The United States Court of Appeals for the Seventh Circuit upheld as "not clearly erroneous" the district court's findings that the plaintiffs had not proved that the Village was administering its zoning policy in an arbitrary manner. However, the court of appeals did not end its inquiry at this point; it proceeded to assess the Village's decision in light of its "historical context and ultimate effect." The court first noted the obvious: pervasive and widespread residential segregation in the Chicago metropolitan area generally and Arlington Heights in particular. Although the court did not suggest that the zoning decisions of Arlington Heights were the primary cause of this residential isolation, it did attach constitutional significance to the fact that the affluent suburb had exploited this situation by not making any attempt to integrate the community. Indeed, the Seventh Circuit noted that Arlington Heights was in this case seeking to avoid its responsibility by rejecting "the only present hope of . . . making even a small contribution toward eliminating the pervasive problem of segregated housing." Unable to find a compelling state interest that would justify the rezoning denial, the Seventh Circuit held that the Village's refusal to rezone constituted a racially discriminatory effect in derogation of plaintiffs' rights under the equal protection clause of the fourteenth amendment.

Mr. Justice Powell, speaking for the majority and relying primarily on the Court's conservative decision in *Washington* v. *Davis,* reversed the court of appeals. In *Davis* the Court reviewed a challenge to the District of Columbia's police recruiting test. Black applicants who had failed the test charged that the general results of the standard examination indicated invidious discrimination because a disproportionately high number of blacks failed it. The Burger Court rejected this argument, and its own earlier logic in *Griggs* v. *Duke Power Co.,* and held that a showing of racially disproportionate impact was inadequate in itself to substantiate a case of unconstitutional discrimination. Rather, a showing of discriminatory intent or purpose was required.

Although the *Arlington Heights* Court admitted that the impact of the Village's decision not to rezone did "arguably bear more heavily on racial minorities," this fact standing alone was insufficient to invoke the prohibitions of the equal protection clause. The Court read *Davis* to require that in order to establish a constitutional violation, the plaintiffs must show that the Village's refusal to rezone the property in question from a single-family to a multi-family classification had been motivated by a racially discriminatory intent or purpose. A review of the records below failed to reveal such a willful scheme on the part of the Village, and the court of appeals' reliance on discriminatory effect was deemed erroneous.

The Court could have simply remanded *Arlington Heights* back to the Seventh Circuit in light of *Washington v. Davis.* Instead, it seized the opportunity to elaborate on the restraintist *Davis* ruling and to indicate clearly the standards of proof that would be imposed on future plaintiffs alleging racial discrimination in the denial of low- and moderate-income housing. In presenting lower courts with guidelines to help determine whether impermissible discriminatory intent was a motivating factor in any official governmental action, Mr. Justice Powell indicated that disproportionate impact may provide a key starting point, but absent a stark pattern of discrimination, "impact alone is not determinative." The Court revealed other factors that might prove highly relevant in an inquiry into discriminatory intent: "a series of official actions taken for invidious purposes"; "the specific sequence of events leading up to the challenged decision"; and procedural and substantive departures from the processes "usually considered important by the decisionmaker." Finally, the Court noted that the legislative or administrative history of the act may be pertinent, "especially where there are contemporary statements by members of the decisionmaking body, minutes of its meetings, or reports."

Turning to the application of these novel principles to the instant case, principles nowhere mentioned in *Davis*, the Court failed to find that the Village had committed any constitutional violations by its failure to grant the rezoning request. Indeed, the Court relied on the district court's finding that racial discrimination had not been a motivating factor in the Village's refusal to rezone. Particular emphasis was placed on the Seventh Circuit's finding that the buffer zone policy had not been applied more stringently in *Arlington Heights* than in most similar cases. Justice Powell further maintained that there was "little about the sequence of events leading up to the decision that would spark suspicion." He noted that the area where MHDC wanted to build the project had been zoned for single-family homes ever since Arlington Heights first adopted a zoning map in 1959 and that the Village was "undeniably committed to single-family homes as its dominant residential land use." No procedural flaws were disclosed by the record, and statements by the Plan Commission and Village Board members "focused almost exclusively on the zoning aspects of the MHDC petition" and did not evince any discriminatory purposes that could be attributed to Village leaders. Having thus disposed of the constitutional issues, the Court remanded the case to the Seventh Circuit to pass on plaintiffs' complaint under the Fair Housing Act.

The Burger Court's restraintist holding in *Arlington Heights* and its reaffirmation of *Washington v. Davis* make a finding of racial discrimination in the denial of low-cost housing extremely difficult, if not impossible, by precluding courts from inferring intent from disproportionate impact except in the most egregious cases, and particularly by requiring a specific showing of intent to discriminate. By predicating a finding of racial discrimination on invidious purpose or motive alone, the Court transformed the slowly evolving trend of increased low- and moderate-income housing in the suburbs into little more than a fanciful pipe dream. The inefficacy of employing the intent test as the primary means for attacking exclusionary zoning is thus readily apparent. The Court held out the possibility that, as one avenue for demonstrating such intent, future courts may undertake inquiries into the actions of governmental officials taken prior to a challenged zoning decision. However, the inevitable difficulties raised by this type of inquiry "cannot be expected to provide much assistance in the determination of discriminatory purpose

or intent." Local legislative and administrative officials are far too clever
to exhibit their prejudicies and malevolent intentions so flagrantly. From
the cases cited by the Court in *Arlington Heights,* it appears that absent
a blatant attempt to discriminate, local zoning actions will be immune
from anything but the most perfunctory scrutiny under the equal protection clause—regardless of how much they in fact burden destitute
minorities.

• • •

53

Interpreting the Constitution: *Roe* v. *Wade*

*[Texas statutes made it a crime to procure an abortion or attempt
one except for the purpose of saving the life of the mother. Mr.
Justice Blackmun delivered the opinion of the Court]*

Jane Roe, a single woman who was residing in Dallas County, Texas,
instituted this federal action in March 1970 against the District Attorney
of the county. She sought a declaratory judgment that the Texas criminal
abortion statutes were unconstitutional on their face, and an injunction
restraining the defendant from enforcing the statutes.

Roe alleged that she was unmarried and pregnant; that she wished
to terminate her pregnancy by an abortion "performed by a competent,
licensed physician, under safe, clinical conditions"; that she was unable
to get a "legal" abortion in Texas because her life did not appear to be
threatened by the continuation of her pregnancy; and that she could not
afford to travel to another jurisdiction in order to secure a legal abortion
under safe conditions. She claimed that the Texas statutes were unconstitutionally vague and that they abridged her right of personal privacy,
protected by the First, Fourth, Fifth, Ninth, and Fourteenth Amendments. By an amendment to her complaint Roe purported to sue "on behalf of herself and all other women" similarly situated.

James Hubert Hallford, a licensed physician, sought and was granted

From *Roe* v. *Wade, Supreme Court Reporter* 93 (1973): 710–711, 726, 727, 730–731,
731–732, 732–733, 733, 763. Footnotes and most references have been omitted.

leave to intervene in Roe's action. In his complaint he alleged that he had been arrested previously for violations of the Texas abortion statutes and that two such prosecutions were pending against him. He described conditions of patients who came to him seeking abortions, and he claimed that for many cases he, as a physician, was unable to determine whether they fell within or outside the exception recognized by Article 1196. He alleged that, as a consequence, the statutes were vague and uncertain, in violation of the Fourteenth Amendment, and that they violated his own and his patients' rights to privacy in the doctor-patient relationship and his own right to practice medicine, rights he claimed were guaranteed by the First, Fourth, Fifth, Ninth, and Fourteenth Amendments.

• • •

The Constitution does not explicitly mention any right of privacy. In a line of decisions, however, going back perhaps as far as Union Pacific R. Co. v. Botsford, 141 U.S. 250, 251, 11 S.Ct. 1000, 1001, 35 L.Ed. 734 (1891), the Court has recognized that a right of personal privacy, or a guarantee of certain areas or zones of privacy, does exist under the Constitution.

• • •

This right of privacy, whether it be founded in the Fourteenth Amendment's concept of personal liberty and restrictions upon state action, as we feel it is, or, as the District Court determined, in the Ninth Amendment's reservation of rights to the people, is broad enough to encompass a woman's decision whether or not to terminate her pregnancy. The detriment that the State would impose upon the pregnant woman by denying this choice altogether is apparent. Specific and direct harm medically diagnosable even in early pregnancy may be involved. Maternity, or additional offspring, may force upon the woman a distressful life and future. Psychological harm may be imminent. Mental and physical health may be taxed by child care. There is also the distress, for all concerned, associated with the unwanted child, and there is the problem of bringing a child into a family already unable, psychologically and otherwise, to care for it. In other cases, as in this one, the additional difficulties and continuing stigma of unwed motherhood may be involved. All these are factors the woman and her responsible physician necessarily will consider in consultation.

On the basis of elements such as these, appellant and some *amici* argue that the woman's right is absolute and that she is entitled to terminate her pregnancy at whatever time, in whatever way, and for whatever reason she alone chooses. With this we do not agree. Appellant's arguments that Texas either has no valid interest at all in regulating the abortion decision, or no interest strong enough to support any limitation upon the woman's sole determination, are unpersuasive. The Court's decisions recognizing a right of privacy also acknowledge that some state regulation in areas protected by that right is appropriate. As noted above, a State may properly assert important interests in safeguarding health, in maintaining medical standards, and in protecting potential life. At some point in pregnancy, these respective interests become sufficiently compelling to sustain regulation of the factors that govern the abortion decision. The privacy right involved, therefore, cannot be said to be absolute. In fact, it is not clear to us that the claim asserted by some *amici* that one has an unlimited right to do with one's body as one pleases bears a close relationship to the right of privacy previously articulated in the Court's decisions. The Court has refused to recognize an unlimited right of this kind in the past. Jacobson v. Massachusetts, 197 U.S. 11, 25 S.Ct. 358, 49 L.Ed. 643 (1905) (vaccination); Buck v. Bell, 274 U.S. 200, 47 S.Ct. 584, 71 L.Ed. 1000 (1927) (sterilization).

We, therefore, conclude that the right of personal privacy includes the abortion decision, but that this right is not unqualified and must be considered against important state interests in regulation.

● ● ●

The pregnant woman cannot be isolated in her privacy. She carries an embryo and, later, a fetus, if one accepts the medical definitions of the developing young in the human uterus. See Dorland's Illustrated Medical Dictionary 478–479, 547 (24th ed. 1965). The situation therefore is inherently different from marital intimacy, or bedroom possession of obscene material, or marriage, or procreation, or education, with which *Eisenstadt* and *Griswold, Stanley, Loving, Skinner* and *Pierce* and *Meyer* were respectively concerned. As we have intimated above, it is reasonable and appropriate for a State to decide that at some point in time another interest, that of health of the mother or that of potential human life, becomes significantly involved. The woman's privacy is no longer sole and any right of privacy she possesses must be measured accordingly.

Texas urges that, apart from the Fourteenth Amendment, life begins at conception and is present throughout pregnancy, and that, therefore, the State has a compelling interest in protecting that life from and after conception. We need not resolve the difficult question of when life begins. When those trained in the respective disciplines of medicine, philosophy, and theology are unable to arrive at any consensus, the judiciary, at this point in the development of man's knowledge, is not in a position to speculate as to the answer.

It should be sufficient to note briefly the wide divergence of thinking on this most sensitive and difficult question. There has always been strong support for the view that life does not begin until live birth. This was the belief of the Stoics. It appears to be the predominant, though not the unanimous, attitude of the Jewish faith. It may be taken to represent also the position of a large segment of the Protestant community, insofar as that can be ascertained; organized groups that have taken a formal position on the abortion issue have generally regarded abortion as a matter for the conscience of the individual and her family. As we have noted, the common law found greater significance in quickening. Physicians and their scientific colleagues have regarded that event with less interest and have tended to focus either upon conception, upon live birth, or upon the interim point at which the fetus becomes "viable," that is, potentially able to live outside the mother's womb, albeit with artificial aid. Viability is usually placed at about seven months (28 weeks) but may occur earlier, even at 24 weeks. The Aristotelian theory of "mediate animation," that held sway throughout the Middle Ages and the Renaissance in Europe, continued to be official Roman Catholic dogma until the 19th century, despite opposition to this "ensoulment" theory from those in the Church who would recognize the existence of life from the moment of conception. The latter is now, of course, the official belief of the Catholic Church. As one brief *amicus* discloses, this is a view strongly held by many non-Catholics as well, and by many physicians. Substantial problems for precise definition of this view are posed, however, by new embryological data that purport to indicate that conception is a "process" over time, rather than an event, and by new medical techniques such as menstrual extraction, the "morning-after" pill, implantation of embryos, artificial insemination, and even artificial wombs.

• • •

In view of all this, we do not agree that, by adopting one theory of life, Texas may override the rights of the pregnant woman that are at stake. We repeat, however, that the State does have an important and legitimate interest in preserving and protecting the health of the pregnant woman, whether she be a resident of the State or a non-resident who seeks medical consultation and treatment there, and that it has still *another* important and legitimate interest in protecting the potentiality of human life. These interests are separate and distinct. Each grows in substantiality as the woman approaches term and, at a point during pregnancy, each becomes "compelling."

With respect to the State's important and legitimate interest in the health of the mother, the "compelling" point, in the light of present medical knowledge, is at approximately the end of the first trimester. This is so because of the now-established medical fact, referred to above that until the end of the first trimester mortality in abortion may be less than mortality in normal childbirth. It follows that, from and after this point, a State may regulate the abortion procedure to the extent that the regulation reasonably relates to the preservation and protection of maternal health. Examples of permissible state regulation in this area are requirements as to the qualifications of the person who is to perform the abortion; as to the licensure of that person; as to the facility in which the procedure is to be performed, that is, whether it must be a hospital or may be a clinic or some other place of less-than-hospital status; as to the licensing of the facility; and the like.

This means, on the other hand, that, for the period of pregnancy prior to this "compelling" point, the attending physician, in consultation with his patient, is free to determine, without regulation by the State, that, in his medical judgment, the patient's pregnancy should be terminated. If that decision is reached, the judgment may be effectuated by an abortion free of interference by the State.

With respect to the State's important and legitimate interest in potential life, the "compelling" point is at viability. This is so because the fetus then presumably has the capability of meaningful life outside the mother's womb. State regulation protective of fetal life after viability thus has both logical and biological justifications. If the State is interested in protecting fetal life after viability, it may go so far as to proscribe abortion during that period, except when it is necessary to preserve the life or health of the mother.

Measured against these standards, Art. 1196 of the Texas Penal Code, in restricting legal abortions to those "procured or attempted by medical advice for the purpose of saving the life of the mother," sweeps too broadly. The statute makes no distinction between abortions performed early in pregnancy and those performed later, and it limits to a single reason, "saving" the mother's life, the legal justification for the procedure. The statute, therefore, cannot survive the constitutional attack made upon it here.

• • •

To summarize and to repeat:

1. A state criminal abortion statute of the current Texas type, that excepts from criminality only a *life-saving* procedure on behalf of the mother, without regard to pregnancy stage and without recognition of the other interests involved, is violative of the Due Process Clause of the Fourteenth Amendment.
    (a) For the stage prior to approximately the end of the first trimester, the abortion decision and its effectuation must be left to the medical judgment of the pregnant woman's attending physician.
    (b) For the stage subsequent to approximately the end of the first

trimester, the State, in promoting its interest in the health of the mother, may, if it chooses, regulate the abortion procedure in ways that are reasonably related to maternal health.

(c) For the stage subsequent to viability, the State in promoting its interest in the potentiality of human life may, if it chooses, regulate, and even proscribe, abortion except where it is necessary, in appropriate medical judgment, for the preservation of the life or health of the mother.

2. The State may define the term "physician," as it has been employed in the preceding paragraphs of this Part XI of this opinion, to mean only a physician currently licensed by the State, and may proscribe any abortion by a person who is not a physician as so defined.

• • •

This holding, we feel, is consistent with the relative weights of the respective interests involved, with the lessons and examples of medical and legal history, with the lenity of the common law, and with the demands of the profound problems of the present day. The decision leaves the State free to place increasing restrictions on abortion as the period of pregnancy lengthens, so long as those restrictions are tailored to the recognized state interests. The decision vindicates the right of the physician to administer medical treatment according to his professional judgment up to the points where important state interests provide compelling justifications for intervention. Up to those points, the abortion decision in all its aspects is inherently, and primarily, a medical decision, and basic responsibility for it must rest with the physician. If an individual practitioner abuses the privilege of exercising proper medical judgment, the usual remedies, judicial and intra-professional, are available.

• • •

[*Justice White wrote a dissenting opinion which Justice Rehnquist joined.*]

• • •

With all due respect, I dissent. I find nothing in the language or history of the Constitution to support the Court's judgments. The Court simply fashions and announces a new constitutional right for pregnant women and, with scarcely any reason or authority for its action, invests that right with sufficient substance to override most existing state abortion statutes. The upshot is that the people and the legislatures of the 50 States are constitutionally disentitled to weigh the relative importance of the continued existence and development of the fetus, on the one hand, against a spectrum of possible impacts on the mother, on the other hand. As an exercise of raw judicial power, the Court perhaps has authority to do what it does today; but in my view its judgment is an improvident and extravagant exercise of the power of judicial review that the Constitution extends to this Court.

The Court apparently values the convenience of the pregnant woman more than the continued existence and development of the life or potential life that she carries. Whether or not I might agree with that marshaling of values, I can in no event join the Court's judgment because I find no constitutional warrant for imposing such an order of priorities on the people and legislatures of the States. In a sensitive area such as this, involving as it does issues over which reasonable men may easily and heatedly differ, I cannot accept the Court's exercise of its clear power of choice by interposing a constitutional barrier to state efforts to protect human life and by investing women and doctors with the constitutionally protected right to exterminate it. This issue, for the most part, should be left with the people and to the political processes the people have devised to govern their affairs.

It is my view, therefore, that the Texas statute is not constitutionally infirm because it denies abortions to those who seek to serve only their convenience rather than to protect their life or health. Nor is this plaintiff, who claims no threat to her mental or physical health, entitled to assert the possible rights of those women whose pregnancy assertedly implicates their health.

54

Interpreting A Statute: Holmes Dissenting

Mr. Justice Holmes, with whom concurred the Chief Justice, Mr. Justice White, and Mr. Justice Peckham, dissenting:

I am unable to agree with the judgment of the majority of the court, and although I think it useless and undesirable, as a rule, to express dissent, I feel bound to do so in this case and to give my reasons for it.

Mr. Justice Holmes dissenting in *Northern Securities* v. *U.S., Supreme Court Reporter* 24 (1904): 468. Footnotes have been omitted.

Great cases, like hard cases, make bad law. For great cases are called great, not by reason of their real importance in shaping the law of the future, but because of some accident of immediate overwhelming interest which appeals to the feelings and distorts the judgment. These immediate interests exercise a kind of hydraulic pressure which makes what previously was clear seem doubtful, and before which even well settled principles of law will bend. What we have to do in this case is to find the meaning of some not very difficult words. We must try,—I have tried,—to do it with the same freedom of natural and spontaneous interpretation that one would be sure of if the same question arose upon an indictment for a similar act which excited no public attention, and was of importance only to a prisoner before the court. Furthermore, while at times judges need for their work the training of economists or statesmen, and must act in view of their foresight of consequences, yet, when their task is to interpret and apply the words of a statute, their function is merely academic to begin with,—to read English intelligently,—and a consideration of consequences comes into play, if at all, only when the meaning of the words used is open to reasonable doubt.

• • •

55

Interpreting A Statute: *Kaiser* v. *Weber*

[*Mr. Justice Brennan delivered the opinion of the Court*]

• • •

I

In 1974 petitioner United Steelworkers of America (USWA) and petitioner Kaiser Aluminum & Chemical Corporation (Kaiser) entered into a master collective-bargaining agreement covering terms and conditions

---

From *Kaiser Aluminum and Chemical Corporation* v. *Weber, The United States Law Week* 47 (1979): 4852–4853, 4853–4855, 4858–4859. *The United States Law Week* is a publication of The Bureau of National Affairs, Inc. Reprinted by permission. Footnotes have been omitted.

of employment at 15 Kaiser plants. The agreement contained, *inter alia,* an affirmative action plan designed to eliminate conspicuous racial imbalances in Kaiser's then almost exclusively white craft work forces. Black craft hiring goals were set for each Kaiser plant equal to the percentage of blacks in the respective local labor forces. To enable plants to meet these goals, on-the-job training programs were established to teach unskilled production workers—black and white—the skills necessary to become craft workers. The plan reserved for black employees 50% of the openings in these newly created in-plant training programs.

This case arose from the operation of the plan at Kaiser's plant in Gramercy, La. Until 1974 Kaiser hired as craft workers for that plant only persons who had had prior craft experience. Because blacks had long been excluded from craft unions, few were able to present such credentials. As a consequence, prior to 1974 only 1.83% (five out of 273) of the skilled craft workers at the Gramercy plant were black, even though the work force in the Gramercy area was approximately 39% black.

Pursuant to the national agreement Kaiser altered its craft hiring practice in the Gramercy plant. Rather than hiring already trained outsiders, Kaiser established a training program to train its production workers to fill craft openings. Selection of craft trainees was made on the basis of seniority, with the proviso that at least 50% of the new trainees were to be black until the percentage of black skilled craft workers in the Gramercy plant approximated the percentage of blacks in the local labor force.

During 1974, the first year of the operation of the Kaiser-USWA affirmative action plan, 13 craft trainees were selected from Gramercy's production work force. Of these, 7 were black and 6 white. The most junior black selected into the program had less seniority than several white production workers whose bids for admission were rejected. Thereafter one of those white production workers, respondent Brian Weber, instituted this class action in the United States District Court for the Eastern District of Louisiana.

The complaint alleged that the filling of craft trainee positions at the Gramercy plant pursuant to the affirmative action program had resulted in junior black employees receiving training in preference to more senior white employees, thus discriminating against respondent and other similarly situated white employees in violation of §§ 703 (a) and (d) of Title VII. The District Court held that the plan violated Title VII, entered a judgment in favor of the plaintiff class, and granted a permanent injunction prohibiting Kaiser and the USWA "from denying plaintiffs, Brian F. Weber and all other members of the class, access to on-the-job training programs on the basis of race." A divided panel of the Court of Appeals for the Fifth Circuit affirmed, holding that all employment preferences based upon race, including those preferences incidental to bona fide affirmative action plans, violated Title VII's prohibition against racial discrimination in employment. We granted certiorari. We reverse.

• • •

The only question before us is the narrow statutory issue of whether Title VII *forbids* private employers and unions from voluntarily agreeing upon bona fide affirmative action plans that accord racial preferences in the manner and for the purpose provided in the Kaiser-USWA plan. That question was expressly left open in *McDonald* v. *Santa Fe Trail Trans. Co.,* which held, in a case not involving affirmative action, that Title VII protects whites as well as blacks from certain forms of racial discrimination.

Respondent argues that Congress intended in Title VII to prohibit all race-conscious affirmative action plans. Respondent's argument rests upon a literal interpretation of §§ 703 (a) and (d) of the Act. Those sections make it unlawful to "discriminate . . . because of . . . race" in hiring and in the selection of apprentices for training programs. Since, the argument runs, *McDonald* v. *Santa Fe Trans. Co., supra,* settled that Title VII forbids discrimination against whites as well as blacks, and since the Kaiser-USWA affirmative action plan operates to discriminate against white employees solely because they are white, it follows that the Kaiser-USWA plan violates Title VII.

Respondent's argument is not without force. But it overlooks the significance of the fact that the Kaiser-USWA plan is an affirmative action plan voluntarily adopted by private parties to eliminate traditional patterns of racial segregation. In this context respondent's reliance upon a literal construction of § 703 (a) and (d) upon *McDonald* is misplaced. It is a "familiar rule, that a thing may be within the letter of the statute and yet not within the statute, because not within its spirit, nor within the intention of its makers." The prohibition against racial discrimination in §§ 703 (a) and (d) of Title VII must therefore be read against the background of the legislative history of Title VII and the historical context from which the Act arose. Examination of those sources makes clear that an interpretation of the sections that forbade all race-conscious affirmative action would "bring about an end completely at variance with the purpose of the statute" and must be rejected.

Congress' primary concern in enacting the prohibition against racial discrimination in Title VII of the Civil Rights Act of 1964 was with "the plight of the Negro in our economy." Before 1964, blacks were largely relegated to "unskilled and semi-skilled jobs." Because of automation the number of such jobs was rapidly decreasing. As a consequence "the relative position of the Negro worker [was] steadily worsening. In 1947 the non-white unemployment rate was only 64 percent higher than the white rate; in 1962 it was 124 percent higher." Congress considered this a serious social problem. As Senator Clark told the Senate:

> "The rate of Negro unemployment has gone up consistently as compared with white unemployment for the past 15 years. This is a social malaise and a social situation which we should not tolerate. That is one of the principal reasons why this bill should pass."

Congress feared that the goals of the Civil Rights Act—the integration of blacks into the mainstream of American society—could not be achieved unless this trend were reversed. And Congress recognized that that would not be possible unless blacks were able to secure jobs "which have a future." As Senator Humphrey explained to the Senate.

> "What good does it do a Negro to be able to eat in a fine restaurant if he cannot afford to pay the bill? What good does it do him to be accepted in a hotel that is too expensive for his modest income? How can a Negro child be motivated to take full advantage of integrated educational facilities if he has no hope of getting a job where he can use that education?"

• • •

> "Without a job, one cannot afford public convenience and accommodations. Income from employment may be necessary to further a man's education, or that of his children. If his children have no hope of getting a good job, what will motivate them to take advantage of educational opportunities."

These remarks echoed President Kennedy's original message to Congress upon the introduction of the Civil Rights Act in 1963.

> "There is little value in a Negro's obtaining the right to be admitted to hotels and restaurants if he has no cash in his pocket and no job."

Accordingly, it was clear to Congress that "the crux of the problem [was] to open employment opportunities for Negroes in occupations which have been traditionally closed to them," and it was to this problem that Title VII's prohibition against racial discrimination in employment was primarily addressed.

It plainly appears from the House Report accompanying the Civil Rights Act that Congress did not intend wholly to prohibit private and voluntary affirmative action efforts as one method of solving this problem. The Report provides:

> "No bill can or should lay claim to eliminating all of the causes and consequences of racial and other types of discrimination against minorities. There is reason to believe, however, that national leadership provided by the enactment of Federal legislation dealing with the most troublesome problems *will create an atmosphere conducive to voluntary or local resolution of other forms of discrimination.*"

Given this legislative history, we cannot agree with respondent that Congress intended to prohibit the private sector from taking effective steps to accomplish the goal that Congress designed Title VII to achieve. The very statutory words intended as a spur or catalyst to cause "employers and unions to self-examine and to self-evaluate their employment practices and to endeavor to eliminate, so far as possible, the last vestiges of an unfortunate and ignominious page in this country's history," cannot be interpreted as an absolute prohibition against all private, voluntary, race-conscious affirmative action efforts to hasten the elimination of such vestiges. It would be ironic indeed if a law triggered by a Nation's concern over centuries of racial injustice and intended to improve the lot of those who had "been excluded from the American dream for so long" constituted the first legislative prohibition of all voluntary, private, race-conscious efforts to abolish traditional patterns of racial segregation and hierarchy.

Our conclusion is further reinforced by examination of the language and legislative history of § 703 (j) of Title VII. Opponents of Title VII raised two related arguments against the bill. First, they argued that the Act would be interpreted to *require* employers with racially imbalanced work forces to grant preferential treatment to racial minorities in order to integrate. Second, they argued that employers with racially imbalanced work forces would grant preferential treatment to racial minorities, even if not required to do so by the Act. Had Congress meant to prohibit all race-conscious affirmative action, as respondent urges, it easily could have answered both objections by providing that Title VII would not require or *permit* racially preferential integration efforts. But Congress did not choose such a course. Rather Congress added § 703 (j) which addresses only the first objection. The section provides that nothing contained in Title VII "shall be interpreted to *require* any employer . . . to grant preferential treatment . . . to any group because of the race . . . of such . . . group on account of" a defacto racial imbalance in the employer's work force. The section does *not* state that "nothing in Title VII shall be interpreted to *permit*" voluntary affirmative efforts to correct racial imbalances. The natural inference is that Congress chose not to forbid all voluntary race-conscious affirmative action.

The reasons for this choice are evident from the legislative record. Title VII could not have been enacted into law without substantial support from legislators in both Houses who traditionally resisted federal regulation of private business. Those legislators demanded as a price for their support that "management prerogatives and union freedoms . . . be left undisturbed to the greatest extent possible." Section 703 (j) was proposed by Senator Dirksen to allay any fears that the Act might be interpreted in such a way as to upset this compromise. The section was designed to prevent § 703 of Title VII from being interpreted in such a way as to lead to undue "Federal Government interference with private businesses because of some Federal employee's ideas about racial balance or imbalance." Clearly, a prohibition against all voluntary, race-conscious, affirmative action efforts would disserve these ends. Such a prohibition would augment the powers of the Federal Government and diminish traditional management prerogatives while at the same time impeding attainment of the ultimate statutory goals. In view of this legislative history and in view of Congress' desire to avoid undue federal regulation of private businesses, use of the word "require" rather than the phrase "require or permit" in § 703 (j) fortifies the conclusion that Congress did not intend to limit traditional business freedom to such a degree as to prohibit all voluntary, race-conscious affirmative action.

We therefore hold that Title VII's prohibition in §§ 703 (a) and (d) against racial discrimination does not condemn all private, voluntary, race-conscious affirmative action plans.

● ● ●

[*Mr. Chief Justice Burger dissenting*]

● ● ●

Until today, I had thought the Court was of the unanimous view that "discriminatory preference for any group, minority or majority, is precisely and only what Congress has proscribed" in Title VII. *Griggs* v. *Duke Power Co.* Had Congress intended otherwise, it very easily could have drafted language allowing what the Court permits today. Far from doing so, Congress expressly *prohibited* in §§ 703 (a) and (d) the discrimination against Brian Weber the Court approves now. If "affirmative action" programs such as the one presented in this case are to be permitted, it is for Congress, not this Court, to so direct.

It is often observed that hard cases make bad law. I suspect there is some truth to that adage, for the "hard" cases always tempt judges to exceed the limits of their authority, as the Court does today by totally rewriting a crucial part of Title VII to reach a desirable result. Cardozo no doubt had this type of case in mind when he wrote:

"The judge, even when he is free, is still not wholly free. He is not to innovate at pleasure. He is not a knight-errant, roaming at will in pursuit of his own ideal of beauty or of goodness. He is to draw his inspiration from consecrated principles. He is not to yield to spasmodic sentiment, to vague and unregulated benevolence. He is to exercise a discretion informed by tradition, methodized by analogy, disciplined by system, and subordinated to 'the primordial necessity of order in the social life.' Wide enough in all conscience is the field of discretion that remains."

What Cardozo tells us is beware the "good result," achieved by judicially unauthorized or intellectually dishonest means on the appealing notion that the desirable ends justify the improper judicial means. For there is always the danger that the seeds of precedent sown by good men for the best of motives will yield a rich harvest of unprincipled acts of others also aiming at "good ends."

Mr. Justice Rehnquist, with whom the Chief Justice joins, dissenting.

In a very real sense, the Court's opinion is ahead of its time: it could more appropriately have been handed down five years from now, in 1984, a year coinciding with the title of a book from which the Court's opinion borrows, perhaps subconsciously, at least one idea. Orwell describes in his book a governmental official of Oceania, one of the three great world powers, denouncing the current enemy, Eurasia, to an assembled crowd:

> "It was almost impossible to listen to him without being first convinced and then maddened. . . . The speech had been proceeding for perhaps twenty minutes when a messenger hurried onto the platform and a scrap of paper was slipped into the speaker's hand. He unrolled and read it without pausing in his speech. Nothing altered in his voice or manner, or in the content of what he was saying, but suddenly the names were different. Without words said, a wave of understanding rippled through the crowd. Oceania was at war with Eastasia! . . . The banners and posters with which the square was decorated were all wrong! . . .
> "[T]he speaker had switched from one line to the other actually in mid-sentence, not only without a pause, but without even breaking the syntax."

Today's decision represents an equally dramatic and equally unremarked switch in this Court's interpretation of Title VII.

The operative sections of Title VII prohibit racial discrimination in employment *simpliciter*. Taken in its normal meaning, and as understood by all Members of Congress who spoke to the issue during the legislative debates . . . this language prohibits a covered employer from considering race when making an employment decision, whether the race be black or white. Several years ago, however, a United States District Court held that "the dismissal of white employees charged with misappropriating company property while not dismissing a similarly charged Negro employee does not raise a claim upon which Title VII relief may be granted." *McDonald* v. *Santa Fe Trail Transp. Co.* This Court unanimously reversed, concluding from the "uncontradicted legislative history" that "Title VII prohibits racial discrimination against the white petitioners in this case upon the same standards as would be applicable were they Negroes. . . ."

We have never waivered in our understanding that Title VII "prohibits *all* racial discrimination in employment, without exception for any particular employees." In *Griggs* v. *Duke Power Co.,* our first occasion to interpret Title VII, a unanimous court observed that "[d]iscriminatory preference, for any group, minority or majority, is precisely and only what Congress has proscribed." And in our most recent discussion of the issue, we uttered words seemingly dispositive of this case: "It is clear beyond cavil that the obligation imposed by Title VII is to provide an equal opportunity for *each* applicant regardless of race, without regard to whether members of the applicant's race are already proportionately represented in the work force." *Furnco Construction Corp.* v. *Waters.*

Today, however, the Court behaves much like the Orwellian speaker earlier described, as if it had been handed a note indicating that Title VII would lead to a result unacceptable to the Court if interpreted here as it was in our prior decisions. Accordingly, without even a break in syntax, the Court rejects "a literal construction of § 703 (a)" in favor of newly discovered "legislative history," which leads it to a conclusion directly contrary to that compelled by the "uncontradicted legislative history" unearthed in *McDonald* and our other prior decisions. Now we are told that the legislative history of Title VII shows that employers are free to discriminate on the basis of race: an employer may, in the Court's words, "trammel the interests of white employees" in favor of black employees in order to eliminate "racial imbalance." Our earlier interpretations of Title VII, like the banners and posters decorating the square in Oceania, were all wrong.

As if this were not enough to make a reasonable observer question this Court's adherence to the oft-stated principle that our duty is to construe rather than rewrite legislation, *United States* v. *Rutherford,* the Court also seizes upon § 703 (j) of Title VII as an independent, or at least partially independent, basis for its holding. Totally ignoring the wording of that section, which is obviously addressed to those charged with the responsibility of interpreting the law rather than those who are subject to its proscriptions, and totally ignoring the months of legislative debates preceding the section's introduction and passage, which demonstrate clearly that it was enacted to prevent precisely what occurred in this case, the Court infers from § 703 (j) that "Congress chose not to forbid all voluntary race-conscious affirmative action."

Thus, by a *tour de force* reminiscent not of jurists such as Hale, Holmes, and Hughes, but of escape artists such as Houdini, the Court eludes clear statutory language, "uncontradicted" legislative history, and uniform precedent in concluding that employers are, after all, permitted to consider race in making employment decisions. It may be that one or more of the principal sponsors of Title VII would have preferred to see a provision allowing preferential treatment of minorities written into the bill. Such a provision, however, would have to have been expressly or impliedly excepted from Title VII's explicit prohibition on all racial discrimination in employment. There is no such exception in the Act. And a reading of the legislative debates concerning Title VII, in which proponents and opponents alike uniformly denounced discrimination in favor of, as well as discrimination against, Negroes, demonstrates clearly that any legislator harboring an unspoken desire for such a provision could not possibly have succeeded in enacting it into law.

--------------------------- **56** ---------------------------

Interpreting A Statute: A Congressman Reacts

SUPREME COURT SAYS CONGRESS IS
WELL INTENTIONED BUT ILLITERATE

HON. JOHN M. ASHBROOK
OF OHIO
IN THE HOUSE OF REPRESENTATIVES
Monday, September 24, 1979

• Mr. ASHBROOK. Mr. Speaker, in the Weber case, the U.S. Supreme Court decided that the Congress, in banning employment discrimination, meant only to ban discrimination against everyone except white males. When we passed title VII of the Civil Rights Act, we are told, we meant to add to that ban the words "except women and nonwhites belonging to groups which, in the opinion of the employer, have been the subject of previous discrimination." That is what we meant, according to the Supreme Court, but we were not capable of saying it.

This is the sort of precedent all of us, liberal, conservative, Republican and Democrat, had better take seriously, because it is an extremely dangerous one. It is true that every Member from time has doubts about the intelligence of some of his colleagues with whom he disagrees, but I do not believe any of us has ever doubted that every Member of this body is quite capable of drafting the exception to title VII which the Supreme

---

Statement of John M. Ashbrook, Representative from Ohio, *Congressional Record,* 96th Congress, 1st Session (September 24, 1979): E4699. Footnotes have been omitted.

Court insists we could not have formulated without its help. If we wish title VII to say something besides what, in the plainest conceivable language, it does say—that all employment discrimination on the basis of race is prohibited—then we can, if a majority so chooses, do so on our own. Every Supreme Court Justice knows such an alteration would be repudiated overwhelmingly. It is not the place of the Supreme Court to unilaterally change the language of the act. That is the business of the U.S. Congress.

If there is one fact of which recent history has made every Member aware, it is that, if we do not defend the authority of Congress, no one is going to protect it for us. While it was not the purpose of the Supreme Court's action, it is impossible to imagine a more direct challenge to our prerogatives than its rewriting of our legislation while we were actually in session less than a block away.

The Supreme Court as a Small Group

57

Courts as Small Groups

Walter F. Murphy

Collegial courts and juries are small groups in a face-to-face relationship that interact under an obligation to solve a specific problem or set of problems. Reliable theories and perhaps even raw data about human behavior in small groups may thus be relevant to the study of the judicial process.

• • •

I

A major stimulus of small group studies of judicial behavior has been the work of C. Herman Pritchett of the University of Chicago. Beginning in the early 1940's Pritchett published a series of articles and *The Roosevelt Court,* demonstrating the existence of cohesive voting blocs on the U.S. Supreme Court during the years 1937–1947. He relied in part on traditional case analysis but also used statistical analysis of the Justices' votes to show consistent tendencies of certain members of the Court to vote together on various classes of issues. The bloc analysis portion of his study depended entirely on the votes of the Justices.

From Walter F. Murphy, "Courts as Small Groups," *Harvard Law Review* 79 (1966): 1565, 1565–1570, 1570–1571, 1572. Copyright © 1966 by the Harvard Law Review Association. Reprinted by permission. Footnotes have been omitted.

In 1958 Eloise Snyder, a sociologist, published an analysis of the Supreme Court which considered whether the Court over a long time span (1921–1953) had divided into persistent subgroups, how changes in alignments occurred, and how new Justices found their position within the larger group. Using as her data the votes of the Justices in all non-unanimous constitutional cases during the thirty-three year period, Snyder found that the Court divided into three subgroups: a liberal group, a conservative group, and a pivotal group that lacked a firm commitment. Snyder reported that these alignments were consistent. While a Justice might switch from a pivotal to a liberal or conservative subgroup or vice-versa, never did a Justice of the liberal subgroup cross over to the conservative bloc, and rarely did a Justice make the conservative-to-liberal transition without a pause in the pivotal group. She noted a general tendency to shift to the right during a Justice's career but attributed this more to the Court moving to the left so as to make a Justice whose views did not change seem to shift to the right than to any change of views by the individual Justice. Newly appointed Justices tended to join the pivotal subgroup, the group that frequently held the balance of power. After a time on the Court they tended to gravitate to the right or left subgroup.

Since Pritchett and Snyder only used voting records they could discover little more than that Justices could be classified; study of groups also requires consideration of interpersonal interaction and influence. The fact that two or more Justices vote together is rather weak evidence that their votes are the result of interaction; standing alone, voting records tell very little about the force or direction of any interpersonal influence that may exist. Small group analysis requires other kinds of data and a more general understanding of the impact of a group decisional situation on individual behavior.

Especially in the postwar period, social psychologists have produced a mass of literature on group decisional situations. Their research was based on observation of people brought together under laboratory conditions and given a specific problem to solve. The experiments were designed to suggest and to test as rigorously as possible general hypotheses about leadership as a function of group interaction. Professor Robert Bales of Harvard, perhaps the leader in this field, developed a concept of the dual character of leadership; task leadership and social leadership. The former seeks to complete the present task in the most effective and efficient manner; the latter seeks to provide the friendly atmosphere that eases cooperation. Experiments indicated that these two functions often are exercised by different persons within the group.

It is difficult to obtain direct observations of the judicial decision-making process. The private papers of deceased judges, however, constitute a fruitful source of information, and various judges have preserved their working papers—including intracourt memoranda, slip opinions as edited by colleagues, and occasionally notes taken during conference discussions—and arranged for their future use by scholars.

David Danelski, a lawyer and political scientist, was the first to utilize both the theoretical constructs of the small group sociologists and the information in judicial papers to apply a small group approach to a court. Relying on materials found in the unpublished papers of a number of Justices, Danelski applied Bales' concept of dual leadership to the Supreme Court under Chief Justices Taft, Hughes, and Stone. Taft, he concluded, was the social leader of his court and relied on his close friend Willis Van Devanter to supply task leadership; Hughes exercised task leadership over his brethren and also offered some social leadership; Stone played neither role and was unable to ally himself with one or more colleagues who could perform these functions.

Danelski concluded that as a result of the comparative ability in social leadership, conflict among the Justices was more muted and cohesion more pronounced on the Taft Court than on the Hughes Court and far more so than on the Stone Court. Danelski ranks the Hughes Court somewhat ahead of that of Taft and well above that of Stone in terms of the effectiveness of task leadership—decisions produced in relation to conference time. Hughes's advantage in playing both roles was offset, Danelski believes, by Taft's greater skill as a social leader.

In a work related to Danelski's, I discussed how a Justice of the Supreme Court could lawfully act to maximize his influence on public policy development through a process of bargaining. My objective was not to demonstrate how the judicial process typically operates but to explain the capability of a single Justice to affect the definition and allocation of values in our society. The Associate Justices of the U.S. Supreme Court are equal in authority, and the Chief Justice has only a small amount of additional authority. It may sometimes happen for a period of time, as with John Marshall, that a judge may by the power of his intellect and the sheer force of his personality lead his colleagues. Certainly one should not underestimate the importance in the judicial process of reasoned argument based on thorough research and grounded in deep learning, nor should one be willing without evidence to deny that even judges may be swayed by a great personality. Yet on many issues a Justice may find himself unable to convince colleagues even after massing all his erudition and dialectical skill, and even after emotional appeals. A Justice may thus find himself either: (a) with the majority on the result but unable to agree with other Justices on the reasoning to support the decision; (b) with the minority on both scores; or (c) with the majority on both points but faced with the publication of an acid dissent. In these situations he can strike out on his own and write his views just as he holds them, or he can negotiate with his colleagues and try to compromise existing differences.

Bickel and Wellington have criticized the Warren Court because some of its opinions appear to be "desperately negotiated documents," but it would seem that many if not most opinions of the Court on major issues are negotiated documents. I would also hypothesize that this kind of bargaining process occurs on any collegial court that follows similar formal procedures of group decision-making. If this is true, close reading of an opinion should include consideration of the compromises it may contain. What may seem inscrutable wisdom to the traditional case analyst may only be deliberate ambiguity designed to accommodate by its very vagueness conflicting doctrines. One would not expect nine or even five intelligent, individualistic, and strong-willed lawyers to agree readily on controversial and significant issues, must less on the doctrines to be established and reasoning to be used to justify any major ruling. As Justice Frankfurter observed after fourteen years on the bench: "When you have to have at least five people to agree on something, they can't have that comprehensive completeness of candor which is open to a single man, giving his own reasons untrammeled by what anybody else may do or not do if he put that out." The bargaining and resulting compromise may be over trivial matters of literary style or over crucial doctrinal issues. The objects which a Justice has to trade are his vote and his concurrence in an opinion; his sanctions are his right to change his vote and his right to write a separate opinion. Quite clearly the effectiveness of the first sanction depends largely on the existing division within the Court and of the second on the Justice's literary skill and legal expertise. Bargaining may be the product of open negotiation or it may be accomplished tacitly. Brandeis, Bickel shows, was a master of the latter technique. Often he would circulate a dissent within the Court, then withdraw it when the conservative majority modified the opinion of the Court.

II

[A] small group approach offers no magic key to understanding judicial behavior. One has to keep in mind, first, that social scientists have so far only a variety of hypotheses about behavior in small groups, most of which have been tested only in experimental, laboratory situations. Clearly one must not uncritically apply to the actions of professional judges concepts derived from the behavior of *ad hoc* groups assembled in a laboratory for the purpose of solving only one problem. The findings of small group sociologists should be treated only as working hypotheses until tested outside the laboratory. And of course no social scientist claims that the group environment is the only factor governing behavior. Small group analysis, as Golembiewski points out, merely supplements understanding of individual psychology and of social forces operating in the larger social environment.

More specifically I have reservations about the orientation of much of the small group literature toward leadership. Stressing leadership as a product of a social situation may leave the impression that because the functions of leadership are needed, they will be performed. But a leadership void may exist and persist, or only be partially filled. Moreover, just as one must be careful not to mistake formal trappings for real leadership, so too one has to be careful not to equate role-playing with effective role-playing. For instance, though Hughes was able to center discussion on the questions he thought important and to conduct that discussion rapidly and efficiently, and though he soothed ruffled feelings and maintained a working level of harmony among the brethren, the vital question remains: having led them to be social and having led them through their tasks, was he able to lead the Justices to vote and to write opinions the way he wanted? The inability of small group theories to provide answers or even a framework for answers to this question detracts from their usefulness; but it would not appear that the future establishment of such a framework is impossible.

• • •

III

Although it may not be of any immediate use in winning a particular lawsuit, small group analysis has already done much to increase understanding—by social scientists as well as lawyers—of the judicial process; and the various approaches have not yet been nearly fully exploited. There have been few investigations of tribunals other than the U.S. Supreme Court. It would be very useful to have comparative studies of the influence of the group situation in courts that follow other kinds of formal decisional procedures. What difference does it make, for instance, that in some states the task of writing the opinion of the court is assigned on a strictly rotational basis? Or if, as in England and Canada, there is a tradition of seriatim rather than institutionl opinions? Or if, as in civil law countries, there is a rule against separate opinions? Do any of these formal practices affect the exercise of leadership and bargaining among the judges? What kinds of informal rules or customs develop to protect the integrity of the court and maintain harmony between the majority and the minority? Most important, what effect do these formal and informal procedures have on the course of the development of law and public policy?

—————————————— 58 ——————————————

Leadership and Group Structure

S. Sidney Ulmer

• • •

Leadership and Group Structure

As soon as decision making is shifted from an individual to a group, a number of immediate opportunities are opened or necessitated. Groups pursuing a task require leadership, and administration of group activities must be coordinated. Recognizing this, all appellate courts have chief judges or justices selected by the groups themselves or by some outside authority.

The chief judges in collegial courts do not all exercise leadership in the same degree. For the question at issue may be not who shall lead, but who in fact gets followed; not how leaders should act, but how they in fact behave. In spite of the designation of a "formal leader" or "head" in a collegial court, the group condition provides the opportunity for any member of the group to exert influence upon his colleagues.

What constitutes evidence of leadership in an appellate court? We cannot answer this question by observing who possesses leadership traits. The trait theory is implausible since research has not been able to establish a set of personality characteristics common to all or even most leaders. Common sense suggests that different situations call for differential leadership, for disparate skills and abilities. One who possesses the qualifications necessary and sufficient to perform brilliantly for the group in one setting may be totally inadequate for a different set of demands or a different situation. It is for precisely such reasons that good field generals in military services are frequently failures in more diplomatic roles. This does not dismiss intelligence, congeniality, analytical skills, and sensitivity to the needs of others as irrelevant for the leader. But it does suggest that a collegial court may have more than one leader and, possibly, that all members of such a group exercise leadership of varying quality and quantity across varying situations.

Leaders may be formally designated or simply followed. Procedure for identifying a leader depends on which approach is followed. Small-group research has shown that the most active member of a group is likely to exert the greatest interpersonal influence on a decision. This finding held for laboratory groups of students and also for mock juries in experiments carried out at the University of Chicago. There the most active jurors were disproportionately powerful in shaping final jury verdicts. But of course this generalization does not always hold, and it is easy to visualize situations in which it would be nonsensical to expect it. Imagine a highly manic or hysterical group member who monopolized the floor in an attempt to displace his own personal drives and problems. We would, in such a case, expect a low correlation between activity and influence.

A modified view combines acts initiated with support received. Where the group is carrying out its work in a glass enclosed laboratory, it is simple to observe who initiates acts and the support or lack of support directed to the initiators. We may expect the same phenomena to occur in collegial courts as in laboratory experiments, but such courts decide cases in private conferences. Thus direct access to multiple judge interaction is not available. To pursue the question further requires some modification in traditional methods. By using surrogate measures of "act initiated" and "support," certain inferences can be derived from indirect observation—retaining at the same time the spirit of traditional small-group research procedures.

Since in many if not all collegial courts, the individual judge is free to initiate a written opinion and to support or oppose opinions written by other judges, opinion initiation and support patterns can be used as indicators to the total activity occurring in the conference. Such a procedure applied to the Michigan Supreme Court by Ulmer . . . has shown a high correlation between leadership so measured and ability to align a majority of the judges in support of an opinion. The most influential Michigan judge was able to get majority support for 97 per cent of the opinions he initiated, but the least effective leader obtained support in only 66 per cent of his opinions.

Since it is the majority opinion alone that furnishes the principal rationale for court decisions and draws the implications of the decision for those in similar litigations, leadership in this instance was highly effective in promoting the leader's point of view in the law.

Danelski . . . suggests that Supreme Court justices engage in "social" and "task" leadership. In social psychology these terms designate a leader who strives to make interpersonal relations congenial to task accomplishment as opposed to one who constantly pushes his group toward completion of the task. The former provides humor in tense situations, interprets conflict as completely devoid of personal considerations, emphasizes common interest and purpose, and generally "strokes" the egos of his colleagues. The task leader, on the other hand, is likely to be more compulsive, efficient at organization and administration, and highly conscious of the responsibility of the group to higher or larger authority.

A single justice may, of course, exercise both leadership functions. Chief Justice Warren was known to take walks with the associate justices around the Supreme Court grounds and on occasion treated them to duck and pheasant luncheons. Yet his court in sixteen years decided more cases than the next three highest courts combined in a period of forty years. But chief justices cannot necessarily be set off from other justices in exercising either task or social leadership or both. Data necessary for comparative evaluation is not available. The associate justices are known to meet socially outside the Court. They lunch together, have cocktails together, and so on. An excellent example of a justice exerting social leadership through humor is represented by a note passed in conference in 1949. In the note, one justice says to another, "I told —— that I would give him a drink if he would discuss Westinghouse with me. There was no chance on you."

As for task leadership, Associate Justice Van Devanter was once described by Justice Brandeis as "like a Jesuit General." Additional examples could be provided quite easily. But the lesson here is not only that both chief justices and associate justices may exercise task and social leadership. It is more important to note that attempts to pigeonhole justices in one or the other category or to characterize individuals as exercising both functions is not at present justified. Until more complete data can be gathered and systematically analyzed, the conceptual distinction will prove to be most useful as a heuristic device.

Whether Supreme Court justices get followed and how those who are influential behave is, of course, a question we can ask. But a formally designated leader in a collegial court influences the behavior of his group not by virtue of his administrative effectiveness or congenial air, not because his colleagues decide he deserves to be followed, but simply because his position carries with it power that can be used effectively to determine certain kinds of issues. This is a direct consequence of group structure and rules of procedure within a structure.

● ● ●

How a chief judge exercises his power is to some extent a personal matter. Consider the use of opinion assignment power. In the Supreme Court, normal procedure calls for oral argument to be followed by a conference of the judges at which a vote is taken. Once the line-up of the justices is known, an opinion for the Court must be written. This opinion should state the decision taken and explain or justify it as against other possible alternatives. It should provide, in other words, the legal reason for the announced outcome. The opinions of the Court are normally written by a single justice in consultation with the other justices on the majority side who join in the opinion with the writer. A consequence of representing a group decision with a single opinion is that a choice of opinion writer from the majority must be made. In a majority of collegial courts in the United States the opinion assignment is made by the chief judge. About a third of such courts use a rotation method. In some courts, including the United States Supreme Court, the assignment is made by the Chief Justice if he is in the majority, otherwise by the senior justice in the majority. Each of these methods has its peculiar consequences for leadership and the exercise of power, but let us consider at a little more length the use of the assignment power by the Chief Justice of the Supreme Court.

This writer has previously suggested . . . that "the power to assign opinions for the court is of no consequence unless (*a*) disparities among the justices chosen occur, (*b*) opinions have substantive significance, and (*c*) the content of opinions reflects the influence of their writers. The second and third conditions can be assumed. Since the meaning of a collegial decision depends, formally, on the interpretation placed on it in the court's opinion, the opinion helps mold the growth of the law and the direction of that growth. And it affects in numerous ways the allocation of values in the American political and social systems. Each judge being unique, each opinion reflects, to some extent, the particular attributes of the writer—his conception of the law, his previous positions, his facility with language and concepts, and so on. Who writes may affect a court decision's acceptability, its value as present or future guideline, and the support of other judges. It is for these reasons, among others, that those who assign opinions may be expected to utilize their power to discriminate among those available for assignment." . . .

This quotation is from a recent study of opinion assignment by Chief Justice Earl Warren to four justices who served with him in the period 1953–60—Justices Black, Douglas, Frankfurter, and Clark. Now it is perfectly possible for a chief justice to view his formally designated authority to choose opinion writers as a mere administrative detail necessitated by the group dimension of the decision processes in the Supreme Court. In a single justice court, the question would not arise. In the multiple judge court, a writer must be picked from the majority. If it were merely a matter of getting the job done, the chief justice could choose his writers at random in such a way as to equalize the work load of each justice. But an examination of 584 assignments by Warren in the eight years studied revealed that Warren assigned opinions *unequally* among his four colleagues. Warren and Black got the most assignments, Douglas and Clark got the next level, and Frankfurter came in a poor fifth.

Since Warren only assigned 80 per cent of the total opinions for the Court, the possibility existed that he varied the quantity of assignments he made so that the total opinion load was equitably distributed. Such a possibility was evaluated by viewing the assignments by Warren to each justice as a percentage of the total times available. Since Warren could only assign the opinion to a member within the majority, such a measure enables one to determine whether Warren discriminated among his colleagues, holding constant the variable of availability.

Results of the analysis showed an overall discrimination in favor of Black and Douglas and against Frankfurter. These justices had opinion assignment rates of 17, 17, and 12 per cent respectively. The same rates from an earlier court (the Stone court) showed Black, Douglas, and Frankfurter with opinions assignment rates of 16, 21, and 10 per cent respectively. When total case data were broken down in terms of the closeness of vote, the significance of the case, and whether the issue was economic (E) or civil liberties (C), it was found that in C cases, Warren's rate of assignment to self was affected by close (5–4) votes and the significance of C cases, but not by E cases. Black's overall rates were not affected by any of the breakdowns; Douglas was consistently favored and Frankfurter consistently disfavored in E cases, with Clark being slightly more favored in C cases. From these results, it was concluded that this formal leadership prerogative—the authority to assign opinions—was used to discriminate among the long term justices in the Court.

Reasons for believing discriminatory assignment of opinions a consequence of attitude may be adduced. But it is more important to observe that phenomena with direct and important consequences for the development and growth of the law stem from the use of the collegial or the multiple judge court to decide and explain the law. By moving from a single to a multiple judge court, we open the possibility that votes may be cast on the same side of an issue for different reasons. Those with disparate reasons may be expected to vary in their notions of how the law should be explained and developed in a given instance. The chief justice, as the formally designated leader of the Supreme Court is, as a result, enabled to choose among competing statements of law.

Certain structural arrangements in collegial courts provide information advantages for a chief judge. The chief is, after all, the administrative head of his court and is saddled with the responsibility of effectively organizing and coordinating the activities of his colleagues. Maximum information flow into his office is essential to his task. Though much of this information may be passed on to the other judges, the chief judge sits "athwart the stream" and is undoubtedly better informed about the overall operation of his court than any of his brethren.

• • •

Thus, the chief has a more complete view of the Court, the current thinking of the associate justices, and the kind of information on which an associate justice may base his argument in a given case (thereby suggesting what other information is needed to effectively undermine such argument).

• • •

The chief justice of the United States Supreme Court speaks first and votes last in the Court's conferences. As a consequence, when he casts his vote, he possesses more information about a case outcome than that available to any other justice at point of decision. He knows, for example, (a) which way the case is to be decided, (b) whether his vote is to be determinative, (c) if he, the chief justice dissents, who will assign the opinion for the Court, (d) whether the case will be decided unanimously, and (e) if nonunanimous, the nature of the voting split. No associate justice has such information at point of voting though they may make guesses or predictions about all of these matters. Thus it is evident that certain structures in collegial courts provide superior data resources for formally designated leaders. While superior resources are not always effectively exploited, the group condition here makes questions of internal informational flow and formal group structure matters to be considered in constructing or modifying judicial systems.

Group Structure and Democratic Leadership: An Example

Though we referred above to the fact that the chief justice in the Supreme Court speaks first and votes last and that this provides leverage for a leader, we have not discussed fully the extent to which this opportunity can be exploited by a strong and determined personality.

A decision usually involves a choice among alternatives. To make this choice the alternatives must be specified, the possible consequences described, and an acceptable set composed of alternative, consequence, and means chosen. Leaders are sometimes distinguished as autocratic or democratic depending on the extent to which these processes are monopolized or shared with group members. A chief justice of the Supreme Court cannot function as an autocratic leader since the option of denying meaningful participation in decisional process is not open to him. However, a democratic leader is not necessarily passive. He may be quite active in indicating alternatives to the group, suggesting those that are preferred, and in urging the group to choose the means he considers most likely to accomplish the preferred end—at the same time emphasizing that it is a group decision that must be made. This type of leadership posture is enhanced for the chief justice by his "right" to speak first in

Supreme Court conferences—a right which if exercised properly may heavily influence the ultimate group action to be taken.

Excellent examples of the use to which the "speak first rule" may be put are found in the Court conferences in the *segregation cases* of 1954 and 1955 [*Brown* v. *Board of Education*]. The complainants charged in these cases that segregation by race in the public schools was a violation of the Fourteenth Amendment to the federal constitution. Yet at this time no previous decision had so stated. In fact from 1896 to May 17, 1954, separation by race was consistently held to be constitutional as long as the facilities for both groups were equal. This is the well-known separate-but-equal doctrine.

By speaking first in two Court conferences dealing with public school segregation in 1954 and 1955, Chief Justice Warren was in a position to define the issues and suggest the action that ought to be taken. It may be noted that he was not required to do either of these things. It would have been perfectly legal and understandable if a chief justice, on such momentous social questions, were to say: "Colleagues, I am at a loss as to what should be done with these cases. What suggestions can you offer?" But if he is a man of force, a man of ideas, a man to whom the exercise of power and influence is neither alien nor uninviting, the opportunity to speak first in the conference will not be wasted.

In fact Warren exploited his opportunity to the full. Speaking first in the 1954 conference, he suggested that the Court could not duck the issue but must decide whether segregation was allowable in the public schools. Taking the view that racial segregation as a policy was based upon a belief in the inherent inferiority of the colored race, he stated flatly that such segregation must be prohbited. For he denied such inherent inferiority and, in his view, separation of the races on such a basis violated the Thirteenth, Fourteenth, and Fifteenth Amendments. As for a remedy, he suggested that the Court avoid precipitous acts that would inflame the situation more than necessary. He recognized the differing conditions in the states and urged the Court to do away with segregation but with minimal upheaval and strife. Thus he said *how* segregation was abolished was vitally important. Subsequent to Warren's opening remarks and discussion in the conference, the Court stood six to three to bar public-school segregation in the states, although no formal vote was taken then.

In May 1954 the Supreme Court unanimously held segregation by race in the public schools to be a violation of the Constitution. As to a remedy, no action was taken then. The immediate cases involved were put down for re-argument, with the Court specifying a number of questions to which it suggested the parties direct their attention. This, along with other internal evidence of conversations taking place in the Court, reflected a gross uncertainty as to how the question of relief should and could be handled effectively.

Throughout the following year, discussion, argument, and debate within the Court continued—primarily on an informal basis. As the time approached for a ruling on a remedy to be chosen, unanimity within the Court was still lacking. Since Warren had worked hard to get a unanimous decision in the first instance, one may assume that he was anxious to have unanimous backing for whatever decrees the Court might issue regarding the cessation of public-school segregation. It is in this context that a formal Court conference on the segregation issue was held on April 16, 1955.

Speaking first, Warren said he had not yet formed a fixed opinion. This statement immediately notified his colleagues in the Court that he was eschewing any kind of autocratic role or posture regarding the segregation remedy. Such a disclaimer suggested to his colleagues that he had not closed his mind on the subject before his associates had spoken. But once having uttered the disclaimer, Warren quickly assumed the role of a positive democratic leader. He flatly and firmly stated his views in the matter—couching them in terms of moral imperatives, by specifying which of the alternative actions available should or should not be taken. Thus he suggested that the Court should not do the following: (a) appoint a master or indicate to the District Courts that they have masters appointed; (b) fix a date for the completion of desegregation nor suggest to District Courts that they set such dates—this to be left up to District Courts; (c) require the District Courts to call for a plan from the school districts, although District Courts might do so; (d) set procedural requirements for District Courts in this, an equity proceeding.

Having stated a list of things that the Court should not do, Warren then urged the Court to: (a) issue an opinion rather than a decree, such opinions stating the factors that the courts below should take into consideration; (b) put into the opinion the principles of the earlier ruling and then a bare-bones decree requiring action in accordance with the opinion of May 17; (c) say something in the opinion that would be of help to the District Court; (d) state that the segregation cases are class actions and as such the Court ruling covers all members of the class; (e) state that the District Courts could take into consideration certain facts, frictions, and problems of compliance; (f) state that in any plans, consideration will be given to whether the plans represent progress; and (g) give the District Courts as much latitude and support as necessary.

Warren's opening statement in this conference suggests that the Court had already decided on a large enforcement role for the Federal District Courts. At the same time, its juxtaposition of alternatives along with

Warren's specific recommendations indicate that a sizable number of issues remained open. Warren's remarks—undoubtedly delivered with vigor and forthrightness—did not, of course, prevent those justices who spoke later from voicing their opinions. But while the chief justice, who speaks first in a group, is excused from unwelcome conflict with or contradiction of the views of a colleague, all the associate justices are faced with precisely that prospect, unless they go along with the chief. Thus freedom of expression in the group is more restricted for the associate justices than for the chief. Moreover, the use of the moral phrases "should" and "should not" rather than a mere listing of possible alternatives increased the pressure on the associate justices to stay in line with the thinking of their leader.

For those associate justices who were uncertain of their position, confused by the complexity of the issues before the Court, relatively neutral as to those issues, or less emotionally involved than the chief justice, such a strong opening statement would be expected to exert great pressure. In the event that the chief justice uttered remarks with which other justices disagreed strongly, the drive to issue defensive remarks or even to consider the alternatives to the justice's own position would provide a distraction and possibly dilute or weaken the associate justice's initial commitments.

While there is no way to prove beyond doubt that Warren's statement was highly persuasive, some of the responses of the associate justices suggest precisely that. The extent to which the other justices expressed disagreement with the Chief, urged conflicting alternatives not listed by Warren, or merely wished to extend the list of actions to be taken by the Court can be viewed as rough measures of Warren's successful exploitation of his "speak first" prerogative.

A justice noted for his strong personality and firm views on many issues, Hugo Black, was the second speaker in the conference. Black was the senior associate justice in the Court at the time. He occupied the end of the rectangular table immediately opposite Warren, and was commonly thought, then and subsequently, to be first in leadership among the associate justices, second only to Warren in the Court. The posture taken by Black was even more democratic—that is, less positive—than the posture assumed by Warren. Black, repeating Warren, said he had no fixed views. But while Warren followed his disclaimer of firm conclusions by a detailed statement of alternatives and recommendations, Black expressed a willingness to do all that was humanly possible to go along with a unanimous action. The record of the remarks made by the associate justices in this conference is almost barren of disagreements with the Chief, new ideas or alternatives, or considerations not covered by Warren's opening statement. Even Frankfurter, who had earlier suggested the appointment of a master, declined to press the point further, given Warren's recommendation that such a path not be pursued.

About the only sticking point that can be found from the record pertained to the recommendation that the cases be specified as class actions. A class action may be brought if the persons constituting a class are so numerous as to make it impractical to bring them all before the Court. In such an event, if one or more of them will insure adequate representation of all, suit may be brought on behalf of the class. The advantages of bringing a class action is that the relief granted will extend to all members of the class rather than being limited to those who individually are identified with the proceeding. Viewing the *Segregation Cases* as class actions would permit the Supreme Court to bar public-school segregation not only of the immediate Negro claimants in the case but for all others across the country who were subjected similarly to such discrimination. The *Segregation Cases* were instituted by the plaintiffs in the District Courts as class actions and were treated as such in the various courts below prior to reaching the Supreme Court level.

Speaking in the second position, Justice Black, in spite of having denied any fixed views, very quickly expressed a preference for treating the cases as individual rather than class actions. He was joined in this position by Justice Stanley Reed who also thought it would be permissible for District Court judges to call for desegregation plans. William O. Douglas preferred individual rather than class actions and would have liked a cut-off date for segregation in the schools, insofar as the plaintiffs in the cases before the Court were concerned. Justice Minton said little beyond the observation that he would go with the majority. Harlan specifically referred to his agreement with Warren and reiterated the view that an opinion and a decree could be issued. In general he expressed the view that Warren's ideas for the content of the opinion were quite acceptable. In commenting on the class action question, Harlan revealingly said that originally he felt that these were not true class suits but now, as a practical matter, thought the class suit decision might be helpful. This suggests the possibility that Harlan shifted his position on the question after hearing Warren's views at the opening of the conference.

On balance, one finds a high degree of acceptance for Warren's opening statement in the expressions of the associate judges in this conference and very little by way of disagreement. Where disagreement was expressed, extended argument was absent. More telling evidence of Warren's influence lies perhaps in the final result of the 1955 case. Such results, of course, did not depend solely on Warren's remarks in conference. But if these results agree with Warren's statement in the conference and are at odds with the few contrary positions expressed by the associate justices at that time, the impact of the Chief Justice in conference, and subsequently, would be underlined.

Considering the final action taken in the 1955 case and comparing the results there with the Conference discussion above is informative. None of the available other possibilities opposed by Warren earlier were adopted in the final solution. A master was not appointed, no date was fixed for completion of desegregation, and detailed procedural requirements for District Courts were not established. Warren's conference recommendations, at the same time, were followed ultimately in great detail. An opinion rather than a decree was issued. As Warren had recommended, the opinion stated the factors that lower courts could take into consideration in enforcing desegregation decrees. These courts could, wrote Warren, "consider problems related to administration, arising from the physical condition of the school plant, the school transportation system, personnel, revision of school districts and attendance areas into compact units to achieve a system of determining admission to the public schools on a non-racial basis and revision of local laws and regulations which may be necessary in solving the foregoing problems. They will also consider the adequacy of any plans the defendants may propose to meet these problems and to effectuate a transition to a racially non-discriminatory school system." . . . The principles of the earlier ruling were put into the 1955 opinion with the statement that "The opinions . . . [of May 17, 1954] declaring the fundamental principle that racial discrimination in public education is unconstitutional, are incorporated herein by reference."

It was not specifically stated in the 1955 opinion, as Warren had recommended in conference, that these cases were class actions. This was undoubtedly a gesture to those associate justices who had objected to viewing the cases as class actions and to those who had some doubt about the matter. But in spite of the absence of a class action statement in the final opinion, Warren's ultimate goal was maintained. The opinion in the *Segregation Cases* decided May 17, 1954, applied the Court's holding in those cases specifically to members of the plaintiff's class. This and other principles of the 1954 decision were incorporated by reference in Warren's 1955 opinion as previously noted. Thus the *Segregation Cases* did not lose their class action context from District Court to final Supreme Court action.

None of the other contrary views expressed by the associate justices in the 1955 conference were carried into the final opinion. Douglas did not get a cut-off date for segregation of the plaintiffs as he had sought. And Reed did not obtain a statement that the District Courts could call for desegregation plans, though Warren did require the lower courts to consider the "adequacy of any plans the defendants may propose to meet these problems and to effectuate a transition to a racially non-discriminatory school system." . . . In sum, there is substantial evidence for the proposition that Warren assumed the role of a positive democratic leader in the 1955 conference on the *Segregation Cases* and that he exploited his formal prerogative to speak first in the conference by specifying precise alternatives and making positive recommendations as to those to be rejected and those to be adopted. Such behavior is commonly associated with the leadership role in small groups in both laboratory and natural settings.

Conclusions

Several general conclusions are indicated by our consideration of small-group concepts and the group condition in the context of collegial courts.

• • •

[O]n the evidence available, we cannot reject the hypothesis that—even in collegial courts—the group condition "makes a difference." Though the evidence on the other side remains largely to be adduced, we have pointed to scattered indications that (*a*) judges behave differently in individual and group settings and (*b*) the structure of collegial courts limits or expands opportunities for leadership and the exercise of power, with comcomitant consequences for decisional output.

Theory and analogy, of course, are not equivalents of verified knowledge. And scattered (and clearly limited) research results do not make a case. We cannot yet be convinced that the group model will enable us to explain large segments of that judicial behavior currently unexplained or inadequately understood. Nevertheless, the work done by social psychologists and the significant implications of their generalizations require that we seek to determine whether and to what extent such propositions are descriptive of behavior in judicial groups. We need to know whether justice is better dispensed through single or multiple-staffed courts, or by courts structured one way rather than another. For unlike laboratory or simulated groups, a collegial court decision may be a means of formalizing fatal error. Thus, by analogy, we are faced with the problem of the statistician who must decide how much error to risk in rejecting his hypothesis. When the consequences of error are trivial a large risk may be acceptable. But if the reverse—caution is the key.

• • •

—————————————— 59 ——————————————

On the Fluidity of Judicial Choice

J. Woodford Howard Jr.

• • •

I. The Evidence of Fluidity

It has long been known, of course, that judges change their votes and permit their opinions to be conduits for the ideas of others. *Causes célèbres* such as the Legal Tender and Flag Salute Cases, or the *Carolene* footnote, come quickly to mind. So does Chief Justice Hughes' pungent expression of willingness to alter language in the interest of harmony: "Justice Holmes used to say, when we asked him to excise portions of his opinions which he thought pretty good, that he was willing to be 'reasonably raped.' I feel the same way."

Walter F. Murphy's excellent *Elements of Judicial Strategy* is replete with examples of how Justices work such changes via internal bargaining. Yet it may come as some surprise to political scientists how commonplace, rather than aberrational, judicial flux actually is. The recently opened papers of Justice Murphy, which contain fairly extensive conference notes for the years 1940–49, as well as docket books for the 1947 term, give a much more plastic impression of judicial choice in the making than the rigidly stratified bloc warfare by which most of us have characterized the Roosevelt and Vinson Courts. Indeed, when meshed with the Stone and Burton papers, which overlap the same period, the Murphy papers tempt one to say that hardly any major decision in this decade was free from significant alteration of vote and language before announcement to the public. Neither was the phenomenon confined to Justices whose overt allegiances were to professional ideologies of law as reason or to philosophies of self-restraint. One of the most striking aspects of the decade is that the most important instances of judicial flux, from the doctrinal standpoint, occurred precisely among those Justices most suspected of ideological automation and in cases that stand as highpoints of their libertarian commitment. From the very human tendency

From J. Woodford Howard, Jr., "On the Fluidity of Judicial Choice," *American Political Science Review* 62 (1968): 44–49, 55. Reprinted by permission. Footnotes have been omitted.

to change one's mind under pressure, no one, and certainly no "libertarian activist," was immune.

Examples of fluctuating options are legion; but for convenience of illustration, certain types of flux may be distinguished from among well-known civil liberties decisions of the day. Without pretending to offer the following categories as a unified theoretical construct, we may classify fluid choices according to certain intervening variables which appear to have been at work. First is the "freshman effect"—i.e., unstable attitudes that seem to have resulted from the process of assimilation to the Court. It is not uncommon for a new Justice to undergo a period of adjustment, often about three years in duration, before his voting behavior stabilizes into observable, not to mention predictable, patterns. Biographical materials suggest the generality of this experience, irrespective of prior background and ranging from Justices as dissimilar as Cardozo and Murphy. Justice Cardozo, according to one clerk's recollection of the docket books, registered suprisingly unstable options as a newcomer. Frequently voting alone in conference before ultimately submerging himself in a group opinion, Cardozo himself confessed discomfort in adjusting from the common law world of the New York Court of Appeals to the public law orientation of the federal Supreme Court. Elsewhere I have documented a similar instability on the part of Justice Murphy. During his freshman years on the high bench, Murphy swung from the wing of Justice Frankfurter, whom he had assumed would be his intellectual mainstay and ally, to substantial agreement with Justice Black, whose views regarding the First Amendment and state criminal procedure, it should be remembered, were also shifting ground at the time. In the process of adjustment, however, Murphy had problems of craftsmanship in the picketing cases and, along with other members of the Court, groped for a coherent position regarding free speech. He drowned a dissent in *Gobitis;* he cast a decisive turnabout vote at the last minute in *Bridges* v. *California;* and he also switched sides in *Hines* v. *Davidowitz.* However contrary to preconceptions, it was the libertarian Justice Murphy who had to be talked out of publishing a concurrence in *Cantwell* v. *Connecticut* (in return for different language) which criticized Justice Roberts' Court opinion for inadequately protecting state power to preserve the peace from clashing religious sects.

Eloise Synder's pioneering study of the Court as a small group supports the hypothesis that the "freshman effect" has been a continuing phenomenon. Parallels in other decision-making groups, e.g., the socialization of freshman Senators, also indicate that the Court is not alone in creating assimilation problems for new members. What occurs is a sort of hiatus between the norms of the individual's belief system and new institutional norms which must be internalized as role expectations unfold. Still, the aggregate effects of such freshman transitions are probably more difficult to trace in the judiciary. Using the concept of cliques, Synder hypothesized that the high court assimilates its new members through a "pivotal clique" in the ideological center, with the implication that uncommitted newcomers on stratified courts are likely to maximize influence at the outset of their judicial careers, before attitudes and bloc alignments jell. The experience of Justices Cardozo and Murphy suggests the need of refining this concept, however, especially the suggestion that fledgling judges with unstable or inchoate attitudes are more influential than senior, committed members. While a pivotal Justice may have a controlling vote in a given five-four situation, the very reasons for the "freshman effect"—inexperience, feelings of inadequacy, hesitation about premature bloc identification, low seniority in assignments, strategies of playing safe, etc.—all point to the opposite direction of freshmen Justices following rather than leading. Further, to the extent that "freshmanness" does cause newcomers to restrain personal preferences and gravitate toward the center, it may retard the absorption of current ideas into the Court's output, which Robert A. Dahl once argued is a prime effect of the appointive system and a means of harmonizing the institution with the outlook of dominant lawmaking majorities. The problem, in brief, is whether the newcomer's influence should be measured in terms of votes or in terms of formulating doctrine and persuading peers. Only a mechanistic view of the judicial process, in my view, would measure influence exclusively in terms of either.

A second cluster of fluctuating choices may be grouped around the familiar strategic variables of massing the Court and of institutional loyalties. Justices frequently compromise personal opinion in order to maximize their collective force and to safeguard the power and legitimacy of the Court among its reference groups. That personal ideology may be qualified or even defined by organizational perspectives is by no means unique to the judiciary. Neither must a judge genuflect at the mere mention of the tribunal, as a friendly wag once said of the agnostic Justice Frankfurter, to be affected by such considerations in the system of expectations within which modern judges operate. The evidence of the 1940's suggests that all of the Justices, at one time or another, were constrained by group and institutional interests. Not only was it common for them to offer helpful suggestions and advice to adversaries, according to the official theory of collective responsibility, but they also sacrificed deeply felt views. For example, Justice Murphy stifled a powerful lone dissent in the first Japanese Relocation Case under the badgering and patriotic appeals of Justice Frankfurter; and Justice Douglas did the same in the second. After finding himself alone, and probably under advice from Justice Rutledge, Murphy also withheld an elaborate dissent in the case of runaway spy Gerhard Eisler, with the result that he left stillborn the first known assault by a Justice upon the House Un-Ameri-

can Activities Committee for violating the First Amendment. Similarly,
Justice Rutledge swallowed personal opinion in order to avoid stale-
mate in *Screws* v. *United States,* an important civil rights decision which
held off an attack on expansive concepts of state action at the price of
enfeebling federal statutory power to punish police brutality in the
states. And in familiar marshalling tactics, Murphy and Rutledge stifled
their prepared dissents in the *Resweber* double execution case by joining
forces with Douglas (who had switched votes) in Justice Burton's libertarian protest. Massing support behind an unexpected ally is not an unfamiliar judicial stratagem, and it may well explain Justice Murphy's
assignments in both *United States* v. *White*, which denied Fifth Amendment privileges to trade union officers in their official capacity, and *Hick-
man* v. *Taylor,* a pathfinding decision regarding pre-trial discovery.

More difficult to analyze is a third class of fluctuating options, those
which appear to have resulted from the changing factual perceptions of
a particular judge. In some cases, the reasons for such a shift may be
indistinguishable from pressures to coalesce. Thus, Justice Douglas' acquiescence in *Korematsu* v. *United States* probably was made easier by
Chief Justice Stone's continuing reminders that opportunity to challenge
relocation orders still remained open to petitioners so long as orders to
report to control centers and actual detention were separable. Lack of
opportunity for individuals to prove their loyalty was what had troubled
Douglas all along. In other cases, shifting perspectives appear to have
been a function of additional thought and homework, by a clerk or a
Justice, into issues that were only partially perceived at first because of
inadequate argument, briefs, or time. The Supreme Court does not follow the practice in some state supreme courts of assigning cases by lot
and of infrequent dissent. But it is not uncommon for a Justice assigned
to express one consensus to reverse field after further analysis, and then
persuade his colleagues to follow suit. Justice Murphy did so with unanimous approval in the complex Chickasaw-Choctaw land claim controversy. An even neater example occurred in *Lawson* v. *Suwannee Fruit &
Steamship Co.,* in 1949. There, after independent research by a clerk in
a poor record showed that a workmen's compensation award for the particular petitioner might jeopardize statutory rights of longshoremen as a
class, Murphy turned tail, reworked the opinion without asking the
Court's leave, and won quick, eight-to-one approval at conference. Justice Frankfurter, at that point, could not resist the "dig":

> It seemed to me a compelled conclusion if due respect is to be given to
> legislation—if, that is, we let Congress make laws and not re-make them.
>   This opinion (and change of Conference vote) ought to be a lesson that
> merely because a particular case is to be decided for a particular employee
> the result on a fair and long view may be a great disservice to labor and to
> Law. I could 'document' this truth.

The difficulty is that the reasons for changing perceptions are not usually so obvious. One may argue that flux of this sort is inevitable in the cross-pressures of a collegial court of last resort whose main business lies at the frontier of legal development. One may speculate further about the competing values, the strategies of avoidance, the problems of obtaining linguistic consensus, the rush of business, and the just plain difficulties of substance which induce perceptual change. Occasionally, one may even suspect Justices of doing the unexpected just to confound bloc identification. Justice Murphy had one clerk who suggested that ploy in close cases after the Black-Douglas-Murphy trio began to form. S. Sidney Ulmer, after publishing an attitudinal study of the Michigan Supreme Court, was later challenged by one of the judges to explain an aberrant vote!

But no outsider really knows why judges change their minds. Seldom do they admit, as Jackson hinted in *Everson* v. *Board of Education,* to having switched their votes. Even when overruling themselves later, seldom do they write with the candor of the Canadian jurist who blandly confessed: "the matter does not appear to me now as it appears to have appeared to me then." Nor, it must be stressed, should judges be faulted either for changing their minds or for lack of complete candor. A major objective of the adversary system, after all, is prevention of premature classification and judgment. That judges may shift position between conference and final voting is not only well understood among themselves, but a testament to the limitations of conference and the effectiveness of the argumentation system. And it is hardly "robism" to suggest that a cloak of secrecy may be just as necessary for judges as for diplomats in making such accommodations possible.

Whatever their causes, however, shifting individual perceptions can significantly affect public policy and the ideological complexion of courts. Consider, for example, the changing positions of Justices Black and Douglas in three of the most ideology-charged decisions of the decade: *Martin* v. *Struthers, Colegrove* v. *Green,* and *Terminiello* v. *Chicago.*

In *Struthers,* the Court faced the question whether an anti-doorbell ringing ordinance designed to protect sleeping night-shift workers in an industrial town violated the First Amendment rights of proselyting Jehovah's Witnesses. Although he too expressed sympathy in conference for the Sunday sleepers of Struthers, Chief Justice Stone at first was unable to attract a majority in support of "preferred freedoms." Justice Black, who saw the scales tipping toward privacy of the home and local control, expressed prophetic fears in conference that the next case might be Jehovah's Witnesses invading Roman Catholic services if no restraints were approved. That view was accepted by a five-four vote; and, after assigning himself the majority opinion, Black circulated a hard-hitting memorandum to the effect that such a community reasonably could forbid doorbell ringing altogether in order to protect privacy. Then, after answering objections in a second circulation, Justice Black suddenly reversed himself. The ordinance was overturned by a five-four vote, and the Chief Justice graciously permitted Black to write a new majority opinion which in effect invited the town to try again with a more carefully drafted ordinance that accommodated privacy and free speech. After all, as Stone argued behind the scenes, some room for accommodation remained before community action, at least until homeowners had an opportunity to listen or object.

Justice Black's about-face in *Struthers* goes far toward explaining some of the puzzles in the opinions. For one thing, it accounted for Justice Murphy's emotional concurrence which replowed the same terrain but had originated as a Murphy-Douglas-Rutledge dissent against their colleague's failure to balance interests. It also made more sense of the Frankfurter-Jackson complaints that the Court was "wanting in explicitness" and attempting to resolve tough practical issues by a "vague but fervent transcendentalism." What the Court had decided was a narrow question of judgment—whether it was possible for a community to accommodate colliding interests by more carefully framed time, place, and manner regulations. What the public read, on the other hand, were heavily rhetorical outpourings from both sides which obscured the precise rights involved and exaggerated the doctrinal split over "preferred freedoms." No one could have guessed until twenty-five years later that privacy of the home and local control loomed so high in Justice Black's scale of values. No one could have guessed that the attitudes he expressed in the sit-in and racial picketing cases of the 1960's represented, not a switch attributable to advancing age, but constancy to prime values which, for two decades, the course of litigation had left unexposed.

Likewise, from reading the opinions in *Colegrove* v. *Green,* no one could have fathomed that Justice Black, author of the three-man opinion which viewed congressional reapportionment as a justiciable issue, had initially expressed contrary conclusions in conference, along with every other Justice but one. Who could have guessed that Justice Black had not only echoed the general fears about entering the apportionment thicket, but himself had attempted to express those sentiments for the Court before he once again changed his mind and wrote the powerful minority opinion which structured a fateful enlargement of judicial power as a supervisor of the electoral process? The answer, of course, is that no one could have inferred such flux from votes or opinions. Having resolved his own misgivings, Justice Black simply advanced his conclusions unencumbered by his previous doubts.

The majority opinion in *Terminiello* v. *Chicago* also provided no clue that its author, Justice Douglas, had followed a parallel course.

Nevertheless, both the Murphy and Burton papers indicate that Justice Douglas had initially perceived Terminiello's speech at a volatile political rally of Gerald L. Smith forces in Chicago as throwing a lighted match into an explosive situation and had cast his vote accordingly. Then, after reversing position and thus the result, Justice Douglas was assigned the majority opinion and defended the choice by arguments that many contemporaries regarded as the apogee of libertarian dogma.

These examples may be extreme because the opinions acknowledged none of the doubts which had been resolved. Yet they serve to make the point. Votes can be a crude measure of attitude. So can opinions, and even the lack of them. The ideological commitments seemingly manifest in both may be lower and the basis of choice far more pragmatic than either imply on their face. Certainly that was true of the 1940's.

• • •

[T]he evidence of the 1940's lends greater support to the lawyer's ideal of the judicial process as a system of reasoning than many legal realists would accept. Clearly, judges of all ideological persuasions pondered, bargained, and argued in the course of reaching their decisions, and they compromised their ideologies, too. No one can plow through the papers of a Stone or a Murphy without coming out with renewed respect for the give-and-take or without appreciation for the multiplicity of variables and constraints, including that old whipping-post, Law, that went into the decision-making of the era.

• • •

Idiosyncratic Factors in Decision Making

60

The Attitudes and Values of Supreme Court Justices

Harold J. Spaeth

• • •

Attitudes

[Attitude is a] key construct. Unfortunately, there are about as many definitions of attitude as there are social psychologists. Rather than add to the clutter, the essence of the definition formulated by Milton Rokeach, a well-known social psychologist, will be used. *An attitude is a relatively enduring set of interrelated beliefs that describe, evaluate, and advocate action with regard to some object or situation.* Two aspects of this definition are crucial. First, attitudes are not ephemeral—at least, not among adults whose status and occupational pattern are relatively stable. Second, the activation of an attitude involves both an *object* and the *situation* in which that object is encountered.

The major deficiency of opinion polling and other attitudinal re-

From Harold J. Spaeth, *Supreme Court Policy Making: Explanation and Prediction* (W. H. Freeman and Company, 1979), pp. 119–123, 125, 129–131, 133, 133–137. Copyright © 1979. Reprinted by permission. Footnotes have been omitted.

search is that they tend to focus upon persons, places, and things without any reference to the context with which the person, place, or thing is associated. In order to explain and predict a person's behavior, one needs to know more than his or her attitude toward such "objects" as blacks, students, indigents, business, and labor unions. It is also necessary to know what the "object" is *doing*. Students studying and students rioting will not likely evoke the same response. A white person's attitude toward a black sitting next to him at a lunch counter may be markedly different from the same person's attitude toward a black who moves in next door, or a black who is employed as his boss.

To a greater extent than the attitudes of the average person, the attitudes of Supreme Court Justices are likely to be "relatively enduring." First, their decisions are a matter of public record. They are published, commented upon, and subjected to close scrutiny by the communications media and the legal profession. Second, all judges, not merely those on the Supreme Court, are expected to decide cases compatibly with what has previously been decided—to adhere to precedent. As a result, judges perforce commit themselves to consistency to a greater extent than they would if their choices and decisions were private.

Apart from the obvious fact that people's actions result from the interplay of their attitudes toward an object and their attitudes toward the situation in which that object is encountered is the norm of judicial blindness: justice is supposed to be blind. Who the litigants are is irrelevant; what the litigants have done is paramount. Though the judicial blindfold may slip occasionally, with results that are less than even-handed, only a cynic would deny that the norm is without a measure of force and effect. Consequently, we may simply assume that the Justices are motivated more by the situations in which litigants find themselves (what they have or have not done) than by the personal characteristics of the litigants.

Rokeach's definition of attitude is purely conceptual. What is now needed is a means to apply it to the Justices' policy making. Such a means exists: cumulative scale analysis.

THE MEASUREMENT OF ATTITUDES.

Toward the end of World War II, a group of Defense Department scientists successfully solved a problem that had long bedeviled social science research: consistency. How, for example, can one know if each of the questions on a test or questionnaire actually bears on the matter being studied? A survey of public attitudes toward crime may be measuring public concerns about violence instead. A test of academic achievement may really be measuring a person's aptitude for learning rather than his or her knowledge of some specific subject. Related to the problem of consistency is ambiguity. Does each question have the same meaning for every respondent? English, after all, is not the most precise language. Clearly, the problem of consistency is basic to a great deal of social science research: aptitude and achievement testing, social status, neurotic behavior, census data, public opinion, and voting behavior.

Cumulative scaling postulates that one way to solve the problem of consistency is to rank order respondents on the basis of how favorable or unfavorable each of them is to the matter being investigated. Consider three questions, to which 75, 50, and 25 percent, respectively, respond favorably. Cumulative scaling simply assumes that if a person endorses an extreme question or statement, that person must also endorse all less extreme statements for the questions to constitute a scale. This merely means that the 25 percent who responded favorably to the one question must be among the 50 and 75 percent who supported the other two statements. The reverse is also necessarily true: a person who replies "no" to the question to which 75 percent said "yes" must also reply "no" to the questions that elicited a less favorable response.

This is the sense in which cumulative scaling solves the problem of consistency. Consistency does not mean that a particular respondent must answer each statement with the same response; rather, it means that once he responds negatively, he must continue to respond negatively to all statements that were supported by a smaller proportion than supported the most extreme statement that he did support. Accordingly, a person may respond "yes" to the statement that was supported by 75 percent of the respondents, and "no" to the other two. He may not, however, say "yes" to the 75 percent statement, "no" to the 50 percent statement, and then reverse himself with a "yes" to the statement that was supported by only 25 percent of the respondents. The pattern must be consistent: yes-yes-yes, yes-yes-no, yes-no-no, or no-no-no.

Now let us apply cumulative scaling to the Supreme Court. Assume that the 10 cases in [Table I] concern federal regulation of public utilities. A "+" signifies a vote favorable to the government and against the utility. A "−" signifies the opposite: an antigovernment, proutility vote. All the Justices supported the government in the least extreme case (Case 1)—the case that was decided 9 to 0. Justice *I* voted against the government in Case 2. He remained consistent, however, by voting against the government and in favor of the utilities in all the other more extremely decided cases. A similar pattern prevails for all the other Justices: once a Justice supports a utility, he continues to do so in each of the more extremely decided cases.

Two things should be noted about the table. First, the cases are ordered solely and simply on the basis of the decreasing proportion of the Justices who voted "+": progovernment and antiutility. Thus, Case 6 is less extreme than Case 7 because 5 Justices voted "+" in 6, 4 voted

TABLE I.

					JUSTICES					
CASE	A	B	C	D	E	F	G	H	I	VOTE
1	+	+	+	+	+	+	+	+	+	9–0
2	+	+	+	+	+	+	+	+	−	8–1
3	+	+	+	+	+	+	+	−	−	7–2
4	+	+	+	+	+	+	−	−	−	6–3
5	+	+	+	+	+	+	−	−	−	6–3
6	+	+	+	+	+	−	−	−	−	5–4
7	+	+	+	+	−	−	−	−	−	4–5
8	+	+	+	+	−	−	−	−	−	4–5
9	+	+	−	−	−	−	−	−	−	2–7
10	+	−	−	−	−	−	−	−	−	1–8

"+" in 7. Case 7, then, is more extreme than Case 6 because fewer Justices voted "+," and not because in some ideal world it ought to be less extreme, or because an expert thinks it should be less extreme. Note that extremeness can be justified just as logically in terms of "−" votes: Case 10 is the least extreme, Case 1 is the most extreme. The order of the cases and the proportion of the Justices remain the same either way.

Second, the voting pattern is not one that is likely to occur by chance. The Supreme Court is a 9-member body and a simple majority of the Justices determines who wins and who loses. Consequently, the Justices may combine in 256 different voting alignments. A unanimous vote can occur in only one way; each of the 9 Justices can dissent alone to produce an 8 to 1 decision; 36 different pairs may dissent to provide a 7 to 2 margin; 84 distinct combinations of 3 dissenters will produce a 6 to 3 vote; and 4 Justices may combine in 126 different ways to provide a 5 to 4 result. But in constructing a cumulative scale, this sum of 256 different combinations must be doubled. The reason for this is that "directionality" is assigned. Each of the decisions in the table, for example, is classified as either progovernment and antiutility or, alternatively, as antigovernment and proutility. Therefore, each of the 9 Justices may dissent alone in an 8 to 1 decision *upholding* the government, and each correspondingly may be the solo dissenter in an 8 to 1 decision *opposing* the government. The result, then, is 512 different combinations (256 × 2).

Given the perfectly consistent pattern of votes displayed in the table, we may reliably infer that the Justices voted as they did in these cases because of their individual attitudes toward federal regulation of public utilities. We need not find an absolutely consistent voting pattern to make such an inference. Assume, for instance, that Justice *G* had voted "−" in Case 2 and that Justice *E* had voted "+" in Case 9. These two votes would be "inconsistencies" or nonscale responses. Too many such votes will destroy the consistent pattern of response, which, as noted, is crucial to cumulative scale construction. How much is too many? To allow us to explain and predict Supreme Court voting, at least 95 percent of the votes in a scale should be consistent; 95 percent, that is, of the votes cast in cases in which there were two or more dissents. Cases decided unanimously and those with only one dissent are excluded from calculation. The former are, by definition, the most extreme items in a scale, and cannot possibly have any inconsistent votes. Solo dissent cases can never have more than one inconsistent vote. Hence, one starts with at least 8 of 9 consistent votes—88.9 percent. This percentage is too close to 95 percent for comfort.

We are now in a position to formulate an operational definition of our basic construct, attitude. *An attitude is a set of cumulatively scaled cases, determined as precisely as the nature of the Court's decisions permit.*

• • •

Values

[*A*] *value may be conceptually defined as simply an interrelated set of attitudes.* This definition arguably accords with a commonsensical understanding of the term "value." Whereas an individual may have tens of thousands of beliefs, he may have only a few hundred attitudes, and perhaps but a few dozen values.

• • •

The cumulative scales that constitute the attitudes that explain the votes of the Justices in both the Warren and Burger Court periods can be divided into three clusters. Each of these clusters is a value, and the three together account for approximately 85 percent of the Court's decisions. Let us examine the contents of each of them.

In the first cluster are the scales that tap such attitudes as those toward involuntary confessions, the right to counsel, double jeopardy, due process of law, freedom of communication, the rights of persons alleged to be security risks, protest demonstrations, the right to confront one's accusers, establishment of religion, trial by jury, self-incrimination, the retroactive application of newly enunciated constitutional guarantees, the rights of debtors and military personnel, abortions, subconstitutional fair procedures, and the Federal Rules of Civil Procedure.

What do these issues have in common? First, many pertain to specific provisions in the Bill of Rights: freedom of speech and press, the establishment of religion clause, due process of law, the right to counsel, double jeopardy, self-incrimination, and the right to trial by jury. Second, these are typically considered civil liberties issues. Third, most of the litigants are persons accused of crime—criminal defendants—or political offenders of one sort or another—security risks and persons expressing unpopular and unconventional points of view. All told, these are situations where individuals are protesting alleged governmental infringements upon their liberty. In a word, what is fundamentally at stake is freedom. This, then, is the label assigned the various attitudes that motivate the Justices' behavior in these sets of cases: the value of *freedom*.

The second cluster of attitude scales taps such attitudes as those toward cruel and unusual punishment (more specifically, the constitutionality of capital punishment); the extralegal influences to which jurors may be subject; the rights of indigent convicts, illegitimates, and juveniles; poverty law; desegregation of schools and other public facilities; sex discrimination; searches and seizures; plea bargaining; the willingness of federal courts to step into allegedly biased state judicial and administrative proceedings; moot questions; the availability of the writ of habeas corpus; and the length of time persons must reside in a state in order to vote, run for public office, or secure state-provided benefits.

What do these attitude scales have in common? First, most of them concern persons who allege discrimination on the basis of race, economic condition, or age, or for political reasons. Second, many of these attitude scales turn on the legal issue of equal protection of the laws: race and sex discrimination; indigent convicts, illegitimates, and juveniles; and residency requirements. This being so, a second label best describes behavior in these sets of cases: the value of *equality*.

In the remaining cluster are attitude scales such as antitrust, mergers, bankruptcy, worker's compensation, state regulation of business, public utilities, federal regulation of securities, the reapportionment and districting of voting districts, natural resources, libel actions alleging defamation of character, the legal rights of unions vis-à-vis business, antitrust activities of unions, the rights of Indians, and the jurisdiction of the federal courts.

The characteristic common to this cluster is economic activity. It is, moreover, economic activity in the context of governmental regulation. Because of this regulatory aspect, it is perhaps most appropriate to label this value *New Deal economics* or New Dealism. This label aptly describes the issues that were raised by the transformation of an agricultural economy into an industrialized economy. For better or for worse, the resolution of most of these issues was the work of the Court of the 1930's and 1940's. The criteria and formulae of those decades still undergird our attitudes and affect our behavior in matters economic.

These, then, are the three values. They explain slightly more than 85 percent of the decisions of both the Warren and Burger Courts. The content of the three values has changed somewhat between the two periods, however. Trial by jury and military personnel, for example, shifted from New Deal economics on the Warren Court to freedom on the Burger Court. This movement of an attitude scale from one value to another can be explained by differences in the content of the cases in these two scales. During the Warren Court, well over one-half of the jury trial cases were civil proceedings in which economic interests were at stake. During the Burger Court, however, three-fourths of the controversies were criminal cases. Similarly, during the Warren Court, many of the cases involving military personnel concerned veterans' benefits. But during the Burger Court, these pertained exclusively to provisions of the selective service statutes—such as draft exemption and conscientious objection—matters that semantically suggest freedom rather than economics.

• • •

The Justices' Value System

A value system [is] defined as the pattern of support or nonsupport of the relevant values that explain a person's decisions.

• • •

As has been noted, analysis has revealed the existence of three major values, each of which a Justice may support or oppose. Eight combinations of support (+) or nonsupport (−) are possible. Each such combination represents a value system. Table 2 lists the eight possible combinations.

One may quarrel with the value system descriptions given in Table 2.

TABLE 2. Values and Value Systems

	VALUES		
VALUE SYSTEM	*Freedom*	*Equality*	*New Dealism*
Liberal	+	+	+
Civil Libertarian	+	+	−
Individualist	+	−	−
Populist	+	−	+
Utopian Collectivist	−	+	−
Benevolent Authoritarian	−	+	+
New Dealer	−	−	+
Conservative	−	−	−

NOTE: A "+" indicates support of the value in question; a "−" indicates nonsupport.

But for the most part they accord with common usage. Liberals support the exercise of civil liberties and an expansion of the rights of persons accused of crime; they also support the demise of racial, social, and political discrimination, and improvement of the economic status of the poor. Liberals also support New Deal economics; that is, they are pro-union, antibusiness, and procompetition, and they favor compensation for injured persons. The value system of Conservatives is opposite that of Liberals. Civil Libertarians support the noneconomic values of freedom and equality. Individualists are the classic nineteenth-century-type liberals—they believe that that government is best that governs least. Government should keep its hands off the economic system, should avoid social engineering regardless of "humanitarian" considerations, and should allow the individual to do his own thing with but a minimum of constraint. Populists are the agrarian reformers of an earlier era. Supportive of personal freedom and economic reform, they had an impact in the West and South from the 1890's to the 1930's.

The next two types, the Utopian Collectivists and the Benevolent Authoritarians, are furthest removed from the mainstream of American politics. (I apologize for the exotic labels, but other existing referents for these types are decidedly uncomplimentary.] Neither supports freedom for others, but both are high on equality. Various Marxist groups, the New Left, student radicals, and some anti-Establishment types might possibly personify them. The New Dealer supports economic reform to the exclusion of personal freedom and political, social, and racial equality. Presumably, the heyday of this type was the Great Depression of the 1930's.

Now that the eight possible value systems that describe the pattern of support or nonsupport of the values of freedom, equality, and New Deal economics have been identified, the voting behavior of the individual Justices can be analyzed. This has been done in Table 3. The table lists all eighteen Justices and specifies what part of the 1958–1977 period each served on the Court. The period of membership is presented in terms rather than years. Thus, Chief Justice Warren served from the beginning of the period being analyzed until the end of the 1968 term, which was June of 1969. The period of service of those Justices who left the Court at a time other than the end of a term is given as the beginning or the end of the term closest to their appointment or departure. The two Justices without a date next to their names held membership throughout 1958–1977.

The three middle columns of Table 3 numerically represent the extent of each Justice's support of or opposition to each of the three values. The scores can range from + 1.00 to − 1.00. The scores for Douglas, Brennan, Marshall, Stewart, and White are based upon their votes in Burger Court decisions only. This was done in order to specify as ac-

TABLE 3.   The Justices and Their Value Systems

| | VALUES AND AVERAGE SCALE SCORES | | | |
JUSTICE	Freedom	Equality	New Dealism	VALUE SYSTEM
Douglas (through 1974)	.73	.76	.73	Liberal
Warren (through 1968)	.65	.61	.43	Liberal
Fortas (1965–1968)	.63	.64	.24	Liberal
Goldberg (1962–1964)	.63	.63	.18	Liberal
Brennan	.38	.58	.37	Liberal
Marshall (from 1967)	.45	.57	.23	Liberal
Black (through 1970)	.53	−.55	.43	Populist
Stevens (from 1975)	.05	.31	−.15	Moderate
Stewart	.09	−.08	−.32	Moderate
White (from 1962)	−.40	−.07	−.02	Moderate
Clark (through 1966)	−.51	−.20	.25	New Dealer
Blackmun (from 1970)	−.34	−.27	−.22	Conservative
Powell (from 1971)	−.26	−.26	−.49	Conservative
Whittaker (through 1961)	−.38	−.67 *	−.06	Conservative
Frankfurter (through 1961)	−.12	−.81 *	−.36	Conservative
Burger (from 1969)	−.49	−.42	−.38	Conservative
Harlan (through 1970)	−.30	−.36	−.64	Conservative
Rehnquist (from 1971)	−.58	−.58	−.55	Conservative

* Based on two scale scores.

curately as possible their current response to the values of freedom, equality, and New Deal economics. The scores of all the other Justices, however, pertain to the part of the 1958–1977 period during which they were members of the Court.

The last column of the table lists each Justice's value system. This column includes a value system not heretofore described: Moderate. Convention decrees that scores occupying the midpoint of a measure that ranges from $+1.00$ to -1.00 lie in a zone of indifference or neutrality with regard to the underlying variables. Persons having such scores are neither pro nor con. Because the scores of Stevens, Stewart, and White (with one exception for each of them) lie in this middle zone between $+.20$ and $-.20$, an additional value system had to be established. The label "Moderate" aptly describes those whose scores fall in that zone.

The ordering of the Justices on Table 3 is from most to least Liberal and from least to most Conservative. This ordering was established simply by totaling each Justice's scores across the three values. Douglas, accordingly, appears most Liberal; Marshall appears the least so. Similarly, Blackmun is the least Conservative; Rehnquist is the most.

All but 5 of the Justices (that is, 13 of 18) have either a Liberal or a Conservative value system. Each group is of approximately equal size— six Liberals, seven Conservatives. Three Justices are neither fish nor fowl—the Moderates (Stevens, Stewart, and White). Justice Clark was apparently the last of the New Dealers, whereas Justice Black, true to his poor rural Southern origins, was very much a Populist.

The identification of Black as a Populist runs counter to the judgment of other observers. During the 1950's, the heyday of McCarthyism, when dirty linen invariably carried Red stains, Black, along with Douglas, was the judicial champion of the Liberal community. But Black did not wax Conservative with age. Prior to the 1960's, the value of equality was not pertinent to the Justices' decision making. Except for the Court's decisions in *Brown* v. *Board of Education,* race relations was not an issue in the Court's deliberations. Concerns that bear on equality, such as sit-in demonstrations; sex discrimination; the rights of juveniles, indigents, and illegitimates; and poverty law did not figure prominently in the Court's decisions until the 1960's. Black simply did not have an opportunity to reveal his true colors until then.

No perceptible shift occurs in the value systems of the Justices who served during both the Warren and Burger Court periods, with the possible exception of Justice White. If separate scores are calculated for the the two periods, White appears to be growing slowly more opposed to the values of freedom and equality, especially the former. If this trend continues, he may not qualify in the future as a Moderate but rather may be classified as a marginal Conservative.

The classification of 16 of the 18 Justices as Liberal, Conservative, or Moderate comports with the value systems that the vast majority of Americans possess. These value systems are commonplace, as even a cursory reading of editorial pages and journals of opinion will reveal. Nor is the New Dealism of Justice Clark, or the Populism of Justice Black, discordant. Clark and Black espoused value systems that were prominent, though at an earlier point in time. On the other hand, who is to say that the economic conditions of the 1980's might not spawn another generation of New Dealers? Especially if freedom and equality become concerns of minor moment, as they already have in some circles?

Be that as it may, these eighteen individuals respond neither to alien nor to inscrutable influences. Their decisions are not dictated by whim, nor by the side of the bed they got up on. The Justices are not motivated by venality or personal aggrandizement. They respond rather to values that are an integral part of our heritage, that touch Americans generally, and that have a fundamental impact upon the character of American life.

● ● ●

61

Values as Variables
in Judicail Decision Making

David J. Danelski

• • •

A Scientific Conception of Values

Values are viewed here as constructs anchored in quantifiable human behavior. Such behavior may be either verbal or nonverbal. In ordinary discourse, we move quickly—almost automatically—from the empirical to the abstract in asserting that a man or a judge possesses certain values. This value-labeling process merits close examination so that we might understand more precisely what we mean when we use the term "values." To begin with, value constructs can be anchored only in a certain class of human behavior—behavior that is perceived and labeled as "evaluations" or "value-facts." Evaluations are defined as units of human behavior indicating that an individual regards a thing, condition, property, event, action, or idea as good, useful, or desirable, in itself, or for the achievement of some purpose he is actually pursuing or may eventually pursue. After evaluations are designated, they are labeled in terms of specific value constructs such as freedom, equality, and tradition. Finally, in the basis of certain criteria—such as the number of evaluations in a specific value category or indication of preference for one value over another—an inference is made that the individual whose behavior is under inquiry possesses certain values, some of which are more salient than others. Values and their relative saliency, it is stressed, are always postulated. They are constructs, not empirical entities; their scientific status hinges entirely upon whether they are validly anchored in evaluations and whether the evaluations are validity designated.

For purposes of developing a theory of judicial decision-making, values are viewed as being anchored in individual evaluations. Although we sometimes speak of the values of a group—we say, for example, that freedom is an important value of the Supreme Court—we are actually either making a complex statement about the values of individual Court

From David J. Danelski, "Values as Variables in Judicial Decision Making." *Vanderbilt Law Review* 19 (1966): 722–727, 737–738, 740. Reprinted by permission. Footnotes have been omitted.

members, or inferring and postulating values from group evaluations (court decisions and opinions), which are the end products of a process we are trying to explain. In either case, we are driven back to the evaluations of individuals. This point has important implications not only in terms of theory building, but also in the selection of data for value analysis.

Evaluations always occur within particular situations—"transactions"—which are circumscribed in time and space. Therefore, any inference leading to the postulation of values must be made in the light of the entire transaction in which evaluations occur. Further, the time-space boundaries of transactions limit generalization of the postulated values to future transactions. If, for example, a judge addresses a group in wartime, a number of evaluations indicating patriotism would be expected; and their presence probably would be relevant in analyzing his judicial behavior at that time. But whether patriotism retained the same high place in his value hierarchy after the war is a matter that would bear inquiry. Other situational considerations must also be taken into account in making inferences from evaluations.

Identification of Values

The conception of values presented above provides a guide for their identification. Evaluations of individual judges constitute the universe of behavior for observation. Once evaluations are designated, specific values can be inferred and postulated. Personal interviews and written questionnaires are possible research techniques in gathering such value data, as well as content analysis of personal documents, speeches, autobiographies, articles, and books. In this regard, the techniques developed by Ralph K. White ("value-analysis") and Charles E. Osgood ("evaluative assertive analysis") are useful.

For purposes of illustration, White's method of value-analysis will be used to identify the top values of Justices Brandeis and Butler. These Justices have been selected as examples because they were known to have had fairly well-defined, stable value systems. In addition, they were perceived by their colleagues as leading proponents of divergent views on the Supreme Court. The basic hypothesis here is that their disagreement was rooted in a fundamental conflict of values—values to which they had been committed long before they came to the Supreme Court.

The universe selected for value-analysis consisted of two addresses by Louis D. Brandeis given in 1915 and 1916 and two addresses given by Pierce Butler in the same years. The 1915 addresses were on essentially the same subject: Brandeis' address, given on the Fourth of July, was entitled "True Americanism"; Butler's address was entitled "Educating for Citizenship: Duties the Citizen Owes the State." The 1916 addresses were both given to bar associations in the Midwest: Brandeis' was entitled "The Living Law," and Butler's was entitled "There Is Important Work for Lawyers as Citizens." Brandeis was appointed to the Supreme Court in 1916; Butler was appointed in 1922.

The results of the value-analysis are reported in Table I. They appear reliable in that they are consistent with independent estimates by contemporaries and scholars. Compare the values indicated in Table I with the following statements from the last chapter of Alpheus T. Mason's *Brandeis: A Free Man's Life:*

1. *Individual Freedom:* "The dominant strain in Brandeis and in his heritage was an urgent zeal for freedom."
2. *Practicality:* "Nor was he carried into ecstacy [sic] by any utopia of what ought to be. His concern was for a society as it is and can be."
3. *Change:* "[H]e knew that social progress, in the very nature of things, demands bold and courageous experimentation, that there must be change. . . . To him, nothing in human affairs is inevitable, save change itself."
4. *Social Justice:* "He was moved by the wrongs of economic privilege, by human suffering and exploitation. . . ."
5. *Knowledge:* "The most significant quality in his career was restless curiosity, thirst for knowledge."

Then compare the values indicated in Table I with the following contemporary perceptions of Butler's values:

TABLE I. Ten Top Values

BRANDEIS		BUTLER	
	(N = 208)		(N = 544)
Value	%	*Value*	%
Individual Freedom	15	Morality	12
Practicality	7	Patriotism	10
Change	7	Tradition	10
Patriotism	7	Individual Freedom	8
Justice	6	Laissez Faire (+)	8
Laissez Faire (−)	5	Religion	5
Social Justice	5	Law	5
Knowledge	5	Safety	4
Unity	4	Justice	4
Equality	3	Order	3

N equals number of evaluation units disclosed by the value-analysis of the speeches mentioned in the text.

TABLE II. Lone Dissents, 1923–1939

VALUE	BRANDEIS (N = 15) %	BUTLER (N = 10) %
Laissez Faire (+)	0	40
Laissez Faire (−)	40	0

N equals the number of cases in which the named Justice was the lone dissenter.

1. *Patriotism:* "Mr. Justice Butler brought to the bench . . . a character . . . fortified by an unfaltering patriotism."
2. *Individual Freedom* and *Laissez Faire:* "He felt that the secret of America's success lay in the opportunity afforded the individual, protected by the Constitution, and that individual enterprise, ingenuity and courage would be undermined and weakened, if not destroyed, by paternalistic government as exemplified by the extension of government power and control over the individual, over private enterprise and over purely state and local matters."
3. *Tradition:* "He believed that only in strict adherence to precedent as established in adjudicated cases could orderly government be maintained and individual right be preserved."
4. *Religion* and *Morality:* "His conservatism was rooted in profound religious convictions."

The value of patriotism in Table I merits special comment. In view of the fact that the speeches were given during the World War I period, and that one of them was a Fourth of July speech, patriotism may have been disproportionately emphasized. Therefore, one might suspect that, if a larger universe of evaluations from other time periods were analyzed, the importance of that value would diminish. A cursory check of subsequent public statements by both men indicates that this was the case in regard to Brandeis but not to Butler. Patriotism was a recurrent value in Butler's addresses even after he came to the Supreme Court.

Table I indicates what appears to be a significant conflict between Justices Brandeis and Butler in regard to laissez faire. Proceeding upon the hypothesis that this value conflict was important in Supreme Court decisions while these two Justices were on the bench, an attempt was made to verify the findings by analyzing individual evaluations of each Justice in the judicial process. This was done by examining the lone dissenting votes of Justices Brandeis and Butler during the period they were together on the Court. If the findings in Table I regarding their respective valuings of laissez faire are correct, the following could be expected: (1) Brandeis would never dissent in favor of laissez faire (+), (2) Butler would never dissent in favor of laissez faire (−), (3) a substantial number of Brandeis' lone dissents would indicate the value of laissez faire (−), and (4) the precise opposite would be true of Butler. That is what Table II shows.

• • •

Toward a Theory of Judicial Decision-Making

Implicit in the discussion of values in this paper is a stimulus-response model of judicial decision-making. Responses are decisions of courts defined in terms of judges' behavior at the end of the decisional process. Stimuli are cases before courts for decision, but precisely what constitutes a "case" raises some difficult problems. Values and all the other postulated variables that connect stimuli and responses in some meaningful way are, of course, only theoretical constructs.

In a strict sense, a case before a collegial court is not a stimulus, but rather a set of stimuli—briefs read by judges, arguments of counsel, conference discussions, comments of law clerks, and so forth. These sets of stimuli are not identical for all judges, partly because each judge perceives stimuli uniquely in terms of his own values, experiences, and needs. Lawyers who argue before collegial courts know this intuitively. Before ascending the bench, Robert H. Jackson, reflecting on his arguments before the Supreme Court, said of Justice Butler:

> He was relentless in bringing the lawyer face to face with the issues as he saw them. I think I never knew a man who could more quickly orient a statement of facts with his own philosophy. When the facts were stated, the argument was about over with him—he could relate the case to his conceptions of legal principles without the aid of counsel.

If the sets of stimuli we call cases are considerably different for each judge, it would be fruitless to use techniques such as factor analysis or cumulative scaling in explaining collegial decision-making, for such techniques assume that the sets of stimuli are the same for all the judges. Discussing this problem, Coombs has written: "An anchor point is needed, and the same stimulus being presented to different individuals provides such an anchor. If a stimulus differs in a significant way from one individual to the next, absolutely nothing can be done with just these observations. . . ." Abandoning the hypothesis that individuals differ in their responses "because they perceive the stimuli differently," Coombs concludes, "we concede that each stimulus is more or less the same thing for everyone, not just in its physical dimensions but in whatever its subjective characteristics might be."

In developing a theory of judicial decision-making, the concession to which Coombs refers cannot be made because we have empirical evidence that judges do, upon occasion, perceive the same cases differently. The problem here is how to specify judges' perceptions. A first step in that direction is intensive study of the judges themselves, using data outside of the decisional process. Value analysis is important in this regard. If judges' values are located in value spaces, inferences can be made about how they perceive value phenomena; then there is some basis for determining whether perceptions overlap. Thus, the exploration of values appears to be a fruitful first step in the development of a theory of judicial decision-making.

• • •

The primary purpose in developing a theory of judicial decision-making is not the prediction of judicial decisions before they occur. Rather it is to understand scientifically the complex phenomena we call the judicial process. Some doubt that this is possible, and they may be correct. However, the scientific student of judicial behavior assumes, with Louis L. Thurstone, "that an unlimited number of phenomena can be comprehended in terms of a limited number of concepts or ideal constructs."

• • •

--- **62** ---

Parabolic Support of Civil Liberty Claims: The Case of William O. Douglas

S. Sidney Ulmer

It is generally conceded that civil liberty claims dimension the behavior of Supreme Court justices. Scales of such cases show that the justices differ from each other in the extent to which they support civil liberty

From S. Sidney Ulmer, "Parabolic Support of Civil Liberty Claims: The Case of William O. Douglas," *Journal of Politics* 41 (1979): 634–639. Reprinted by permission. Footnotes have been omitted.

claims. And these differences have been found to be stable over relatively short periods of time. What we do not know is whether the same degree of equilibrium occurs over more substantial periods. That question has been explored for Justice Hugo Black over a career span of 34 Court terms. From the research, one may infer that Black's support for civil liberty claims underwant some metamorphosis and that a parabola accurately depicts the contours of that change.

In this note, we examine the question with reference to Justice William O. Douglas. Douglas is a prime candidate for analysis given his long tenure on the Court. Moreover, he is an interesting candidate since the observed change in Black's behavior was said to be more significant in the absence of similar change by his close liberal colleague.

The analysis of Douglas' support pattern over the same length of time used in examining Black may be given focus by posing two orienting questions: (1) if Douglas is compared to himself over 34 terms, is change in the trend of his support for civil liberty claims observed? and (2) if change in trend is found, can it be attributed to change in theoretical variables?

The Research Design

For analytical purposes, we identify three predictor variables: support of civil liberty claims by the Court majority, the subject matter mix of the cases, and the cumulative service of Douglas on the Court. The dependent variable is defined as the support of civil liberty claims by Douglas over the first 34 years of his tenure.

The predictor variables are derived from what is basically theoretical reasoning, though we make no claim to anything other than partial theory here. First of all, the Supreme Court is a small group and has been shown to conform to some of the tenets of small group theory. One of these is that small group members tend to conform to group norms or the will of the majority. Thus, we expect some significant correlation between the support patterns of the Court and those provided by Douglas. Secondly, if the predisposition of a justice to support a civil liberty claim is variable across claims—which it certainly is—a change in the subject matter mix of the case load should produce a change in support patterns. Finally, the factor—cumulative service—is justified on the ground that service on the Court is a learning process and that learning promotes behavioral change over the long run. It should be noted here that we do not get into the complex linkages inherent in this relationship. But it is a matter for further investigation, should the suggested relationship hold.

Operationally, the dependent variable may be measured by the percentage of claims supported by Douglas in each of 34 terms. The action taken by the Court may be measured in a similar fashion. The indicator to subject matter mix is more laboriously derived. Essentially, we conceptualize four sub-categories of issues in the civil liberty case pool. Variation of each category as a percentage of total cases in each term may serve as a measure of subject matter mix.

Findings

Figure 1 verifies that the support for civil liberty claims offered by Douglas across 34 Court terms did in fact vary, and in the same parabolic fashion as that depicted earlier for Hugo Black. However, variation does not establish change in the trend of behavior—our fundamental interest. To make such a determination objectively, we have run regression lines from the apex of the parabola portrayed in Figure 1 and evaluated the angle formed at the intersection of the lines. Since the probability of the angle derived for Douglas occurring by chance is less than one in a hun-

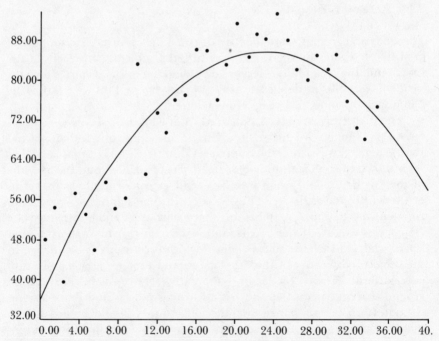

FIGURE 1. Regression of support for civil liberty claims (y) on cumulative years of service (x), for William O. Douglas, 1937–1971 terms.

dred, we infer that change in the trend of Douglas' support behavior did occur.

What we wish to know is whether the change observed in support behavior is subject to explanation by the three factors discussed above. Specifically, we hypothesize that these three variables will account for a significant amount of the variation seen in the Douglas support curve. The hypothesis will be rejected, however, unless the relationship between predictor and dependent variables is statistically significant at .05 or better and the variance accounted for exceeds 50%. Moreover, we shall use an adjusted formula for R^2 which gives a more conservative estimate than R^2.

The analysis shows that using the modified formula for R^2, the subject mix variable explained 47% of the variance in the Douglas support curve. When Court action was added, the cumulative variance accounted for dropped to 45%. But when we added service on the Court, total explained variance increased to 86%. Since this association is significant at .01 and the variance accounted for exceeds 50%, we cannot reject the hypothesis.

Significance of the Findings

The support accorded civil liberty claims by Justice Douglas not only changed substantially over time but did so parabolically—i.e., the change took the same form as that established earlier for Justice Black. Douglas has not been subjected to the same kind of critical commentary which Black's performance drew over the last years of his tenure. Yet if support for civil liberty claims measures "liberalism," both Black and Douglas were less liberal early and late and most liberal in the middle years of their service.

The substantive significance of our findings are several. We now appoint Supreme Court justices for good behavior (essentially life) and screen them only at the beginning of their service. Apparently this reflects a belief that if a nominee can pass muster once—he will provide competent service for as long as he remains on the Court. If the patterned changes in behavior established for Douglas (and Black) were to characterize all justices and competent service includes the reflection of attitudes suitable to the problems of the times, certain Court structures may be candidates for modification. Instead of lifetime tenure, we may wish to limit a justice to a specific term (say 8 to 10 years) so that periodic review of performance could be had.

If long service in the Court is associated with basic modifications in the attitudes or outlook of a justice—or in what he thinks the Constitution requires—organizations that attempt to influence Court policy making through nominating/advise and consent processes may have to rethink their strategies. It may not be enough to look at the past decisions of say a Court of Appeals judge in order to predict his subsequent decisions—except in the short run. The same consideration applies to a president who seeks to control Court policy-making or reverse it in selected areas via the appointment process. Moreover, those interested in obtaining preferred policy outputs from the Court must be sensitive to what Irving Lefberg has called "incipient change." For a litigant who can anticipate the Court's changes in direction or read the signs of change early, the ability to shape or influence the Court's future policies is enhanced. Lower court judges are in a similar situation. Indeed, such judges have been criticized, on occasion, for failing to anticipate changes in the direction of Supreme Court policies and ruling accordingly.

Lefberg points to several other reasons why change in the behavior of Supreme Court justices is important. One is a moral reason. Since consistency in Court made policy is the norm, inconsistency may invite our attention to make sure that it is not venal. Another reason pertains to the general problem of inferential statistics. If one would explain Supreme Court behavior by studying variation on assorted dependent variables, it is essential that such variation occur. Leaving aside the question of the specific factors used in the present investigation, the approach is salutary and will take us a step beyond inferences about relative liberalism/conservatism typically drawn from multi-dimensional scale models.

Finally, the support of civil liberty claims by the Court contributes to the social climate in which the interface of individual aspiration and governmental authority is embedded. Variation in those factors that shape the tenor and tone of that climate must interest those of us who are committed to the maintenance of a democratic political system or the kind of "Constitutional Republic" we have known.

— 63 —

Social Background as an Indicator to the Votes of Supreme Court Justices in Criminal Cases: 1947–1956 Terms

S. Sidney Ulmer

Writing in the May 1968, issue of *Law and Society Review,* the editor of that journal, Richard D. Schwartz, declared ". . . We know of enough major changes in orientation by Judges once on the bench to be very doubtful that background analysis will carry us very far. The influences that operate toward uniformity . . . very likely constitute a powerful counterweight to variations based on background." This statement came three years after Bowen's research on 373 state and federal Judges sitting in 1960. Bowen's study led him to conclude, *inter alia,* that variation in decisional output was associated in some patterned way with variation in the sociological characteristics of the Judges, that the social backgrounds of the Judges ". . . affects the output of decisions."

Bowen found, however, that none of the sociological variables examined explained more than 16 percent of the variance when other variables were controlled and that social background for the most part ". . . explained somewhat between 20 percent and 30 percent of the total variation in . . . different case areas." As a result, he went on to say that "A final inescapable conclusion about the explanatory power of the sociological background characteristics of these Judges is that they are generally not very helpful."

Sheldon Goldman, on the other hand, has observed that "there is abundant evidence that attitude/value variations among Judges is primarily responsible for non-unanimously rendered decisions." The present author, in a 1970 paper, suggested that attitudes/values are a consequence of social/experiential background. But attempts by Schmidhauser, Nagel, Adamany, Beiser, and others to connect the social backgrounds of judge to their voting behavior have produced mixed results.

In the present note, we wish to add to the picture some results from research on 14 justices who sat in the Court in the ten terms, 1947–56.

The selection of the decade, 1947–57, for analysis was an artifact of a separate research project for which this period was relevant. In that separate project it was found that the justices varied considerably in the rates at which they supported government and failed to support individuals in criminal cases decided during the decade. Using rate of support for government as a dependent variable, we selected (from social background studies) 12 possible indicators to support rate. These were the following: age at appointment, highest degree received, status of school granting L.L.B., size of place of birth, size of place of last law practice, state legislative experience, federal legislative experience, prior service on a appellate bench, federal administrative experience, religious affiliation, public office immediately prior to appointment, and party affiliation.

These 12 variables, collectively, were found to account for 91.8 percent of the variance in support for state and federal governments in criminal cases. But since the number of independent variables almost equalled the number of observations, this finding is of no great moment. Close analysis, however, led to the identification of three factors that appear to have some explanatory power. These variables are age at appointment, federal administrative experience, and religious affiliation.

Age at appointment was operationalized in years; federal administrative experience was coded as present or absent; a similar dichotomization was used to separate protestants from non-protestants on variable three. For the dependent variable, we calculated the percentage of criminal cases, per year, in which each justice supported government. Table 1

TABLE 1. Raw Data Matrix *

JUSTICES	x_1	x_2	x_3	y	N
Douglas	40	2	2	19	217
Rutledge	48	1	2	22	58
Jackson	48	2	2	56	149
Murphy	50	2	1	20	58
Brennan	50	1	1	23	38
Clark	50	2	2	59	174
Black	51	1	2	21	237
Reed	54	2	2	67	214
Harlan	55	1	2	50	62
Frankfurter	56	2	1	39	239
Vinson	56	2	2	69	136
Burton	57	1	2	54	238
Minton	58	2	2	77	133
Warren	62	1	2	32	93

* Variable identification: (x_1) age at appointment; (x_2) federal administrative experience, 1 if absent, 2 if present; (x_3) religious affiliation, 1 if nonprotestant, 2 if protestant; (y) percentage of criminal cases decided favorably for state or federal government, 1947–56 terms; N = total number of cases.

portrays the raw data matrix to which a step-wise multiple regression routine was applied.

As shown in Table 2, our three independent variables, collectively, can account for 70 percent of the variance in the rate at which these 14 justices supported state or federal governments in criminal cases during the 1947–56 terms of the Supreme Court. Initially, the variable most highly correlated with support for government is age at appointment. By starting with that variable, adding additional variables one at a time, and observing the changes in R^2, we find a fairly sizable jump in the "explained variance" at each step. Each of our three independent variables makes a contribution. Using age at appointment and federal administrative experience, we can explain 49 percent of the variance. And if we also consider whether the justice's religious denomination is Protestant or non-Protestant, we improve our level of explained variance another 21 percentage points.

The six sociological characteristics in the Bowen study accounted for only 20 to 30 percent of the total variance in the decisions made by a population of lower court judges. For 14 Supreme Court judges, three social background variables explain between three and four times the variance accounted for in the Bowen study. This suggests, at a minimum, that Bowen's findings are not necessarily conclusive for all judges or all courts.

In the stepwise multiple regression analysis, the variable—age at appointment—was entered first since it exhibited the highest simple correlation (.506) with the dependent variable. But that does not indicate that age at appointment was, relatively, the most important of the social background characteristics examined. The reason is that the simple correlation between any single factor and decision is affected by the extent to which other factors influence output. In terms of the ability of any single variable to reduce the variance left unexplained by any combination of two variables, the order of importance is: (1) age at appointment, (2) federal administrative experience, and (3) religious affiliation. The data supporting this conclusion are presented in Table 3.

Table 3 shows that if we control for various combinations of two variables, age at appointment alone will reduce unexplained variance by 77 percent while federal administrative experience, after other variables

TABLE 2. Multiple Regression Analysis of Data in Table 1

VARIABLES ENTERED IN EQUATION	MULTIPLE R	R^2
x_1	.51	.26
x_1, x_2	.70	.49
x_1, x_2, x_3	.83	.70

TABLE 3. Correlation Analysis of Data in Table 1

VARIABLE	PEARSON r (rx₁ y, rx₂ y, etc.)	PARTIALS (rx₁ y · x₂ x₃, (rx₂ y · x₁ x₃, etc.)	PERCENT REDUCTION IN UNEXPLAINED VARIANCE
x_1	.51	.88	.77
x_2	.37	.81	.66
x_3	.43	.63	.40

have accounted for all the variance they can, will account for 66 percent of the remaining variance. In these terms, then, religious affiliation is the least important of our independent variables, age at appointment the most important, with federal administrative experience between the two extremes.

The same order of relative importance is maintained when we determine the proportion of the variance explained by each of the input factors in the regression equation. This determination is made by utilizing net regression coefficients, standard partial regression coefficients, standard deviations and Pearson product moment coefficients. Application of the appropriate formula shows that in the prediction equation, 30 percent of the variance is explained by age at appointment, 20 percent by federal administrative experience, and 19 percent by religious affiliation.

When the same analysis was applied to state and federal cases separately, similar results were produced. In federal criminal cases only, our three factors accounted for 70 percent of the variance in support for the federal government. In state cases, R^2 was reduced to 58 percent. Calculation of the relative contribution of the input variables to the regression equation revealed the same relative importance of the variables in federal cases as in combined cases. But a separate analysis of state cases ranked federal administrative experience as most important, accounting for 27 percent of the variance as against 22 percent for age at appointment and 10 percent for religious affiliation. Thus, a "federalism" variable appears to exert some influence. But our overall finding is not appreciably disturbed.

There is no attempt in this note to suggest that starting from some complete theory, we have derived three empirical indicators to decision patterns in criminal cases and successfully confirmed a theory. The effort reported here is strictly exploratory. It is reported for two reasons. First, recent writing dealing with social background theory seems sufficiently pessimistic to risk premature closure of this kind of research in the judicial area. We do not believe such closure is warranted at this time. Second, we subscribe to the view that attitudes influence decisions of judges and that socialization patterns help determine attitudinal structure. Consequently, our inquiry is not without a theoretical base. It is legitimate, however, to ask whether the exploration reported here is suggestive.

If "age at appointment," "federal administrative experience," and "religious affiliation" are indicators to socialization patterns which shape attitudes, it should be possible to identify plausible linkages. Nagel has shown that, in 11 state supreme courts, protestants were more likely than catholics to support government in criminal cases. This is consistent with our findings for the 13 Supreme Court justices who fall in these two categories. Nagel also reports that protestants from the "high income" denominations are more likely than "low income protestants" to support government in criminal cases. This, also, is consistent with our findings. Of eight protestants from high income denominations, six supported government between 50 and 77 percent of the time. Of three protestants from low income denominations, two supported government at rates of 21 and 32 percent. The linkage between religious affiliation and voting in criminal cases may, therefore, be socio-economic class and the influences emanating from the disparate socialization patterns which characterize different classes.

Federal administrative experience may progressively socialize the bureaucrat to support the government which employs him and, via metastisization, governmental authority in general when in conflict with alleged criminals. For every Ramsey Clark that comes to mind, there are a number of Tom Clarks, J. Edgar Hoovers, and Robert Jacksons. Serving the federal establishment is not known to be a liberalizing experience. One can surmise, of course, that ardent activists for individual rights against government are not rewarded with high federal administrative posts in the first place. Thus, the possibility exists that federal administrative experience is a surrogate for other earlier socialization patterns yet to be identified.

Age at appointment is not the same as age at point of decision. And the same theoretical considerations do not apply. If one assumes that, subsequent to appointment to the Court, all justices undergo common in-Court socializing experiences, then differences in certain areas of judicial behavior may result from initial differences in the "subjects." One such initial difference is age at appointment—a rough measure of the total impact of other socializing experiences prior to those encountered in the Court. Our data suggest that the greater the number of years to which the individual is subjected to these "other" experiences before coming to the Court, the more likely he will support government in criminal cases after getting there.

The discrepancies between the high level of explanation offered here (in terms of variance explained) and the relatively low levels produced by earlier studies underline our 1970 suggestion: *i.e.*, that it is premature to rule out the social background model as a useful device for explaining judicial behavior.

64

"That Word" and the "Bad B's"

Bob Woodward, Scott Armstrong

Harlan's view of the First Amendment was not always . . . expansive. Paul Cohen, a young antiwar protester, had been sentenced to thirty days in jail for disturbing the peace by wearing a jacket with the words "Fuck the Draft" inscribed on the back. Harlan termed this case (*Cohen* v. *California*) a "peewee."

When they had first granted cert on the case, Black had vehemently disagreed with Harlan. His interpretation of the First Amendment was literal: "Congress shall make no law . . . abridging the freedom of speech."

"I read 'no law . . . abridging' to mean *no law abridging*," he had stated emphatically in a 1959 opinion (*Smith* v. *California*).

Black found the conviction of Cohen so outrageous that he insisted that the Court summarily reverse the conviction without even holding oral argument. Harlan's strong opposition prevented the summary reversal, and only reluctantly did he agree to have it argued.

Many clerks, however, saw the case as symbolically important. Sentiment against the Vietnam war was at its height. Many of the clerks opposed the war, and felt a little guilty that they had signed up for a year with an establishment institution like the Supreme Court. Most agreed with the sentiments on Cohen's jacket, and one way or another many had themselves avoided military service. In a vote on whom to invite to a question-and-answer lunch, one of their top choices had been the outspoken antiwar activist and actress Jane Fonda.

From Bob Woodward and Scott Armstrong, *The Brethren* (Simon & Schuster, 1979) : 128, 128–133. Copyright © 1979 by Bob Woodward and Scott Armstrong. Reprinted by permission of Simon & Schuster, a Division of Gulf & Western Corporation. Footnotes have been omitted.

The antiwar movement was part of the clerks' culture, and its slogans part of their politics. The obscenities used to denounce Vietnam and the draft were important political expressions. Clearly, if the First Amendment protected speech of any kind, it protected political speech. Abrasive, outrageous expressions were sometimes called for. "Fuck the Draft" was hardly the most extreme. A decision against Cohen, in essence banning "Fuck the Draft" from the jackets and posters of the antiwar movement, could have deeper ramifications, some clerks believed. Police throughout the country were looking for grounds on which to curtail the activism unleashed by the war.

In Stewart's chamber, it looked to the clerks as if the Court was about to say that vulgar antiwar protests were not protected speech. Both flag sculptures and jacket slogans would be banned. The Court was desperately out of touch with the times. And, perhaps, with the Constitution. One of the clerks fashioned a makeshift patch combining the themes and put it on the back of his suit coat. "Fuck the Flag," it said. He wore it for several hours around the chambers before deciding that he did not want to test the Court's tolerance for political speech in its own building.

At oral argument on February 22, the Chief attempted to signal Cohen's attorney to not use the vile slogan in the courtroom. ". . . You may proceed whenever you are ready," Burger said. ". . . the Court is thoroughly familiar with the factual setting of this case and it will not be necessary for you . . . to dwell on the facts."

But Cohen's lawyer, Melville B. Nimmer, acting on behalf of the A.C.L.U., thought that the case would be lost if he didn't say the word at least once. To not utter it would be conceding that the word was or should be unspeakable.

"At Mr. Chief Justice's suggestion," the lawyer responded, "I certainly will keep very brief the statement of facts. . . . What this young man did was to walk through a courthouse corridor . . . wearing a jacket on which were inscribed the words 'Fuck the Draft.' "

The Chief's irritation was evident in his tone for the rest of oral argument. The Justices avoided using the word *fuck* in their questioning of the lawyers, referring instead to "that word."

The ritual that Harlan enjoyed most was sitting with his clerks on Thursday afternoons, reviewing the cases argued that week in preparation for the Friday conference. The afternoon of February 25, the clerk he had assigned to the Fuck-the-Draft case reviewed the details at length, pointing out that according to Harlan's prior opinions, the slogan was clearly protected by the First Amendment. Cohen's conviction was for the content of the message on his jacket, for his opposition to the war, and not for some disruptive conduct.

For Harlan, and for all of his colleagues except Douglas and Black, there were exceptions to what was protected speech under the First Amendment. The clerk went down the list to assure Harlan that none was involved.

Did the words advocate an insurrectionary act—the overthrow of the government or interference with the draft? No, they merely conveyed Cohen's view of the war and of the draft.

Did the words immediately endanger observers—like shouting "Fire!" in a crowded theater? No, of course not.

Did the words incite a noisy disruption? No, the only one in the courthouse apparently bothered by them was the arresting officer.

Did the words provoke a violent reaction from observers, so-called "fighting words"? No, again only the arresting officer seemed concerned. He had tried and failed to get the judge to hold Cohen in contempt.

Were the words "offensive" to unconsenting viewers? This was the most difficult problem for Harlan. Some passersby in the corridor might have been offended. But they could have limited their exposure by moving away, the clerk argued. The only captive audience would have been the one in the courtroom where Cohen appeared, but there he folded his coat over his arm, so that the spectators were not exposed. Moreover, the clerk reasoned, a certain amount of "offensive" exposure had to be expected in public.

Were the words themselves "obscene"? Certainly the use Cohen had made of the word *fuck* was not meant to be erotic, or to appeal to "prurient" interests. It did not depict explicit sexual activity. Surely, the state of California could not purge the word from public discourse.

Harlan was still not sure how he would vote the next day, but he admitted that he now saw the case in a different light. The war was a continuing subject of protest. That protest was an exercise of free speech. And the various levels of government—federal, state and local—were doing their best to curtail that protest. Why should a jacket be different from a flag sculpture? Perhaps he was being inconsistent.

At conference the next afternoon, the Chief referred to the case as the "screw the draft" case. He voted to uphold the conviction. To everyone's surprise, Black's position had changed drastically. He did not offer his absolutist position. Instead, he agreed with the Chief: this was a question not of political speech but rather of the pernicious use of a vile word. Cohen's jacket slogan was not protected "speech," but unprotected "conduct," he said. Cohen could be prosecuted.

With his most boisterous drawl, Black claimed that he was not deviating from his absolutism. Conduct was different from speech. His favorite example was picketing a courthouse. It was unacceptable *conduct,* not speech. People could not "tramp up and down the streets by the thousands" and threaten others, for example.

Douglas and the other First Amendment liberals—Brennan, Stewart and Marshall, who grumbled that it wasn't a case worth "giving blood on"—all lined up in favor of reversing the conviction. White and Blackmun sided with the Chief and Black.

Harlan provided the day's second surprise. He had thought it over, and he was now leaning toward overturning the conviction. But he was still not sure. He wanted the case put over for a week. He needed more time to consider it.

The others agreed.

Douglas's clerk joked about how the "magic word" set off such severe reactions in the "Bad B's," as he referred to Black, Burger and Blackmun. Douglas was disappointed that Black had deserted his long-standing First Amendment position. Perhaps Black was simply too old to understand these issues any more, to pursue the reasoning necessary to draw consistent parallels. But Harlan's hesitation offered little encouragement. He would likely end up voting to uphold the conviction. He too was out of touch with the country. The key would be Black, Douglas figured.

Black's clerks kept a constant pressure on their boss to revise his stance, but the word *fuck* offended Black's moral sensibilities. For all the freedoms he espoused, Black was priggish, especially about vulgar language. Never had his son heard him utter an obscene word. "Crook" was his strongest expletive. "What if Elizabeth [his wife] were in that corridor." he asked. "Why should she have to see that word?" Wearing the offensive jacket was conduct, not speech. The clerks could not move him.

The day before the next conference, Harlan's clerk mentioned the Cohen case. "We don't have to spend time on that," Harlan said. "I've made up my mind." He was now firm to reverse Cohen's conviction. He was determined to be consistent; the slogan was no less speech than the flag sculptures were. He could not understand Black's sensitivity to the word. "I wouldn't mind telling my wife, or your wife, or anyone's wife, about the slogan," Harlan told his clerks.

At the Friday conference, the voting went quickly, since everyone had had a week to consider. Harlan indicated that he had switched his position and would vote to reverse. Douglas, the senior member of the new 5-to-4 majority, realized that Harlan was the shakiest vote. Over the course of thirty-two years on the Court, he had learned that the best way to hold a swing vote was to assign that Justice to write the decision. "John, I'm assigning the opinion to you," Douglas said.

Harlan then said that he would prefer a narrow ruling, not one broadly declaring the use of these particular words to be protected speech.

"That's not enough for me, John," Stewart said. Like Douglas he wanted the slogan declared to be speech that was protected by the First Amendment.

Harlan assented quickly. If he wrote the decision on narrower grounds, Stewart and Douglas would concur separately and Brennan and Marshall might well join one of them. Harlan's majority would soon become a concurrence to someone else's majority.

Harlan and his clerk were pleased to have the opinion. They turned immediately to the drafting. Traditionally the Court had held that expletives like *fuck* were devoid of any social value. Suddenly to say that the word had value would certainly go beyond Harlan's previously expressed views and those of the other members. But if the slogan itself were protected, there must be some basis for protecting the words individually. The person expressing his political views ought to be able to choose from his own lexicon of expression. "One man's vulgarity is another's lyric,'" the clerk wrote.

When he had completed the draft, the clerk read it to Harlan and they discussed each section as they went. Harlan was generally pleased, though slow to warm to the protection afforded the word itself. He did not want to move recklessly in such a delicate field. He said that he would take the draft home overnight and reread it in his study. The next morning, Harlan announced that the draft was fine as it was. He was taking a major step, but he was behind it wholeheartedly.

The draft circulated shortly thereafter. The Chief was less than pleased when he read it in late May. He never expected to see Harlan glorifying such filth. Cohen should be spanked, and here Harlan was congratulating him.

"This case may seem at first blush too inconsequential to find its way into our books, but the issue it presents is of no small constitutional significance," Harlan's draft began.

Worse still, Harlan repeated the facts in detail, including the offending phrase, by quoting the lower court opinion. Raising such a word to a level of protected speech was more than the Chief could stomach. He sat down and scrawled out a short dissent. It helped blow off steam, but it also let his colleagues know about his strong feelings. On May 25, he sent his dissent to the conference. "I will probably add the following, which is the most restrained utterance I can manage," the Chief's memo began. His dissent was typed on the bottom half of the page. "I, too, join in a word of protest that this Court's limited resources of time should be devoted to such a case as this. It is a measure of a lack of a sense of priorities and with all deference, I submit that Mr. Justice Harlan's 'first blush' was the correct reaction. It is nothing short of absurd nonesense that juvenile delinquents and their emotionally unstable outbursts should command the attention of this Court."

Blackmun too was deeply offended by Cohen. "Cohen's absurd and immature antic, in my view, was mainly conduct and little speech," he wrote.

Sensing the exaggerated tone of reactions, Black decided not to write an opinion; Burger dropped his own opinion and joined Blackmun's instead; White found even Blackmun's opinion too severe and joined only part of it.

Burger was still angry on June 7 when the case was set for announcement. In the light-oak-paneled robing room, a messenger—selected for the task because he was taller than any of the Justices—was helping Harlan into his robe.

"John, you're not going to use 'that word' in delivering the opinion, are you?" Burger asked.

Harlan had been deeply amused at Burger's concern. He had no intention of utering the word aloud in open court, but he sidestepped the question. He enjoyed "twitting" the Chief, as he called it.

"It would be the end of the Court if you use it, John," the Chief asserted.

Harlan chuckled. It was time for Court. They paraded out the door after the Chief in order of seniority—Black, Douglas, and then Harlan—along a red carpet placed in the hall between the robing room and the courtroom. As the case was announced, Harlan bent over in his chair to review his notes, his forehead almost touching the bench as his eyes strained to read. He straightened up and repeated most of it from memory. His occasional sideways glances to see if the Chief was still paying attention were almost imperceptible. The Chief sat in rigid and pained stoicism, waiting for the offending word. Harlan paused, glanced again at the Chief, and proceeded, still without uttering the word. Finally, he finished without ever using it.

PART V

Interaction of Courts with Their Environment

Since courts do not exist in a vacuum, they cannot be understood out of context. In a democratic political system, all courts are subject to the vagaries of public opinion. At the level of the U.S. Supreme Court, public opinion may feed into the political branches of government and affect the support which those branches provide for the Court. At least, that is the theory. It undoubtedly has validity in times of crises—as in 1937 when President Franklin Roosevelt tried to "pack" the institution with justices favorable to the "New Deal." At the time public opinion favored the Court and Roosevelt's plan was not adopted. In general, however, the Court does not fare too well at the hands of the public. At any given time, less than 10 percent of the public is likely to think the Court's work "excellent." And most people view the institution unfavorably most of the time. At the same time, the Court is salient for less than a majority of the American public. And most Americans are ill informed about its day to day function. Thus, as Wasby puts it, given public ignorance of the work of the Court and the fact that the implementation of Court decisions does not normally require public involvement, public opinion may be irrelevant for much of the Court's work.

At the level of state courts, public opinion looms somewhat larger. This is because state court judges are usually elected periodically whereas federal judges are appointed by the president with the consent of the Senate. A judge who must face periodic election is not a judge who will lightly dismiss the views of the public vis-à-vis his work.

The tension between the election and the appointment of judges directs debate to judicial accountability. In democratic political systems, policy makers are expected to account to those for whom the policies are made. As judges come to be perceived more and more as policy makers, the pressure toward accountability is enhanced. The counter argument is that the judge must be somewhat insulated from societal and political pressures if he is to act impartially in resolving disputes. Moreover, it is said, the need for accountability can be served indirectly and, indeed, is enforced through the psychological influence of public opinion and peer groups. One may, in other words, want approval from such sources in spite of the fact that disapproval will not jeopardize employment. The checks and balances in the federal system are also said to promote a responsible relationship between the Court and its publics.

In electoral systems in which political pressure can be brought to bear, courts might develop "client" groups whose awards from the courts simply reflect their political power. In a life tenure, appointive system, in which a court is relatively isolated from direct political influence, certain exchange relationships between a court and a particular interest group or class are not ruled out. Two of the readings in Section seventeen focus on the possibility that the relative decline in black support for the Supreme Court in recent years might be a function of declining support for black claims by the Court.

In addition to public opinion, courts may be influenced by the general environment in which they operate. The three readings in Section Eighteen explore this possibility in the context of economic, social, political, and structural conditions. Atkins and Glick reveal that the distribution of issues decided by state courts of last resort are affected by the presence or absence of intermediate appellate courts in the jurisdiction. The reason for this is unclear. But the result in many cases is that the highest state court functions as a criminal court of last instance.

In a study of draft cases, Cook reveals a great disparity in the sentences dispensed by federal district court judges. While some judges consistently gave the maximum five-year sentences, a majority always gave probation. How can we account for the difference? Cook explores the possibility that environmental, demographic, and political culture variables are responsible. The explanation offered is basically suggestive, but a finding of particular interest is that neither political party can be associated with racism in draft case sentencing.

The findings on school district desegregation reported by Giles and Walker clearly establish the impact of environmental factors on judicial decision making. Combining theory and practical political questions, these authors ask whether in the 1970s, 151 Southern school districts differed in the extent to which they had been required to desegregate by a federal judge. Finding that the districts did differ, the authors then inquired as to why—suggesting the possibility that the social background of the judge, and environmental or community linkage variables may provide explanations. While social background was not an effective explanation, a combination of school district size, black enrollment, court location, and judicial education explained 39 percent of the variation in level of segregation. Of particular interest here is the fact that the most important "explainer" was the location of the relevant court. Federal district court judges in these Southern districts appeared less willing to enforce desegregation strictly in the district where the court was located than in other districts. One implication is that community pressure on the judge is greater in his "home" district.

Section nineteen presents five readings dealing with the impact of court decisions on those publics and officials to whom they are directed. The study of impact is a fairly recent development. It grew out of a recognition that once a court has decided a case, automatic compliance cannot be assumed. Many court decisions are not implemented or are implemented in some fashion other than that intended by the deciding court. Effective communication is essential for the implementation of a Supreme Court decision. While communication may not be a major problem in the case of most lower court judges, for lawyers, prosecutors, policemen, and lay public, an unambiguous understanding of what the Court is doing and what it means can be a hit-or-miss matter.

Assuming that a decision is fairly well communicated and fairly well understood does not guarantee that action consistent with it will be taken below. As Canon points out, lower court judges may resist

Supreme Court instructions or commands for any number of reasons, from dislike of an opinion to concern for "victims" where the ruling is favorable to criminal suspects. Canon's study of four major Supreme Court cases turns up resistance to implementation in thirty-two of fifty states.

Other selections in this section suggest the variety of impacts made by court decisions. Policemen may respond to a search and seizure decision by exercising more care in their investigations, thereby reducing arrest rates. Or state legislatures may change the direction of their expenditures in response to a reapportionment decision. A particularly interesting kind of response to a Supreme Court decision is discussed by Birkby. Failing to show that urbanization, religious pluralism, and other factors account for disparity in procedures adopted after Abington v. Schempp, *he suggests that affected parties may respond procedurally without engaging in substantive change in the behavior which the high Court found objectionable.*

Our general understanding of the way in which courts interact with their environment and of the specific cause and effect relationships is incomplete. But such interactions are clearly in the realm of processes that explain court actions.

Courts and Their Constituencies

65

The Supreme Court and Public Opinion

Stephen L. Wasby

• • •

Early History and Editorial Reaction

In earlier times, even though we did not have available public opinion polls and other relatively sophisticated instruments for recording public opinion, it was clear that the Supreme Court's decisions had an impact on opinion. The decisions often produced mixed reactions. When the Court invalidated state fugitive slave statutes, "the decision was equally unsatisfactory to both pro-slavery and anti-slavery men" because the former were upset at the blow to states' rights and the latter, who disliked the federal fugitive slave law, thought the Court was backing the South. The Court also suffered in the public eye when, shortly after being enlarged and only a year after it had held in the first Legal Tender Case that the Union government could not require that debts made before the passage of the Legal Tender Act be paid in paper money, the Court

From Stephen L. Wasby, *The Supreme Court in the Federal Judicial System* (Holt, Rinehart and Winston, 1978), pp. 44–53. Copyright © 1978 by Holt, Rinehart and Winston. Reprinted by permission of Holt, Rinehart and Winston. Holt, Rinehart and Winston footnotes have been omitted.

reversed itself. Although the legal community felt that the Legal Tender Act was constitutional, the reopening of the case was "a mistake which for many years impaired the people's confidence, not in the honesty, but in the impartiality and good sense of the Court."

In the New Deal period, divided reaction was again evident. When the Court invalidated the National Industrial Recovery Act, "the more conservative sections of the press welcomed it as putting an end to unsound experiments in government regulation of industry," labor opposed the decision, and the business community was divided. However, more and more elements of the public were alienated by the Court's continued striking down of New Deal legislation, and "each new adverse decision in the winter and spring of 1936 brought new bursts of hostility." The farmers were upset about invalidation of the Agricultural Adjustment Act, the voiding of the Bituminous Coal Act irritated workers, and the minimum wage rulings "alienated nearly everybody"—including supporters of earlier decisions. Only ten of 344 editorials approved the decision on the minimum wage, with some sixty papers, including a number of conservative ones, calling for a constitutional amendment on the subject.

Editorial reaction to decisions is one measure, although an indirect one, of public opinion, and it has thus received some attention. Twenty-four large-circulation newspapers generally favored separation of church and state after three of four major Supreme Court church-state decisions; the exception was the *Zorach* ruling upholding New York's released time program, which the papers favored. The *McCollum* ruling striking down religious classes on school property was the most favorably received (eight papers favoring and two opposing), with editorials on the school prayer case closely divided (thirteen favoring, nine opposing). Support for the released time ruling may have resulted from that program's milder link between church and state, more conservative public attitudes toward civil liberties in 1952, liberal Justice Douglas's authorship of the Court's opinion, and the general tendency of newspapers to support the Court. Newspapers' editorial positions on church-state matters were affected by the city's political climate (the more Democrats, the more likely a paper to favor church-state separation), the publisher's politics (same relationship, but stronger), and the publisher's religion (higher support for the Court if Catholic or Episcopalian).

A study of a much larger number of papers—sixty-three—revealed that twenty-seven had opposed the school prayer ruling in editorials while sixteen had favored it, and editorial cartoons were also more likely to be critical of the ruling than to favor it. These proportions were more in line with general public opinion than the more favorable reaction of the big-city papers just noted. Opposition to the ruling was strongest in the upper Midwest, with more southern papers neutral or favorable. Editorial reaction to the Court's first reapportionment decision was generally favorable, with thirty-eight editorials favoring, ten opposing, and another twelve neutral or confused; sixteen editorial cartoons were favorable, while only four were opposed. The newspapers' editorial position on reapportionment affected news coverage: those supporting the Court presented a more restrained account of the Court's rulings in both headlines and reportage of critical reaction to the decisions than did those papers opposed to the decision.

Public Opinion Polls

Other evidence about public opinion has come from questions asked of the general public by the national commercial polling organizations, from studies by political scientists of particular groups in the population, and (to be discussed in the next section) from intensive analysis of state and national surveys carried out by university polling units. In part because the polling organizations and social scientists have examined public opinion among a variety of different populations, no unified statement about public opinion and the Supreme Court has yet been developed. Differences in the results reported in the remainder of this chapter may be somewhat confusing, but they are only an indication of our relatively underdeveloped understanding of the subject.

In the 1960s, national polling organizations began to ask how people rated the Supreme Court. Overall ratings remained fairly constant in the 1963–1967 period. A November 1966 Harris Poll showed the public giving the Court an overall negative rating (46 percent–54 percent). Younger people, the better educated, and blacks backed the Court, while southerners, older people, and the less well educated were the Court's severest critics. Similar results appear in a 1967 Gallup Poll. The Court's work was rated excellent by 15 percent, good by 30 percent, fair by 29 percent, and poor by 17 percent, leaving an almost even balance between favorable and unfavorable reactions. The June 1968 Gallup Poll showed how quickly opinion can change. Evaluations had shifted to 36 percent favorable, 53 percent unfavorable, with only 8 percent rating the Court's work as excellent. Republicans were most critical of the Court, and those with less than a college education were also negative; Democrats and those with a college education were evenly divided.

Although the Burger Court's criminal procedure rulings were more in tune with public opinion, they did not produce an improvement in the Court's overall rating. The Court received only a slightly higher Gallup Poll in 1973 than it had received in 1969—a rating much lower than the Court's mid-1960s ratings. In 1973, 37 percent rated the Court's work good or excellent, but only 6 percent rated it excellent. Thirty-five percent thought the Court too *liberal,* while 26 percent thought it too conservative. Who liked the Court had also changed. Decreased approval of the Court was shown by the college-educated, those twenty-one to twenty-nine years old (who showed the greatest drop), westerners and easterners, and Democrats, but ratings were up among those age fifty and over, southerners, and Republicans (up 12 percent).

Information concerning opinion about the Supreme Court among specific groupings in the population is much more sparse, but also provides evidence of difference among groupings in views of the Court. A 1970 poll of Providence, Rhode Island, lawyers showed they were more dissatisfied with the Court than the Gallup Poll's national sample. They were also more undecided than the national sample's college-educated and business and professional groups, with their indecision coming from indifference rather than ambivalence. The criminal procedure decisions seemed most important for the lawyers who criticized the Court; they tended to hold a "traditional" attitude toward the Court—including the idea that the Court only finds law—and wanted "strict constructionist" judges. Those favoring the Warren Court were more likely to approve of judges engaging in lawmaking. Another "special population," small-town police chiefs in southern Illinois and western Massachusetts, perceived changes in the Court's direction. However, some of the Illinois chiefs, who were not favorably disposed toward the Warren Court and gave the Supreme Court only a marginally positive overall evaluation in 1972, seemed unaware of changes the Burger Court produced. Massachusetts chiefs, who gave the Court a generally favorable evaluation and who were more knowledgeable about it, felt that the changes were favorable to the police.

More than three of four federal judges, state supreme court judges, and lawyers surveyed in early 1977 preferred the Burger Court to the Warren Court. Almost all (98.8 percent) thought the Burger Court to be more conservative than the Warren Court, and 78.4 percent approved of this conservative position. Although two-fifths thought the Court was still taking questions the respondents felt better left to the legislative or executive branches of government, 84.2 percent thought the Burger Court less likely to do so than the Warren Court, and only 2.4 percent thought the Burger Court *more* likely to do so. Over half of those in the poll approved of the Court's making it more difficult for citizens to use the federal courts to obtain redress of grievances and just under half (48.4 percent) said that the Court *was* making it more difficult. The quality of the Burger Court's written opinions was thought to be better than the quality of the Warren Court's opinions by 33.6 percent, with over half (51.9 percent) saying the quality was the same and 14.5 percent saying it was worse. Despite the perceived improvement, almost two-thirds (65.3 percent) said that the Court's opinions were often unclear and over three-fourths said they were often too long.

The national polls reported above showed not only changes in overall ratings of the Supreme Court but also shifts in confidence in the Court as an institution. In 1966 a Harris Poll majority (51 percent) expressed a great deal of confidence in the Court. This was almost 10 percent more than expressed comparable regard for either Congress or the executive branch but less than for medicine, colleges, or the military. A Gallup Poll the next year indicated that almost half the American public thought the Court had been impartial, but 30 percent—particularly older citizens, Republicans, and southerners—believed the judges showed some group favoritism.

Confidence in the Court had decreased noticeably by 1972, only 28 percent of a Harris survey expressing a great deal of confidence in it. Yet this figure was up from 1971 (21 percent) and was about the same as the confidence shown in the executive branch but more than was shown for Congress. Confidence in the Court then rose for two more years—to 33 percent having a great deal of confidence in 1973 and to 40 percent in 1974—but then decreased substantially to only 28 percent in 1975 and to 22 percent in 1976. This drop was part of the overall decrease in public confidence in its leaders, but the Court remained considerably ahead of the other two branches of government. In the 1975 survey, 38 percent said that those in charge of the Supreme Court "really know what most people they represent or serve think and want," somewhat better than Congress, the White House, or the executive branch. However, more— 43 percent—said the Court was out of touch with those it served. (Nineteen percent did not know, higher than for any other institution.)

In addition to their general evaluation of the Court, the public expressed reaction to specific decisions. Thus the 1966 Harris survey showed the public, despite its overall negative rating of the Court, favoring rulings on reapportionment (76 percent–24 percent) and desegregation of schools and public accommodations (both 64 percent–36 percent). Only reapportionment received approval in the South, where only 44 percent of the public supported school desegregation. Opinion was evenly divided on the Court's having forbidden the State Department to deny passports to Communists, but the school prayer and *Miranda* rulings were disliked (30 percent–70 percent and 35 percent–65 percent). A 1973 Gallup Poll revealed that 58 percent favored the Burger Court's conservative ruling on obscenity, but roughly the same percentage disapproved of the Court's 1972 invalidation of the death penalty. (President Nixon's appointees, who had dissented, were closer to public opinion.) The rulings denying news reporters a First Amendment right to protect confidential sources and invalidating aid to parochial schools were also opposed by majorities of those questioned.

Reactions of specific groups to particular decisions have been little studied. Examination in 1967 of the impact of *Miranda* showed that four-fifths of all police officers in four Wisconsin medium-sized cities disap-

proved of the ruling. There was no relationship between attitude and
amount of formal education, but those with least police experience approved of the decision the least. Five years later, Illinois and Massachusetts small-town police chiefs did not show this same resistance to
Miranda, as most officers had learned to live with the ruling. However,
although Massachusetts officers generally favored the *(Mapp)* rule excluding illegally seized evidence from trials, it was hard to find an Illinois officer who could say anything good about that doctrine. The chiefs'
views were not related to their formal education, but those who had had
law enforcement training before becoming officers were somewhat more
likely to view the rule positively. A study of officers in twenty-nine St.
Louis area police departments carried out at the same time, however,
showed weak relationships between training and attitudes. Officers with
a college education were somewhat less likely than others to see the
Supreme Court's criminal procedure rulings as harmful, but some findings ran counter to the hypotheses that officers with higher levels of education and training would "have a view of the goals of law enforcement
which includes the protection of civil liberties even of persons suspected
of criminal acts" and would "be less critical of Supreme Court decisions."

A 1975–1976 study of University of Tennessee Law School students
showed general agreement that five major cases—*Brown, Miranda, Engel
v. Vitale* (school prayer), *Roe v. Wade* (abortion), and *Furman v. Georgia*
(the 1972 death penalty ruling)—were "basically good . . . , involved
reasonably practical solutions to the problems presented to the Court . . . ,
and were appropriate decisions for the Court to be making." *Miranda*
received the most positive rating on a "good-bad" dimension, *Furman*
the least positive rating (marginally positive). *Furman* was also seen as
the least effective of the five on the "practical-impractical" dimension,
with the abortion ruling first and *Miranda* next. *Miranda* also received
the highest rating on the "appropriate-inappropriate" dimension, despite
criticisms that the Court had been "legislative" in its action. The respondents' responses across all three dimensions were significantly affected by the law students' legal values; those adhering to a "social welfare" view of the law were uniformly more positive about all five cases
than were those adopting a more traditional "entrepreneurial" view of
the law and the lawyer's role. (Political party leanings and party activism
helped explain differences, but to a lesser extent.) In the above-noted
survey of federal and state judges and lawyers, a majority of those surveyed approved of the Burger Court's recent decisions and direction in
all areas except obscenity/pornography, where 51.4 percent disapproved.
Highest approval—80.4 percent—came in the area of racial discrimination. Also receiving over 70 percent approval were the Court's decisions
and direction in the areas of criminal defendants' rights, sexual discrimination, labor union law, environmental protection, and free speech and

freedom of the press. The Court's abortion rulings received approval from almost two-thirds (65.3 percent), and its work in the states' rights-federalism was approved by 68.7 percent. Only 57.5 percent approved the Court's death penalty decisions, and the smallest favorable majority (51.1 percent) approved the Court's rulings with respect to mandatory busing to alleviate segregation.

More Extensive Surveys

A more detailed picture of the structure of public opinion about the Court and particularly about "public orientations toward courts [which] apparently change slowly over time if at all, as decisions and popular policy preferences (and other factors) interact," is provided by systematic opinion surveys conducted during the 1960s. These avoid the problems of the forced-choice responses of the Gallup and Harris polls, which allow people to answer without knowing about the decisions on which they are commenting. The principal extensive surveys, all undertaken during the Warren Court, were conducted in Seattle (1965), Wisconsin (1966), and Missouri (1968), and nationally by the University of Michigan Survey Research Center (SRC) as part of its 1964 and 1966 postelection surveys.

Seattle residents had relatively little information about the Supreme Court. However, they were supportive of the Court's work, although those with negative views held them somewhat more intensely. People's limited awareness appeared in the national survey through inability to name good or bad things the Court had done and through the attribution to the Court of cases it had not decided. In a test of knowledge about decisions, only 2 percent of the Wisconsin sample had all items correct and only 15 percent had more than half correct; 12 percent had every answer wrong. One-fourth of the Missouri sample declined to comment on the Court or pled ignorance. Lack of awareness in Wisconsin extended even to criminal procedure decisions which had been the subject of open controversy and to reapportionment despite the redistricting in the state. The prayer rulings were among the most salient decisions and, along with civil rights decisions, accounted for more than two-thirds of the 1964 likes and dislikes about the Court; by 1966, however, most likes and dislikes were accounted for by criminal procedure decisions. The school prayer decisions were "unknown only to the same seemingly irreducible number of persons who have managed to remain unaware of the segregation decisions." A majority of blacks, however, were in such a category. It thus appears that people have difficulty relating decisions to their personal lives and that "only a few cases are sufficiently dramatic to rise above the public's threshold of attention." Yet because some in the Missouri survey who did not read newspapers knew of at least one of the Court's decisions, it appears that "issues which gain the Court renown (or notoriety) are so salient that they come through even to people virtually isolated from the printed word."

If we move from awareness to support, we find that in the 1964/1966 SRC surveys, those giving the Court diffuse (general) support outnumbered by four to one those giving the Court specific support (that based on particular decisions). Only about 20 percent were negative as to diffuse support, but one-third were negative on specific support. Thus, despite the unpopularity of recent decisions, the Court seemed to retain a "substantial reservoir" of general support, some of which came from those opposed to particular decisions. (Among small-town police chiefs, negative evaluation of the Court did not prevent agreement by substantial majorities that the Supreme Court should be the "final judge of law enforcement and police matters.") Some of those least knowledgeable about the Court, who also seemed most trusting of government, were among those giving the Court diffuse support, while those aware of the Court were more likely to distrust government and not to find it responsive.

Higher knowledge about the Court seemed to correlate with greater *dis*approval of the Court in Wisconsin. Similarly, in Seattle, "critics are more likely to have paid some attention to the Court than its supporters" did. Those with college degrees were more likely to be strong supporters or critics, while those with little education were likely to be weak supporters, weak critics, or neutral. Favorable prior information about the Court had an independent effect on support, while favorable attitudes and belief in specific procedural rights affected what a person heard and read about the Court and reduced the effect of communication concerning the Court. In the Seattle and Wisconsin studies, but not in the Missouri survey, political party identification affected a person's attitudes. Being a Republican affected reactions to Court rulings, but being a Democrat influenced what one heard, leading to maintenance of current attitudes. In Wisconsin, although approval of the president was positively related to approval of the Court, regardless of one's party, part of Republicans' unhappiness with the Court seemed to stem from Democratic control of the White House. (Republicans and Democrats also differed more than did conservatives and liberals.) In the SRC national surveys, respondents' "attitudes toward public policy as measured by the scale of liberalism/conservatism" was the single factor best able to assist in explaining support for the Court, even among those most active politically, although specific support by those knowledgeable about the Court also helped explain their general support. Congruence between liberals' political positions and the Warren Court's decisions meant that liberals gave the Supreme Court more support at that time.

To what extent does the public believe in the myth that the Court is a legal rather than a political body? When the Missouri sample was asked the Supreme Court's main job, only 8.1 percent associated the Court directly with the Constitution (references to constitutionality increase the figure to 16.6 percent). Thirty percent of the responses contained references to law, and courtlike functions were mentioned by an equal number. Less than half of the comments (46.7 percent) contained positive symbols regarded as legitimators of the Court's authority, although a majority of the respondents (60 percent) did see the Court in terms of symbols and beliefs. In less than one-fourth of all the responses was the Court seen primarily as a political institution. This data led to the conclusion that "the Court's myth enjoys widespread diffusion," although members of the public were not fully dependent on external symbols to legitimate their belief in the Court. However, education increased rather than reduced belief in the myth, which was not disturbed by the Court's exercise of its political role. That those of higher social status have a greater belief in the myth helps to explain its "cultural dominance"; those who do not believe in the myth were not more politically sophisticated but actually were less well socialized into prevailing norms. The Wisconsin data suggests that, although myth acceptance may result from satisfaction with the Court, "mythification" increases support for the Court.

A related important question explored in analysis of the SRC national surveys was whether people thought it proper for the Court to produce changes in governmental structure or process—like those required by the reapportionment decisions—that is, whether the Court could "legitimate regime change." A Supreme Court ruling can perform this function only for those who perceive the Court, recognize that it may properly interpret and apply the Constitution, and feel that the Court was acting competently and impartially. Forty percent of the population satisfied neither of the first two conditions, while roughly one-fourth satisfied both; only about one-eighth satisfied all three. (Local leaders in Wisconsin were far more likely than the average citizen to satisfy comparable criteria.)

The Court's ability to legitimate change for only a few supports Adamany's assertion that the Court does not perform the legitimating role. However, we also need to know whether those opposed to the Court will act on their beliefs. Those who think the Court's performance is poor are "most likely to act to change a decision" but "they are neither numerous nor particularly rebelliously inclined." In Wisconsin only a few of those who said they would do something to change a Supreme Court decision they disliked would try to develop further opposition to those decisions among the public. Half would work through their congressmen, and another one-fourth would "act within the established legal processes." Virtually no Illinois or Massachusetts small-town police chiefs said they would refuse to go along with a court ruling. Over half the Illinois officers said, however, that they would do something about a decision they disliked, but for most this was only to talk about the disliked decisions, complain, and "gripe." In Massachusetts, most spoke of writing to the authorities, including their commanding officers or other chiefs, in order to express their opinions, while a couple would have acted through the legal system.

These responses lead to the remark made about the Wisconsin sample: "This is quiescence indeed" and to the conclusion that "the decisions of the Supreme Court have had more effect on the reputation of the Court than the activities of its antagonists." However, it is also clear that acquiescence rather than active approval has served to produce compliance with Court decisions. Because the public becomes aware of so few decisions and because public officials can often put the Court's commands into effect without involving the public, the public's views of the Court often are irrelevant to much of what the Court does. Public opinion on the Court's actions and overall estimates of the court are responses to factors external to the Court, including partisan and ideological predispositions. If the Court's doctrines become more consonant with elements of public opinion, it is likely to happen more because new justices themselves embody the changing trends in public opinion than because the Court responds directly to public opinion as registered in Harris and Gallup polls or in elections. However, the Court's strategy is to some degree affected by public opinion, as the justices try not to stray too far from that opinion and particularly from the views of its special attentive audiences.

• • •

——————————— **66** ———————————

The Accountability of Judges
David W. Adamany and Philip Dubois

• • •

A. Should Judges Be Accountable?

There is no escaping that judges make policy. Since any judicial decision involving broad policy questions advantages some interests far beyond the immediate litigants and disadvantages other interests, one scholar has argued that "a judge is in the political process and his activity is interest activity not as a matter of choice but of function." The mere act of deciding is inherently policy formulation in such cases. But judges make policy as a matter of choice as well as function, for most know that sweeping public issues are involved and they act upon their personal values in resolving those issues.

Since judges make public policy, it follows that, like other policymakers, they should be accountable to the people in a representative political system. Accountability usually means that those who lead policymaking departments are subject to direct, periodic popular review in elections. In some cases, accountability may be achieved indirectly through the appointment of policymakers by those who are periodically subject to voter approval.

Accountability has several conditions. First, policymakers must be accountable, either directly or indirectly. Second, accountability must be regular and periodic. Officials' terms should not be so long as to thwart the public's real ability effectively to revise or reverse disfavored policies by replacing those who promulgated them. Third, the procedures used to hold policymakers accountable should not obscure the public's choices. Officials should in some general way be identified with the policies they have made; and the alternatives to those officials and their policies should be generally known.

American practice reveals a substantial commitment to the principle that judges, like other policymakers, should be accountable to the public. Yet it reflects also significant hesitations about judicial accountability.

From David W. Adamany and Philip Dubois, "Electing State Judges," *Wisconsin Law Review* (1976): 768–769, 770–776, 778. Reprinted by permission. Footnotes have been omitted.

Only the national government and four states name judges for life terms. All the others require either direct or indirect judicial accountability. Eight states favor indirect accountability—two by initial selection and subsequent gubernatorial appointment, three by gubernatorial appointment from a list of nominees submitted by a "merit plan" commission, and three by legislative selection. The remaining 38 invoke some type of electoral review. Fourteen states favor partisan elections and an equal number nonpartisan ballots. The remaining 10 employ some variant of the Missouri plan, requiring at a minimum that justices must submit themselves to the voters for approval or disapproval on a retention ballot that carries the name of no opponent.

The commitment in 46 states to some element of direct or indirect electoral review in judicial selection and retention is diluted by particular procedures found in several states. At the outset, most Missouri plan states diminish the effectiveness of voter choice. In an unopposed retention election, there is little need for a sitting judge to explain and defend his policies. And there is no opponent to challenge those policies, advance a contrasting program, or offer an alternative set of qualifications for the bench. Long tenure is the other major hesitation about popular review reflected in contemporary American practices. In the 46 states shunning life tenure, high court judges serve terms ranging from 2 years to 15 years. The average state grants an 8-year term to justices, 2 years longer than the tenure of United States Senators. But 18 states grant terms of 10 years or longer, which may substantially diminish the public's opportunity to hold judges accountable.

Despite the philosophic argument for holding judges publicly accountable in a representative system and the widespread state practice of incorporating elements of voter review in judicial selection systems, there is a powerful strain of American thought that rejects the argument for judicial accountability. This debate has tended to rage around the national judiciary, because its judges make highly visible and controversial policy but are subject to neither direct nor indirect popular review.

● ● ●

Defenders of life tenure for federal judges have insisted that it allows judges fearlessly to protect minority rights in a majoritarian system. But with the exception of the Warren Court era, the performance of the national courts has not validated this claim. Scholars have pointed out that the Supreme Court has most often invoked the Constitution to safeguard the prerogatives of advantaged and privileged minorities, while ignoring the pleas of and striking down legislation aiding the poor, racial minorities, women, and other disadvantaged classes. Even if the judiciary vigilantly protected minority rights, it has been argued that this erodes the will and the responsibility of the Congress to do so, with adverse long-term effects upon the Nation's respect for civil liberties."

Second, it has been argued that the appointment process, the judges' reliance on executive enforcement of their decrees, congressional authority over judicial structure and organization, the amendment power, the authority to impeach, and similar checks upon the judiciary are sufficient to bring it into line with the popular will. At the outset, several of these checks—more notably the amending and impeaching powers—require extraordinary legislative majorities, thus failing to vindicate the majority rule principle of democracy. Further, the checks and balances within the legislative process—such as bicameralism, the filibuster, the decentralized committee system, and the seniority rule for selecting committee leaders—have made it difficult for majorities to prevail. Some state judiciaries have greater constitutional independence and many state legislatures are not characterized by such extensive dispersion of power; but the essential point remains that decentralization of power between and within the other departments reduces their ability to impose checks upon the courts. Hence judicial policy initiatives often may be sustained by the support of well-placed and determined legislative minorities.

Even if checks by the popular branches were less cumbersome, they are blunt instruments at best. They do not reverse particular constitutional interpretations but rather alter the organization, personnel, or function of the courts. Many who disagree with specific judicial policies may hesitate to invoke such sweeping checks. Finally, of course, such blunt tools for court-curbing do not enjoy wide public acceptance.

Third, it is argued that the main function of the judiciary is not to check the popular branches, but to legitimate their work. Since the judges sustain far more legislation than they strike down, their real impact is to signal the public—especially those who oppose the policies involved—that the elected branches have acted within their constitutional authority and their decisions should therefore be respected. Public opinion studies show very low public knowledge of the Supreme Court's work. What is known are those highly controversial cases in which the justices overturn decisions of other decisionmakers—cases involving school desegregation, obscenity, defendants' rights, regulation of subversive speech and organizations, and school prayers. The Court's decisions affirming actions of the popular branches are not even a whisper in the winds of public opinion. The state judiciaries are far less visible to the public than is the Supreme Court, and any approval they may give to policies of the popular branches can have no significant impact on public opinion.

Even if the courts had a legitimating capacity, this would raise a barrier to accountability at critical moments in American history. During those periods of social and economic upheaval when voters reject the long-standing dominant party coalition and install a new party in power to address urgent national issues, the federal courts will still be staffed by life-tenured judges named by the old regime. Invoking the power of judicial review and expressing their disapproal in other, more indirect ways, the courts cast a shadow upon the constitutionality of the work of the new majority coalition. The power to legitimate is also the power to delegitimate. And it will most often work its negative effects in moments of high controversy and sweeping change, when the elected departments—struggling to meet a national crisis—are most vulnerable to the shadowing of their policies by constitutional doubts.

Finally, it is argued that judicial decisionmaking, insulated from elections, is a more rational and neutral process than occurs in the political branches. A closer examination does not support that proposition. Scholars have discovered that judges vote their values, and that liberal and conservative blocs form on the Supreme Court. Moreover, Justices maneuver for votes, in the assignment of opinions, and in the shaping of policies. From the inside, the Court bears strong resemblance to a legislative committee.

In all, the controversy has revealed few persuasive reasons for insulating judges from public accountability. It would, of course, be impossible to elect judges nationwide. And it would be undesirable to elect them by district or state, lest their implementation of national legislation and the Constitution take on a local rather than national perspective. But these practical objections do not apply to the selection of state judges. (Nor do they preclude periodic indirect popular review of federal judges by appointment for fixed terms only, thus vesting the elected departments with power to replace judges whose policies are far removed from the popular will with others whose views are more nearly consistent with it.)

B. Making Judges Accountable By Appointment

Since judges make policy, it follows that, like other policymakers, they should be accountable to the people in a representative political system. No persuasive reason has been advanced for insulating state judges from accountability. The primary question is how to make them accountable. It is sometimes argued that indirect accountability by appointment is preferable to direct accountability by popular election. The main arguments for appointment do not, however, withstand close scrutiny. And in the absence of some strong reason for policymakers to be only indirectly accountable to the people, there ought to be a preference in a representative democracy to allow voters directly to name those who head one of the three independent policymaking departments of government.

One argument advanced for the appointment of judges, rather than their election, is that governors, legislatures, or Missouri plan nominating commissions are more likely to name higher quality judges than will judicial electorates. But there remains the threshold difficulty of specifying the qualifications of a "good" judge. Herbert Jacob, using gross characteristics such as graduation from an out-of-state law school, holding a prior college degree, winning law school honors, and attending a substandard law school, found very few differences between trial court judges appointed by the executive, named by the legislature, selected under the Missouri plan, or chosen in partisan or nonpartisan elections.

A similar study of state supreme courts discovered few educational differences among justices named through differing selection systems. All selection systems produced about the same percentage of justices with law degrees. Where Governors named judges, a somewhat higher percentage had a bachelor's degree and a somewhat smaller percentage had earned their law degrees at an in-state university. But other systems did not differ significantly in these ways.

It had also been suggested that gubernatorial appointment or Missouri plan selection are desirable because they reduce partisan considerations in appointments. But it is not clear, at the outset, whether the elimination of partisanship is desirable. Since it is usually improper for an executive to quiz potential appointees about their stances on judicial questions, party affiliation may be a useful surrogate for predicting how a judge will vote. If it is argued that appointive judges are made accountable by appointment, then it makes sense for an elected executive to name judges from his own party, because they are more likely to reflect the values that the voters endorsed when they elected the executive.

Furthermore, it is well known that partisanship is a major influence in the executive appointment of judges. Of 103 Justices named to the United States Supreme Court, only nine have been appointed from outside the President's party. Since the end of the Civil War, 95 percent of lower federal court judges were named from the President's party. There is less evidence on the party affiliation of gubernatorial appointees to the bench. But an overwhelming majority are from the Governor's party. Even in Missouri plan states, the selection commissions which submit lists of judicial candidates for gubernatorial consideration are usually dominated by members of the chief executive's party. Hence, the Governor is ordinarily able to name one of his fellow partisans to the bench. It is not clear, therefore, that direct gubernatorial appointment or the Missouri plan in fact reduce partisan considerations in naming judges, or indeed that they should do so.

C. Making Judges Accountable By Election

Since no persuasive argument can be advanced for indirect accountability of judicial policymakers, direct accountability through elections is a preferable means for giving the public control over the third branch of government. And partisan elections seem preferable to nonpartisan ballots. At the simplest level, partisan elections are much more likely to assure the existence of opposition, vigorous criticism of those in power, and effective presentation of alternative policies. Political party leaders feel an obligation to recruit qualified candidates for each partisan office contested in an election, if for no other reason than to fill out and balance the party ticket. Further, party organizations provide some of the campaign resources necessary to promote a candidate and his program.

Herdon has shown that effective public participation in selecting judges is diminished in nonpartisan elective systems because the political advantages of incumbency and the lack of an organized party opposition easily allow judges to be reelected. In nonpartisan systems, a judge typically serves until retirement age, which usually occurs in mid-term, and the Governor then appoints a successor until the next election. The appointed successor enters the lists with all the advantages of incumbency, is usually reelected, and initiates another cycle which terminates upon his retirement and a new gubernatorial appointment.

In states with partisan judicial elections, this cycle is often broken when an out-party landslide defeats incumbent judges along with other officials. Fewer judges serve until retirement, and fewer judges therefore initially take office by gubernatorial appointment. If direct public accountability is desirable for judicial policymakers, partisan elections effect this result better than nonpartisan systems, by reducing the frequency with which judgeships are initially filled by appointment rather than election.

Partisan judicial elections allow voters to make more intelligent decisions at the polls than do nonpartisan ballots. The evidence that voters switch parties or stand pat in response to the records and platforms of Presidential candidates is probably not duplicated in judicial elections. Supreme court contests have low visibility, and it is unlikely that voters know much about judicial candidates. In Wisconsin's 1965 nonpartisan judicial contest, only 44 percent of those who voted and only 30 percent of the whole sample knew that Nathan Heffernan was the incumbent justice. Only 21 percent of the voters and 12 percent of the whole sample had any correct information about Justice Heffernan. And only 17 percent of the voters and 10 percent of the whole sample gave any correct information about Howard Boyle, his opponent, who had also waged a vigorous race for the high court in the previous year.

Similarly low levels of information were found in a 1954 study of New York's partisan judicial election. Only 1 percent of voters in New York City, Buffalo, and rural Cayuga County could recall the name of Chief Judge Conway, who had been reelected that year. Only 5 percent of the Buffalo electorate recalled voting for Judge Desmond, a local resident. Not more than 30 percent could recall the name of any judicial candidate, and not more than 20 percent could name any court for which an election was being held.

If the public knows little about judicial candidates, they might nonetheless cast intelligent votes in a partisan election. At the simplest level, party labels permit voters, especially the "have-nots," to identify those in power, to fix responsibility by party, and to make retrospective judgments on judicial conduct. But more important is the correlation between party affiliation and policy preference. Voters' party allegiances are not random; there is a high correlation between party identification, ideological outlook, and issues preference. Overall, Democrats lean toward liberal postures, Republicans toward conservative stances. The same correlation is even more pronounced among political activists. Partisan values are reinforced when officeholders must anticipate seeking renomination in partisan primaries or conventions and reelection on partisan ballots. Their need to maintain the support of party activists also strengthens partisan values.

Party labels may, therefore, provide useful guidance to voters, who can usually be confident that a Democratic judicial candidate will favor liberal decisions on the bench and Republican aspirants conservative positions. Democratic and Republican voters who share their respective parties' usual postures will not have difficulty casting an intelligent judicial ballot; moreover, independent voters can at least identify the competing outlooks of judicial candidates from their party labels.

• • •

Modern legal scholars and social scientists no longer deny that judges make policy. In a republican system, policymakers must be accountable to the people, either directly or indirectly. This principle is affirmed by the large number of states that either elect judges initially or retain them by balloting after some type of "merit plan" appointment. Accountability requires institutional arrangements that strengthen voters' ability to select officials who will, in the main, govern consistently with the majority's policy preferences. Concurrently scheduled partisan judicial elections more readily allow voters to hold judicial policymakers accountable than do nonconcurrent or nonpartisan voting arrangements, separately or combined.

• • •

———————— **67** ————————

Black–White Differences in Attitudes Toward the Supreme Court

Lee Sigelman

Do black and white Americans hold dissimilar attitudes toward the Supreme Court? In a study published in 1968, Hirsch and Donohew found that blacks were much more positively oriented toward the Court than were whites; favorable attitudes toward the Court were expressed by less than 30% of the white sample, but by almost 72% of the blacks. This racial difference withstood controls for several other factors, including education, region, income, party identification and sense of political efficacy.

Hirsch and Donohew's findings concerning racial differences in Court-related attitudes are hardly unique. . . . Nor are their findings very surprising. In fact, they originally decided to focus on the Supreme Court precisely because it was an institution for which race seemed to play an especially significant role in structuring popular evaluations. . . . At the time the data were gathered for this analysis (1964), the Court was still in the midst of a long and dramatic series of decisions that put it, in Hirsch and Donohew's . . . words, "in the forefront of the civil rights revolution." Since the mid-1960s, though, the United States has undergone massive racial protest and violence, popular disaffection with a long and unsuccessful war effort, and devastating revelations of government corruption. Moreover, the Supreme Court itself has undergone considerable changes of personnel and doctrine, evolving from the activist tradition of the Warren Court to the more restrained course followed by the Burger Court.

Has support for the Court continued at mid-1960s levels despite the turbulent events of the late 1960s and early 1970s? Or has the pervasive political malaise of the 1970s undermined confidence in the Court? If so, has this impact been felt more or less equally by blacks and whites, so that Court support, although perhaps lower for both groups than it was in the 1960s, continues to be higher among blacks? Or, to take another possibility, have the changes in the Court eroded confidence among blacks in particular, to the point that racial differences in Court support have diminished?

We now have a great many studies of recent trends in the general dimensions of political support, confidence and trust . . . as well as confidence in the executive and legislative branches in particular. . . . We also have a wealth of information on racial differences in political attitudes. . . . But far less is known about recent attitudes toward the Court, especially as they relate to Hirsch and Donohew's conclusions about racial differences. In the only relevant study of which I am aware, Miller, Brudney and Joftis found that between 1972 and 1974 both blacks and whites became less likely to cite either Congress or the presidency as the "part of government you trust most often to do what's right." . . . As a result, the percentage who named the Court as the most trustworthy branch increased between 1972 and 1974, especially among whites. In 1972, almost 50% of the blacks but barely over 20% of the whites had selected the Court; this margin narrowed considerably, to approximately 52% for blacks and 45% for whites, in 1974. Unfortunately, the manner in which trust in the three branches was measured makes it difficult to interpret these findings. Rather than posing independent questions about trust in each branch, Miller, Brudney and Joftis in essence measured "relative trust," i.e., trust in any branch compared to trust in the other branches. Thus, one could be counted as a supporter of the Court simply because of one's greater antipathy toward the other two branches, both of which are more salient than the Court for most people. . . . As confidence in the executive and legislative branches declined in the early 1970s, then, increased confidence in the Court became a mathematical certainty, given the relativistic nature of Miller, Brudney and Joftis' trust measure. If, as in the present case, we are concerned with popular evaluations of one particular institution, the Supreme Court, then the nature of Miller, Brudney and Joftis' trust measure makes their data and findings ill-suited for our purposes.

Data

In the yearly General Social Surveys it has conducted since 1973, the National Opinion Research Center (NORC) has asked random samples of Americans about their confidence in a number of key social, cultural, economic and political institutions. NORC's confidence question is the same one that the Harris Poll introduced during the 1960s:

> I am going to name some institutions in this country. As far as the people running these institutions are concerned, would you say you have a great deal of confidence, only some confidence, or hardly any confidence at all in them?

After having this question read to them, NORC respondents are handed a card that lists the executive branch of the federal government, Congress, and the U.S. Supreme Court, along with ten other institutions. NORC also gathers a full complement of supportive background information and a wide variety of other attitudinal data, so variables similar or identical to the control factors introduced by Hirsch and Donohew can also be employed here. Each yearly NORC sample numbers approximately 1,500 respondents, of whom an average of between 11% and 12% are black. Pooling the yearly samples over the entire 1973–77 period produces an omnibus sample of 6,644 whites and 900 blacks, although missing data reduce these numbers to approximately 6,300 and 770, respectively, in the analyses reported below.

• • •

Findings

The NORC question relating to confidence in the Supreme Court is not the same one that Hirsch and Donohew (1968) used to make racial comparisons. As a result, it is impossible to draw any firm conclusions here about changes in absolute levels of support for the Court since the mid-1960s. The NORC data do, however, permit a follow-up comparison of relative levels of Court support among blacks and whites.

In this regard, the first, and in many respects most important, conclusion to be drawn from the five years of NORC surveys is simply that by the mid-1970s there was no longer any substantial black-white difference in confidence in the Court. As Table 1 reveals, during this period the very same proportion of blacks and whites (15.6%) expressed "hardly any confidence at all" in the Court, and blacks and whites differed very little from one another (by only 4.2%) in the tendency to express "a great deal" or "only some" confidence in the Court. As a re-

TABLE 1. Black and White Levels of Confidence in the Supreme Court, 1973–77 (%)

| | RACE | |
| | White | Black |
CONFIDENCE	(N = 6,334)	(N = 776)
A great deal	35.3	31.1
Only some	49.1	53.4
Hardly any	15.6	15.6
	$V = .029$	

flection of these minimal differences, Cramer's V for the relationship between race and Court support between 1973 and 1977 is only .029, which, even with the huge sample sizes that are involved here, falls short of statistical significance at the .01 level.

Table 1 also reveals that, in direct contrast to the situation a decade or more ago, whatever racial difference existed in the mid-1970s was in the direction of greater confidence in the Court among whites than blacks. Obviously, however, too much should not be made of this, given the small and statistically insignificant size of the differences involved. Incidentally, it is also true that Court support was slightly higher in 1976 and 1977 for both blacks and whites than it had been between 1973 and 1975. Moreover, while whites expressed slightly greater support for the Court than did blacks in each yearly survey from 1973 through 1976, the 1977 results indicated a slight (2.1%) tipping back toward blacks over whites in the tendency to express "a great deal" of confidence in the Court. Of course, whether these represent the beginnings of new long-range trends or are only momentary aberrations remains to be seen. Here again, however, it should be borne in mind that these differences are extremely small and statistically insignificant ones. Accordingly, rather than focusing on any changes within the period or even on the direction of the race-Court support relationship through this period, let me emphasize that at no time during the period examined here was there any appreciable black-white difference in confidence in the Court.

It is nonetheless possible that the same sort of racial difference in Court support that was uncovered by Hirsch and Donohew in the 1960s could emerge if certain other factors were held constant. This proved not to be the case, however, when control variables similar or identical to the ones that Hirsch and Donohew employed were introduced in the present analysis. Although the controlled relationships summarized in Table 2 tend to be somewhat more substantial than the simple relationship detailed in Table 1, they are far too small to justify concurrence with Hirsch and Donohew's (1968:559) earlier conclusion that there is "a large difference" in black and white attitudes toward the Court. In fact, not a single one of the 28 V coefficients in Table 2 is significantly different from 0 at the .01 level of probability. Moreover, even these negligible black-white differences tend to run in the direction of greater confidence in the Court among whites than blacks, a pattern that holds within no fewer than 20 of the 28 categories in Table 2.

Discussion

These findings suggest that the sizable black-white differential in support for the Supreme Court that was uncovered in the 1960s by Hirsch

TABLE 2. Relationships between Race and Confidence in the Supreme Court, by Various Control Factors

CONTROL FACTOR	CATEGORY [a]	V
Education	Grade School	.081 [b]
	Some high school	.021
	High school graduate	.040
	Post–high school	.057
Region	New England	.115
	Middle Atlantic	.067
	East North Central	.032
	West North Central	.026
	South	.031 [b]
	Mountain	.090
	Pacific	.064
Income	$0–$3,999	.047
	$4,000–$7,999	.053
	$8,000–$9,999	.048
	$10,000–$14,999	.040
	$15,000–$19,999	.047 [b]
	$20,000 +	.031
Party	Strong Democrat	.082
	Not very strong Democrat	.056
	Independent, closer to Democrat	.016
	Independent	.034 [b]
	Independent, closer to Republican	.054
	Not very strong Republican	.029 [b]
	Strong Republican	.039 [b]
Anomia	0	.049
	1	.039
	2	.024 [b]
	3	.055 [b]

[a] Categories are self-explanatory except for region and anomia. See NORC (1977:35) for a listing of states within each geographic region. Anomia items were introduced as substitutes for the efficacy scale employed by Hirsch and Donohew (1968). The three items that were repeated in four of the five NORC surveys were used to form the anomia scale, with each person's score calculated as the number of times he or she agreed with the anomic position.

[b] Within these eight categories, blacks expressed greater confidence in the Court than did whites.

and Donohew, among others, had faded to insignificance by the mid-1970s. How and why did this happen? The answer to this question must be somewhat speculative, but two different types of explanation seem especially plausible.

First, previous research . . . has established that diffuse support for the Court is shaped by evaluations of specific Court decisions. As the Warren Court of the 1950s and 1960s evolved into the Burger Court of the 1970s, it seems understandable that black confidence in particular would have waned, thereby lessening or perhaps even reversing the racial differential in Court support.

But while evaluations of the Court may in part be built from the bottom up (i.e., from support for specific actions to general affect for the institution), they may also represent specific applications of a more general attitudinal set. In this respect, it should be noted that among both blacks and whites, evaluations of the Court are fairly closely tied to evaluation of the other two branches of the federal government, Bearing this in mind, it seems entirely possible that the Court was a victim of the more general decline in political trust that occurred during the late 1960s and early 1970s—especially among blacks. . . . According to this interpretation, the lack of differentiation between blacks and whites in levels of confidence in the Court during the 1970s reflects the fact that political support declined among whites and virtually bottomed out among blacks. Congress or the President may more often than the Court have been the true focus of this mood of disenchantment; and, indeed, among both blacks and whites during the 1970s there was greater confidence in the Court than in either of the other branches. But the Court appears to have paid the price of the generally bleak atmosphere as well. In sum, the fact that during the 1970s blacks were no longer more supportive of the Court than were whites seems likely to reflect both a lessening of support for specific Court (in) actions, and the more pervasive political mood that enveloped the nation at mid-decade.

--------------------------------- 68 ---------------------------------

Supreme Court Support
for Black Litigants: A Comparison
of the Warren and Burger Courts

S. Sidney Ulmer, Michael Thomson

Introduction

It is well known that the support given certain litigant classes by the United States Supreme Court varies across classes and within classes over time. Thus, aliens are unlikely to fare well during wartime, while business corporations might find less support from the Court during periods of economic distress. The federal government, on the other hand, is likely to fare better than other litigants whether appearing as direct litigants or as amicus curiae.

As a litigant class, Negroes have received different levels of support depending on the historical period examined. During the era of the Warren Court, the chief justice supported the claims of Negro litigants 94 percent of the time. Warren's predecessor, Vinson, supported such claims in only 64 percent of the opportunities presented to him (Ulmer 1970). Comparable figures for the Warren and Vinson Courts are 83.9 and 73.5 percent respectively.

The reasons for such differences across and within classes are varied. The mood of the country, the configuration of political and economic interests within the United States at a given time, the persistence of certain litigant classes during particular historical periods, and the variation in resources available to those who press the Court for relief from one era to another undoubtedly have some impact. But whatever the changes in Court response to particular litigant classes, such changes do not occur in a vacuum. Court support is not a one-way street.

In a recent study, Sigelman found that the sizable black-white differential in support for the Court in the 1960s faded to insignificance in the 70's. By way of explanation Sigelman suggests (among other things) that ". . . diffuse support for the Court is shaped by evaluations of specific Court decisions. As the Warren Court of the 1950's and 1960's evolved into the Burger Court of the 1970's, it seems understandable that black confidence in particular would have waned, thereby lessening or even reversing the racial differential in Court support" (Sigelman, 1979). However, no evaluation of this hypothesis is offered.

To infer that relative black support for the Court has lessened as a direct response to a waning support for black claims in the Court requires analysis of support patterns on both sides of the equation. Sigelman has conveniently provided the first. In this paper we address the second—Court support for black claims. We wish to know whether black claimants have fared better in the Warren Court than in the Burger Court. If so, then the Sigelman hypothesis that waning relative black support for the Court merely reflects a lessening sensitivity to black claims in the Court may be entertained.

For purposes of analysis we have identified two periods. The first (t_1) covers the 1964–68 terms; the second (t_2) the 1972–76 terms. The first period represents the last five terms of the Warren Court prior to the appointment of the first Nixon justice—Warren Burger; the second period represents the first five terms of the Burger Court subsequent to the completion of the four Nixon appointments. The analysis is carried out at two levels: Court decision and decisions of selected justices.

Hypotheses

Our inquiry may be addressed through three hypotheses:

1. If t_1 is compared to t_2, a statistically significant reduction in support for Negro claims will be observed at the level of the Court itself.

2. If the support accorded Negro claimants in t_1 by the Warren Court justices is compared to the support accorded such claims by the justices who replaced them in t_2, a statistically significant reduction in support rate will be observed in t_2.

These hypotheses suggest that any variation in support rate that might turn up will be due to change in the personnel of the Court. If that were the only source of such variation a third hypothesis should hold—to wit:

3. If the support accorded Negro claimants in t_1 by the holdover justices from the Warren Court is compared to the support provided for such claims in t_2 by the same justices, no statistically significant reduction in support rate will be observed.

The justices exchanged between 1968 and 1972 were Burger, Rehnquist, Blackmun, and Powell for Warren, Black, Fortas, and Harlan, respectively. The holdover justices were Douglas, Brennan, Stewart, Marshall, and White.

Data and Methods

A Negro claimant case is one in which a Negro or organization representing a Negro cause, (such as the NAACP), is a litigant. We assessed our three hypotheses by collecting all Negro claimant cases in the 1964–68 and 1972–76 terms respectively. In this ten-year span, we collected votes in support (or nonsupport) of Negro litigants for the Court and for each justice specified in hypotheses two and three. We derived a support score by taking the case in which support was forthcoming as a percentage of all cases involving Negro litigants.

We evaluated the difference between t_1 and t_2 support scores with a Mann-Whitney U statistic (Blalock, 1960). We decided to reject hypotheses one and two if U would be expected by chance more than five times in a hundred. For hypotheses three, the rule was to reject only if the probability of U by chance was less than five times in a hundred. It may be noted here that these hypotheses have been evaluated for each justice separately. Thus, hypotheses two and three may be rejected for some justices, but not for others.

Primary Findings

Table I provides a summary of the support given Negro claims by the Warren and Burger Courts and by the eight justices involved in the 1964–68/1972–76 exchange. As the table shows, the Burger Court supported the claims of Negro litigants in t_2 at about half the level recorded for the Warren Court in t_1. Since the probability of such a difference is only six times in a thousand, hypothesis one cannot be rejected.

A comparison of the Warren Court justices and those who replaced them shows reductions in Negro claimant support of a similar magnitude—each Warren Court justice suporting the claims at about double the rate of their replacements. The only exception to this generalization is the Warren-Burger comparison that reveals that Burger reduced Warren's rate of support by 62 percent. Clearly, hypothesis two cannot be rejected for any of four comparisons.

The calculations for evaluating hypothesis three are presented in Table II. It is to be recalled that hypothesis three predicts no change in support rate for the five holdover justices. An impressive fact about Table II is the high level of support revealed by Douglas, Brennan, and Marshall—from 7 to 14 percentage points above the high level provided in the Warren years by the Court itself. Equally striking is that while the Burger Court cut the support rate in half, these holdover justices maintained almost identical rates in both periods. This suggests that for these justices, level of support was not a function of the environmental, attitudinal, or fact—law variables that might have affected level of support by the Court in the 1972–76 terms. But, in any event, hypothesis three cannot be rejected for these three justices.

TABLE I. Comparing Negro Claimant Support Scores for the Warren-Burger Courts and for Warren Court Justices and Their Replacements, 1964–68 and 1972–76 Terms

WARREN COURT			BURGER COURT					
Justice	N	Mean Support Score (%)	Justice	N	M Support Score (%)	Diff.	U	P
Warren	65	89.2	Burger	65	33.8	55.4	0	<.004
Black	63	55.6	Rehnquist	64	28.1	27.5	0	<.004
Fortas	46	89.1	Blackmun	65	44.6	44.5	0	<.004
Harlan	65	63.1	Powell	62	32.3	30.8	0	<.004
Warren Court	65	80	Burger Court	65	41.5	38.5	.5	.00

TABLE II. Comparing Negro Claimant Support Scores For Holdover Justices, Warren to Burger Courts, 1964–68 and 1972–76 Terms

Justice	WARREN COURT YEARS		BURGER COURT YEARS				
	N	Support Score (%)	N	Support Score (%)	Diff.	U	P
Douglas	65	93.8	33	87.9	5.9	5.5	>.650
Brennan	65	87.7	65	87.7	00	12.5	>.500
Marshall	24	87.5	58	86.2	1.3	6.5	>.571
White	65	75.4	64	43.8	31.6	1.5	<.016
Stewart	64	67.2	65	44.6	22.6	1.5	<.016

The cases of White and Stewart show a different pattern. Indeed, we must reject hypothesis three for these two justices since the difference in the rate of support provided across the two time periods could occur by chance much less than—"five times in a hundred"—the traditional cutting point in social science research. The finding here requires some rethinking of hypothesis three for White and Stewart. Our initial reasoning was that if variation in support was a function of compositional change in the Court, a justice serving across both periods should show no change. It now appears that the validity of such reasoning depends on the justice and the basis of his support in the first instance—i.e., the extent to which support is based on favorable predispositions toward Negro claimants.

If one were to assume that the Court is objectively responding to the facts and law of each Negro claimant case, a rough indicator of a justice's sympathy for Negroes is the difference between the justice's support score and the score compiled by his Court. Comparing Douglas and Brennan to their Courts in the Warren and Burger years, we find them responding respectively at rates of 13.8 and 7.9 percentage points above the level of the Warren Court. During the Burger years, these justices increased the disparity to 34.7 and 38.5 percentage points respectively. Marshall, who supported Negro claims at the same level reached by the Warren Court, increased his support to a level of 43.1 percentage points above that of the Burger Court in t_2. These dramatic changes relative to the Court of service may be compared to those of Stewart and White, both of whom were slightly below the level of the Warren Court and slightly above the rate attained by the Burger Court. Given a Court swing of 41.5 points, swings of 7.8 for White and 15.8 for Stewart suggest that these justices are "swing" justices in a sense not fully appreciated earlier.

During and subsequent to the Warren years, these two justices have been viewed as centrists, occupying a middle position between ideologically conservative and liberal justices. But given the dramatic reduction in support for Negro claims during the Burger era, if ideology explained White and Stewart's sympathy for Negro claimants, swings in support greatly exceeding 15.8 percentage points should be observed. The failure of the data to reveal such swings may be due to either of two factors. First, it may be that ideological commitment to support Negro claims underwent some major modification between 1964–68 and 1972–76. Given that attitudes and predispositions change slowly, such a proposition is hardly plausible. The second possibility is that the swing of these two justices in the Warren Court was influenced considerably by the actions of their majority brethren—that is, these justices were majority prone. This is a more satisfying explanation than the first. But until further research is done, the explanation is speculative.

Controlled Analysis

While we have established eight of ten relationships predicted by hypotheses one through three, we have not shown that the associations discovered are due only to the factors incorporated in the analysis. For example, one might think that whether a case is state or federal will affect the relationships on which we have focussed. Or perhaps as case issues vary from civil to criminal, civil rights to non-civil rights, or constitutional to statutory, support for Negro claimants also varies. Moreover, we have not established the strength of the relationships revealed in the Mann-Whitney analysis. A partial Gamma analysis will provide additional insights into both these matters.

Gamma is a PRE (proportionate reduction in error) statistic. It measures the probability that knowing the order of a randomly chosen pair of cases on one variable, one can predict the ordering on a second variable (Kirkpatrick 1974). While zero Gamma measures the relationship between two variables without consideration of other possible intervening factors, partial Gamma measures the same relationships while controlling statistically for N other variables. In Table III, we present both the zero Gamma between support for Negro claims and Court/justice, as well as the partial Gammas for the same associations controlling for variation in state-federal, civil-criminal, civil rights-non-civil rights, and constitutional-statutory characteristics of the cases.

Table III reveals that the association between support and Court or justice, as measured by the zero Gamma, is quite strong. Whether exchanging Court or justice, knowledge of the elements in the exchange enables us to predict support for Negro litigants at accuracy levels rang-

TABLE III.   Zero Gammas and Fourth Order Partial Gammas for Relationships Between Support for Negro Claims and Justice/Court Controlling, for State-Federal, Civil Rights-Non-Civil Rights, Constitutional-Statutory, and Criminal-Civil Characteristics of the Cases

Comparison	Zero Order Gamma	Fourth Order Partials
Warren Ct.-Burger Ct.	.609	.763
Warren-Burger	.864	.912
Black-Rehnquist	.435	.742
Fortas-Blackmun	.775	.729
Harlan-Powell	.451	.654
Douglas t_1-Douglas t_2	.532	.846
Brennan t_1-Brennan t_2	−.028	.333
Marshall t_1-Marshall t_2	.165	.128

ing from 43 to 86 percent. The highest figure is associated with the exchange of Warren for Burger. When four selected variables are controlled, the accuracy level increases to better than 91 percent. In only one of five exchange situations (the exchange of Fortas and Blackmun) does the control analysis result in a lower Gamma, but even there, the dip is so slight that it can be ignored safely. We infer in all five instances that the relationships established in the Mann-Whitney analysis are of considerable strength.

As for the three holdover justices compared to themselves in two Court time periods, the picture is more mixed. Knowing whether Douglas is in period one or two enables us to predict his support for Negro claims with a probability of 84.6 percent—a very strong relationship under controlled conditions. For Brennan, the relationship is moderate and for Marshall quite weak. The relative figures for the three justices reflect the fact that under controlled conditions, Douglas and Brennan show more change in their support patterns than does Marshall. If Marshall's ratio of support to nonsupport in the first Court was identical to his ratio in the second, Gamma would be zero. The partial Gamma of .128 simply reveals little change in Marshall's support for Negro litigants across two courts in spite of dramatic changes in the Court's personnel.

Summary and Conclusions

Our analysis has revealed that the Nixon justices are supporting black claimants at a significantly lower level than that associated with the justices they replaced. It has also revealed that black claimants are being supported by the Burger Court significantly less than they were supported by the Warren Court. Indeed, the rate of support in the Burger Court is only one-half that of its predecessor. Undoubtedly, such a precipitous drop in support for Negro litigants has not gone unnoticed in the Negro community. Given these findings, the hypothesis that the relative decline in black support for the Court is a function of the waning support for black claims by the Court is both plausible and worth further investigation.

References

BLALOCK, HUBERT M. *Social Statistics*. New York: McGraw-Hill, 1960, pp. 197–203.

KIRKPATRICK, SAMUEL A. *Quantitative Analysis of Political Data*. Columbus, OH: Charles Merrill, 1974, pp. 47–53.

SIGELMAN, LEE. "Black-White Differences in Attitudes Toward the Supreme

Court: A Replication in the 1970's." *Social Science Quarterly* (June 1979), pp. 113–119.

ULMER, S. SIDNEY. "The Saliency of Negro Claims for Earl Warren's Response Behavior, 1953–1968." Panel paper presented at the annual meeting of the Southern Political Science Association, Atlanta, GA, 1970.

Environmental Influences
on Decision Making

——————————— 69 ———————————

Environmental Factors
in State Court Decisions

Burton M. Atkins, Henry R. Glick

• • •

Multiple regression models were used to examine the relationship between
environmental variables and the issues decided by state supreme courts.
The first model tests the total effects of environmental variables upon
the distribution of issues and assumes a linear effect of the independent
variables on each of the issue categories. This model hypothesizes that
much of the variation in issues decided by state supreme courts can be
accounted for by the state's environmental characteristics which shape
the conflicts requiring political and judicial resolution. Moreover, it is
hypothesized that criminal law, civil liberties, and government economic
regulation decisions will be positively related to economic development
and political competition, positively related to expenditures on health
and welfare services, but negatively related to expenditures on Highways-
Natural Resources. Private litigation, both economic and noneconomic,

From Burton M. Atkins and Henry R. Glick, "Environmental and Structural Variables as Determinants of Issues in State Courts of Last Resort," *American Journal of
Political Science* 20 (February 1976): 103–105, 106–108, 111–113, 114. Copyright ©
1976 by The University of Texas Press. Reprinted by permission of The University of
Texas Press, publisher. Footnotes have been omitted.

should occur most frequently in states low on Affluence and Industrialization, low on Professionalism and Competition, low on Welfare, but high on Highways-Natural Resources.

These hypotheses, however, do not presume that there is a direct correspondence between socioeconomic and political conditions on the one hand, and issues resolved by state courts on the other; numerous processes can divert certain types of controversies from the judicial system and thereby skew the distribution of issues. Insofar as a state supreme court is concerned, one particularly important variable is whether or not the court system of which it is a part contains an intermediate appellate court.

Intermediate appellate courts are usually established to reduce the case load of courts of last resort. In practice, however, the effect of intermediate appellate courts is not so much to reduce the case load as it is to redistribute the types of issues decided by the court of last resort. Cases not raising fundamental issues are left to the intermediate appellate court, thus allocating the supreme court's time more effectively by reserving their attention to issues perceived to be more critical to the political system. The second regression model tests for effects of state intermediate appellate courts upon the distribution of issues decided by courts of last resort by adding Court System as a dummy variable to the equation, with a value of zero when no intermediate appellate court exists, and a value of 1 when the intermediate appellate court does exist.

For the purposes of this study, criminal law issues were analyzed in a third regression model. While we have hypothesized that the distribution of criminal cases decided by state supreme courts is a function of environmental variables and the court structure, one would obviously expect that the amount of criminal litigation would be a reflection of the number of cases prosecuted by the state. Since information on the number of prosecutions was not available, a measure of reported crime in the states was used as a surrogate and added as a separate variable in the regression equation.

The final regression model tested for an interaction effect between crime rate and the presence or absence of an appellate court upon the distribution of criminal law cases decided by state supreme court. This was done because the continued increase of criminal litigation in state and federal judicial systems, recognized as placing severe strains upon the legal systems, has spawned attempts to shield state supreme courts from routine criminal appeals. One tactic often used to divert criminal appeals is to create an intermediate appellate court between trial and supreme courts. Thus, the joint effects of high crime rates and intermediate appellate courts were added to the stepwise model as a separate interaction term.

TABLE 2. Regression Coefficients of Six Environmental Variables on State Supreme Court Decisions

	Civil Liberties					Private Suits (Noneconomic)					Private Suits (Economic)				
		Model 1		Model 2			Model 1		Model 2			Model 1		Model 2	
	R	b	BETA	b	BETA	R	b	BETA	b	BETA	R	b	BETA	b	BETA
Economic Component	.20					.35					.34				
Affluence		.81	.33	.95	.39		−6.63	−1.01	−6.19	−.94		−5.31	−.58	−4.93	−.54
Industrialization		−.85	−.33	−.80	−.33		1.52	.23	1.70	.26		.12	.01	.27	.03
Political Component	.31					.29					.29				
Professionalism		.71	.30	.96	.41		.78	−.12	.02	.003		−.48	−.05	.21	.02
Competition		.00	.00	−.01	.00		.87	.14	.81	.12		−1.92	.22	−1.98	−.22
Policy Component	.25					.21					.20				
Highways		−1.04	−.45	−1.20	−.52		4.28	.68	3.77	.60		3.56	.41	3.12	.35
Welfare		−.20	−.08	−.46	−.19		2.85	.45	2.01	.32		3.56	.41	2.84	.32
Court System				−1.37	−.28				−4.46	−.34				−3.82	−.21
		R = .40		R = .47			R = .60		R = .67			R = .44		R = .47	
		p = .27		p = .162			p = .003		p = .001			p = .15		p = .14	

457

TABLE 2. (continued)

ECONOMIC REGULATION

	R	Model 1		Model 2	
		b	BETA	b	BETA
Economic Component	.47				
Affluence		2.46	.406	3.76	.619
Industrialization		3.53	.581	2.56	.421
Political Component	.26				
Competition		−.918	−.158	−.952	−.164
Professionalism		−1.86	−.316	−1.43	−.243
Policy Component	.42				
Highways		−2.82	.487	−3.09	−.533
Welfare		−.922	−.158	−1.36	−.234
Court System				−2.34	−.195
		R = .575		R = .598	
		p = .008		p = .009	

Continued

TABLE 2. (continued)

CRIMINAL LAW

	R	Model 1 (Environmental) b	BETA	Model 2 (Court Structure) b	BETA	Model 3 (Crime Rate) b	BETA	Model 4 (Interaction) b	BETA
Economic Component	.16								
Affluence		2.11	.146	.379	.026	−6.21	−.43	−6.175	−.42
Industrialization		−.520	−.036	−1.22	−.085	−1.68	−.11	−1.626	−.11
Political Component	.19								
Competition		2.56	.186	2.82	.204	4.62	.33	4.265	.33
Professionalism		.937	.067	−2.19	−.157	−3.10	−.22	3.11	−.22
Policy Component	.13								
Highways		−1.61	−.117	.358	.015	1.23	.08	1.25	.09
Welfare		1.55	−.112	1.70	.123	4.00	.29	3.92	.28
Court System				17.32	.608	14.56	.51	13.57	.47
Crime Rate						.158	.45	.155	.44
Crime Rate × System								9.56	.03
		R = .210		R = .551		R = .63		R = .63	
		p = .925		p = .03		p = .006		p = .01	

459

Results of Aggression Analysis: Model 1

The data in Table 2 report the contribution of each of the three pairs of indicators as well as the explanatory power of all six. The correlation between each environmental compound and each issue, it should be observed, is the R between the two factors comprising the dimension and each issue. For example, the R representing the relationship between economic conditions and civil liberties decisions (.20) is the multiple correlation between affluence and industrialization, on the one hand, and civil liberties decisions on the other. Likewise, the R representing the relationship between the political dimension and civil liberties decisions (.31) reflects the multiple correlation of each of the two dimensions within that environmental descriptor and that issue. Since the two dimensions within each environmental component are uncorrelated, there is no statistical redundancy within this multiple correlation. Also reported in Table 2 are the regression coefficients for each environmental dimension. Finally, at the bottom of each column are the R and statistical significance for each model. These data show that no one set of environmental factors is primarily responsible for the variance on the issues, although the economic descriptors are marginally stronger correlates with private litigation and government economic regulation suits.

Another basis for comparing the relative effects of the environmental indicators is their explanatory contribution in the regression equations. Table 2 shows that affluence is the most important variable affecting civil liberties, private economic, and private noneconomic litigation, whereas industrialization is the most important predictor of economic regulation controversies, and almost as important as affluence in the civil liberties equation.

• • •

Effects of Intermediate Appellate Courts: Model 2

Since economic and political development is associated with an increase in litigation, . . . intermediate appellate courts would presumably be established in states having complex socioeconomic and political structures. To test this hypothesis, Table 5 compares the mean factor scores of states with and without intermediate appellate courts. As anticipated, the characteristics of the states do differ. In particular, states with intermediate appellate courts tend to score high on Professionalism, high on Industrialization, and low on Highways-Natural Resources (a negative correlate of economic development).

The fact that the establishment of intermediate appellate courts is

TABLE 5. Mean Factor Scores by Type of Court System

	STATES WITH INTERMEDIATE APPELLATE COURT	STATES WITHOUT INTERMEDIATE APPELLATE COURT
Professionalism	.561	—.310
Competition	—.271	.173
Welfare-Education	—.121	.084
Highways-Natural Resources	—.528	.322
Affluence	—.172	.092
Industrialization	.455	—.250

related to socioeconomic and political diversification suggests a certain restructuring of issues in supreme courts with an appellate court below. In particular, it would be expected that supreme courts with the appellate court below would decide fewer cases involving personal justice, these having been siphoned away by the lower appellate court, and would decide larger proportions of criminal law, civil liberties, and government economic regulation cases.

The regression coefficients for the Court System variable entered into the equations for each issue show the effect of intermediate appellate courts upon the distribution of issues. Some of the results are startling. The negative signs of the coefficients indicate that the appearance of four of the issues is inversely related to the presence of an intermediate appellate court. However, supreme courts with intermediate appellate courts below are not necessarily deciding fewer cases, since the sign and magnitude of the regression coefficient for Court System on criminal appeals (17.32) shows that the existence of an intermediate appellate court is associated with substantial increases of criminal decisions rendered by the supreme court. The effect of intermediate appellate courts on the appearance of criminal law decisions is also apparent in the substantial increment of the R from .210 to .551 when that variable is added to the regression equation. The empirical significance of the marked increase in criminal litigation decided by supreme courts with intermediate appellate courts below is difficult to ascertain without data on the flow of litigation at all tiers of the state judicial systems. In other words, it is impossible to ascertain whether or not these court systems have so much criminal litigation that the intermediate appellate courts cannot effectively shield the supreme court from them, or whether or not the appearance of these cases represent a policy by the supreme courts to devote their attention to criminal law cases. In either event, the data do show that some supreme courts, by necessity or design, are functioning primarily as criminal courts of last resort.

• • •

Conclusions

The data reported in this study demonstrate that environmental variables are important predictors to the types of issues resolved through state supreme court decisions. Court System, it has been shown, is an important structural variable shaping the distribution of issues as they emerge in state courts of last resort. Although our emphasis has been upon the effects of the environmental variables, the fact that the presence or absence of an intermediate appellate court affects the distribution of issues on supreme courts suggests the need to incorporate additional court system variables into models seeking to account for the types of conflicts found in courts of last resort. By examining aggregate relationships between judicial decisions and environmental conditions, we naturally bypass some of the more subtle relationships between courts and other governmental institutions and environmental conditions that bear upon the types of issues resolved by supreme courts. For example, in-depth case studies exploring links between supreme courts and other political subsystems would provide important information. Additionally, there may be considerable variation among states in judicial roles, norms, and decisionmaking processes that affect the range of issues resolved by courts of last resort. Finally, the complex maze of jurisdiction woven into state constitutions and statutes probably explains some of the variation, and future research would need to examine the impact of formal rules as inhibitors of issues in courts.

------------------------------ 70 ------------------------------

Sentencing Behavior of Federal Judges:
Draft Cases—1972

Beverly Blair Cook

Judicial decision-making is of interest to the political scientist and the lawyer, and of significance to the public, where the judge exercises choice: at the appellate level in making new law and at the trial level in making

From Beverly Blair Cook, "Sentencing Behavior of Federal Judges: Draft Cases—1972," *University of Cincinnati Law Review* 42 (1973) : 597, 601–602, 602–603, 610–615. Copyright © 1974 by the *University of Cincinnati Law Review*. Reprinted by permission. Footnotes have been omitted.

discretionary decisions. In areas of discretion such as the management of the trial and the selection of the sentence, the trial judge utilizes his own experiences, preferences, and common sense. Where law and precedent provide weak guidelines rather than mandates, the chief factors associated with the judge's choice may be discovered in his personal history and in his political and social environment. This study seeks such explanations for judicial discretionary behavior by examining the choice of sentences for 1,852 draft offenders by 304 federal district judges in 1972.

Sentences are treated as policy decisions.

• • •

The set of draft sentences treated as the dependent variable in this study are those decided in the forty-eight continental states in 1972 by federal trial judges sitting in their own districts. District judges serving as visiting judges heard 95 cases. Since some propositions in the research required the judge to act within his local environment, these cases were excluded from the analysis. During 1972 seven appellate judges on assignment decided draft cases in district courts. Their sentences also were eliminated from the set, leaving 1,852 cases.

Data on the cases was supplied by the Administrative Office of the United States Courts. The Administrative Office collects data from the clerk of each district court on criminal case forms and transfers the data to tape for computer analysis. A code is employed to preserve information: the identification of the circuit and district, the city of decision, the docket number of the case, the number of defendants in the proceeding, the filing and termination dates, the interval in months, and the offense number. Other information reported includes the type of counsel (*i.e.*, appointed, hired or none), the judge code number, and the disposition of the case—whether dismissed, acquitted or convicted by judge or jury. Personal data available on the defendant include sex, race, year of birth, and prior record. Finally, the print-out describes the exact type of sentence, including the amount of fine, length of probation, and length of prison term.

A severity index of draft sentences ranging from 1 to 99 is the specific dependent variable employed in this study. The index is based on the weighting scale first developed by the Administrative Office in 1964. The weighting of each kind of sentence, whether fine, probation, prison, or other, allows the formation of a single scale. The draft severity index was created by the multiplication of the Administrative Office weights by four and the assignment to the highest statutory sentence for a draft offense, five years in prison, the value of 99. . . . The translation of a sentence into an index can be followed in this example: a draft sentence of three years in prison and a $500 fine with one year of probation upon release involves the addition of the weights of 48 and 3 and 12 to form an index of 63.

TABLE 1. Disparities of Draft Sentences, 1972

Severity Index	Number of Cases	Percent of Cases	Percent of Judges	Number of Judges
Under 10	326	18%	10%	29
10–19	938	50%	51%	156
20–29	203	11%	20%	61
30–39	164	9%	7%	22
40–49	140	8%	6%	18
50–59	66	3%	3%	10
60–69	1	—	—	1
70–79	0	—	—	1
80–89	0	—	—	0
99	14	1%	2%	6

The analyses in this study use case indices and judge indices as dependent variables (*i.e.*, measures of the sentencing events to be explained). Each judge has a severity index which is the average of all his case indices for the year. The range of the case and judge indices is shown in table 1. The table indicates that ten percent of the judges have routinely issued a nominal sentence which appears to be a rejection of the legislative and bureaucratic draft policy. Six of the trial judges followed a settled policy of five-year prison terms and two judges a pattern of four-year terms, both likely indicators of strong support for the selective service system and its affective penumbra of patriotism and national security consciousness.

A majority of the judges limit their sentences to probation only. Approximately the same percentage of judges and cases are in the index category of 10–19, which gives only lip-service to the draft policy. One-third of the judges employed a range of sentences between the moderate majority and the extremely punitive minority. Evidently these judges were individualizing punishment of the offender according to some pattern. The "correlates" of factors associated with these various sentence choices will be the topic of the next section.

• • •

Environment

Social, economic, demographic and political variables of the environment within which the court operates have seldom been used as predictors of criminal case output, although they have been utilized extensively in studies of legislative output. Students of judicial behavior have tended to treat judges as if they worked in a subsystem with impermeable boundaries, isolated from any outside pressures, affected only by their internalized norms and the review power of the appellate judges. Although the interrelatedness of the judicial and political subsystems, with their entrenchment in a social milieu, have often been discussed in a theoretical context, research designs have seldom incorporated such environmental variables. Environmental factors have been treated in an impressionistic way in conventional studies dealing with periods of executive or congressional attack on the Supreme Court and apparent changes in the direction of common law development. Only a few attempts have been made to study the effect of environmental variables on trial courts.

1. Economic-Social Variables

In his study of the 1965–1969 draft cases, Markham employed social-economic and educational variables. He concluded that "while punitive policy associated with run-of-the-mine criminal activity is measurably influenced by the economic-social indicators, this influence, though still present, is much less pronounced in the special case of draft offenders."

In the study of the 1972 cases reported here, two economic-social variables are introduced: Poor, operationalized by the percentage of families with less than $5000 per year income in the city where the case was decided; and Crime, operationalized by the 1971 FBI crime index for that city. In every analysis the same relationship appeared: the more poor families in the city, the more severe the sentence; the more crime in the city, the more mild the sentence. The correlations, however, were very low, and the two variables combined contributed only one percent to the explanation of severity.

Evidently, the environmental variables are more useful in a comparison of district performance (Markham's study) than individual judicial performance. These variables may belong in a causal chain, their vitality not obvious without a subset analysis. The sentence severity of judges with Republican party affiliation showed a stronger correlation with the environmental variables. The explanatory power increased to two percent. Subset analysis revealed that Democratic judges' severity varied only slightly with Crime, and the environmental variables had no explanatory power. Judges serving in metropolitan areas (over 500,000 population) were examined separately and the severity of their sentences varied significantly only in relation to the poverty of the city. It should be noted, however, that their populations included more blacks and more criminals than the cities with a lower Poor factor. The Poor variable added four percent to the explanation of the sentencing severity of metropolitan judges. It is possible that poor draft offenders are treated like ordinary criminals, particularly by Republican judges in metropolitan areas.

2. Demographic Variables

The two demographic variables of concern in this study are the size of the population and the size of the black population. Markham discovered that the size of the district population correlated positively and significantly with the percentage of offenders sentenced to prison, but not with the length of the prison term nor the disparity of sentences within the district. With a single severity index, the present study tends to support the opposite conclusion. The severity indices of the judges themselves differed according to the population of the city in which they decided the case, with the judges in the smallest cities giving the most severe sentences.

TABLE 4.   Severity of Sentencing by Population

No. Judges	City Pop.	Av. Severity Index
20	Under 50,000	29.9
117	50–500,000	23.5
167	Over 500,000	20.2

Racial composition is a demographic variable suggested by Vines as a predictor of case disposition involving racial discrimination in Southern federal districts. Vines reported that the relationship between the black percentage of the population and the percentage of cases decided in favor of the black party was inverse. The higher the proportion of blacks in the city of decision, the lower the percentage of cases decided in favor of the black party. Markham discovered that when he examined the treatment of non-white draft offenders separately, the disparity of the sentence length increased with the size of the non-white population. The population size and the black population were the two significant variables in his demographic regression analysis, explaining 26 percent of the disparity between districts. The Vines and Markham works suggest that racism affects judicial policy in both Northern and Southern federal courts.

In this study a variable, Black, was operationalized by the percentage of the black population of the city where the case was decided. Since federal judges, particularly in the more decentralized Southern districts, often sit at different court locations within the district, this indicator measures more precisely the immediate demographic setting of the deliberating magistrate. On a regression analysis of all 1,852 cases, the Black variable did not correlate at all with severity of sentences. The results of the three studies taken together suggest that the racial variable comes into play only in cases with black defendants and perhaps with particular judges.

When senior judges were examined separately, their severity correlated negatively and at a significant level with the size of the black population, despite the fact that the average percentage of blacks was slightly higher in the cities where senior judges sat. The Black variable (inverse) combined with the Poor variable (direct) explained 13 percent of the severity of senior judges. Evidently the senior judges do not give disproportionately severe sentences to black defendants.

Democratic and Republican judges were randomly scattered in areas with various racial population distributions. As in the universe of cases, those cases decided by Democratic judges had zero correlation between black population and severity, and those decided by Republican judges had a small and insignificant negative correlation. Neither party can be associated with racism in the judiciary.

3. Political

The thesis that judges respond to the political culture is part of our conventional wisdom, but selected features of the political system have not been measured and related to judicial output. Political competition has been carefully operationalized in an attempt to explain legislative policy. Markham used political competition as a variable in his regression analysis without any theoretical basis for inclusion. Although the political competition variable correlated positively and significantly with ordinary criminal sentencing, it failed to vary with indicators of draft sentences.

In this 1972 study two political variables are introduced: one, an indicator of political party dominance; and another, an indicator of pressure group strength. The party indicator is based on the party affiliation and percentage of voters for the United States senatorial candidate who received a plurality in the city where the case was decided. The preappointment party affiliation of each judge is compared with that of the winning local candidate to generate four subsets for analysis: Republican judges in congruent and incongruent partisan milieus; and Democratic judges in congruent and incongruent partisan milieus. The percentage of voter support is used as a variable to test the impact of the intensity of local partisanship upon the judge's sentencing.

Table 5 shows that judges vary their sentences to some extent in relation to the political dominance in their environment. About one-

Interaction of Courts with Their Environment

TABLE 5. **Severity of Draft Sentences by Political Environment, 1972**

	DEMOCRATIC JUDGES (165)		REPUBLICAN JUDGES (128)	
	Democratic Environment	*Republican Environment*	*Republican Environment*	*Democratic Environment*
Percent of Judges	65%	35%	31%	69%
Mean Severity Index	19.6	21.7	19.9	23.4

third of the Democratic judges sit in a Republican environment and two-thirds of the Republican judges sit in a Democratic environment. The severity of the sentences given by Democratic judges is two points higher in Republican territory. Apparently, the Democratic judge responds to the poll power of the Republican party with more severe sentences. The Republican judges, however, do not temper their severity to suit the Democratic milieu and the correlation between severity and the size of the vote for the opposite party shows that they are not influenced by the strength of the opposition. The judges were not affected by the relative strength of their own parties among the voters.

The second political culture variable, AmLeg, was intended to measure the strength of political pressure groups. The American Legion, a pressure group with an intense commitment to national security was chosen as an indicator for the variable. The supportive attitude of the American Legion toward the selective service system is exemplified by the fact that more than 70 percent of the local draft board members came from the Legion. The indicator was operationalized by the percentage of veterans in the state who belonged to the Legion. A positive correlation between the AmLeg variable and the severity index was expected based on the hypothesis that local judges would adjust their behavior to the preferences of the most relevant organized interest in the policy area of the case.

The correlates showed that the size of American Legion membership in the state did not vary significantly with the severity indices of most judges. There was no correlation for the universe of cases. A number of subset analyses were performed. The severity of sentences of senior judges and all judges over 65 varied positively but not significantly with Legion membership. Judges with national associations rather than local cultural and civil memberships had higher sentences in proportion to state Legionnaire strength. The sentences of judges who had never served in the armed forces ranged higher in proportion to AmLeg, but only in comparison with judges who had service experience. The latter's sentences showed no relationship. Only Democratic judges serving in a Republican environment revealed a significant relationship between severe sentences and state Legion size. On the whole, the judges appeared unaffected by pressure group preferences. The Legion evidently provides policy cues only to judges without other sources of input, *e.g.,* from their political party, court cohort group, service experiences, or local reference groups.

• • •

―――――――――――― 71 ――――――――――――

Judicial Policy-Making
and Southern School Segregation
Micheal W. Giles, Thomas G. Walker

• • •

In this study we will examine the policy-making behavior of Southern federal judges in school segregation controversies in 1970. The desegregation of public schools provides an excellent subject for study because this category includes the most frequently heard and publicly sensitive of the race relations disputes. In 1954, Southern school systems were totally segregated by law, but by 1970 some level of desegregation was evident in every school system in the region.

As the judiciary learned from painful experience the school segregation question was not one which could often be resolved by a single hearing or judicial decree. In most instances once a school district's desegregation efforts were challenged in court as being inadequate it marked

From Micheal W. Giles and Thomas G. Walker, "Judicial Policy-Making and Southern School Segregation," *Journal of Politics* 37 (1975): 922–924, 925, 926, 927, 927–928, 928, 928–929, 929–934, 935–936. Reprinted by permission. Footnotes have been omitted.

only the beginning of long and continuous litigation lasting in some districts for more than a decade. In such circumstances the district judge having jurisdiction over the case maintained constant surveillance over the district to insure adequate compliance with constitutional standards.

The basic unit of analysis in the present study was the combination of a school district and its supervising judge. In order to gather the necessary data to conduct the designed research, we began with the approximately 400 Southern school districts listed by the U.S. Department of Health, Education and Welfare as being in compliance with court ordered desegregation in 1970. Officials in each of these school districts were contacted and asked to supply information regarding the legal status of desegregation disputes in their districts in 1970. A total of 288 school districts responded and of these 151 provided complete information including verification that they were operating under active court supervision in 1970 and the name of the district judge involved.

The basic unit of analysis, therefore, became the 151 school district/ supervising federal judge combinations. Of the 95 United States district judges serving the South in 1970, 42 (44 percent) were supervising at least one school district in the sample.

Dependent Variable

To measure the level of enforcement of desegregation an index of school segregation was computed for each of the 151 school districts. This index was adopted from Taeuber's index of residential segregation. The index measures the amount of departure of each school in a school district from the racial balance for the entire district. The index varies from zero, signifying that each school in the district mirrors the racial balance of the district as a whole, to 1.00, indicating that a school district is totally segregated with no racial heterogeneity in any of its schools. The value that the index attains between these extremes may be interpreted as the percentage of Black and/or White students who must be transferred in order to obtain district wide racial balance. The information necessary to compute the index for each of the 151 districts was drawn from racial/ ethnic surveys of the public schools conducted in 1970 by the U.S. Department of Health, Education and Welfare.

The dependent variable, then, represents the degree of segregation remaining in the sampled Southern school districts in 1970. Because each of these districts was operating under court issued desegregation orders, the dependent variable also represents the amount of deviation from perfect racial balance which the supervising judge has allowed. This can be interpreted as the district judge's policy decision in implementing the *Brown* mandate at the local level. Operationalized in this manner, judicial policy-making is studied not in terms of the words the judge uses in his opinions but on the basis of the actual level of desegregation he enforces on the litigated school district.

• • •

For the 151 sampled school districts the mean index of segregation was .3227, with a standard deviation of .2145. Individual school district segregation levels ranged from a low index score of .0111 to a high of .8640.

Independent Variables

In order to explain the desegregation policies imposed by district judges in the sampled school districts we tested the impact of twelve independent variables which have been suggested as possible determinants of judicial behavior in this area of litigation. These independent variables can be classified into four categories: social background variables, environmental variables, community linkage variables and school district variables.

(1) SOCIAL BACKGROUND VARIABLES.

As we noted in earlier sections of this paper, social background experiences which indicate a judge's degree of association with the traditional Southern culture may be related to how vigorously he enforces desegregation policy. In order to test this proposition we selected six judicial social background variables for analysis: birthplace, location of higher education, religious affiliation, political party identification, local political office held, and state political office held.

• • •

(2) ENVIRONMENTAL VARIABLES.

In order to consider the impact of community opinion on desegregation policy, some measure needed to be devised to tap the local cultural ethos within a judge's jurisdiction. Given the importance in the literature placed on this variable, a study of Southern desegregation would be incomplete without including it. For this reason we examined the impact of two environmental variables. The first of these was the proportion of Blacks among the general population in the judge's district or division.

• • •

The second environmental variable was the percentage of total 1968 presidential election votes within the judicial district or division which were cast for George Wallace. The degree of support for the Wallace candidacy would appear to give a good indication of public attitudes toward desegregation. As Wallace support increases so too should a lack of community sympathy for court imposed segregation.

(3) COMMUNITY LINKAGE VARIABLES.

. . . For purposes of analysis we isolated two possible indicators of a judge's relationship with the community. First, a judge's linkage to local attitudes may be reflected in the number of associational memberships he holds within the community.

• • •

As the number of associational ties increases we would expect the district judge to pay more attention to community pressure. The second community linkage variable involved the location of the judge's court vis-a-vis the school district being desegregated. A judge's regular jurisdiction, be it an entire district or a division, generally encompasses several cities and counties and, therefore, several school districts. A judge, however, will usually hold his court in a single location within the judicial district, although he may occasionally hear cases throughout his jurisdiction. Judges are likely to live and develop associations in the area immediately surrounding the established locations of their courts. Therefore, we might expect that a judge would be more reluctant to impose activist desegregation policies on school districts which envelop the judge's court than if the schools are located in an outlying area. The pressure of the local community would appear more immediate and pertinent to the judge if it originated from his "home" area than if it came from a more remote portion of his jurisdiction.

• • •

Two school system variables were used in the present study. The first was the percentage of students in the school district who were Black. The influence of this variable theoretically is similar to that of percent Black among the general population. As the concentration of Blacks increases in the schools so, too, may White fear of the consequences of integration. Sending White students to fully integrated schools which have ten percent Black enrollment may be much easier to accomplish than ordering White children to attend integrated schools composed of 60 percent Black enrollment. Not only would we expect resistance to increase as Black enrollment increases, but also as the percentage of Black students grows it may be more difficult to carry out desegregation for technical reasons. Using desegregation tools such as busing or altering attendance zones may be relatively easy when the goal is integrating the district's ten percent minority enrollment, but extremely difficult as minority enrollment approaches majority status. The second school district variable examined was the size of the educational system (measured in terms of total district enrollment). Recent studies have suggested that school district size may be related to segregation levels.

• • •

Findings

In order to evaluate the explanatory power of our independent variables, we first tested the association of each with the levels of segregation which existed in the 151 school systems and then analyzed the combined impact of these variables.

Zero-Order Relationships

For the most part, our analysis of social background characteristics contributed little to an increased understanding of judicially imposed desegregation policy. The expectation that those judges most closely tied to the South would allow the highest levels of school segregation received little support. The relationships between two of the social background variables (birthplace and party identification) and level of school segregation are in the predicted direction, but fail to reach statistical significance. The level of segregation in school districts under the surveillance of judges born outside the South is only slightly lower than that allowed in districts supervised by judges of Southern origin. The utility of the birthplace variable, however, is severely restricted by its lack of variation. Only four of the 42 judges were born outside the South. Similarly, the correlation between party identification and school segregation is in the expected direction with Democrats approving higher levels of segregation than non-Democrats, but the relationship is quite weak. The analysis of three social background variables yielded unanticipated results. Although not statistically significant, holding a state or local political office and membership in a low status Protestant faith are negatively correlated with segregation. What makes this result particularly important is that Vines previously found the political office and religious affiliation variables to have a significant *positive* relationship with segregationist decisions.

Among the background variables only the location of a judge's edu-

Table 1.   Zero-Order Correlations (r) of Social
Background, Environmental, Community
Linkage, and School District Variables to
Segregation in 1970

Social Background Variables	
Birthplace	.022
Education	.160 [a]
Religion	—.028
Political Party	.086
Local Political Office	—.026
State Political Office	—.032
Environmental Variables	
Percent Black	.095
Percent Wallace Vote	—.096
Community Linkage Variables	
Organizational Memberships	—.018
Court Location	.448 [b]
School District Variables	
Percent Black Enrollment	.125
School District Size (in hundreds)	.537 [b]

[a] $p < .05$
[b] $p < .01$

cation is related to school segregation in the predicted direction and at
a statistically significant level. The mean level of segregation allowed by
the policies of judges who received non-South college *and* law school
education is .233; for judges attending non-Southern schools for *either*
college *or* law school the segregation level rises to .304; and the segregation index increases to .345 for judges obtaining *all* of their advanced
education from institutions within the region. From these data we may
conclude that the years spent by judges in non-Southern educational institutions expose them to national norms of race relations and mollify
social attitudes acquired during the course of a Southern upbringing.
This, of course, does not mean that Southern schools indoctrinate their
students with racist attitudes; rather it indicates that Southern judges
who attend only schools within the region receive less exposure to non-
Southern views toward race.

The environmental variables fare little better than the social background characteristics in predicting desegregation policies. Black concentration within the judicial district or division is positively associated
with segregation levels, but the relationship may easily be attributable to
chance. The community's support for the 1968 Wallace candidacy, surprisingly, is negatively associated with the amount of school segregation
tolerated by federal judges, albeit the association fails to reach conventional levels of statistical significance.

The lack of predictive ability provided by the environmental variables does not necessarily preclude the possibility that the analysis of community linkage may yield productive results. The first community linkage variable analyzed the number of local organizational memberships held by the supervising judge, exhibited no relationship whatever to the level of segregation permitted. The court location variable, however, provided altogether different results. As hypothesized, a judge's policy will allow significantly higher levels of segregation if the court is located within the school district under supervision than it will if the school system is geographically divorced from the location of the court. This demonstrates that federal judges tend to be more vigilant in enforcing national desegregation standards in remote areas than when similar issues arise within the judge's immediate work/residence locale. This finding might lead one to speculate that while a judge may not generally be affected by hostile community pressures, such factors are relevant when a judge must desegregate his own community. This, however, is not the case. When we examined only those school district/judge combinations in which the court was located within the school system, the percent Black, Wallace vote and organization membership variables remained non-significant.

There are three possible explanations for the significance of the court location variable. First, the court location variable may link the judge to environmental forces not included in the present study. Second, a judge's personal attitudes against massive social change may be greatly activated when he is desegregating his own community, whereas he is able to maintain greater detachment in litigation involving communities in which he has little personal stake. Finally, when faced with desegregating his own community a judge may be more concerned with public reaction than when dealing with an outlying area. Consequently, he may perceive a hostile environment—which may or may not exist.

School district variables provided additional insight into the desegregation policy process. While the percentage of Black enrollment in the school district was positively associated with segregation, the relationship failed to attain statistically meaningful levels. However, the size of the school district was substantially associated with the level of desegregation enforced by the supervising judge. As the size of the school district increases so too does the existing level of racial segregation within that education system.

The Combined Model

While the zero-order relationships tell us a great deal about possible determinants of court ordered desegregation policy, they do not provide a complete account of the explanatory power of the variables under analysis. First, zero-order relationships do not demonstrate the combined impact of the independent variables on Southern school segregation. And second, zero-order relationships fail to give adequate warning of the possible effects of inter-correlation among the independent variables. For example, two independent variables used in the present analysis, court location and school district size, are significantly correlated ($r = .575$). This should not be surprising because of the fact that most district courts are located in urban centers with large school systems. Therefore, the previously discussed relationship between court location and school segregation levels may simply be an artifact of the size of the school districts in which the courts are located. In order to deal with the question of spuriousness and assess the combined explanatory power of the independent variables, the data were examined using multiple regression. The results are presented in Table 2.

With one exception the results of this analysis are consistent with the zero-order correlations presented in Table 1. Percent Black enrollment is not statistically significant in Table 1, but does make a significant contribution to the multiple regression. This inconsistency arises from the fact that Black enrollment and school district size are negatively correlated and, therefore, the size variable suppresses the zero-order correlation between Black enrollment and segregation. Apart from Black enrollment, none of the independent variables which had non-significant zero-order correlations with segregation make a significant contribution to the regression equation.

The combined efforts of school district size, Black enrollment, court location, and judicial education explain 39 percent of the variance in Southern school segregation. An examination of the standardized betas shows school district size to have the largest independent effect of any of these four variables. But even with the effects of size accounted for, court location remains significantly related to segregation levels. Indeed, court

Table 2. Partial Regression Coefficients and Standardized Betas for Selected Variables with Segregation in 1970

	b	STANDARDIZED BETA	F
School District Size (in hundreds)	.00048	.42000	26.861 [b]
Percent Black Enrollment	.00251	.25914	14.923 [b]
Court Location	.13949	.23861	8.936 [b]
Education	.04946	.15490	5.273 [a]
(Constant)	.05518		

[a] $p < .05$ $R = .624$ $R^2 = .389$
[b] $p < .01$

location, a previously unexplored variable, appears to have independent effect comparable to percent Black enrollment, a variable that has received considerable attention. Southern education, while making a significant contribution to the regression equation, is the least helpful of the four independent variables in explaining the desegregation policies of federal judges.

Although explained variance is the most common means for interpreting regression, the "dummy" variable structure of the court location variable permits another interpretation. The regression coefficient for court location is the difference between the mean segregation index scores for the dichotomized observations on this variable, adjusted for the effects of school district size, Black enrollment, and judicial education. Thus, when the school district encompasses the location of the district court, the level of segregation averages 14 index points higher than when the court is not held within the school district boundaries. This means that in these school districts an average of 14 percent more of the Black and/or White students would need to be transferred to achieve racial balance than in those school districts geographically separated from the supervising judge. Similarly, the adjusted average difference between judges who received college and law school training in the South and those who received both outside the region is ten index points. These are not trivial differences from either a practical or statistical standpoint.

• • •

Conclusions

A number of conclusions may be drawn from the data analyzed in the present study, especially when considered in light of previous research. First, the influence of judicial social background characteristics, which were found to be significantly related to district court race relations decisions by Vines, was minimal on the desegregation policies examined here. This may well be due to the fact that by 1970 a new generation of federal judges was staffing the Southern courts. Of the judges in our sample, a few two-thirds took office after the period studied by Vines and almost 80 percent were appointed after the original publication of Peltason's study. Apart from the education variable, none of the social background factors were found to be significantly related to school desegregation levels.

Second, the environmental factors examined in the present study demonstrated no substantial relationship with school district segregation. This again is in conflict with studies conducted during the years immediately following *Brown* which generally linked the district's racial climate and public attitudes to race relations decisions of local federal judges.

Third, the community linkage yielded mixed results. The number of organizational ties which the judge had with his community showed no relationship to the degree of school desegregation imposed. Once again much of the literature on Southern school integration efforts would predict otherwise. The linkage variable which does have a demonstrated impact is court location. Judges tend to allow substantially more segregation in their own communities than when implementing desegregation policy in other areas. What makes this variable particularly intriguing is that its influence occurs independent of environmental factors or the number of community associated memberships held by the judge. The differential application of law indeed appears to be worthy of more extensive analysis than we are able to provide here.

Finally, the school district variables yielded the greatest amount of explained variance. Both the Black concentration within the schools and the size of the school district were significantly related to the level of segregation allowed by district court orders. The Black enrollment variable may suggest the continuing impact of public resistance to desegregation. On the other hand, the combined importance of Black enrollment and school district size may well signify a substantial change from the original round of Southern desegregation efforts. Emphasis appears to have shifted from intense battles over the principle of integration to a judicial analysis of conditions within the schools. The prominence of these variables indicates that desegregation may be in the process of becoming a more technical procedure. The primary question (both legally and behaviorally) may now focus on how much desegregation can be practically ordered by the judge given extant school district characteristics, rather than whether integration should occur at all. This interpretation is consistent with the tone of Supreme Court desegregation precedents handed down in the late 1960s and early 1970s. The evolution of the desegregation process may be following the same pattern as exhibited in the reapportionment cases—that is, an intensely political question gradually eroding into technical applications of Supreme Court established national legal policy. The history of desegregation, however, has been a much more lengthy and painful one.

The Impact
of Court Decisions

72

Communication of Decisions

Stephen L. Wasby

• • •

Several relevant "populations," identified in terms of their roles and thus varying from issue to issue, are involved in the process by which Supreme Court rulings are communicated. The populations are an "interpreting population," usually a lower court, which refines—makes clearer—the higher court's policy; an "implementing population" which applies the Court's basic policy directive; a "consumer population" for whom the directive was intended and to whom it is applied; and a "secondary population." This last grouping includes the general population not included in the consumer population—for example, for school desegregation, perhaps those without children in schools, as well as both governmental and nongovernmental "attentive publics"—those interested in but not directly involved in the particular policy and its implementation.

There are several types of behaviors which occur during the communication process and which follow from it. These are the "acceptance decisions," in which populations decide whether or not to comply with the policy; "subsystem adjustment," in which behavioral norms and formal rules may be changed to accommodate the new policy and mechanisms for implementation may be developed; "compliance behavior," as the implementing and consumer populations in particular act on the policy which has been transmitted to them; and finally, "feedback behavior," the transmission of reactions to policy back in the direction from which the policy came. In this context, feedback behavior would include public opinion and the bringing of new litigation to enforce or alter the Supreme Court's directives.

The most obvious means of communicating the Supreme Court's rulings are its own opinions, available in several forms, including the "slip opinions" handed out on Decision Day, the advance sheets published by private companies soon thereafter, and, in due course, bound volumes. These circulate among at least some attorneys and others interested in the Court's work. The actual availability of the decisions at the local level where people might want to use them is generally unsatisfactory, particularly in the more rural states, where a set of the *United States Reports* may be found only in the few larger cities. In many counties in the United States, a set is simply not available—and the reported decisions of the courts of appeals and district courts are even less likely to be accessible. However, even in larger cities, only a few of the larger law offices—and the county law library—may have copies.

The court system itself can serve as a means of communication. The decision in a case is generally sent to a lower court for "proceedings not inconsistent with this opinion." As a result, "the formal judicial structure . . . provides an important channel through which a ruling is transmitted to those directly under obligation to act." But Supreme Court decisions often are not communicated directly to others, instead slowly working their way down to implementing populations through intervening layers of federal and state courts. The relationship of the highest court and the courts below it, despite the court system's official structure, is not hierarchical and bureaucratic. Indeed, "communication channels may be so poor that subordinates do not become aware that a superior has issued a directive," particularly the further away they are from the Supreme Court. Thus first-instance trial judges are not likely to obtain information through vertical channels, but may learn about them "horizontally" or laterally from fellow judges at the same jurisdiction level. Because the decisions of some state courts are cited or adopted more often than those of others, they can play an important role in this process to the extent they contain discussions of Supreme Court opinions.

With few judges monitoring higher court decisions, a Supreme Court ruling may come to a judge's attention only when a lawyer presenting a case cites it. Indeed, many judges, partly because of work pressures which limit their reading, intentionally wait until attorneys bring new legal doctrine to their attention. Yet if attorneys are unaware of cases and thus do not cite them, the judges may never be apprised of new rules, and trial lawyers' negative feelings about their clients do serve to limit their learning about the rulings. Where a substantial number of attorneys practice a particular specialty, they may have an informal organization for circulating information about relevant cases, and lawyers arguing appellate cases are particularly likely to know about relevant higher court decisions. (Nonlawyers generally must rely on the interest groups to which they belong to provide such information, but most interest groups do this only sporadically.)

The basic "interpreting population," judges of courts nearer the implementing population, can be exceptionally important in transmitting information about the Supreme Court. Even when they correctly apply the Supreme Court's rulings, they do so narrowly. Lower court judges who did not like the *Escobedo* ruling—that a suspect being interrogated had to be allowed access to his lawyer—refused to apply *Escobedo* to anyone who did not already have a lawyer; similarly, judges who did not like the *Miranda* ruling did not require warnings to be given to those not in custody, and then defined "in custody" as narrowly as possible. Only four state supreme courts followed the letter and spirit of *Escobedo,* while thirty-seven followed the letter but violated the spirit by refusing to extend the ruling beyond its specific facts; five openly criticized the decision. On the other hand, all but two of the courts interpreting *Miranda* complied, with fourteen classified as "liberal" in their interpretations.

While showing appropriate respect for the U.S. Supreme Court, judges have engaged in sarcasm or injected "organizational contumacy" into communication channels by criticizing the rulings, by stating concern for the effect of those decisions upon the safety of the public, and by challenging the factual premises underlying the rulings, at times even going beyond criticism to urge lower state courts not to extend disliked Supreme Court rulings beyond absolute necessity so as not to unsettle the state judiciary. This failure to be more positive about the cases they were applying, with enforcement based less on "genuine enthusiasm" than on "a sense of hierarchical duty" with the courts indicating they were acting because they had to, is not likely to kindle much enforcement activity by implementing populations.

Despite such "organizational contumacy," seldom does criticism become organized as it did in 1958, when the Conference of Chief Justices of the States adopted resolutions criticizing the Supreme Court for its tendency to adopt the role of policy maker without proper judicial restraints and stating that the basis of the Supreme Court's decisions should be the Constitution and not what temporary majorities might deem desirable. Lower courts have, however, openly resisted Supreme Court rulings, particularly over school desegregation and other civil rights matters. This may require that cases be appealed several times from the lower courts before compliance occurs, as with the admission of Virgil Hawkins to the University of Florida Law School or of James Meredith to the University of Mississippi. Similarly, Alabama's effort to prevent the NAACP from operating in that state brought the case to the Supreme Court on four different occasions before the matter was settled—but not before the organization had effectively been prevented from operating during the intervening time.

Despite the visibility of Southern resistance and the fact that resistant judges were unwilling to penalize those engaged in violation of people's rights, not all southern judges acted this way. A few were aggressive, active enforcers of individual rights, while others, more gradualist, while probably having personal attitudes not congruent with the rights required by the Constitution and statutes, would enforce the law if they were given enough evidence. Similarly, while some state supreme court judges (States' Righters) have emphasized local needs and problems and stressed the primacy of state law and state judicial processes, others (Federals) have been willing to take their cues from higher federal courts and from the Supreme Court's interpretation of the national constitution. If some local judges were to do what the Supreme Court wanted and to resist pressures from the communities to which they had ties, they needed a "hierarchy of scapegoats" as well as more specific guidance as to how to achieve desegregation. In this situation, the Supreme Court's making a virtue of district court discretion in implementing desegregation was thus counterproductive. It was also easier for state judges to sustain civil rights where they could avoid mentioning the U.S. Constitution and could emphasize state legal symbols and could cite state cases in preference to federal ones.

Trial court judges are crucial in the transmission of the Supreme Court's decisions to some groups, such as the police. "To the average officer 'the law' concerning arrest, search, and other police practices is in large measure represented by his direct and indirect knowledge of the attitudes of the local judiciary." Yet the trial judge seldom explains his decision, most trial court decisions are either unwritten (announced from the bench) or unpublished, and few local government units have established methods for systematically gathering and transmitting information from the courts. Furthermore, trial judges may not even pay much heed to the Supreme Court, particularly if they have adopted a position on an issue before the Supreme Court has spoken or if their attitudes are "unfavorable to the intrusion of 'law' into court proceedings which are highly routinized."

Attorneys general and prosecuting attorneys are among the lawyers playing a most important role in the communication process. State attorney generals' advisory opinions, which may incorporate Supreme Court rulings, do not have the force of law but are often given great weight by officials contemplating the legal ramifications of proposed actions. However, the advisory opinions usually are issued only on request by a public official and are not widely circulated, thus limiting their use as a means of communication. More important are informational meetings on new developments in the law and bulletins published for law enforcement officials, in which Supreme Court decisions are related to state statutes and judicial rulings and thus made more relevant to local officials' immediate concerns.

Local prosecutors, while they could play a large role in the communications process, may not be knowledgeable even on the subjects of cases they have tried. For example, Wisconsin district attorneys involved in obscenity cases felt some books and magazines "cleared" by the Supreme Court were obscene and other prosecutors gave many wrong answers to factual questions about Supreme Court obscenity cases; only 20 percent were rated as having high perception of Court policy (medium perception: 42 percent, low: 20 percent). However, regardless of their knowledge, even where the police would like them to do so, prosecutors rarely undertake the task of telling the police about Supreme Court decisions or about how police practices might be altered to comply with those decisions. Similarly, a regular link with local police departments through which the information could be transmitted is likely to be lacking, so that officials who obtain legal information from the prosecutor usually must do so informally. This lack of legal information from the prosecutor has led an increasing number of large police departments to hire police legal advisers—lawyers whose task includes interpretation of Supreme Court decisions, the development of teaching materials, and training within the department. Small departments, which cannot afford to hire these advisers, are thus left without systematic means of acquiring appropriate legal information.

Although sources of legal information inside the legal community are quite important, there are others outside the judicial system and the legal community. The mass media serve as an important initial source of information about cases, with television being the principal—as well as the most credible—source of news for the general public and newspapers providing greater detail. In the 1960s reporters covering the Court were frequently criticized for not being well trained, and for being passive and uncritical in their reporting of the Court. Since then, however, the accuracy of reporting has increased; most reporters covering the Supreme Court for major newspapers, the wire services, and the television networks either have law degrees or have spent some time studying law. This results in greater legal sophistication in coverage of the Court and one no longer finds such errors as reporting a denial of review as a full decision of the Court.

The media do not transmit Supreme Court decisions intact, few even printing portions of the most important cases. Nor could they, not only for reasons of space but because the Court's opinions are too complex in their original form to be understood by most people. The wire services have been and continue to be the principal source of information about the Court for newspapers and to some extent for television as well. A study of *Baker* v. *Carr* and the School Prayer Cases in the early 1960s showed that twenty-three of twenty-five papers carried reports of the reapportionment ruling on Decision Day, with fourteen stories coming from AP, five from UPI, one from the *Herald Tribune* News Service, and only two from the papers' staff writers. The picture was roughly the same for the school prayer rulings. However, starting with the second day after the opinion, although wire service domination continued, more stories were written by staff writers.

The media do not treat all decisions the same. Some are dealt with more carefully or more sympathetically than others. Some are not treated at all, being lost in the "deluge" of rulings, particularly toward the end of each term of Court. Because the rulings are not directly reproduced, much of the "richness"—including the rationale or reasoning—of the Court's opinions is lost during transmission. The media are thus part of a translation process in which changes are introduced and different elements of a decision and its context are emphasized. Each medium differs in what it emphasizes about what happens at the Court. The wire services, which cover the Court on more days than the newspapers (relatively close behind) or the television networks, appear to have the greatest capacity to handle "raw word flow." Although individual newspapers vary considerably, wire service and newspaper coverage is closely related to the Court's output, but television coverage is not. When output increases, changes in the pattern of coverage occur, with more attention paid to impact and somewhat less to legal principles; television is more affected by increase in output than are the other media. However, when output reaches a certain level, the ability of the media to expand coverage to match that output ceases and coverage loses most of its "depth," tending to summaries of individual cases.

Each medium also seems to have a different "profile" in relation to "Court time": wire services and television give relatively greater emphasis to predecision coverage; newspapers, more to postdecision coverage. Television seems to add more "contextual information" than do the other media, and to report "informational content" about the decisions least; the newspapers, on the other hand, seem to be most balanced in coverage of various elements—including not only predecision material and the decision itself, but also material on the Court as an institution and trends in the Court's decisions. The inclusion of all this other material makes it difficult for people to find out what the Court has said: they may be able to read about the decision's impact without knowing what it is that is having the impact. Yet if a decision is to be applied to a variety of circumstances, its rationale—not merely the facts and the holding—must be communicated.

For specialized audiences, television is clearly inadequate as a source of needed operational information and even newspapers are likely to have insufficient material about the Court's decisions. Because of these inadequacies, specialized magazines must perform an information-communication function about judicial decisions. However, while most occupational groups' "trade journals" can carry such information and some do, it usually is not well developed and is available only sporadically. Another, related source of information about legal decisions is the specialized material prepared for use in training. An advantage of such material is that the law is related to problem situations which those who must implement the rulings will face. Such details, although quite necescary, are not likely to have been provided by the courts. Such material must be written so that it can be understood; for example, materials for police officers must be written without a "dumb cop" image but so that those with a high school education or at most a couple of years of college can understand it.

As this suggests, training serves as a major means of communicating the law (statutory materials as well as court cases) to specific occupational groupings like police officers, who tend to rank training as the most effective means of learning about the law. Training takes a variety of forms, including degree programs at two-year and four-year colleges and much shorter two- or three-day or one-week in-service programs. These education and training programs must cover many subjects, so that coverage of legal matters is likely to constitute only a very small percentage of a total program unless, as is rarely the case, it is devoted solely to the law.

Another sort of educational program potentially important in communicating the Supreme Court's decision is the general education through which most citizens pass. Like many of the others, however, it is underdeveloped or underutilized. High school courses in civics or Problems of Democracy usually contain some mention of the Supreme Court but little systematic examination of the law. Until recently, there has been very little "law-related" or "law-focused" education at the secondary level. Such courses, even if they do not contain information about specific Supreme Court rulings, may expose students to basic information about the Court and particularly to attitudes about the Court's decisional trends—exposure which will later serve as background when a person is exposed to other material about specific rulings.

The few studies we have of how people actually find out about those Supreme Court decisions intended to affect them have been carried out in the area of criminal procedure. A study of the impact of *Miranda* in four medium-sized Wisconsin cities included an examination of the ways in which patrolmen, their superior officers, and detectives found out about the case, how they rated their sources, and the relationship between these and a department's professionalism. In the least professionalized of the departments, Green Bay, more than a third of the police officers found out initially about the decision from the newspaper, an eighth from the opinion itself, and another 10 percent from training sessions; others discovered the ruling from television and radio, magazines, superior police officers, and the state attorney general. With both initial and later sources combined, about 75 percent heard about it from a superior officer and about the same proportion read about it in a newspaper, with only slightly fewer having some television exposure to the case; somewhat over 60 percent heard of the case in training sessions. This evidence confirms that "people who have no formal connection with the judiciary may be a more important source of information than any judiciary authority." A full 40 percent, however, ultimately read the opinion itself. In Racine, a more professionalized department with a captain of detectives who was relied upon for legal information, a high percentage of police officers received their first information about *Miranda* from superior officers, who were also the predominant overall source of information about the decision in the department. In the most professional department, Madison, the most common initial source was the newspaper; however, more than 90 percent of the Madison officers were exposed to the decision in conference-and-training, while roughly three-quarters heard about the decision from the newspapers, a superior officer, and the attorney general.

The greater the professionalism of the department, the larger the number of sources of information and the greater the percentage of officers who received information from training sessions. Formal law enforcement sources were stressed more in the more professionalized departments. However, none of the departments had much contact with "outside" information which might have proved helpful in understanding the decision. Professionalization did not bring increased contact with nonpolice groups, but instead tended to bring about well-developed intradepartmental communication lines. Outside groups were listened to more frequently in the more professionalized departments, but that was because the groups furnished information which reinforced professional ideology. In all four departments, conference-and-training was rated the best source of information by the most people, with opinions as to the next best source varying. Those approving and those disapproving of the decision did not differ much in selecting the best source of information. However, those approving of the decisions were more likely to have received information at training sessions than were those who disapproved. While professionalization affected the way *Miranda* was communicated and received, after the decision as before, "there was no real hierarchy through which binding directives regarding the implementation of the *Miranda* decision could flow." Thus *Miranda* "did not basically change the decentralized and often unsystematic communications processes used to inform police departments about innovation."

In a subsequent study, on how small (two- and three-officer) police departments in two Wisconsin counties found out about the Court's decisions, the officers seemed more aware of particular areas of the law related to their local enforcement problems although their levels of knowledge of the law were not high. Most often mentioned as the first source of information about an opinion was the newspaper, which was also most often mentioned as a general source and as the best source; second in all three categories was radio and television. The only other sources mentioned consistently were police magazines and the attorney general's office, although the officers in these small towns lacked direct contact with that office. Conferences and training sessions, which received high ratings and attendance at which gave the officers prestige, were mentioned in connection with *Miranda,* probably because of the large number of FBI-conducted sessions on it.

Small-town police chiefs in southern Illinois and western Massachusetts were particularly likely to have found out about Supreme Court decisions from bulletins and other specialized or professional literature, with media (particularly newspapers) next; law books and the Court's opinions were mentioned in Massachusetts but barely noted in Illinois. Few chiefs mentioned training programs as a primary source of information about the Supreme Court. However, when queried, they said such programs had provided some information about the Court's decisions. Particularly in Illinois, where training did not become mandatory until 1976, the chiefs felt they had not learned enough about the Court through training. In large city departments throughout the country, three types of sources of information about Court decisions—the decisions themselves, specialized police publications, and the district attorney—predominated, with the media accounting for only about 10 percent of the responses.

The most effective means of communication were thought by the small-town chiefs to be published federal and state court decisions; state and/or local prosecutors followed close behind in the rankings, and bulletins were also frequently mentioned as helpful. The mass media and personal friends were thought to be highly ineffective; opinion about specialized police publications was divided. Written communications were seen by most as more effective than oral communications in helping the officers learn about Supreme Court rulings, although some suggested that a combination of the two, e.g., training materials discussed at a conference, was better still. The officers seemed to want something like a regular (monthly) free bulletin or newsletter which came to the individual officer and which digested cases and updated information the officer already possessed.

The small-town chiefs unanimously felt it was important for police to know about the U.S. Supreme Court's decisions. Virtually all the chiefs said their men wanted to know about Supreme Court rulings, although they made distinctions between officers who were serious about their jobs and other, less interested officers. In both states, the local prosecuting attorney was seen as having responsibility for providing legal advice to the police, for example, by preparing bulletins on the law and having meetings with the police on changes in the law; in Massachusetts the attorney general was seen as sharing responsibilities. Almost all chiefs said that advice about the law was available to them, but many said they were not provided sufficient material or access to it, although the situation was seen as more favorable in Massachusetts than in Illinois. For example, two-thirds of the Illinois chiefs did not know where published versions of Supreme Court decisions were available, indicating that they made little or no use of the decisions themselves. Massachusetts chiefs, however, had both the Supreme Court and state court decisions available to them, often in their own offices, and furthermore read the decisions although they generally felt that there was not enough time to do so. Evaluating the material, a majority of the chiefs in both states said such materials were understandable by nonlawyers, although at least some officers would need assistance if they were to understand them.

• • •

---------- 73 ----------

Organizational Contumacy
in the Transmission of Judicial Policies
Bradley C. Canon

I

• • •

This article focuses upon the organizational contumacy provoked by
three criminal policies established by the Supreme Court in the 1960s.
The first was *Mapp* v. *Ohio* which held that evidence obtained by unconstitutional searches and seizures was inadmissible in state criminal
trials. The second policy was initially developed in *Escobedo* v. *Illinois*
and further expanded and clarified in *Miranda* v. *Arizona*. In these decisions, the Court ruled not only that an accused, while in police custody,
must be provided with an opportunity to consult with counsel, but also
that incriminating statements made by the accused during police interrogation were inadmissible at trial unless he had been informed that he
had the right to remain silent, that anything he said could be used
against him in court, and that he was entitled to have a lawyer (including an appointed one if the accused were indigent) present during questioning. The third policy was announced in *In re Gault,* where the Court
held that defendants in juvenile court proceedings in which the institutional commitment of the juvenile might result were entitled to adequate notice of specific charges, the presence of counsel (including an
appointed one if the child was indigent) at trial, the right to confront
and cross-examine adverse witnesses, and the privilege against self-
incrimination.

A survey of state supreme court decisions through 1972 disclosed approximately 1800 decisions in which the aforementioned cases were discussed in some detail. In most instances the state supreme court applied
or distinguished the Supreme Court decisions without inserting into its
opinion any evaluation of the decision's merits or consequences. However, in 91 opinions the state supreme court negatively evaluated one or

From Bradley C. Canon, "Organizational Contumacy in the Transmission of Ju-
dicial Policies: The Mapp, Escobedo, Miranda, and Gault Cases," *Villanova Law
Review* 20 (1974): 58–59, 61–70, 76–77. Copyright © 1974 by Villanova University.
Reprinted by permission. Footnotes have been omitted.

more of the decisions. It is these instances of organizational contumacy which are to be analyzed here.

• • •

II

The most frequent examples of organizational contumacy among state supreme courts were decisions deploring the adverse impact of the Supreme Court's decisions upon public safety. Those taking this approach seemed to identify less with the values ascribed to courts in determining constitutional policy than with values held by those outside the judiciary. They denigrated the judicial traditions of isolated detachment and concern for proper procedures; on the contrary, there was an almost open identification with law enforcement agencies and their values. "Government is constituted to provide law and order. The Bill of Rights must be understood in the light of that mission," the Supreme Court of New Jersey announced. In other cases, the same court argued that the judiciary needed more "realism" and admonished it to attune itself to "the tumult of the streets, [not] abstract contemplation." Sometimes organizational contumacy appeared to reflect the political pressures surrounding the judiciary. Reminiscent of former Vice President Spiro Agnew's or Governor George Wallace's rhetoric, some courts publicly eschewed "the effete attitude" or "the soft approach" to criminal justice.

In particular, state supreme courts evinced considerable sympathy for the police. At best, the Supreme Court's rulings were charged with being too complex or confusing to warrant instant or complete police compliance. As the Indiana court stated, officers could not be expected to "conduct a course in constitutional law" every time they had to make a decision. At worst, the decisions did not make good sense to the police. Judicial rebuke by reversal of convictions was viewed as an unwise policy which would further alienate law enforcement personnel from the courts. According to the Washington Supreme Court, "The constant arching of the judicial eyebrows at the police and routine investigations conducted by them does little to advance the cause of civil liberty and much to endanger the public safety."

Underlying this concern was a belief that the Supreme Court's decisions seriously limited the ability of law enforcement agencies to solve crimes, that they "handcuffed and shackled" the police. In the opinion of some courts, large numbers of criminals were escaping justice. Utah's high court believed that the Supreme Court had so "exaggerated" the defendants' rights "as to give licentious protections to criminal conduct," while the New Jersey court asserted that "[I]t is idle to suppose, as some do, that those decisions have no impact upon law enforcement or at the worst only a minimal one."

Victims of crime were also an object of judicial concern; one court called them "forgotten people." "The law abiding citizen should not be forgotten," echoed another. This concern extended to future victims: the Georgia court prayed that the Supreme Court's concern for individual rights not overrule "the superior rights of the public to be protected against rapists, robbers, kidnappers and murderers." And the New Jersey court warned, "To set criminals free is to exact a price, not from some pain-free societal entity, but from innocent individuals who will be their next victims."

For some courts, the lack of full identification with the judiciary's own organizational values caused them to "distort" considerably the communications of the Supreme Court. Some of their opinions conjured up the spectre of an almost Hobbesian world as the logical progeny of decisions such as *Escobedo* or *Miranda*. Mississippi's highest court prophesied that soon "nothing will remain for the citizen, save to convert his home into a fortress, and go armed for his own and his family's protection." Others noted the rising crime rate or resorted to painting emotion-arousing portraits of murderers going unpunished or rapists roaming the streets at will. Not all were as dramatic in their description and downward communication of the Supreme Court's opinions, but some spoke fearfully of such things as the danger to the social fabric stemming from the High Court's decisions.

For some state supreme courts, organizational contumacy arose not so much from an identification with groups outside the judiciary as from an identification with the lower echelons of the judicial organization. The gravamen of their resistance was not the adverse substantive impact of the Supreme Court's policies, but the adverse organizational impact. These courts were reacting to the seeming uncertainty and instability into which the four High Court decisions had placed a good part of the law of criminal procedure. Uncertainty about organizational policy is a major source of intraorganizational tension. As with the higher echelons in all hierarchical organizations, a primary function of appellate courts is the maintenance of stability and predictability in policy output. Indeed, some appellate judges accord this function greater weight than that assigned to the quality of the law. Changes in the law occur, of course, but ideally they should come slowly and incrementally. Because *Mapp, Escobedo-Miranda,* and *Gault* constituted significant and sudden shifts in the law, some state supreme courts became visibly upset. They worried about the rapidity with which "far-reaching and revolutionary" changes were enervating the criminal justice system and sought an opportunity for the "proper digestion by society of the radical departures" from past law. To other courts the considerable ambiguity which always accompanies great changes was most bothersome; some openly complained of having to engage in "second guessing future Supreme Court decisions," or confessed to "wishing we had a crystal ball."

Another cause of uncertainty was the clouded future of the Warren Court's criminal justice decisions—particularly the exclusionary rule and the interrogation doctrines. Several state courts noted that *Mapp, Escobedo,* and *Miranda* had been rendered by close votes. While none explicitly argued that a 5–4 decision was less authoritative than a unanimous one, a few suggested that when cases were subject to severe political and professional criticism, they might not have a long legal life. Others expressed the hope that changes in Court personnel and viewpoint would limit their expansion or sap their vitality. Particularly after the advent of the Nixon administration and its appointment of several justices, some state high courts began to look openly for an overruling of *Miranda* and *Mapp.*

Sometimes the vertical communications of state supreme courts transmitted organizational contumacy in direct messages to their hierarchical subordinates. The Pennsylvania Supreme Court pointedly admonished trial judges not to "jump on their . . . horses and ride [off] in all directions" in response to *Escobedo.* Several state courts announced that these Supreme Court decisions should be applied "in the interest of realistic administration of criminal investigations," so as to avoid a "devastating impact on the administration of criminal law," "disastrous social consequences," or "extraction of a price from society grossly exorbitant . . . compared to the value likely to be received." Logical constructions or extensions were to be rejected if they produced unwise or impractical results. To this end, several state supreme courts proudly refused to "be presumptuous," "lead the way," or "attempt to outrun the Supreme Court of the United States."

Moreover, messages designed to keep the judical bureaucracy as stable as possible were sent to the lower rungs of the organizational hierarchy. Several courts admonished defense lawyers against relying on a particular Supreme Court decision too often and warned that "to press the . . . language of our Highest Court to its fullest meaning" might endanger the smooth functioning of the criminal justice system. Where such explicit warnings seemed inappropriate, sarcasm was employed. A Texas appellate court, for example, referred to the criminal defense bar as having "greeted the *Miranda* decision with such exclamations as 'Isn't it wonderful.' "

Organizational contumacy also took the form of disputing the Supreme Court's reasoning in one or more of its decisions. Here the subordinate court's behavior did not reflect a loss of loyalty to the judiciary's values and procedures. Organizational identification was present in the abstract, but the organization's highest policy makers were viewed as incompetent. Even so, it must be recognized that public pronouncements to this effect represent a potential threat to hierarchical authority as serious as that resulting from organizational alienation.

A number of state supreme courts found the Supreme Court's factual premises to be in error. For example, the Supreme Court of New Jersey argued that the absence of the exclusionary rule would not lead to unbridled police discretion because "[i]t would be a bit absurd to say ours was a 'police state' before . . . [*Mapp*]." By the 1970's some courts were questioning whether the exclusionary rule did in fact curtail illegal police searches. With regard to *Miranda,* some argued that the High Court was misinformed about the tactics and behavior of police in interrogation situations. Furthermore, in the view of the New York Court of Appeals, the circumstances in *Gault* were atypical and unusually dramatic, and it was quite unfortunate that the Supreme Court had based sweeping conclusions about the nature of the juvenile system upon the facts of that one case.

Criticism was also directed at the Supreme Court's heavy emphasis upon the adversary system. It was argued that this system was a means to an end, not an end in itself. The ultimate goal was justice and "[i]t was consonant with good morals, and the Constitution, to exploit a criminal's ignorance or stupidity in the detection process." As Nebraska's highest court stated, "an anticipatory and enthusiastic expansion of the Miranda holding" would defeat "an honest endeavor to find out if the accused is guilty or innocent." In stronger language, the Court of Appeals of Maryland charged the Supreme Court with having turned the criminal trial into "a sporting event, to be governed by the Marquis of Queensbury Rules, [rather than] a practical and actual determination . . . of guilt. . . ."

A few courts disagreed with the Supreme Court's interpretations of the Constitution. To them the fourth amendment was never meant to apply to rules of evidence and the fifth amendment was never intended to cover interrogation by law enforcement officers. Such requirements were thought to be products of an ideological judicial activism. In the analogy of Michigan's highest court, Supreme Court justices went "to even further reaches [than the astronauts] to put under foot precedents making constitutional interpretations."

Most of the challenges to the Supreme Court's reasoning were cogently developed and not openly disrespectful. Sometimes, however, state supreme courts indulge in sarcasm—one caustically announced that the Supreme Court had not yet gone so far as to require a policeman to gag a suspect to keep him from confessing—or unelaborated pejoratives, such as musings that the reasoning in *Escobedo* involved "a kind of judicial legerdemain."

Another alternative available to a hierarchical subordinate who dislikes his superior's policy is to question its legitimacy per se. This can be accomplished by asserting or implying that the policy is beyond the superior's legal or traditional authority within the organization. Even more so than questioning a superior's competence, challenging his authority poses a fundamental threat to the organization's hierarchical structure. Appellate judges fully expect that trial judges will accord legitimacy to their rulings, and, consequently, they are aware of the dangerous precedent which is established by undermining the legitimacy of the decisions of their own superiors. For this reason, this alternative was resorted to rather infrequently.

Echoes of such sentiments could be heard in the Deep South, historically the center of states' rights advocacy. Opinions in several states bemoaned the High Court's lack of comity for state courts and protested against federal court "onslaughts," "manipulations of the Fourteenth Amendment," and decisions which "have no basis in law." However, their tone was one of resignation; the impassioned arguments and defiance so characteristic of that region's political rhetoric were absent.

It was a court far outside the South—in Utah—which issued the most straightforward challenge to the legitimacy of the Supreme Court's decisions. In a case governed by *Miranda*, the Utah Supreme Court stated flatly that the Court had misconstrued the sixth amendment's right to counsel provision and then fired off a more general indictment:

> The United States Supreme Court, as at present constituted, has departed from the Constitution as it has been interpreted from its inception and has followed the urgings of social reformers in foisting upon this Nation laws which even Congress could not constitutionally pass. It has amended the Constitution in a manner unknown to the document itself.

While the opinion fell one step short of a clarion call to revolt in that the court reluctantly conceded its obligation to comply, it was certainly one of the most dangerously contumacious opinions to emanate from the state supreme courts in the wake of the United States Supreme Court's criminal justice decisions of the 1960s.

III

Infrequently, state supreme courts would positively evaluate *Mapp, Escobedo-Miranda,* or *Gault.* There were perhaps two dozen such occurrences, or about one-fourth the number of negative evaluations. A few of these opinions demonstrated a genuine enthusiasm for the Court's new policies. This was particularly true on the *Mapp* decision, where the Supreme Court's reasoning had previously been adopted by almost half the state supreme courts. More often, however, the positive evaluation seemed to come from a sense of hierarchical duty. Its most common impetus was a critical dissenting opinion which would often cause the majority to adopt a defensive posture while attempting to rationalize its position. Even when a direct stimulus was not present, positive evaluatory opinions seemed to be shaped by anticipated criticism from the bar or the public.

Occasionally a state court would articulate its sense of hierarchical duty and broadly endorse a seemingly unpopular High Court decision. Equally often, however, the notion of hierarchical duty was employed to dramatize the state court's disagreement with the Supreme Court in such prefatory statements as: "Because of *Miranda* [or *Mapp*], we are compelled to. . . ." The most frequent appeal to hierarchical duty, however, came from dissenting justices who believed that the majority's decision "ignored" or "rejected" its "constitutional duty" or the "abundantly plain" intention of the Supreme Court. In most such cases, it appeared that the dissenters not only believed in hierarchical duty, but positively approved the Supreme Court policy which their colleagues presumably were not applying.

IV

What has been termed "organizational contumacy" occurred in nearly two-thirds (32) of the 50 state supreme courts during the 1961–72 period. The phenomenon was found in all the populous, industrial states; many of the states which had no such occurrences are sparsely populated and had very few cases involving the four Supreme Court decisions. Otherwise, there were no pronounced regional proclivities for negatively evaluating the Supreme Court and its criminal justice decisions (although the courts in Western states did seem to demonstrate a greater inclination toward positive evaluation).

• • •

V

The occurrence of organizational contumacy in the judiciary's formulation and implementation of constitutional policy comes as no great surprise. Presumably it is present at least to a minimal degree in most political organizations; moreover, there is salient historical precedent for it in the American judiciary. Nonetheless, discussions of this phenomenon are few and attempts to ascertain its dimensions are almost nonexistent. While the judicial impact studies have illuminated the area somewhat, their analyses tend to be haphazard and illustrative rather than systematic. Moreover, as noted earlier, many impact studies seem to leap over the judicial hierarchy to concentrate upon the ultimate or penultimate recipients of policy, such as school teachers or policemen. Obviously this attention is necessary, but such findings might be placed in a clearer perspective if we also explore the organizational links between the United States Supreme Court and those charged with the final administration of its decisions.

In this article, an attempt has been made to fill a portion of this void. It is by no means a complete effort. Exploration of the relationship between organizational contumacy and the actual nature of state supreme court decisions relating to *Mapp, Escobedo-Miranda,* and *Gault* has not been performed. Nor has direct investigation been made of the relationship between this phenomenon and the behavior of persons "in the field" who are ultimately charged with implementing Supreme Court decisions. Hence, conclusions about the importance and impact of organizational contumacy must be viewed as rather tentative.

• • •

———————— 74 ————————

The Impact of the Exclusionary Rule
on Arrest Rates
Bradley C. Canon

• • •

Arrest in Search-and-Seizure Types of Crimes

Oaks,[1] it will be recalled, compiled arrest statistics from Cincinnati for the 1956–67 period and concluded that the imposition of the exclusionary rule in 1961 had virtually no effect on the propensity of the police to make arrests for narcotics and weapons offenses, although he con-

From Bradley C. Canon, "Is the Exclusionary Rule in Failing Health? Some New Data and a Plea Against a Precipitous Conclusion," *Kentucky Law Journal* 62 (1973): 703, 703–707, 707. Copyright © 1973 by the *Kentucky Law Journal*. Reprinted by permission. Footnotes have been omitted.

Figure 1. Arrests in Cincinnati, 1956–67

	STOLEN PROPERTY	WEAPONS	NARCOTICS	GAMBLING
1956	180	382	97	894
1957	169	380	84	879
1958	231	337	77	891
1959	198	216	59	699
1960	235	237	70	858
1961	328	220	52	586
1962	313	189	72	369
1963	340	202	53	500
1964	381	194	54	385
1965	326	185	45	296
1966	251	219	45	408
1967	390	270	82	204

SOURCE: Cincinnati Police Department, *Annual Reports.*

ceded some likelihood that the decision reduced the number of gambling arrests. [W]e have gathered similar data for 14 cities which did not have the rule prior to *Mapp*. In addition to the three crimes Oaks used, we have recorded arrests for possessing or receiving stolen property, an offense for which evidence is often obtained by search and seizure.

The data show that the Cincinnati experience relied upon by Oaks is not necessarily typical. Contrast the arrests there (shown in Figure 1) with those in Baltimore (shown in Figure 2) or those in Buffalo (shown in Figure 3). In Baltimore, the decreases in arrests following *Mapp* were both dramatically sudden and truly spectacular; one would be hard pressed to attribute them in large measure to anything but the imposition of the exclusionary rule. Even in 1965 the arrest rates for all crimes

Figure 2. Arrests in Baltimore, 1956–65

	STOLEN PROPERTY	WEAPONS	NARCOTICS	GAMBLING
1956	166	1341	324	434
1957	144	1324	239	512
1958	241	1343	435	849
1959	350	1452	239	577
1960	488	1559	502	623
1961	294	936	221	345
1962	274	1031	275	467
1963	163	1120	314	328
1964	171	1326	368	192
1965	168	1030	378	996

SOURCE: Baltimore Police Department, *Annual Reports.* Data for 1966 are unavailable.

Figure 3.   Arrests in Buffalo, 1956–66

	STOLEN PROPERTY	WEAPONS	NARCOTICS	GAMBLING
1956	41	148	76	91
1957	46	137	62	90
1958	68	152	68	93
1959	67	108	87	126
1960	72	125	112	171
. . . .	. .	. . .	. . .	. . .
1962	57	97	69	222
1963	44	94	110	137
1964	65	113	80	154
1965	81	127	83	102
1966	81	147	173	92

SOURCE: Buffalo Police Department, *Annual Reports*. Data for 1961 are un-available.

except gambling were significantly less than they were in 1960 (and for gambling they were significantly lower in 1962–64). In Buffalo the decreases in arrests were not so spectacular but were quite noticeable. More importantly, it is apparent that a monotonic increase in arrests for all crimes except weapons offenses was halted in 1962 (except for gambling where the decline began in 1963). By 1965, arrest figures for two crimes were considerably lower than those for 1960, and the arrests in the other two were only slightly above those in 1960. The conclusion that police behavior in Buffalo was affected by the imposition of the exclusionary rule is certainly tenable.

It should be understood that Baltimore and Buffalo are not being paraded as "typical." Baltimore is probably an extreme case and is illustrated to counter Oaks' generalizations about the efficacy of the exclusionary rule from the presentation of Cincinnati's arrest figures. Buffalo is less extreme, but not necessarily typical. Indeed, it is not at all clear that there is a typical response to the exclusionary rule. Rather, if the arrest figures we have gathered are indicative, response patterns vary considerably from city to city. Moreover, there is variation from crime to crime: arrests for gambling and weapons offenses seem to have been frequently affected, but stolen property and narcotics arrest rates were impaired in fewer locales. Space precludes setting forth the arrest figures for each of the 14 cities here, but Figure 4 gives a summary account of their relationship to the imposition of the exclusionary rule. A look at it shows that only four other cities, Boston, Dayton, New Orleans and New York have the rather minimal response pattern that Cincinnati has. At the other end of the spectrum, *Mapp* apparently had a significant impact in Baltimore and Buffalo (as we have seen), as well as Philadelphia and perhaps Akron. The remaining five cities show differentiated results;

Figure 4. Relationship Between Arrest Rates and Imposition of the Exclusionary Rule in 14 Cities

	STOLEN PROPERTY	WEAPONS	NARCOTICS	GAMBLING
Akron	*	A	*	A
Atlanta	X	C	X	A
Baltimore	A	A	A	C
Boston	X	X	X	A
Buffalo	B	C	B	A
Cincinnati	X	X	X	A
Cleveland	B	X	X	C
Columbus (Ohio)	X	A	X	A
Dayton	X	X	*	X
Denver	C	X	X	C
Newark	X	A	C	A
New Orleans	X	A	X	X
New York	X	C	X	X
Philadelphia	A	A	X	A

Key

X = No clear effect. Includes declines in arrest rates where trend began prior to 1961.
A = Permanent decrease. Arrest rates following *Mapp* average at least 10% less than those before *Mapp*.
B = Levelling off. Arrest rates increase in years preceding 1961 and remain steady (perhaps increasing slightly by 1965 or 1966) thereafter.
C = Impermanent decrease. A decline of 20% or more in arrest rates in 1962 or 1963 and lasting at least two years, but with an increase substantially above the pre-*Mapp* rates thereafter.
* = Indeterminate. Too few arrests for analysis or change in reporting format makes comparison impossible.

figures for some crimes lend support to arguments for the rule's efficacy while others support the opposite contention.

This discussion should not be read as an argument that a leveling-off or decline in arrest rates was necessarily caused by imposition of the exclusionary rule. Obviously, arrest rates are affected by changes in local crime situations or law enforcement priorities. Gambling in particular is subject to such factors. (Gambling arrests declined, usually rather substantially in 11 of the 14 cities, however, and it is unlikely that such a widespread phenomenon was the chance product of entirely local factors.) [W]e could not fairly expect police behavior to change radically in the years immediately following *Mapp,* and a before and after type of comparison using arrest rates is not particularly adequate for our purposes. Consequently, our argument is negative rather than positive; we are maintaining that the evidence from the 14 cities certainly does not support a conclusion that the exclusionary rule had no impact upon arrests in search-and-seizure type crimes in the years following its imposition.

• • •

Note

1. Dallin Oaks, "Studying the Exclusionary Rule in Search and Seizure," 37 *University of Chicago Law Review* 665 (1970).

──────────────── 75 ────────────────

The Supreme Court and the Bible Belt: Tennessee Reaction to the Schempp Decision

Robert H. Birkby

[*In 1963, the Supreme Court held that the required reading of the Bible in the public schools violated the "establishment of religion" clause of the First Amendment* (Abington School District v. Schempp *374 U.S. 203). Prior to that time, Tennessee statutes required that a selection from the Bible be read in class at the beginning of each school day. The following selection reports the reaction of Tennessee School districts to the Schempp decision.*]

I

• • •

If the *Schempp* decision had any effect in Tennessee it should be noticeable in the policies adopted and enforced at the school district level. The State Commissioner of Education was reported as saying that it was permissible to read the Bible in public schools despite *Schempp* but he left the final decision to local school officials. The school boards were left free to continue the practice required by state law or to comply with the Court's ruling. This study was undertaken to determine what the school boards did and, if possible, why. Even though it was expected that, in Gordon Patric's words, the "decision was put into effect in diverse ways

From Robert K. Birkby, "The Supreme Court and the Bible Belt: Tennessee Reaction to the 'Schempp' Decision," *Midwest Journal of Political Science* 10 (August 1966) 307–310, 311, 312–317, 318–319.

and 'obeyed' to varying degrees," board action in response to *Schempp* was classified as changing or not changing policy. All districts reporting a departure from the pre-*Schempp* provisions of state law were considered changing districts. It was believed that one of several factors could be used to explain the differences between changing and non-changing districts. These were degree of urbanization, extent of religious pluralism, articulate opposition within the district to devotional exercises, or differences in the socio-economic composition of the school boards.

To test these suppositions three questionnaires were prepared and sent out in late 1964 and early 1965. One was mailed to each of the 152 superintendents of schools in the state. The second was mailed to the chairman and two other randomly selected members of each school board. The third was sent to the remaining school board members in those districts from which responses were obtained to either or both of the first two questionnaires. The superintendents were asked what the policy on Bible reading and devotional exercises had been in their district before June, 1963, and what it currently was. They were asked to identify any factors inducing change and to describe, in each time period, the policy-making role of the board, superintendent, principals, teachers, parents, religious groups, and any other participants. The first group of board members was asked about current (post 1963) policy, how it differed from that of the past, what groups or persons made policy suggestions to the board, and what groups or persons were consulted by the board. The second group of board members was simply asked to supply information on age, occupation, education, income, religious affiliation, length of service on the board, and length of residence in the school district of its members. Response to the first and third questionnaires was good. Ninety-two (60.5%) of the superintendents responded; ninety-seven (21.2%) of the first group of board members representing eighty-four of 152 districts replied; and 237 (56.1%) of the second group of board members from 109 out of a possible 121 districts returned the questionnaire. By combining the reports of the superintendents and the first group of board members (cross-checking where possible) the policy currently in effect in 121 of the state's 152 school districts was determined.

Of the 121 districts, 70 were reported to be still following the requirements of state law. The other 51 districts were reported to have made some changes in their policy but only one of these completely eliminated all Bible reading and devotional exercises. The other fifty merely made student participation voluntary and left the decision whether to have devotional exercises to the discretion of the classroom teacher. Thus 42 percent of the reporting school districts no longer adhere strictly to the provisions of state law even though all but one could have some form of classroom devotional exercise.

The most reasonable explanation for these differences in response to *Schempp* seemed to lie in the extent of urbanization. Table 1 shows

Table 1.   Relationship of Urbanization and School Religious Exercise Policy Change

% OF DISTRICT POPULATION URBANIZED	NUMBER OF DISTRICTS	
	Changing	*Not Changing*
90–100	17	19
80–89	1	0
70–79	0	0
60–69	0	0
50–59	1	0
40–49	3	1
30–39	2	0
20–29	5	9
10–19	3	4
0–9	19	37
Totals	51	70

the distribution of changing and non-changing districts according to this factor.

Using the point bi-serial correlation the relationship between urbanization and tendency toward partial compliance with *Schempp* was found to be practically non-existent ($r_{pb} = -0.08$). Thus, on the basis of questionnaire responses, school boards and superintendents in urban areas showed no greater tendency to change Bible reading and devotional exercise policy than the respondents from rural areas.

The possibility that increasing religious pluralism may account for objections to religion in the schools must remain largely in the realm of speculation since accurate figures on denominational membership by school district or even county do not exist. The National Council of Churches has issued a rough compilation by counties and in lieu of anything else these figures were used to test this possibility. Only those counties with a single area-wide school district (no city districts) and those counties in which the county district and the city district took the same position could be used. This distorts the results somewhat but was made necessary by the impossibility of breaking county religious affiliation figures down into smaller units. On this rough test there is only slight correlation between religious pluralism and tendency to change ($r_{pb} = 0.02$). The pattern of change classified by total population of the district was also checked on the theory that heavily populated districts would be more likely to be religiously heterogeneous; again only a slight correlation was found ($r_{pb} = 0.24$).

The other two possibilities advanced above are equally ineffective in explaining the pattern of change. From only one of the eighty-four districts represented by responses from the first group of board members

Table 2.   Occupation of School Board Members

Occupation	Non-changing Districts	Changing Districts
Attorney	7	12
Professional and Banker	19	33
Self-employed	46	34
Managerial	15	12
White Collar	16	12
Skilled and Semi-skilled	18	4
Farmer	38	32
Retired	4	9
Other	15	11
Totals	178	159

$X^2 = 18.76$; $p > 0.05$

was there a report that the board had been approached by an individual who objected to a continuation of the Bible reading and devotional exercises. In this instance the protester's efforts were in vain since that district still complies with state law. Either there was no significant opposition to devotional exercise or else no board member wanted to admit that there had been any.

Using the chi square test and rejecting the null hypothesis at the 0.01 level of significance, tabulation of the responses of the second group of board members produced no significant differences in socio-economic characteristics between changing and non-changing boards. Tables 2 and 3 show the distribution and significance level of occupation and religious affiliation.

Table 3.   Religious Affiliation of School Board Members

Denomination	Non-changing Districts	Changing Districts
Baptist	55	39
Methodist	49	42
Church of Christ	20	17
Presbyterian, Congregational, and Episcopalian	14	28
Christian and Lutheran	22	12
Unspecified Protestant	12	10
Jewish	0	2
Totals	172	150

$X^2 = 11.84$; $p > 0.10$

In each instance the null hypothesis must be accepted.

II

• • •

The reported response by Tennesseee school districts to *Schempp* might be explained by one other hypothesis. There is in the question- naires some support for it but not enough to make it possible to assert that it is correct. What follows then is largely speculative. The line of reasoning starts with a distinction between procedural and substantive change in policy. Policy change in any situation may take the form of (1) altering procedure without altering the policy goal, (2) changing pro- cedure to reach a new policy goal without, however, making the new goal explicit, or (3) changing the policy goal with or without a change in procedure. Although we cannot be sure, it seems fairly safe to say that in the fifty school districts which overtly changed their policy on Bible reading and delegated the decision to the teachers there has been little change in fact. That is, it is suspected that the classroom teachers are "voluntarily" conducting Bible reading and devotional exercises just as they did before *Schempp*. One might go a step further and assert, without being able to prove it, that the school boards were aware that this would probably happen. I am suggesting that the board members acted con- sciously either to save the substance of the program or to avoid upsetting the community status quo by making slight procedural changes. In the language of Sayre and Kaufman, the contestants who had the prizes of the game were able to keep them by responding to a rules change with a rules change of their own. A comment by a lawyer on the board of a changing district indicates the compromise nature of the policy adopted:

> My personal conviction is that the Supreme Court decisions are correct, and I so told the Board and Superintendent; but I saw no reason to create controversy. If the Board had made public a decision abolishing devotional exercises, there would have been public outcry. I believe all staff members understand that the continuance of devotional exercises in their schools and in their rooms is entirely voluntary and subject to discontinuance upon objection of any individual or minority group.

There are other reasons that a board might adopt this strategy of procedural change. It could be used to reduce disagreement within the board itself. It could be suggested by an individual as a means of re- ducing his own tensions between a desire to comply with the Court's decision and a desire to retain perceived advantages of devotional exer- cises. Finally, change in procedure without change in substance might be made to forestall demands for even greater change. There is nothing in the questionnaire responses to indicate which of these alternatives is correct and it is possible that all were present to some extent. If any or all of these suppositions are correct, a desire to retain the program rather than religious pluralism and urbanization would be responsible for the formal change. To this point the hypothesis does not provide an answer to the question of why the form was changed in some districts and not in others. It does emphasize that the answer must be sought in psychological rather than in demographic or socio-economic factors.

The question being asked in any impact study is why the Court's decision is not self-executing. In a different context Richard Neustadt has concluded that a self-executing order must have five characteristics: (1) the issuer of the order must be unambiguously involved in making the decision, (2) the order must be unambiguously worded, (3) the order must receive wide publicity, (4) those receiving the order must have control of the means of implementation, and (5) there must be no doubt of the individual's authority to issue the order. Neustadt was speaking of orders issued by the President but there is no reason that the same analysis cannot be applied to Court decisions. In this instance, there was no doubt that the Court did in fact make the decision though one school board member suggested that the Court was "controlled by small pressure groups." When applied to the Tennessee statute the wording of the order, although negative in content, was clear enough. There was wide publicity. The members of the boards of education had control of the means of implementation. However, the fifth factor was not so obviously present.

There was some confusion about the Court's decision. It was clear enough that required devotional exercises were forbidden but the Court did not commit itself on the status of voluntary programs such as those adopted by the fifty changing districts in Tennessee. This ambiguity caused one superintendent to assert confidently "we believe our policy [voluntary participation] is an accordance with the ruling of the Supreme Court and in accord with the desires of the people in this community."

More important is the question of the Court's authority to issue the order. The policy maker's reaction to a judicial decision will be conditioned by his perception of the Court's role in general, his beliefs concerning the importance of the challenged activity or program, his perception of the attitudes of his reference groups and constituents on the issue, and his perception of his role. The differences in policy position may be the result of a general attitude toward the Court and its role in the American system of government. The following comments are typical in content and intensity.

Changing Districts

A Surgeon: We must conform with Federal law. If we are to teach our children to obey laws we must set an example.

A Farmer: We did not want to violate any federal law.

A Superintendent: I think the Supreme Court is correct. Very few people understand the religious issue, less seem to understand what is meant by religious freedom, and relatively few seem to understand the Supreme Court's role in our government.

A Farmer: We are commanded by the Bible to be subject to civil powers as long as their laws do not conflict with laws of God.

Non-Changing Districts

A Superintendent: Impeach Earl Warren.

A Housewife: The decision of the Supreme Court seemed senseless and I could see no advantage in making changes.

A College Professor: The Supreme Court decision didn't mean a damn.

A Banker: The general public in this country do not have the respect for the U.S. Supreme Court as they once did. They think it is packed, so to speak, and doubt very much if all are qualified and unbiased and listen to the whims of the President that gave them the appointment. The standards are on a lower level than back several years ago.

A Superintendent: I am at a loss to understand the necessity for this survey. I am of the opinion that 99% of the people in the United States feel as I do about the Supreme Court's decision—that it was an outrage and that Congress should have it amended. The remaining 1% do not belong in this free world.

A Lawyer: We felt that in the absence of some good specific objection, there was no compelling reason to change previous policy.

If one had these comments without information on the policy adopted, it would not be too difficult to predict the position taken by each of these school boards.

The Court-attitude is only one of the variables affecting the impact of a judicial decision. The other major variable is the policy maker's assessment of and commitment to the challenged program or activity. Comments on the benefits and value of Bible reading and devotional exercises came only from the school board members and superintendents from the non-changing districts. These are typical:

A Farmer: I believe that if the Bible is removed from our schools and is not read that would be the first step toward removing the Holy Bible from our free society. Then we would eventually drift into heathenism.

A Merchant: This nation was founded and has grown under the firm belief in God. For those who do not believe it, there are places where they do not believe. Let them go there if they choose.

A Locomotive Engineer: I thought the Bible should be read and prayer held on account this was the only time some of our students ever had any spiritual guidance.

A Surgeon: This is a free country. If Bible reading is offensive to a very small minority then this minority may do homework or look out the window. However, we shall not discard Bible reading in order to coddle them.

A Bookkeeper: While this is a federal law, we do not intend to stick strictly to same. We permit Bible reading and devotional exercises in our school. If it was not being done, I would insist that it be done, bearing in mind that perhaps this is the only place some children are exposed to same. I cannot bear to think of communist atmosphere being exercised through our schools and children.

A Superintendent: Political leaders should read Bible and quit playing politics.

In some of these instances the belief in the importance of the program was sufficiently intense to override any desire to comply with the decision. In other instances, respondents combined attacks on the Court with a defense of the program. It seems reasonable to assume that the relative intensities of the Court-attitude and the program-attitude determined in large part the policy position taken by the school board. In changing districts the board must have felt a greater obligation to follow the Court ruling than to continue to enforce their beliefs in the value of devotional exercises. In the non-changing districts *Schempp* was repudiated either because of a pre-existing negative attitude toward the Court or because of a strong belief in the value of the program, or both.

Perceptions of the attitudes of constituents or clientele are important but seem to be secondary. They play the role of reinforcing or modifying the Court-attitude and/or the program-attitude. A dentist on the board of a changing district observed that "we thought public opinion would want us to comply with Federal Law," while a chairman of a non-changing board (who did not indicate his occupation) said that the most important factor influencing him was that "we would have had complaints if we did not have Bible reading." Both of these board members were reacting to their perception of constituent attitude. The officials' constituents or clientele are not the only reference group they have. Other official bodies, such as the State Board of Education and the Commissioner of Education, may constitute another while non-official groups and opinion leaders could make up a third. The Commissioner's statement that Bible reading was permissible was not mentioned by any respondent but undoubtedly played a part in the making of decisions. The state has also continued to print the statutory requirement in the handbook of regulations for teachers. This prompted one superintendent to remark that "most teachers consider Bible reading a state law since it is still in their register." And a merchant in a non-changing district said that he was influenced by the necessity of "complying with the laws of the State." Another superintendent indicated his valuation of the Court's decision by reporting that he "suggested teachers continue practices of past until forbidden by law." While official reference groups, constituents, and perceptions of the ranking of state law and Court decisions played an admitted role in the policy making process, no board member indicated that he had been influenced by any non-official reference group. However, the possibility cannot be ruled out. One superintendent justified the lack of change in his district by pointing out that the county education association had adopted a resolution favoring continued compliance with state law.

On the basis of the information available, it is impossible to weigh the value of the perceptions that went into the making of the policies. But one might hazard a guess that in the changing districts a perception of the Court as an authoritative body exercising legitimate power was strong enough to override any commitment to devotional exercises. The reverse, of course, would hold true in non-changing districts. The weight given to reference group attitudes and the direction of those attitudes probably, though not necessarily, varied in the same direction as the final policy decision and served to reinforce attitudes toward the Court or beliefs in the value of devotionals. That is, public opinion in changing districts probably was perceived by the board as favoring or at least not opposing compliance with *Schempp* and strengthened the board's desire to comply.

III

• • •

One must conclude with Robert A. Dahl that "by itself, the Court is almost powerless to affect the course of national policy." It may delay or accelerate adoption of policy but cannot impose or reverse policy. Court decisions, therefore, will increase in effectiveness as those who have to implement them are either in accord with the Court's position or are sufficiently convinced of the legitimacy of the Court's exercise of power that this conviction overrides any prior commitment to an alternative policy. A limit is thus placed on the ability of the Court to make policy and this impales the justices on the horns of a strategic dilemma. Their decisions have the greatest effectiveness when the policy laid down is non-controversial and the Court's prestige is high. But in a period of massive social (and therefore legal) change the justices' policy choices will be controversial and as a result the Court's prestige will be lower than in quieter periods. The options available are to deal with one problem area at a time in an attempt to maximize effectiveness by minimizing controversy or to take the problems as they come since any decision will have some, even if not total, effect. Unless we are to counsel judicial abdication the only way to resolve this dilemma is for the Court to utilize every legitimate means at its disposal to convince other policy-makers and the general public that its policy choice is the best of the possible alternatives.

--------------------------------- 76 ---------------------------------

The Policy Impact
of Reapportionment

Roger A. Hanson, Robert E. Crew, Jr.

• • •

The findings of . . . current research are that reapportionment is associated with important policy changes in the 1960's. By means of a longi-
tudinal analysis, evidence is gathered which can be interpreted as showing that reapportionment preceded changes in the pattern of policy
outcomes.

Research Design

The basic function of the design is to provide a valid test of the association between reapportionment and policy outcomes. Because the authors
of prior studies claim that malapportionment index scores are not highly
related to policy outcomes, it is reasonable to suppose that reapportionment might not be a causal determinant of interstate variations in such
outcomes. With that presumption, a research format is developed which
permits us to determine if an adjustment in apportionment precedes any
major policy changes within a given state. The verification of hypothesized connections between reapportionment and variation in intrastate
policy outcomes is a basic step in obtaining knowledge about the impact
of the judicially ordered changes in the legislative structure.

The methodological framework selected for the purpose of examining
the causal efficacy of reapportionment within the boundaries of the individual states is a before and after test. In this context, reapportionment
is conceptualized as an event which occurs within the broader time frame
of the ongoing process of policy-making. The before period includes observations about the policy outcomes prior to the date of the application
of a reapportionment plan. The after period takes in measurable decisional outcomes which happen subsequent to the implementation of the
structural reform. The first task of the empirical analysis is to ascertain

From Roger A. Hanson and Robert E. Crew, Jr., "The Policy Impact of Reapportionment," *Law and Society Review* 8 (1973): 72, 72–75, 76–77, 77–78, 78–82, 82, 82–86,
90. *Law and Society Review* is the official publication of the Law and Society Association, Copyright Holder. Reprinted by permission. Footnotes have been omitted.

whether any significant changes in policy outcomes are evident after re-apportionment is introduced. The second task is to ascertain whether it is reapportionment or some other antecedent condition that is the source of any observable policy change. In order to attempt to satisfy these research goals, the data are analyzed in a manner approximating the standards of inference that have been proposed for quasi-experimental designs.

Forty-eight states (Hawaii and Alaska are excluded) are the subjects for comparisons of intra-unit variations in policy outcomes. By looking at forty-eight units, this research effort complements the scope of prior analyses of the impact of reapportionment which are close examinations of legislative roll call voting and legislative committee occupancy in a single state. . . . Each state is examined for the *first* state election held under the guidelines of a reapportionment plan. Because reapportionment plans are not necessarily adopted simultaneously for both houses of a state legislature, we consider a change in *one* house to be sufficient for a state to be classified as reapportioned. Since state governmental expenditures are adopted as the indicators of policy outcomes, the fiscal year expenditures that are the result of legislative activity prior to reapportionment are the data set of the before period. Those fiscal year expenditures that are the result of legislative activity under the reapportioned districts form the data base of the after period.

In order to undertake appropriate quantitative analysis, there must be a sufficient number of observations of policy outcomes during both periods. This requirement eliminates most states from being classified as reapportioned because many did not hold an election under a reapportionment plan until 1968. After the election of 1968, there were, at the time that this study was completed, data for only two fiscal years. Thus, all of the states classified as reapportioned underwent the treatment of reapportionment in a state election before 1966. In spite of this common feature, not all of these states received the same dosage of reapportionment. Some states experienced major shifts in district boundaries and the number of urban legislators increased significantly while other states experienced only minor rearrangements. In future studies of the effects of reapportionment, it will be important to estimate the association between the degree of structural modification and the variation in governmental outlays. However, in this exploratory study, attention is not given to this problem. The states in which the legislatures were reapportioned to some degree are listed with the fiscal years for the respective time periods.

The non-reapportioned states are defined as those states in which a reapportioned legislature was not elected during the first five years of the 1960's. This time dimension is imposed because any state legislature elected after 1965 under a reapportionment plan would make allocations

	Before	After
New York	1958–66	1967–69
Massachusetts	1958–63	1964–68
Oregon	1958–63	1964–68
South Carolina	1958–63	1964–68
Kentucky	1959–64	1965–68
Delaware	1959–64	1965–68
Georgia	1958–63	1964–68
Mississippi	1959–64	1965–68
Virginia	1959–66	1967–69
Kansas	1958–66	1967–69
West Virginia	1958–65	1966–69
Wisconsin	1958–66	1967–69
Michigan	1958–65	1966–69
Wyoming	1958–65	1966–69
Oklahoma	1958–66	1967–69

beginning with the fiscal year 1968. Since fiscal year 1969 is the last year for which data are available, the limited number of observations obviate classifying such a state legislature as "reapportioned." Instead, those states that did not experience the election of a reapportioned legislature before 1965 are utilized as a control group. Since the states are not randomly assigned to the control group, it is not possible to assume that all features of state political systems other than the dates of reapportionment are randomly distributed across all the states. The lack of random assignment of states into the control group brings impurity into an assumption about the variables that are not controlled statistically. Nevertheless, the policy outcomes of the states in the control group are analyzed in order to determine if the patterns of policy outcomes without the intervention of reapportionment are similar to, or different from, the patterns exhibited in reapportioned states. The nonreapportioned states are divided artificially into before and after periods. The control group can be examined for evidence of policy changes between the two time periods. If factors other than reapportionment are the foundation for policy changes, then such events would be equally probable in both reapportioned and nonreapportioned states. (The assumption of equal probability can not be made because of the nonrandom selection of units for the control group.) Since factors other than reapportionment, such as a sudden influx of federal aid or a social commitment by a governor to a new program area, can occur in between the before and after period, the existence of any policy changes in a reapportioned state cannot be immediately attributed to reapportionment.

The states that are included in the nonreapportioned category include Alabama, Arizona, Arkansas, California, Colorado, Connecticut, Florida, Idaho, Illinois, Indiana, Iowa, Louisiana, Maine, Maryland,

Minnesota, Missouri, Montana, Nebraska, Nevada, New Hampshire, New Jersey, New Mexico, North Dakota, North Carolina, Ohio, Pennsylvania, Rhode Island, South Dakota, Tennessee, Texas, Utah, Vermont, and Washington. The before period for all of these states is 1958–63, and the after period is 1964–67. By using 1967 as the end point, there is no state in which a fiscal year expenditure is the product of a legislature reapportioned after 1965.

• • •

There are two sets of data to be used as the bases for tests of verification of the hypotheses. The first set consists of state governmental expenditures for various areas of policy outcomes. These data represent the total amount of state expenditures in a given fiscal year for specified functional areas. The areas selected are the following per capita spending items: higher education, inter-governmental expenditures for education (local schools), highways, public welfare, and hospitals.

• • •

The second set of data is the amount of money that state governments allocate to municipal corporations. This set of data provides a more valid measure of the policy impact of reapportionment than the first set. Since the alleged effect of reapportionment is to make the legislature more responsive to urban needs and demands, it is imperative to measure the level of state expenditures committed to their major cities. Prior studies that use expenditures as measures of policy outcomes do not include any indicators of state allocations to cities. To fill that gap, the total expenditures allocated to municipal corporations over 100,000 in population by state governments are used. Specific functional areas such as welfare and education are not used since there is no one area funded by all of the states for all of the cities. The periods of the allocations to municipal corporations in the nonreapportioned states are 1959–64 for the before period and 1965–68 as the after period. For the reapportioned states, the time periods are the same as in the first set of data.

• • •

Some mention needs to be made about the meaning of the term "policy change." For both sets of data, if the trend of yearly governmental expenditures increases, a policy change occurs. Generally, the level of expenditures rises in an absolute amount year after year. Given that basic fact, important changes in expenditure patterns are evidenced by increases in the rate of change in levels of expenditures. Since the levels before and after a particular point in time are being compared, it is necessary to compute the rate of change of expenditures for the fiscal years in each period. It is not appropriate to compare rates of change for each year because there is only one breaking point (reapportionment).

Measurement Technique

The measurement technique used to determine the presence of before and after policy changes is the comparison of unstandardized regression coefficients. To ascertain the intrastate policy impact of reapportionment, regression equations are computed for each state. For every state the independent variable is the set of fiscal years included within the respective period. As an illustration, with a 6 year time period, the values of the observations of the independent variable are 1,2,3,4,5,6. The expenditure items are the dependent variables. The regression coefficients are in this instance measures of the average rate of change in the dependent variable as a function of time. They can be interpreted as trends in expenditures because the regression coefficient determines the trend line's slope which is the most important aspect of a trend line. The particular trend in expenditures for each state's before and after period is found by computing regression coefficients for each period. As an illustration, see Table 1. For Massachusetts there are two comparable regression coefficients each time a different dependent variable is regressed on fiscal years. In the case of the first set of data there are five dependent variables. Looking at one dependent variable, higher education expenditures, the rate of change in expenditure levels before reapportionment is .492 and after reapportionment it is 3.647. In order to determine whether or not this difference between the regression coefficients is significant, a test is made of the statistical null hypothesis that $b_1 = b_2$, where b_1 is the regression coefficient of the before period and b_2 is the regression coefficient of the after period. This procedure generates a t-value, which is a measure of the statistical difference between the two coefficients.

Applied to the substantive problem of the current research, the null hypothesis *(H.O.)* is as follows: *H.O.* for every state, the regression coefficient in the before period is equal to the regression coefficient in the after period. This hypothesis is similar to the claim that only minimal policy changes will accompany reapportionment. If the t-value generated by the analysis is not statistically significant, *H.O.* cannot be rejected. In that case, the forecasts of Dye, Hoffebert, Jacob, Brady and Edmonds are confirmed. On the other hand, those individuals who maintain that reapportionment can produce increases in expenditure levels suggest an alternative hypothesis. Their hypothesis (H.1) is as follows: H.1. for every state, the regression coefficient in the after period is a

TABLE 1. Trends in Governmental Expenditures Before and After Reapportionment

STATE	POLICY AREA	HIGHER EDUCATION b1	b2	LOCAL SCHOOLS b1	b2	HIGHWAYS b1	b2	PUBLIC WELFARE b1	b2	HOSPITALS b1	b2	t-VALUE AT .01 LEVEL	NUMBER OF POLICY CHANGES
Delaware		4.113	8.391	10.450	−.676	1.380	5.243	.382	1.705	−1.50	15.665	d.f. = 6	1
	t =	−2.788		1.134		−3.304*		−2.971		−.687		3.143	
Georgia		1.285	5.947	3.671	7.930	3.049	3.371	.925	1.759	3.986	15.981	d.f. = 7	3
	t =	−9.091*		−2.542		−4.141*		−1.623		−10.168*		2.896	
Kansas		3.099	5.215	2.885	1.05	1.031	6.465	.759	1.345	6.155	7.21	d.f. = 8	1
	t =	−1.227		.407		−10.417*		−1.965		−.193		2.896	
Kentucky		3.062	7.896	3.715	8.303	5.657	11.592	9.006	5.740	7.306	17.695	d.f. = 7	4
	t =	−4.916		−3.391*		−6.063*		1.211		−6.419*		2.998	
Massachusetts		.492	3.647	.630	5.175	.371	5.194	.389	1.548	2.303	9.678	d.f. = 6	4
	t =	−15.626*		−3.027		−6.543*		−3.737*		−5.277*		3.143	
Michigan		2.709	5.314	2.23	7.459	1.155	8.764	6.28	2.603	5.095	15.095	d.f. = 8	3
	t =	−2.024		−5.378*		−15.787*		1.462		−4.876*		2.896	
Mississippi		1.496	2.921	.098	7.949	1.683	1.391	.754	1.147	1.737	12.695	d.f. = 6	2
	t =	−2.906		−9.211*		−2.783		−.861		−9.643*		3.143	
New York		1.851	.94	5.242	13.25	.2832	4.15	2.868	27.675	5.23	4.56	d.f. = 8	4
	t =	.79		−3.3*		−21.948*		−12.619*		−5.919*		2.896	
Oklahoma		3.243	5.865	1.366	2.177	1.827	4.023	2.748	6.229	.612	1.722	d.f. = 8	1
	t =	−1.424		−1.138		−.658		−2.177		−4.742*		2.896	

											d.f.	
Oregon	3.605	8.440	2.023	5.291	3.205	1.044	.716	.877	5.741	14.580	d.f. = 6	2
t =	-7.507*		-2.650		-.716		-.764		-5.957*		3.143	
South Carolina	1.085	4.583	1.285	7.804	1.026	.135	.883	1.382	2.897	17.659	d.f. = 6	3
t =	-6.977*		-6.115*		.980		-2.207		-9.859*		3.143	
Virginia	1.90	6.01	2.071	11.748	.445	1.436	.329	1.799	3.481	20.559	d.f. = 8	5
t =	-15.725*		-10.089*		-5.141*		-5.936*		-18.304*		2.896	
West Virginia	1.66	9.082	1.894	5.962	3.065	2	.588	1.789	3.903	16.998	d.f. = 8	4
t =	-6.596		-7.191*		.754		-11.469*		-9.465*		2.896	
Wisconsin	5.001	5.68	2.621	3.14	1.323	9.86	1.182	2.365	7.859	9.825	d.f. = 8	1
t =	-.202		-.516		-9.787*		-1.906		-.459		2.896	
Wyoming	3.139	5.876	2.195	2.936	.208	1.622	.266	.061	5.466	10.711	d.f. = 8	1
t =	-1.153		-.500		-3.917*		.325		-1.583		2.896	

* The results of the regression analysis for each expenditure variable are listed for each individual state. The regression coefficient in the before period is the set of numbers in the upper left hand side of a cell. In the upper right hand side is the regression coefficient in the after period. Below the period is the t-value. Significant t-values at the .01 level of significance are asterisked.

positive increase over the previous regression coefficient. With this hypothesis, the regression coefficients are predicted to be different and the difference is in a particular direction. If the t-value obtained from the calculations is *negative* and statistically significant with a one-tailed test level of significance, then *H.1.* can be accepted. Let us examine briefly the findings in order to illustrate the utilization of these hypotheses. In the case of Massachusetts, a comparison of the regression coefficients .492 and 3.647 yields a t-value of − 15.626, which is significant at the .01 level of significance. On the basis of the high negative t-value, we infer the existence of an important policy change.

• • •

Findings

A blunt manner of interpreting the results of the regression analyses is to calculate the relative frequency of policy changes across all of the units within each of the two groups of states. The operational meaning of the term "policy change" refers to a negative t-value that is statistically significant. Such a t-value which is predicted by *H.1.* indicates that there is an upswing in the trend of state expenditures when compared to the trend in expenditures during a preceding period of time.

• • •

Tables I and II list the regression coefficients and t-values from operations performed on the five state expenditure variables for reapportioned and nonreapportioned states, respectively. H.1 is supported in 39 of the 75 possible instances for the reapportioned group. The 52 percent level of corroboration of *H.1.* suggests that reapportionment accounts for changes in the direction of expenditures. The occurrence of policy changes in the nonreapportioned states is not as frequent. On the basis of the figures displayed in Table 2, policy changes happened in 62 of the 165 possible instances. The relative frequency of policy changes among all of the nonreapportioned states is 37 percent. A comparison of the two groups of states reveals that the percentage of changes in the reapportioned states is nearly one and a half times greater than in the nonreapportioned states. While a higher proportion of policy changes exist in the reapportioned states, it is clear that reapportionment is not a necessary condition for increases in the trend of state expenditures. Policy changes, as they are defined in this research, are produced in the absence of legislative reapportionment. The fact that a higher proportion of policy changes takes place in states that are reapportioned than occur

TABLE 2. Trends in Governmental Expenditures for Non-Reapportioned States

STATE	POLICY AREA	HIGHER EDUCATION b₁	b₂	LOCAL SCHOOLS b₁	b₂	HIGHWAYS b₁	b₂	PUBLIC WELFARE b₁	b₂	HOSPITALS b₁	b₂	t-VALUE AT .01 LEVEL	NUMBER OF POLICY CHANGES
Alabama		1.844	4.8	.041	7.363	1.305	1.383	.862	.128	.670	−.022	3.143	1
	t =	−1.100		−6.404*		−.032		.639		1.953			
Arizona		2.361	9.503	3.065	8.577	1.912	12.917	.503	.603	.114	.355	3.143	2
	t =	−7.092*		−2.746		−6.081*		−.353		−.769			
Arkansas		.999	4.267	.672	8.934	3.785	4.793	1.739	3.462	.655	.058	3.143	2
	t =	−3.914*		−3.791*		−.576		−2.063		2.353			
California		1.647	−670	.340	5.987	285	3.605	1.167	15.07	2.49	.679	3.143	2
	t =	.880		−1.317		−1.752		−7.240*		−1.190			
Colorado		3.661	8.154	1.714	7.043	−.998	3.567	.605	1.793	1.318	.758	3.143	1
	t =	−2.860		−5.385*		−3.219*		−1.305		1.331			
Connecticut		.126	1.403	−9.662	1.996	−8.171	−5.959	1.559	−.442	1.539	−.11	3.143	2
	t =	−3.286*		−.959		−.226		1.989		.657			
Florida		.499	3.757	.257	10.908	.129	−1.225	−.146	1.155	.067	.737	2.896	1
	t =	−15.142*		−3.938*		1.011		−5.246*		−9.066*			
Idaho		1.999	5.174	1.907	8.044	2.838	2.411	.980	1.8	.673	.435	3.143	4
	t =	−2.870		−4.307*		.142		−.791		.571			
Illinois		2.002	3.48	2.194	6.384	−1.804	−.761	3.5466	2.011	.371	1.671	3.143	1
	t =	−2.155		−2.887		−.640		1.463		−2.568			
Indiana		2.872	5.513	1.538	6.646	3.347	.469	.484	.806	.401	1.591	3.143	0
	t =	−2.386		−6.078*		1.650		−1.900		−3.571*			

517

TABLE 2. (continued)

STATE	POLICY AREA	HIGHER EDUCATION b₁ b₂	LOCAL SCHOOLS b₁ b₂	HIGHWAYS b₁ b₂	PUBLIC WELFARE b₁ b₂	HOSPITALS b₁ b₂	t-VALUE AT .01 LEVEL	NUMBER OF POLICY CHANGES
Iowa		2.885 5.889	.882 6.496	−.132 6.188	.957 1.567	.717 .993	3.143	2
	t =	−5.221*	−6.395*	−2.904	−1.437	−1.489		
Louisiana		1.317 5.994	2.038 8.178	.289 2.92	1.526 .675	7.64 1.783	3.143	2
	t =	−3.214*	−5.285*	−.863	2.126	−2.267		
Maine		2.282 5.268	1.305 4.501	.867 2.418	1.618 1.672	.399 .958	3.143	2
	t =	−2.100	−5.392*	−.863	.107	−3.367*		
Maryland		1.432 3.378	3.440 7.265	.251 −.276	.912 5.214	1.167 −.178	3.143	2
	t =	−5.419*	−1.347	.222	−4.118*	2.337		
Minnesota		1.447 7.99	2.697 5.988	.296 5.183	1.394 3.792	.404 .699	3.143	3
	t =	−15.048*	−3.901*	−2.025	−4.760*	−1.218		
Missouri		.912 5.261	2.355 6.576	2.430 −.621	.464 .957	.517 1.12	3.143	2
	t =	−6.815*	−1.469	1.971	−.841	−3.880*		
Montana		1.861 5.789	1.749 5.79	3.737 −.704	−.435 1.986	−.18 .578	3.143	4
	t =	−3.823*	−12.314*	1.533	−4.962*	−3.819*		
Nebraska		1.751 6.392	.260 2.231	3.807 3.359	.733 3.142	.363 2.02	3.143	3
	t =	−4.187*	−2.826	.183	−5.311*	−5.323*		
Nevada		4.175 9.032	4.044 5.441	.761 −5.057	.968 2.34	.290 −.089	3.143	0
	t =	−2.124	−.747	.719	−1.355	.507		
New Hampshire		.392 7.84	.419 −.32	.172 .979	1.078 2.161	.165 1.439	3.143	2
	t =	−3.912*	.188	−.406	−2.037	−6.201*		
New Jersey		1.513 1.893	.452 6.688	1.903 2.486	.84 1.774	.575 1.087	3.143	2
	t =	.491	−4.448*	−.671	−9.253*	−1.185		
New Mexico		3.433 12.87	2.614 11.255	−4.097 6.422	4.305 2.59	.010 11.063	3.143	3
	t =	−5.657*	−3.246*	−2.089	.538	−9.303*		

518

State		(1)	(2)	(3)	(4)	(5)		
North Carolina		1.569 4.904	11.502 10.053	.924 4.787	1.047 1.13	.661 .838	3.143	2
	t =	-8.248*	.304	-3.165*	-.481	-1.315		
North Dakota		1.088 4.4	-.156 3.497	1.193 -1.925	3.193 -1.925	1.148 1.358	3.143	0
	t =	-.689	-.982	.596	.604	-.342		
Ohio		.965 6.754	.657 5.562	.218 3.752	1.630 1.143	-.028 .621	3.143	2
	t =	-4.659*	-4.043*	-2.452	.274	-2.538		
Pennsylvania		.879 2.091	1.639 5.140	2.020 3.962	2.053 1.78	.616 .828	3.143	2
	t =	-3.482*	-3.394*	-1.107	.983	-.433		
Rhode Island		1.264 6.325	2.471 5.312	.673 8.084	1.623 1.226	.839 2.16	3.143	3
	t =	-3.482*	-3.235*	-3.219*	6.783*	-2.908		
South Dakota		1.567 8.34	.44 6.422	2.165 11.231	.718 5.871	.367 .725	3.143	3
	t =	-6.375*	-3.854*	-1.237	3.945*	-2.243		
Tennessee		1.215 7.35	1.573 8.4	3.342 1.986	.375 2.727	-.048 1.326	3.143	2
	t =	-6.906*	-1.072	.748	-7.461*	-1.975		
Texas		1.09 .169	2.325 6.434	.012 1.558	.707 .185	.210 .059	3.143	0
	t =	.386	-.829	-.741	.829	.428		
Utah		3.772 13.202	4.374 7.258	3.835 2.113	1.059 2.557	.1 2.1	3.143	3
	t =	-6.884*	-1.488	.433	-3.610*	-3.552*		
Vermont		4.077 7.837	.133 5.2	7.014 15.45	1.212 2.457	.850 .472	3.143	0
	t =	-1.172	-1.920	-2.064	-.877	.306		
Washington		4.066 6.543	4.825 9.105	1.293 9.105	1.648 1.675	.677 .673	3.143	1
	t =	-3.418*	-.970	-2.347	-.952	.007		

519

* The results of the regression analysis for each expenditure variable are listed for each individual state. The regression coefficient in the before period is the set of numbers in the upper left hand side of a cell. In the upper right hand side is the regression coefficient in the after period. Below the two regression coefficients is the t-value. Significant t-values at the .01 level of significance are asterisked.

in nonreapportioned states offers the possibility that reapportionment is a sufficient condition for increases in the trend of expenditures.

•   •   •

Conclusions

The foregoing research has provided empirical support for the hypothesis that legislative reapportionment is related to changes in state public policy. The nature of the data examined and the test utilized allows us to speak with some confidence to one of the major questions posed by political scientists: "How does governmental organization (and reorganization) affect governmental policy?"

The specific nature and the strength of the relationship remains unclear. Legislative reapportionment is not a necessary condition of policy change. There is a possibility that it is a sufficient condition. It clearly has different effects in different policy areas. However, there is a relationship. Future research may want to focus on the variables which intervene between the act of reapportionment and public policy change.

•   •   •

PART VI

Current Problems
in the Courts

In this part, we consider case load problems in federal courts. The increased number of disputes the federal courts are being called on to resolve has far outstripped the resources available for the job. This leads to delay in the district courts, and it also invites short cuts in the disposition of cases resulting in a threat to the quality of justice being meted out in these courts. As Goldman points out, Congressional attempts to speed up legal processes in some areas may produce greater problems in those areas that are less salient for the Congress.

In the federal courts of appeals, problems of a different nature can be traced to increases in case load. These courts serve eleven different circuits. A decision of such a court is binding only in its particular jurisdiction—that is, it is regional law. It is possible that courts of appeals in different circuits will decide the same issue in two or more ways. That can be a problem, since an individual's legal rights may depend on jurisdictional (and thus, geographical) location.

The remedy for such a "balkanization" of federal law lies with the Supreme Court, which can review and resolve circuit court conflicts where national law or policy in the area seems dictated.

This remedy is sufficient to the task in a system in which case loads are moderate. But the tremendous increase in circuit court business in recent years has steadily eroded the ability of the high Court to review appeals courts decisions. Thus the appeals courts increasingly become the courts of final decision. Moreover, as Howard points out, the Supreme Court appears to be using its limited opportunities for review not to resolve conflict but to secure "the supremacy of highly selective policy values irrespective of levels." While Howard's paper is a study of only three circuits, other research reveals that the problem is systemwide.

Recent case loads in the Supreme Court have created the most concern. It is a matter of considerable moment to Chief Justice Burger and several of the Court's associate justices, and to the legal profession generally. The magnitude of the problem, its consequences, and suggested reforms (as well as responses to them) are dealt with by Casper and Posner. In addition to the reform proposals discussed there, a more recent one has been put forward by the Commission on Revision of the Federal Court Appellate System. The Commission was appointed by Congress to study and make recommendations in this area.

In its report, the Commission recommended the establishment of a National Court of Appeals consisting of seven Article III judges appointed by the President with the advice and consent of the U.S. Senate. The court would have jurisdiction to hear any case referred to it by the Supreme Court (reference jurisdiction) and any case transferred to it by any federal court of appeals (transfer jurisdiction). Its decisions would be precedential for all the courts of appeals and all state courts, insofar as federal questions are concerned, unless modified by the Supreme Court itself. While such a new court might address some of the questions raised by the readings in this part, it would not appear to be a timesaver for the Supreme Court. Casper and Posner estimate that it takes a Supreme Court justice ten to fifteen minutes to decide whether to grant review of a paid case. It seems highly unlikely that a decision whether or not to "refer" a case to a National Court of Appeals could be taken in less time. In any event, at this writing, Congress has yet to adopt this or any other major reform of Supreme Court jurisdiction.

In the final reading in this part, attention is given to the possibility that courts contribute to their own caseload problem—that is, the actions taken by a court in deciding cases can invite or discourage litigation in the same area. But, as Friedman makes clear, it is too simple to assert that demand is created solely by the actions of courts. The demand for legal service may also be created by society. Since a court does not control its society, its potential docket is not—in the broad sense—subject to its complete discretion.

Case Flow and Caseloads

───────────────── 77 ─────────────────

Criminal Justice
in the Federal Courts

Sheldon Goldman

• • •

Until the fourteenth amendment became part of the constitution in 1868, the constitution imposed few criminal justice standards on the states. With the adoption of the fourteenth amendment, in particular the due process clause ("No State shall . . . deprive any person of life, liberty, or property without due process of law"), the potential for federal court supervision of criminal justice in the states was established. At about the same time, Congress passed legislation giving the federal courts jurisdiction to entertain habeas corpus petitions from state prisoners. However, in the last third of the nineteenth and the first third of the twentieth century, the federal judiciary included judges who were concerned not with civil liberties but with the attempts of government (both state and national) to regulate the economy. Nonetheless, these judges developed doctrines that enabled the federal courts to exercise vast supervisory powers over the actions of the states. Once the judiciary was staffed by judges more sympathetic to civil liberties, these doctrines provided the basis for overseeing criminal justice.

From Sheldon Goldman, "Criminal Justice in the Federal Courts," *Current History* (June 1976): 258–259, 259–260, 271. Reprinted by permission of *Current History*, Inc. Footnotes have been omitted.

Gradually, during the second third of the twentieth century, most of the basic rights guaranteed to federal criminal defendants in the Bill of Rights became "incorporated" within the fourteenth amendment's due process clause and provided the basis for the federal judiciary's supervision of criminal justice in the states. Much of the incorporation of criminal procedural guarantees occurred during the 1960's, when the Supreme Court, under Chief Justice Earl Warren, for the first time in its history had a liberal activist majority intent on elevating the standards of criminal justice. Significantly, a 1963 decision of the Warren Court made it easier for state prisoners to pursue habeas corpus relief in the federal district courts.

The expansion of federal court supervision over criminal justice in the states resulted in a caseload explosion at every level of the court system. Although under Chief Justice Warren Burger the Supreme Court has been dominated by a new majority considerably less sympathetic to the claims of criminal defendants or prisoners than the Warren Court majority, the caseload problem has persisted to the present.

The federal courts have a dual responsibility for overseeing the administration of criminal justice. They are concerned with those accused of violating federal law; they also oversee the criminal justice standards used by the states particularly (but not exclusively) through the habeas corpus process. Table 1 presents the criminal as well as civil caseload figures for five selected years over the recent 15-year period.

It is clear from Table 1 that the total business of each court level has increased dramatically from fiscal 1960 through fiscal 1975; the greatest increase occurred at the appeals court level. By 1975, the appeals courts had more than five times as many cases as they had 15 years earlier. It is reasonable to conclude that the Warren Court's assumption of responsibility for elevating criminal justice standards in the states played a significant part in increasing court business at every level. The increase in state prisoners' habeas corpus petitions is most startling at the district and appeals court levels. Over the 15-year period, the district courts experienced almost a ninefold increase in habeas corpus petitions from state prisoners, while the appeals courts had close to eight times the petitions it had 15 years earlier.

Even at the Supreme Court level, state and federal prisoner petitions placed on its miscellaneous docket approximately doubled. Clearly, the Warren Court's deep concern with criminal justice standards provided a profound challenge to the administrative abilities of the federal courts. This has been particularly true in the appeals courts and the Supreme Court. If it is assumed that they were not underworked in 1960, the question must be raised as to the impact of this greatly increased workload on the court's ability to administer justice.

This becomes even more important when federal criminal prosecu-

TABLE I. The Business of the Federal Courts—Cases Begun (Filed) during Fiscal Years 1960, 1964, 1968, 1972, and 1975

	Fiscal 1960	Fiscal 1964	Fiscal 1968	Fiscal 1972	Fiscal 1975	Percent Increase from Fiscal 1960 to Fiscal 1975
U.S. District Courts:						
Criminal cases	28,137	29,944	30,714	47,043	43,282	54%
Habeas corpus, federal prisoners	861	1,045	1,202	1,429	1,687	96%
Habeas corpus, state prisoners	872	3,531	6,331	7,868	7,838	799%
Other civil cases	57,551	62,354	63,916	86,876	107,795	87%
Total criminal and civil cases	87,421	96,874	102,163	143,216	160,602	84%
Number of authorized judgeships	245	306	341	400	400	63%
U.S. Courts of Appeals:						
Criminal cases	623	1,223 *	2,098	3,980	4,187	572%
Habeas corpus, federal prisoners	65	104 *	118	234	207	218%
Habeas corpus, state prisoners	111	571 *	1,069	1,319	871	685%
Administrative agency cases	737	1,106 *	1,545	1,509	2,290	211%
Other civil cases	1,409	1,981 *	4,286	7,493	8,414	497%
Total criminal and civil cases	2,945	6,766 *	9,116	14,535	16,658	466%
Number of authorized judgeships	68	78	88	97	97	43%
U.S. Supreme Court:						
Appellate Docket	857	1,017	1,540	1,708	1,768	106%
Miscellaneous Docket	1,005	1,276	2,036	1,930	1,891	88%

Sources: Annual Reports of the Director of the Administrative Office of the U.S. Courts; Supreme Court Reporter; U.S. Law Week.
* Fiscal 1965 figure; the fiscal 1964 breakdowns were not provided in the Annual Reports of the Administrative Office.

tion figures are considered. Thanks to the liberal criminal justice rulings of the Warren Court and to the Criminal Justice Act of 1964 (under which the federal government picks up the tab for a lawyer for indigent defendants for the trial and for an appeal as well), appeals from criminal convictions in the district courts have increased close to sevenfold from fiscal 1960s to fiscal 1975. Questions can be raised with regard to the extent to which these caseload pressures impede the administration of justice. To be sure, the caseload crunch has motivated the federal judiciary to develop stopgap measures in order to stay afloat. But it is fair to ask whether litigants are receiving the same consideration of their claims and counterclaims that they would receive if the proportion of cases to judges were the same today as it was 15 years ago. This takes us more directly to a consideration of some of the problem areas of criminal justice administration and selected proposals aimed at correcting present deficiencies. The focus will be more on a description of some major problems and considerably less on proposed solutions. . . .

There is no doubt that the increased caseloads of the federal appellate courts and the district courts (particularly in the lage metropolitan areas) present problems of court management or administration and fundamental problems of achieving justice. Logjams in the courts create backlogs in court calendars that delay the resolution of some cases (particularly civil cases) several years. In the Speedy Trial Act of 1974, Congress sought to guarantee a speedy trial to those accused of violating federal law by requiring the government either to bring the accused to trial within a specified time period or to drop the charges. By 1980, the period between arraignment and trial can be no longer than 60 days. What this means for the district courts is that criminal proceedings will have the highest priority; as a consequence, the backlog of civil suits, including habeas corpus proceedings, can be expected to increase, unless a host of minor and probably major "reforms" are instituted.

The case crunch can not only delay justice; it can also affect the quality of justice. A greater caseload per judge obviously means that less time is available for each case. This means that less time can be given to research and deliberation.

What can be done to remedy the problems associated with the case crunch? Some relatively minor remedies have frequently been suggested in recent years, including proposals for more judges, more supporting court personnel, and more courts. More fundamental proposals with broad implications for the workings of our criminal justice system have also been discussed seriously. One such proposal actively promoted by Chief Justice Burger (among others) is the elimination of the diversity of citizenship jurisdiction, whereby matters ordinarily settled in state courts go to federal court if they involve plaintiffs from one state suing respondents residing elsewhere. In these cases, federal courts are obliged to apply state law; it has therefore been argued that state judges who continually work with state law, rather than federal judges who do not, are best able to interpret and apply state law. Chief Justice Burger has pointed out that diversity cases represent about one-fourth of all civil cases handled by the district courts each year. Were the civil docket reduced, federal judges would have more time to devote to criminal matters.

Another fundamental proposal is to limit the use of habeas corpus by state prisoners by lowering the standards of criminal justice that the states are required to follow, thus contracting the grounds for pursuing habeas corpus. Indeed, this approach has characterized much of the Burger Court's decisionmaking in the area of criminal procedures. Habeas corpus relief could also be denied state prisoners if the federal courts were instructed to defer to the state courts' adjudication of the federal questions at issue. Narrowing the conditions under which habeas corpus petitions from state prisoners can be entertained by federal district judges would not only reduce the case crunch but would fundamentally alter the role the federal courts have played supervising criminal justice in the states. This would have serious implications for another problem area, the achievement of uniform standards of justice throughout the country.

The criminal law case crunch would also be lessened (although more in the state judicial systems than in the federal judicial system) if some types of behavior were not considered criminal by law. In particular, it has been frequently suggested that with few exceptions, crimes without victims, in which there is no complaining party aside from the government, should no longer be considered criminal. It is argued that consenting adults' sexual acts and their access to pornography, gambling, and narcotics use and small-scale sales, while they may raise serious moral issues, are best dealt with by institutions other than the criminal justice system; cluttering the courts with such victimless crimes is said to make it more difficult to administer justice in cases with real victims.

• • •

For a variety of historical reasons, the federal courts are now deeply involved in the administration of criminal justice across the entire nation. The problems and challenges have proved to be immense. Whether or not there are "solutions" to the problems of administration of criminal justice remains to be seen. It is not yet clear how far the federal courts, and particularly the Supreme Court, will go on the recent course of lowering standards of criminal justice (from the standpoint of the rights of defendants) and reducing federal oversight of criminal justice in the states.

——————————— 78 ———————————

Litigation Flow
In Three United States
Courts of Appeals

J. Woodford Howard, Jr.

[*The following selection reports the results of research on the U.S. Courts of Appeals for the District of Columbia, the Second, and Fifth Circuits. The goal of the research was to determine just what these three courts decided in the federal judicial system.*]

• • •

I

The first task is to describe briefly the business of the three courts of appeals. Table 1 provides the gross caseloads and the criminal portion of each circuit court during fiscal years 1965–67. Habeas corpus petitions, following AO practice, are considered civil actions. Note that the Fifth Circuit had almost as much volume as the other two circuits combined. Together, the three circuits handled approximately 40% of all cases disposed of by the eleven courts of appeals after hearing or submission of briefs. By 1970, in fact, the 15 judges of the Fifth Circuit alone decided almost one-fourth of the cases disposed of after hearing or submission in U.S. circuit courts.

TABLE 1.

CIRCUIT	1965	1966	1967	TOTAL	% CRIMINAL
D.C.	457	468	411	1,336	39.0
Second	430	445	482	1,357	21.7
Fifth	669	727	852	2,248	16.1
Sums	1,556	1,640	1,745	4,941	23.8

Three things become noteworthy when these data are considered in conjunction with AO reports on the nature of circuit cases disposed of after hearing since 1950. First, civil litigation, which constituted three-fourths of this sample, dominated the dockets of the three circuits and of courts of appeals generally. But, second, there have been major shifts in appellate business over time. For example, criminal appeals for all circuits rose from 10.6% of total volume in 1950 to 28.9% in 1970, while "private civil" remained substantially unchanged (42.1% to 40.7%). Criminal justice is no longer a minor courts of appeals function. If prisoner petitions are taken into account, 35.8% of this sample dealt with criminal disputes. Third, although the rising criminal trend is reflected in all three circuits, there are significant variations among them. In our data the D.C. Circuit's 1967 rate of criminal appeals (39.0%) was far higher, and the Fifth Circuit's rate of 16.2% was lower, than the AO's rate of criminal appeals for all circuits (22%). Indeed, AO data shows that the D.C. Circuit's rate of criminal appeals jumped dramatically in one generation—from only 7.1% of its total volume in 1950 to 56.2% in 1970—while its "private civil" rate fell from 47.1% to 16.3%. . . . It goes too far to suggest a displacement of roles for any circuit court. Comparisons among circuits and over time nonetheless suggest that federal appellate courts are better reflexes of society than is sometimes supposed. . . .

A related comparison concerns who uses the courts of appeals. Table 2 distinguishes the appeals according to governmental, nongovernmental, and other (usually missing information) categories of litigants which appeared in the case citations. These data underscore the theme that the three courts of appeals, though forums for private litigation, serve primarily to enforce federal law. The U.S. government, both as appellant and appellee, was their prime consumer. The federal law enforced, moreover, was largely statutory in character. Classified by subject-matter, only 9.3% of this litigation involved constitutional questions while 62.5% involved statutory or federal rules questions. Appeals from administrative agencies, half of them from the N.L.R.B. and U.S. Tax Courts, consti-

TABLE 2. Governments as Parties to Litigation (Appellant or Appellee, N = 4,941)

CIRCUIT	NONE %	U.S. %	STATE %	OTHER %	TOTAL N	TOTAL %
D.C.	28.2	70.5	1.0	0.2	1,336	100.0
Second	39.9	51.7	8.0	0.4	1,357	100.0
Fifth	36.2	48.5	14.4	0.9	2,248	100.0
Sums	35.1	55.3	9.0	0.6	4,941	100.0

tuted only 12.8% of the total sample. However important administrative review may be politically, that function rests on a select sampling of administrative disputes.

These characteristics of federal appeals have basic implications for analysis of judicial policy functions. One is that recognition of the resistance-potential of lower federal courts should not obscure the underlying premise that *both* Congress and the Supreme Court depend on these tribunals for enforcement of federal policy. Innovation by either is difficult to imagine without their support. . . . Another implication is that intermediate federal courts have acquired new roles in national law enforcement without discarding old, private-law responsibilities. For chronically overloaded circuits, one or the other may have to give.

Table 2 also reveals variations among the three circuits which tend to confirm traditional functional descriptions. That is, the D.C. Circuit is primarily a U.S. government tribunal having little to do with states, though in one-fourth of its business in this period it served uniquely as the equivalent of a state supreme court for the District of Columbia. The Second Circuit tended to have a larger share of private litigation. The Fifth Circuit had the largest share of cases involving states or state agents as parties. To determine whether the three circuits concentrated on different subjects, Table 3 classifies the litigation according to 12 broad fields which summarize 62 subjects in the original data.

At first glance, the spread of business within the three circuits appears

TABLE 3. The Business of Three Circuit Courts

	D.C. N = 1,336 %	Second N = 1,357 %	Fifth N = 2,248 %
Contracts	10.3	9.3	12.9
Torts	7.1	13.8	14.8
Commerce	13.8	16.3	9.1
Labor	7.3	11.5	10.8
Taxation	2.5	10.8	12.4
Personal Status *	9.1	12.9	23.0
Crimes against Persons	8.8	0.3	0.2
Crimes against Property	18.7	5.5	6.8
Morals Offenses	6.9	9.4	1.8
Miscellaneous Crimes	1.4	2.7	1.1
Local	4.0	0.0	0.0
Other	10.2	7.6	6.9
Sums	100.0	100.0	100.0

* "Personal Status" includes civil rights, immigration, and suffrage cases, plus prisoner petitions.

remarkably even; but closer analysis supports conventional wisdom about their differences. There are some surprises, too. As expected, the Fifth Circuit had the largest share of personal status cases while the D.C. Circuit had relatively little tax litigation and the heaviest concentration of crimes against persons and property. Yet the Second Circuit heard relatively more morals offenses (mainly narcotics) than the others and concentrated less on tort and contract cases than anticipated from its reputation as the nation's "top commercial court. . . ." Despite the Fifth Circuit's disproportionate share of civil liberties claims, that court as well as the Second Circuit had more cases concerning economic issues than personal status and crimes. Similarly, the D.C. Circuit dominated appeals from the FCC (60 of 61), CAB (24 of 25), and other regulatory agencies while the Second Circuit and Fifth Circuit carried a larger burden of appeals from the NLRB, Tax Courts, and Immigration and Naturalization Service.

Location and social conditions probably account for these differences, just as the D.C. Circuit's monopoly of rape and FCC licensing cases can be attributed to its special jurisdiction. Still, more than location and jurisdiction are required to explain intriguing variations which appear within specific subjects. Why, for instance, did the D.C. Circuit have no bankruptcy or selective service appeals? Why did the Fifth Circuit have such a large workload in the fields of insurance, social security, and workmen's compensation? Why did the Second Circuit have the smallest share of patents? Interview data suggest ideological explanations, such as the hospitality of Texas courts to workmen's compensation awards and the relative inhospitality of the Second Circuit to patents. Our space and sampling are too brief to confirm such answers, but they sustain one warning: Beware of generalization about *the* policy role of courts of appeals. Regionalization of appellate structures, for some subjects at least, may well mean regional specialization and regionalized national law.

II

• • •

Table 4 reports how the circuit courts decided all appeals in our sample. The "Mixed" category includes decisions affirmed in part and reversed in part. "Avoid" means the issue on appeal was avoided, usually by procedural techniques. "Other" is a residual category for appeals that were dismissed or had missing information. Although Table 4 includes appeals from administrative agencies as well as from district courts, the reversal rate 21.1% is similar to the estimate for district courts only. Together

TABLE 4. Circuit Court Decisions

Circuit	Affirm %	Mixed %	Reverse %	Avoid %	Other %	Total N	Total %
D.C.	68.9	2.9	19.6	3.6	4.9	1,336	100.0
Second	73.6	5.8	17.2	1.7	1.6	1,357	100.0
Fifth	63.9	6.0	24.4	1.5	4.3	2,248	100.0
Sums	67.9	5.1	21.1	2.1	3.7	4,941	100.0

these estimates of appeal to and reversal by the circuit courts show that district courts and agencies formally decide a large majority of federal adjudications.

Though litigants appealed up to half of the district court decisions in this period, the courts of appeals reviewed less than a third of them after hearing and disturbed only about one-fourth of those they heard.

The opportunity of circuit courts to interpret national law, while substantial, is therefore limited to a select group of cases whose character largely depends on the strategic choices of litigants and tribunals below.

• • •

[A] simple reverse rate does not reveal the *degree of finality* of appellate decisions. It fails to distinguish flat reversals, which officially preclude further lower court discretion, from remands, which often leave some degree of lower court discretion intact. Given the special opportunities for resistance by lower courts after remand, we distinguished remands from flat affirmances, reversals, and other disposition of the caseload in Table 5.

Since most remands are reversals, and vice versa, the primary result of distinguishing flat decisions from remands is a sharp drop in the reversal rate from 21.1% to 7.7%.

TABLE 5. Circuit Court Finality

Circuit	Affirm %	Reverse %	Remand %	Other %	Total N	Total %
D.C.	68.7	8.8	18.6	3.8	1,336	100.0
Second	73.1	7.4	13.6	5.9	1,357	100.0
Fifth	63.1	7.1	24.5	5.3	2,248	100.0
Sums	67.4	7.7	19.9	5.1	4,941	100.0

• • •

TABLE 6. Supreme Court Review of Circuit Decisions (N = 4,945)

CIRCUIT	TOTAL N	%	No APPEAL %	DECLINED OR DISMISSED %	GRANTED %	(N)
D.C.	1,337	100.0	88.3	10.5	1.3	(17)
Second	1,359	100.0	70.3	26.7	2.9	(40)
Fifth	2,249	100.0	80.3	18.2	1.6	(35)
Sums	4,945	100.0	79.7	18.4	1.9	(92)

Now let us contrast these circuit decisions with their fate in the Supreme Court. Table 6 distinguishes circuit decisions which were not appealed from those which were appealed and declined or accepted by the Justices.

• • •

The most striking pattern is how little direct supervision the Justices exercised over the three courts of appeals. Litigants appealed 1,004 or 1-in-5 of these circuit decisions to the Supreme Court, which granted certiorari in 9.2% of those appealed. Discounting 11 dismissals, the court intervened in 92 cases or 1.9% of the entire sample of 4,945 cases.

• • •

The rate of appeal to the high court (20.3% of the sample or 30.4% if we adjust for consolidation and certiorari petitions without circuit citations) was far higher than the classic hunch estimate of 10%. The Court's decisions also confirm the expectation that Justices grant certiorari primarily to reverse decisions below. Table 7, which presents the Supreme Court's decisions according to the same categories as in Table 4 for the circuits, including "Other" cases, shows that the Supreme Court disturbed more than two out of three decisions it heard. This disturbance rate was triple that of the three circuits.

Table 7. Supreme Court Decision in Circuit Cases Reviewed (N = 103)

CIRCUIT	AFFIRM N	MIXED N	REVERSE N	AVOID N	OTHER * N	TOTAL N
D.C.	3	1	13	0	1	18
Second	11	0	28	1	8	48
Fifth	11	4	20	0	2	37
Sums	25	5	61	1	11	103

* Assorted dismissals

Similar contrasts prevail across a wide spectrum of decisional characteristics. Including "Other" cases for consistent comparison (N = 103), the rate of decision by full opinion (60%) was slightly larger than in the circuits (50%). The in forma pauperis rate was 12.6% compared to 1.0% for the circuits. Amicus briefs appeared in 27.2% as compared to 1.4% for the circuits. Dissents occurred in two-thirds of the cases as compared to 8.3% for the three circuits.

• • •

As expected, the Supreme Court had a higher mix of constitutional questions (32%) than the three circuits (9.3%), relatively more criminal cases (30%) than the circuits (23.8%), and a larger share of administrative appeals (22.3%) than the circuits (12.8%). Of the 33 constitutional cases, 25 concerned criminal procedure, only four involved the first amendment, and not one involved elections or civil rights. In cases rising through the three federal circuit courts during this period, the Warren Court clearly concentrated on economic regulation and criminal law. And unlike circuit practices, the Justices affirmed only one criminal case.

These contrasts among circuit and Supreme Court decisions run counter to casual assumptions that intermediate appellate courts are mirror images of Mt. Everest. A comparison of the business of the Supreme Court and the three circuits combined in Table 8 is also at odds with the popular notion that the Warren Court in this period was essentially a civil liberties tribunal. Over half of the Court's cases from these circuits were economic in character, not counting ten criminal cases in taxation and commerce. Though that distribution resembled the circuits', the Court came closer to mirroring their business within personal

TABLE 8. Comparison of Appellate Court Business

| | Three Circuits | | Supreme Court | |
	N	%	%	N
Contracts	554	11.2	3.9	4
Torts	615	12.4	8.7	9
Commerce	613	12.4	27.2	28
Labor	497	10.0	6.8	7
Taxation	459	9.3	14.6	15
Personal Status	814	16.5	15.5	16
Crimes against Persons	125	2.5	0.0	0
Crimes against Property	477	9.7	8.7	9
Morals Offenses	261	5.3	2.9	3
Miscellaneous Crimes	81	1.6	5.8	6
Local	54	1.1	0.0	0
Other	395	8.0	5.8	6
Sums	4,945	100.0	100.0	103

status and criminal categories than within the economic sector. The Justices decided both a lower rate of contract and tort cases than the circuits and a surprisingly higher portion of commerce and tax cases.

The upshot is uneven supervision of circuit courts by the Justices, which suggests a division of labor among appellate tribunals that needs to be explored. . . . For three years, these courts of appeals were left to their own devices in broad ranges of litigation. The Justices exercised no review at all over their treatment of insurance and marine contracts, workmen's compensation, fair labor standards, parole, social security, suffrage, and school desegregation. The Justices heard only one appeal in negotiable instruments, patents, and copyrights. Their remand rate (34%) was also twice as high as the circuits'. Notwithstanding the high court's propensity to reverse, the Justices intervened so rarely and selectively in these federal appeals that controls on the discretion of circuit judges would appear to depend less on fear of formal reversal than on the informal constraints embodied in the notion of "judicial role." Interviews with 35 judges from the three circuits support that inference; Supreme Court review looms as too irregular for rotating circuit judges to worry greatly about reversal or second-guessing Justices.

• • •

III

In a leading study of the Supreme Court's certiorari jurisdiction, Joseph Tanenhaus and his students developed the theory that certain "cues" in certiorari petitions guide the Justices in narrowing their grants of certiorari to a select few. The cues found were dissension within lower courts, civil liberties issues, and the federal government's seeking review. No attempt was made in this sample to replicate Tanenhaus' method or to isolate the same variables. But certain characteristics of these appeals bearing on the Supreme Court's responsibility to control dissension among lower courts were compared to explore the screening process. . . . The hypotheses are that the Justices were inclined to hear reversed decisions more than affirmed decisions, non-unanimous decisions more than unanimous decisions, and en banc decisions more than panel decisions. The comparative rates of certiorari petitions granted in these situations, reported for the 92 writs granted in Table 9, support each hypothesis.

The hypothesis for reversed decisions received weaker support than the hypotheses for split and en banc decisions. A related reason may be that reversals were weaker "cues" to appellants than split and en banc decisions. Reversals, unexpectedly, were appealed at a lower rate than affirmances.

TABLE 9. Supreme Court Certiorari

TYPE OF CIRCUIT DECISION	CIRCUIT DECISIONS APPEALED		CERTIORARI PETITIONS GRANTED	
	Total Decisions N	*Rate Appealed* % of N	*Total Certiorari Petitions* n	*Rate Granted* % of n
Affirmance	3,357	23.0	772	7.9
Reversal & Mixed	1,300	16.2	211	13.7
Other & Avoid	288	7.3	21	23.8
All Cases	4,945	20.3	1,004	9.2
Unanimous	4,535	18.7	848	7.5
Split	410	38.0	156	17.9
All Cases	4,945	20.3	1,004	9.2
Panel	4,903	20.1	987	8.9
En Banc	42	40.5	17	23.5
All Cases	4,945	20.3	1,004	9.2

Disagreements between levels in a circuit may project weaker signals of relevance to the Supreme Court than disagreements within courts of appeals. Since the data in Table 9 mix the motives of appellants and Justices, it is impossible to unravel them conclusively. However, the results after certiorari was granted in these cases reinforce the significance of the screening process. There was little difference in how the Supreme Court treated circuit decisions once certiorari was granted. The Court disturbed reversals and mixed decisions at about the same rate (72.4%) as affirmances (71.9%). No difference existed between its rate of disturbing unanimous (71.9%) and split (71.4%) decisions. Thus a relationship between intracircuit disagreement and Supreme Court judgments did emerge by what the Justices decided to hear. Cue theory, on the other hand, probably should be expanded to include decisions of appellants which, after all, determine the appeals that Justices see. These litigants were surprisingly persistent. The rate of appeal from the litigants from the circuits to the Supreme Court (20.3% or 30.4% adjusting for consolidated and uncited cases) did not fall as much below the estimated rate from district courts to the circuits (48.7% total or 30.2% after hearing) as one would expect from 9–1 odds against acceptance. Affirmed decisions also were appealed at a higher rate than disturbed decisions in face of a 2–1 lower chance of acceptance. Are judges right about the waste of resources on unnecessary appeals?

Additional light on intercourt relations is provided by Table 10, which juxtaposes all decisions at both appellate levels in order to discover who supported whom. The nebulous data in "Avoid" and "Other"

TABLE 10.   Intercourt Relations

	CIRCUIT DECISIONS (N = 4,842)		SUPREME COURT DECISIONS (N = 103)			
	No Appeal	Review Declined	SC * Affirm	SC Disturb	SC Avoid/ Other	Sums
CA** Affirm	2,585	708	16	41	7	3,357
CA Disturb	1,089	177	8	21	5	1,300
CA Avoid/Other	267	16	1	4	0	288
Sums	3,941	901	25	66	12	4,945

* SC = Supreme Court
** CA = Court of Appeals

columns are excluded from much of the following analysis. Both "disturbed" decisions and "conflicts" between levels are composed of mixed decisions and reversals.

Our conclusions are, first, that the Supreme Court disturbed more circuit affirmances (41) than it reaffirmed (16). Hence, the Supreme Court injected more court-conflict into this stream of litigation than it averted or resolved (34). Second, the Supreme Court disturbed more circuit reversals and mixed decisions (21) than it affirmed (8). Hence, when conflict already existed between district courts or agencies and the circuit courts, the Supreme Court disturbed more circuit resolution of conflict than it sustained and sided more often with original than with appellate tribunals.

But third, the Justices also disturbed more district court and agency decisions (41) than they affirmed (37). Hence, we cannot leap to the conclusion that the Supreme Court was basically supportive of original tribunals. Rather, the first two conclusions (which confirm those of Richardson and Vines) and the third resolve into a final and deceptively simple conclusion that the Justices supported whoever agreed with them in whatever interested them in appeals before them. A 100% reversal rate, the theoretical optimum use of Supreme Court resources, is unlikely for the same reasons. Hence, amending some implications of cue theory, the Supreme Court was less interested in resolving intracircuit disagreements per se than in resolving the policy disputes with which those disagreements correlated. In other words, Supreme Court review of the three courts of appeals in this period was less the resolution of lower court conflicts than "applied politics"—securing the supremacy of highly selective policy values irrespective of levels.

● ● ●

[Remarkable] growth has enlarged the capacity of circuit courts to influence public policy, because it has increased the Supreme Court's reliance on the circuits to enforce national law while decreasing the Court's ability to insure uniformity among them. To enforce national law under present growth trends, in short, the Supreme Court must increasingly rely on the very courts in a position to Balkanize federal law. The same forces also tax the ability of courts of appeals to maintain uniformity within the circuits and to adjudicate the increasing volume without resort to mass-production techniques that are the bane of American trial courts. All the more important, therefore, become: (1) the screening process by which Supreme Court Justices select their targets, and (2) the decisional relationships within and among the eleven courts of appeals.

• • •

79

A Study of the Supreme Court's Caseload

Gerhard Casper, Richard A. Posner

• • •

V. The Impact of the Caseload Increase on the Effective Functioning of the Court

The increase in the Court's caseload could affect its operations in three ways: it could reduce the time available to the members of the Court to screen applications for review; it could reduce the time available to them for deciding on the merits the cases that they do take for review; it could

---

From Gerhard Casper and Richard A. Posner, "A Study of the Supreme Court's Caseload," *Journal of Legal Studies* 3 (1974): 362–364, 364–366, 366–371, 371–374. Copyright © 1974 by the University of Chicago Law School. Reprinted by permission. Most footnotes have been omitted.

prevent the Court from accepting for review cases that would have met its standards for review when its caseload was smaller. We discuss the first two effects together.

A

Unless every case tendered to the Court is identical with respect to the difficulty of deciding whether to grant review—as of course it is not—one is on treacherous ground in using caseload statistics to estimate the actual workload that the cases represent. Standardizing for difficulty is out of the question. One can, however, make one simple correction, which is to deflate the indigent cases in recognition of the fact that on average they are less meritorious than the paid cases and so should require less screening time. Table 16 uses as the deflator the ratio of the percentage of indigent cases granted to the percentage of paid cases granted, as computed from Table 14. The deflator is used to transform the indigent cases into "paid equivalents."[34]

The next step is to estimate the average time necessary to decide whether or not to accept a case for review. Table 16 uses alternative assumptions—that each Justice spends an average of 15 minutes of his own time on a paid case (including discussion with the other Justices in conference) and that he spends just 9.5 minutes. The second assumption is derived from Professor Hart's study of the Court's workload.[35] If our estimates seem very short, it must be remembered that each Justice has the assistance of law clerks[36] and that many cases are either clear grants or clear denials and hence require little time to decide.

TABLE 16. Estimated Time for Deciding Applications for Review

Terms of Court[a]	Paid Cases	Paid Equivalents[b]	Total	Hours Required Per Week @ 15 Minutes per Case[c]	Hours Required @ 9.5 Minutes[c]
1957–58	1746	505	2251	5.4	3.4
1959–60	1757	610	2367	5.7	3.6
1961–62	1900	677	2577	6.2	3.9
1963–64	2060	631	2691	6.5	4.1
1965–66	2427	1062	3489	8.4	5.3
1967–68	2644	1284	3928	9.4	6.0
1969–70	3097	1396	4493	10.8	6.8
1971–72	3474	1454	4928	11.8	7.5

a Pairs of terms.
b Term explained in text.
c We assume a 52-week work year. This assumption is discussed below in the text.

Table 16 reveals significant but seemingly tolerable increases over the period covered by this study in the amount of time required by each Justice to screen applications for review. The increase between the beginning and end of the period is either four or six and one-half hours per week, depending on which assumption concerning the time required to dispose of the average case is made.

Our confidence in these figures was bolstered by discovering that our estimate that the screening function takes approximately one working day a week is identical to a figure (unknown to us when we made our estimate) arrived at by Nathan Lewin after interviewing recent law clerks. Still, various objections can be made to our figures.

1. Some Justices may spend fewer than 9.5 minutes per case. This would imply that the screening function was less burdensome than we have found—but also that the importance of the function to the Justices is less than is suggested by those who have objected to the . . . proposal to shift part of the function to another court. If Justices spend only a few minutes deciding whether to take a case, it is difficult to maintain that they are engaged in making complex and subtle strategic judgments that are important to the Supreme Court's effectiveness.

There is a related point. Faced with a choice between devoting more time in the aggregate to screening and less to their other duties, or reducing the average screening time per case, the Justices might elect the latter course. In that event, statistics of the actual time spent by the Justices on screening, were they available, might show no increases. But it would not follow that the increase in the caseload had had no adverse effect on the Court. The reduction in the average time spent on screening a case below a 15-minute or 9.5-minute threshold might well result in an increase in the rate of error in screening—*i.e.*, in an increase in the probability that a case will be accepted for review, or rejected, where the contrary result would have been reached had the Court devoted more time to examining the appropriateness of reviewing the case. In Part VII we suggest how such a hypothesis might be tested.

2. There are questions concerning the allocation of work time among the weeks of the year. The estimates in Table 16 are based on a 52-week work year, which may seem excessive. However, since at present about 25 per cent of the applications for review are screened during the summer months, and the summer recess (now about 13–14 weeks long) is about 25 per cent of the year, the weekly time estimates in Table 16 would be unaffected by treating term time and summer recess time separately. If, however, we assume that the percentage of cases screened during the summer recess was substantially lower in earlier years, the increases in time revealed by Table 16 would be reduced. We have no basis for such an assumption, but we shall consider its implications anyway. Suppose the Court in the 1957–1958 terms screened only 10 per cent of its cases during

the summer (assumed to be 13 weeks long). Then the number of hours devoted to screening per week *during the term* would be, not 5.4 or 3.4, as shown in the first row of Table 16, but 6.5 or 4.1. This is not a large change, and in any event its significance is not obvious. The increase in the time devoted to screening during the term is smaller, true, but the difference is made up out of the Justices' vacation time and for all one knows a significant reduction in that time could reduce the Justices' productivity (not to mention their welfare) significantly.

3. As the percentage of cases granted declines over time with the increase in the caseload, a larger fraction of the cases filed can be expected to have some merit. This implies a reduction in the fraction of cases that can be decided in a minimal amount of time.

Consider two hypothetical cases in which the gain to the claimant if the Court accepts his case for review and reverses the judgment of the lower court is $10,000 and the cost of Supreme Court review to the claimant (in attorney's and filing fees, etc.) is $1000. Assume that the probability of reversal, if the Court takes the case, is 60 per cent and the probability that the Court will take the case, computed solely as a function of the intrinsic appropriateness of Supreme Court review and without regard to any caseload pressures on the Court, is 50 per cent in the first case and 30 per cent in the second. Then the expected value of seeking Supreme Court review is $2000 to the first claimant (10,000 × .60 × .50 − $1000) and $800 to the second claimant ($10,000 × .60 × .30 − $1000), and both will seek review. Now assume that, solely because of the interaction of increased case filings and limited capacity for deciding cases, the probability of the Court's accepting a case for review is half of what it would be in the absence of any time pressures. Then the expected value of seeking review in the first case drops from $2000 to $500 ($10,000 × .60 × .50 × .50 − $1000) but it is still positive, while the expected value in the second case drops to − $100 ($10,000 × .60 × .30 × .50 − $1000), so the second case will not be filed. This example suggests that the pool of cases from which the Court draws those that it decides to review will becomes richer in cases appropriate for review as increased filings force down the percentage of cases taken. If so, the time required to make the selection of cases from the pool will presumably increase—a larger percentage of cases are plausible candidates for review.

This conclusion may not be obvious, so we will elaborate it a bit. We assume that the cases filed with the Court in any term can be arrayed according to their merit. We further assume that the Court, in deciding which cases to accept for review, examines carefully all cases above some point on the merit scale—call it the "merit threshold." If the average merit of the cases filed with the Court increases, more cases will be found above the merit threshold, and therefore the Court will examine carefully more cases in making its selection of (a fixed number of) cases to review. To be somewhat more realistic, we must also assume that some cases have such obvious merit that the Court spends little time in deciding whether to review them. Clearly the number of these cases will rise too. This effect leads to a reduction in screening time, but we assume that it is dominated by the effect of an increase in average merit of cases filed in enlarging the pool of cases that the Court sifts carefully in deciding which cases—a fixed number—to accept for review.

We need to examine a little more closely the premise that the average merit of the cases filed has probably increased through deterrence of marginal cases by the decreased probability that an application for review will be granted. In many cases, perhaps, the benefits to the applicant for review if he obtains a reversal of the lower court's judgment are so great, or the costs of applying for Supreme Court review so small, that even a substantial decline in the probability of obtaining review will not deter the application. A good example is provided by applications submitted by prisoners. The benefits to the applicant if his case is accepted for review and the judgment reversed may be very great—his liberty—and the cost of seeking review, which consists primarily of the opportunity costs of the prisoner's time, may be very low. Another example might be the repeated efforts by an organization such as the NAACP to get the Supreme Court to adjudicate a question of great importance to the organization.

The issue raised by these examples is the magnitude rather than existence of the effect we have described. No one, we take it, would disagree that if the probability of the Supreme Court's taking a case fell from .05 to zero, the number of cases filed with the Court would decline. It would be arbitrary to assert that if the probability fell from .05 to .00001, or from .9 to .1, the number of cases would be unaffected. The number of cases may, however, be *relatively* insensitive to changes in the probability of review, in which event a substantial decline in that probability might have little impact on the number of cases.

[Earlier analysis] revealed a decline, over the period 1956–1971, of roughly 50 per cent in the probability of obtaining review. Table 17, using a different method of computation, tells the same story. For the reason just explained we do not know by what amount this decline has increased the difficulty of deciding which cases to accept for review, but our analysis suggests that it must have increased it to some extent.

B

Tables 14 and 17 also bear on the second type of cost associated with an increase in the caseload—reduction in the number of meritorious cases that are actually accepted for review. The decline in the proportion of cases accepted for review revealed by these tables would have little significance if one believed that it reflected a decline in the average merit of

TABLE 17. Percentage of Cases Accepted for Review

Terms [a]	Total [b]	Accepted for Review [c]	Percentage
1957–58	2251	297	13.2%
1959–60	2367	279	11.8
1961–62	2577	288	11.2
1963–64	2691	266	9.9
1965–66	3489	281	8.1
1967–68	3928	320	8.1
1969–70	4493	295	6.6
1971–72	4928	354	7.2

[a] Pairs of terms.
[b] From Table 16.
[c] We use number of cases argued orally, from Report of the Study Group on the Caseload of the Supreme Court, p. A7 (Fed. Judic. Center, Dec. 1972), as our proxy for the number of cases accepted for review.

applications for review. But there is no basis for such a belief after the correction for the presumed lesser merit of the average indigent case made in Table 17. On the contrary, theory suggests that the average merit of the applications for review has increased over the period covered by our study. If the percentages in the last column of Table 17 had not declined, the number of applications for review would probably be even greater today than it is and the average merit of the applications the same as at the beginning of the period. Thus, caseload statistics probably understate the true increase over time in the demand for Supreme Court review.

To summarize, we have found a significant but not extremely large increase in the amount of time that the Justices are required to devote to the task of screening applications for review, and we have found that the Court is probably refusing to review cases that would have met its standards for granting review at a period when its caseload was substantially smaller than it is today. But we cannot conclude that the caseload has become so heavy as to undermine the Court's effectiveness seriously. Conceivably the Court in 1957 was devoting too much time to screening cases or was accepting too large a fraction of the cases tendered to it for review. We have not investigated these questions.

VI. Proposals for Alleviating the Caseload Problem

Although its findings are modest and tentative, this study may be helpful in evaluating the proposals now under consideration for reducing the

Court's workload. These proposals take many forms. Some involve changes in the method of screening cases for review; some involve changes in the Court's jurisdiction; some involve administrative changes (number of Justices, etc.). Some involve a combination of these approaches.

The Freund Study Group [a study group on the caseload of the Supreme Court, appointed by Chief Justice Burger in 1971], while also recommending certain jurisdictional reforms, focused on a new screening mechanism:

> We recommend creation of a National Court of Appeals which would screen all petitions for review now filed in the Supreme Court, and hear and decide on the merits many cases of conflicts between circuits. Petitions for review would be filed initially in the National Court of Appeals. The great majority, it is to be expected, would be finally denied by that court. Several hundred would be certified annually to the Supreme Court for further screening and choice of cases to be heard and adjudicated there. Petitions found to establish a true conflict between circuits would be granted by the National Court of Appeals and the cases heard and finally disposed of there, except as to those petitions deemed important enough for certification to the Supreme Court.

We put to one side the question—crucial though it is—whether the increase in the Supreme Court's caseload in recent years has, as assumed but not established by the Freund Group, weakened the Court. Even if the answer is "yes," the Freund Group's proposal should be rejected because it is unsuited to the character of the caseload problem. Our study found that the rise in the caseload has increased—but not by a great amount—the time that the Justices spend (or should spend) on screening. The National Court of Appeals would enable only a modest saving in that time because the Supreme Court would still be required to screen the nonobvious cases and these presumably take most of the time allocated to the screening function today.

The Freund Group estimated (on what basis is not revealed) that 400 cases would survive the initial screening by the National Court of Appeals. Assume that each Justice would spend an average of half an hour in the study and discussion of such a case. Then the total hours devoted to screening would be four a week, resulting in a time saving of only three and one-half hours a week if one accepts the lesser of our two estimates of the time currently allocated by the Justices to screening cases (see Table 16).

A more serious consequence of the caseload increase, we said, was the probable reduction in the number of meritorious cases accepted for review. The only proposal of the Freund Study Group specifically addressed to this problem is the proposal to empower the National Court of Appeals to resolve conflicts among the federal courts of appeals. This treats only one small aspect of the problem. The other classes of case in which the size of the Court's caseload may be forcing it to decline to review cases that should receive further review are ignored.

However, other proposals of the Study Group bear indirectly on the problem. For example, the elimination of direct appeals from district courts, a proposal discussed below, would enable plenary review by the federal courts of appeals of many decisions that the Supreme Court today disposes of summarily (which we consider to be the equivalent, in general, of no review). And relevant here is the question left unanswered by the Freund Report of what the Supreme Court would do with the time saving effected by the creation of the National Court of Appeals. If the time saved were used to hear and decide cases denied review today because of limitations of time, the problem of nonreview of worthy cases would be less severe. Conceivably, too, the time the Court spends on screening would be reduced—it would not have to be quite so selective since it was taking more cases. But one doubts that the time saving would be large enough to produce significant effects along these lines. And it is of course possible—and we think envisaged by the members of the Freund Study Group—that the Court would devote all or most of any time saved to additional deliberation in cases accepted for review rather than to deciding additional cases.

The jurisdictional changes recommended by the Freund Group include, as just mentioned, the elimination of direct appeals from three-judge district courts (which would be abolished) and from one-judge district courts in government antitrust cases. Appeals from three-judge district courts were less than three per cent of all the cases filed with the Court during the 1971 term but they were 22 per cent of the cases argued orally before the Court, which suggests that this jurisdictional change could have as much impact on the Court's workload as the proposed National Court of Appeals. A simple calculation yields a better idea of the potential effect. Using the 22 per cent figure, and treating the number of cases decided with full opinion during the 1971 term (151) as approximately equivalent to the number of cases argued orally, we calculate that 33 of the cases argued orally that term were appeals from three-judge courts. Since 120 such appeals were filed in the 1971 term, it follows that about one-fourth of all appeals from three-judge courts were set for oral argument, the rest being disposed of summarily. This suggests that the Court is already fairly selective and hence that many cases from three-judge district courts would be accepted for review if brought to the Court by writ of certiorari. Suppose that half of the 33 cases would survive. Then the proposed jurisdictional change would eliminate 17 cases, or 11 per cent of those argued orally—a figure by no means negligible, although small. Since this proposal is relatively uncontroversial we shall not discuss it further here. And for the same reason we shall not discuss the proposal to move the remaining appeals to the discretionary jurisdiction of the Supreme Court. The Freund Group rightly assumed that this reform would be more in the nature of a ratification of existing practice than a change in it.

A more radical jurisdictional proposal is that of Judge Haynsworth, who favors "the creation by the Congress of a national court of appeals having jurisdiction to review on writs of certiorari federal question issues in convictions in the state and federal systems and in all postconviction proceedings in those systems in which a conviction or a sentence is called into question." Petitions for certiorari would be allowed to the Supreme Court when the National Court of Criminal Appeals decided a case on the merits or when one (or more) of its members dissented from that court's denial of certiorari. The proposal could in theory eliminate a large percentage of the Supreme Court's cases . . . , but the effect in practice would depend on the new court's certiorari practices, on the degree of unanimity among the members of the court, and, most important, on the congruence between the new court and the Supreme Court on the questions of law raised by criminal defendants—all imponderables.

Another radical jurisdictional proposal is Professor Kurland's suggestion that the Supreme Court be limited to constitutional cases . . . today 58 per cent of the cases on the Court's appellate docket (*i.e.*, paid cases) raise constitutional issues. If the proportion of constitutional cases were the same for unpaid as for paid cases, the result of the proposal would be to reduce the Court's present caseload by 42 per cent. But in reality the fraction of unpaid cases that are constitutional must be greater than the fraction of paid cases that are constitutional, since currently 83 per cent of the unpaid cases are criminal and therefore more likely to raise constitutional issues. If we assume—arbitrarily, to be sure—that the percentages of criminal and of civil cases on the miscellaneous docket that are constitutional are the same as on the appellate docket, then it would follow that currently 75 per cent of the cases on the miscellaneous docket are constitutional cases, in which event limiting the Supreme Court to constitutional cases would have reduced by only 1218 the number of cases filed in the 1972 term. Using the methods of calculating the time devoted to screening that underlie Table 16, we calculate that the elimination of these cases would have saved the Court between 2.8 and 4.4 hours a week. And some of the time saving might prove illusory, because litigants would have an even greater incentive than at present to characterize issues as constitutional, in order to invoke the Court's jurisdiction.

The greatest impact of Kurland's proposal would be on the cases decided with full opinion. As shown in Table 18, 55 per cent of such cases in the 1971 and 1972 terms were constitutional cases. For the reason just stated, some of what are now nonconstitutional cases might reappear as

TABLE 18. Cases Decided with Full Opinion

Type of Case	Terms of Court,[a] and Numbers of Cases/Proportion Constitutional							
	1957-58	1959-60	1961-62	1963-64	1965-66	1967-68	1969-70	1971-72
Federal Taxation	15/.00	20/.05	10/.00	15/.00	8/.00	6/.00	7/.14	11/.00
Review of Administrative Action	27/.00	34/.09	28/.00	34/.00	42/.02	28/.04	22/.05	29/.07
Antitrust	5/.00	4/.00	12/.00	7/.00	8/.00	6/.00	4/.00	7/.00
Criminal	68/.52	57/.51	57/.61	68/.78	77/.81	83/.80	71/.80	101/.78
Other	116/.24	128/.31	106/.28	117/.46	91/.37	124/.46	112/.46	167/.54
Total	231/.28	223/.30	213/.31	241/.43	226/.43	247/.50	216/.51	315/.55

[a] Pairs of Terms.
SOURCE: Computed from Harvard Law Review, Supreme Court Note, vols. 72–87.

constitutional cases if the Court's jurisdiction were limited to constitutional cases. Still, there seems little doubt that the proposal would rid the Court of a large number of time-consuming cases and also enable it to review a larger number of constitutional cases than at present. This could, by our earlier analysis, result in a larger number of constitutional cases filed. Nonetheless, the Kurland proposal would probably be a more effective remedy for an excessive caseload than the other proposals that we have considered. Of course, it raises many problems (as do the less effective proposals), but since they are not illuminated by our statistical analysis we do not consider them here except to note that the proposal would require the creation of a new court to resolve definitively questions of federal statutory law—these would no longer be within the Supreme Court's jurisdiction.

The final proposal that we shall discuss was made recently by the American Bar Association's Special Committee on Coordination of Judicial Improvements. It has become known as the Hufstedler proposal and variants of it are supported by Professor Rosenberg, Dean Griswold, and others. The proposal is complex and its consequences difficult to predict:

> The key features of the proposed national court of appeals are these: (1) Congress creates a national court of appeals, (2) the judges of which are selected from active United States Circuit judges with not less than a specified number of years service, (3) it grants power to the Supreme Court, by Supreme Court rules, to confer jurisdiction on the new court, (4) within boundaries set by Congress, (5) to hear and to decide classes of litigation, or individual cases referred to it by the Supreme Court, and to recommend to the Supreme Court hearing or denial of hearings in such cases, (6) subject to the continuing power of the Supreme Court to accept or to reject any case for hearing, and further subject to the requirement, (7) that no decision of the national court shall become final until the elapse of a specified period of time after the records, decisions and recommendations of the national court have been received by the Supreme Court, and the Court has not taken active action thereon, (8) Congress creates new circuit judgeships to replace the circuit judges who will be assigned to the national court.

It does not seem that the proposal would reduce the Supreme Court's burden of initial review substantially. Its potential lies, rather, in enabling the Court to delegate decision in certain case categories to the national court of appeals. In recent testimony before the Commission on Revision of the Federal Court Appellate System, Judge Hufstedler suggested the following specific jurisdictional changes in implementation of the proposal: Congress would empower the Supreme Court to transfer to the national court of appeals (1) all tax cases, (2) all patent cases, (3) all petitions to review decisions of state courts of last resort in criminal cases, (4) petitions to review decisions of cases to which certain administrative agencies are parties (NLRB, SEC, FCC, FPC, ICC, and FAA), (5) nonconstitutional federal-question conflicts between federal courts of appeals, and (6) categories specifically designated by Congress.

The effect of the Hufstedler proposal on screening is similar to that of Kurland's constitutional-court proposal. From the 3,749 new cases filed in the 1972 term, the Hufstedler proposal would eliminate roughly 1100. One must emphasize, however, that the Hufstedler proposal, which in this respect is very different from the Kurland proposal, provides only for "initial decision" by the new court. Supreme Court review would remain possible.

There are, of course, many other possibilities for reducing the Court's workload. Higher filing fees, or delay, could be used to reduce the demand for Supreme Court review. The number of Justices could be increased and the screening function delegated to panels of the enlarged Court. These are far-reaching proposals and we shall not attempt to assess their merits here.

• • •

Notes

34. The ratios, for the four terms reported in Table 14, are .29 (1956), .25 (1961), .34 (1966), and .37 (1971). To derive the "paid equivalents" in Table 16, we multiplied the number of miscellaneous cases by .29 for the 1957–1958 and 1959–1960 terms, by .25 for the 1961–1962 and 1963–1964 terms, by .34 for the 1965–1966 and 1967–1968 terms, and by .37 for the 1969–1970 and 1971–1972 terms.

35. Henry M. Hart, Jr., *supra* note 10. The average time we derived from Professor Hart's estimates was actually 10.4 to 11.4 minutes depending on the precise mixture of cases in the Term. We reduced it to 9.5 minutes after adjusting downward, from 30 minutes to 15, his estimate of the time required to dispose of a nonfrivolous appeal (as contrasted with a petition for certiorari). We made the adjustment to reflect the fact that, by all accounts, the Court does not differentiate between appeals and certiorari petitions in deciding whether to grant review.

36. The number of law clerks rose from two to three during the period covered by this study. We have not assumed that this increase enabled the Justices to reduce the amount of their personal time spent on screening: the 9.5-minute estimate would appear to be the minimum amount of time that the Justices must personally spend on the screening function if they—rather than their law clerks—are to discharge it. [In 1979, all justices had 3 or 4 law clerks to assist them.]

—————————— **80** ——————————

Judicial Rules and Caseload

Lawrence M. Friedman

• • •

Judicial Rules and the Volume of Business

Institutions have normal expectations with regard to their work load. They expect to meet with certain kinds of problems in the course of a day: they expect a certain amount of work, and no more. The number of employees, the equipment available, the organizational structure are all based on these expectations. If radically new problems arise, the institution may find it hard to adapt. Equally, if too many problems of a familiar kind arise, the institution faces a crisis.

An increase in volume is not necessarily trouble. For a department store, more business—up to a point—is a blessing. The store may hire more workers, open new branches, and add on to its buildings; however, if there were a severe labor shortage or floor space could not be added at a given location, then customers might be alienated by unpleasantness, crowds, poor service, and parking troubles.

The American judicial system is in the position of the department store that cannot hire new staff easily or expand its plant. It cannot, in other words, react to increased demand simply by giving additional service. This characteristic is generally true of *all* American courts, from the United States Supreme Court to the lowest trial court. The court system responds to new demands at a tortoise-like pace. For one thing, control over personnel is not vested in the courts themselves. The labor force is relatively fixed; a court cannot reproduce; it cannot expand out of "profits." Those who control the statute books and the purse strings have allowed court systems to grow only slowly over the years and have not allowed them to grow at all to meet the total *potential* demand for adjudication of disputes.

In the long run it is at least theoretically possible to multiply courts to keep up with changing demand. In the short run the difficulties are

From Lawrence M. Friedman, "Legal Rules and the Process of Social Change," *Stanford Law Review* 19 (1967) : 798–800, 804, 807–810. Copyright © 1967 by the Board of Trustees of the Leland Stanford Junior University. Reprinted by permission. Footnotes have been omitted.

immense. The process of creating a new federal judgeship is laborious and delicate; it takes formal or informal action by the President, the Senate, the Senators of the proposed judge's state, and (in recent years) a committee of the American Bar Association. Sometimes a nomination is blocked or a new seat left vacant because of political quarrels not easily resolved. Even if all goes well, pressure on the docket is only slowly translated into new jobs. State court capacity is generally as difficult to expand as federal court capacity. An increase in the number of judges may require authorization from the legislature, a good deal of political jockeying, new elections, and sometimes even a constitutional change. Moreover, judgeships are typically local in their jurisdiction, and there is no bureaucratic, rational management of the work load and the staff. If the docket in a rural county is virtually empty, what could be more logical than to shift the local judge, at least part-time, to the big city, where there is tremendous congestion in the courtroom? Yet, well into the second half of the twentieth century such responses were the exception rather than the rule; until recently no state was willing to create any central coordinating body to do this.

Since the number of workers (judges and clerks) is fixed, in the short run at least, courts do not have defenses against sharply rising demands. They cannot expand and contract automatically in response to the ebb and flow of litigation. Nor has there been any significant technological improvement to help the courts handle classic kinds of cases in mass. The legal system has therefore had to evolve devices and strategies to prevent a crisis in numbers.

A. Costs of Litigation

It is worth dwelling on gross historical changes in the character of court dockets in order to illustrate the means of meeting excessive demands for judicial services. A century ago commercial litigation made up much of the ordinary work of both trial and appellate courts. The tremendous growth in population, wealth, and commercial-industrial activities that occurred from 1850 on created such a potential for overburdening the courts that one of the following events had to happen: (1) expansion of the court system; (2) routinization and mass handling of commercial matters in the courts; (3) routinization and mass handling of commercial matters *outside* the courtroom; (4) use or expansion of a policy in favor of settlements to control the volume of litigation; (5) development of efficient dispute-settling mechanisms external to the judicial system; (6) adoption by courts or the imposition upon courts of substantive rules whose effect would be to discourage litigants from using the courts; or (7) increases in the costs of litigation sufficient to reduce its volume.

The first alternative was never adopted. No radical expansion of the court system occurred. The second was adopted where appropriate (in garnishment and collection actions, for example). The third alternative was in some ways the dominant response of the business world—the rationalization of business practices through the development of standard forms and patterns of doing business. The permissive attitude of the courts toward these devices made good sense ideologically, economically, and institutionally.

The effective use of the fourth alternative is difficult to measure. Its existence is evidenced, however, by the constantly enunciated proposition that the law favors settlement rather than litigation and by the fact that it is an unethical—even criminal—act to stir up lawsuits. It is somewhat paradoxical for an institution to declare so emphatically that public policy favors avoiding its use. There are many reasons other than caseload reasons why noncoerced settlements are preferable to trials. Yet it is also true that if no cases were settled out of court the judicial system as presently constituted could not sustain its share of the dispute-settling business.

The fifth solution, development of extrajudicial mechanisms for settling disputes, is exemplified by the rise of commercial arbitration. The sixth solution, adoption of "hostile" substantive rules, is far more difficult to attest. The seventh, increases in the cost of litigation, is often overlooked, but its institutional impact has been very great. Yet the trend toward judicial substitutes, and the acceptance by the courts of commercial routinization and extrajudicial settlement, is not related to this final factor, the rise in the cost of litigation.

• • •

The price device has on the whole been useful, however. The price of the law is a factor which, along with the formal and technical structure of the legal system, tends to keep legal and social change relatively even-paced, orderly, and free from caprice. In addition, the cost of litigation has tended to increase the predictability of the consequences that will flow from the acts of private parties.

• • •

B. *Jurisdictional and Procedural Rules*

Up to this point, we have discussed how increases in the price of litigation are related to the specific institutional problem of volume of business. Jurisdictional and procedural rules also control the volume of business in courts. Procedural formality adds to the cost of litigation by making lawyers necessary and by requiring time-consuming effort on the part of litigants. A trial of an issue in court results in the risk of public condemnation as well as the chance of public vindication. Procedural technicality increases the difficulty of winning a lawsuit, adds an element of chance to litigation, and in turn increases the uncertainty of outcome, which is a critical element in cost. Procedural technicality as a cost-producing device characterized English royal law in the medieval period. It is much less tolerated in modern law, which has an ideological commitment to rationality and efficiency.

Jurisdictional rules are widely used to control directly the volume of upper-court business. The United States Supreme Court keeps its work load within bounds through its power over its docket. Since 1925 the case load of the Court has been almost completely discretionary. The Court may turn down cases which it deems too trivial, as well as those it deems too controversial to handle at the moment. The Court's right to refuse to hear controversial cases is the right to prevent substantive institutional crisis; the right to refuse to hear vast numbers of trivial cases is the right to prevent a crisis in volume.

The Supreme Court's freedom to choose its cases is unusual, corresponding to the unusual demands which potentially might be made upon the Court. In some states, statutes define which types of cases appellate courts *must* hear and which are discretionary. The lower the court, the less in general its leeway. As we have mentioned, courts (high and low) have been relatively inflexible institutions; they have been unable to increase productivity or staff. Limitations on the docket, or discretionary control of the docket, have allowed upper courts to retain their classic style of weighty deliberation and reasoned opinions. Lower courts, lacking the freedom of their appellate brother and more vulnerable to the pressures of excess business, have had to countenance more and more informal processes, which—whatever other virtues they may have—succeed in limiting the docket to manageable size.

Of course, judicial institutions are not inherently incapable of handling great quantities of "cases." Mass-handling techniques can indeed be used for some kinds of business. If the social interest in rapid, efficient processing is superior to the social interest in carefully individuated justice, it is certainly possible to devise mass-production legal methods. The traffic courts, for example, handle a tremendous flow of business. Their work is mostly quite routine. The "trial" has been reduced to a formula, a vestige. Parking tickets can be paid by mail in many cities. Other lower courts handle garnishments, debt collections, and wage assignments in fantastic numbers. Probate judges in urban centers sign hundreds of routine orders and forms each session; simple hearings on heirships and intermediate accounts are delegated to clerks or assistants.

The procedures used by courts in "trials" of this kind resemble more

the procedures of record-handling and processing offices than the procedures of a court handling a murder trial or a large antitrust suit. The
traffic ticket is processed on as perfunctory a basis as the recording of a
deed in a county recorder's office. That one task is handled by a "court"
and the other by an "office" is not often a fact of much functional importance. If one defines a court as an institution which weighs evidence,
hears disputes, and renders carefully reasoned judgments, perhaps traffic
and probate courts are not courts at all, but the epigones of courts, retaining from a more vital day their titles and customs. If so, then these
"courts" represent not so much an adaption of judicial institutions to
mass processing of routine matters, but rather an abandonment of the
judicial system. The difference depends solely upon one's definition of a
court.

Abandonment of the judicial system, or at least of traditional judicial
procedures, has indeed been historically one major social response to the
pressures of increasing business. Some work has been transferred to private institutions of conciliation; some to different agencies of government. The boards and commissions than handle industrial accident or
social security claims, for example, are dealing with matters that at one
time were handled, if at all, through litigation initiated by private parties. In most cases of removal of jurisdiction to administrative bodies, the
courts retain a right of review—prestigious, but relatively powerless. Of
course, a shift in institutional locus is more than a matter of jurisdiction.
As industrial accident law shifted from court to commission, the substantive content of the rules changed too. Indeed, that was one point of the
transfer. But the new rules were such that the courts would have been
hard pressed to administer them without severe distortion of their classic
structure.

Courts also have the power to shut off litigation by adopting a *rule of
refusal*—that is, a rule refusing to acknowledge as valid a particular
cause of action. Frequently, judges defend a particular rule by arguing
that to abandon it would bring on an unmanageable flood of new cases.
This argument can be and no doubt often is nothing more than a rationalization disguising some judicial policy choice that remains unarti-
culated, but it is heard so frequently that it must be at least sometimes
honestly put forth. At least *sometimes* courts must deliberately adopt a
rule of refusal precisely because they fear being "overwhelmed." The unspoken premise is that society will suffer if the courts are overwhelmed.
A further premise is that society will be unable to rescue the courts from
suffocation. Yet society certainly has the power to create an unlimited
number of bypass institutions. What the courts may mean (even if they
do not say so) is that a rule of refusal will preserve the institutional integrity of the courts as they now exist.

To a limited degree, such fears are justified. Rules of refusal may be needed to keep the flow of work through courts in a manageable state. Whether society benefits is another question; perhaps it is good, in some instances, to avoid short-run dislocations and institutional imbalance. Conversely, rules of refusal are harmful if the court's perception of the volume of potential business is wrong, if the claim which has been refused is otherwise justified, and if other institutions are incapable of meeting the demand in the short run. Thus, the Supreme Court might have made a dangerous mistake had it adopted a rule of refusal in the school segregation cases, fearful of the institutional consequences of so grave a decision. The Justices probably believed in their hearts that segregation was morally wrong and constitutionally unsupportable; civil rights groups had failed to get satisfaction in the legislatures; and the Court in fact weathered the crisis. Of course, it is easy to see now that twelve years have passed that the Court survived the crisis stronger than ever. It was not so easy to predict at the time.

Brown v. Board of Educ. is an excellent example of the impact of a rule of *reception* (as opposed to *refusal*) on litigation. Since the Court in effect opened up a whole new area of law, it invited Negro organizations and individual Negro plaintiffs to use litigation for an attack on this or that aspect of segregation. Such litigation had already been frequent, but the frequency now increased. Federal dockets, particularly in the South, were materially affected by many complicated, controversial cases on segregation in schools, parks, and other public facilities. It can truthfully be said that the result of the rule of reception was to create an additional demand for court services. We must be careful, however, not to overemphasize the word "create." Demand is created, not by the courts, but by society. Certainly, a Supreme Court decision which puts in question the validity of certain kinds of criminal convictions will induce numbers of petitions for redress on the strength of the new doctrine, but the basic desire of prisoners for release was not created by the Court's decision. Nor is the Court to be praised or blamed for such important social events as the rise of Negro protest movements or the sexual frankness of the modern novel. Obviously, specific Supreme Court and state court decisions strongly influenced some strategies taken by the Negro protest movement, and others encouraged bold publishers to print increasingly erotic works. Obviously, too, specific court actions play a role in social movements by sharpening public perception of problems and solutions and by directing attention to the subjects of particular litigation. But the underlying drives come to and not from the courts.

In an important—even vital—sense, a court does not control its potential docket, simply because it does not control its society. It is a member-institution in society, but not the guiding one. To do its job a court must walk a tightrope. It must be able to cope with crises or to avoid them, but it must not evade and avoid so ruthlessly as to diminish its reason for survival and lapse into ceremonial triviality (like the English sovereign). Nor must it grapple with crises in such a way as to arouse forces powerful enough to destroy it. The United States Supreme Court is in a particularly delicate position compared to other courts. It has controlled its volume of work to the point that ordinary litigation no longer reaches it. Its normal docket consists of extraordinary cases, and the necessity for striking a balance between too much avoidance and too much boldness is all the more delicate.

• • •

Index